Schools, pupils, and teachers

Volume III explores the basic units in the educational system: student, teacher, and school. It examines the aims of education, historically and philosophically, and describes the development of various types of schools. The book provides an analysis of the use of educational media, a description of school buildings and equipment, among many other topics. An important part of the volume is a description of the evolution of the curriculum from the nineteenth century, with a detailed analysis of the changes made in such areas as science, the social sciences, and French.

W.G. FLEMING studied at Queen's University and the University of Toronto (MEd, Ed D). He has taught elementary (1941–3) and high school (1948–54) and was principal of an intermediate school in the province of Quebec (1943–5). He joined the faculty of the University of Toronto in 1954 and since that time has been a researcher and instructor in the graduate school. He was assistant director of the Department of Educational Research from 1962 to 1966 and was the first coordinator of research and assistant director of the Ontario Institute for Studies in Education. At present he is professor of education at the University of Toronto and at OISE. He has travelled widely, studying and making recommendations on educational planning, and other matters.

ONTARIO'S EDUCATIVE SOCIETY / III

Schools, pupils, and teachers

W. G. FLEMING

UNIVERSITY OF TORONTO PRESS

Toronto and Buffalo
Reprinted in paperback 2017

Volume III
ISBN 978-0-8020-3269-0 (cloth)
ISBN 978-1-4875-9862-4 (paper)

Volumes I-V (set)
ISBN 0-8020-3258-3
Microfiche ISBN 0-8020-0079-7
LC 77-166928

Preface

The series entitled ONTARIO'S EDUCATIVE SOCIETY, of which this volume is the third, deals with many formal and informal aspects of education as they have developed in Ontario in recent years. The province of Ontario is particularly suitable for a study of this kind. Its population of approximately 7.5 million, the largest of any Canadian province, demonstrates a rich and varied mosaic of cultures and traditions. Its extended territory includes a wide range of topographical and climatic features shaping the lives of its people in many different ways. During the post-war period it has surged with unprecedented life and vitality, striding ahead in population, in resource development, in technology, and in culture. As both a highly developed and a rapidly developing society, it offers examples of many of the problems and difficulties involved in meeting the challenges of the modern world.

Recent educational progress in Ontario has been impressive in both quantity and quality. Such a judgment has been made by numerous observers from other provinces and from abroad. This does not mean, of course, that the province has become the universal model; in some respects it is in the process of catching up with developments already completed elsewhere. It is perhaps not unreasonable to suggest, however, that many of its achievements are at least worthy of attention, if not of emulation, in other parts of the world.

Education is defined in a broad sense to include training activities of many kinds, even those with very limited goals. Such treatment does not imply that there is no value in distinguishing between education and training as concepts. The danger in dwelling excessively on such distinctions is that it becomes difficult to discern the larger pattern in which both types of activity have a part. They are often in practice so inextricably intertwined that any effort at separate treatment becomes highly artificial.

The reader will be conscious of two somewhat different approaches, one for the great majority of events and developments, where I have been largely or exclusively a bystander, and the other for situations where I have had some significant personal involvement. Examples of the latter are the operation of the departmental grade 13 examination system and the origin and early expansion of the Ontario Institute for Studies in Education. No matter what the topic, I have attempted to present an objective factual account. However, where direct experience has seemed to justify it, I have been much freer about offering opinions and assessments than where my material has been obtained at second hand. I trust that I have been successful in keeping fact separated from opinion. A second feature distinguishing the two types of material is that I have presented a relatively large amount of information about the developments in which I have had a substantial role. As a result, my attempt to present a fairly complete overview of education in Ontario has perhaps been somewhat distorted. I can only hope that there is value in the more thorough treatment which I have felt particularly qualified to provide.

For the whole series, I have used the title ONTARIO'S EDUCATIVE SOCIETY. In doing so, I have deliberately obscured a valid distinction between the ideal and the actual. Imperfect human society will not soon be truly educative in the sense that education in all its manifestations is universally accepted as the central activity to which all others are subordinated. Yet if modern civilization, and even humanity itself, is to survive, I firmly believe that there will have to be a strong and consistent move in that direction. Future generations, if any, will have to ask themselves first of any activity: "Is it educative?" Only when they have answered affirmatively will they then be justified in asking: "Is it productive of material goods?" "Is it entertaining?"

If Ontario does not yet, strictly speaking, have an educative society, a study of the record of recent years suggests that remarkable strides have been made toward that objective. The extension of formal opportunities for learning has been impressive enough in itself. When one also considers the multiplicity of informal influences that are actually or potentially educative, the over-all effect is awesome. It is possible to feel in moments of optimism that the ultimate ideal is not completely unattainable.

Volume I, *The expansion of the educational system*, provides an introduction to the whole series, in which some of the major contemporary issues and problems in education are discussed briefly, followed by seven chapters containing most of the quantitative information in compact form. For many readers it may serve chiefly for reference purposes. Volume II, *The administrative structure*, deals with the development and functions of the Department of Education and of local school systems, the financing of education, and the educational activities of the provincial and federal governments. Volume III, *Schools, pupils, and teachers*, covers the evolution of the school structure and curriculum, and attempts to show how the process of education has operated up to the end of secondary school. Volume IV, *Post-secondary and adult education*, deals with the development and activities of universities, colleges of applied arts and technology, and other institutions of post-secondary education, as well as with public and private training activities in business and industry. Volume V, *Supporting institutions and services*, relates to a variety of institutions and activities such as teacher preparation, research and development, educational television services, and externally administered examinations. Volume VI, *Significant developments in local school systems*, indicates some of the educational contributions arising chiefly from local initiative. Volume VII, *Educational contributions of associations*, attempts to demonstrate the extent to which educative activities in Ontario are initiated and conducted through voluntary effort as a supplement to formal and official services. A companion volume to the series, *Education: Ontario's preoccupation*, contains a review of the main highlights of educational development in Ontario, with less emphasis on fact and more on interpretation.

The main focus of the series is on the recent period. An attempt was made to record developments of major importance up to early 1970, just before the first five volumes were delivered to the publisher. Volumes VI and VII, which were written during the latter part of the same year, contain a certain amount of more recent material. Very few additions or changes were made during the editorial stage. The result is that a number of the speculations about future developments have already lost some of the value they might have had earlier.

The treatment of the topic is essentially descriptive. As a means of conveying a reasonable understanding of recent developments, it was thought desirable to trace the origins of many current institutions and practices back into the nineteenth century. For the relevant material in the earlier period, I have relied almost exclusively on secondary sources. Treatment of the last four decades, particularly the period since the Second World War, involved increasing use of primary data.

Acknowledgments

I am deeply indebted to the Honourable William G. Davis, Minister of Education and of University Affairs at the time of writing, for providing me the full co-operation of his departments in the production of the series of volumes constituting ONTARIO'S EDUCATIVE SOCIETY. In this task I was given access to all pertinent material in the two departments under his direction. His officials at the time of writing, headed by Dr J.R. McCarthy, Deputy Minister of Education, and Dr E.E. Stewart, Deputy Minister of University Affairs, were also extraordinarily co-operative and helpful. I am particularly grateful to these officials for enabling me to pursue the work in a way that most appeals to a member of the university community: that is, I was completely free to choose, present, and interpret the facts according to my own best judgment. I did not feel the slightest pressure to adapt or modify the material in any way so as to present an "official" version of educational developments in Ontario. As a consequence, I am completely responsible for any opinions or interpretations of the facts that the work contains. The generous assistance for the project provided by the Ontario government, without which publication would have been impossible, does not involve any responsibility for the contents.

I would like to express my particular gratitude to those who assisted me so devotedly in the project: Miss L. McGuire, my loyal secretary, who served from the time the work began in the spring of 1968, Mrs E. West, who also served with extraordinary devotion and competence during most of the same period, and Mrs S. Constable, Miss D. McDowell, and Mrs G.J. Moore, each of whom participated during an extended period. Mr C.H. Westcott, who served as Executive Assistant to the Minister of Education and University Affairs, gave me continuous encouragement and helped to deal with practical problems relating to production and publication. Particularly helpful advice and information were given by Dr C.A. Brown, Professor E.B. Rideout, and Dr J.A. Keddy. Arrangements by Dr G.E. Flower to relieve me of the majority of my other professional obligations during most of a three-year period are also greatly appreciated. In addition, I would like to acknowledge my general indebtedness to the hundreds of people who supplied information so willingly in a variety of forms. That I am unable to name them all individually does not mean that I am any the less grateful for their contributions.

W.G. FLEMING
July 1971

Contents

ONTARIO'S EDUCATIVE SOCIETY / III

Schools, pupils, and teachers

ONE

Aims of education

Since its release in June 1968 the report *Living and Learning*, produced by the Provincial Committee on Aims and Objectives of Education in the Schools of Ontario, has played a dominant part in the discussion of educational aims. The present chapter is largely restricted to a treatment of the question of aims as seen during the period before that impressive document appeared.

As a passing comment, it may be noted that the close association of "aims and objectives of education" and "the schools of Ontario" seems to imply that the two are inextricably linked. In fact, schools may under certain circumstances have little part to play in the attempt to achieve educational aims. The committee itself apparently entertained the idea that desirable aims might be most effectively pursued if the schools were abolished and full dependence placed on other educative influences.

PHILOSOPHICAL ISSUES

Aims of education cannot properly be considered except in terms of educational philosophy. It is impossible in the present context to identify the distinguishing features, gross or subtle, that characterize the specific intellectual structures built up by the major contributors to human thought in this field. But any intelligible discussion of the role of aims in the development of education in Ontario must recognize the nature of the assumptions that underlie fundamental differences among adherents of different schools.

There are two opposing propositions which broadly categorize educational thinkers: 1 / that the child can best attain self-realization as an individual and a social being if he is shaped by experiences selected and organized by competent members of adult society; 2 / that he has within himself the urge toward growth, of which learning is a natural part, and that this impulse, if properly nourished, will carry him to the realization of his full potentialities for individual and social development. There is room among the adherents of the first position for those who believe that the values of the culture can be inculcated by physical torture or hardship. Others in the same camp scorn such tactics as sadism and accept a responsibility for making the educational prescription as appealing as is humanly possible. Many believe in capitalizing to the maximum degree on the student's interest. All, or at least all who have thought their position through clearly, are convinced that there are times when the student's own ultimate welfare demands that he be required to continue with boring or unpleasant tasks when his own free choice would lead him to drop them. They believe that he lacks the capacity to select, even with the most adequate guidance, those learning experiences that will ultimately prove to be in his own best interests. They believe that externally imposed activity leads to the internal motivation that will induce the adult to seek a continuation of such activity on his own initiative – or at least they believe that it happens often enough to justify the approach as a valid educational procedure. A large proportion, further, accept the view that the best way to ensure that the adult will be able to cope with social realities such as competition, frustration, and failure is to experience them to some degree in childhood. The distinction between the harshness of reality that no individual is in a position to mitigate and the unpleasant experiences designed deliberately by an adult "for the child's own good" is not usually regarded as one of major importance. In modern parlance, those who have chosen to be counted in the camp just described are called traditionalists or essentialists.

A leading exponent of traditionalism, George S. Counts, wrote that he was "prepared to defend the thesis that all education contains a large element of imposition, that in the very nature of the case this is inevitable, that the existence and evolution of society depend upon it, that it is consequently eminently desirable, and that the frank acceptance of this fact by the educator is a major professional obligation."[1] He offered a set of propositions to support his views. 1 / Man is not born free but attains freedom as an individual and as a race through culture, which adults impose on him when he is young. Such imposition releases his energies, sets up standards of excellence, and makes great achievement possible. 2 / The child is neither good nor bad by nature, but merely a bundle of potentialities. If he is to be a good adult, he must be moulded in the context of a good society, which is strictly a human creation. 3 / The child lives in the same society as that of adults, and not one of his own. School and society must be bound together if the educational program is to have meaning and vitality. 4 / Education must be adapted to time and place. Where disintegrative forces are strong, it must be imposed with special firmness. 5 / It is impossible for the school to achieve impartiality, and it should not try to do so. It should shape attitudes, develop tastes, and impose ideas. 6 / Education should produce people who have the capacity to act, rather than waiting in a paralysis of will for the perfect solution to social problems. 7 / The processes and goals of education should be concerned with faith and human purpose as well as with intellectual development. 8 / The best way to educate for change is to develop qualities of steadfastness and loyalty rather than mere agility.

At one extreme among the adherents of the second point of view are those who regard the child's growth impulse as so pure and so adequate that the educator's chief responsibility is to avoid interfering with it lest he distort or corrupt it. Although some of Dewey's disciples, including Kilpatrick, have found this notion appealing, it seems appropriate for the most part for the mythical society in which Rousseau's "noble savage" was imagined to have existed. Confronted by the complexities of current civilization, most of those who are prepared to be called progressives have emphasized the necessity of selecting and making available those experiences that will provide a satisfactory introduction to the many facets of living. Realizing that the provision of only one possible course of action for the individual to choose gives him no choice at all, their stress is on the range of activities that will permit the exercise and development of every constructive human talent and capacity. Those who are realistic recognize quite frankly that the preservation of human society requires the acceptance of certain values and of certain restraints on individual freedom. While they accept the necessity of imposing these with force where reason fails, they expect them to be defensible on rational grounds. Within the minimum of necessary restraints, the learner makes the essential choice of his own experiences. When these are selected on the basis of his own growth needs, the result is true learning which becomes a part of himself. What is imposed in the absence of these conditions is not regarded as learning at all, but as a fraud. The progressive is willing to concede that many an individual, if left to make his own choice, will reject the strongest inducements and refuse to learn. The reason, they claim, is that his natural drive toward growth has been perverted, atrophied, or destroyed by repressive and hostile influences. If he has indeed reached this state, however, they see nothing to be gained by using compulsion.

The progressive does not believe that the proper way for the child to develop the capacity to tolerate discomfort, frustration, and failure is by experiencing them at the dictate of an adult or of an artificial system. If he is ever going to take them in his stride, he will do so because of the sense of self-confidence and mastery that come from achievement within the limits of his ability.

While acknowledging the variations among the schools of progressive thought, Paul Goodman has claimed that all of them encompass the following positions:

To learn theory by experiment and doing.
To learn belonging by participation and self-rule.
Permissiveness in all animal behavior and interpersonal expression.
Emphasis on individual differences.
Unblocking and training feeling by plastic arts, eurhythmics and dramatics.

Tolerance of races, classes, and cultures.
Group therapy as a means of solidarity, in the staff meeting and community meeting.
Taking youth seriously as an age in itself.
Community of youth and adults, minimizing "authority".
Educational use of the actual physical plant (buildings and farms) and the culture of the school community.
Emphasis in the curriculum on real problems of wider society, its geography and history, with actual participation in the neighboring community (village or city).
Trying for functional interrelation of activities.[2]

John Dewey, the leading contributor to progressive thought in education, depicted an ideal school, which would have many of the characteristics of life outside, including opportunities for democratic co-operation with fellow pupils under the guidance of teachers. Each pupil would have contacts with a variety of teachers while engaged in various activities. The whole atmosphere would be one of informality and spontaneity. Discipline would be intrinsic rather than being imposed by a teacher. Each pupil would be encouraged to attain the highest standards of achievement, not by studying subject matter organized in its traditional forms, but as adapted to meet his own recognized needs. Wholesome play would be regarded as an integral part of the learning experience. The school would absorb an increased part of the child's life with fewer holidays and shorter vacations. There would be no segregation on the basis of intellectual and practical tasks.

Central to Dewey's educational philosophy was his statement that

> This educational process has two sides – one psychological and one sociological – and neither can be subordinated to the other, or neglected, without evil results following. Of these two sides, the psychological is the basis. The child's own instincts and powers furnish the material and give the starting point for all education. Save as the efforts of the educator connect with some activity which the child is carrying on of his own initiative independent of the educator, education becomes reduced to a pressure from without. It may, indeed, give certain external results, but cannot truly be called educative. Without insight into the psychological structure and activities of the individual, the educative process will, therefore, be haphazard and arbitrary. If it chances to coincide with the child's activity it will get a leverage; if it does not, it will result in friction, or distintegration [*sic*], or arrest of the child-nature.[3]

The differences between the traditionalist and the progressive approaches to educational aims and methods are a product of the complexities of civilized life. Under primitive conditions, the experiences the adult chooses and the skills he prescribes for the child are so obviously useful and necessary in the latter's eyes that he does not question his obligation to acquire them if he wishes to survive. He has the strongest possible motive for learning to gather and preserve food and to defend himself against animals or enemies from other tribes. When a margin of safety and security develops, alternatives become possible and freedom is a reality. Educators can then divide themselves on the basis of their opinion on how much freedom the immature child should be accorded and on the relationship between his exercise of freedom in childhood and his performance as an adult. They can argue about the validity of trying to prepare him to attain remote or intangible goals which have no bearing on his immediate sense of reality.

In the entire history of civilization, there has been little evidence of a serious effort to depart from the traditionalist approach to formal education. The traditionalists are often tempted to say that what has been so obviously prevalent is more likely than not to have been right. The progressives can maintain that man has limped along his erratic upward path carrying a great deal of useless baggage, but that the perilous conditions of modern life demand something better. The very continuation of civilization may hinge on the more effective tapping of creative and dynamic human forces that have hitherto been only partly utilized.

Many educators have a strong antipathy to the idea of being identified with a particular camp. Their inclination is to soften the edges of theory in the conduct of practical affairs. Dewey observed that much of the conflict between the traditionalists and the progressives was to be attributed to the extremes of practice adopted by each group. The subject matter chosen by the traditionalists was static, remote from the learner's view of reality, and taught as a finished product. It exerted so little intrinsic appeal, even though artfully disguised by good teachers, that it had to be imposed with great firmness and resolution. The situation demanded an attitude of docility and obedience on the part of the learner. On the other hand, he thought it a great mistake for progressive educators to proceed on the basis of a negative reaction to everything related to traditionalist practice. They should be asking about the meaning of subject matter and of organization within experience. While rejecting the ready-made organization of the past, they must not reject the principle of organization. While opposing external control, they must look for the factors of control that were inherent within experience. External authority should be replaced, not by chaos, but by a more effective form of authority. The fact that the knowledge and skills of the adult were not to be imposed arbitrarily on the child did not mean that they had no value for the child. The necessity of looking to the future did not negate the value of a study of the past.[4]

To suggest that the extremes can be softened in practice does not, of course, constitute a defence of an educator whose views are a mere hodgepodge of vague notions without any coherence or logical consistency.

However effectively the extremes may be compromised, there is a clear distinction between learning experiences chosen by the adult on the basis of external criteria and those selected in response to the learner's identifiable needs. A teacher who wavers back and forth between the two positions can hardly be an effective exponent of either and is likely to succeed only in appearing to be shallow or hypocritical. Whether an educational system can operate successfully according to progressive principles at one level and traditional principles at another also seems problematical. Some further observations on this point are reserved for a discussion of the views of the Royal Commission on Education, which reported in 1950.

No less an authority than Bertrand Russell seems to have taken a view that is diametrically opposed to that just offered and to have claimed that a good school system must have elements of conflicting philosophies.

> Three divergent theories of education all have their advocates in the present day. Of these the first considers that the sole purpose of education is to provide opportunities of growth and to remove hampering influences. The second holds that the purpose of education is to give culture to the individual and to develop his capacities to the utmost. The third holds that education is to be considered rather in relation to the community than in relation to the individual, and that its business is to train useful citizens. Of these theories the first is the newest while the third is the oldest. The second and third theories have in common the view that education can give something positive, while the first regards its function as purely negative. No actual education proceeds wholly and completely on any one of the three theories. All three in varying proportions are found in every system that actually exists. It is, I think, fairly clear that no one of the three is adequate by itself, and that the choice of a right system of education depends in great measure upon the adoption of a due proportion between the three theories. For my part, while I think that there is more truth in the first theory, which we may call the negative view of education, I do not think that it contains by any means the whole truth.[5]

It could hardly have been by offering the kind of opinion contained in the second last sentence that Russell won his reputation as a philosopher.

WAYS OF DEFINING AIMS

The traditionalist educator has a characteristic way of approaching the definition of educational aims. He identifies a series of spheres in which he expects the educated adult to operate and simply states that the educational process must ensure that the child is equipped, intellectually, physically, morally, and socially, to perform with maximum effectiveness in each sphere. Thus if he is to be a parent, a citizen, a worker, a beneficiary and transmitter of culture, a member of various social groupings, a child of God, etc, he must be educated to do all these things successfully. The task for the educator, unless he unthinkingly perpetuates practices handed down to him, is the straightforward, although never easy, one of deciding what kinds of behaviour will lead to the achievement of each aim. This process usually involves listing numerous goals with varying degrees of specificity which constitute components of, or half-way stations to, the aim. To be a good citizen, for example, one needs to know one's legal rights and obligations, one needs to know the issues relating to voting for representatives at various levels of government, one needs a healthy attitude toward authority, including an understanding of when to obey and when to criticize. A curriculum is then devised to enable the learner to acquire the skills, knowledge, and attitudes to become a good citizen. Different societies will define different aims with different priorities, sometimes by a conscious, but often by an unconscious, process. A rapidly changing society needs to subject its educational aims to constant scrutiny to ensure that they remain appropriate. More and more commonly, it also evaluates the process by which it tries to achieve these aims.

The progressive may be equally concerned that the child will emerge as an effective adult in various roles which his own nature and his social milieu demand. He places much less stress, however, on the definition of these roles and does not attempt to mark out in detail the paths by which they are to be reached. He possesses a faith and, if he is honest, he will admit that it is faith rather than the fruit of some specially brilliant logical deduction, that the individual's impulse to growth, if sympathetically nourished and stimulated, will lead him to become a good parent, citizen, friend, and whatever else is desirable in the civilized human being.

THE INFLUENCE OF SPENCER ON THE PROCESS OF DEFINING EDUCATIONAL AIMS

Herbert Spencer exerted a great deal of influence on attempts to define educational aims during the nineteenth and twentieth centuries. His approach was related to his classification, in order of importance, of the leading activities constituting human life: 1 / activities directly ministering to self-preservation; 2 / activities which, by providing the necessities of life, indirectly contribute to self-preservation; 3 / activities directed toward the rearing and discipline of offspring; 4 / activities involving the maintenance of proper social and political relations; 5 / miscellaneous activities which make up the leisure part of life and are devoted to the gratification of the tastes and feelings. Aims of education formulated in accordance with these principles were highly utilitarian. Spencer placed strong emphasis on the practical and consigned cultural subjects to the leisure part of education.

There are obvious dangers in the way utility is defined. It has become increasingly evident in modern industrialized society that the most direct and straightforward occupational preparation may actually minister much less effectively to self-preservation than a less obvious route through a more highly intellectual or cultural program. There is certainly no room in Spencer's approach for studies that are judged worthy of inclusion in the curriculum only through blind faith. It has been suggested, however, that he was so preoccupied with the means of creating civilization that he overlooked the question of the values by which it was to be justified.

AIMS IN PIONEER ONTARIO

There is not much evidence of deliberate soul-searching about the aims of education in Upper Canada in the early part of the nineteenth century. There is no doubt, however, that there were definite expectations of the schools. They would not otherwise have been maintained at a far greater relative sacrifice on the part of the pioneer settler than the vastly more expensive institutions of today impose on the presumably overburdened taxpayer. Quite different sets of aims underlay the earliest grammar and common schools. The first were quite deliberately designed to produce educated gentlemen to participate in the administration of the colony according to the paternalistic procedures that were employed at a time when democracy was inclined to be regarded as a dangerous virus. Since the means of producing the desired product had been completely worked out in the old world, it was necessary merely to arrange for the transplantation of the heavily classical curriculum in use in Great Britain. The common schools, in contrast, were designed for the settler who would normally be expected to earn a livelihood in farming, in other extractive industries, in transportation, or in uncomplicated commercial activities. The understood aims of the common school were to give him such skills to communicate and calculate as were needed in these activities. The ability to read the Bible enabled him to keep his moral standards on a high level and thus merited the encouragement of those in authority. Apart from these factors, there was a general respect for learning which no doubt stemmed from an awe of the social elite, who had special opportunities to acquire it. It is also not beyond belief, even in a cynical age, that many had a high regard for learning simply for its own sake.

There were certain breezes of thought blowing in the young republic to the south which failed to raise much dust across the Canadian border. Thomas Jefferson, for example, saw education as a means of raising up a citizenry that would appreciate, expand, and defend freedom. He saw a study of history, for example, as contributing to this end. In Upper Canada, the prevailing virtue was not a love of liberty but loyalty to existing institutions and values. Education often seemed to resist the democratic transformation of society rather than to aid it.

For decades there was little sign of a modification in the traditionalist orientation of the school program. This does not mean, of course, that there was no change in the atmosphere of the school. Reports from teachers' conferences and topics chosen by speakers on educational matters indicate a weakening of confidence in the value of abstract precept, and there was less empty moralizing. Handling of pupils' transgressions reflected the growing humaneness of Canadian society. Yet the school program continued to be made up of a set of prescriptions consisting of what adults thought best represented the culture or what they thought most useful for the child to learn. There was little evident attempt to organize subject matter in accordance with the child's interests or psychological make-up.

AIMS IDENTIFIED IN THE PROGRAM OF STUDIES FOR 1937

The *Programme of Studies for Grades I to VI of the Public and Separate Schools, 1937* demonstrated a highly progressive orientation and might have set the schools of Ontario on an entirely new path had certain circumstances been more propitious. The main reason why the point of view expressed in the document was "ahead of its time" was that the short period of preparation for elementary teachers during the post-war years made it impossible to induce them to abandon the patterns by which they themselves had been taught.

In the *Programme*, evidence about the nature of the child's development was said to support the conviction that the child develops by virtue of his own activity. This activity consisted of both knowing and doing, which were to be regarded as synonymous terms, each implying purposeful effort. Each child's plan of development was to be determined by his own nature. The realities on which the school was urged to build were described as follows.

> Children of elementary school age are active and inquisitive, delighting in movement, in small tasks which they can perform with deftness and skill, and in the sense of visible and tangible accomplishments which such tasks offer. They are intensely interested in the character and purpose of the material objects around them. They are at once absorbed in creating their own miniature world of imagination and emotion, and keen observers who take pleasure in reproducing their observations by speech and dramatic action; and still engaged in mastering a difficult and unfamiliar language, without knowing they are doing so, because it is a means of communicating with others.[6]

The school was to achieve its aims by stimulating the child through his own interests and by guiding him into experiences that would help him to satisfy his own needs.

There was said to be no use in teaching the child things which had no immediate value for him. His own needs and capacities were to be the criteria by which appropriate educational experiences were to be selected. Account was to be taken of his need to live with others and to live as they approved. The writers did not seem overly apprehensive about overdoing social adjustment at the expense of individuality. The aims of the curriculum were "to develop in the child his physical powers and to train him in their proper use and control, to awaken him to the fundamental interests of civilized life so far as they lie within the compass of childhood, and to encourage him to attain to the orderly management of his energies, impulses, and emotions which is the basis of desirable attitudes."[7]

The physical welfare of the child was identified as fundamental because he was, first of all, a growing organism. As part of the human family, he was to learn to be an active, co-operative, and intelligent member of society. The curriculum was to give him the means of thought and communication in language and number. Through reading, he would come in contact with other minds and discover that life has a past and future as well as a present. He would acquire some information about the physical environment as the home of man. He would develop the capacity to create and appreciate beauty through participation in a variety of aesthetic activities. While the attainment of adult standards in various areas of study would not be demanded, he would be expected to develop habits of thoroughness and honesty in his work:

> ... in the elementary school a child should learn, within the limits of his experience, to use the noble instrument of his native language with clearness and dignity; that he should acquire simple kinds of manual skill and take pleasure in using them; that he should admire what is admirable in form and design; that he should read some good books with zest and enjoyment; that he should acquire bodily poise and balance, a habit of natural and expressive motion, not merely as physical accomplishments, but as the outward sign and symbol of our common culture and civilization; and that he should learn that the behaviour of the physical universe is not arbitrary or capricious, but governed by principles some at least of which it is possible for him to grasp.[8]

The Hall-Dennis Committee later declared that there was only one immediately noticeable exception to the general observation that virtually every idea in the *Programme* might have been expressed by educationally enlightened and advanced authors in the current period. That exception was apparently the recommendation that the curriculum be pervaded by religion, which was not, however, to be taught as a separate subject. While the individual teacher was to determine how religious attitudes could best be developed, it was suggested that school activity should include the reverent singing of simple hymns, and that the parables of Jesus and the great human stories of the Old Testament should become the familiar possessions of every child.

The *Programme* had a number of suggestions about how the recommended aims might be realized. The grade system was not to be rigid or inflexible. The work of any particular grade was not necessarily to require the work of a full school year. Some bright children might cover the six grades in five years, or even four, while in other cases provision was to be made for enrichment. The organization of three streams might be feasible in some of the large urban schools. In some courses, the work of two or three grades might be combined and arranged in successive cycles. The elementary school was said to have no business with uniform standards of attainment. "The only uniformity at which the elementary school should aim is that every child at the end of the course should have acquired the power to attack new work and feel a zest in doing so."[9]

The teacher, and not the child, was to select the topics for study within the broad areas outlined by the curriculum. In this sense, the *Programme* did not advocate a thoroughgoing progressive approach. The fact that the selection was not made by a departmental official and prescribed for the teacher to follow was as advanced a position as one could expect for that time. It was at least possible to make adaptations to suit the interests and capacities of individual pupils. That this could be done would obviate the unwholesome pressure of an examination for the purposes of promotion. Frequent tests were to be used as a basis for the modification of teaching and for remedial work. "What is necessary ... if we wish children to retain certain 'facts' is not to require that they be memorized for an examination, but to clothe those facts with interest and provide opportunities for their use – this, we think, teachers can and will do if given the necessary freedom."[10]

Attention was called to a circular issued a short time earlier which advised inspectors to discourage unreasonable amounts of homework for elementary school pupils. Children at that stage were said to be consuming most of their energies in physical development and to need time for rest and recreation. Between grades 1 and 6 they were considered to have ample time during the school day to cover their work satisfactorily without having the burden of additional school work to be done at home. It is perhaps worth observing that this exhortation was not being universally heeded in Ontario schools even in 1970. Certain traditional practices indeed die hard.

CONTRIBUTIONS OF THE ROYAL COMMISSION

The Royal Commission on Education devoted an early chapter to aims of education, a subject on which it made a much greater effort to accommodate all its members than it did in tackling the separate school question. It proclaimed the virtues of understanding different points of view rather than of selecting a consistent and coherent set of principles and acting in accordance with them.

> Experienced educators and thoughtful parents ... realize the difficulty of applying any one theory ... under all circumstances and to all young people. They have studied the views of others with an open mind and have come to appreciate the reasons for views which modify or are contrary to their own.[11]

The commissioners apparently refused to recognize the possibility that serious thought about issues might produce irreconcilable differences rather than a happy consensus, and that a conscientious and sincere person might not be able to submerge his convictions in a flood of sentimental good will.

The commissioners attempted a layman's definition of the two basic philosophical orientations. The oversimplified result of their efforts came out this way: "We may think of the traditionalist as one who believes in strict discipline and the mastering of school subjects, and of the progressive as one who puts emphasis on interest and learning by experience."[12] If strict discipline is to be thought of as the kind that is imposed by irrational authority with the possibility of physical force constantly hovering in the background, the progressives, of course, would want none of it. But they would certainly want to be counted as favouring the development of strong self-discipline in the learner. They might also be positively impressed to see children mastering school subjects, in traditional form or otherwise, provided that such activity was in response to a recognized need. In fact, they might suggest that effort to fill a felt need is the only real way to master school subjects or anything else. For his part, a traditionalist might place a high value on learner interest and go to great lengths to arouse and sustain it, although he would insist that effort continue even when interest has palled.

The paragraphs that followed in the commission's report presented a much more satisfying elaboration of the two fundamental orientations than was afforded by the initial definition. The particular syndrome that gives rise to the traditionalist approach to education was described in this way:

> ... some people are influenced more consistently than others by anything which has deep personal significance for them. Nearly everyone holds his own life dear, has loved-ones whom he regards with peculiar affection, and sets a special value on his own possessions. But people vary in the degree of their personal attachment, especially when the list is extended to ideas, habits, and institutions: the church and tenets of faith; the school attended and type of schooling received; one's native or adopted country; and any way of doing things that has brought success or satisfaction ...
>
> With this background, it is not difficult to understand why some people are insistent that a greater effort should be made in school to ensure a passionate love of country, strong personal attachment to established ways of living, knowledge and appreciation of cultural achievements, and acceptance of recognized values and articles of faith. Strict discipline is frequently demanded because it is needed to achieve these specific ends.[13]

The progressive point of view was subsequently explained with the attention to the pragmatic view of truth that the later Hall-Dennis Committee neglected to, or dared not, give it.

Many others ... are reluctant to assert the universal or abiding truth of any belief, principle, or criterion of value. They regard it as self-evident that learning is essential to life, and they assume that free access to facts and ideas, and the disclosure of full information, are at once rights and obligations. But they do not believe that it is possible to make any general statement that must always be accepted by others as true. They may assume that fullness of life is good, and that what restricts or curtails life is bad. They refuse, however, to prescribe any set pattern of living for others, or to limit the meaning of "good" or "bad" by prescribed rules of conduct. From their assumptions it may follow that deception and violence are wrong and that honesty and equity are right. But they prefer not to speak in terms of "should" and "ought", or "sin" and "evil", because they believe that values have meaning for others only as they arise in experience and operate in practice.[14]

This passage, along with the subsequent references to the progressive's faith in democracy as an ideal and a way of life and to his confidence in the results of the application of scientific method to human affairs, is a good interpretation within a very restricted space, of the fundamental tenets of Deweyism.

Coming closer to the specific approaches to education which the progressive supports, the section continued:

Instead of insisting on a knowledge of history, civics, and national literature to inculcate patriotism, they would have pupils investigate modern problems in social studies in order to extend their understanding of the world. Instead of requiring acceptance by young persons of values, beliefs, and modes of behaviour, they would encourage critical and honest inquiry in every field. They would rely chiefly on the inherent interest of students in their work, and they would allow the learners to discipline themselves. In their opinion, no subject or organized scheme of knowledge should be held to be of value in itself. They maintain that the important thing in the learning situation is what happens to the learner and that, unless the pupil sees a genuine need for learning what is taught, he may acquire notions and attitudes decidedly at variance with the course of study and the teacher's intentions. It is as vain, they say, to expect that insistence on memory of organized facts will result in predictable knowledge and wisdom as it is to think that mental gymnastics in a subject such as mathematics will train the mind to cope with any problem of life. Accordingly, they contend that the school should broaden its scope to provide for the full development of the whole child and to meet the needs of different individuals. From this point of view, the content and method of instruction should have all the vitality of out-of-school experience; for learning is the reconstruction of experience and not merely the memory of facts and mastery of skills.[15]

Despite their pose of benevolent tolerance of opposing points of view, the commissioners did not manage to stay on the fence but rather slid off on the traditionalist side as if not quite fully aware of what they were doing. Their position became clear when they supplemented their declared allegiance to individual rights by a reference in support of obligatory subject matter and other external controls on the school and pupil: the schools were trying to "produce" a certain type of pupil; "some young people are ready to accept any statement without question, prefer to be told what to do, and need to be compelled to do it."[16] At this point, they seemed close to the absurdity of suggesting that the progressive orientation is appropriate for some individuals and the traditionalist for others.

They singled out two cardinal virtues which they identified as beyond dispute: honesty and Christian love. Apparently Jewish love or Buddhist love would not do. These virtues were to be taught, by precept and example, as absolute truths or eternal verities which everyone must accept, defend, and strive to practise. The school's obligation to inculcate them was justified on the grounds that they were essential for the preservation of our society. Those who later applied the term "sermon" in a derogatory fashion to the Hall-Dennis report should review passages like this.

The enemy of honesty and love in action is the ubiquitous demon named selfishness. The church, in particular, must build and continuously strengthen the spiritual foundations of the basic virtues. The home must provide security for their growth in understanding and practice. School, home, and church should stand together to counteract more effectively those influences in society which offer rewards for selfishness.[17]

The present generation, no less than any other, is calling out for more love and more honesty in personal and social relationships. However, the threat of destruction from man's treatment of his physical environment and other consequences of ignorant behaviour, well-intentioned or otherwise, may have shifted the emphasis in recent years in the direction of such qualities as intelligence and foresight.

The commission declared that the pursuit of truth must be the main purpose of education in a democracy. This is not quite the same as the Hall-Dennis committee's later assertion that the underlying aim of education is to further man's unending search for truth, since it lacks the individual emphasis. The commission demonstrated clearly that it had no confidence that the exercise of freedom in childhood would lead to right actions. It declared on the one hand that the learner's loyalty (a major virtue) would have "the strength of sincerity" if an object were accepted as good after thorough and frank investigation. Yet honesty and Christian love, being absolutes of a free society, were to be taught by the strongest means at the school's command – by indoctrination, if necessary. Since these absolutes were justified by reason, the fact that each new generation had to be induced to accept them through indoctrination suggested that adults had the power to reason while children did not. Yet adults could go astray, as the report suggested the Nazis and Communists had done. Again it appeared that a democratic system would ensure that the true virtues would be identified, and selfishness recognized as the main threat to organized society. Some of the commission's confidence in its proposals seem, in the light of its evident lack of awareness of the complexities of the problems it was supposed to be grappling with, more than a little naïve.

On the issue of the interests of society versus the child's exercise of freedom, the commission had quite unequivocal advice. The school was to declare in effect:

> These are the standards and rules of conduct of the society to which we belong. Some you will recognize as unquestionably right, binding at all times on all of us, and therefore to be followed regardless of consequence. About others there will be disagreement. Some of these you should examine carefully to see where and how they should apply, some you will have to accept tentatively as right until you are in a position to decide for yourself. But, in every case, whatever other sanction they may have, these are rules which most people have declared to be necessary for living together. They make our way of living possible. Therefore, even where there is no clear issue of absolute right and wrong, everyone is obliged to obey these rules or pay the penalty of social disapproval ... Those in charge of this school are bound to tell you about these standards and rules of conduct, and to insist that you learn in the beginning to live in the way that society approves and not in a way that will certainly be to your disadvantage and that, indeed, may be disastrous.[18]

One may well agree with the commission that this approach is heavily weighted on the side of conformity. It sounds archaic, also, in that it shows little sign of recognizing the dilemmas of life in the society of twenty years later. The school loses the child's respect if it assumes a certainty about the rules of conduct that is not reflected in practice outside. It is often found enforcing conformity to customs that are generally being abandoned.

The commission's proposals for curricular organization were an apparent attempt to compromise between opposing orientations by employing a relatively progressive approach in the early years and a traditional approach later. Society's requirements of the beginner would be held to the bare minimum of mastery of the ordinary means of communication to the extent employed in everyday affairs. These means would include spelling and arithmetic and the ability to use and understand direct and simple English. Apart from these basics, the child would have wide freedom of choice in the world of ideas, the arts, and physical activities. The imposition of rigid methods of teaching and of examinations would not be allowed to stifle the growth of desirable attitudes and abilities. Between the "small enclosure of necessary skills" and the broad range of varied interests would be a "middle ground where obligation and freedom must blend." This meant that the teacher would encourage a choice of learning activities connected with human relations through a study of history and literature and through practice in living and working together.

> To an increasing degree pupils should be able, as they mature, to choose their reading material and, in social studies, to carry on their own investigations, conduct their own conferences, and keep their own records. In all subjects and activities they should grow in capacity to evaluate their own achievement. As powers such as these are acquired, the need for external pressure grows less and less.[19]

Even the most permissive educator could hardly but be happy with this passage. It turns out, however, that the commissioners were discussing an educational diet that was to be confined to childhood. By the age of sixteen, they suggested, students should spend nearly all their time studying subject matter according to the conventional organization. The reason for the change? The commissioners offered no better answer than that it would be rash to suggest any radical departure from the established trend. The best they could do was to recommend a less sudden shift away from the experience concept than was currently taking place in the schools.

As they themselves described it, existing practice does not sound very prepossessing. By the time the pupil reached grade 7, he and the teacher were so occupied with subject matter organized into separate categories that they had "little time for thinking of life situations in school." Motivation had "changed from an interest in life and a desire to learn something obviously worth while, to a desire to please, or to escape trouble, by learning something which the teacher says has value."[20] As we read such an account, we wait for the denunciation that we think must surely follow; but what we get is a feeble statement that at least the child, by this procedure, learns something of the accomplishments of man in the past, of current practice, and of facts or values arranged in an accepted pattern. The commissioners expressed approval of the satisfaction gained from examination marks.

We can almost tell at this stage what to expect of the commissioners in the way of a list of educational aims. As such lists go, it is quite a satisfactory one. The Hall-Dennis committee expressed approval, despite the fact that its educational prescription, at least at the higher age levels, was entirely different. The list was given as follows:

A. To develop capacity to apprehend and practise basic virtues.
B. To develop the power to think clearly, independently, and courageously.

C. To develop talent to understand the views of others and to express one's own views effectively.
D. To develop competence for a suitable occupation.
E. To develop good health.
F. To develop aptitudes for recreation.
G. To develop characteristics for happy family relations.
H. To develop good citizenship.
I. To develop the concept that education is a continuing process beyond the school.

In the subsequent pages, the home and the church were recognized as the essential allies of the school in realizing aims such as the first. In that sense, it may be said that some limit on the school's capacities was acknowledged. Yet there was no critical estimate of how far the school could reasonably be expected to go, such as that contained in Bereiter's appraisal of the Hall-Dennis report (see chapter 14). The committee offered instead a flood of sentimental moralizing.

TRENDS IN THE EARLY POST-WAR PERIOD

Views of J.G. Althouse

J.G. Althouse, an undisputed educational leader of his day, was a voluble exponent of the old-fashioned virtues that characterized pioneer days, or at least later perceptions of them. He proclaimed in one of his Quance Lectures in 1949:

> These are grim days; we must not shrink from bringing young people to the discovery that everything worth while involves a cost as well as a reward, and that the cost comes first. For this reason the high school, especially in the higher grades, must demand a measure of practical success that may appear harsh and exacting. The high school pupil is to be taught to achieve, not to account for failure; he is to be led to exert effort, not to be politely idle or to simulate interest with no real enthusiasm ...
>
> Self-expression is a necessary step in development, but the school must be quite as much concerned about the kind of "selves" to be expressed as about the opportunities for expressing them. Our national tradition and the present world situation both suggest strongly that we need a host of "selves" which can find true expression in the performance of many unobtrusive, often distasteful, and sometimes dangerous tasks which must be done if we and our way of life are to be preserved. It is in our high schools and in our homes that these "selves" are best developed.[21]

There is something extremely impressive, even awesome, about the old-fashioned educator who had not yet passed from the scene even a generation ago. It was no discredit to him that he was hardly aware of the intellectual cross-currents of his own day. He had a serene confidence in the basic virtues, which he had little trouble identifying or defining. The freedom of the individual meant, in the ultimate sense, freedom to choose right. Such an educator, who often radiated compassion and concern, left a profound influence on many a student. What might otherwise have appeared to be a boring or distasteful task became a heady challenge, because success was crowned with his approval. A compliment from him was more than an indication of personal benevolence, but carried with it the assurance that one was really on the right path.

While Althouse's views were the antithesis of radicalism, he saw the school as a disturbing influence in society. With its unrelenting insistence on the highest ideals, it could not help drawing attention to social and economic practices which did not measure up. He seemed to feel that this influence would prove to be a constructive one. There was possibly little reason to foresee, even twenty years ago, that a considerable group of young people would conclude that adult society, including the school, was too corrupt to be worth saving.

The Dunlop philosophy

W.J. Dunlop, a contemporary of Althouse, was known for his stress on the fundamentals and for his belief in the necessity of inculcating the pioneer virtues. The following passage, which appeared under his signature in the *Report of the Minister, 1953*, is a fairly good résumé of his attitude toward the aims of education.

> Special attention has been given to thorough instruction in the basic fundamentals of education – those skills with which every citizen should be familiar if he is to be equipped to make a good living and to live a good life. For this type of instruction there can be no substitute. Pupils must have plenty of hard work in school if they are to be qualified to undertake in adult life those difficult tasks which they confront as they travel the road to success. Boys and girls must learn that they owe a duty to the country in which they are privileged to live – a duty which can best be fulfilled by working as the pioneers worked, by having regard to the rights of their fellow-citizens, by striving to be strong, healthy, loyal, and religious men and women. Such citizens the schools of this Province are endeavouring, with a great measure of success, to produce.[22]

It did not take any Russian successes in the scientific field to produce an extreme traditionalist approach, at least at the top, in Ontario. At a time when the schools were barely being kept open with the aid of ill-trained teachers, there was little strength in the system to oppose Dunlop's views, nor even much sign of a desire to do so.

VIEWS EXPRESSED IN CONNECTION WITH THE SECOND CANADIAN CONFERENCE ON EDUCATION, 1962

The preparations for the Second Canadian Conference on Education in 1962, which spawned a number of other gatherings of greater or lesser importance, including the Ontario Conference on Education in November 1961, gave rise to an orgy of writing and speaking on a great many matters of educational concern. The decision to devote the first day of the conference to the discussion of aims gave that topic an unusual degree of attention. The preliminary booklet and the conference addresses were prepared by a series of educational leaders deliberately selected for their different points of view. Thus a brief review of the major contributions will give some impression of the range and nature of the ideas being propounded at the beginning of the decade.

Contribution of C.E. Phillips

In preparing a paper for the publication, *The Aims of Education*, designed to give participants in the conference some food for thought before their momentous deliberations, C.E. Phillips left no doubt about his Deweyite orientation. His first paragraph scorned the whole process in which he had agreed to engage.

> Statements of educational aims have little effect on classroom practice of teachers, who are kept busy doing what they have to do. Effective aims are worked out and made explicit (if at all) through the operation of the school in its social setting. But discussion of aims is a pleasurable exercise. People enjoy what they do well, and we in the modern western world may claim without boasting to be pretty good at anything which calls for a large measure of hypocrisy, as does the formulation of lofty objectives.[23]

Phillips declared himself unable to distinguish clearly or sharply between the physical and the mental, the intellectual and the emotional, or the functions of the school and the home. He saw education as the modification of human behaviour, its success to be measured, not by what a person is, or claims to be or believe, but what he does. In this light, knowledge seemed most appropriately considered in terms of whether or not it is operative in the life of the pupil.

While acknowledging that aims are determined mainly by values, he declared that values do not exist at the beginning of experience but arise out of experience. They are adopted as they are tested in practice. Initially, at least, the pupil's values are different from those of the teacher. The teacher can make the pupil go through the motions, but he cannot effectively impose a set of values. Phillips condensed his ideas about educational aims.

The chief educational aim of the Canadian people should be to get teachers for publicly supported schools who can and will use the school curriculum effectively to help young people realize their full potentialities and, specifically, to achieve the following purposes:

1. To have pupils learn the means of communication.
2. To develop responsibility.
3. To encourage some knowledge of the past and an alert understanding of current developments.
4. To encourage active participation in aesthetic and social activities.[24]

These same aims were to apply to the majority of pupils in higher secondary grades who were continuing a general education. For those specializing in an academic program at this level, a fifth aim would be to acquire scholarly knowledge of academic subjects. For those specializing in non-academic vocational programs, the alternative would be to develop the will and ability to do conscientious work in the occupations for which they were prepared.

Lest anyone get the impression that he was of the extreme permissive school, Phillips emphasized that there was no argument about the value of high achievement in comprehenison of the native language and in arithmetic. Disagreement had to do with methods of teaching and with subsidiary content. The teacher had a difficult task in getting the pupil to appreciate the subtleties of language and to strive for excellence in using it as a means of communication. Arithmetic would be taught as a means of enabling the pupil to deal with the problems he encountered in life. Phillips saw considerable value in the skill of working quickly with approximate numbers – the kind of thing that could not be taught by drill. Consistent with the principle that learning should be functional, he rejected the idea that children who had no opportunity to practise a second language should spend their time learning it in preparation for some remote occasion when they might have an opportunity to use it. Such a notion ignored the deterioration that rapidly destroys unused skills. Thus he stood against the enthusiasm being expressed at the time for teaching French to children in areas where the language was seldom or never spoken.

Responsibility was to be developed as the child increasingly managed his own affairs in accordance with his capacity. The process was to be guided by parents and teachers who were themselves sincere and honest. Phillips warned that the goal of responsibility was not to be attained without cost.

Upbringing for responsibility releases the child from obligation to conform in particular ways, so that there can be no assurance that he will learn to play the piano, choose law as his profession, or be a continuing Presbyterian. Individuality is encouraged. Adults who above all want the younger generation to adhere to cherished patterns must aim at conformity, not at responsibility.[25]

Phillips had strong criticism for those who advocated that the child be taught to think and yet were prepared to allow him to arrive only at predetermined conclusions. He found it particularly reprehensible on the part of the public to persecute teachers who actually encouraged original thought.

Beyond the basic elements of communication, Phillips thought it a mistake to strain for exacting standards as measured by examinations. To do so would be to encourage teaching for factual recall and run the risk of killing potential interest in such subjects as history, geography, and literature. There was a good chance that the pupil would develop the desire to learn more if he began with "spectacular developments which fire the imagination." As to the balance between past and present, Phillips acknowledged the forces that were tending to swing the emphasis away from the former but managed to find a good word for the study of ancient history. He was not ready to repudiate his earlier career as a teacher of the classics.

He was not in favour of the balanced program for everyone. He could see no reason why a high school student should not be permitted to specialize in some area of aesthetic interest such as music if he had little talent for academic work. Conversely, there seemed to be no special virtue in his continuing a mediocre performance in art or music if he preferred to pursue intellectual interests.

The means by which Phillips would ensure the attainment of exacting standards in scholarship was to postpone scholarly work until those with the requisite aptitudes and interests had sorted themselves out. He claimed that academic subjects were "debased by insistence that all, or nearly all, pupils attempt to pursue a scholarly discipline on the ground that only such subjects are truly educative."[26] It did no harm to those who developed an aptitude for them to delay entry into a specialized program. They could quickly make up for any deficiencies as a select group at the higher levels. In the meantime, they needed the benefits of association with those having a wide range of abilities and interests.

Contribution of J.F. Leddy

J.F. Leddy, a Roman Catholic who became president of the reorganized and secularly controlled University of Windsor, was later a member of the Hall-Dennis Committee, and as such put his name to a report that was permeated with progressive ideas. One wonders about his opinions at this time in view of his presentation of a set of premises on the aims of education in 1962 which he frankly identified as traditional. Did he have a change of heart in the intervening years? Did he regard the committee's concern with schools, rather than with all types of educational institutions, including universities, as placing him on the periphery, where it would have seemed presumptuous to dissent?

His opposition to pragmatism as a philosophy was demonstrated in his affirmation of the belief that truth exists and that man is capable of apprehending it through the exercise of reason. He saw the individual as having his own destiny in a life endowed with direction and meaning in a larger design. He was undoubtedly correct in his assertion that these ideas appealed instinctively to most of his fellow countrymen, whether or not they had given much specific thought to the question.

Leddy thought it necessary to reject the extreme emphases on anarchic permissiveness and on excessive conformity, which he said had found a certain favour among professional educators, although never popular with the general public. He did not say whether the educators he had in mind had won acclaim in Canada or not. It is singularly difficult to think of any outstanding Canadian who has expounded either extreme.

After demanding that children be taught to think, Leddy was unprepared to accept the full consequences:

> ... rejections of free will and of an ordered meaning in life – and both denials are common with certain social scientists and philosophers of the moment – are destructive of sound educational practice, since they undermine any solid motivation on the part of student or teacher. Such perverse notions are sometimes taken seriously, especially by bright students at the university level who are attracted by the appeal of apparent novelty, and when this happens the student is likely ... to suffer considerable disintegration so far as his work and ambition are concerned.[27]

He found it disconcerting that so many European and North American writers were enthralled with the idea that life was meaningless and completely lacking in reason and dignity. Pressing on to identify the full dimensions of the menace, he wrote:

> The influence of this literary philosophy, for such it is, although it is unfortunately not generally recognized as such when it is encountered, should not be underestimated by the educator, for it is very damaging. If you wish to test this assertion, then recall the last best selling novel you have read or some recent much advertised film you have seen. Almost certainly the characters were portrayed stripped of any dignity, at the complete mercy of the emotion of the moment, acting on whim and impulse, carried along by the situation to a conclusion which was irrelevant and pointless in a story which was deliberately contrived to have no significance. Such is a major literary fashion of the day, artificial and affected, but at the same time corrosive, casually undermining by indirection every proposition which justifies education.[28]

One might have expected this account of the intellectual perils besetting modern man to be followed by some specific suggestions for containing or eliminating the threat. Instead, Leddy was immediately off on another line, proclaiming that the first aim of education should be to enable the student to communicate effectively with others, and delivering an old-fashioned lecture on the low state into which the arts of speaking and writing had fallen. It does not seem to have occurred to him that the spread of the corrosive ideas with which he was apparently so concerned might have been counteracted by preventing the development of the ability to communicate rather than by fostering it.

As a major aim, Leddy approved of the preparation of the student for the environment in which he lived, provided that environment was given a very wide interpretation, including a temporal as well as a spatial dimension. He deplored the general indifference of Canadians to the past. His reasons for advocating a study of history were familiar: it provided depth and perspective for the study of other subjects; it helped one understand the source and nature of the swift changes which the modern world was undergoing. Science was also important as a route to an understanding of many aspects of the environment and as a means of modifying and controlling natural processes and of acquiring a technique for problem solving. Space apparently prevented Leddy from reviewing all the conventional reasons for studying each element in the traditional curriculum.

In a more general realm, Leddy advocated the negative aim that education should give the student an awareness of how much he does not know. If the matter were handled in the right way, he would derive intellectual stimulation from this realization without being overwhelmed by it. A somewhat related point was that he should come to realize how great were the potentialities of man: "To establish this confidence in the great possibilities which lie ahead of mankind is probably the most important single purpose of education."[29]

Contribution of Northrop Frye

Northrop Frye, a noted literary scholar, has been an exponent of an especially coherent traditionalist point of view. Particularly concerned with the educative role of the university, he has often sounded as if he saw the work of the junior grades primarily as a preparation for work at more advanced levels.

For Frye the primary school should not be a place where the child is encouraged to follow his natural impulses and attempts to solve problems arising out of his own limited interests. It should concern itself, rather, with giving him the specific skills and information on which later education will be based. It represents the alien cultural life into which he must be initiated if he is to become truly civilized. He cannot be expected to begin the arduous process of real thought until he has undergone a long apprenticeship designed to give him the necessary equipment. The primary school, although basing its approach on sound principles of learning (a contradiction, the progressives would say), should be highly structured and prescriptive. As the child proceeds to secondary school, the controls should relax as he moves toward intellectual self-motivation, a process that he carries to completion in the university. Frye deplored the policy of covering a quantity of subject matter in preparation for an examination but suggested rather that, by the time he reached grade 13, the student should be developing the ability to organize a program of study.

In certain respects, Frye's student reaches a point where he bears considerable resemblance to the type of individual who is supposed to emerge from a progressive educational program. He is self-reliant and pursues learning because he enjoys it. Frye would say his protégé differs from the other in that he alone has a basis for appreciating standards of intellectual excellence. An absolutely irreconcilable difference between Frye and the progressives has to do with the question of social involvement. Frye maintains that it is impossible to get an objective view of society without withdrawing physically and mentally from it in order to contemplate it, as it were, from the outside. From his cloistered position, the university student can distinguish between what the world is and what humanity can do in the higher realms of art and science. The progressive, on the other hand, usually maintains that learning has meaning only in terms of its social relevance. Frye condemned this aspect of progressive theories on the following grounds.

Education ... became a matter of social adjustment to the world one must live in. But this world, in itself, provides no real standards or values. It stands for immaturity and a cult of youth, for social values rooted in entertainment and advertising, and for emotions rooted in the erotic. Besides, the world, unlike nature, always betrays the heart that loves her. It changes very rapidly, driven on by forces that the socially adjusted cannot comprehend, and can only cope with by the fixations of prejudice and stock response. Thus understanding the world, if it is to be made the goal of education, becomes acceptance of the world, and that in turn becomes increasingly an acceptance of illusion. The forms of illusion are familiar: there are the illusions of advertising and its status symbols; the illusions of slanted news, and the illusions of entertainment, where the "fixing" of a television programme or ball game is so much more emotionally disturbing than major corruption or crime. What started out as a fearless grappling with the conditions of present-day life finishes in a neurotic prison of credulity, bewilderment, and cynicism.[30]

Even below the university level, Frye sees the school fighting the rest of the student's environment to pull him toward higher educative experiences.

On one side of him is his ordinary social environment, the world of his television set, his movies, the family car, advertising, entertainment, news, and gossip. On the other side is the school, and perhaps the church, trying to dislodge him from this lotus land and prod him into further voyages of discovery ... The school has only five hours a day in which to fight the influences which keep soaking into the student from the rest of his experience, and which usually command an authority that the school cannot command. As a rule, therefore, the world of technology and rhetoric wins out, whether the student goes on to university or not. In moments of depression one feels that the majority of university students have already been conditioned beyond the point at which the university can effect [*sic*] them at all.[31]

Frye's university student does not look upon the study of a particular subject as a means to an end but rather as a worthy end in itself. In association with a respected teacher, he becomes absorbed and consumed by it. The ultimate result is a flexible and dispassionate mind capable of dealing effectively with the problems of society.

P.D. Lawlor, member of the Legislature for the Lakeshore, once delineated the educated man in terms that Frye would surely approve.

The proper education would be such as to range beyond contemporary norms ... The truly educated man would be like a man from Cassiopeia or out of the distant Arcturus, who would visit us as a stranger. He would not only be completely at home where he was born and where he was educated, he would also be a stranger in our midst. He would look at things with a cold eye, he would be able to judge them from enormous distance. The business of establishing distance, of getting away from the acceptable, of being able to make a critique of that which is offered in a spoon – that is the business of education ... [32]

Jacques Maritain seems at first glance to take a view of the relationship between education and society in direct opposition to that of Frye. He reproaches the earlier form of education for its abstract and bookish individualism and commends the more recent trend toward experience, concrete life, and social concern. He asserts, however, that the inner centre of the individual must receive primary attention if the potentialities of concrete and social experience are to be realized. For him "the pursuit of concrete life becomes a decoy if it scatters the attention of man or child among practical trifles, psychotechnical recipes, and the infinity of utilitarian activities, while disregarding the genuine concrete life of the intellect and the soul."[33] Thus his educational prescription is not so very different from Frye's after all.

Contribution of Father Marcel de Grandpré

The educational philosophy of the Roman Catholic Church as it had shaped the lives of French Canadians was explained by Father Marcel de Grandpré in the fourth essay of the collection. His treatment of the role of education in the lives of the early settlers of Quebec and his general handling of the question of aims provided a considerable contrast to the contributions of the other three authorities.

Father de Grandpré looked back with considerable nostalgia to an earlier society in which religion permeated practically every activity and event of importance in the lives of the people. The parish priest, invariably the most cultured and the best educated individual in the community, was at the centre of all the concerns of his parishioners. Not only did they bare their souls to him in the confessional, but they also went to him for assistance in civil matters in the absence of conveniently located notaries.

From infancy the child was surrounded by influences that combined to inculcate a religious outlook on life. Whether or not there was anything else to read in the house, there was always a copy of the *Catéchisme du diocèse du Québec,* composed by Monseigneur de Saint-Vallier and first printed in 1702. It contained a holy history with a summary of all the great biblical narratives and detailed references to the text of the Bible; an exposition of Christian doctrine in questions and answers, with the answers accompanied by biblical references; instruction in the meaning of fifty-nine liturgical feast days and ceremonies; Christian devotional exercises for every occasion such as before work, before and after meals, and on the stroke of the hour; and a "little catechism" consisting of the whole in abridged form. Every child learned the little catechism long before he went to school. He participated in the forms of Christian observance before he could understand their full meaning. He learned to express himself in biblical terms. From the smaller catechism, he proceeded to the larger, which he also studied intensively in the family circle. He spent the whole of every day for about two months before his first communion, which he celebrated at about eleven years of age, studying the catechism. After the ceremony, which marked his full incorporation into the religious and social community, he participated in the "catechism of perseverance" class and was given various religious duties to perform. As de Grandpré expressed it, the catechism exercised "an essential influence, and extremely profound educative action, as everyone drew from it his conception of life."[34] In short, it would be harder to imagine an example of a more effective process of indoctrination, a concept which so many modern English-speaking educators profess to find unattractive.

As the powers of his mind developed, the French Canadian found in the catechism, according to de Grandpré, considerable food for the intellect in "abstract formulas of great theological and philosophical precision." During the happy and sorrowful occasions of their lives, the successes and disappointments, they had recourse to these formulas which were registered in the memory and encountered repeatedly in Sunday sermons. They were thus assisted in forming judgments, regulating their conduct, and deriving a motive for living. De Grandpré claimed "that intellectual training extended beyond religious thought. It gave more maturity to the mind, made the intellect more supple and capable of grasping the abstract side of a problem."[35]

The passage of time greatly increased the complexity of life and involved the individual in a network of activities extending beyond the parish and the diocese. De Grandpré, however, saw the changes as only superficial. There were underlying permanent values, "an explicit philosophy of life and of society which is at the same time a philosophy of education."[36] A central reality was that man was both flesh and spirit, tending toward a beyond that was already part of existence. He developed the potentialities of his nature by life in society and by service to others. He participated simultaneously in two complementary societies, civil and religious, the respective goals of which were temporal and eternal happiness.

De Grandpré asserted that everything essential in education was produced at the individual level. He asked rhetorically how one human will succeeded in moving another and how a human intelligence caused another to understand. In answer, he declared that the teacher was powerless to communicate a good habit directly to the will of the pupil or an idea to his intellect. Education thus had to be transmitted through intermediaries. It was the personality of the teacher that constituted the educative influence.

> What takes place, first of all, in the education of the will? Let us observe, at the outset, that the teacher's behaviour translates his philosophy of life, as well as his moral value, into concrete, particular actions. This manifestation expresses not what he knows he should do, nor what he thinks, but exactly what he is, what he is worth. Through the lessons in morality, where in the teacher presents the ideal order to the intellect, the pupil is sensitive to what the teacher truly loves, to what he really feels. Therefore, it is the personality of the teacher that acts upon that of the pupil. The child's still plastic sensibility is moulded by that of his educator. It then presents to the will the external world garbed in the colours thus perceived. The natural inclinations of the will are thus favoured or hindered.[37]

De Grandpré recognized the awesome responsibility placed on the educator to be the kind of personal model that the moulding of the pupil's will required. He saw some protection against a mediocre teacher in the fact that the pupil was subject, not merely to the influence of one personality, but to that of the whole environment.

In de Grandpré's paper, we have a powerful exposition of the reason Roman Catholic educators, in provinces other than Quebec, have insisted so firmly on having their own separate schools. The formation of certain attitudes and the acceptance of certain values is seen as dependent on the whole environment of education rather than being identifiable with specific provision for religious instruction. The desired attitudes and values are absorbed rather than being directly taught. Thus Roman Catholic aims cannot be realized in secular schools. This view does not, of course, answer the question of how minority separate schools should be financially supported.

In certain respects, the educational philosophy outlined by de Grandpré showed a certain similarity to that earlier identified as progressive. He saw the pupil's own activity of mind as the prime factor in the acquisition of knowledge. The teacher's essential task was to feed his internal dynamism. It was quite possible for the learner to instruct himself by discovery and observation and dispense with the teacher altogether. Yet the latter could be of great assistance in speeding up the process and making it more certain. De Grandpré apparently entertained no doubt that an honest and sincere approach would lead unerringly to absolute truth. In this respect, of course, he was completely at variance with the pragmatists.

Address of N.V. Scarfe

At the conference itself, Neville V. Scarfe, Dean of the Faculty of Education of the University of British Columbia, gave an address on "The Aims of Education in a Free Society." His main thesis was that "schools and institutions of higher learning must primarily be places where young people are encouraged to think creatively and constructively for themselves in ways that will deal effectively with the novel and challenging problems which they must face in the future."[38] He felt that the school was a place where unorthodox ideas could be debated without the conformist restrictions of society at large.

What Scarfe saw in the schools was not very encouraging. He found them dominated by traditional, authoritarian educators who still laboured under the impression, formed in the nineteenth century and the early part of the twentieth, that the great responsibility of education was to unify the country and weld together diverse groups of people. In fact, mass production, mass media of communication, and improved transportation had produced conformity much more effectively than the schools could do. Now it was far more important for the schools to promote diversity, ingenuity, novelty, and research.

The progressive nature of Scarfe's views is indicated by his summary of his convictions about the aims of education in the schools.

1. The function of the teacher in school is to select and arrange materials and conditions which encourage and stimulate future citizens to reflect, contemplate, reason, cogitate, and think diligently, critically, constructively, and creatively for themselves and by themselves about the the world of men and nature.

2. In order to think effectively future citizens need (a) to be alertly aware of and curiously inquisitive about the world of nature and man around them; (b) to acquire the mental skills necessary to face *new* problems courageously, constructively, and creatively.
3. In order to become effective future citizens, schools should encourage the maximum development of initiative, independence, and responsible use of freedom in their pupils.
4. In order to promote maximum mental growth and health, schools should concern themselves with the all-round development of the child – in particular, much care must be taken of emotional, aesthetic, and artistic development. Intellectual, physical, and spiritual growth depend on the care devoted to emotional harmony, balance, and well-being.
5. Education is an active, exploratory, discovery process of self-development and fulfilment. It is stimulated by using the child's native curiosity, love of adventure and experiment, and his desire to create and construct for himself. Education is stimulating chiefly when it deals with modern problems which have real and immediate significance for the child. The emphasis must always be on treading new ground, on possible future problems rather than on going over well-trodden ground or recounting past difficulties.
6. Education implies the development of future citizens who welcome change and are willing and able to modify society progressively and intelligently for the benefit of all mankind.
7. Education is not *primarily*: (a) handing on the heritage of the past; (b) moulding citizens to a type; (c) acquisition of factual information; (d) testing, by recall, of acquired facts; (e) training of regimented minds who accept traditional behaviour and thinking uncritically; (f) a passive absorptive process.
8. An educated person is one for whom facts, knowledge, and particularly experience have stimulated thinking so that independent ideas, conclusions, attitudes, and wisdom have developed to produce a harmoniously balanced personality devoted to freedom, honesty, impartiality, tolerance, and human virtue. An educated person not only knows facts, but has thought about them, has associated them into ideas, patterns of thought, connected argument and generalizations. Further the educated person has assimilated the ideas and principles derived from thinking about facts and experiences and is able to use and apply these ideas to understanding the world and himself. He has further developed attitudes[,] character, culture, maturity and wisdom. His mind has developed power, efficiency and humanity.[39]

REACTIONS TO THE AMIDON CONCEPT IN THE EARLY 1960s

In 1963 the *Toronto Education Quarterly* devoted space to a discussion of certain fundamental issues, thus helping to give an indication of the view of educational aims held at that time by five leading Toronto educators.[40] These were by no means typical or "average" teachers, supervisors, and administrators, as proved by the sensitivity and thoughtfulness of their comments. Since all five were intimately involved in practical educational affairs, it is reasonable to suppose that they had a good understanding of the prevailing attitudes among local members of the teaching profession.

The matter was introduced by F. Henry Johnson of the Faculty of Education in the University of British Columbia in an article entitled "Amidon: a Return to Essentialism?" In this article he outlined views which had been used by Carl F. Hansen as the basis of the Amidon Plan introduced in a school in Washington, DC. These views had been offered, not as a return to anything, but as a new advance in educational ideas. In actual fact, they sound remarkably like extreme essentialism. As reported by Johnson, they were covered in ten points.

1. The primary responsibility of the school is to educate for intellectual behaviour rather than for "life adjustment".
2. The basic subjects should be emphasized and taught as clearly defined subjects rather than through integration into amorphous activity units. Activity units would not be abolished entirely, but used subordinately as a means of "cross-pollination of disciplines".
3. The curriculum must be pre-planned by scholars, specialists and educators and presented by informed teachers. Such planning opposes the practice prevalent in many American school systems of a curriculum devised from day to day on the basis of impromptu pupil-teacher selection.
4. Children should be grouped at each grade level by "ability", taking into account intelligence, achievement, attitude and age factors.
5. Where possible this ability grouping should be into full classes rather than into small groups within a class. Too many within-class groups tend to wear the teacher out, to place too much reliance on workbooks for seat work and "to fractionate teaching time to the point that each student enjoys very little direct instruction in the course of day".
6. The Readiness Theory may sometimes be used as an excuse for poor teaching. Readiness need not always precede teaching but wise teaching should be an accompaniment of the maturation process. Such a concept rejects the common conviction in America that reading should not be taught to five-year-olds. There is mounting evidence that children can learn much more at an earlier date than has been currently believed possible.
7. In the modern debate concerning the teacher-centred versus the child-centred school, the evidence is unequivocally on the side of the elementary teacher as the "reactor centre" of the learning process.
8. Phonics should be taught consciously from the earliest stages of reading instruction. The Phonovisual Method which has been adopted in the District of Columbia schools incorporates concurrent instruction in sight reading and phonetic analysis.
9. It is not the responsibility of the school to supply all the educational needs of the child (i.e. *Teach the Whole Child*). When the school encroaches

upon home responsibilities it thereby contributes to the weakening of the home. At the same time it over-extends itself beyond its most effective field, namely, the teaching of basic subjects.

10. The school should concentrate on teaching "the basic subjects" but these should be taught with practical purposes in mind.[41]

In discussing these ten points, Johnson commented on their resemblance to views expressed by William C. Bagley in 1938 in his "Essentialist's Platform for the Advancement of American Education."[42] Both Hansen and Bagley had placed high value on basic learning, ordered and sustained effort, discipline, and the central role of the teacher. Both were opposed to an emphasis on immediate interests, a laissez-faire atmosphere in the classroom, psychological versus logical organization of subject matter, and the discrediting of such ideals as effort, discipline, and the cultural heritage.

In Johnson's opinion, the only surprise the Amidon Plan might occasion among the general run of Canadian teachers would be that it was considered in any way unusual. He believed that most of them had continued, despite the existence of progressivism, to retain beliefs and to follow practices that were largely essentialist. He assumed that they would approve of the emphasis on intellectual behaviour as the main responsibility of the school while acknowledging that all the educational devices of society should contribute to the development of moral, ethical, and social values. They would support the stress on basic subjects and, in view of their familiarity with provincially organized curricula, would wonder why anyone would insist on a pre-planned curriculum and a definite timetable.

In a subsequent issue, the *Toronto Education Quarterly* submitted three of Hansen's premises to the five Toronto educators for their comments. A brief review of their reactions to the first of these will offer a general indication of their views. The proposition read as follows: "The primary responsibility of the school is to educate for intellectual behaviour rather than for 'life adjustment.' "

Lloyd Dennis, later a leading member of the Provincial Committee on Aims and Objectives, did not argue with the claim that the primary responsibility of the school was in the area of the intellect. He took issue, however, with the dichotomization of intellectual behaviour and life adjustment. He felt that the former had to take place within cultural terms of reference. Further, he characterized the development of intellectual behaviour as a kind of adjustment to life. The same definition could be applied to the prevailing system of education, with its subject matter, timetables, methods, and textbooks. Although Dennis did not appear to be quite as progressive as he did after the completion of the later report, he ended his comments thus: "It is as a man that he will live when he leaves his school, and one would hope that the institution has found it possible to develop more than his intellectual power."[43]

Miss Gertrude Fatt, principal of Eastdale Vocational School, found that the terms "intellectual behaviour" and "life adjustment" bordered on jargon. Like Dennis, she doubted the validity of trying to separate them, in terms either of the aims of education or of the business of living. She also questioned the idea that the school had the same responsibility toward all students. If education for intellectual behaviour was a useful term, it could best be applied to the intelligent, well-adjusted child from a prosperous and stable home. He needed the basic learning tools that would enable him to acquire knowledge, the ability to reason, the recreational and cultural interests that would round out his life, and vocational skills. On the other hand, the child who was deficient in intelligence, emotionally disturbed, or culturally deprived was hardly receptive to education for intellectual behaviour. If the home was incapable of meeting his needs, the school must attempt to do so.

Duncan Green, head of the English Department of Jarvis Collegiate Institute, asserted less equivocally than either of the other two that he saw no conflict between education for intellectual behaviour and for life adjustment. The apparent discrepancy seemed to have grown out of an increasing tendency to "educate directly" by substituting training for education. Thus the response to a high divorce rate was a course in family living; the response to excessive buying on the instalment plan, a course in credit buying; and the response to an excess of traffic accidents, a course in safe driving. He was opposed to this kind of education for life adjustment, feeling that a constant study of literature, history, and mathematics was the best ultimate solution to life problems. These views appeared, as far as they went, to be substantially in agreement with those of Hansen.

R.E. Jones, Inspector of Special Education, was, not suprisingly, very much concerned with the group Miss Fatt identified as not being in a position to profit much from education for intellectual behaviour. He wrote sympathetically of teachers in the primary grades who favoured the abandonment of the formal curriculum and concentrated instead on the development of good work habits, the stimulation of interest and imagination, and the establishment of positive attitudes. This kind of treatment, which might be considered life adjustment, would produce accelerated intellectual development at a later stage. He also questioned the value of academic learning that proceeded in spite of poor adjustment. A study of gifted secondary school students in Toronto had shown that many who were "overachieving" suffered from severe emotional disturbance. Intellectual development was also illusory for young people classified as schizophrenic, gifted underachievers, drop-outs, juvenile delinquents, and other alienated youth. Jones asserted that the great legacy of the progressive movement was the clear knowledge that a child's mind could not be trained apart from his person.

L.A. Shore, Assistant Supervisor of Arts and Crafts, flatly disagreed with Hansen's proposition. He did not consider that intellectual development deserved first rank in the contemporary educational system. He endorsed the aim of educating each person to realize his fullest potential as an individual and as a participating member of many groups. In the light of this aim, intellectual development was to be regarded as a component rather than the core. Like Green, although for quite different reasons, he refused to look upon education for life adjustment and education for intellectual development as a real dichotomy.

VIEWS ON AIMS HELD BY W.G. DAVIS

In view of his dominating position in the evolution of education in the 1960s, the opinions of W.G. Davis about the aims of education are of particular significance. Davis can hardly be called an unequivocal exponent of the precepts of any single philosophical school. His orientation has, however, been basically progressive, as indicated by his consistent support for programs that attempt to relate school experience more closely to life and his advocacy of the maximum of individual freedom for the learner at whatever age. His views have obviously evolved in a liberal direction as he has observed the undesirable effects of structural and curricular rigidities in the system which he took over early in the decade.

Davis has always been noted for his keen interest in various technological developments that promise to make education more efficient. He has found it necessary on occasion, however, to claim adherence to certain human values. He made these comments in the Legislature in 1965.

> Despite my keen interest in these new developments, I would emphasize that all is not new in education. The experience of centuries in guiding the development of children and youth in body, mind, and character is not being discarded because a number of fascinatingly intricate machines have been invented ... the qualities of diligence, honesty and dependability will still be in demand as long as human beings work together. These are among the qualities that are best fostered in the life of the home, the church and the school. In our inquiry into the ways of tomorrow we must be on our guard against neglecting or discarding the valuable truths that mankind has learned through its long history and experience.[44]

SPECIAL EMPHASES IN RECENT DEFINITIONS OF AIMS

Education for flexibility

Recent preoccupation with the speed of material and social change has resulted in an emphasis on the development of qualities that are supposed to be particularly effective in coping with uncertainty and instability. It is no longer supremely important that modern man be firm and steadfast;

he should be flexible. He must be able to shake off the tyranny of the customary and the habitual. Rather than depending on a fixed route outlined for him by previous generations, he must be able to plan his own course.

The progressives and the traditionalists discover as much basis for disagreement on the way to attain this goal as they do with respect to most others. The progressive finds the rigidities in organization and procedure in the conventional school most unpropitious. He would expose the child to as wide as possible a variety of life situations in the hope that lessons learned from direct experience can be generalized to meet new circumstances. Sceptical that the historical development of the race has major relevance, he tends to focus attention on the events and conditions of the present. When history is taught, the record is combed for parallels to modern "problems." The traditionalist usually seeks a less direct route to the attainment of flexibility. He expects the quality to emerge from absorption in and appreciation of the best in human culture. The truly flexible man is Frye's scholar who has stood outside society and examined it from a dispassionate and disinterested point of view. He studies history for its own sake rather than perverting it to serve some ephemeral ulterior purpose. This approach is thought to give him the best chance of seeing his own era in perspective and of anticipating, as far as humanly possible, the problems and opportunities of the future.

The ability to respond flexibly to new circumstances rests to a large extent on the individual's sense of confidence and security. The early atmosphere of the home clearly has more to do with the development of this quality than anything that is likely to happen in the school. The school can, however, make a major contribution by giving the pupil a sense of achievement and mastery. The actual task he performs may be less important than that it is within the limits of his capacity while stretching his capacity to the limit. Flexibility as a by-product of the strengthening of self-confidence is a goal that offers a realistic hope of attainment.

Mental health

Seymour L. Halleck, professor of psychiatry at the University of Wisconsin, has defined a set of aims most of which are concerned with mental health.[45] His list, summarized briefly, includes the development of the capacity to share strong feelings of affection with another person, and the related feeling of compassion; openness to experience, which means the ability to seek and evaluate without prejudice the wide variety of experience possible within the limits of one's commitment to others; the ability to find an optimum amount of freedom; an ideology that one can value; a sense of mastery over the environment; an appreciation of the value of order; the capacity to assume responsibility for one's own behaviour; honesty with oneself and others; the rejection of violence as social behaviour; and respect for elderly members of society.

The mental health element was strongly in evidence in a set of aims, ostensibly for the class of 1984, expounded by Bruno Bettelheim.

The class of '84 will need to learn all we know about the true nature of man, his external appearances and his inner turmoil; the prevalence of the powerful forces of his social and his asocial tendencies, and how the latter can be domesticated by the former without destroying his freedom, his self respect, his self love, his autonomy. Young people will have to learn that nobody can love well who cannot recognize his occasional wish to hate; nobody can love others well who does not love himself in the first place. They will have to learn that, while hating is natural, they must be able to hate without resorting to acts that might harm other persons, since in harming others they harm themselves.[46]

The person who places priority on mental health is inclined to see good mental health as the key to the attainment of desirable aims in the intellectual, social, and moral spheres. The mentally healthy person is the one most capable of enjoying the stimulation of further learning. He can best adapt to the exigencies of the existing social order and benefit from human associations, while at the same time maintaining an awareness of anomalies and evils in his environment and a willingness to work for their eradication. Certain research studies have tended to show that values prevailing in many schools are in conflict with those associated with good mental health. Children who are quiet and docile may be contrasted favourably with those whose spontaneity or boisterousness brings them into conflict with the regulations but may, in the long run, be headed for serious trouble. The mental health enthusiast is convinced that educational aims in general must be brought into harmony with principles of good mental health if they are to be realized effectively according to any criterion. He may even believe that the future of the human race is at stake.

Changing attitudes toward national aims

Concern with certain chauvinistic national aims reached a peak at the National Conference on Engineering, Scientific and Technical Manpower at St Andrews-By-The-Sea, New Brunswick, in 1956. Whether the delegates all accepted what they were told or not, they sat and listened to ringing assertions that the nation's educational systems must be mobilized to produce more engineers, scientists, technologists, and technicians to avoid defeat in the competition with the Communist world. If the battle for supremacy in industry and commerce were lost, military conquest appeared to be an ultimate probability. Perhaps in view of the recency of the Korean War, such an eventuality was plausible.

Well before that time, a message of quite different import was being delivered by those who saw the chief danger to the future of man in the peculiarly self-righteous propensity for aggressiveness that had characterized his behaviour throughout recorded history. Almost immediately after the end of the Second World War, Brock Chisholm, at one time Director of the World Health Organization, began warning of the danger of perpetuating certain myths. His chief immediate reward among the general public was to be identified as the would-be slayer of Santa Claus.

In material prepared for the Second Canadian Conference on Education, Chisholm wrote on the earlier role of group loyalties.[47] National survival depended on the maintenance of sufficient force to repel an attack. Security was bound up with the ability to kill members of the rival group. Under such circumstances, the agressive qualities of the group were regarded in terms of high moral principle. It was a virtue to destroy the lives, property, and power of outsiders, and any feeling of concern for their welfare had to be discouraged. Every war in which one's own nation engaged was a just one. Chisholm went on to describe the bearing these attitudes had on educational aims.

> Incorporation of these values into consciences in early childhood was a necessary and effective way of ensuring that the strictly limited loyalty on which the effectiveness of the system depended would be accepted. This indoctrination has been effected by the use of biased history and news, the setting up of noted killers as heroes for our children's admiration and emulation, nationalistic rituals, myths and songs, depreciation of the cultures, civilization, and accomplishments of rival groups and misinterpretation of their motives.[48]

The limits of acceptable group loyalty were quite precise. Anyone who identified himself with interests beyond those of his own survival group was treated as a traitor and a criminal. Much the same applied to one who identified himself exclusively with some lesser group and thus could not be counted on to help defend the survival group. It was demanded of each individual that his loyalties grow to a certain specified limit and stop there. Chisholm defined the dangers of the situation in a world suddenly transformed by advances in weaponry.

> The survival unit suddenly has become the human race itself, but we have no tradition of concern for the survival of the human race, and no moral values to support such necessary concern. Many of the moral values we have learned from our parents and ancestors suddenly have become exceedingly dangerous, even suicidal. Our ancestral feeling, thinking and behaviour patterns produced, or failed to prevent, warfare in every generation of our past history. Many of our ancestors survived those wars, but only because they were relatively inefficient in killing as compared with ourselves.[49]

Chisholm did not dismiss the difficulty of taking the long step toward the development of a primary loyalty to the new survival unit, the human race. Children would have to acquire the attitudes that would prepare them to forego a certain amount of national economic advantage in order to reduce the disparities between the prosperous minority and the poverty-stricken majority of the world population. They would have to get over the current generation's delusion that security and freedom could be bought cheaply. Chisholm did not actually go beyond the exhortation that new ways of thinking and new values were needed. The educational world was left with a monumental task in devising the means to meet his challenge.

Moral development as an aim

Whatever responsibility they are prepared to assign to the school, practically all those who attempt to formulate a comprehensive set of educational aims include moral development among the most important. Typically, however, they leave the term only vaguely defined, if at all. Considerable clarification of the issue was provided by the Committee on Religious Education in the Public Schools of the Province of Ontario, which reported in February 1969.[50]

The committee took some pains to define what it did not regard as effective moral development. No value was seen in merely changing overt forms of expression. Obedience to a precept or a command had no value apart from the quality of the thinking that underlay a moral judgment or decision. The committee also warned against absolute standards of morality, which it pointed out were not a normal part of human experience. To pretend that they were was to run the risk that the child would, at a later stage, reject the whole system. Good deportment was said to be of value only if it resulted from a process of reasoning. To give the learner the freedom to arrive at his own conclusions meant that he might adopt a hedonistic philosophy that was likely to lead to moral bankruptcy. A mature person, however, had to reach this conclusion independently; it could not be imposed on him. "It must always warm our hearts to encounter politeness or goodness in others; but the greater joy is to know that these qualities flow from the mind and the soul, and not from sterile conformity to imposed rules of conduct."[51] The rejection of absolutes in favour of conclusions based on moral reasoning was said to have widespread implications for all phases of social living. Some examples given by the committee were the ethics of driving, the salesman's duty to tell the truth about his product, the public's attitude toward law-enforcement officers, respect for the democratic process in meetings, sportsmanship on the playing field, courtesy in the shopping centre, and the peer-group influence in relation to the new morality.

TWO

The development of different types of schools

In *The Development of Education in Canada*, C.E. Phillips described a first stage of educational development lasting to about 1840 in eastern Canada, when the list of types of schools for the people included church or parish schools, charity schools, Sunday schools, monitorial schools, and infant schools operated by organized philanthropy. The privileged few had access to Latin grammar schools and private schools. As a result of the efforts of enterprising middle-class people, and occasionally of a religious denomination, there were some academies, which appealed somewhat more widely than the grammar schools because of the practical subjects on their curriculum.[1]

ELEMENTARY SCHOOLS

Origin of the common schools

At the beginning of the nineteenth century in pioneer Upper Canada, pressure for the provision of elementary education came from the public. In scattered places throughout the province, small schools, largely operated by clergymen, were opened in private homes. There, for small fees, children were taught the three RS, sometimes supplemented by geography, bookkeeping, and the classics. The Legislature demonstrated its indifference or hostility to popular education between 1800 and 1806 by refusing to approve the establishment of schools in Glengarry County.[2]

The attitude of the legislators seemed to have become somewhat more favourable by 1816, when the Common School Act provided for a grant of £6,000 a year, to be divided among elementary schools where there was a minimum attendance of twenty. This amount of money was too small to be of much practical assistance. The main importance of the act was that it enabled communities to elect a board of trustees with power to employ and dismiss a teacher, to select textbooks from a prescribed list, and to make rules and regulations. The typical common school established at this time had a single room and teacher.

By the 1830s the condition of the common schools was deplorable. The grant of 1816, small as it had been, was now only half the original amount. In 1832 a select committee of the Assembly reported that the Legislature was spending less for the education of the youth of the population of 300,000 than for the contingent expenses of one of its own sessions.[3] The result was that only the dregs of the population, or those prepared to spend a year on the way to a better job, could be persuaded to teach. Enthusiasm for education was by no means uniformly high among the population.

Upper Canada, like other colonies, had to shake off the idea that education was a benefaction to be provided by philanthropic organizations established for that purpose or by churches. As long as this impression was rife, the people were not prepared to accept full responsibility for providing for their own needs. Phillips stressed the importance of the final withdrawal of the Society for the Propagation of the Gospel from educational operations in North America in 1836 as marking "the almost complete disappearance of paternalistic charity, which had to cease before schools of the people could be fully established."[4]

In rural communities there was unlikely to be any alternative to the common school. In the towns, particularly as the payment of taxes was substituted for fees or support by subscription, the stigma attached to attendance at free schools induced many from the more prosperous class to send their children to private schools. In Toronto, most of the children who attended the first "public" schools were from the working class and were expected to find jobs as soon as they could read, write, and cipher. This influence is said to account for the small number who went beyond the intermediate division, the still smaller number who tried the final examinations, the extreme caution with which the board introduced anything that might be considered a frill, and the reluctance to permit school time to be used for anything but classroom lessons.[5]

After his year of travel abroad as Assistant Superintendent of Education, and his subsequent appointment in 1846 as Superintendent, Egerton Ryerson persuaded the Legislature to pass a series of acts which had the effect among other things of greatly improving the quality of education in the public schools. Provincial regulations eventually ensured the maintenance of minimum standards by providing for financial support through local taxation, compulsory attendance, systematic inspection, professional training for teachers, and the use of textbooks of better quality.

Central schools

The term "central school" has been applied to the rural elementary schools with two or more classrooms which gradually replaced one-room schools after the Second World War. The movement was made possible by the improvement of highways, public acceptance of the transportation of pupils, and the formation of larger units of administration. While the establishment of graded programs does not appear to be the tremendous step forward that it did a few years ago, now that non-grading has become such a major manifestation of progress, there is no doubt about the advantages the central schools provided in terms of improved facilities and a better quality of teaching. The new schools provided much more attractive surroundings than the ancient relics that many of the children attended earlier.

By May 1953 it was reported that 164 central schools had replaced 426 smaller schools. The average central school contained four classrooms, accommodated 130 pupils, and served four former school sections. Six years later the total had risen to 459 schools replacing 1,035 one-room schools. Since there were 2,426 classrooms, the average size had evidently increased. The *Report of the Minister, 1959* indicated that, since 86 of these schools had been built in the 1958–9 school year, the trend toward centralization was gathering momentum. Thus, in fairness it could hardly be said, as some did, that W.J. Dunlop's regard for the graduates of the little red schoolhouse of pioneer days involved any major effort to preserve such schools. By 1960 the minister was able to report that less than 8 per cent of the province's elementary school enrolment was found in one-room schools and less than 4 per cent in two-room schools. In 1963 an estimated 60 per cent of the pupils in rural and suburban areas were attending central schools, of which there were over seven hundred.

Facilities for early childhood education

Kindergartens were introduced into the province in 1882 and made part of the elementary school system by legislation passed in 1885. School boards have added them by gradual stages, until they have come close to being universal. The expansion of kindergarten enrolment since the end of the Second World War was indicated in volume I, chapter 2. The extent to which Roman Catholic separate schools have been able to add such a service has been a particularly significant development during the recent period.

Junior kindergartens, admitting children at the age of four, have been provided to a very limited extent for many years. It has been the policy in Metropolitan Toronto to make them available only for children who are particularly in need of a stimulating environment. For the most part, local school systems have made no substantial effort to provide for the pre-kindergarten age groups, despite mounting evidence of the importance of an adequate emotional, social, and intellectual environment at this stage of development. Such facilities as are available are mostly provided by private individuals, voluntary associations, and educational institutions including Ryerson Polytechnical Institute, certain colleges of applied arts and technology, and university agencies such as the Institute of Child Study of the University of Toronto. Nursery schools maintained by the latter institutions are intended primarily for experimental and practice teaching purposes. Generally speaking, schools and classes under these auspices, as well as those operated by private agencies, do little for those who most need them, since the fees they charge ensure that they serve the needs of the more prosperous families. A few culturally deprived children are recruited where there is a particular desire to experiment with them, but the numbers are infinitesimal in relation to the total need.

The Royal Commission of 1945–50 looked with favour on the assumption of public responsibility for pre-school education, recommending

(a) that, conditional upon maintenance of a required minimum standard of education in grades I to VI inclusive, as determined by the Minister, local education authorities be permitted to establish nursery schools and classes for 3-year-old and 4-year-old children;
(b) that attendance at such schools or classes be voluntary and on a half-day basis;
(c) that the full cost of the establishment and operation of such schools or classes be a responsibility of the local education authority;
(d) that, for pupils attending such classes, local education authorities be authorized to charge such fees as they may deem necessary.[6]

As Education Minister, Davis showed some interest in the possibility of exerting a greater effort in this area. On June 2, 1965, he stated in the Legislature:

Perhaps we should be giving much more attention to the implications of what we used to think of as "pre-school" education, that is, education in nursery schools and in kindergartens. Training at this early level is of particular importance in the case of our young children who, through unfortunate circumstances, have suffered cultural deprivation and live in disadvantaged areas. Examples may readily be found in some Eskimo and Indian communities, and even in some of the downtown parts of our large urban centres. Earlier experience with school life might do much to prepare such children to profit more effectively from regular grade work, and to compensate for unfortunate environmental conditions over which neither they, nor we, have too much control.[7]

The chief justification for lack of any conspicuous action since that time has been the amount of funds required for other programs and activities. It may well be, however, that the dividends from higher expenditure at this level would ultimately be much greater than from comparable investment somewhere else. The Provincial Committee on Aims and Objectives intimated as much in declaring that it had come to view pre-kindergarten schooling as valuable, if not vital, for all children.[8]

Tim Reid, Liberal education critic and member of the Legislature for Scarborough East, has emphasized the importance of adequate education at the pre-school level, especially for disadvantaged children. On June 5, 1968, he said in the Legislature: "A child born into a slum has its intelligence deteriorate absolutely. It is on the basis of this premise, as applied to humans, that the advocates of pre-primary school education for children born into the 'poverty syndrome' largely rest their case."[9] On that occasion he spoke approvingly of the Head Start program in the United States. He offered the opinion that the province might eventually save millions of dollars in adult retraining costs if an adequate pre-kindergarten course were provided for children from low-income families.

On March 5, 1969, Reid expanded on the same theme, with the additional plea that the federal government interpret its responsibility for manpower development to cover assistance for pre-kindergarten programs.

> It is my opinion that pre-primary and primary school education is the area in which a substantial upward shift in expenditures could have the greatest long-run individual, social, economic and political return in Canada.
>
> On the one hand, there is the question of preparing individuals for the world of work and of maximizing their contribution to economic growth in this era of a permanent scientific and technological revolution, commonly called the age of automation ...
>
> On the other hand, there is the belief that it is good for an individual, however gifted, to be able to develop and use the gifts with which he was born. Related to this is the belief that social and economic barriers which stand between a child and the development of his inherited, creative, intellectual and physical gifts, ought to be eliminated.[10]

SECONDARY ACADEMIC SCHOOLS

The district schools

Recent years have been marked by frequent wringing of hands over the sharpness of the distinction between elementary and secondary education in Ontario. Sporadic efforts have been made for over twenty years to break down the barriers, but these have had only limited and local success. The situation is not, of course, peculiar to this province. It is rather to be regarded as the normal state of affairs throughout a large part of the world. Where the great majority of young people are expected to obtain at least a secondary education, however, the existence of the traditional distinction appears more and more anomalous.

It is hardly surprising that some of the current difficulties can be traced to the way in which the secondary schools were established and operated in pioneer days. Interest has often been expressed over the reversal of what seems a normal procedure in that they originated before the common schools. The first step was taken in 1797, when the Legislative Council asked that certain waste lands be set aside to support a grammar school in each of the eight districts into which the colony was divided. This appeal was coupled with a request for a similar grant for the establishment of a college or university. In acquiescing, the Colonial

Secretary, the Duke of Portland, referred to "free" grammar schools. When the eight schools, designated at first "district schools," were organized in 1807, the colonial aristocracy managed to ensure, however, that fees were required and that the schools were of an exclusive character. The District Public School Act of that year provided for the appointment of five "fit and discreet persons" as trustees for each district who were to hire a teacher and make regulations. The act also made available the sum of £100 per year for the teacher's salary. The fees collected from the pupils were to meet other expenses.

At first the schools had a rather precarious existence. For a time after 1823 they were under the supervision of the General Board of Education. A committee of the Legislature, appointed in 1829, found them inefficient, partly because of high tuition fees, the unwise selection of teachers and trustees, and sectarian influence, but mainly because of the backwardness of the province and the poverty of the people.[11] It was some time, however, before this condition underwent any substantial change. The main provisions of the District Public School Act remained in force until 1853.

The academies

An alternative form of secondary education began to be provided in the academies, which were founded in part as a reaction against the exclusiveness of the district schools. This feeling does much to account for the establishment of Upper Canada Academy by the Wesleyans in 1836. While taking full advantage of the common schools, they found themselves without sufficient opportunities beyond that level. There were implications of disloyalty if they resorted to the practice of sending their children to educational institutions across the American border.[12] Thus there was no reasonable alternative to providing a school of their own.

Phillips pointed out that, while the academies were less numerous and influential in Upper Canada than they were in the United States, they played a similar role in the two places in the evolution of the secondary school. By admitting pupils from the common schools and offering instruction only at the secondary level, they provided a discrete section of the educational ladder. In offering a co-educational program that was broader than that required for university admission, they set a pattern for later secondary schools.[13] One of the eleven that appeared before 1850 evolved into a university, one into a private school, and others into publicly controlled high schools, while others disappeared.

The imposition of public control

An important step was taken in 1853, when the Grammar School Act gave the central authority the right to regulate the courses of study provided by the grammar schools and, in general, to control them in the same way as it did the common schools. While their offerings are said to have improved, a considerable amount of confusion was caused by their practice of controlling elementary pupils in order to qualify for larger government grants. By 1865 Ryerson apparently felt that he had other matters well enough in hand to justify concentrating his attention on this area and began the preparatory work that led to the passing of An Act to Improve the Common and Grammar Schools of the Province of Ontario in 1871.

The foundations of the pattern of publicly supported secondary education

This act assigned full responsibility to the common schools, henceforth called public schools, for elementary education. Secondary education was to be provided by high schools and collegiate institutes, both of which would receive financial support from local taxation. In 1873 the high school entrance examination, based on the work of the fourth form, was introduced to ensure that only properly qualified candidates were admitted to secondary schools. This device had obvious advantages at the time but had outlived its usefulness by a considerable span of time before it was abolished in 1949. The right of girls to attend institutions of secondary education, which according to Robin Harris remained in doubt in the grammar schools until 1869, was now clearly established.[14]

Distinction between high schools and collegiate institutes

Ryerson intended that the collegiate institutes would constitute the link between the common schools and the universities and that they would offer for this purpose a program of classical and modern languages. In order to qualify for collegiate institute status, they originally had to have at least four full-time masters and a minimum of sixty boys studying Latin and Greek. Later the prescription was changed so that they had to have at least five specialists teaching the basic academic subjects as well as a science laboratory and specified equipment. They received a special financial grant that in the early years amounted to $750 per annum.

The high schools were intended to provide a general course for those not bound for the university, including English, commercial work, and natural science, with emphasis on agriculture. The distinction between the two types of secondary school did not develop. The high schools took advantage of the opportunity afforded them to offer the classical program, and the collegiate institutes acceded to pressure to establish the general course. Observers do not agree about the relative amount of emphasis placed on the university-bound and the non-university bound student.

Guillet comments on the state of the high schools as seen in 1878.[15] Of the 107 of these which had existed in 1871, very few had had more than one master; the 103 in current operation had an average of three masters. The entrance examination had done its work in keeping out unqualified pupils. The introduction of the intermediate examination had made possible the ill-fated experiment with payment by results, as explained in volume v, chapter 15. At the time there also was comment on the need for a leaving examination to provide for university admission.

Secondary education in Ontario for the next few decades is generally considered to have been predominantly oriented toward university preparation, however small the proportion of young people who actually succeeded in attending university. The view seems to underlie a passage from *The Structure of Post-Secondary Education in Ontario*, one of the earlier publications of the Committee of Provincially Assisted Universities and Colleges of Ontario. After referring to the academic program of the collegiate institutes leading to university matriculation, it went on:

By 1883 the academically-oriented programme was dominant in both, and the only differences between them were that the high schools had smaller enrolments and the collegiate institutes had a specified number of specialist teachers on their staffs. Whether the reason for the breakdown of this distinction was a desire for the greater prestige (and larger subsidy) that accrued to the collegiate institute, or a determination in the smaller towns to prevent the larger ones from supplying more than their share of the university students, or a deep-rooted belief in academically-oriented secondary education, or a combination of all these, the consequence was that the collegiate institute pattern became the norm, and for over twenty years no attempt was made to develop any of the secondary schools into the type of institution that combined general education with some vocational elements.[16]

Harris disputes the impression that secondary education in Ontario since the 1870s has been primarily a matter of providing an academic course for students who intend to proceed to university. He asserts, in fact, that "nothing could be further from the truth."[17] In his opinion, the significant fact about the failure of the two types of schools to develop in different ways is not that the high schools assumed the task of teaching the classical course, but that the collegiates offered the general course. This view neglects the extent to which the general course evolved in an academic direction.

Continuation schools

Continuation schools played their part for a considerable period in the educational history of the province as a means of providing some of the benefits of a high school education for those to whom a full-fledged high school was inaccessible. After declining to a remnant of their former numbers, they disappeared with the legislation of 1968 which established the reorganized school systems. In a sense, however, they survived as grade 9 and 10 classes in Roman Catholic separate schools, where the students were treated as elementary school pupils for provincial grant purposes.

Continuation schools apparently originated rather informally during the latter half of the nineteenth century when enterprising teachers, particularly in rural schools, encouraged some of their better pupils to continue their studies in fifth book classes.[18] Provision was made in 1889 for such classes to be set up under the management of a school board in any municipality where there was no high school. The privilege was extended to separate school as well as to public school boards, and both were entitled to grants from the Legislature for the support of the classes.

Legislation of 1908 divided the continuation classes into continuation schools and fifth classes. Further reference to legal provisions may be found in volume II, chapter 5. As a type of institution, the continuation school differed little from the smaller and less adequately endowed high schools. Its fate was usually to become a regular high school or to disappear as better alternative facilities became available.

District high schools

Until the end of the Second World War, opportunities for secondary education in the rural areas of the province were far from satisfactory. Pupils who completed grade 8, or in some cases grade 10, in their local school might proceed to a continuation or high school in the area, where their fees were paid by the county council. Under the circumstances, it was hard to avoid the impression that they were outsiders. Few schools had programs that catered adequately to the needs of the rural community.

Just about the time the war ended, a vigorous campaign was launched by the Department of Education, with inspectors as front line troops, to persuade local citizens to support the organization of high school districts and to construct new and more adequate district high schools. Besides providing a higher quality of education, these schools were promoted as community centres for adults. The campaign represents one of the success stories of the development of education in the province. Twenty years after the movement began Harris was able to report that the entire populated area of the province was divided into high school districts and that there were no fewer than 170 district high school boards.[19]

The *Report of the Minister, 1953* contained the following description.

A typical District High School, the result of the reorganization of a school area, and the product of a well-planned building programme, may be described in general terms which would apply to a number of modern schools in Ontario. Its territory probably covers about 400 square miles and it is administered by an appointed board representative of all the municipalities served, all of whom have an equity in the school property. It has a comprehensive system of transportation of pupils by bus, together with adequate lunch-room facilities in the school building. Modern and attractive accommodation, usually on one floor, include [*sic*] well-lighted and acoustically treated classrooms, and special rooms for subjects such as Music, Art, Commercial work, Home Economics and Industrial Arts, and a gymnasium auditorium. For a curriculum it offers, within the framework of the General Course, the required subjects of English, Social Studies, and Physical Education, the traditional options of Latin, French, Mathematics, and Science, and such of the more recently introduced optional subjects as are suited to the needs of the community. In addition, a district school quite often offers a commercial course as distinct from the commercial option in the General Course.[20]

The modern buildings, higher salaries, and larger staffs tended to attract more capable teachers. There were increased opportunities for specialization, which were said to improve the general level of instruction. For the students there were opportunities to participate in a variety of extracurricular activities not available in smaller schools. The extension of such opportunities, along with the improved program and level of instruction, resulted in substantially better retention rates.

ROLE OF JUNIOR HIGH SCHOOLS AND SENIOR PUBLIC SCHOOLS

A number of reasons have been given for the establishment of separately organized and administered junior high schools. They provide a means of concentrating on the particular needs of the pre-adolescent and early adolescent, which differ substantially from those of the child at the elementary level and the full-blown adolescent or early adult in the senior high school. They may be so organized and administered as to ease the transition between assignment to a single teacher, except for peripheral activities, and the complete rotary system, where there is a change of teachers for almost every subject. They make it possible to provide some of the more expensive facilities and equipment at the level of grades 7 and 8 that could not be supplied to every elementary school. On the other hand, students in grades 9 and 10 can be handled at less expense in the junior high school than in the regular high school. If grades 7 and 8 are removed from the elementary school, there are considered to be more opportunities for leadership for the grade 6 pupils.

Recent theories enjoying support among Ontario educators tend to deny some of these advantages. The idea of continuous progress, with each student engaging in activities cutting across the old grade structure, seems to call for either a single school housing pupils from kindergarten to grade 13, or at least a complex of adjoining buildings. This concept has been propounded in particular by supporters of the extension of the Roman Catholic separate school system to the end of high school. It is possible that the advantages of continuous progress do not entirely negate the arguments in favour of separating certain age groups.

The village of Forest Hill established a junior high school as early as 1932, an action which demonstrates the power Ontario boards of education have had to adopt the physical and administrative arrangements for different grade levels according to their preferences. It was not until the Porter Plan was introduced in 1949, as dealt with in chapter 5, that a real attempt was made to organize a coherent program of studies for the intermediate level. It might have been expected that administrative changes would have followed and that, as the need for new buildings arose, junior high schools with grades 7 to 10 would have appeared all over the province. Eventually, new teaching certificates, valid at the junior high school level, would have been introduced. In fact, only a few systems such as those in East York, North York, and South Peel saw fit to adopt junior high schools. The K–6, 7–9, and 10–13 organization found more favour than one that would have corresponded to the intermediate division defined by the Department of Education. School systems such as that of Toronto preferred to leave their secondary school structure intact and placed their grade 7 and 8 pupils in senior public schools.

Junior high schools began to appear around 1910 in the United States and were widely adopted in many parts of the country. In some cases, junior and senior high schools were operated in separate buildings, and in others, although they were organized separately, they occupied a single building. Junior high schools offered a general program, emphasizing the "core" curriculum and avoiding any pressure to induce the student to make a career choice. In the late 1950s and the 1960s, there was a beginning of a swing away from the junior high school in favour of the middle school, which combined grades 5 to 8 or grades 6 to 8. In the view of many authorities, this division corresponds better to the psychological realities of children's development. The middle school is said to reflect dissatisfaction with the self-contained classroom of the traditional elementary school and to represent an attempt to provide for more specialization from grade 5 or 6 on.[21]

According to a report in 1969, the junior high school promised to remain a dominant form in the United States for some years.[22] After surveying 449 school systems, the Educational Research Service found that 68 per cent had a 6–3–3 grade plan, a reduction from the 71 per cent reporting the same plan in 1963. At the same time 4 per cent of the systems were using a middle school plan, as compared with fewer than 1 per cent in 1963.

CHARACTERISTICS OF SENIOR PUBLIC SCHOOLS

In practical terms, it has been much easier for urban school systems to establish senior public schools than junior high schools, at least as long as departmental organization, supervision, and teacher preparation remain divided on the basis of elementary and secondary levels. Also, few elementary school buildings would have been altogether satisfactory if converted to junior high schools. For a built-up area with a fairly stable population, the easiest course of action has been to designate certain strategically located schools as senior public schools.

Having conducted a study of the senior public schools in Hamilton, the results of which were published in 1965, the principals of these schools claimed that adolescent and pre-adolescent children had been encouraged to progress more quickly than in the traditional setting.[23] The adjustment from grade 8 to 9 had been facilitated as they had moved from a modified rotary plan of instruction to the full rotary organization of the secondary school. The schools had been able to provide an enriched program developed around individual talents and social behavioural patterns. Special classes had enabled slow learners to remain with their own age groups. Guidance had assumed special significance, with an orientation toward the three streams provided in the secondary schools. There had been financial advantages in that classrooms for science, music, industrial arts, home economics, art, and speech had provided accommodation for children from several feeder schools, thus preventing unnecessary duplication. The senior school teaching assignment was an incentive for those whose interests, abilities, and talents fitted them to teach the adolescent.

The schools had been able to provide a productive set of "co-curricular" activities to meet the young adolescent's awakening need for a purpose in life. These included student councils, assemblies, concerts, sports and athletics, clubs, and choirs. The principals thought student publications a good means of improving English but suggested that they be kept simple because the "senior school should not pre-empt the pleasures and greater responsibilities of the secondary school." The Hamilton student must have been a particularly angelic breed, since at the senior school level he was said to have reached the age at which he welcomed the opportunity to set an example of acceptable behaviour.

VOCATIONAL SCHOOLS

Definitions

The term "vocational education" has been used to describe more than one concept, with a certain amount of consequent confusion. In many minds, it has meant preparation to carry on a vocation. But those who formulate statements of educational aims usually prefer to designate this process as training and to consider it inadequate or even misguided as a process meriting public support in a school system. They think of vocational education as a means whereby broader aims are realized in part through the study of procedures and the acquisition of certain skills used in commerce and industry. The student who works in wood, metal, fabrics, or foods is learning about society and his potential role in it. He is acquiring moral values, including an appreciation of the virtues of sound, honest, competent work; he is becoming a better potential citizen by gaining an increased understanding of how he can contribute to the welfare of his fellow citizens as well as to his own. By working in a vocationally oriented atmosphere, he is physically and emotionally prepared for the specific training that will be required of him when he actually becomes employed. Further, although it may not actually be essential to his preparatory educational program, he may have developed to a fairly high level some of the skills that can be used on the job.

The proponents of vocational education, as opposed to vocational training, in the public school system have been able to cite as support for their position the fact that most people are employed in jobs that require only a few months, weeks, or even days of specific preparation. The growing complexity of industry and the increase in service occupations have not necessarily tended to lengthen this period. In fact, some industries have recorded a sharp drop in the average amount of training required. Employers are much more interested in character, attitude, and potential for acquiring skill than in developed skill itself. That is, they look for employees who are vocationally educated rather than vocationally trained. If the qualities they seek are most likely to be found among those with a strictly academic education, they will choose such individuals over those whose preparation seems at first glance to be much more relevant.

Vocational education tends to seem easier to provide in some respects than vocational training. If experiences are to be offered for their general educative value rather than for the sake of skill development, one can continue woodworking classes long after industry has ceased to offer many opportunities in this field; one can let the students dismantle and reassemble a 1955 automobile in 1970. However, the attitude that teachers do not need to keep up with industrial advances in fact involves serious fallacies. The teacher who cannot speak with confidence about current developments in a particular field is not likely to be an up-to-date interpreter of modern society either, and students will react unfavourably to his obvious obsolescence. Also, education is so expensive in any case that it seems unjustifiable to refuse to spend the extra amount required to ensure that it is as closely related as possible to current realities.

The Ontario Department of Education has quite consistently followed the proclaimed policy of providing vocational education rather than vocational training. Observers have frequently noticed, however, how difficult it has been to follow the former as a live and meaningful concept. There have been many teachers in vocational schools who have made no pretence at anything other than instructing in a specific skill. Students themselves have often regarded the general or academic component of a prescribed course as so much useless baggage to be lived through somehow and dropped as quickly as possible. The best use they have been able to think of for the final years of compulsory education has been to pick up something saleable on the job market. Thus there tends to be constant pressure to reduce vocational education to training. If the school persists in excessively lofty purposes, the students drop out.

The term "technical education" is commonly associated with vocational education. It may be used as a subcategory of the latter, paralleling agricultural, commercial, home economics, and other forms, and is quite often employed interchangeably with "industrial education." Technical high schools in Ontario have been considered a type of vocational school along with high schools of commerce, and the technical course was at a certain stage called "industrial." When the term is used in this way, the same distinction applies to technical education and training as to that between vocational education and training.

In certain circumstances, a distinction has been made between technical and industrial education on the basis of level. John Seath recognized the use of the former term to apply to courses that were more concerned with theory and led to the higher directive positions in industry, while industrial education, although also involving both theory and practice, placed more emphasis on practice. In a sense the difference shaded into that between education and training.

First provision for vocational courses

The first tangible evidence of concern for the provision of appropriately oriented education for workmen is to be found in the establishment of mechanics' institutes in the 1830s. These were based on a distinctly over-optimistic view of the desire for learning among the working class and survived mainly as libraries. It was one of Ryerson's hopes that agricultural and technical schools would become part of his educational system, but the time was apparently not ripe for such a development. According to McCutcheon, the period between 1870 and 1900 was marked by the establishment of private agencies for those entering mechanical and commercial occupations. He commented, however, on the lack of attention given to the educational needs of those entering the lower occupational fields.[24]

During that period, some commercial work was offered in the high school program. When the bookkeeping option was made compulsory in 1882, every high school student was given a measure of commercial education for the first time. The Department of Education offered a Commercial Diploma, beginning in 1885, for which the requirements were a large number of academic subjects along with writing, bookkeeping, commercial transactions, and précis writing. During the 1890s a two-year commercial course was being offered in the schools, and commercial teachers were being prepared at the School of Pedagogy in Toronto. Shortly after the turn of the century, the course was extended to three years.[25]

According to Harris, the following developments after that period were major steps in the increasing activity in the vocational field: the authorization of commercial departments in secondary schools in 1891; the introduction of manual training and household science at the turn of the century; the authorizing of school boards to establish technical schools in 1897; the listing of manual training, household science, art, and agriculture as secondary school subjects by 1904; the placing of agriculture on a solid footing as a two-year course at the Essex High School and at the collegiate institutes in Lindsay, Perth, Morrisburg, Collingwood, and Galt in 1907; and the appointment of a departmental Director of Elementary Agricultural Education.[26] The first technical night classes were begun in Toronto in 1891. Technical schools were shortly opened in Hamilton and Toronto. The first day classes in the latter, dating from 1901, consisted of drafting and industrial design, physics, chemistry, commerce and finance, mathematics, and domestic science.[27]

The Seath report and its aftermath

The production in 1911 of the report of John Seath entitled *Education for Industrial Purposes* was a major landmark in the development of vocational education in Ontario.[28] McCutcheon was unabashedly enthusiastic about it: "[it]is perhaps unexcelled as a treatise on technical education. It covers the subject in a most skilful, scholarly, and comprehensive manner."[29] Bascom St John later commented that the report was "still remarkable for its insight into what was needed in this field."[30]

Seath's recommendations were, of course, attuned to the general level of education prevailing at the time. He recognized, first of all, two basic categories of individuals needing industrial or technical "training": those in attendance at public, separate, or high schools, and those actually employed who would benefit from part-time courses. The first of these categories consisted of two subgroups: the "very large number" who left school for various reasons at or below the age of fourteen, and those who remained, or might be induced to remain, at school beyond that age. For the first of these subgroups, Seath's prescription involved courses in the elementary school: manual training, art work, and drawing for boys, with household science substituted for manual training for girls. The purposes to be achieved were indicated in part by the following passage:

> Before this age [i.e., fourteen], the boy is not ready for industrial training, but he can be taught to use his hands properly making things in which he is interested; he may be trained so that his hand and his brain may work together; he may learn the value of accuracy and the result of miscalculation; he may also learn that nothing but good handiwork will do and nothing but the best is good; he may be taught to express himself with his pencil as well as in language, and in particular to make and to work from simple plans; he may increase his power of invention by designing objects in wood or metal; and, under the influence of a competent teacher and suitable environment, he may even realize that some forms are more beautiful than others. And the knowledge and skill he acquires by the above processes he may turn into power in dealing with the handiwork of his future trade.[31]

For the small number of boys and girls with an interest in vocational education who remained in school after the age of fourteen, Seath recommended three types of day schools: the general industrial school, the special industrial school, and the technical high school and high school department. The general industrial school was to offer a two-year course, to be increased or diminished according to local conditions. Its curriculum would consist of general shop work in wood and metal for about a third of the time, and drawing, English, bookkeeping, practical mathematics, and science, all closely related to the shop work, as well as courses in civics, history, and literature taking up the remainder. Actual trade training would be given subsequently in industry. The special industrial school, as Seath envisioned it, would be a kind of trade school, to which a student would proceed after leaving the general industrial school. At that institution, he would learn the theory and processes of the trade without aspiring to become fully skilled. It would be especially important to relate the learning program closely to the needs of the locality in which the school was situated. The length of the period of study would depend on the nature of the trade. Recognizing that certain pressures would force a modification of what he considered ideal, Seath suggested possible variations in his general-special sequence. One of these was a special school at his proposed general level, and another was a co-operative program combining work and formal study. Seath's third type of school, the technical high school, would prepare students for positions in industrial life requiring special technical knowledge and of greater importance and responsibility than those held by skilled mechanics. It would offer a uniform two-year course followed by two years of specialized courses. Seath did not see much prospect of a demand for the product of such schools in Ontario for a number of years.

Seath asserted that, for many years to come, men and women who were employed during the daytime would be the most numerous of the claimants for industrial instruction. Although the establishment of the other types of schools he advocated would ensure that more of these people entered their trades with formal prior preparation, even the most proficient would benefit from supplementary instruction. For those who never had the opportunity for daytime instruction, special systematic training would be indispensable. Seath recommended three types of schools for these groups: the apprenticeship school, the evening industrial and technical school, and the correspondence industrial and technical school.

The Industrial Education Act of 1911 represented an attempt to implement some of the recommendations of the Seath report. It authorized municipalities to levy taxes for the establishment and support of day and evening industrial and technical schools. They might also establish commercial and agricultural high schools or such departments in ordinary high schools. Progress as a result of the legislation is usually considered to have been slow, although McCutcheon observed that, within two years, twenty-nine evening technical and industrial classes and six technical and industrial day schools were in operation.[32] Action was delayed during the years of the First World War but accelerated with the assistance of federal funds under the Technical Education Act of 1919. According to the terms of this act, $10 million was made available to all of the provinces, to be spent over a period of ten years. Ontario claimed over $3 million of this amount. By 1921 there were thirteen vocational schools in the province.

The Seath report made some recommendations for commercial as well as for industrial education, including provision for a general business course and an office course. The Department of Education was influenced to publish an outline of a suggested four-year general commercial course in 1913. Commercial departments were put under advisory commercial committees, which were prototypes for the advisory vocational committees added later.[33]

The Industrial Education Act of 1911 was superseded by *The Vocational Education Act* of 1921. Two years later, according to a description supplied by Harris, the sixteen existing schools had a full-time enrolment of nearly seven thousand and a part-time enrolment of a little less than one thousand. There was also an enrolment of 33,000 in the evening classes offered in these vocational schools and in thirty-four collegiate institutes or high schools.[34]

The technical schools gained in prestige in 1926 when the University of Toronto established a matriculation course for students in them who desired admission to the Faculty of Applied Science. In 1927 and 1928 respectively, the university took similar action with respect to matriculation candidates for admission to the Faculties of Household Science and Commerce. Comparatively few students, however, took advantage of these provisions.

The passing of *The Apprenticeship Act* in 1928 gave the technical schools the responsibility for offering the formal aspect of the training provided for those registered in the so-called designated trades. The first classes under the provisions of the act were held in 1930 at the Hamilton Technical Institute and the Central Technical School in Toronto. With the opening of similar classes in Ottawa and Windsor the following year, a total of 314 apprentices were enrolled for eight-week courses.[35] These programs expanded until after the war, when the responsibility for formal apprenticeship training was assumed in succession largely by the provincial trades institutes and vocational centres and by the colleges of applied arts and technology.

Regulations which came into force in 1936 determined the pattern of development for vocational schools during the subsequent period. They specified the types of vocational schools and departments, the courses of study, and the requirements for admission. The program was to consist of a broad foundation of general education along with special training in industrial, applied arts, commercial, agricultural, and homemaking occupations.

Trend toward composite secondary schools
During the period following the Second World War, there was an increasing tendency to establish composite schools rather than schools for strictly vocational courses. These had separate departments for the general course and whatever vocational courses, technical or commercial, the board saw fit to offer. The advantages leading to the choice of a composite school rather than separate academic and vocational schools might be seen in terms of financial savings, particularly in communities where the high school population was not large. There was also a growing feeling that there were social advantages in having students with varied interests and in programs of varied types mingling with one another. Transfer, where appropriate, was easier when the process meant moving from one department to another rather than from school to school.

Situation before the Technical and Vocational Training Assistance Act, 1960
The situation as it existed before the major changes brought about by the federal *Technical and Vocational Training Assistance Act* is described in material prepared by the Education Division of the Dominion Bureau of Statistics.[36] A high school board or board of education might, with the approval of the minister, establish a vocational school, or a vocational program in a composite school, providing some or all of the following: 1 / pre-vocational school courses; 2 / general full-time courses; 3 / part-time day courses; 4 / special full-time day courses; and 5 / evening courses. Pre-vocational courses, where offered, might be entered by pupils at the end of grade 7. Special vocational schools or classes could be established for pupils aged thirteen or over who had been in auxiliary classes. Full-time industrial courses, the main feature of the program, were being offered in 1960 in fifty-seven vocational and composite secondary schools. The four-year course led to a diploma in one of twenty-five shop subjects related to trades. Most of the schools were said to be offering between five and fifteen of these courses.

At that time evening courses were being offered in a wide variety of academic, cultural, hobby, and trade subjects. Of the sixty to seventy thousand enrolled, about a third were estimated to be taking industrial courses. Advanced Technical Evening courses, initiated in 1952, were being given in nineteen centres by 1960. Those offered in technical high schools were parallel to the ones offered in the provincial technical institutes and were given in recognition of the fact that these institutes were too few to be accessible to more than a part of the population of the province. An Advanced Technical Evening course might be offered by a high school board or board of education on condition that 1 / a request was made to the advisory vocational committee of the board by a local firm or a group of such firms; 2 / the advisory committee, after a survey of local conditions, recommended the establishment of such a course; and 3 / the minister approved the content of the proposed course and the qualifications of the proposed staff. The courses were offered on two levels, the grade I and grade II certificate courses. In each there were obligatory and optional subjects. Nine units of at least fifty hours each of in-school study were required to qualify for the provincial certificate.[37]

In September 1961 the H.B. Beal Secondary School in London began offering a course that was equivalent to that of the first year in the provincial technical institutes. This temporary provision was extended during the next two years to secondary schools in North York, Sarnia, Sault Ste Marie, and Toronto. Successful graduates were acceptable for the second year in certain diploma courses in the institutes.

Members of advisory vocational committees were appointed for terms of up to three years. Each committee consisted of 1 / the chairman and between three and five members of the board including, where appropriate, representatives of the public and separate school boards and county councils; and 2 / two or three employers and the same number of employees from industry. Members were appointed initially by the school board, and vacancies were filled according to the position of the former member. The committee might select a suitable site, erect a building, and purchase equipment, or arrange for the program to be conducted in another school. It defined the courses, approved the selection of teachers, determined the salary schedule, reported on the activities of the school, fixed fees, and submitted estimates annually to the board. The latter could not withhold approval of the estimates without giving the committee a hearing. The committee was authorized to appoint co-ordinating officers with the responsibility of informing employers and employees about the work of the school, arranging for part-time classes, and choosing vocational guidance officers.[38]

Significance of Federal-Provincial Technical and Vocational Training Agreement

The implications of the Federal-Provincial Technical and Vocational Training Agreement, signed in 1961 in accordance with the terms of the Technical and Vocational Training Assistance Act passed by the Parliament of Canada in December 1960, are dealt with in a number of sections of the present series, including volume I, chapters 2, 3, and 7; volume II, chapter 11; volume III, chapter 5; and volume IV, chapter 19. The large amount of funds made available for the construction of schools and additions to schools and for some aspects of the maintenance of facilities for vocational education helped to shift a substantial proportion of young people into programs that were better suited to their needs, capacities, and interests. Vocational schools and departments gained in prestige during the period when the Reorganized Program or Robarts Plan was operative. Whether or not the latter was a necessary step, it indisputably facilitated the movement, well under way in 1969–70, toward individual programs that might consist of various combinations of academic and vocational courses cutting across the old barriers.

While most people were prepared to agree that substantial benefits resulted from federal assistance in vocational school building, there were widespread doubts that a shared-cost program of this type was a very efficient way of attaining the objective. Walter Pitman expressed some of these misgivings.

I can remember in 1960, when the legislation came down from Ottawa entitled, The Vocational Training Act, and millions of dollars were poured into the provincial system, there was no one who made any philosophical decision as to the effect this would have on the educational experience of the children of the province. If you went to the federal government, all they said was, "All we do is to hand money to the municipal authority". If you went to the provincial authority, they said, "We have nothing to do with it, all we do is to approve the buildings which have been financed by the federal government, and requested by the municipality". And, if you went to municipalities, they were not very sure essentially what it was all about but they did know that they were getting a great deal of money for nothing.[39]

If matters worked out reasonably well, it was certainly not because they developed according to plan. The federal authorities originally intended to stimulate activity on the part of provincial governments and not school boards. They had in mind assistance with the construction of provincial institutes of technology and trade schools. On the basis of an initial estimate received from Ontario, that province was expected to receive about $15 million over the six-year period during which the agreement was in effect, while the total cost for all the provinces was estimated at about $90 million. A short time after the act was passed, however, the federal government agreed to include provincial grants to school boards for the construction of vocational high schools and of vocational facilities in composite high schools in its definition of recognized provincial expenditure. Under that interpretation, Ontario was able to claim nearly $230 million of the $333 million worth of projects approved for the whole of Canada in 1961–2 alone. The federal government had to seek approval for more than one set of supplementary estimates during the first year. It had stumbled into a policy that transformed the secondary school system in Ontario and to a lesser extent in other provinces.

Special vocational schools

The 1960s saw a rapid increase in the number of special vocational schools designed mainly for students who lacked the capacity to handle the regular programs in the Arts and Science, Business and Commerce, and Science, Technology, and Trades Branches, but who had reached an age where retention in elementary school was considered inappropriate. They were transferred rather than being promoted from grade 8 (a practice that perhaps indicates a surviving remnant of the mentality that insisted on a high school entrance examination up to 1949). The special vocational schools also accepted some students who won promotion to grade 9.

J.F. McGivney, a leader in the development of facilities for this group, and for a time Principal of Parkway Vocational School in Toronto, described this group.

> What are these pupils like? They are more like normal pupils than they are like anything else. They have the same wants, habits and appearance. The differences, significant though they may be, are a comparatively small part of the total individual. They are *not* bad or delinquent children or behaviour problems. They are probably slightly below the norm of the population in this regard. They are *not* mentally disturbed children but a larger proportion than average of mentally disturbed children can get into this group through poor academic performance and faulty diagnosis. They are not people who can't learn. They have learned more already than many people will learn in the last nine tenths of their lives. They do not learn, however, according to the speeds and patterns usually expected by educators. The paths they take to learning are not the ones that we as educators think are the simplest, most direct or most economical. The shortest distance between two learning points is not, for them, the straight line we pedagogues expect. It may be a long, tortuous and complicated track to us, but perfectly logical and acceptable to an individual and perhaps, for him, the only way. For this reason they have presented educators with a problem that educators, being what they are, have been, perhaps unwilling, but apparently unable to solve.[40]

As McGivney described them, these young people have a great many problems arising out of the way they have been treated. They suffer one defeat after another in the conventional school program. They are left behind by their peers and associates. Parents have expressed disappointment in them and often held them up to ridicule. They have developed very low opinions of themselves, unless taught by exceptional opportunity class teachers. They have responded to external hostility by setting up behavioural defense mechanisms, such as an apparently cheerful, passive acceptance of an inferior status, partial or complete withdrawal, belligerence, or a tendency to show off.

Successful operation of the school program obviously called for teachers with exceptional personal qualities and training. The students were usually given special academic and remedial instruction for half their time and vocational subjects for the remainder. During the first year, they took introductory courses in a number of trades and occupations and later specialized in a vocational subject appropriate to their talents and inclinations. While most of the courses led to service occupations, some of the more able students were accepted into apprenticeship.

In his annual report for 1965–6, G.E. Price, Director of Education for the City of Hamilton, referred with pride to the development of junior vocational schools in his system. This was representative of what was happening in the major centres of Ontario. The first school of the junior vocational type in Hamilton had been organized thirty-five years earlier in an old, unassigned building. Since 1963 the two older schools, one for boys and one for girls, had been replaced by modern structures, and a third had been built. Three others were on the drawing boards, and a complement of ten was foreseen for the future. In addition to an academic program, the boys' schools offered courses in auto servicing, auto body repair, sheet metalwork, building construction, trowel trades, shoe repair, tailoring and dry cleaning, business and merchandising, appliance repair, chef training, and restaurant services. The corresponding courses in the girls' school were in beauty culture, homemaking and hospital care, home economics, restaurant services, textiles and sewing, floral design, merchandising, and others. The students were given instruction especially adapted to their needs in classes that were always kept smaller than the average.[41]

PRIVATE SCHOOLS

Private schools in Canada have never attracted as large a proportion of total school enrolment as have those in Great Britain, the United States, or Australia. Phillips reported that, during the first half of the twentieth century, they just about held their own. In 1921 one pupil attended a private elementary or secondary school for every twenty-three who attended publicly controlled day schools; in 1948 the ratio was one to twenty-two. Two-thirds of the private school enrolment was in Quebec, where the ratio was one in ten. In the rest of Canada, it was one in thirty in 1921 and one in forty in 1948.[42] Chapter 2 of volume I of the present series indicates a substantial decline in this ratio in Ontario in recent years. Only schools at the elementary level have recorded substantial gains, but these have not been sufficient to counteract the general trend.

Part of the reason why so few children in Ontario attend private schools is that the Roman Catholic separate school system is classified as public. Thus dissent from the "public" system does not force a parent to seek a private alternative for his child. This difference does a good deal to invalidate direct comparisons with the United States, where parochial schools are private.

Types, purposes, and contributions

Private schools are maintained in Ontario for a variety of reasons: 1 / to offer an education in a particular religious atmosphere; 2 / to perpetuate an understanding and appreciation of a minority culture; 3 / to provide an alternative in aim or method to the kind of education offered in the publicly supported system; 4 / to supply facilities and opportunities that are not available in the publicly supported system; 5 / to provide an amount or quality of individual attention beyond that offered in the publicly supported system; 6 / to cater to children who have become behaviour problems. 7 / A less openly acknowledged factor on the part of many parents who send their children to the more prestigious schools is the desire for social or economic privilege.

In a brief to the Ontario cabinet in July 1968 the Ontario Alliance of Christian Schools clarified its reasons for insisting on the maintenance of its own particular type of private schools.

Christian schools as operated by the societies affiliated with the Ontario Alliance of Christian Schools are schools where children receive an education based on the Bible. We believe that the Bible reveals that man has been created in the image of God to live and labour as his servant in this world. We feel that our children must be taught to understand life as the service of God. They must be prepared to take their place in society as citizens equipped to serve God and their nation. It is obvious that religion is not a mere addendum, something which can be added at will to education. Christian education does not merely consist of reciting prayers, reading Bible passages, or telling Bible stories. Important as they are, by themselves they do not make a school system christian [*sic*]. Christian education takes it [*sic*] starting point in the Word of God and in that light seeks to instruct students. Hence we assert that the purpose of education, its contents and methods must be scripturally directed.[43]

Except for differences in doctrine, the case is quite similar to that made by Roman Catholics for their own system.

The Parents' Committee of Jewish Day Schools of the Province of Ontario stated its case to the Prime Minister and to the Minister of Education in a submission dated January 1968. It referred to a question that had been frequently asked: "Why Jewish day schools?" Their response was, in part, that

... many Jewish parents desire and yes, are entitled to a more intensive Jewish religious program for their children than can be obtained by having their children educated in the normal public schools and attending the afternoon Jewish schools upon completion of their regular school day.

Jewish parents, who have over the years wanted their children to get a general education as provided by the best public schools, found that there was only one way to supplement this general education with a thorough grounding in the rich lore and culture of Judaism and that was by setting up an integrated school with a dual program of secular and Jewish learning. The Jewish Day Schools in Ontario follow the prescribed Ontario curriculum in their general studies and have set standards as high as any school in the Province. At the same time, the level of achievement in Jewish studies is no less gratifying.[44]

Jewish spokesmen have claimed that there is no long-term hope for the survival of their distinct cultural heritage unless they can maintain their private schools.

A brief was submitted to the Ontario Committee on Taxation on behalf of a group of independent secondary schools, including non-denominational or Protestant church affiliated schools, Roman Catholic private schools, and Jewish schools. The educational contributions of such schools were indicated as follows.

To varying degrees the independent schools attempt to offer a more closely supervised and more extensive program than is usually provided by the tax dependent schools. The schools themselves and the individual classes are as a rule smaller than is found in the tax supported schools, and there is more emphasis on participation in sports and cultural activities. In addition, the independent schools usually have religious associations and attempt to encourage an appreciation of spiritual and moral values. They do a particularly good job for students who need more specialized instruction, and in rounding out the interests and personalities of the unusual or gifted students. The residential schools are able to go even farther than these basic objectives by giving the students experience in responsibility, leadership, and the application of citizenship principles in their school commmunity.

... Some have been pioneers in new teaching techniques and all secondary education has benefited from their experiments.

... They provide the community with a choice in its educational facilities and thus give meaning to the principle of freedom of choice which is a fundamental of our democratic society.[45]

The brief classified the independent schools of the province into three categories: 1 / schools in large communities such as Toronto, Hamilton, and Ottawa, which were primarily for day students in the community and included, as examples, St Michael's College School, Upper Canada College, Havergal College, and the Jewish secondary schools; 2 / schools in smaller communities catering almost exclusively to students in the community, of which Roman Catholic private secondary schools were typical; and 3 / schools in smaller communities which accepted boarders from outside the community as well as some local day students, examples of which were St Andrew's College, the Ontario Ladies' College, and Lakefield Preparatory School.

Eric LeBourdais surveyed the opportunities offered by the independent boys' schools within reach of Toronto and reported the results in *Toronto Life* in 1967.[46] His appraisal covered the Little Big Four – Upper Canada College, Trinity College School, Ridley College, and St Andrew's College – as well as Appleby College, Pickering College, Lakefield Preparatory School, and Hillfield College. On the basis of the fact that they had room at the high school level for a total of 2,776 boys, of whom 1,1621 were boarders and a large contingent came from other provinces and countries, he concluded that there were roughly nine hundred places accessible to boys from Metropolitan Toronto. Thus the schools were clearly very exclusive. All of them boasted of the heterogeneity of their enrolment, with all races and religions welcomed. But, while their ethnic and religious composition came close to that of English Canada as a whole, their high fees restricted the mixing of social levels. Even considering financial assistance, which was provided for a percentage ranging from below 10 at Upper Canada to over 22 at Lakefield, LeBourdais concluded that the number of parents who would even consider sending a boy to a private school comprised a tiny layer at the top of society.

LeBourdais found that, while only a decade earlier the staffs of the private schools had suffered in comparison with those in the public schools, they were currently as good and possibly in some ways better. Their students, who were selected either for their academic ability or their broad interests and talents, did much better than the provincial average on the grade 13 departmental examinations. The fact that the schools were not tied to the provincial curriculum and textbooks gave them an opportunity to "experiment, innovate, modify and embellish." They all provided classes of fifteen to twenty students. Tutors, advisers, or counsellors were assigned to small groups of boys. At all schools, sports and other activities, of which there was a very wide range, were compulsory. There was thus a basis for the claim that the schools provided a more rounded education than did schools which left such matters to chance. Cadets and religion were strongly emphasized, although specific religious affiliations were played down. Discipline was strict, and a great deal of attention was given to manners and appearance.

An undated brief to the Minister of Education lists a number of unique services performed by boarding schools. They are said to be particularly useful under the following circumstances: 1 / when one or both parents are dead; 2 / when parents are posted overseas for temporary periods; 3 / when parents live permanently outside Canada and want their children to have the advantages of a Canadian education; 4 / when parents living in isolated areas of Canada where facilities for a good education are lacking want their children to be educated in an environment where they may eventually be earning a living; 5 / where both parents work and cannot provide a normal home life; 6 / where parents are separated; and 7 / where there are other unusual conditions in the home, such as a lone son among daughters or an only child.[47]

A private school with a unique purpose and program was the National Ballet School, founded in Toronto in 1959. It recognized that a child must begin training at about the age of ten in order to achieve maximum excellence as a ballet dancer. After some nine years of practice and development, he was ready for the relatively short career in dancing. The school propounded the principle that a professional dancer should have a first class academic and aesthetic education. Also, since some children of ten might not develop adequate talent for dancing, it was considered important that they not be handicapped from choosing a more satisfactory alternative. In 1969 the school followed the educational program set out by the Toronto Board of Education and the Department of Education from grade 5 through grade 12, except that science was taken by special arrangement at Jarvis Collegiate Institute. Strong emphasis was placed on music and art. In the specialized field of ballet, an attempt was made to secure the short-term services of outstanding teachers from various parts of the world. Talented children were recruited from all across the country and, where necessary, assisted with bursaries. Residences were provided for students from out of town, while those from Toronto were able to live at home. In addition to the regular program, there were provisions for a post-graduate year of ballet training, for the training of ballet teachers, and for classes for part-time students from the Toronto school system. While the school was founded as an independent private school under a board of directors, the Ontario government had not discovered the same barriers to supporting it as it had with respect to other types of private schools. Contributions were also received from the Canada Council, the Ontario Council of the Arts, and the Metropolitan Toronto Council.

A type of school embodying the desire to seek education through approaches that differ more or less radically from those followed in the public system is Superschool, operated briefly in Toronto from 1968 on. Its manifestation of freedom was to ensure that what was taught was approved by students, teachers, and parents. Teachers were called resource persons and acted as partners with the students in running the school. Funds were adequate only for the provision of the simplest accommodation and the most modest of facilities, and staff served because of their devotion to the cause despite salaries that seemed a pittance in comparison with those paid to teachers in the public system. Schools of this type, in addition to whatever benefits are received by the small number who attend them, perform a valuable general service in demonstrating how educational theories work out in practice. Some of them will undoubtedly turn out to be prototypes for the future.

Financial status

The main purpose of the brief from the independent schools to the Ontario Committee on Taxation was to present arguments against the proposition, which the committee nevertheless accepted, that the independent schools should lose the tax exemption they enjoyed on their property. It was estimated that the savings to the provincial and local governments resulting from the contributions of the schools in the first two categories amounted to over $17 million in 1961 alone. Even those in the third category (in small communities catering largely to outsiders) were an asset to the communities in which they were located that more than outweighed the loss attributable to tax exemption. The suggestion that the independent schools should be subject to property taxes or payments in lieu of taxes and reimbursed by provincial grants was labeled impractical in application. Among the disadvantages of such a procedure, it was suggested that political discussions of the virtues of different religious and racial groups be invited, and discriminatory legislation might ensue.

On logical grounds it is as easy, or as difficult, to justify tax relief for the supporters of one type of private school as it is for those of another. Up to 1970 none of the three major political parties in Ontario had adopted a policy that involved providing such relief. As observed in volume II, chapter 6, the Liberal and New Democratic Parties advocated extending financial support for a Roman Catholic separate school system to the end of secondary school. They insisted, however, on defining this system as an alternative public system and disapproved of granting assistance to private Roman Catholic high schools. The Conservatives had not, at the time of writing, been able to grasp the distinction between a "public" system maintained for the children of one particular religious group and a private system designed for the same purpose. Neither had some supporters or potential supporters of the other parties.

If the government maintains the policy of refusing all assistance to private schools, the disproportionately rapid rise in educational costs is likely to eliminate most of those designed to provide a particular religious atmosphere or to perpetuate a specific culture. Parents who want such special schools are not necessarily particularly prosperous and will not be able to support the facilities and amenities that public systems can afford or to pay their teachers at the levels prevailing in the latter. On the other hand, the schools with high prestige based on long tradition will probably be able to maintain themselves by appealing to a narrowing group of the economic elite, who may be expected to pay higher and higher fees as places grow increasingly scarce. The price these schools pay for survival will be a growing estrangement from the ordinary life of the community. If Ontario is indeed set on a course that will reduce or eliminate private schools as a significant educational influence, it will be extremely important to encourage variety within the public system itself. The alternative to some provision for variety is to accept schools as one of the major dehumanizing influences of modern society.

Departmental supervision

The fact that private schools receive no financial support from the government does not mean that there is no official interest in them. They are required to register with the Department of Education and to submit their students and teachers in grades 11 and 12 to departmental inspection in order to be able to recommend students for the Ontario Secondary School Graduation Diploma. The department also has a general right of inspection at any level. When departmental inspection of publicly supported schools ceased in 1968, it was still maintained for private schools, which paid a fee for this service. In addition to submitting to inspection, they are required by *The Department of Education Act* to furnish statistical information regarding enrolment, staff, courses of study, and other matters as required by the minister. Buildings must meet the standards established by the Ontario Department of Health and the Ontario Fire Marshal.

Profit-making vocational schools

A type of private school which has diminished in relative importance with the expansion of offerings in the public secondary and post-secondary systems is the private profit-making vocational school, one of the most important types of which is the business college. These institutions are in business to sell a commodity, that is, a specific skill or set of skills such as typing, shorthand, bookkeeping, or data processing. Market conditions demand that they utilize the most efficient methods available and achieve their purpose in a minimum period of time. They must be flexible in terms of enabling a student to begin a course when it suits his convenience and in offering courses of varying lengths. They ordinarily do not claim to offer an "education" but devote their attention solely to the improvement of the student's value on the job market. While this field of private endeavour may have fallen on lean days, there is no immediate prospect that it will disappear. It would seem desirable to have public institutions kept constantly aware that they may face the loss of their students if they do not provide for their practical needs and interests.

THREE

School organization and administration

THE PRINCIPAL'S ROLE

J.G. Althouse, discussing the structure and aims of education, presented a highly idealized concept of administration in his Quance Lectures in 1949.

> Sometimes it is stated as the release of power for a given purpose. In education, it would be the release of the power of intelligent self-determination in the local school authorities, the release of the power of well-informed goodwill among the members of a community, the release of the power of stimulating instruction among the teachers, the release of the power of interested industry and honest thinking among the students. For all of these powers do exist; they are latent in our communities.
>
> If administration goes no farther than to release these powers, no farther than to protect good teachers and good students from outside interference and from themselves, it can raise school efficiency to a new high level. Yet I believe that even this is not a satisfactory goal for administration. It must not only release power; it must augment power and even generate power where now so little exists as to be almost negligible. The administrative structure must, if you like, be a power-house of energy at the disposal of all who seek it.[1]

In an article in *School Progress* in 1965, W.W. Worth expressed the same idea in more prosaic terms.[2] He observed that teachers improved by being challenged by the job and by being stimulated to put into practice their knowledge of good teaching. He identified a considerable measure of agreement that the motivating function was the primary responsibility of the school principal. As an integral part of the social system of the school, the principal was considered to be in the best position to provide the continuous, sustained leadership that was closely associated with effective teacher motivation. Worth noted that the motivation function was poorly understood and very difficult to perform. While he found it impossible to offer a list of the techniques that might be employed, certain insights and generalizations might be identified from social-psychological findings relating to organization and leadership. Most of the article was devoted to a review of different ways in which members adapted to the organization in which they made their living, as described by Robert Presthus in *The Organizational Society*. The three types of personality identified were labeled the upward-mobile, the indifferent, and the ambivalent. Worth suggested that success in performing the administrative function depended on an understanding of the characteristics of these basic types.

The task of defining the type of person who makes the best principal is as difficult as it is to determine the ideal candidate for any other role. It is easy to fall into the trap of making a compendium of all the virtues one can think of, with a result that is pleasant to contemplate but of little use in sorting out real human beings for available tasks and obligations. On the other hand, an attempt to compile a brief list of the really essential qualities usually fails in the face of the complex interrelationships that are characteristic of human personality. What may appear to be a serious strength or weakness when considered in isolation may be of no great significance when juxtaposed with some other quality. It seems much simpler to most people to recognize the individual who is fitted for administrative responsibility than it is to generalize about the traits needed for success.

Regardless of other considerations, one factor of supreme importance to the health of the school as a truly educational institution is the nature of the principal's will to power. Frank MacKinnon observed that

> Just as the consumption of alcohol is motivated by various desires – thirst, celebration, stimulation or imitation – so the exercise of power may result from a real desire to do something that is right and do it well, or from a tendency to boost the ego or to mind other people's business. As with alcohol, power can be divorced from responsibility: those who wield it are often too fond of exercising it independently and tend to judge their importance by the amount of power entrusted to them. When people, even the most powerful, get too intoxicated with it, power becomes illusory, and they, like the great pre-historic monsters or the powerful dictatorships, give way to others.[3]

Unfortunately, principals whose motives for exercising power are to boost their ego or to mind other people's business are not immediately swept aside. They remain to establish an atmosphere where things are not done because it is obviously logical or right to do them but because they say so. Under such circumstances, the teachers may be respectful and the students obedient, and the whole operation may be such as to appeal highly to a lover of order. But in terms of relevance to their interests and aspirations, the students may have long since swept the school aside, and the principal and all he stands for may be as obsolete as the dinosaur. Regrettably, while legal means may be used to oust an administrator who proves to be grossly incompetent or who offends the moral sensibilities of the community, there are no comparable sanctions for the love of irrational and destructive power. Student rebels who try to organize active resistance usually find themselves cast as subversives.

The Schools Administration Act assigns to the principal a considerable list of duties in addition to those he assumes as a teacher:

(a) to maintain proper order and discipline in the school;

(b) to register the pupils, classify them according to the courses of study prescribed, and record their progress through school;

(ba) to ensure that the attendance of pupils for every school day is recorded in the register supplied by the Minister in accordance with the instructions contained therein or in such other manner as is approved by the Minister;

(c) to prepare and conduct the school according to a timetable which shall be accessible to pupils, teachers and the inspectors;

(d) to hold such examinations as may be required by the inspector for the promotion of pupils or for any other purpose as the inspector may direct and report the progress of the pupil to his parent or guardian at least for each school term;

(e) subject to revision by the inspector, to make at the end of each school term such promotions from one grade to another as he may deem expedient;

(f) to prevent the use by pupils of text-books that are not approved under the regulations;

(g) to furnish to the Minister and to the inspector any information that it may be in his power to give respecting the conditions of the school premises, the discipline of the school, the progress of the pupils and any other matter affecting the interests of the school, and to prepare such reports for the board as are required by the regulations.

(h) to give assiduous attention to the health and comfort of the pupils, to the cleanliness, temperature and ventilation of the schoolhouse, to the care of all maps, apparatus and other school property, to the preservation of shade trees and the orderly arrangement and neat appearance of the playgrounds;

(i) to report promptly to the board and to the municipal health officer or to the school medical officer where one has been appointed, when he has reason to suspect the existence of any infectious or contagious disease in the school, or the unsanitary condition of the schoolhouse, outhouses or surroundings;

(j) to refuse admission to the school of any pupil who he believes is infected with or exposed to communicable diseases requiring quarantine and placarding under regulations made pursuant to *The Public Health Act* until furnished with a certificate of a medical officer of health or of a duly qualified medical practitioner approved by him that all danger from exposure to contact with such pupil has passed;

(k) to suspend any pupil guilty of persistent truancy, or persistent opposition to authority, habitual neglect of duty, the use of profane or improper language, or conduct injurious to the moral tone of the school, and to notify the parent or guardian of the pupil and the board and the inspector of the suspension, but the parent or guardian of any pupil suspended may appeal against the action of the principal to the board which has power to remove, confirm or modify the suspension; and

(l) to keep a visitors' book and make it available for visitors to sign.[4]

These statutory obligations could clearly stand some revising in terms of their references to such matters as the inspector's role and grade promotion.

SELECTION AND PREPARATION OF SCHOOL PRINCIPALS

There are continual complaints that the best members of the teaching profession are drained away to fill the ranks of the principals and of other administrators. Hardly anyone appears to be willing, however, to accept either of the alternatives: that the poor teachers be given the administrative jobs, or that administrators be selected from outside the ranks of the profession. Education Minister Davis discussed this problem in the Legislature in 1965 and, while he had no radical solutions to offer, he felt that the best course of action was to free the principal from as many as possible of his administrative tasks so that he could be the intellectual leader of the school.[5] Davis believed that a principal should have a good deal of time to devote to staff development. In some ways this function paralleled that of superintendents and inspectors. Davis thought it would be possible in this way to justify the fact that a good teacher had been lost from the staff.

Secondary schools

Prior to 1952 a holder of a High School Assistant's Certificate was eligible for a High School Principal's Certificate after three years of successful experience and on recommendation of an inspector. Such certificates were often awarded without too much restriction, and many of those who qualified applied for them as a matter of course without necessarily having much expectation of moving into administrative work. As far as elementary schools were concerned, there was no formal requirement for holding the principalship.

The first formal training for principals of academic high schools began in 1951 with a five-week summer course. Similar arrangements were made for vocational principals the following year, when award of the certificate was made contingent on successful completion of the course. Selection of suitable applicants was considered to be a crucial part of the process. Those who participated heard presentations from a variety of educators, not only on problems relating specifically to administration, but also on a considerable range of issues of current interest. An extremely flexible procedure allowed for informal discussions, question-and-answer sessions, and the like. There was no final examination.

A new secondary school principal's course was introduced in 1957 leading to a Secondary School Principal's Certificate, which was valid in a high school, collegiate institute, vocational school, or composite school. It consisted of two parts, each of five weeks' duration, offered in consecutive summers. An applicant for admission to the first part of the course had to 1 / hold a Permanent High School Assistant's Certificate or a High School Specialist's Certificate; 2 / have a minimum of five years of teaching experience, at least three of which had to have been in an Ontario secondary school; 3 / have been rated a better-than-average teacher for at least the last two years of his teaching experience; and 4 / pass an oral examination. Oral examinations were conducted by a committee appointed by the Superintendent of Secondary Education.[6] To qualify for the second session, an applicant had to have completed the first session or else to meet the conditions for admission to it, as well as hold a High School Principal's Certificate or a Vocational School Principal's Certificate. The holder of either of these latter certificates had to take the second session in order to obtain the Secondary School Principal's Certificate, which was required before appointment to the principalship of a composite school. The holder of both the High School Principal's Certificate and the Vocational School Principal's Certificate continued, however, to be eligible for such a position without taking a summer course.

Requirements for admission to the second session were raised in 1959. Now five years of successful teaching experience had to be completed in Ontario secondary schools before the year of application, and the candidate had to have taught one or more subjects of grades 11, 12, or 13 for at least three years. The Secondary School Principal's Certificate was to be granted to those who held positions as principals or vice-principals in the school year after completion of the course. Others received an Interim Secondary School Principal's Certificate valid for five years.

Further changes were made in 1965. Two first-year sessions, each restricted to an enrolment of eighty, were offered in different university centres. Requirements for admission to the first session were unchanged, except that the Vocational Specialist's Certificate with an acceptable degree was mentioned as an alternative to the High School Assistant's Certificate. On successful completion of the first session, the candidate was granted an Interim Secondary School Principal's Certificate, Type B, which qualified him to be a vice-principal of any provincial secondary school, a principal of a provincial secondary school with an enrolment of fewer than five hundred students, or a principal of a special vocational school of any size. After two years or more in one of these positions, and on the recommendation of the district inspector or municipal superintendent, the holder of the Interim Type B Certificate could apply to have his certificate made permanent. He might then be admitted to the second session of the course and, on completing it successfully, would be granted a Permanent Secondary School Principal's Certificate, Type A, which was valid for the principalship of any provincial secondary school.[7]

Elementary schools

As of 1961 all new appointees to the principalship of an elementary school having an enrolment of three hundred or more were required to hold a BA degree as well as a Permanent First Class Certificate or a Permanent Elementary School Teacher's Certificate. This change was made in recognition of the more active part such a principal was expected to take in the supervision of instruction. After that date, a Letter of Permission was required for the employment of a principal of a school of the specified size who lacked the requisite qualifications. Boards were advised that they might retain such a principal without advertising his position if he had completed two university courses during the preceding calendar year. Where the enrolment of a school increased from less to more than three hundred, and thus rendered a principal unqualified for his position, a Letter of Permission might be issued at the discretion of the Department of Education. School boards and inspectors were asked to urge principals who did hold the necessary minimum qualifications to improve their effectiveness by taking a summer course each year in such areas as primary methods, junior education, intermediate education, and auxiliary education.[8]

An elementary school principal's course, leading to the Elementary School Principal's Certificate, was begun in 1966. One of its announced purposes was to give added recognition to the role played by the principal. During the first summer, the elementary course and Part I of the secondary course were offered at Queen's University, the University of Waterloo, and the University of Western Ontario, with enrolment limited to eighty elementary and eighty secondary candidates in each centre. In the interests of further integration of the two levels, joint sessions were held on suitable topics, and facilities were shared. An applicant for the Elementary School Principal's course had to 1 / hold a Permanent Elementary School Teacher's Certificate, Standard IV, 2 / be a principal or be appointed to the principalship of an Ontario elementary school as of September 1966, and 3 / have been considered to be above average in competence as a teacher for at least the last two years of his teaching or principalship experience. On successful completion of the course, the candidate was eligible for an Interim Certificate valid for a period of five years from the date of issue. According to the original announcement on December 3, 1965, the certificate was not to be required for appointment as a principal without adequate notice being given.[9] Naturally it would take some time before such a change could be made without rendering most of the existing principals unqualified for their current positions. In order to qualify for a permanent certificate, a candidate had to have two years of successful experience as a principal after receiving his certificate. The notice warned that he might also have to attend a second session of the course or submit evidence of standing in certain specified units of graduate study in education.

Both levels

At the same time requirements for admission to the Secondary School Principal's course were somewhat modified. The Occupational Specialist's Certificate with an acceptable degree was added to the list of acceptable certificates. As an alternative to three years' teaching of one or more subjects of grades 11, 12, or 13, the candidate might hold a Specialist's Certificate in Auxiliary Education with secondary school options and have at least two years' experience teaching general or practical subjects in the Occupational program. He did not require the latter certificate, however, if he had an Occupational Specialist's Certificate.

For 1967 the requirements for making the Interim Elementary School Principal's Certificate permanent, in addition to two years of successful experience, were specified as follows: successful completion of one of 1 / a departmental summer course of five weeks' duration or an equivalent winter course for which a Department of Education certificate had been granted, but not a course required for a basic teaching certificate; 2 / two units of graduate study toward the former B Paed, B Ed, or M Ed degree taken at the College of Education of the University of Toronto, or the equivalent; 3 / two half-courses of graduate study in education from the Ontario Institute for Studies in Education, or the equivalent.

One occasionally encounters an acid appraisal of the content and approach used in some of these principals' courses. H.L. Willis, writing as Assistant Superintendent of the Collegiate Institute Board of Ottawa, undertook an evaluation of the performance of the Canadian superintendent.[10] He felt that it was time to develop educators who were "students of their craft and scholars in their profession." Unfortunately, most Canadian superintendents and directors of education lacked the kind of training that would make them either students or scholars in educational administration. Against the background of his own direct experience with principals' training courses, Willis continued:

> *The only organized training that many of them have had is the Mickey Mouse courses offered for the preparation of principals. Such training, composed of caveats and shibboleths, is simply not good enough.*
>
> Modern education has become too complex to be run on a notebook list of do's and don'ts for pupil behaviour and discipline, for grading of students, for handling the recalcitrant, the lazy and the incompetent teacher, for building timetables. These are like the popular "do it yourself" routines that have made temporary fixers out of harried husbands and are likely to make the same kind of temporary fixers out of harried principals and superintendents.

SECURITY FOR PRINCIPALS

The teachers' federations in Ontario have campaigned successfully for the unity of the profession in that membership has included both practising teachers and those appointed to administrative positions. The official contract form has covered the employment of teachers only, and status as an administrator has been conferred subsequently and additionally. It has been said that the arrangement has tended to elevate the status of the classroom teacher or, conversely, to keep administrators from becoming too much of a group apart. By providing for the involvement of administrators in their discussions of policy issues, teachers have ensured that their official attitudes will reflect a comprehensive point of view. Impartial observers are impressed by the argument that this approach moderates the teachers' position and prevents them from drifting into the extreme forms of self-centred and militant unionism that have developed in some parts of the United States. Because the arrangement has appeared to increase the power of the teachers in relation to the boards, trustees have exerted pressure to separate the two groups. There is a distinct possibility that the attainment of this objective would create new and formidable problems for them.

The theory is that school boards and teachers are partners in a great co-operative enterprise, making their respective contributions to the attainment of one common goal. However, there are not only possibilities of misunderstanding between them but genuine sources of conflict as well. In such circumstances boards feel that principals, as a part of management, must be on their side and may not regard themselves as supporters of the teachers' interests. Boards have also tended to insist that they have the unequivocal right to appoint, promote, or dismiss a principal without having to account in any way to the teachers' federations. In the world of business and industry, it has generally been accepted as a fundamental right of the employer to control employment at the managerial level.

Quite clearly the boards would have their ability to control school systems seriously weakened if the federations were able to demand an accounting every time a principal was demoted, as long as his basic contract as a teacher continued to be honoured. The federations have understandably been antagonized, however, when there was serious doubt that the basis for demotion was real incompetence on the job. Before they established their positions securely, it was not unknown for a principal to be dismissed because he had been too active in promoting federation affairs. In other cases, the action appears to have been taken on the basis of a board's prejudice or misjudgment of the circumstances. The most successful federation tactic under such conditions has been through pressure to have the situation examined impartially and fairly. There remains some vagueness about a board's right to dismiss a principal completely, as opposed to restoring him to a position as a classroom teacher.

CLASS SIZE

There are few aspects of the organization and operation of schools that have been more discussed, and with fewer definite conclusions, than that of the ideal class size. There are obviously many specific factors to be considered, such as the purpose of the instruction, the characteristics of the group, and the techniques and media to be used. The recent tendency has been for some of these to vary so much that the attempt to arrive at meaningful figures apart from the context has seemed rather futile. Yet the question of the optimum pupil-teacher ratio, or perhaps the best that can be managed under a given set of economic circumstances, remains highly relevant. The over-all figures do much to determine the kind of specific groupings that can be arranged for particular purposes.

Those who support the idea of having classes of relatively large size usually do so on the basis of economy. They have tended to derive a certain degree of satisfaction from research studies, which have often failed to uncover any significant difference related to this factor. The case for increasing class size was taken up by Don O'Hearn in an article printed in the *Windsor Star* in May 1968.[11] He noted that there were 27.5 pupils for every elementary school teacher in Ontario, a decrease from 30.2 in 1963. He did not go into the question of the extent to which the change could be explained by the increase in supervisors, administrators, and consultants who did not teach regular classes; that is, he did not indicate to what extent the actual size of the class faced by the average teacher had been affected. He observed, however, that Ontario teachers enjoyed one of the most favourable ratios in the world. He proceeded to show the savings that would have resulted had one pupil been added to the numerator of the ratio. Under such circumstances, 1,718 fewer teachers would have been needed in the province and, with the average teacher's salary estimated at $5,000 a year, the saving would have been $8.5 million. If the ratio were restored to that of 1963, the saving would have been over $20 million.

Small classes are favoured by those who stress the complexity and the intensely personal nature of the learning process. Arguing from the principle that the teacher's influence is a key element, they reason that true education must diminish if this influence is dispersed beyond a certain point. Large classes and individualized instruction are seen as contradictory. Large classes also tend to demand regimentation and conformity and to inhibit constructive pupil interaction.

Paul Goodman has condemned large classes in the most emphatic terms: "Terrible damage is done to children simply by the size and standardization of the big system. Suppose a class size of 20 is good for average purposes; it does *not* follow that 35 is better than nothing. Rather, it is likely to be positively harmful, because the children have ceased to be persons and the teacher is destroyed as a teacher."[12]

Writing in 1966, B.L. Cox, Vice-Principal of Earl Haig Secondary School, was able to cite previous research to support the idea of small classes.[13] He cited Hollingsworth's report on fifteen years of studies at Teachers College, Columbia University, where "on every criterion used, the small classes had the advantage over the larger ones." The reasons for the difference were attributed to group work and interaction between teacher and pupils in the small classes. In most of the latter, the use of a variety of enrichment materials was observed, while the larger classes relied almost totally on the textbook. Cox pointed to the particularly strong case for small classes in English. If a teacher is to accept the obligation to appraise one essay a week from each student, obviously the classes must be small or else the teacher must have relatively few of them.

Translation of the over-all student-teacher ratio into actual class figures has been difficult in Ontario secondary schools. During the late 1950s, the provincial figures were about twenty-three or twenty-two to one, gradually declining during subsequent years until the ratio in 1968–9 stood at approximately seventeen to one. But the proliferation of administrative positions and supporting services has been particularly great during this period. At the Annual Assembly of the Ontario Secondary School Teachers' Federation in Hamilton for 1968–9, one lady is said to have exclaimed: "Seventeen to one? Why, I had no idea that classes were that small. I remember 40 in one of my classes."[14] A report delivered at the Annual Assembly in 1965 urged the following maxima for class size: academic, thirty-three; shop academic, thirty; shop, twenty-two; and occupations, seventeen. The same report suggested a goal of no more than thirty periods a week for teachers and considerably less for department heads.[15] In 1967 a policy statement suggested that normal class size should be a maximum of thirty for academic subjects, twenty for technical subjects, and fifteen for occupational and special classes. The federation also expressed disapproval of the practice of combining small technical classes into large groups for their academic subjects.[16]

In March 1969 the minister announced that class sizes would probably have to be increased in 1969–70 in some secondary schools. There was no doubt a hope that such a measure would result in financial savings. The main reason, however, was that the elimination of the special summer courses, except in modified forms, promised to leave the schools with a temporary shortage of teachers. The minister had effected the change after years of urging from the teachers' federations and after the most thorough consultation with them. He had received their assurance, along with that of other groups, such as the trustees, that they would co-operate to get over the transitional period, which would necessarily be somewhat painful. In view of this fact, it was surprising to hear many teachers interpret Davis's warning as if it represented a deliberate policy of attempting to increase their work load.

LENGTH OF THE SCHOOL YEAR

The nine- or ten-month school year, with time off during the summer months, traditionally accommodated the work rhythm of the farming community by ensuring that the children would be available at home when they were most needed. There was perhaps some consideration given also to the difficulties of studying during the hot months, but this factor probably did not weigh heavily in view of the widespread notion that hardship strengthened the moral fibres. In recent years, a number of people have called attention to the anomaly of maintaining a practice for which the original justification is gone. They point out that if education is essentially a pleasant process of growth in knowledge, skill, and personal realization, there is no good reason why it should be interrupted for a long period of time during the middle of the year. The trend for certain boards to establish summer schools, not only for those who need extra help to make up for deficiencies, but also for those who seek new and challenging experiences, is a practical demonstration of this concept. It is often pointed out that such a practice involves a more adequate use of buildings and facilities that must be paid for in any case.

The official length of the school year in Ontario is ordinarily a little less than ten months, beginning the day after Labour Day and continuing until a date near the end of June established annually by departmental regulation. The elementary schools have traditionally adhered to this scheme but, because of complexities attributable to the final examinations, particularly those surrounding the grade 13 departmental examinations as administered until 1967, secondary students have normally been released earlier. In theory, the departmentals began about the second week in June and continued until almost the end of the month. In fact, the papers written by most of the candidates were scheduled for the beginning of the examination period, and the less frequently chosen papers for the latter part of the month. Thus many grade 13 students were finished by the middle of the month or shortly thereafter. Students in other grades were also released long before the end of the month. Many of them were excused from writing the final examinations by virtue of recommendations based on their year's work. The period of time during the latter part of the month in which teachers were free of instructional obligations provided them with an opportunity to mark examination papers and to hold promotion meetings.

In June 1968, the year after the elimination of the departmental examinations, grade 13 students could be excused from writing those subjects in which they had obtained at least 60 per cent on their year's work. Since a major proportion were able to qualify for exemption under this provision, their school year in fact ended on June 3, while a small percentage remained to write examinations. Thus the school year was effectively reduced to nine months, and the period of instruction to 179 days. In reviewing the situation, the minister observed that some schools were able to complete all promotion meetings and mail reports to students by June 18.[17] As a means of restoring conditions comparable to those of 1967 and previous years, the department announced in December 1968 that classes would continue until June 13, 1969, after which those not required to write examinations might be excused. Thus the period available for instruction was 184 days, five days longer than in 1967–8.

The subsequent furor over what was originally regarded as a routine announcement must have astonished all those concerned with it. For months afterwards, the media were full of reports of student protests, threats of strikes, and rallies in front of the Parliament Buildings to confront the minister. His action was interpreted as a lengthening of the school year and was labeled as arbitrary, dictatorial, and demonstrative of a contemptuous attitude toward the students. Many of the latter were thought to have spent far more than the five days' worth of extra school time in campaigning on the issue.

There was little variety in the arguments offered. The general nature of the case may be illustrated from a presentation in the Legislature by Tim Reid of the views of a group of students from Woburn Collegiate Institute.[18] Their first objection was to the short notice to students, teachers, and employers of students who, in order to be financially able to attend post-secondary educational institutions, had to work during the summer. Students from universities and colleges of applied arts and technology, who were formerly released three weeks earlier than secondary school students, now had a five-week head start. No explanation was offered as to why a five-week advantage would have made any difference to a student who had not already secured employment during a three-week interval. In any case, the petitioners felt that, if they had to attend school until June 13, there should be a change in the current Ontario Student Aid Program, which assumed that a student would have saved $250 from summer earnings to qualify for a student award.

The students' second objection was on behalf of the teachers as well as of themselves. They attributed to an Ontario Secondary School Teachers' Federation spokesman the statement that the arrangement would make accurate evaluation almost impossible, as a result of the fact that time for the meetings of the promotion committees would be cut in half. Also, because of the shortness of the available time, the examinations were not apt to be marked so carefully. There was no reference to the fact that the marking applied, not to the whole secondary school body, but only to those who failed to secure recommendations based on their year's work.

The students supposed that the purpose of the regulation was to enable or force them to learn more. If so, they were sure that it would fail. In their words: "It is our feeling that a student will not learn that much more by wasting his energies, and the teachers', in a hot classroom for an extra ten school days." They were sure that most of the students would demonstrate a flippant and languid attitude. This particular point was significant in demonstrating how far away the students were from feeling impelled to learn for learning's sake. They were seemingly still dominated by the view that school was a pill that society forced them to swallow but, since even adolescents had some democratic rights, they would be pushed only so far. Perhaps nothing that happened during the year revealed quite so effectively how far the secondary schools still had to go to attain some of the aims being so vigorously propounded in the wake of *Living and Learning.*

DISCIPLINE

The present context does not permit a thorough analysis of the psychological or social bases for discipline of the young. It is possible only to identify a few of the most obvious trends in thinking and practice characteristic of Ontario schools in recent years. The following extract from an article written by Emerson Lavender as Principal of Central High School in Burlington represents what might be called a traditionalist point of view.

> Establishing a teacher's authority and a student's duties and responsibility in a classroom has to come before friendship, popularity and understanding. Only in firm adherence to specific rules and restrictions can a class achieve that freedom which is required for academic progress ...
>
> The teacher's first duty to his class is to outline to it the basic assumptions on which the class operates and the student's responsibility to the class and to the teacher. These regulations must be specific, positive and reasonable. They should be based on the assumption that the majority of people in the class are young ladies and gentlemen in a place of business. A class must know what is expected of each member on such mundane matters as the method of entering the classroom, how to prepare for the beginning of the class, the student's responsibility during the class, homework – how much and how it is to be done, note making, homework correction, how free time, if any, is to be spent in the class at the end of the period, how the room is to be left at the end of the period, what arrangements are made for extra help after school, what is expected of the student in the way of talking or not talking, what is expected of the student in the reporting of defacement of the desks, the correction of examinations, the asking and answering of questions, and participation in the development of a lesson.[19]

This is an exceptionally lucid exposition of the authoritarian point of view. It gives clear precedence to the formulation of a detailed set of regulations governing practically every one of the student's classroom activities. Although these are to be "reasonable," it appears that the criterion of reason is solely defined by an adult whose supreme value is order. The assumption is that the teacher's main obligation is to make sure the rules are thoroughly understood, and that once this is done, he has every reason to expect and to exact obedience. The status of a young lady or a young gentleman does not confer any privilege of making any decision of the slightest importance about one's conduct.

The continued existence of this attitude does much to explain why many Ontario secondary schools are facing problems of crucial importance in coming to terms with their students. These problems are quite different from those encountered in earlier years because the dissidents are not largely confined to the irresponsible, the lazy, and the chronic malcontents but involve many of the most thoughtful and able of the student group. The essence of the conflict is that students are rebelling against the concept of irrational authority, of the rule that must be obeyed simply because it was prescribed by an adult in a position of power. They want regulations subjected to scrutiny in terms of their own ideas of logic and common sense. They are demanding limits to the areas of their personal lives in which the school may prescribe their behaviour. Failing to see any relationship between the achievement of educational goals and the styles of dress they adopt or the way they choose to wear their hair, they are insisting on the right to their own decisions about such matters. They refuse to accept the dichotomy between the teacher who seeks popularity and the one who does his conscientious duty. They reject the teacher who sets out to establish his authority before attempting to develop friendship and understanding but rather expect him to justify his leadership through these means. The image of the young lady or gentleman in a place of business has little appeal when the school is obviously not a place of business, and there is no reason why it should be. But if the analogy were pursued, they might ask what modern place of business imposes the kind of prohibition against talking on young people of eighteen or nineteen years of age that schools have typically done.

It may be that student malaise and dissatisfaction are rooted in causes that go much deeper than the way particular principals and teachers interpret their role and obligations. Edgar Z. Friedenberg observed and analyzed the situation in two American high schools and concluded as follows:

In my judgment, the kind of tutelage and status that the high school assigns students affects their lives and subsequent development far more crucially than the content and quality of formal instruction. What is learned most thoroughly by attendance at Milgrim or Hartsburgh is certain core assumptions that govern the conditions of life of most adolescents in this country and train them to operate as adult, if not as mature, Americans. The first of these is the assumption that the state has the right to compel adolescents to spend six or seven hours a day, five days a week, thirty-six or so weeks a year, in a specific place, under the charge of a particular group of persons in whose selection they have no voice, performing tasks about which they have no choice, without remuneration and subject to specialized regulations and sanctions that are applicable to no one

> else in the community nor to them except in this place. So accustomed are we to assuming that education is a *service* to the young that this statement must seem flagrantly biased. But it is a simple statement of what the law provides. Whether this provision is a service or a burden to the young – and, indeed, it is both, in varying degrees – is another issue altogether. Compulsory school attendance functions as a bill of attainder against a particular age group, so the first thing the young learn in school is that there are certain sanctions and restrictions that apply only to them, that they do not participate fully in the freedoms guaranteed by the state, and that, *therefore, these freedoms do not really partake of the character of inalienable rights.*[20]

Canadian schools operate within a social and legal framework that is very similar to that characterizing their American counterparts, and if Friedenberg's observations are true of those in one country, they probably apply equally to the other. The situation seems to call, not for a democratization of the operation of the school in the sense that the students' council should be assigned the responsibility for running it, but for a revolutionary change in the way society defines, through law and custom, the status and rights of the adolescent.

The issue of corporal punishment was of particular concern in the Ontario system in 1968–9. While the practice has not been specifically authorized by legislation, it has been condoned under section 40 (1b) of Ontario Regulation 339/66, which states that "a pupil shall submit to such discipline as would be exercised by a kind, firm and judicious parent." Such provision means that the action has to be judged in the light of the prevalent social customs and attitudes.

There was a good deal of discussion of the extent to which corporal punishment survived. Betty Lee reviewed the situation in June in the *Globe Magazine.*[21] She quoted the sales manager of the Ontario Rubber Company as saying that two thousand straps had formerly been shipped from the factory every couple of months, and that they still sold about one thousand a year. A.S. Milloy, Superintendent of Secondary Schools for the Toronto Board of Education, had said that the strap was still in use, but to a diminishing extent, paralleling the declining reliance on corporal punishment in the home. A Toronto-based clergyman, K.T. Smits, had said: "I go into the schools of this city all the time. And I know children are being regularly strapped, sometimes for petty offenses." The writer of the article probed the theory that strapping was reserved for serious misbehaviour. She reported one case where a thirteen-year-old boy in an Ontario school who committed the offense of chewing gum was strapped eighteen times on each hand until he bled. In another school, a girl was reputedly strapped severely to induce her to reveal the name of a boy who was flipping paper wads around the classroom.

The article quoted some strong views against the idea of corporal punishment. The late Karl S. Bernhardt, once director of the Institute of Child Study at the University of Toronto, reputedly said that most of the children at Juvenile and Family Court were there because of the strappings they had had, and not in spite of them. Donald Urquhart, principal of Jesse Ketchum School in Toronto, had said that the philosophy of the correction strap was as outdated as the rack. Robert H. Hemstreet, a Hamilton Unitarian minister, was quoted as saying: "When are we going to emerge from the dark ages? Canadians have at least done something about outlawing capital punishment. Ontario has banned flogging as a disciplinary measure in the province's reform institutions. But it's apparently quite all right to whack little kids in school."

Davis has been known to oppose the use of corporal punishment and to feel that it has no place in a modern school system. Near the end of 1968, he took a rather mild action to have it stopped. Speaking in the Legislature, he first noted the legal situation, and continued:

> Without commenting in any way on the responsibilities or prerogatives of parents, it is suggested that this regulation should be interpreted as providing within the context of the schools, an atmosphere of respect, and trust between students and teachers with the cultivation of individual responsibility as a major goal.[22]

He observed that the Hall-Dennis committee had commented adversely on the use of punishment in the area of behavioural learning. His subsequent pronouncement fell short of a prohibition of corporal punishment.

> Consequently, it is considered that the use of corporal punishment, in any form is not appropriate in the schools of Ontario and it is recommended that principals and teachers refrain from its use.

Tim Reid, his Liberal critic, expressed the view that this kind of action was ineffective and that if the minister really wanted corporal punishment stopped, he should change the regulations so that it would be absolutely banned.

There is a possibility that, once the practice has been officially condemned and considerable adverse publicity has been focused on it, it will gradually die out. Some of the private schools may prove an exception, but the trend there is in line with that in the public system. An article in the *Toronto Daily Star* reported attitudes expressed by some of the headmasters subsequent to the minister's announcement.[23] The headmaster of Upper Canada College had instructed housemasters the previous summer that he felt that corporal punishment was inappropriate, and there had been no caning since September. The question was somewhat more in doubt at Ridley College, where the cane had been used once or twice a term for the "dreadful act" of smoking. The principal was not sure whether the practice would continue, although he reputedly said that he thought there was still room for the sensible use of the cane in the development of the adolescent. The headmaster at Appleby College had not yet found it necessary to apply the strap, but the possibility of resorting to it had not been abandoned. The headmaster at Ashbury College saw no reason to change the school's policy. The strap was used about a dozen times a year for such offences as bullying and malicious damage.

The departmental announcement elicited considerable support for strapping. Its defenders used two basic arguments in its favour: that it was good for the child and that it was necessary to maintain order. The following extracts from a letter written by a *Toronto Daily Star* reader contain some elements of both:

> Does the minister realize the disciplinary problems teachers are confronted with by the "take-over generation"?
>
> It is incongruous that parents with the most unruly children are the agitators for the removal of the strap. A few sharp whacks on the palm of the hand which should have been exercised at home in the first place, never hurt a child, but teaches [*sic*] him to respect authority ...
>
> I have had the ultimate in devilish pupil behavior – they have cheated, lied, stolen money off my desk, written disparaging notes, swore [*sic*], screamed, were insolent and slovenly, and refused to work.
>
> I cajoled, threatened, tried to use kindness but to no avail: their minds were geared to revolt – and they were only 10 years old in Grade 4.
>
> I really don't blame the children – they are victims of our perverse society and so-called advanced education.[24]

The possibility of backtracking was demonstrated by the Renfrew County Board of Education which, after prohibiting all forms of corporal punishment in 1969, authorized the reinstatement of the strap in elementary schools at a meeting in May 1970.[25] According to a press report, the action was taken at the request of the consultative advisory committee and of a number of parents. The views of 440 teachers had been sought by means of a mailed questionnaire. Of the 362 who replied, 322 favoured the restoration of strapping; 214 of those in favour wanted the strap administered only by the principal or vice-principal and witnessed by another staff member. One trustee was quoted as saying: "I don't think teachers want to make use of the strap, but by removing it we've killed the only deterrent we had." Another who opposed the board's decision said: "I guess discipline means a strap in public school, a hickory stick in high school and a club in university."

Defence of the use of the strap as beneficial to the child has no support whatever from current studies of human behaviour. The teacher who uses it deliberately as an instrument of education is expressing a particularly reprehensible form of hostility against a victim who is helpless to retaliate. The latter is perfectly aware of the real motive and reacts with corresponding hatred. The social environment may force him to repress his feelings, but they will ultimately manifest themselves in anti-social acts. The educational system should rid itself as quickly as possible of any remaining exponents of the virtues of inflicting pain. Unfortunately, the great problem is not with them, but rather with those who inflict pain by indirect and disguised means often without themselves realizing what they are doing.

The teacher who uses the strap to keep order may be in quite a different category. It is easy for a theorist outside the school, or even in a school where relationships between teachers and pupils are harmonious, to say with the writer of another letter to the *Toronto Star*: "Now, more than ever, it will become the duty of every teacher to become vitally involved in the task of finding the why behind the unacceptable behavior. The individual problems of the misbehavers must be discovered, and the needs of these children must be met."[26] This is, of course, a statement of unimpeachable validity. But it must also be remembered that, in an imperfect system, teachers are not infrequently put in charge of large classes of children already rendered intractable by years of parental indifference, by the influence of cynical companions, and by unsympathetic treatment by former teachers. The principal's instructions may well be to keep the class under control at all costs and by any available means. Whether the children learn anything or not is a secondary point. The consequence for the teacher who fails in the primary task of keeping order is professional failure. Under these circumstances, the exhortation to study the child's motives for misbehaving may ring a little hollow. Practical means must be provided for the advice to be carried out, and these means include such a public attitude that the principal too will see his professional rewards in constructive measures rather than in repression.

An increasing number of people have seen a possible solution to the problem in the relaxation of compulsory education up to sixteen. There would be provision for those between the ages of fourteen and sixteen to be released from the obligation to attend school if, in the opinion of responsible authorities, they had ceased to benefit from the experience. In 1969–70 the Scarborough Board of Education appealed to the Department of Education for a relaxation of the sixteen-year-old limit so that a fifteen-year-old student might leave school upon written application by his parent or guardian and with the approval of the principal. The department did not, however, respond favourably. In June 1970 the Metropolitan Toronto School Board gave its support to the same proposal. While care would need to be taken to ensure that a change did not lead to abuse, it would appear that teachers' demands for instruments of control that are suitable for penal institutions would be removed if arrangements were made for the release of students who had come to regard the school as a kind of prison.

Abolition of the use of the strap has tended to force schools to rely more on suspension as the last resort in dealing with the most serious misbehaviour problems. Suspension is seen as a means of involving the parents, who may be asked to accompany the child to the school to discuss his difficulties. A certain proportion of parents refuse to assume any responsibility and throw the onus back on the school. Thus little is gained except perhaps to impress upon the child that his offence is indeed regarded as serious.

An experimental school in South Dakota allowed half of the students in one class to do anything they wanted for two weeks. As many cynics would have predicted, they promptly abandoned classes for the entire period. Less in accordance with expectations, however, they wrote the same examinations as the other students when they came back and did better. As a result attendance restrictions were removed from the entire school. After a chaotic period of another two weeks, the students began to return to classes. However, they selected only those that were related to their own goals. If a person believes that the immature young person cannot be expected to select the important and vital as opposed to the trivial, the shoddy, and the sensational, he presumably thinks that a regime of the kind described will inevitably lead to disaster. And there are many leading educators in Ontario who view things in exactly that way. The notion is gaining ground, however, that the adolescent will act in a much more mature fashion than has been traditionally supposed if he is given the obligation and the opportunity to do so.

FOUR

The organization of the school program

THE DEVELOPMENT OF THE GRADE SYSTEM

Elementary level

In the pioneer schools of Upper Canada, instruction was highly individualized. The lack of an organized grade structure depended to a large extent on the absence of enough copies of a single textbook to enable a group of children to be handled as a class. Also, in the typical one-room school, with the extended age range of the pupils and the comparatively small number at any given stage of development, the advantages of organization by grades were not overwhelming.

As larger concentrations of school children became more common, the apparent efficiency of dealing with groups at approximately the same level of achievement exerted increasing appeal. The trend was reinforced by the growth in popularity of formal examinations and certificates, which called for relatively uniform preparation. The pioneer fondness for having pupils recite lessons in chorus no doubt also exerted an influence in the same direction.

The examinations that came to be held in certain communities were very much a public function. The children were put through their paces in front of assembled dignitaries, and those who excelled were awarded with books or other prizes and made very conscious of the honours they had won. Naturally this kind of ceremony could be held only on infrequent occasions, and when promotion came to be associated with it, that too became attainable at relatively rare intervals. Those who were not promoted had nothing to do but go back and cover the same ground in preparation for another attempt. The earlier belief in the particular virtues of failure as a means of developing character made its own contribution to the establishment of the system.

There were factors other than any peculiar advantages of the grade system that tended to make the early graded school synonymous with superior education. This type of school tended to appear in towns and cities where there was a relatively high level of wealth available for the support of education. It was thus better endowed with equipment and supplies and could attract the better teachers. As teaching came to be increasingly associated with active performance in front of the room, those pupils who belonged to a class consisting of a single grade seemed to enjoy obvious advantages in the increased attention they received as a group. Also, a teacher who had fewer individual lessons to prepare beforehand could quite obviously be expected to achieve a higher level of performance. In fact, as long as education is equated with overt teacher activity, the superiority of a strictly graded system is overwhelming. It is only when the focus shifts indisputably to individual development that its weaknesses become evident.

When textbooks in series came into more common use, it became customary to speak of a pupil as being in the first book, the second book, and so on. Where a book was considered sufficient reading matter for a year, the latter term was often substituted. A form, as applied to the elementary school, most commonly covered two years, and junior and senior forms were recognized. By 1870 smaller schools had generally adopted an organization by books or grades, and fully graded schools were found in cities and larger towns.

While an average child was expected to spend two years in each of the four forms, there was for the most part provision for many reasonably bright children to proceed at a faster rate. The course of study issued by the Department of Education in 1936 specified that, for pupils of average ability, the course in each of forms I to V was intended to take two years, with the exception of form II, which might be completed in one year. However, "throughout the school, pupils shall be classified by the Principal in accordance with their aptitudes and attainments and the organization shall be flexible enough to allow within the school year the promotion of capable pupils, in all or any of the subjects of the grade."[1]

The Royal Commission on Education recommended that the elementary school program consist of nursery schools and kindergartens, where established, along with a six-grade program ending at about age twelve. The six grades would consist of two divisions, which the commission called for convenience junior and senior, each of three years' duration. It would be possible, although the reasons why it might be desirable are not too obvious, to organize a separate department in the school for each division. The two divisions would have the same general aims and would shade into one another.

The commission further recommended

> ... that in the elementary and secondary stages provision be made:
> (i) for classification of children according to needs, ability, and achievement at each level of the programme;
> (ii) for promotion according to individual achievement, evaluated in terms of capacity and total development;
> (iii) for programmes arranged on the following basis:
> (1) a minimum core of skills and knowledge to be attainable with reason-

able success and to be taken by all pupils;
(2) a supplement to be taken by pupils of average ability;
(3) an enriched supplement to be taken by pupils of higher than average ability;
(iv) for special educational treatment of markedly atypical children in separated classes.[2]

Secondary level

It took many years for the secondary school program in Ontario to settle into a stable pattern. Some of the developments that occurred between 1876 and 1921 are described by R.S. Harris in *Quiet Evolution.*[3] In 1876 the first two forms were called lower school and the last two, admission to which depended on passing the intermediate examination, were called upper school. Form III, the first of upper school, was at the level of junior matriculation, which was required for admission to the first year of a university course. The work of form IV led to senior matriculation, which entitled one to enter the second year of certain university courses.

By the mid-1890s most of the Ontario universities had developed honours as well as general BA programs and were requiring junior matriculation with honours for admission to certain honours courses. At that time the junior matriculation examinations were divided into two parts, with both honours and pass papers being provided in some subjects in part II. The two parts of the examination were offered at different times. In 1904 the work leading to the part I examination was assigned to the newly introduced middle school, and that leading to part II was combined with senior matriculation work in upper school. Within a decade, there were two-year programs in each of lower, middle, and upper school.[4]

The recommendations of the Royal Commission on University Financing in Ontario in 1921 led to a reduction of the six-year secondary school program to five years by limiting upper school to one year. The distinction between honour junior matriculation and senior matriculation disappeared. The main reason for shortening the program was said to be to encourage more of the students who were not bound for university to complete upper school. With the changes of 1921 the grade pattern that has existed throughout the modern period was complete.

The status of grade 13 was affected significantly in 1930 when the University of Toronto announced that it would no longer offer the first year of the four-year BA program, which had up to that time paralleled the upper school course. Thus after that time the only route to the university was through upper school. In subsequent years other universities adopted the same practice, although some continue to offer preparatory work in a preliminary year parallel to grade 13 for specific categories of entrants. The move on the part of the University of Toronto emphasized the role of upper school as a university preparatory year.

PROPOSALS TO REDUCE THE LENGTH OF THE THIRTEEN-YEAR PROGRAM

The Royal Commission declared flatly that the period of time required to complete the elementary and secondary school program was unnecessarily long. It found the condition aggravated by the frequent addition of content, with no corresponding deletion of obsolete material; the adoption of teaching methods that were more time-consuming than the old (one wonders what these time-wasting methods were); the repetition of courses in successive grades; and the practice of extending the work of grade 13 over two years, or that of grades 12 and 13 over three years. As was noted in volume I of the present series, the latter practice diminished after the 1950s.

The commission was particularly unhappy about the fact that the division between the two stages of the educational program came at about age fourteen, "almost exactly in the middle of the period of early adolescence."[5] The proposed restructuring of the program according to a 6–4–3 pattern, which was a major recommendation of the commission, would both have shortened the combined elementary and secondary stages to ten years and ensured that the dividing line came at what it considered a more appropriate age. The final stage would be junior college, which would offer the equivalent of grade 13 and a further year of the existing university program as well as certain terminal courses. These proposals were coupled with the observation that the successive stages of the system needed to be better integrated.

In part as a means of ensuring that the transition to secondary school was not too traumatic, the commission opposed carrying rotation of high school classes too far. It claimed that nearly all the evidence on the subject strongly supported the practice of having pupils receive instruction in the majority of subjects from a home-room teacher. The necessity of having other teachers involved in the process was acknowledged with some apparent reluctance. These teachers were to be confined to such subjects as general science, home economics, industrial arts, physical education, and possibly music. The number of such subjects might be modified along with the range of options, but the arrangement was not to be substantially changed throughout the secondary school. Advantages were seen in the close relationship that would be facilitated between student and teacher.[6]

A resolution was passed at the annual convention of the Ontario Educational Association in 1963 calling for a reduction in the length of the school program from thirteen years to twelve. The change was to be effected by eliminating one year at the elementary level. It was pointed out that a considerable proportion of the pupils already managed to cover the program in seven years, and it appeared quite feasible to make further modifications to enable the majority to follow the same pattern.

Bascom St John examined the question in his column in the *Globe and*

Mail on April 23, 1963.[7] He observed that a number of people supported the change from economic rather than educational motives; the average child took a year longer than his counterpart in most other provinces in getting to university and a year longer getting to work. Others felt that the existing program contained a good deal of unnecessary repetition, particularly in social studies and the natural sciences. Teachers were said to be complaining that opportunities for learning outside the school, including those provided by television, were making it unnecessary to teach some of the traditional parts of the school program.

Much of the discussion at that time was based on a view of the school program as so much ground to be covered rather than as a means of facilitating the attainment of a certain level of development. The fact that the children were bored by repetition of the same subject matter was far more of a condemnation of inept teaching than some of the critics appeared to realize. Official programs of the time could certainly not be held entirely to blame if teachers could find nothing to do but go over the same ground in successive years.

ORGANIZATIONAL IMPLICATIONS OF THE PORTER PLAN

What was known as the Porter Plan was important both because it represented an attempt to recognize an intermediate level in the Ontario school system and because it involved a new approach to curriculum development. These two features were, of course, closely interrelated. In the present chapter, it will suffice to deal with the first. The decentralization of curriculum development is reserved for fuller treatment in chapter v.

The Honourable Dana Porter, Minister of Education, was known to be eager to make certain structural and curricular reforms in the school system from the time of his appointment in 1948. He was hoping to be able to base the desired changes on the recommendations of the Royal Commission, which had been at work since 1945. He and J.G. Althouse, the Chief Director of Education, are said to have become quite impatient over the length of time being taken by the commissioners and to have decided that certain actions could not wait. The abolition of the high school entrance examination in 1949 was a case in point. On November 3 of that year, Porter proceeded to unveil his plan in an address at St Thomas. He thus angered Justice Hope, chairman of the commission, who did not hesitate to express his displeasure to certain departmental officials, whom he blamed for exerting pressure behind the scenes. In fact, few officials knew any more than did local administrators, the teaching profession, or the general public; the announcement came to them as a complete surprise.

According to Porter's announcement, the school curriculum was to be organized in four divisions: the primary, from grades 1 to 3; the junior, from grades 4 to 6; the intermediate, from grades 7 to 10; and the senior, from grades 11 to 13. An effort was to be made to develop a new focus in the primary division by having children from all of the first three grades, or years, in a single class, where they could be grouped and regrouped to engage in different kinds of activities according to their interests and capacities. No drastic changes were planned for the junior division. The intermediate grades were to be considered as a single unit, with the former sharp division between elementary and secondary school disappearing. Throughout the grades of the division, the rotary system was to be used, to some extent at least. In the senior years new course options were to be available, and the number of obligatory subjects reduced.

In an address to a group of school principals on April 10, 1950, Althouse identified the problems resulting from the lack of continuity between the elementary and secondary school levels as the failure to articulate the courses of study, the sharp differences in organization, and the ignorance on the part of the staff at each level of what went on at the other level. He declared that these barriers would be broken down mainly by the joint action of the local school boards and local teaching staffs. But this prescription was more than a little unrealistic. Local action could do nothing to weaken the separate traditions and procedures of teacher preparation at the two levels. Nor could it change the organization of the Department of Education, which was particularly reflected at the local level by different supervisory practices. Even a firm resolution on the part of teachers to co-operate in the development of co-ordinated curricula could only have continued to succeed had there been a continuation of the initial leadership provided at the top. W.J. Dunlop, who became minister on October 1, 1951, failed to give unequivocal support to the plan, and his later performance suggested indifference, if not actual opposition. A permanent change in the organization of the learning program would have required the construction of a network of intermediate schools to bridge the old gap. The appearance of a few of these in expanding suburbs of Toronto did not make any drastic change in the provincial system as a whole. A few years after the announcement of the Porter Plan, the sharpness of the elementary-secondary division was being deplored in the old terms.

PROVISION FOR INDIVIDUAL DIFFERENCES WITHIN THE GRADE STRUCTURE

Although the length of the basic program of the Ontario school system was established by 1921 at thirteen years, it was commonly considered unreasonable to insist that every pupil be forced to take that long between entrance to grade 1 and graduation from grade 13. Thus the brighter pupils were often encouraged to skip at least one grade, or to cover the work of one form in a single year, as the 1936 course of study suggested with respect to form II. The success of acceleration depended a good deal on how well the learning sequence was organized. In some cases grade skipping meant simply omitting part of the work. In a skill subject such as arithmetic, the child might easily encounter later difficulties which he could not readily overcome. Sometimes, also, the sudden shift to a higher age group involved psychological and social disadvantages. Although for a time there was a pronounced reaction against the practice of grade skipping, the 1950s saw a swing back in that direction, and by the end of the decade about two-thirds of the larger systems permitted one or two years of acceleration.

There was no comparable provision in the secondary schools, and only in unusual circumstances were students permitted to cover the program in less than five years. Several other methods existed for allowing for differences in students' capacity to handle the work. One factor that tended to narrow the range of ability was failure and withdrawal. There were cases of schools maintaining their standards by withholding promotion from more than 30 per cent of the students in their grade 9 classes in the General course. The level of effort that could be demanded of those who were left made acceleration a less urgent question than it might otherwise have been.

The range of ability in the Technical and Commercial courses was restricted by the tendency of the brighter students to enrol in the General course. A very high proportion of the technical and commercial students left at the end of grade 9, and only a minor proportion were left after grade 10 (see volume I, chapter 2 of this series). The fact that the problem of individual differences was dealt with in this unsatisfactory manner was one of the reasons why a new organization emerged in the 1960s.

Some schools streamed their General course students, at least after grade 9, by grouping them from high to low according to their previous year's achievement. The logic of this arrangement would seem to have called for the adoption of a different set of goals and the use of a different set of techniques and examinations for each group. In fact, however, only the techniques tended to be subject to modification. The class at the lower end might be offered extra assistance and assigned more homework in order to improve its members' chances on the same final examination as the other wrote. The bright class, on the other hand, might have opportunities for enrichment. There were certain disadvantages in the arrangement that typify any procedure that involves labeling groups on the basis of achievement or capacity. Despite occasional attempts to disguise the situation, the lowest group soon identified itself, or was identified by others, as the "idiots" or the "dummies." With more gusto than pleased some of the teachers the members often wore this label as a badge of honour and did their best to live up to it. Their performance reflected the teachers' low expectation of their capacities. Many teachers regarded it as a kind of penance to have to teach them and even frankly regarded their segregation as a means of getting them out of the way so that they could devote their real efforts to the more talented. Others, however, accepted the challenge of teaching the lower group and sometimes achieved startling results.

During the 1950s the concept of enrichment enjoyed a great deal of popularity as a means of providing for the needs of the particularly able or "gifted" student. This term usually referred to some kind of addition to the regular program designed for all pupils at a particular age level; in same cases it tended to mean more work of the kind required of the average student. Where school work means a rather unpleasant obligation imposed by an authority on the basis of unknown and little-understood criteria, this kind of "enrichment" is not received with any great amount of enthusiasm. It tends to be seen as a penalty for being bright and ensures that many possessors of unusual ability will do as much as they can to conceal the fact. A somewhat more attractive form of enrichment involved the opportunity to pursue areas of special interest not offered as part of the regular program. In elementary school, provision was sometimes made for extra field trips, advanced reading programs, "research" studies in certain areas of science, and opportunities for participation in musical or dramatic performances. Critics have wondered whether these activities are not of sufficient educative value to be offered to all children rather than to a minority of those judged to be extra bright.

The typical method of enriching the secondary school program has been to provide options. In accordance with the trend toward the elimination of very small secondary schools in the post-war period, the number of these available to the average student has been greatly extended. It has been customary to confine a student of average or below-average achievement to the compulsory subjects and the minimum number of options and to permit the brighter student to take one or more extra options. Before the 1960s the three-option diploma represented a minimum effort at the end of grade 12, and more capable students took four or occasionally more options. At the beginning of the decade, four options became the minimum requirement.

THE REORGANIZED PROGRAM OR ROBARTS PLAN

For a number of years, S.D. Rendall, Superintendent of Secondary Education, pressed his departmental colleagues for a reorganization of the secondary school structure. The evidence of this pressure is to be found in the records of the proceedings of meetings held by officials at his level. The opportunity came with the passing of the *Technical and Vocational Training Assistance Act* by the federal government at the end of 1960. It was immediately obvious that the programs for which federal funds would be available must be put on a new and more attractive basis if the potential benefits were to be realized.

As announced by the minister, J.P. Robarts, in August 1961, the three branches, at that time called General, Commercial, and Technical, were to be redesignated Arts and Science, Business and Commerce, and Science, Technology, and Trades (at first called tentatively "Engineering, Technology, and Trades"). Besides providing the branches with a new image, something which the second and third particularly needed, the new terms were designed to indicate the probable destination of successful students. All three branches would be offered in the majority of secondary schools, which would thus have composite status. Although some of the existing schools in large municipalities did not lend themselves to the inclusion of more than one or two branches, they would nevertheless be part of a composite system.

There were to be three programs within each branch: a five-year program for those with the capacity and desire for post-secondary education, a four-year program for those who would end their formal education and seek employment on completing grade 12, and a modification of the four-year program in the form of a two-year program, to be offered in the larger schools, for those determined to leave when it became legally possible at the age of sixteen. There was also to be an Occupational program for students aged fifteen or sixteen who were transferred rather than promoted to the secondary school. In addressing the Legislature on April 10, 1962, Robarts explained that this program was for "pupils of limited ability who can at best become only semi-skilled in any branch where applicable, and this will permit all these pupils to remain profitably for a longer period in school."[8]

A departmental memorandum explained that students in classes organized in the Occupational program in any school system under an advisory vocational committee would be considered to be vocational pupils. The courses, of short duration, would be designed to meet local needs in the service occupations. It was regarded as desirable to place the program under the supervision of a subcommittee of the advisory vocational committee, which would include trustees having a special interest in fitting courses to the needs of students with limited ability. The department expected that no more than 10 per cent of the enrolment of a school district would be classified in the Occupational program.[9]

The four-year program of the Arts and Science Branch was considered to be the major innovation of the scheme. It was intended to provide a basic education followed by training on the job, an objective that rapidly became less realistic for many students as the level of preparation demanded by employers tended to increase. The development of the system of colleges of applied arts and technology was thus rushed in the latter part of the decade to help meet the demand for further education among this group, as well as among those in the five-year program who did not proceed to university. The curriculum in this particular program and branch was used for experiments and innovations such as the course Man and Society, which proved so attractive in some quarters that agitation developed to have it introduced into the five-year program as well. A major effort was to be made to improve the quality of the offerings in the four-year program in the Business and Commerce and the Science, Technology, and Trades Branches to improve their appeal to students who wanted to combine a good basic education with the acquisition of certain practical skills. Between 55 and 65 per cent of the time would be spent on basic subjects and the rest on practical and related subjects. The minister declared that the business courses, which had hitherto attracted mostly girls, would be redesigned to meet the interest of boys. They would deal with the distributive processes of the business community, advertising, display, and merchandising. The agriculture option in district high schools would be completely revised to include a good deal of agricultural economics.[10]

In the five-year program, at least 80 per cent of the student's time was to be spent on the traditional subjects of English, French, other languages, history, geography, mathematics, and science. It was in this form that basically the old General course was continued. Although a good deal was said about opening the route to university more widely for Business and Commerce and Science, Technology, and Trades students, these branches never provided more than a very small proportion of university entrants.

The five-year program in the Science, Technology, and Trades Branch was designed particularly for students wishing to prepare for a university engineering course or to enter an institute of technology. It was intended to be very similar to the pre-engineering course which had been offered for a number of years in Central Technical School in Toronto. In addition to the obligatory academic subjects, the latter had offered a machine-shop option for those planning to take mechanical engineering and electrical theory for those aiming at electrical engineering.

A good deal of emphasis was placed on what seemed at that time to be the flexibility of the scheme. On entering grade 9 the student would have to make a choice only among branches, but even that would not be final. During his grade 9 year he might take one option from another branch and transfer at the end of the year. A choice of program would be made in grade 10, but a student who could meet the academic requirements might move at later stages.

The minister indicated some of the thinking behind the plan in an address to the Legislature in November 1961.[11] The first consideration had been a recognition of the inadequacies of the curriculum in relation to the diverse needs of young people. The second consideration, actually an aspect of the first, had to do with the need to give secondary school students better occupational preparation in the light of the employment situation and changing procedures in industry. "It appears to me to be fundamental that we must keep our educational system completely flexible so that it may not only provide our young people with the basic education required for a happy and contented life in our society, but also, we must educate them to fill the needs in industry as it develops." If these objectives seem to lean rather heavily toward conformity, it must be remembered that they were spoken in 1961. The third point that Robarts made was that there had been concern for several years over the number of drop-outs from the secondary schools, with consequent loss to those withdrawing and to society as well. Fourthly, it seemed increasingly desirable to shift the emphasis from what had been in many schools a single course option.

The appropriate discussion group at the Ontario Conference on Education, which met two months after the announcement of the Reorganized Program (Robarts never wanted to hear it referred to as the Robarts Plan), went on record as being in full accord with its "intent and philosophy." It was a much-neeeded attempt to provide for individual differences at the secondary school level. Reaction over the way in which the scheme had been introduced was not, however, entirely favourable. H. Pullen, then Deputy Business Administrator of the Ottawa Collegiate Institute Board, declared that he had no quarrel with the outlined pattern. Time would tell whether or not it was good or bad. He objected, however, to its hasty conception and premature announcement. While haste could be defended on the basis of the urgency of taking advantage of federal funds for school building, there was no excuse for the failure to consult headmasters, superintendents, directors, or members of the teachers' federations. The plan had merely been announced to them.

The Reörganized Program was introduced, where practical, in September 1962 and continued as the students proceeded to higher grades. School boards were, however, permitted to defer it in full or in part until a later year at their discretion. In such cases the students continued to be classified in the General, Commercial, and Technical courses, and proceeded to the Secondary School Graduation Diploma in its existing form. Very small schools which had too few students to justify differentiating between students in the four-year and five-year programs in the Arts and Science Branch were asked to offer only the five-year program so that their most capable students would be able to proceed to post-secondary education. Those schools having enough students in grades 10, 11, and 12 to set up a class with a minimum of twenty students in each program might offer both programs.[12]

The introduction of the plan created a staffing problem of considerable proportions, which was met in the long run with the assistance of federal funds. The Department of Education took steps to provide emergency training for prospective teachers of technical subjects. Summer courses leading to the Interim Vocational Certificate, Type B, in Occupational Training, were offered for the first time in Toronto in 1962. Further information about these developments is given in volume V, chapter 6.

Robarts pointed out that the year-by-year introduction of the plan was at least a partial answer to the charges of undue haste. The course introduced in September was merely one for grade 9. Final details of the grade 10 program would not be worked out before 1963, nor those for grade 11 until 1964. Robert Nixon, however, saw the possibility of considerable waste.

The teachers concerned are being asked to buy equipment and prepare budgets for their industrial chemistry laboratories, for example, and these budgets were in many cases supposed to be ready before Christmas of this year, before any courses were available. There may have been some misdirection here, but I know that this is so. No courses were available, nobody was even ready to tell us what was to be taught, yet we were preparing budgets amounting to thousands of dollars, and I have no doubt but what the orders based on these budgets have gone in, to buy equipment that will be put into buildings that will not be used for two or three years. It seems to me there is some disorganization here.[13]

The situation was perhaps an inevitable result of having federal and provincial fingers in the same educational pie.

Not much was said about viable alternatives to the plan. John Wintermeyer suggested the possibility of giving all young people an academic education to the maximum of their ability to the end either of grade 10 or of grade 11. After that those so inclined would receive a vocational training limited to basic information about trades and then go into industry, where they would receive training under the aegis of a government-sponsored program.[14] Robarts pointed out, in response, that only about 55 per cent continued in grade 11 under the existing scheme, and asserted that it was impossible to hold a great many of the drop-outs in the schools for a straight academic program.

By Donald MacDonald's calculations, a large proportion of the students of the province would be denied access to the full scheme, which would be available only in a school accommodating one thousand or more students.

Their break-down works something like this. For a school of up to 200, they could only have one programme. In other words, there is absolutely no possibility at all of implementing anything but a fraction of the Robarts plan. For a school from 200 to 400 pupils, they could have two programmes. In a school of 400 to 600 pupils, they could have three programmes, that is, they could have the five-year course and the four-year course in the academic stream, and one course in the commercial stream. In a school of 600 to 800, they might have the four programmes and, perhaps, the limited technical course, and for a school of over 800 – up into the 1,000 range – there would be a possibility of implementing the whole of the Robarts plan.[15]

To point out this problem was not, of course, to correct it. As noted in volume I, chapter 3, however, there was a marked trend toward the elimination of the smallest schools. The government's policy of consolidating local school systems has been conducive to such a development.

In January 1964 T.L. Wells reviewed the degree of success achieved by the Reorganized Program up to that time. During its second year, between 90 and 95 per cent of the secondary school boards of Ontario had adopted some features of it. These included all city boards, all schools with fifteen teachers or more, and 95 per cent of the students. In grade 10 the percentage of students in the Arts and Science Branch had been reduced to 55, while the remaining 45 per cent were in the other two branches. Occupational programs were established quickly and seemed to be filling an urgent need in a very satisfactory manner. In the township of Scarborough, part of which he represented in the Legislature, the retention rate in secondary schools had risen from 73.7 per cent in 1959 to 79.9 per cent in 1963.[16]

In the issue of the *Toronto Education Quarterly* for the winter of 1963–4, Gertrude M. Fatt wrote that the changes brought about by the Reorganized Program had been little short of revolutionary. The new courses had succeeded in their objective of making the schools more flexible and of offering something of value to the non-academic student. New status had been given to the commercial and technical schools by providing courses leading to post-secondary education, including university. But she felt it necessary to warn about the way the four-year program should not be handled.

> The whole purpose in introducing them will be defeated if teachers look upon these four-year courses as merely watered-down versions of the five-year courses, and regard this stream in their school as the repository for the dullards. These courses are not this and were never intended to be. If the new four-year courses are properly organized, and if the right people are directed into them, they can be interesting, rewarding, enriching and even exciting to the student who does not want to go on to college but who needs to remain in school to gain maturity before he goes out to become a salesman, an interior decorator, a super-market manager, an hotelman, an actor, a musician, a commercial artist, a theatre producer, a restaurant operator, or a recreation director, to name only a very few of the many useful, nay, necessary occupations in our community which do not require a college education.[17]

DISSATISFACTION WITH GRADE 13 AND EFFORTS AT REFORM

A good deal of dissatisfaction developed during the 1950s over the quality of the educational experience offered in grade 13. This dissatisfaction involved the status and purposes of the year, its curriculum, the prevailing methods of instruction, and the departmental examination system, which was abolished in 1967. These different aspects are treated more fully in other parts of the present series. Attention at this point is focused on grade 13 as an element in the secondary school structure.

For several successive years, the annual conference of the Ontario Association for Curriculum Development recorded comments about the situation in grade 13. In 1957 there was said to be a need to bring secondary teachers and university professors closer together so that grade 13 in particular would provide a better link with the universities. In 1960 one of the study groups suggested that the existing thirteen-year program be reduced to twelve-years with externally administered content-style examinations at the end. Grade 13 would become an exploratory year for those bound for university, during which they would consider the broad sweep of human knowledge. The group studying university problems at the Ontario Conference on Education in 1961 observed: "Other provinces and countries have only four years of high school." It then asked rhetorically: "Should grade 13 be abolished and the four years preceding be strengthened?"

In 1961 the University Matriculation Board set up a committee to study certain aspects of admission requirements. Chaired by President G.E. Hall of the University of Western Ontario, it also included H.S. Armstrong, Dean of the Faculty of Arts and Science at McMaster University, A.R.C. Duncan, Dean of the Faculty of Arts and Science at Queen's University, H.F. Légaré, Rector of the University of Ottawa, and R. Ross, Registrar of the University of Toronto. This committee decided that it could not fruitfully discuss the possibility of reducing the number of papers required for university admission without first making clear its views on what it regarded as necessary reforms in the secondary schools. Implying blithely that the schools were wasting a good deal of time, it urged that "much more work" be given in grades 9, 10, and 11, so that the existing thirteen-year program could be covered in twelve years. A uniform external examination would establish grade 12 as the effective end of secondary school, and grade 13 would become a really superior year of pre-university educational experience. The students would study four instead of five subjects and treat them in greater depth than under current conditions.

In 1964 C.T. Bissell offered some thoughts about grade 13 to the North York Junior and Senior High School Principals' Association. He referred with disfavour to the suggestion that the grade be taken away from the secondary schools and offered in community colleges. He felt that such a move would damage the prestige and teaching power of the school system. As to the proposals to abolish it, the universities had depended on grade 13 graduates for their honours courses in particular and would suffer "appalling" dislocation if it were "re-structured" out of existence. He was rather scornful of the idea that thirteen years' work could be covered equally well in twelve. Such a proposition reminded him of the claim that two could live as cheaply as one.

Prophesying the demise of the grade 13 departmental examinations, he repeated what was by now a familiar view that the year should offer opportunities for deeper concentration on fewer subjects, thus constituting a better preparation for university work. There would be more time for exploration, for essay-writing, for becoming acquainted with appropriate scholarly journals, and for "the extra-curricular activities of the intellect." More selective admission would make possible a high quality of work. There would be incidental advantages in providing closer liaison between school teachers and their university colleagues in the same discipline.

The minister took into account the recommendations of the University Matriculation Board committee and of other groups in establishing the Grade 13 Study Committee in 1964. Representative of the Department of Education, the schools, the universities, and the school boards, it was given the following terms of reference.

1. The Committee is asked to inquire into and report upon the nature and function of the Grade 13 year in the Ontario educational system, particularly in the light of opinions expressed frequently by responsible persons that, despite the fact that much can be said in its favour,
   (a) Grade 13 is a cram year with too much emphasis upon the memorization of factual information and upon preparation for the final Departmental examination;
   (b) the year should provide a richer educational experience than it does for all students, whether they propose to go either to universities and other institutions of higher learning or directly to some form of employment; and
   (c) the year should be a better liaison between the school programme and the programmes of the universities and other institutions of higher learning.
2. While it is not intended to restrict the Committee's authority to look into any matter which it considers relevant, to the extent permitted by the time available, the members are asked to keep in mind that the following programmes have been initiated, after considerable study in each case:
   (a) the Reorganized Programme in the Secondary Schools;
   (b) the curriculum revision programme in most subjects in all grades; and
   (c) the progressive reduction in the number of Grade 13 papers to be written by each candidate, through the replacement, in several subjects, of two papers by a single paper and of three papers by two in Mathematics.
3. Specifically, if the situation as outlined in section 1 is found to exist, the Committee is asked to recommend for the Minister's consideration,
   (a) changes which might be made immediately to improve the situation;
   (b) an ideal solution for the problems presented by the situation; and
   (c) successive steps which might be taken to implement the ideal solution, including means of determining whether the candidates concerned have met satisfactory standards for (i) graduation from secondary school, and (ii) admission to universities and other institutions of higher learning.[18]

While the establishment of the committee met with general approval, there was some feeling that its scope was too limited. In the Legislature, Donald MacDonald pointed out that grade 13, rather than being an isolated problem, was only the most controversial link in the whole educational chain from grade 1 to the increasingly diversified field of higher education. He suggested that the entire system should be examined.[19]

The Grade 13 Study Committee actually did look at the structure to some extent, although mainly as the framework in which the successor to the existing grade 13, the matriculation year, would be contained. It offered an ideal and an interim solution. The first of these would depend on two developments: 1 / the establishment of community colleges offering "valid and attractive" courses in a number of centres, and 2 / the complete revision of the curriculum from grades 1 to 12. The committee suggested that it would take ten or fifteen years to attain these objectives. Steps to implement the interim solution could begin immediately.

The essence of the recommended change was that the secondary school program should conclude at the end of grade 12. The twelve-year program up to that stage might be organized on any one of a variety of bases: 8–4, 7–5, 6–2–4, or 6–3–3. When the ideal solution was established, the matriculation year would be offered as one of a number of programs in grade 12 – distinguished from the others in preparing students for university. At the post-secondary level, the range of possibilities would include two-year community colleges, teachers' colleges, and polytechnical institutes, in addition to universities. During the interim period, the matriculation year would continue to be offered between grade 12 and university entrance.

Admission to the matriculation year, which was to be introduced in September 1966, would be based on the possession of the Ontario Secondary School Graduation Diploma and the recommendation of the principal and staff of the school attended by the candidate. This recommendation was to take account of the previous academic record, the results of a scholastic aptitude test similar to that being administered currently in grade 12, and marks in examinations on a limited number of subjects, perhaps two or three, set by secondary school teachers under the direction of the Department of Education and marked by the teachers in the schools in accordance with a scheme prepared by those who set the paper.

The normal program of the matriculation year would consist of not more than four subjects, two at the general and two at the advanced level. There would be provision for a certain amount of flexibility with respect to combinations at the two levels. English or Français would be compulsory at one level or the other for all students.

To carry out its recommendations the Grade 13 Study Committee proposed the formation of an Implementation Council, with a well-qualified and experienced official as executive officer. Among immediate steps, the minister was urged to appoint a representative committee in each of the major subject areas to submit, not later than August 31, 1964, a list of the topics to be deleted from the grade 13 courses for departmental examination purposes in 1965 and 1966 and a brochure indicating how teachers might make use of the three weeks of additional time at their disposal. The universities would be asked to consider a reduction in the number of grade 13 subjects required for admission in September 1966 without reference to general and advanced levels of instruction. During the four-year period between 1967–8 and 1970–1, they would be asked to consider an admission scheme consisting of 1 / provisional admission based on the recommendation of the principal and staff and the results of objective tests of aptitude and achievement and 2 / final admission based on results in work at the advanced and ordinary levels. In each advanced level subject, half the mark would be based on the recommendation of the principal and staff and half on the results of an external examination. In each general level subject, credit would be based entirely on the recommended mark. A system of accrediting schools would ultimately be worked out. A further recommendation was that the minister appoint a representative committee to study the implications of the proposals for courses at the general and advanced levels and to report to the Implementation Committee by November 1, 1964. The minister was also to appoint representative committees to organize the content of the general and advanced courses in various subjects, their work to be completed, at least in experimental form, by December 1, 1965.

The various committees were set up largely as recommended and carried out their tasks in preparation for the proposed changes. For a time the whole scheme seemed to be viewed with general favour. On January 12, 1965, the Ontario Teachers' Federation submitted a brief to the Grade 13 Implementation Committee (as it was called, instead of the proposed "Council") and to the Grade 13 General and Advanced Committee.[20] The federation spoke of the proposals of the Grade 13 Study Committee as imaginative and bold, but it had a few reservations. For one thing it suggested that the recommended introduction of the matriculation year in September 1966 left very little time to revise the curriculum for grades 1 to 12, to prepare the necessary textbooks, and to organize the courses at the general and advanced levels. Concern was also expressed about the lack of uniformity that might be expected to result from the use of recommended marks in the departmental examinations. It was suggested that these marks be adjusted in the light of the class performance in relation to a provincial standard. The federation was, on the other hand, wholeheartedly in favour of reducing the number of subjects required for admission to the university. It expressed approval, also, of having papers at different levels, which would correct the existing anomaly of requiring the same mathematical efficiency of prospective science and moderns students alike.

The brief identified with the following problems to be dealt with in establishing the matriculation year.

1. With grade 12 proposed as the year of decision, steps must be taken lest the pressure presently felt at the Grade 13 level simply drop a grade.
2. Smaller classes will necessarily follow from the introduction of two levels of instruction in the matriculation year. While this is all to the good, can this year survive in smaller and more remote centres? It is urgent that these centres receive all the consideration they deserve.
3. Accreditation has its merits, but will it tend to breed its own special problem? Non-accredited schools will, of necessity, be regarded as second-class institutions.
4. It is doubtful whether existing school library facilities will be adequate to cope with anticipated requirements of the advanced level of instruction. Once again, smaller centres, with less ample public facilities for reference, will be at a disadvantage. Our libraries must grow with the new concept.

The essence of the proposal of the Grade 13 Study Committee for the establishment of the matriculation year was abandoned when the universities registered their opposition to the idea of having general and advanced courses, as recounted in volume v, chapter 15. A number of the less important recommendations were carried out: for example, an attempt was made to shorten the grade 13 courses and the universities reduced their admission requirements from nine to seven credits. The possibility that the length of the school program may ultimately be reduced to twelve years, however, by no means died.

RECENT PROPOSALS TO SHORTEN THE GRADE 13 PROGRAM

On February 10, 1967, the Senate of the University of Toronto passed a resolution which was reported to the Department of Education:

> ... the Senate wishes to inform the Department of Education that the University of Toronto is generally favourable to the idea of a 12 grade school system, provided that the level of preparedness reached at the end of the new 12th grade be equal to that presently reached at the end of the 13th grade. The University would further urge that as much of this compression as possible take place in the lower grades and that there be no reduction in the number of years spent in the secondary schools.[21]

This kind of resolution was obviously a safe one to make. After all, who could object if the schools mended their ways and ceased wasting a year of the pupils' time, as they obviously must have been doing?

The Provincial Committee on Aims and Objectives supported the move to eliminate a year of the total program by advocating a learning continuum covering a period of thirteen years, including kindergarten.

This recommendation was coupled with the proposal to eliminate horizontal or vertical divisions of pupils into such groupings as elementary, secondary, vocational, and academic, or into streams differentiated according to ability. Extraordinary arrangements for pupils in special learning situations would still be possible.

On June 5, 1968, the minister expressed several reactions to what was becoming a frequently heard proposal to shorten the program.[22] He pointed out that it was not a question of lopping off a grade, but of restructuring the entire system from kindergarten through grade 13. In claiming that between 40 and 45 per cent of the students actually completed the thirteen-year program in twelve years, he did not make it altogether clear whether he was suggesting that a change was not particularly urgent or whether he meant that it could be accomplished with relative ease. He mentioned the experiments involving individualized timetables and partial non-grading then being conducted in certain high schools and expressed the view that the general adoption of this approach would make it less important whether a particular student took twelve, thirteen, or fourteen years to cover the program.

In the same debate, Walter Pitman declared that grade 13 was on its way out. He saw it being eroded by practices recently introduced by certain universities. Guelph was admitting students to its spring semester before they had completed the grade 13 year, and Brock was accepting a selected group of grade 12 graduates into first year after a six-week summer course. If this process continued, grade 13 would become a repository for those who could not make it to university from grade 12.[23] Davis responded that there was still something to be said for grade 13. There would always have to be a final year of secondary school, and if a fifth year could offer a valid educational experience, there was a good deal to be said for retaining it. He asked why it should be transferred to the universities if it could be successfully offered in the secondary school program.[24]

In the *Globe and Mail* on August 23, 1968, it was reported that Donald Ivey, principal of New College at the University of Toronto, offered reasons why the school program could be reduced by a year. He was reputed to have said that 95 per cent of the body of factual material could be cut out of any given grade without any loss. Secondly, the number of subjects a student had to deal with could be reduced – a trend which had already begun. Finally, the length of the school year could be increased. If the Christmas and Easter vacations were added to the two months of idleness during the summer, elementary school facilities were unused for almost three months of the year. With students out during part of June, the situation in secondary schools was even worse. It was seen as desirable to have children receive more intensive instruction during "the irreplaceable years when their ability to absorb is greatest."

THE MOVE TOWARD NON-GRADING IN ELEMENTARY SCHOOLS

There was clear recognition before the 1960s of the contradiction between the grade system and the genuine recognition of the individual. W.H. Swift, Deputy Minister of Education for Alberta, said in his Quance Lectures in 1958:

> The artificiality of the grade system has long been recognized. Everyone knows that there is an optimum rate of learning for each person. But schools are so organized that each is expected to learn at the same rate as others in his grade, despite the great range of capacities to learn. So the really bright are doing that which is too easy for them, and the slow are doing things that are beyond their capacity to do properly.[25]

Swift asked why the lock-step in education had not been broken. He referred to the Dalton and Winnetka plans introduced as early as thirty years before which had enabled each child to proceed by completing units of work at his own speed, but had not been generally adopted. He offered three reasons for the lack of significant progress. 1 / It was easier for the teacher to handle the class as a body rather than to try to deal with each pupil individually. 2 / Any scheme that required more individual instruction would necessitate smaller classes and thus more staff and facilities, neither of which society had been able or willing to provide. 3 / There was some question whether it was desirable for children to be thrown in with those of a different age group. In connection with this latter point, one wonders whether Swift really undersood that a genuine individualized program does not lead to segregation by age group but determines a child's associations only in terms of specific pursuits.

Saskatchewan introduced a so-called non-graded plan in 1964–5 which provided for the reorganization of the existing twelve grades into four divisions based on the idea of continuous growth. Each division consisted of a number of work units through which the individual child proceeded according to his ability and aptitude. At the end of the school year, he was credited with completing a certain number of units, and the following September he proceeded from where he had left off. There was no such thing as failing or skipping a year, but only continuing progress.[26]

In 1966 New Brunswick announced the replacement of the formal grade system by a scheme of continuous progress and subject promotion. In the six-year elementary school program, units or levels of work were substituted for grades. A system of Opportunity classes was provided for those who could not be expected to complete the regular program within a reasonable period of time. The junior high school program offered units of work in various subject areas in Regular and Modified programs and could be completed in either three or four years. The system of Opportunity classes was continued at this level. The senior high school offered three programs: College Preparatory and Technical, General Educational and Occupational Preparatory, and Practical, for which the Regular, Modified and Opportunity programs in junior high school provided the minimum respective qualifications. The three senior high school programs offered four types of programs in subject fields.[27]

Authorities on the subject are not inclined to accept schools with units or levels as truly non-graded. Madeline Hunter, principal of the University Elementary School at the University of California, said that a non-graded school must satisfy three criteria. 1 / There must be individual diagnosis of each learner. 2 / There must be a prescription for the learner generated by such a diagnosis and not by curricular demands imposed from outside. 3 / The school must be organized as a pharmacy from which these prescriptions can be filled. She says that if children are organized for reading into groups determined by their achievement level, there is no pharmacy for alternatives but simply patent medicine to fill the prescription.[28] In a genuine non-graded system, the criteria for pupil placement and mobility are 1 / the kind of teacher that a child needs at any given moment and 2 / the kind of peer group in which he works best. Academic achievement and intelligence are not considered as criteria for placement in instructional teams. A child seldom needs to be moved during a school year because provision is made for him to proceed to a new concept as soon as he learns the previous one. The idea is that he is continuously working at "that critical point where his knowledge leaves off and his new learning needs to begin."

The non-graded system makes very great demands on the teacher's intelligence, ingenuity, knowledge, and sensitivity. The intelligence required must be of a practical type that implies that ability to assess the important factors in a situation and to arrive at sound judgments about the relationship between cause and effect. Ingenuity is needed to produce novel and original solutions in the light of each child's particular needs. The teacher must have a large fund of general knowledge, not because he must be able to answer every question the child may ask, or precede him into every area where his curiosity impels him, but because it is impossible to be a sound guide without having an understanding of the nature of knowledge, of its organization, of the basis for its current subdivisions, and of the forms in which it is stored and made available to those who wish to use it. The teacher's sensitivity must be supplemented and refined by a knowledge of the main psychological principles underlying motivation and learning as far as these are known. The whole set of requirements points emphatically to the need for a much more lengthy and comprehensive program of teacher preparation than Ontario has so far provided. Thus it may be assumed that non-grading will go hand in hand with the implementation of the recommendations of the Minister's Committee on the Training of Elementary School Teachers, and that it has little chance of success unless the latter is also successful.

The Ontario Department of Education moved cautiously in 1967 in recommending a relaxation of the grade system in elementary schools. In reviewing the continual process of adaptation and revision of the curriculum, a bulletin of the department re-stated the emphasis on modifying the grade system in citing an extract from a 1937 bulletin.

If the organization by grades, or the practice of sending children on to a new teacher at the end of each school year, tends to prevent the children from progressing at a rate that is natural to them, or to perpetuate the evils of 'lockstep' promotion, as it may in some schools, thought should be given to modifying the grade organization.

The most frequent cause of retardation in the past has been failure to meet grade requirements arbitrarily set up, particularly in the fields of reading and arithmetic. It must be recognized that there is no set time or grade level at which every child can be expected to develop the ability to master an arithmetical process or to reach a given standard of reading achievement. The wisdom of retarding a child for a year because of failure in these respects is open to grave questions.[29]

The 1967 bulletin also noted that it was suggested in 1965 that "the grade system *has* tended to prevent far too many children from progressing at a rate that is natural to them."[30] It pointed out that "some communities have devised modifications of the grade system that have considerably reduced 'failure rates.' Some schools have maintained the grade system in the flexible manner in which it was originally conceived."[31] Some systems are now trying truly non-graded patterns of organization.

The report of the Hall-Dennis Committee added greatly to the impetus toward non-graded schools. The following extract shows how explicitly it recommended this form of organization.

... children come to school mentally, physically and emotionally different, and they mature at varying rates in each of these areas. Furthermore, there is a wide diversity in their intellectual, social, cultural and economic backgrounds. It is irrational and unfair to require all children to start in school at a common level or to expect them to reach standards of achievement with any great degree of uniformity.

The obvious corollary is that the curriculum must provide for the individual progress of pupils. To make this possible, two major innovations are indicated: complete abolition of the graded system throughout the school; and the use of individual time-tables at the senior level ... During the last fifty years, as it has become increasingly difficult to retard and eliminate pupils at an early age by failure, the graded system has become an anomaly.[32]

RECENT MOVES TOWARD FLEXIBILITY IN SECONDARY SCHOOL ORGANIZATION

It was customary in most secondary schools in Ontario until very recently to provide each student in grades 9, 10, and 11 with a full timetable at his particular level. At the end of the year, he was either promoted or required to repeat the entire year. Writing in the *Bulletin* in 1966, K.N. Craig, a teacher at the Oakville-Trafalgar High School, commented that repeating a year was such a devastating experience that students were promoted whenever possible.[33] If a good enough average was obtained, failure in some subjects was permitted or marks were adjusted to permit promotion. But Craig pointed out some undesirable results from these practices 1 / A marginal student promoted under such circumstances undertook work in certain subjects for which he was not properly prepared. The difficulty would be compounded in subsequent years. 2 / A student who failed found himself among younger students facing subjects in which he had succeeded as well as those in which he had not. He lost interest in his better subjects throught boring repetition and tended to withdraw from school with a negative attitude toward education. While he was in attendance, his lack of enthusiasm was detrimental to teaching and to the standards attained by the rest of the class. The obvious solution to these problems seemed to be promotion on the basis of success in individual subjects. A full realization of the advantages of this procedure depends, of course, on reasonable flexibility in terms of compulsory subjects and requirements for entry into post-secondary institutions. There is something a bit ludicrous in the idea of a student's being forced to return to school for another futile effort to pass grade 10 history after completing the rest of his program up to the end of grade 13.

During the 1967–8 school year an experimental organizational project was introduced in six secondary schools: Parkside High School in Dundas; Newtonbrook Secondary School in North York; Oakville-Trafalgar High School; Fisher Park Secondary School in Ottawa; Sir John A. Macdonald Collegiate Institute in Scarborough; and Malvern Collegiate Institute in Toronto. The schools tried various modifications of the regular program, involving individual timetables, subject promotion, and additional optional courses. Some moves were made toward bridging the gap between the four-year and five-year programs as well as in breaking down the barriers between the three branches. In commenting on the program in the Legislature, Davis expressed his hopes: "It may well be ... that in the future the traditional distinction between the arts and science, business and commerce, and technical and vocational programmes will decrease and that students will be offered a much wider selection of interests, regardless of their ultimate choice of career pattern."[34] An incidental purpose of the experiment was to demonstrate that there was more flexibility within the existing high school regulations than a number of people thought. Departmental officials were hoping to discover what additional changes needed to be made in these regulations.

The program was under the supervision of a twelve-member School Program Organizational Committee, consisting of four members of the Program Branch of the department and a group of principals who had demonstrated a special interest. Assistance was also supplied by members of the Ontario Institute for Studies in Education, particularly with the designing of timetables and with the evaluation of the effects on the students' interests and motivation. Each school worked out its own particular approach.

The scheme as worked out in Fisher Park High School involved the use of the diploma credit system. A credit was awarded for the successful completion of work in a subject extending over five periods a week throughout the school year. The grade 12 diploma required twenty-seven credits, of which thirteen were compulsory and fourteen optional. At least six credits had to be at level 4. The standard grade 13 program was defined in terms of seven credits at level 5. In order to make the scheme work effectively, at least in larger schools, there were two outstanding requirements: 1 / the availability of a computer for use in timetabling and 2 / adequate counselling to ensure that students made an intelligent selection of options.

A rapidly increasing number of secondary schools later attempted to introduce some form of "non-grading." There were about twenty of these in 1968–9, with an estimated eighty added in 1969–70. Guidelines for the new system were provided in Circular H.S.1. for 1969–70, although it was suggested the principals should not proceed with undue haste. Under these guidelines, a student was to choose a minimum number of subjects from four study areas: communications, social sciences, pure and applied sciences, and arts. An area of study was defined as a "broad segment of man's knowledge and enquiry, characterized by a unity of orientation and comprising a number of subject disciplines." According to an interpretation offered in *New Dimensions in Education,*

> What this means in effect is that students will get a balance of basic education in certain broad subject areas, as well as choice outside the basic minimum. This increased flexibility in curriculum development will place the emphasis on skills and understanding rather than content. It will make possible new interest courses ranging, for example, from beginner's geology offered at Thornlea High School, Thornhill, to philosophy and logic taught at Port Credit High School.[35]

It was also a basic aim of the guidelines to enable a school to organize instruction in semester, trimester, or summer school blocks and to abandon the year as the only unit of time. Thornlea High School was the first to operate on a trimester system, with provision for students to change levels in mid-term and to choose different subjects each term.

Some further consideration of the program as worked out in a typical high school may help to clarify the nature of the changes being made. This program provided for each student, within certain restrictions, to pursue his own interests at an appropriate level of difficulty. Subjects were offered at up to five "phases" or levels of difficulty. Those who pursued work at the higher phases completed their course with a wider range of available opportunities for post-secondary education and employment.

Phase One was confined to first year English and mathematics and was offered only to those who had had considerable difficulty with these subjects in elementary school. Phase Two contained the core subjects carried through four years of high school and prepared a student for the Ontario Secondary School Graduation Diploma. It was the normal preparation for certain types of employment at that stage. In some cases a student might choose Phase Two in his weak subjects while taking the remainder of his work at Phase Three or Phase Four. Success in Phase Three of a subject was required for study of the same subject in the fifth year of high school. Those who sought the Ontario Secondary School Honour Graduation Diploma had to achieve success at Phase Three or Phase Four. Phase Four was an advanced course designed for students who demonstrated a high level of interest and ability in the area in question. Phase Five was restricted to students with intensive interests who wished to pursue independent study in one or more subjects. Such students had to present a program of study and find a staff sponsor. Certain courses which depended mostly on student interest, such as art, were unphased.

A first-year student was required to take English, history, geography, physical and health education, reading, mathematics, science, and three optional subjects. He might choose any phase, presumably with the advice of a guidance counsellor. In subsequent years he had to take at least one subject from each of four categories corresponding to those referred to in the departmental guidelines – in this case labeled Language, Social Sciences, Mathematics, Science and Skill Subjects, and Cultural Subjects. English was the only specifically compulsory subject. A credit was awarded, in line with practice in general, for a subject taken one day a week for a school year, with provision also for half credits. For the purposes of the Ontario Secondary School Honour Graduation Diploma, a student met the minimum requirement in a subject category by the time he had taken four credits, which he might do before the end of the fourth year. His total requirement for the grade 12 diploma was twenty-seven credits, of which at least thirteen must be third- or fourth-year courses.

A restriction on the student's choice was that he have the necessary background to undertake study in a particular area. Prerequisites for each course were shown in course outlines. There was provision for these to be waived in certain cases: for example, a French-speaking student entering secondary school might be allowed to take third-year French. In order to continue the study of a particular subject in the same phase during the following year, a student had to attain D standing or an average of 50 per cent. Consideration was given to requests from honour students to be allowed to take a subject in a higher phase and year. In the first and second years, a student with an average of 55 per cent and one failure or 60 per cent and two failures was given the following choices: repeat the subject in the same phase; drop the subject but be granted credit; continue the subject in the next year in a lower phase; take a course in summer school, if offered.

Evaluation practices were an important part of the scheme. The school took the attitude that the formal examination was not an adequate method of determining mastery of a subject, and in many subjects no final examinations were held. Evaluation depended mainly on tests, class work, reports, assignments, and performance at seminars. A student might be exempted from mid-term examinations, final examinations, or both.

At a meeting of the Ontario Secondary School Headmasters' Council in March 1969, the minister explained the department's current policy with respect to secondary school programs. He spoke appreciatively of the experience gained from the Reorganized Program and declared that the following guiding principles had emerged.

(1) The education of a student should progress along a continuum.
(2) Choice of experiences for the student within that continuum should depend on the student's needs and interests.
(3) The student's need is probably best served by providing some balance of basic education over certain broad subject areas and providing choice beyond and outside the basic minimum.
(4) The student's progress into higher levels of experience should be geared to his own rate of maturing.
(5) School experience should provide the opportunity for a student to concentrate to a greater extent on those subjects to which his interests and needs point. In general, however, concentration on narrow areas of study belongs in the later years of school experience.
(6) The handling of information is at least as important as its accumulation.
(7) The student's intense and co-operative involvement at each place and at each stage of the continuum is of prime importance.
(8) Restriction of a student's program to a narrow channel of subject experience chosen narrowly to provide for some ultimate employment or further education is manifestly unfair, not only because of a student's divergence of competence among subjects but also because it fails to provide for variety of experience and choice of interest.

Davis declared that each student was to have a program suited to his individual needs and aspirations. In order to achieve this purpose, it was necessary to take the following steps.

(1) To remove the present restrictions that force any pupil to obtain all of his school experience within the narrow confines of Two-year, Four-year, and Five-year Programs, or of any one of the three Branches.
(2) To facilitate the development of an organization that will allow individual scheduling according to a student's area of interest and level of competence.
(3) To provide guidance to the principal on the provision of a balance of program among broad areas of study, and to limit these requirements to a minimum so that the principal is free to provide a variety of electives according to the needs of his students and based on the resources of his school in terms of staff and facilities.
(4) To limit requirements for Departmental diplomas to a minimum so that the principal is free to arrange a school program to meet the individual needs of each student both as to choice of study units and rate of progress.
(5) To free the school from the previous requirements based upon 40-minute class periods in order to make possible and encourage the use of different period lengths to provide for alternative patterns such as seminars, variable group instruction, individual study or research, or concentrated group projects represented by excursions, and the like.
(6) To free the school from the previous requirements of time to allow instruction in semester, trimester, or summer school blocks.

Branch or program classifications were to give way to curricular choices based on broad areas of study. The use of the credit system was to facilitate flexible schedule patterns to give the student greater freedom of choice among an expanding range of subject offerings. Course outlines supplied by the department would constitute a framework upon which courses of study could be developed at the local level to meet the needs, aptitudes, and interests of individual students. While great demands would be made on teachers with limited training and experience in curriculum building, the departmental program consultants would be available to provide assistance.

Davis indicated the extent of official support for the breaking down of organizational and procedural rigidities.

Conventional period-packaging and even the rather standardized commencement and ending of the school day are being seen as local variables. To provide a greater breadth of program some schools have lengthened their operating day. Others are moving into various forms of modular scheduling or similar devices designed to relate the time-unit to the nature of the learning process. In providing students with time for independent study during school hours, many schools are now enabling students to make more effective use of our library, laboratory, and other resource facilities. Such a provision represents a major educational advance which may well reach fruition in most of our schools in the foreseeable future.

Davis was not eager to push schools into the new plan before they were ready. If planning was not already well advanced, he suggested that implementation might well be deferred until 1970–1. He called particular attention to the need for additional student counselling as a result of the extended freedom of curricular choice. Efforts would have to be made to find new methods of providing this counselling as well as to obtain more counselling personnel.

PUPILS TRANSFERRING FROM OUTSIDE THE PROVINCE

One of the chief reasons for criticism of the existence of a different school system in each of the Canadian provinces has been that it is quite difficult for many pupils to make a smooth transition from one to another. They are typically faced with different organizational patterns, courses of study, textbooks, examination systems, and to some extent of instructional approach and methodology. The effects have been considered bad for the pupils' intellectual and emotional development and to some extent disruptive of the school's program. Population mobility has been impeded because many parents have preferred to stay where they are rather than force their children to confront so many problems. The results are said to delay the breakdown of parochial attitudes and to prevent the unification of the country.

A solution that has held attractions for certain people is to have a single national system of education for the entire country, which would obviously mean the substitution of federal for provincial control. The political facts of life do not, of course, give such a scheme the slightest chance of being adopted (see also volume II, chapters 14 and 15). Even if the possibility existed, the inevitable inflexibilities in a system managed on such a scale in a country with such great social, cultural, and geographical diversities would be appalling.

It has been suggested more seriously, particularly by the news media, that the provinces should make serious voluntary efforts to standardize their programs and practices. Such a task is suggested as a suitable one for the ministers of education to undertake as part of their program of co-operation. In view of the long history of independent action, and of each province's assumption of the superiority of at least some aspects of its own educational system, this expectation appears distinctly unrealistic. And even if it were possible, the same inflexibilities would appear as if the enterprise were placed under federal control. Uniformity could be maintained only at the expense of suppressing innumerable initiatives and local departures from standard patterns. The desired objective could be attained under conditions of educational stagnation.

The traditional Ontario method of dealing with the transfer problem has been, as in the case of so many other matters, by detailed regulations. A departmental memorandum in 1963 called attention to section 67, subsection (2) of *The Secondary Schools and Boards of Education Act* which stated that "an applicant who has not been promoted from Grade 8 to Grade 9 in the manner prescribed by the regulations shall be admitted to Grade 9 if the principal has satisfied himself that the applicant is competent to undertake the work of that grade."[36] The memorandum indicated that students from other provinces would be admitted to the same grade under this provision. Those applying for admission to other grades would be considered in terms of a table of equivalent standing. Principals must have been pleased to hear that they were not required to obtain the minister's approval for the admission of each applicant. But they had to ensure that some quite specific requirements were met before the student could be recommended for the Ontario Secondary School Honour Graduation Diploma.

The Ontario Secondary School Graduation Diploma can be granted only where the candidate completes successfully at least the Grade 12 portion of the Grades 11 and 12 course at an Ontario secondary school or an inspected private school as a regular or private-study candidate and obtains Ontario Grade 12 standing in every subject required for the diploma, except as noted below.
NOTE 1. If in the opinion of the principal the candidate holds equivalent standing from another province in History (an obligatory subject in Ontario) or in one of the Parts of the subject comparable to that prescribed in Ontario, he need take only the ONE history subject which he needs (World History Part I or World History Part II in the case of the General Course) which is being taught in Grade 11 or Grade 12, to meet the history requirements for the diploma. The principal may take into consideration the fact that in some provinces one History is taken in Grade 10 and the other in Grade 11.
NOTE 2. The same ruling as in Note 1 may be applied to such optional subjects in the General Course as Mathematics (Geometry and Algebra), Science (Physics and Chemistry), Geography (Geography Part I and Geography Part II), and to the obligatory and optional subjects of the Vocational Courses where the subject is divided in Grades 11 and 12 and is not considered to be cumulative.
NOTE 3. A pupil may be admitted to Grade 12 in Ontario only in the same course (General, Commercial, Technical, Home Economics, or Art) which he has taken in Grade 11 in his former school. If a pupil transferring to Ontario wishes to finish his instruction in another course, he may be accorded the same privileges of taking a special one-year course as are accorded to pupils enrolled in Ontario secondary schools.

These detailed instructions are of interest for reasons other than that they reveal the regulation mentality that dominated the department at this time. They also show great confidence in the particular subject prescription authorized in Ontario and an apprehension lest the Ontario diploma be awarded on the basis of any inferior preparation. Perhaps nothing more effectively demonstrates the contrast between the inflexibility of the old approach and the recent attempts to design programs to meet individual needs.

FIVE

The evolution of curriculum

The present chapter is an attempt to trace the evolution of the major curricular practices and concepts prevailing in Ontario schools down through the years. The story is made rather complex by the number of different aspects of the main theme, including the identity of subjects taught at different levels of the system, the general methodological approach used in instruction, the type and degree of control exercised by the central authority and the amount delegated to local agencies or individual teachers, and the ideas held and expressed by prominent educators about what should be taught and how.

NINETEENTH-CENTURY CURRICULA

The early common schools

In his *Documentary History of Education in Upper Canada*, Hodgins has described the curriculum and instructional procedures followed in the common schools in the early part of the nineteenth century.

After the letters were thoroughly learned, the first step in advance was promotion to the class which was engaged in the study of the New Testament, the Bible being then the standard test book [*sic*] for reading. The scholars were thoroughly drilled in the teachings of Bible truths for a long time after learning to read fairly well. Cobb's spelling book was introduced. Not until the scholar could read and spell well was he allowed to begin to write, and a good deal of pains was taken to teach the scholar to write well. The pens used were made of goose quills, the ink also was made of soft maple bark, oak galls or something of that nature. To buy ink was impossible at that time, and steel pens had not come into general use. The copy books were often made of wrapping paper, foolscap paper being very scarce and expensive. A little arithmetic was also taught, and this, in the majority of cases, was the total amount of education which the pupils, as a general rule, had the chance to receive, more advanced pupils were taught a little grammar, geography and history.[1]

C.E. Phillips has also provided a vivid description of the approach to teaching and learning that prevailed in the schools of the same period.

... one has only to realize what reliance was placed on set forms – on crystallized articles of belief, on fixed codes of conduct, on the concept of a static society, on shibboleths about the propensities and treatment of the young, on rules of thumb for this and rules of thumb for that, on standard remedies, on made-up prescriptions of subject matter, and on traditional methods of teaching. To have a child read a sentence in praise of virtue must have a good effect; to have him memorize the sentence must make that effect more permanent. Who could think otherwise when to doubt was a major offence and to test such assumptions a process almost unknown?

The adult formulae for the improvement of the young were applied without thought of the reaction of the child. His only virtue was receptivity and obedience. With the intention of facilitating the learning process, material was arranged in the logical order helpful to those who have knowledge to organize but often meaningless to the youthful learner. Hence formal content without significance had to be memorized, not understood. For this uncongenial task there could be only one motivation – the fear of punishment. It was not the difficulty of the work which made the rod necessary, but the complete absence of any other motivation.[2]

Common schools in the Ryerson years

Centennial Story provides considerable information about the program followed in the common schools of Toronto during the period around 1850 and for the next two decades or so.[3] Boys and girls were divided into separate departments, and these in turn had three divisions: the first or junior division took the smallest children through the first book; the second or intermediate division covered the second and third books; and the third or senior division, the fourth and fifth books. The books referred to were the Irish National Readers, which had been authorized as a result of the favourable impression Ryerson formed of them during his visit to Europe at the beginning of his long career as Assistant Superintendent and then Superintendent of Education.

Centennial Story also tells of a typical timetable followed in the third or senior division. The boys were given a more demanding program than the girls, obviously on a basis other than observation of the relative capacities of the two sexes. From 9:00 to 10:00 a.m. both the male and the female departments had reading, with the addition in the male department of scripture and sacred geography on Monday, history or political economy on Tuesday, dictation or science on Wednesday, and history or political economy on Thursday. The girls received instruction in spelling and history as well as reading. From 10:00 to 10:50 both sexes were taught writing on three days of the week and drawing on one; on Friday boys got bookkeeping and writing of figures, while girls got arithmetic. After a ten minute recess the boys had an hour of arithmetic every day and the girls, arithmetic on three days and dictation on two. The first class in the afternoon consisted of grammar and composition for the boys and grammar only for the girls. Geography or history followed for both departments, supplemented by map drawing for the boys. On four days of the week, the boys ended with algebra, geometry, arithmetic, or science, while the girls had sewing or natural philosophy. Friday was devoted to review until the last hour, when the boys had singing and recitation of poetry and the girls, singing and sewing, and library books were distributed to both groups.[4]

The same source tells of Ryerson's attempt to add new subjects to the curriculum. These included agriculture, mechanics, and chemistry, while at the same time composition was defined as a separate subject. The additions were in line with Ryerson's observation that there were new opportunities developing in railways, manufacturing, and mining. Not only were Toronto teachers entirely unprepared to teach these subjects, but there were also many complaints that the children's minds would be overburdened, and they would have no opportunity to learn anything really well. The increased cost of books was also an important consideration. Along with the recent provision for music and drawing, there were now nineteen subjects in the program; these did indeed prove to be too many and the number had to be reduced.[5]

At the time of the School Act of 1871, the number of subjects taught in the common schools again rose to nineteen, with the addition of natural history and natural philosophy (mechanics). While individual pupils did not take all the subjects, the teachers were supposed to be able to teach them.[6] Given the nature of teacher preparation in those days, the results may well be imagined. A great deal of learning consisted of rote parroting of facts from a textbook.

Post-Ryerson changes in the elementary schools

In 1884 the elementary school program was reduced to twelve subjects: reading, writing, arithmetic, history, geography, composition, grammar, music, drawing, temperance, drill and calisthenics, and agriculture. At the same time, school boards were given the right, subject to the approval of the public school inspector, to modify the course to meet local needs. This was a concession which the Toronto authorities had long sought in vain. Among the curriculum changes recorded by McCutcheon during this period, English was made compulsory, while bilingual readers were authorized for use by French- and German-speaking pupils. Physiology was added in 1886 and made compulsory for high school entrance in 1893. A course in the teaching of domestic science was introduced into the normal schools in 1898, and the subject, along with manual training, became optional in the elementary schools two years later. During this period, Canadian history became compulsory and agriculture optional.[7]

While there was undoubtedly no dearth of backward practices in the period before the turn of the century, many concerns of educators had quite a modern ring. The following topics were dealt with in addresses delivered at annual meetings of the Ontario Educational Association before 1900: the importance of character training; the value of precept and example; evidence of the acceptance of faculty theory; the possibility of separating religious principles from dogma; the uselessness of dull, routine teaching of facts; the ideas of Pestalozzi, Froebel, Horace Mann, and others about developing the child's innate capacities; the harm done by too much stress on examinations, despite their value in maintaining standards; the importance of teaching the love of good literature; the undesirability of too much teaching of formal grammar; the importance of avoiding excessive spoon-feeding and of developing student self-reliance; the need to avoid dispersal of effort over too many subjects in high school.[8]

Grammar schools

Before the reorganization of 1853, the grammar schools (earlier called district schools) were primarily boys' boarding schools for the sons of the wealthy. Latin and Greek had a predominant place in the curriculum, while other subjects such as English, mathematics, history, geography, writing, drawing, and vocal music were also offered. A new program of studies was issued in 1854, changing the emphasis from classics to English. The other subjects were continued; physics, chemistry, geology, and physiology were introduced under the name "natural philosophy"; and bookkeeping and French were optional. Ryerson hoped that the course would have practical value for students not intending to go further, as well as for students bound for university.[9] According to George Paxton Young, who was provincial Inspector of Grammar Schools from 1864 to 1871, the new curriculum was not followed. Stress was still placed on the classics, to the neglect of English.

An attempt was made in 1867 to provide two courses for the grammar schools, a classical course for university matriculation and an alternative for those who might wish to matriculate in the University of Toronto as students of civil engineering. The latter course substituted English and French for Latin and Greek. It attracted almost no students, no doubt largely because provincial grants were based on the number taking the classical subjects.

Before 1865 only a few of the grammar schools admitted girls, and then only to classes taking the elementary subjects. In that year trustees were authorized to admit them if they passed the admission examination prescribed for boys. They were not, however, permitted to study Latin and Greek, to be designated as grammar school pupils, or to be counted in the calculation of enrolment for grant purposes.[10] These restrictions were removed by the Act of 1871.

Secondary schools after 1871

A concerted effort was made in 1871 to reduce the influence of the classics, which were now made optional. This measure was partly counteracted, however, by the requirement that sixty boys take Latin and Greek as a condition for the granting of collegiate institute status. Along with a new effort to emphasize English, mathematics, history, and geography received more attention, and provision was made for French, German, commercial subjects, and science.[11]

During the remainder of the century there was some progress in reducing the number of compulsory subjects, a trend that was probably even more of a blessing to the small number of teachers in most of the schools than it was to the students. In 1871 there were eleven of these subjects in the first form, and by 1897 only seven. In the third form the comparable reduction was from twelve to six, and seven were required in the fourth. In the larger schools there was increased flexibility with the provision of a wider range of options, of which there were six in the third and fourth forms in 1897, as compared with two in 1871.[12]

DEVELOPMENTS IN THE EARLY TWENTIETH CENTURY

Elementary curriculum

At the beginning of the twentieth century there was a move in the direction of a stronger cultural emphasis. McCutcheon reported that a year of study preceded the revision of 1904, which emphasized nature study, art, music, "constructive work," and physical culture. At the same time, manual training, domestic science, and agriculture were made optional, while elementary science, stenography, and typewriting were made available for form V.[13] These changes did not prevent continued attention to what were regarded as essential subjects, which John Seath defined as English, mathematics, geography, and history.[14]

Emphasis is placed in *Centennial Story* on the influence of Johann Friedrich Herbart on educational thought in the United States and Canada during the early years of the twentieth century. Textbooks following his inductive-deductive methods were introduced in the Ontario normal schools about 1910. The complete revision of school textbooks between 1908 and 1910 showed strong Herbartian influence, particularly those dealing with grammar and arithmetic. Little change in method characterized the further revision of 1920.[15]

There was no change of major proportions in the departmental prescriptions until 1937, as shown by the course of study issued in 1936. The curriculum for kindergarten had the most modern ring, mainly, no doubt because the enlightened principles defined by Froebel had become so firmly established. The program consisted of "gifts," occupations, games, and stories. The kindergarten gifts were defined as "plays leading to a recognition of the qualities and possibilities of the various Gifts and of objects related to them." Occupations consisted of sewing, art, folding, cutting, weaving, modeling, bead stringing, and exercises with pegs and tiles.

There were also certain activities common to the kindergarten and kindergarten–primary forms. These included manners and morals, which were to be taught incidentally through songs, games, talks, and stories, and by example; nature study, to be taught through songs, conversations, and observation; vocal music; physical culture, to consist of simple games with a minimum of attention and fatigue; and hygiene. The kindergarten-primary form was also to have literature; language, including reading and spelling; reading (by word recognition); oral and written phonics concurrent with, and supplementary to, reading; writing, with muscular movements taught in games with emphasis on rhythm; arithmetic; art; manual training; and sewing.

For the same year the course of study for forms I to IV consisted of obligatory and optional subjects. In the first of these groups were reading and literature, composition and spelling, writing, arithmetic, history, geography, grammar, hygiene and physical culture, art and constructive work (minimum course), nature study and agriculture (minimum course), and vocal music (minimum course). The optional courses were art and constructive work (supplementary course), nature study and agriculture (supplementary course), vocal music (supplementary course), manual training, and household science. The school board might, on the recommendation of the inspector, select "such subjects ... and such topics of these subjects as in its judgment are desirable and practicable in the condition of the school."[16] Other suitable optional subjects that met the needs of the locality might be added with the approval of the minister. In all the courses, the teacher was to give instruction in moral principles and practices and in good manners. Opportunities for attaining such objectives were to be found in current incidents, in lessons in literature and history, in anecdotes and didactic talks, and in personal example.

For form V, the obligatory subjects were reading and literature, composition and spelling, British history, geography, grammar, and arithmetic. The optional subjects were physiography, algebra, geometry, art , botany, zoology, agriculture and horticulture, Latin, French, German, manual training, household science, music, business practice, stenography, and typewriting. These courses were the same as those prescribed for the lower school of the high school. Students could receive credit for lower school subjects by fulfilling the examination requirements. Teachers of form V were to give instruction in manners and morals by the methods used in the first four forms.

Secondary curriculum

In his report of 1911, Seath referred to two types of secondary school courses: the General course, taken by those who sought a general education, and the Special courses. The latter consisted of seven subclassifications: the courses for university matriculation and the preliminary examinations of the learned professions; the courses for admission to the normal and model schools and the faculties of education; the Household Science course; the Commercial course; the Agricultural course; the Manual Training course; and the Middle School Art course.[17] According to C.A. Brown, there is little evidence of any major official attempt to provide two types of courses, one for those bound for university and one for the others.[18] Pullen's verdict is also that the distinction was largely fictitious.[19] The insistence of the universities on the classics as a prerequisite for admission had resulted in a failure to develop any real alternative.

An attempt was made in 1913 to infuse new vigour into the General course. The lower, middle, and upper school divisions were established, each of two years' duration. The two mainstreams were the General and Special courses, with the Special courses consisting, as in Seath's description, mainly of the Matriculation and Normal Entrance courses. The subjects offered differed little from one stream to another. In lower school, all students took geography, reading, English composition, English literature, and history. During the first year, arithmetic and grammar were uniformly compulsory, but could be dropped by students of the Matriculation course in the second year. Art and elementary science were prescribed for the General course in lower school. Subjects for both main streams in middle school were English composition, English literature, ancient and British history, algebra, geometry, Latin, Greek, French, German, physics, chemistry, art, agriculture and horticulture, and industrial arts. Upper school offerings were English composition and rhetoric, English literature, medieval and modern history, algebra, geometry, trigonometry, French, German, physics, chemistry, mineralogy, and biology. Two languages were compulsory for the Matriculation course, but not for the Normal Entrance course. In practice, students tended to take the options that enabled them to qualify in both courses.[20]

By 1920 it was evident that nearly all the students were enrolling in the Matriculation or the Normal Entrance course. As might be expected, there were complaints that there were too many subjects and that the courses were too heavy. There were also objections to the requirement that all the subjects be passed in one year.[21] The effect was that general interest in secondary education increased very slowly.

Revisions made in 1921 included the abolition of the three distinct courses and the reduction of the secondary school course to five years by the elimination of one of the two years of the upper school. A limit on the number of compulsory subjects also lightened the burden in lower and middle school. The obligatory subjects in lower school were English literature and composition for both years and each of Canadian history and civics, physiography, and algebra for one year. The optional subjects were arithmetic, grammar, art, geography, botany and zoology or agriculture and horticulture, Latin, French, Greek, German, Spanish or Italian, manual training, household science, music, business practice, and stenography and typewriting. School boards were authorized to add subjects to the list of options, with the approval of the minister, in order to meet the special needs of the local community. This arrangement paralleled that for vocational courses, which had existed since 1911. Students in the lower school had to take at least two and not more than eight optional subjects along with the compulsory subjects. The compulsory subjects in middle school were English literature and composition, and the options were algebra, geometry, physics and chemistry or agriculture and horticulture, British history, ancient history, Latin, Greek, French, German, Spanish or Italian, manual training, household science, art, music, bookkeeping and penmanship, stenography and typewriting, and additional subjects requested by the school board and approved by the minister. The number of options to be taken at this level ranged between four and seven. In addition to the academic subjects, physical culture was compulsory for both lower and middle school students. Subjects offered in upper school were English literature, English composition, algebra, geometry, trigonometry, modern history, physics, chemistry, biology, Latin, Greek, French, German, Spanish or Italian, and additional subjects chosen in the same way as those for lower and middle school. There was no minimum or maximum number of courses to be taken. It became common practice for students to take certain upper school subjects in their fourth year.[22] A further measure to lighten the burden on students was the provision that they could write one or more examination papers at a time instead of all at once. The universities adopted the same arrangement with respect to matriculation examinations.

Pullen has provided evidence of how the curriculum revisions of 1921 were brought about. The minister appointed a special committee consisting of representatives of the provincial universities, the Ontario College of Education, the collegiate institutes and high schools, the continuation schools, the public and separate school inspectors, and the Department of Education.[23] These individuals were instructed to review the courses of study and the examination system and to consider any other matter that affected the organization or efficiency of the schools. The committee was reported to have met frequently and to have made a very thorough study of the situation.

REFORMS IN THE ELEMENTARY SCHOOL PROGRAM INITIATED IN THE 1930s

Program of 1937

The appearance of the *Programme of Studies for Grades I to VI of the*

Public and Separate Schools, 1937 was an event of considerable importance in the evolution of curriculum in elementary schools in Ontario because of the progressive outlook defined in the introduction and embodied in the recommendations. Certain aspects of the work were discussed in chapter 1 on aims of education. Many of the ideas and some of the wording were taken from the reports of the Consultative Committee of the Board of Education in Great Britain, commonly known as the Hadow reports, which between 1927 and 1934 dealt successively with the education of the adolescent, the primary school, and nursery and infant schools. The Ontario program was drawn up by a committee of teachers under the guidance of Thornton Mustard and S.A. Watson of the Department of Education.

Health

As a component of the curriculum, health was to include school experiences which favourably influenced habits, knowledge, and attitudes that related to individual and community health, such as health service, health education, and physical training. The first of these covered the maintenance of healthful surroundings, the provision, where feasible, of regular health examinations, morning inspection, the control of communicable diseases, and the availability of first aid in emergencies. Health education was designed to produce good health habits and desirable attitudes toward personal and community health. Knowledge of scientific principles underlying these habits and attitudes was to be introduced where appropriate. The third element, physical education, included free play, games, drills, dances, and exercises designed to develop and maintain physical efficiency. Health was not to be isolated as a subject but was to be regarded as a practice and an ideal permeating the whole life of the school.

The children's mental health was to be regarded as equal in importance to their physical health. The objective of good mental health was to be attained by preventing injurious practices and by cultivating happiness through activity accompanied by a reasonable degree of success. For the most part, this aspect of the program was left rather vague.

English

English was identified as occupying the first place among the intellectual exercises of the elementary school. The course consisted of oral and silent reading and oral and written language exercises. Oral reading was to include informal conversation, story-telling, reporting on private reading, and, where necessary, corrective exercises. Written language was to include training in sentence and paragraph structure, the writing of simple letters, exercises in verse-making and play-writing, and the gradual acquisition of skill in the mechanics of punctuation, spelling, and writing. Those who drew up the curriculum apparently had no particular sympathy with the idea that the all-important objective in written work was to encourage a spontaneous flow of expression, since the teacher was enjoined to ensure a high standard of neatness in arrangement, legibility, and accuracy in spelling in all the written work of the school through careful supervision, judicious commendation, and, if necessary, remedial exercises. On the other hand, creative efforts in the form of writing or telling original stories or composing verse were not to be judged by adult standards.

Supplementary reading was described as the most important phase of the English course. With enough suitable books and proper guidance and encouragement in their use, the child would almost be able to educate himself. Extensive reading was also to be regarded as a desirable form of recreation. One wonders to whom the advice to have a small library of attractive, well-chosen books in each classroom was directed. Teachers in the depression years were not usually in a position to do much about such an exhortation.

Performance expected of the child in handwriting had been considerably eased in comparison with earlier years. The use of print script, which had become almost universal in primary classes, was strongly recommended. As muscular control developed, ordinary cursive writing might be introduced. The difficulties of joinings, suitable slant, the use of the pen, and rhythm were to be mastered one by one so that by the age of twelve the child could be expected to write in ink with reasonable speed and legibility.

Social studies

The purpose of social studies was said to be to help the child understand the society in which he lived and the duties and responsibilities of its members to one another. The course consisted of a blending of geography, history, and citizenship. As the child proceeded through the primary grades, he was to work his way outward through concentric circles. In grade 1, he was to study his home and school; in grade 2, his community of town and country; in grade 3, similar communities in other lands; in grade 4, contemporary and, subsequently, ancient, primitive, and medieval communities where he could see the evolution of social life; in grade 5, the great discoverers; and in grade 6, Canada, with attention to the beginnings of social life in various parts of the country.

The formal approach was to be supplemented by the discussion of such current events as were of interest to the children. Opportunities were to be provided for visits to places of local interest, which would help them to visualize past events and understand the relationship between environment and social life. Teachers were not to worry too much if the children accumulated knowledge in a rather unsystematic fashion. The important thing was not to amass facts but to develop interests and form desirable attitudes. Yet the hope was expressed that, if the child proceeded on the basis of interest, he would learn more and better facts than by memorizing second-hand compendiums.

The enterprise method was strongly recommended for social studies. A dramatization of the visit of Marco Polo to the court of Genghis Khan was suggested as an opportunity for making costumes, arranging the stage, writing the dialogue, searching for information, tracing the route, and writing letters of invitation and thanks. Above all, the children would have had an opportunity to work together on constructive activities. The progressive point of view was particularly strong in the following passage.

> The social virtues of the good citizen are not things merely to learn about. They are to be achieved by practising them. The development of qualities of co-operation, respect for the rights and feelings of others, willingness to accept responsibility, and other attributes of the good citizen can be developed only by exercising them in situations that demand their practice. They are to be accepted willingly as desirable forms of conduct; they cannot be developed by coercion. The school must, therefore, be so organized as to permit of their growth and exercise in situations that require their practice.[24]

Natural science

Topics for study in natural science included features of plant and animal life; first-hand natural phenomena such as the changing weather, the apparent movement of the heavenly bodies, and the sequence of day and night and the seasons; and an exploration of the principles of physiology and hygiene to give support to the health habits which the school attempted to establish. The purpose of the course was to produce an appreciation of science and to enhance the children's natural desire to know more about the world around them. They were to learn to observe carefully and dispassionately and to make proper inferences from their observations.

As much as possible of the study of plants and animals was to be conducted in their natural habitat. Where that was impossible, the fullest use was to be made of window boxes, nature tables, insect cages, wormeries, aquariums, and vivariums. The construction of such receptacles would give the children valuable training in handwork, and the care of the occupants would teach them lessons about plant and animal husbandry. Other desirable activities included drawing and modelling of objects or living creatures and the making of portfolios and notebooks.

Individual differences were to be provided for in that the same activities would not be prescribed for every child. Outside a common core of knowledge, each was to be encouraged to follow his natural bent. Obviously this meant that a large part of the program was to be conducted in some manner other than that of the formal lesson.

Arithmetic

The purpose of teaching arithmetic in the elementary grades was to give the child an understanding of the significance of number in the ordinary affairs of life and to provide him with numerical skills for his own practical use. He was to acquire a knowledge of our system of notation and numeration for integral and fractional numbers, skill and accuracy in the application of the four fundamental processes to the solution of problems arising out of experience, and a familiarity with the meaning and use of the units of measure employed in ordinary life. The reformed curriculum had resulted in a new grade placement of certain topics, the elimination of others, and the exclusion of excessively unwieldy numbers and involved problems.

It was suggested that new facts and mechanical processes could be presented most effectively in problem situations that had reality for the child, rather than those having only adult application. The teacher was urged to try to create a felt need for the new fact or skill. Yet, while the solution of problems arising out of real situations was said to offer the best arithmetic training, these opportunities were not regarded as sufficient to make the use of the fundamental processes automatic. Short periods of practice were considered necessary. Mental computation was highly commended.

Music

Music was identified with the other arts as an expression of deep-seated instincts in human nature. While it was considered to appeal primarily to the feelings and emotions, it was said to have an important intellectual side as well. Desirable training would include rhythmic expression, the correct and pleasing use of the voice in singing, the "concerted rendering" of worthwhile music, and the appreciation of great musical compositions. The use of national and folk songs was urged as a means of developing a sound melodic taste. Children were to be encouraged to read stories about music and music-makers. Appreciation was to be developed by actual hearing of expert performance and by the use of good records.

Art

As defined in the elementary school curriculum, art was to include graphic, plastic, and industrial arts. Recognition was to be given to the importance of both appreciation and creation. The school was to provide experience in and training for both the emotional and intellectual phases of appreciation, as well as the emotional, intellectual, and physical phases of creation. The broad purposes were to develop in children the ability to see and enjoy the beautiful in art and nature and to cultivate their capacity to express their own ideas through various media. Technical instruction was to be given in response to a felt need and was not to be offered before there was evidence of such a need. Children were to be encouraged to find their best mode of expression, whether drawing, carving, modelling, or construction. There was said to be no reason why all the children in a class should be working on the same subject or with the same medium at the same time.

Artistic appreciation was to be taught in a variety of indirect ways. The teacher was to be constantly on the alert to direct the child's attention toward beautiful things in his surroundings. These would include both natural phenomena and articles of human creation such as paintings, sculpture, lettering, stained glass windows, rugs, fabrics, china, and glassware. The classroom was to be made aesthetically pleasing by the use of harmonious colour combinations, the careful arrangement of furnishings, and the use of displays of illustrative material.

Formal picture study, requiring a knowledge of standards of beauty, and of principles of design, colour, and tonal values, was not to be included in the course for elementary grades. It was recommended, however, that pupils be brought into contact with some of the world's great pictures. These were to come within the interests and experiences of the child. The collection of appealing pictures, suitably mounted and preserved, was a recommended activity.

Apportionment of time

The program of studies warned that rigid time limits for different subjects must be abandoned. Allowing for the possibility of overlap and the need for flexibility, the following balance was suggested: English – 30 per cent, social studies – 20 per cent, health – 10 per cent, natural science – 10 per cent, arithmetic – 10 per cent, music – 10 per cent, art – 10 per cent.

Class organization and management

Age was suggested as a good guide for the grading of pupils. It was also permissible to place them in accordance with their progress in arithmetic or by reading ability as determined by one of the familiar standardized tests. Informal tests were to be given freely in skill areas such as reading, writing, arithmetic, spelling, and language. In social studies and natural science, where interests and attitudes were more important than the acquisition of facts, tests were to be de-emphasized in favour of encouragement to read, explore, discover, record, and create.

Promotion by age was recommended for the junior grades. The work of each grade was said to constitute a reasonable program for the average child. Slower children were to have a modified program and special attention from the teacher to enable them to progress with their social group. Bright children were to be accelerated or given an enriched program. For most children, acceleration was to be regarded as inadvisable because it would remove them from a physically or mentally appropriate environment.

It was suggested that reports contain the necessary information about the child's attendance and punctuality, his progress, his attitudes, and his interests. The use of letter grades might indicate unusual excellence, satisfactory progress, or unsatisfactory progress. These ratings were to be determined in relation to natural capacity and not to an absolute standard. Attitudes and characteristics such as courtesy, helpfulness, co-operation, and leadership (and presumably their absence) were to be reported in brief comments. A report of this kind would demand that the teacher make a careful study of each child.

Modifications during the war

Change in emphasis

The outline of 1937 was revised somewhat in successive years in the light of suggestions by teachers and inspectors. For the most part, the changes were quite minor, and the general nature of the recommended approach remained essentially the same. The introduction was rewritten in 1941 with much greater stress on the objective of preparing children to live in a democratic society and correspondingly less emphasis on individual development. The increasing menace of the war was possibly responsible for the assertion that democracy demanded "the finest service of which [the child] is capable, and a willingness to make sacrifices for the common welfare."[25]

Advice on means of developing effective behaviour for democratic living was completely in the progressive tradition. Reliance on the verbal teaching of precepts was dismissed as valueless. The proper habits were to be learned through meaningful social experiences which required the exercise of qualities of helpfulness, self-direction, and the acceptance of responsibility. "The school must set up for its pupils an environment in which, through use, they may learn the social techniques, derive the attitudes and beliefs, and develop the abilities and skills that social life in a democratic society requires."[26]

Activity and learning

The program reaffirmed the premise that learning is an active process. Possibly reflecting a tendency on the part of some teachers to interpret this expression too narrowly, it emphasized that activity did not refer only to physical movement, but also included such mental processes as thinking, reflecting, and planning. Learning was said to take place most efficiently, although not necessarily only, when the learner's interest was aroused. External motivation became "less necessary" rather than "unnecessary" when the pupil's actions were directed by a continuing purpose. Somewhat after the manner of Dewey's strictures, immediate and transitory interests were distinguished from enduring purposes.

The program of 1937 and each revision in subsequent years contained a section on the enterprise. There may or may not have been real significance in the fact that, in 1941, this section was moved up ahead of the treatment of different subjects rather than being dealt with at the end. There was particular stress at this stage on having the enterprise arise from needs or purposes felt strongly by the children. Although it might be inspired by the teacher, the children were to accept it as their own and plan it co-operatively. While it might provide opportunities for improving spoken or written English, for using books or other sources to obtain information, and for extending knowledge, its main purpose was to develop the children's ability to live and work together.

The educational value of the enterprise was said to be dependent on the following of an orderly procedure in its conduct. It was to begin with the arousal of interest, followed by a planning period during which the teacher and pupils co-operatively selected goals and determined the activities to be carried out. The work period would be devoted to investigation and research, and then to the production of drawings, plays, and other tangible results. In the culmination stage, the work of different individuals or subgroups would be brought together for others to share, possibly in the form of a display. Teachers were urged to keep in mind that the value of the enterprise did not lie in the final product, but in the interest and stimulation inherent in the process itself. A particular warning was offered against allowing the approach to become formalized or stereotyped.

Quite obviously, no aspect of the program outlined at that time depended more on the imagination, creativity, and maturity of the teachers. They had to be able to strike out in new directions without the props of textbooks and detailed study outlines. If they lacked the requisite ability and experience, they often produced either sterile exercises, following the form of a model without the spirit, or else let their classes dissolve into chaos. The concept of the enterprise was never discredited, but it fell into disrepute in many quarters because of teacher incompetence.

REFORMS IN THE SECONDARY SCHOOL PROGRAM

The revision of the secondary school program in 1937 was much more moderate than that in the elementary schools. At this time the use of the term lower school was dropped, and a common grade 9 program was introduced for all courses. The compulsory subjects were English, social studies, health and physical education, business practice and writing, mathematics, general or agricultural science, French, general shop for boys and home economics for girls, and music and art. In 1950 this common course was dropped and options were again introduced.

According to the arrangements made in 1937, English, social studies, and health were compulsory in grade 10 of the General course and in all the vocational courses. General course students also took any four of mathematics, science or agriculture, shop work or home economics, commercial or German or Greek, music and art, Latin, and French. Students in the Industrial and Agriculture courses took as additional obligatory subjects mathematics, science, and shop or agriculture, with music or art as options. In the Home Economics course, home economics was an additional obligatory subject and mathematics, science, and music or art or French were optional. In the Commercial course, commercial was an additional obligatory subject and mathematics, French or home economics or shop, and music or art were optional. In the Art course, art was obligatory and mathematics, science, shop or home economics, French, and music were optional.

To continue with a rather tedious litany for the sake of a complete record, English, history, and health were obligatory in grades 11 and 12 of the General course and in all vocational courses. The options in the General course, of which four were required, were mathematics, science or agriculture, French, Latin, German, Greek, Spanish, Italian, commercial or shop or home economics, and music and art or music or art. In the Industrial course, shops or agriculture, mathematics, and science were obligatory and music or art optional. In the Art course, art and crafts were obligatory, and music, French, science, and mathematics were opitonal. In the Home Economics course, science or art and practical work were obligatory and French, mathematics, music, and business practice were optional. In the Commercial course, commercial was obligatory and mathematics, French, art, music, science, home economics, and shops were optional.

Among subsequent changes up to 1950 which Pullen considered worthy of attention were the following: in 1939, the introduction of the Intermediate Certificate for those successfully completing any course to the end of grade 10; in 1940, the first appearance of geography as an option in grades 11 and 12 and the requirement that health and physical education be taken in grade 13; in 1942, the addition of defence training to health and physical education; in 1943, the addition of music as a grade 13 subject; in 1941 and 1942, the beginning of the departmental practice of issuing the Ontario Secondary School Graduation Diploma and the Ontario Secondary School Honour Graduation Diploma respectively; in 1945, the addition of occupations as a compusory subject in grade 9, and the adoption of agriculture as a separate option above grade 10; in 1949, the addition of accountancy, secretarial practice, and mathematics of investment in grade 13.[27] No really fundamental change was made in the subject offerings, however, until the 1960s.

SIGNIFICANCE OF THE 1930S AND EARLY 1940S

Phillips showed that what happened in Ontario in the 1930s, and continued in some respects in the 1940s, was a phenomenon that was occurring all across Canada.

... the first real curriculum revision in Canada, in contrast with accretions in earlier years, occurred in the depression years. Saskatchewan set a pattern in October, 1929, and by 1937 every province had re-written its curriculum. Some provinces completed the revision in a year, some took several years. Nova Scotia published the revision and related suggestions in one handbook of 655 pages. Ontario covered Grades I to VI and subsequently Grades VII and VIII in booklets of about 150 pages each, and issued brief pamphlets on each of the secondary school subjects. British Columbia turned out voluminous publications which dwarfed all others. The new programs were based to an unprecedented degree on the concept of education as development and aimed primarily at socially desirable qualities and abilities rather than the amassing of knowledge. They raised music, art, home economics, and shop work from the status of optional subjects or extra-curricular activities to the importance of the traditional subjects. They placed great emphasis on health and physical education. Reflecting new educational thought in the United States under a veil of acknowledgments to Hadow in Britain, they provided for enterprises and limited activity programs. They sought to remove restrictions on teachers and pupils by providing latitude for selective emphasis and variation in methods of treatment at the teacher's discretion. These changes were limited to elementary and junior high school grades.[28]

EVOLUTION OF VOCATIONAL CURRICULUM FROM THE 1920S

From the time the first vocational education act was passed, the Department of Education assumed no responsibility for prescribing vocational courses. According to Pullen, the practice around 1921 was for tradesmen to be selected to teach their own specialities, and each teacher's course existed mainly in his own head.[29] Inspectors increasingly tended to ask for written outlines, and the best of these were circulated by the department on a suggestive basis in 1935. In 1946 a revised outline of industrial courses was edited by Inspector A.M. Moon.

RECOMMENDATIONS OF THE ROYAL COMMISSION

Elementary schools

The Royal Commission disclaimed any intention of outlining in detail the curricula for the reorganized system which it recommended. Possibly reflecting some idea of what was coming in the Porter Plan, it expressed a conviction that, if individual needs were to be met, the courses should be suggestive rather than prescriptive and should be developed through co-operative effort by all who were concerned with the educational development of the child.[30] What the commission was apparently eschewing was the specification of topics to be covered and the level of difficulty in each subject, since it did not hesitate to prescribe specific subjects or even to hint at the method of teaching it thought appropriate.

The basis for a curriculum for nursery school and kindergarten was embodied in the following aims:

(1) To assist in the development of fundamental habits of living through the acquisition of proper health habits associated with rest, play and exercise, eating, and toilet practices.
(2) To develop and improve the use of language through listening to stories told by the teacher, relating personal experiences, looking at and discussing pictures, and communicating with fellow-pupils in play and other school situations; and gradually to develop "reading readiness" through these and similar exercises and experiences.
(3) To assist informally in the growth of the number sense through games and special activities appropriate to particular times of the day and seasons.
(4) To introduce aesthetic training by learning and appreciating simple tunes and rhythms; and, in art, by enlarging the appreciation and thoughtful use of different kinds of materials.
(5) To assist moral and spiritual development through morning prayer, sacred songs, verse speaking, and Bible stories.
(6) To provide an environment in which the child may develop a feeling of security and gain a sense of "belonging", so that he becomes less and less dependent on the teacher.
(7) To develop in the child a feeling of adequacy in meeting ordinary situations appropriate to his age by mastering the use of, and gaining confidence in his ability to handle, selected play equipment.
(8) To teach the child to work and play with others of his own age in an acceptable manner; to respect the rights of others and to await his turn; to select materials for games and activities, to use them, and then to replace them in their storage places.[31]

For the junior and senior divisions of the elementary school, the commission recommended that the curriculum consist of English, social studies, arithmetic, natural science, music, art, physical and health education, and religious education. As at the secondary level, the school program was to encourage the idea of temperance in living. The commission gave the reformed curriculum of 1937 a good deal of encouragement by advocating a progressive approach to teaching at the elementary level.

Secondary schools

The commission made some critical comments about the existing secondary school program. There was said to be little more adaptation and selection of courses than there had been in the grammar schools of the previous century. In Ontario, as elsewhere, the program was dominated by university admission requirements. The commission declared that it was impossible to have a common course that would do justice both to those who were bound for university and to those who were not.

In the commission's scheme, the four years of secondary school would cover approximately ages twelve to sixteen, extending to the end of the period of compulsory attendance. For many children, it would be the final stage of formal education. It was thought appropriate to emphasize general education, with a basic core of English, social studies, physical and health education, and religious education or ethics. All subjects would be obligatory in the first two years, while in the last two there would be options introducing specialized academic training and exploratory vocational courses. Content was to be adapted to suit the interests and capacities of individual students. The commission was apparently thinking in terms of streams rather than of genuinely individualized programs.

In more detailed terms, the obligatory program for the first and second years was to consist, in addition to the basic core, of general mathematics, general science (including agricultural science), home economics or general shop work, oral French or special courses in French, art, and music. For the third year, compulsory subjects added to the basic core would be general mathematics, general science (including agriculture), and occupations. Cadet training for boys and "its equivalent for girls" were to be included with physical and health education. In addition to the compulsory part of the program, students would take three or four options from among agriculture, commercial work, home economics or general shop work, art or music or art and music, French or special courses in French, and one of Latin, German, Spanish, and Greek. For the fourth year, mathematics and science would be added to the optional list, which would otherwise be the same as for the third year.

The commission felt it necessary to give some passing attention to work-study programs in which a student divided his time between school and employment. Such programs were said to have valuable features, but their general history had not been encouraging. There were difficulties in arranging for the necessary co-operation among school authorities, organized labour, and employers.

THE PORTER PLAN

Mention was made in chapter 4 of the introduction in November 1949 of the Porter Plan by Dana Porter, at that time Minister of Education. Of the organizational and curricular aspects to the plan, the latter are of chief concern at this point. The main focus of attention was the new intermediate division, which was to combine grades 7 to 10 for curriculum purposes. The abolition of the high school entrance examination was a major step in facilitating articulation between grades 8 and 9. The senior years of the new division were to have fewer obligatory subjects and more options. Terminal courses were to be provided for students who wished to leave school at the age of sixteen. There was also to be some attention given to the senior years of secondary school, where an attempt was to be made to redistribute part of the grade 13 program through grades 11 and 12.

What was really significant about the Porter Plan was that it involved an unprecedented effort to decentralize the process of curriculum construction in Ontario, and to give a major part of the responsibility to local authorities and to teachers. Under the supervision of a curriculum co-ordinating committee, the latter were authorized to revise earlier courses, to adapt new departmental courses, or use new departmental courses in their original form.

H. Pullen became the chief chronicler of that particular phase of educational experimentation in his doctoral thesis, "A Study of Secondary School Curriculum Change in Canada with Special Emphasis on an Ontario Experiment," which was accepted at the University of Toronto in 1955.[32] Pullen gave particularly detailed information about developments at Ottawa, where he was a prominent educational administrator. He referred to two different methods by which courses were revised. 1 / For English, mathematics, and social studies, an organization was set up to enable every teacher to make suggestions. 2 / The second method, introduced after a year's experience, applied to science, home economics, industrial arts, physical education, and art and involved the establishment of selected committees with the direct responsibility of revising the courses.

The first of these methods involved the establishment of a city committee in each of the three subject areas operating under the supervision of the central co-ordinating committee. Each subject committee consisted of seventeen members, one from the central co-ordinating committee, eight chosen by the public or separate school inspectors, and eight appointed by the Superintendent of Secondary Schools. The city subject committee appointed members to district subject committees, which in turn had liaison members in school committees. The latter brought the opinions and criticisms of classroom teachers to the district committees. The second method involved an approach that was structurally much simpler.

Apparently there was a feeling that a good deal of useful work was accomplished. The committees began their activities in early 1950, and by September the revised courses were in use in grade 7. In successive years, these were extended to grades 8, 9, and 10. The co-ordinating committee also established a special committee to deal with terminal programs. Under its guidance, courses were developed in carpentry, homemaking, and commercial work.

Pullen conducted surveys to determine the extent to which local officials and teachers had been involved in the program throughout the province. He found more than twelve hundred revised courses being used in the secondary schools and commented: "Certainly this is no mean achievement and demonstrates a large measure of initial interest and enthusiasm for local curriculum work."[33] About 77 per cent of the revisions in grades 9 and 10 were in English, social studies, mathematics, and science, while the remaining 23 per cent were in shops, languages, art, home economics, music, and physical education, according to reports of committee chairmen and principals. Pullen estimated that about 16 per cent of the public school teachers and 18 per cent of the secondary school teachers in the province had some hand in the work in 1952. In relation to those actually teaching in the intermediate division, the proportion involved was obviously much higher.

A poll of teacher opinion not surprisingly indicated definite support for local control over curriculum to the end of grade 10. Teachers in Toronto expressed the view that the revised courses were better suited to meet the needs of the pupils than were the former courses. The majority were not, however, prepared to claim that teachers alone should have the right to determine what to teach. Those who had served as chairmen of curriculum committees felt that training was essential for curriculum workers. The need to free teachers to work on new courses and course revisions was also stressed.

Pullen conducted his study at a time when the initial inspiration for the plan in the Department of Education had largely disappeared. He later supplied information showing the rise and fall of activity at the local level. The number of curriculum committees formed in successive years was as follows: in 1950, eighty-two; in 1951, twenty-five; in 1952 and 1953, two. In 1950 two committees disappeared; in 1951, twenty-one; and in 1952, twenty-eight. By 1960 there were not more than half a dozen left in the province. Pullen's explanation centred around the lack of enthusiasm for the scheme on the part of W.J. Dunlop, who became minister in 1951, and whose attitude was soon reflected in the behaviour of the departmental inspectors. Pullen was also critical of the haste in which the scheme was apparently conceived, the lack of consultation with school officials when it was introduced, and the meagreness of departmental guidance from the beginning. L.S. Beattie and S.A. Watson, who were at that time Co-chairmen of Curriculum, were assigned to work with the local committees and were kept extremely busy meeting requests for assistance, but pressures of other duties soon reduced the time they had available for field work, and neither was given adequate assistance. A further negative influence on local initiative was exerted by the department's issuance soon after committee work was begun of a guide called Curriculum I:1. As Pullen expressed it: "To many it was the same as a teacher asking a pupil to solve a problem in mathematics and, just as soon as a good start had been made, to thrust the complete answer upon him. Such a practice does not provide the pupil with much incentive to go ahead on his own solution."[34]

As to the proposed reorganization of the primary division under the Porter Plan, some initial hope was expressed that it would succeed. According to the *Report of the Minister, 1951*, experimental classes set up during the previous year were in their second year of operation. It was said to be impossible at that stage to evaluate the results, although it appeared that the learning of the fundamenal skills, particularly reading and handwriting, was improved when children remained with a good teacher for a second year. The scheme foundered, at least for the time being, in part because of the lack of adequate and sustained support by the department and because of inadequate teacher preparation.

Donald MacDonald undertook an evaluation of some aspects of the Porter Plan in 1956. He declared that a departmental statement about the freedom of teachers to construct courses of study pretended to be a statement of reality, but was actually only an expression of hope. He conceded that there were some schools in the province where new courses had been worked out, but not on a wide enough scale to justify the implication that the over-all problem had been met. Apparently opposed to the idea of local curriculum development, he asked: "Why do we continue to 'pass the buck' to an unknown and undefined local level of administration regarding curriculum planning?"[35] He felt that it was time to have a director of curricula for the province, with a qualified assistant from each of the academic, technical, commercial, and trade training branches to perform the function in a competent fashion.

Bascom St John evaluated certain aspects of the Porter Plan in 1964.

> The formation and use of these committees depended chiefly on the degree of progressive leadership available in the communities, and most of the cities and some of the smaller towns eagerly accepted the opportunity.
>
> The chief point of doubt was the Grade 7 to 10 period, which required close consultations between elementary and secondary teachers. In some areas these were difficult to organize because of the deep-seated prejudices that had remained through the years.
>
> Where the prejudices were overcome, some highly productive collaboration was achieved, to the great benefit of the children of that community.[36]

There is room for doubt that local factors vary enough to justify any wide differences in curricula from one part of the province to another. There is, of course, good reason for children to devote attention to the physical and historical features of their own area, and to study local phenomena in certain branches of science. There is also an argument for vocational courses based on occupations available within the community, although with increasing population mobility, that proposition is gradually weakening. In general, the argument for decentralizing curriculum development is not so much that it is likely to produce better courses as that it improves the quality of the teachers. The exercise of thinking about aims and objectives, about the organization of content, and about appropriate teaching methods is an extremely stimulating experience, and one that builds a sense of professional responsibility. Engaging in this kind of activity with one's fellow teachers is a most effective means of developing a healthy *esprit de corps*. One of the chief dangers in decentralization is perhaps that it may not go far enough and involve a wide enough spectrum of practising teachers. In some communities, the Porter Plan is said merely to have substituted a local department of education for the one with headquarters in Toronto.

DEPARTMENTAL CURRICULUM POLICIES IN THE 1950s

Successive reports of the Minister of Education give certain clues about the official attitude toward curriculum development during the 1950s. It usually appeared to be a matter of pride to the anonymous writer of the section on curriculum to mention revisions that had taken place or were in progress at one or more levels. There is little indication of how great some of the modifications were, but an examination of published courses of study suggests that many of them were minor. In grade 13 the departmental examination continued to be the dominant influence. The report for 1954 mentioned that new or revised courses of study were introduced for most of the subjects at this level. The revisions had been made by curriculum committees composed of representatives of the universities and the Department of Education who, in their work, had consulted representatives of various educational organizations as well as individual teachers. The hope was expressed that the new courses would be kept under continuous review.

The reports usually mentioned that the department retained the responsibility for determining the content of courses in grades 11 and 12. Following experimental revisions which had been in progress for some time, new courses were issued in 1952 in English, history, Latin, mathematics, and science. The changes could, in fact, have legitimately been described as minor tinkering. In the report for the same year, credit for revising the curriculum in the vocational schools was given to the Commercial Teachers' Association and the Technical Research Council. The next year reference was made to the close contact maintained by these schools with the leaders of commerce and industry in their immediate localities; this contact was said to be keeping the courses and methods of instruction in harmony with local needs and conditions. Acknowledgment was made of the co-operation of such bodies as the Canadian Manufacturers' Association, the National Office Management Association, boards of trade, and chambers of commerce. In 1954 new courses in commercial work and industrial arts were introduced.

Throughout most of the decade, mention was made in successive reports of the right of local authorities to prepare their own courses for grades 9 and 10 as an alternative to using the courses suggested by the department. The report for 1956 called the establishment of local co-ordinating committees with the power and responsibility of appointing curriculum committees to make revisions "an extreme of freedom for teachers." The development was said to have been generally approved, and the teachers were given credit for responding to the new challenge with commendable professional zeal.

> At the local level, curriculum committees have been formed to study and report on special educational needs of the community; to set up special courses to meet local needs, e.g., terminal courses, courses for slow learners; to construct courses or to modify for local use course outlines provided by the Department of Education. As an example of the last-named type of activity, a revision of the Social Studies Courses, Grades 1 to 6, for use in the schools of Toronto, has been completed by committees of teachers. Similar revisions have been made in Hamilton and Windsor. These courses have been made within the framework of the course outlined by the Department. Elements of the Departmental outline which seem to have little relevance to the local situation have been omitted. Topics not specifically referred to in the Departmental outline but seeming to meet local needs have been included.[37]

There was little hint of the extent to which the original inspiration of the local curriculum movement had faded, although it was clear that the department was keeping initiative within definite limits.

The report for 1959 indicated that local co-ordinating committees continued to exercise the powers granted to them in 1950 to make adjustments in existing courses to meet local requirements. The admission was made, however, that the divergence of these courses from those outlined in departmental circulars was not great because the available textbooks were related to the departmental courses. If there had been any genuine desire to encourage local initiative, obviously an appropriate policy on textbooks would have been developed. At this time departmental activity in course revision was increasing. In 1959 new courses were introduced in physical education in the junior division, history in grades 7–9, art in grades 11 and 12, the technical course in secondary schools, and history and geography in the senior grades. Work was being done on science in the intermediate division and on senior mathematics and biology.

The report for 1957 gave an account of the responsibilities of the Curriculum Branch of the department. These included supervision of all departmental work relating to curriculum revision, recommendations for final approval of curricular materials including textbooks, and maintenance of contact with outside agencies interested in curriculum development. Emphasis was placed on the importance of the provision of textbooks to meet the requirements of the courses of study, particularly those for elementary schools.

The latter part of the 1950s was characterized in the United States by a great deal of talk about getting back to the fundamentals and raising standards to the level they had presumably attained before the schools were swamped with courses in basket weaving and other such nonsense. By American standards Ontario schools had taken only the most timid and halting steps, mainly under the influence of the 1937 revision of the elementary curriculum, in a progressive direction. There was nevertheless a counterpart in Canada to the American anti-progressive movement – a trend that was in evidence before the Soviet Union began its most impressive triumphs in space.

Opposition comments in the Legislature presented a sharp contrast in tone to those that characterized the debates of a decade later. On February 11, 1958, Farquhar Oliver, Leader of the Opposition, described the curriculum as completely flexible, with almost all control left in the hands of pupils and teachers. He declared that the minister only suggested to them in a very broad, general sort of way what the curriculum should be. This permissive approach, as he perceived it to be, did not please him at all. While he did not advocate going back to the rigid curriculum and examinations of a number of years before, he thought it was time for the department to return, to some extent at least, to departmental examinations, and to "exercise much more control over, and direction of, the curriculum in our elementary schools than they do now."[38]

The following month Dunlop hastened to align himself with Oliver's views about curriculum, which he said were exactly the same as his own. By implication he condemned the innovations of the 1930s.

> Let me tell the hon. members about the curriculum. For the past 25 years the curriculum was just not all that we would want it to be. It takes some time to get it back, and we are getting it back to fundamental education, getting it back to stress the subjects that are really essential, in order to equip young people for the work they have to do.[39]

One of Dunlop's methods of restoring the old standards had been the establishment of the Curriculum Branch, which he said was responsible for a continuous revision of the curricula in the elementary and secondary fields, and would produce "great results in the reformation ... of the curriculum." He explained how one of his favourite objectives would be achieved.

> For instance, we can offer to the schools not only the old course that they have had for 25 years in social studies but we will say to them: "If you want that, carry it on for a little while, but take rather if you will history, geography and government instead, and have some real work done in those standard subjects of history, geography and, as we used to call it, civics."[40]

Dunlop did not reveal any awareness of the irony of appointing S.A. Watson as Superintendent of Curriculum. Along with Thornton Mustard,

Watson had been a prime mover in the development and promotion of the very ideas that Dunlop looked upon with such disfavour.

CURRICULUM ISSUES RELATING TO SECONDARY EDUCATION IN THE 1950s

It was evident during the 1950s that the rising trend of enrolment in secondary school would probably continue until the overwhelming proportion of young people in the appropriate age group were in attendance. One might have expected that, as a result, very serious thought would have been given to the question of how a wider spectrum of needs and interests might have been met. Vocational programs of various kinds might seem to have called for greater emphasis, and a concerted effort to enhance their prestige might appear to have been in order. In actual fact the predominance of academic studies increased.

A departmental official with a responsible position at the end of the 1960s recalls that the 1950s were a grim time for vocational education. In his opinion Dunlop saw no educational value in the program. There was very little money for equipment, teaching was concentrated on trade aspects, and morale was low. Donald MacDonald was critical of the high drop-out rate. In March 1956 he declared that, out of every hundred who enrolled in grade 9 of the industrial course, only twenty-two graduated from grade 12. His explanation was that they were being driven away by the excessive rigour of the academic courses, in which failure rates were sometimes as high as 53 per cent in grade 9 and 88 per cent in grade 12. The result of their frustration was that many of them were turning to delinquency and even crime.[41]

In his review of trends in Canadian education in the Quance Lectures of 1958, W.H. Swift observed that, as the secondary school population expanded, there was an increase in course offerings.[42] These consisted, however, largely of courses already established and recognized in official programs, such as shop work, drama, and commercial work. British Columbia had established a course in forestry, Ontario had recognized geography as a suitable subject for study in grade 13, and here and there driver education was "knocking at the door." For the most part, though, students were taking "a crack at" the academic subjects that remained the central core. Swift did not feel that the continued stress on these subjects was at all inappropriate. In fact, he assumed that members of his audience would be saddened to hear that the study of Latin was on the decline all across the country. He declared that almost all of his generation had studied the subject, and he did not think they regretted it.

Swift observed that there had been talk of instituting a two- or three-stream pattern with rigid selection, following the European tradition. This was apparently only a trend in thinking, since there was no sign of such a pattern being adopted anywhere in Canada. Although the Robarts Plan was introduced into Ontario a short time later, it could hardly have been described as involving rigid selection. The significance of Swift's observation is that there were no practical efforts of any importance to adapt a curriculum designed for a minority to fit the abilities or interests of the great mass of young people.

Trends of thought in the early 1960s

By the beginning of the 1960s, some of the deeper concerns about the fundamentals of curriculum were beginning to become more noticeable in Ontario. The ideas of Jerome Bruner seemed to have considerable attraction for those who advocated higher levels of achievement and wanted some plausible and respectable psychological theory to back it up. Bruner emphasized the importance of understanding the structure of the disciplines and of adapting them to facilitate maximum learning. Instead of waiting for readiness, which often involved a waste of time, the educator was to seek a productive way of approaching the child at his particular stage of development. If, for example, he was at the stage of concrete reasoning in Piaget's terms, there was said to be some way of laying the foundation for a later grasp of the relevant concepts on the abstract level.

Bruner explained his hypothesis by referring to certain subjects.

> If the hypothesis ... is true – that any subject can be taught to any child in some honest form – then it should follow that a curriculum ought to be built around the great issues, principles, and values that a society deems worthy of the continual concern of its members. Consider two examples – the teaching of literature and of science. If it is granted, for example, that it is desirable to give children an awareness of the meaning of human tragedy and a sense of compassion for it, is it not possible at the earliest appropriate age to teach the literature of tragedy in a manner that illuminates but does not threaten? There are many possible ways to begin: through a retelling of the great myths, through the use of children's classics, through presentation of and commentary on selected films that have proved themselves. Precisely what kinds of materials should be used at what age with what effect is a subject for research ... Nor need we wait for all the research findings to be in before proceeding, for a skillful teacher can also experiment by attempting to teach what seems to be intuitively right for children of different ages, correcting as he goes. In time, one goes beyond to more complex versions of the same kind of literature or simply revisits some of the same books used earlier. What matters is that later teaching build upon earlier reactions to literature, that it seek to create an ever more explicit and mature understanding of the literature of tragedy. Any of the great literary forms can be handled in the same way, or any of the great themes – be it the form of comedy or the theme of identity, personal loyalty, or what not.
>
> So too in science. If the understanding of number, measure, and probability is judged crucial in the pursuit of science, then instruction in these subjects should begin as intellectually honestly and as early as possible in a manner consistent with the child's forms of thought.[43]

Bruner may have had some real influence on the development of the new science course for the intermediate division which was introduced in 1960. At least this course was said to have adapted some of the subject matter formerly taught in the higher grades. The report of the minister declared that it emphasized the experimental method and demonstrated the interrelationships among several branches of science. It had the very commendable objectives of encouraging the student to make accurate observations, to suspend judgment until the evidence was in, to draw only such conclusions as were justified by the evidence, and to develop all other aspects of critical thinking.

Some people with a progressive orientation were sceptical about Bruner's ideas. At the Ontario Conference on Education in 1961, J.R. McCarthy voiced his reservations.

There are a number of questions which are raised by Bruner's book. For example, to what extent is his position a re-statement of an emphasis on subject matter for its own sake? Is this really a new approach or is it the same one clothed in a new respectability? Is there really only one structure within each discipline or are several possible? Is there even any structure in the discipline of English? An outstanding professor of English has said that he cannot recognize a structure in his field and says that a person can dip into it at many points to achieve valid educational objectives. Does the structure of a discipline developed by scholars in the field mean that teachers and others who work with boys and girls will no longer be able to select from that discipline what they know, to be within the range of their students' abilities, interests and aptitudes and leave out the rest? If not, some of the major gains in education over the last half-century will be threatened. One wonders if a design based on one structure isn't just as slippery as some of those we've had in the past.

Another point worth consideration is whether the relationships within each of several disciplines are the only ones to which students in elementary and secondary schools should be directed. Isn't it the basis of education to teach the selection of knowledge to solve problems? Isn't the teacher's hardest task that of helping children relate knowledge from different areas? Can this be left to the student to manage for himself?[44]

McCarthy had a few other observations to make on the same occasion with respect to new developments with a bearing on curriculum. He referred to programmed instruction materials and teaching machines, language laboratories, educational television, the introduction of modern languages at the elementary level, modern mathematics, classes for the gifted, and the ungraded primary. He conceded that one or several of these developments might prove to be of major significance for the curriculum, but he thought evidence should be assembled before they were embraced too enthusiastically. A look back over the period suggests that such advice was well heeded. While the mathematics curriculum was gradually changed over a period of years, partly as a result of the efforts of the Ontario Mathematics Commission, and although elementary school children from the upper grades down were gradually introduced to a smattering of French, the changes could hardly have been considered revolutionary.

The English Study Committee of the Joint Committee of the Toronto Board of Education and the University of Toronto, chaired by Mary A. Campbell, observed with respect to structure in English:

> The curriculum is at best, however, a design to be interpreted by teachers, for children – by teachers with varying degrees of ability and insight, for children with differing equipment in intelligence and language background. In raising the question of the possibility of sequential programmes in English, the committee would warn against a neat formula, or any interpretation that might result in a rigid curriculum with a lock-step treatment. The ideas of sequence and integration should be interpreted broadly, to give reasonable freedom to individual school systems and schools. Indeed, no other approach is suitable for this subject.[45]

W. R. Wees, in an address to the Second International Curriculum Conference in 1966, sounded a note that was strongly at variance with much of the curriculum work that had been done during the previous few years.

> Today the doctrinaires of the various disciplines, with that patriarchal authority which we have mentioned, extract what they confidently call the known facts, organize them and reorganize them to suit themselves, and then produce them as "new curricula" in the schemata of "curriculum development." Because of their prestige in the various disciplines these curriculum committees, as they are euphemistically described, are able to apply their authority in an overwhelming majority of classrooms and thus assume the status of oligarchies of education.[46]

Bruner was invited to Toronto at the time of the discussions that led to the formation of the Ontario Curriculum Institute, the development of which is dealt with in volume v, chapter 11. His influence was evident in the studies of science and social sciences, in addition to that in English already referred to, conducted by the Toronto Board – University of Toronto Joint Committee. It would be difficult to establish any claim, however, that there was a coherent or consistent philosophical orientation running through the numerous publications of the successor institute that continued to be issued over the next several years. A conservative influence was exerted by the university representatives on the study committees who, for the first time in the educational history of Ontario, participated significantly with teachers and officials in coming to grips with curricular issues at the elementary and secondary school levels.

SIGNIFICANCE OF THE CONTRIBUTION OF THE ONTARIO CURRICULUM INSTITUTE

To comment at any length on the contributions of the Ontario Curriculum Institute at this point would be to repeat the more thorough treatment of the topic undertaken in volume v. It is impossible, however, to deal with the highlights of curriculum development in the 1960s without reference to this organization. It originated as a genuine grassroots movement, although it soon attained at least the official blessing of the educational establishment. This statement takes no credit away from Roy C. Sharp, whose vision and drive made it a reality. His success was, however, made possible because the spark he lit fell on dry tinder. There was growing awareness of the rate at which new knowledge, or perhaps awareness of changing ways of organizing and interpreting knowledge, was challenging the validity of the school program. The increasing extent of departmental activity in curriculum development seemed to many critics to involve too much moving around of old furniture and not enough examination of fundamental principles and concepts as illuminated by recent advances in psychology, sociology, and other disciplines. The idea of the institute was accepted eagerly by teachers and by enough members of the university community to ensure that there would be a genuine infusion of scholarship.

The existence of the institute seemed to have a highly stimulating influence on the Department of Education itself. This result was not achieved by the working out of any genuine partnership between the Curriculum Branch and the institute. In fact, the two agencies never did manage to clarify the basic differences between their respective functions. This uncertainty probably exerted a salutary influence on department officials, who understandably did not want to risk turning over the responsibilities which they were legally obligated to discharge. The departmental committees which prepared courses of study certainly took an increasingly serious look at fundamental curricular issues. The breaking of the old department custom of refusing to pay expenses to any official travelling further than the Rocky Mountains or going anywhere else by any but the cheapest method of transportation short of an ox-cart, helped to enable committee participants to gain a better understanding of what was happening elsewhere.

The institute had time, during its brief existence as a separate entity, and for a short time while its spirit was being strangled by the professional educators after its merger with the Ontario Institute for Studies in Education, to produce analyses of all the major subject areas covered by the school curriculum. The resulting reports were known to have been widely read and, if reading can influence the behaviour of educators, they may be assumed, in the absence of absolute proof, to have had an effect. It would be less safe to speculate on results achieved by some of the studies that were not tied to particular subjects but dealt with more basic problems or more fundamental issues. Had the institute survived in its original form, its natural direction of development would have been toward this type of study. Thus it is a question of how the vital and thoroughgoing participation of teachers in partnership with university faculty members from the fundamental disciplines would have fared. Despite this uncertainty, it seems unfortunate that the potentialities inherent in this relationship were not fully realized.

THE REORGANIZED PROGRAM OR ROBARTS PLAN

The major development in the curriculum field during the early 1960s was the Reorganized Program or the Robarts Plan. Its objectives and its structural aspects were outlined in chapter 4. Mention was made of the haste with which it was introduced and of the confusion that resulted. From the government's point of view, there were some very good reasons for prompt action. By 1963 the federal government's contribution to vocational school building was to drop from 75 to 50 per cent, and it thus seemed only good business to get as many projects as possible under way. There had, however, to be some additional justification for a construction spree apart from the fact that there were funds to be used up. The existing commercial and technical programs were hardly in sufficiently good repute that a frantic effort to make them more widely available would have seemed plausible. Education Minister Robarts thus acted quite logically in announcing that the secondary program would have a facelift, while leaving the details of course coverage to be worked out later. The consultation that was lacking in the planning of the basic framework was very much in evidence during the major part of the 1961–2 school year as departmental officials hastened to ask the advice of teachers, university professors, trustees, parents, and business and commercial interests.

The four-year Arts and Science program

The time had not yet come when the five-year program in the Arts and Science Branch could be liberated from the dominating influence of university entrance requirements. It was the four-year program in the same branch where the real challenge to the innovators lay. Although some opportunities for further education would be open, many of the students were presumed to be headed for the completion of their formal schooling at the end of grade 12. If the Reorganized Program were to achieve one of its major objectives, they would have to be enticed to remain voluntarily after they reached the end of the period of compulsory education around grade 10. There was thus a challenge to produce the kind of optional courses that would appeal to their interests and be within their capacity to handle with a sense of gratification. Educators with reasonable foresight also realized that grade 12 was quickly becoming less satisfactory as a terminal point, and that more post-secondary educational opportunities, other than university, would have to be opened.

Some of the less imaginative planners could think of nothing better than to make the four-year program a watered down copy of the five-year program. They simply thought that the amount of content should be reduced, that the more difficult concepts should be omitted, or that a lesser level of proficiency should be accepted. This approach was at least an improvement over the one so often encountered in earlier decades, when classes were occasionally streamed according to previous achievement, but were expected to pass the same examinations at the end of the year. Yet it left a good deal to be desired. There was not even a very good chance that the distinction between levels could be maintained unless different sets of textbooks were available, particularly if the same teachers were expected to switch back and forth from one program to another.

Fortunately there were educational leaders with the vision to see that the four-year program could be made the testing ground for new content patterns and emphases. Courses were developed in theatre arts, speech arts, modern literature, geology, politics, and economics. Most symbolic of the fresh approach being taken was the Man in Society course, which cut across traditional social science disciplines to produce a new focus for young people with a profound interest in the meaning of contemporary life. While singling out a particular individual always involves the risk of slighting others who play a significant part in a given cause, it is perhaps safe to give a great deal of credit for realizing the potentialities of the four-year program to M. B. Parnall, whose services were available for an all-too-brief period as Superintendent of Curriculum and as Director of the Program Branch in the Department of Education. A contemporary official declares that S.D. Rendall devised the structure of the Reorganized Program and Parnall put in the humanity. While tradition obstructed any immediate drastic change in the five-year program for the university bound, Parnall is said to have realized that there would soon be a clamour from that quarter for courses like Man in Society if they turned out to be the success he expected in the four-year program.

While the present chapter is not intended to provide detailed coverage of course content, some information from official announcements will indicate the kind of thinking that lay behind the curricular provisions of the four-year program. Man in Society was to involve a study of some of the forces in contemporary life, with attention to their influence on man's behaviour and his effort to control them. There was to be a descriptive survey of the current scene and a study with some historical dimensions of such institutions as the family, the state, the courts, and the government. The course would touch on psychology in dealing with hereditary and environmental influences, learning, remembering, conditioning and habit formation, reasoning, and problem solving. There would be treatment of such social issues as adjustment to cultural change, freedom and responsibility, emotions and thinking, propaganda and the transmission of ideas, changes posed by technology, community planning, minority groups, and the welfare state. There would be no particular encouragement for students to exchange ill-informed opinions on such questions as "Should Canada have capital punishment?" Instead, they would be led "to identify and define some of the issues involved, to study the history of the relationship between society and the criminal, and to examine arguments favouring and opposing capital punishment."[47] Through an appreciation of the complexities of the problem, a recognition of the need to assess the attitudes of subgroups in society, and an examination of theories and practices of the past and present, they would be expected to learn to recognize bias, emotion, the social conscience, and prejudice. It would be most important that each student be made aware, within the limits of his capabilities, of his need for knowledge and objectivity in playing his part as a citizen.

Another innovative course, which might be taken in grade 11 or 12, was one in World Politics, designed for students who wished to know more about the background and issues involved. Official literature gave as the aims "to enhance the students' understanding of the world situation, to foster a continuing interest in such study, to produce students who will enter the world of work better qualified to appreciate the problems of, and to make judgments about, national and international affairs."[48] There would be some treatment of the historical background of influential political movements in the modern world. Reliance was to be placed on headline events of the day, as well as on texts and reference books, in order to maintain the quality of timeliness. Opportunities would be provided for discussion of problems of the emerging and established nations in the contexts of nationalism, regional or racial affiliation, and internationalism.

The courses in speech arts were intended to help students to develop in a wide variety of ways: "to assist them in their social and business life; to foster their creative and appreciative talents; to aid them in their ability to think rationally, to express their thoughts clearly; and to listen with understanding; and, finally, to encourage those students with latent powers of leadership."[49] As much attention was to be given to content as to technique. Students were to analyse and discuss the speech patterns of radio and television, to listen critically to recordings of the spoken word, and to attend public meetings, the law courts, and the Legislature. Classroom time would be devoted to the study of voice quality and practice of voice control, delivery, platform behaviour, types of addresses, logic and argument, debate, rules of procedure, and evaluation.

The purpose of the course in modern literature, which was to be provided in addition to the regular compulsory course in English, was to encourage broad interests in reading "through extensive reading and comparative study of the drama, the novel, and other contemporary prose works."[50] A list of titles for study was suggested, representing a wide variety of interests and reading levels, which would enable the teacher to begin at the students' level of interest and competence. While there would be selections from the best of contemporary writing, the course was not to be considered one in twentieth-century classics. By a judicious selection of additional titles, the teacher would be able to bring the students' interests under classroom study and discussion.

In the May 1967 issue of the *Bulletin* of the Ontario Secondary School Teachers' Federation, M. Doyle, Principal of Neil McNeil High School in Scarborough, expressed his enthusiasm for the program.

> Rarely in recent years has our Ontario Department of Education devised a programme which offers as many possibilities as 4 Year Arts & Science. Here at last is the programme which accomplishes at a stroke what a generation of teachers have sighed for. Here at last is a curriculum without pressure; a course of studies which does not demand early specialization, without the threatening spectre of exams at the end of the road. We are given a course of studies which not merely permits but specifically requests the teacher to experiment. Here too is a selection of material wider and more varied than anything a student's time-table can accomplish in the more conventional confines of the 5 Year programmes. He can study the best in modern literature, the finest in Theatre. He can discuss thorny political problems, dig into Psychology and come to grips with the sociological factors influencing our society. His study of history is rounded out by exposure to economics and if he is scientifically inclined he can plunge into Biology and Geology in addition to Physics and Chemistry.[51]

Despite such favourable reactions to the content of the four-year program, there was increasing dissatisfaction over its terminal quality. The occupational world was changing so quickly that what appeared in 1960 to be a satisfactory formal education for a major proportion of young people seemed by 1965 to be anything but adequate, at least for those who were capable of going further. A realization of this fact produced one of the most rapid changes in the post-secondary field ever experienced anywhere. Such was the creation of the system of colleges of applied arts and technology.

Science, Technology, and Trades programs

As indicated earlier, the dark days through which vocational education had passed had seen a good deal of unadulterated skill training, and much of that of poor quality, as opposed to a more sophisticated effort to educate through the practical arts. The curriculum development activities inspired by the Reorganized Program provided a new opportunity to pursue the objectives which had been effectively articulated for decades. While technical courses continued to aim at the development of certain basic skills, the emphasis for the bulk of the students swung toward technology in the broad sense. There was stress on principles and concepts with transfer value. These changes did not come immediately with the introduction of the new plan in 1961; for a time, the main change was quantitative. It was not until 1965 or 1966 that the qualitative differences really became evident. The creation of the colleges of applied arts and technology did much to further the idea that secondary school courses were intended, not primarily to prepare the student for a job, but rather to give him an appreciation of the role of the machine and a reasonable feeling of self-confidence in the face of technology.

The hope for real vigour in technical courses lay in the interest and participation of individual teachers in course development. The old advisory vocational committees were assessed as completely ineffective because the members usually did not know enough about technical matters to make a worthwhile contribution. On the other hand, good results were said to have been obtained by subject committees which, by the end of the 1960s, had been established in many schools. Younger teachers have been impressed by techniques such as the so-called integrated program, which involves the use of one basic theme around which are grouped a number of subjects such as science, mathematics, technology, and communications. The old project or enterprise method keeps reappearing under a number of guises.

G.H. Peck, member for Scarborough Centre, commented on February 11, 1965 on the success achieved in the Science, Technology, and Trades Branch.

> From this programme and from the changed emphasis on the needs of modern society, we find that what used to be known as a technical education at one of our technical institutions no longer bears the stigma that it traditionally did. Parents often hesitated to send their children to technical school, as it was regarded as a dumping ground for those students who had limited possibilities. The programmes of study were such that they held little challenge to the majority of the students. Under the reorganized programme, I feel that this has changed. The need for technicians has upgraded the public acceptance of these courses to almost the same status, or even as great a status, as that of the academic arts and sciences programmes.[52]

The Occupational program

In an article by Walter Chlystyk published in the *Bulletin* of the Ontario Secondary School Teachers' Federation in January 1963, the Occupational program was described during the early experimental stages.[53] Training was being offered to give the slow learner an insight into a basic skill that could be sold to an employer. The skills that were to be provided by a particular school were to be determined by a survey carried out in the surrounding community to identify existing job opportunities. These might include service station work, restaurant service and cooking, machine operation, lawn and garden upkeep, and many other related occupations.

Approximately 50 per cent of the Occupational program consisted of academic classes and 50 per cent of practical work. Chlystyk warned that the academic work should be carefully selected to meet the needs of the students and that rigid adherence to a course of study could be fatal. He urged that wherever possible the academic work should be related to the practical work so that the students would have an understanding of the reason why they needed to know reading, arithmetic, history, geography, and other subjects. The demands on the teacher's ingenuity were obvious. During the year, or in some cases two years, in which the student attended, he was expected to spend some time in actual employment. Chlystyk's suggestion was that the work period on one particular job should not exceed two weeks. An employer was expected to pay for the student's lunch and transportation, but whether or not he offered any remuneration was left to his own discretion. Among early problems of school boards instituting the Occupational program was that of determining how to insure students against accidents, since Workmen's Compensation did not provide coverage.

A departmental memorandum of 1966 indicated that the Occupational program would subsequently include the Occupations course and the Services course. Students in the first of these would be allowed to specialize in a trade requiring an indentured apprenticeship provided that they reached a level of achievement in mathematics, science, and English equivalent to grade 10 standing. The weekly program suggested for this group consisted of seven periods of English and library work, five periods of history and geography, three periods of science, five periods of mathematics, one period of group guidance, four periods of physical and health education, and twenty periods of practical work. Students who were unable to reach the required level in the basic subjects had to seek employment in non-apprenticeship occupations.[54]

In 1966 a consultative committee was formed to study the Occupational program and to clarify the needs of its students. Members were drawn from the School of Social Work of the University of Toronto, the Adult Training Counselling Centre of the Toronto Board of Education, and the Social Planning Council of Metropolitan Toronto and also included teachers and officials of the Department of Education. Presentations were heard from school administrators, officials of the Canada Manpower Centres, and recruiters from the Ontario Civil Service. Material was prepared for use in the Occupational program and television programs were designed to inform educators and members of the public about the scope and nature of the program. Research was conducted into the differences between students in the program and those in the other streams.

PROPOSALS FOR THE REVISION OF THE K–6 CURRICULUM

Shortly after his appointment as minister in 1962, W.G. Davis repeated a suggestion made earlier by Robarts that the department would undertake a revision of the curriculum from grades 1 to 6. Planning was strictly in the preliminary stage, and before any definite positive action was taken there would be widespread consultation, and all groups and organizations with an interest in education would have an opportunity to make their views known. Davis indicated that the actual work of revision would include classroom teachers, inspectors, and members of the staffs of teachers' colleges.

It would be impossible to identify a single, or even a main, reason for the pressure to take a new look at curriculum at this level. For some, presumably the fact that there had been little fundamental change in the course prescriptions during the preceding twenty-five years was sufficient justification for a thorough appraisal. Among those who had specific reasons for dissatisfaction, there were some who felt that too little was being demanded of children and that the requirements should be stiffened and standards raised. It is rather surprising in retrospect that W.J. Dunlop, despite the fact that he championed this point of view, never erased the imprint of departmental courses of study made by the progressives of the late 1930s.

Robarts had apparently counted himself among those who favoured a greater intellectual challenge in the early grades. In April 1962 he said it was his own personal opinion that there should be a good deal of stiffening in the courses of study. He attributed the lack of challenge to "a hang-over from what might be referred to as Deweyism or progressive education."[55] Although he did not hold Dewey responsible for everything done in his name, he felt that progressivism was associated with the idea that young people could teach themselves, and that they were not to be pushed. Robarts thought it would be desirable to stiffen the elementary school program, not only because such an approach would be educationally desirable at that level, but also because the secondary school load was becoming heavier as a result of the pace at which knowledge was accumulating, and pupils might be better prepared for it if more work were demanded of them at the elementary school level.

Robert Nixon, Liberal education critic, expressed a point of view that was, by implication, based on a similar philosophical orientation. Having recently abandoned high school science teaching for politics, he was still vividly conscious of how little science many of the students knew when they reached the lower high school grades. On the basis of his experience, he felt that much of the time spent in the early grades was wasted. One of his reasons for concern was the lack of consistency in elementary school preparation. For some the high school work was new and for others it was boring repetition, simply because there was insufficient curriculum control at the lower level.[56]

Dissatisfaction also existed in the opposite camp, that is, among those who felt that the spirit of the 1937 course had never been realized in practice, and that traditional teaching routines were being pursued under a progressive guise. The question seemed to be whether new forms of organization, teaching methodology, and teacher attitudes could not produce a more successful effort to attain the desirable goals defined so long before. Whatever the balance of forces in 1962, this group was dominant by the end of the decade.

In reacting to the minister's announcement, Bascom St John entered a plea for a very thoroughgoing approach.

Curriculum reform in the present stage of social development is not a preserve of a professional clique in education. It is of profound interest to almost everybody.

For one thing: this matter falls into two very different but equally important phases. The first is to decide what is to be taught in the elementary schools. The second is the actual course of study and the teaching methods to be used. The first of these is a primary interest of parents and wise thinkers in the social sciences. This is difficult for some educators to accept, but accept it they must. This is a self-governing society, and education, as a public service, ought to be responsive to what the people want.[57]

While it would be difficult to quarrel with St John's basic thesis, he was somewhat unrealistic in his expectation of the ability of many parents to articulate a point of view of what should be taught. If professional educators do not provide leadership in this area, the results are quite likely to be unsatisfactory in the extreme. Yet there can be no defence of a group of officials who claim the right of ultimate decision regardless of a clear expression of popular wishes.

The proposal to revise the program up to the end of the first six grades met with criticism even before Davis became minister. On April 10, 1962, Nixon accused the Department of Education of compartmentalized thinking. He thought that what was needed was a far-reaching revision of courses from one end to the other, and he was not sure that the universities should be left out. Bascom St John berated the department for the same reason in considerably stronger terms. He thought it deplorable to continue the piecemeal revision of the course of study which had involved the intermediate level a number of years earlier, recent changes in history and geography at the same level, and the current activity in connection with the Robarts Plan, which appeared to take no account of the reforms in grades 7 to 10, or of any others.

There ought to be an overall pattern and structure in the scheme of knowledge offered in the schools, from beginning to end. By using the piecemeal method of curriculum reform, by maintaining the old splits between elementary and secondary, even with the overlaid transition of the intermediate courses from Grades 7 to 10, we are perpetuating the limitations and inadequacies of our primitive beginnings.

To be more specific, it is very bad policy to reform the first grades unless there is to be an integration with the others, in both philosophy and matter, which will be carried right through. The curse of the existing program of studies in Ontario is the dreary repetition, not only between grades in the primary division (Grades 1 to 6), but between these and in the intermediate group. This is a major reason why so many children in our schools are bored, at a period in their lives when new knowledge should be a source of continuous excitement.[58]

The *Report of the Minister, 1964* declared that major revisions of the K–6 curriculum had been well launched. Five inspectors and teachers' college masters had been attached to the Curriculum Branch to serve as curriculum consultants. Educational information on aims, organization, research findings, methods, and content had been compiled from a variety of sources. Plans had been made to approach major educational organizations for information and consultation. It was intended that courses of study developed by local curriculum committees would be analysed and evaluated as the revision proceeded.[59]

Performance fell somewhat short of promise, as indicated by a departmental memorandum of May 10, 1966.

1. The first of the updated courses of study for Kindergarten and Grades 1 to 6 will be mailed to the schools shortly. Others will follow during the Spring and Fall terms.
2. These are interim statements only, and with few exceptions, will not suggest major changes in the program. They attempt to update course content within the general aims of the former program of studies and are intended for use pending the report of the Provincial Committee on Aims and Objectives of Education (the Hall Committee).[60]

Emphasis was placed on the fact that the courses were optional and that any part of them might be introduced. Study and discussion by teachers were strongly recommended, as was the preparation of curriculum guides.

Curriculum Bulletin 5, issued in January 1967, contained a statement of ideas behind the interim courses. 1 / The courses stated the ideas that were basic to the purposes of the elementary school program. An attempt was made to outline the fundamental concepts of each discipline. 2 / While some suggestions relating to methodology were included, the teacher was expected to adapt, amend, adjust, and augment the fundamental concepts of the courses to meet the needs of each pupil. 3 / The courses might be adapted to grades, units, levels, or non-graded organization. No prescribed attainment at specified times was to be demanded of children. It was observed that even the establishment of average levels of achievement created goals against which unwarranted judgments had been made about young children. 4 / The courses were not to be used in daily planning.

Textbooks, films, television, etc., all provide more than enough help with the transferring of content to children. It is with the processes of learning, of the social, ethical and intellectual attitudes that develop in the minds of children, that teachers are really concerned. This concern cannot be translated into practice if your daily routine is prescribed by detailed and prescriptive courses.[61]

5 / Teachers were urged to work together to study the courses and to exchange ideas about them. 6 / The courses were said to need new methods of evaluation. Teachers were warned that achievement tests in current use needed to be re-examined in each school and school system to ensure that they related to the aims of the course. They were also advised to exercise care in using learning capacity tests to ensure that the results did not become expectations.

The following statements about the elementary program show quite clearly that the report of the Hall-Dennis Committee, then in the process of preparation, was part of a trend of thought that was already well established in the Curriculum Branch of the department.

1. These children (pupils in the elementary school) are at a period when vital energies are largely consumed in physical development, and consequently they must have time for rest and recreation. The school has no excuse for infringing upon the right of the children to sufficient time for sleep and play and the right of the home to direct their activities outside of school hours. There can be no doubt that both of these rights are seriously encroached upon by the prescription of homework, ill-chosen in character and excessive in quantity. *For pupils in Grades 1 to 6 there is ample time during the school day to engage in the necessary activities satisfactorily without burdening them with additional school work to be done at home.*
2. This should not, of course, prevent out-of-school pursuits taken up by children in their own time as an extension of interests generated in school. But such undertakings should be on a purely *voluntary* basis and motivated by *genuine interest.*
3. All children have the desire to gain recognition in some aspect of school activity. *The school must see to it that every child achieves success in some respect.* The sense of achievement must be put within reach of even the least responsive child. Failure to provide the climate for a pupil's expression of the best of which he is capable will likely result in frustration and consequent aggressiveness. Teachers who think more of their pupils and less of the curriculum will find something to praise in each child's work. A child, by right, has the respect of his teacher, but he needs also to feel that he enjoys the respect of his classmates.

4. It is important to emphasize that the experiences provided for in the elementary school must be designed to meet the psychological needs of the child. They must be designed also to prepare him to meet the situations that will confront him in life. They are intended to aid him in the process of becoming mature, of growing up physically, mentally, and emotionally. The best preparation that the child can have for the demands of later life is a store of individual and group experiences acquired during life at school.[62]

Despite urging from a number of quarters, there was no attempt comparable to that undertaken in some parts of the United States to stiffen the elementary school program. An article in the *New York Times* in September 1966 referred to a revolution in the three RS which would require further improvement at the junior and senior high school levels to keep the pupils interested. A child entering the first grade that fall would study the new science for eight or nine years at the elementary and junior high school levels. He would thus find the existing high school courses in biology, chemistry, and physics too simple. Children in the first three grades were being introduced to algebra and geometry. A growing number of schools were teaching first graders to read and enjoy Aesop's fables and the children's classics. Improved reading ability alone would have a tremendous effect on every part of the curriculum. A restraining note was sounded with a quotation from John Goodlad, who pointed out that tens of thousands of schools remained untouched by the swing toward more effective teaching and higher standards of achievement.[63]

THE PROGRAM IN GRADE 13

Criticisms and proposals before 1964

The influence of the departmental examinations on the grade 13 program in the years up to 1967 was so great that any attempt to deal separately with examinations and curriculum, as is done in the present series, must necessarily be artificial. The story of the evolution of the examination system is recounted in volume V, chapter 15. References to that development in the present chapter are kept to a minimum in order to avoid unnecessary repetition.

It is ironical that much of the malign influence exerted on the grade 13 curriculum by the departmental examination could be attributed to what was considered one of the latter's greatest virtues – its "fairness" to all candidates. This fairness was interpreted in terms of objectivity, although the term "objective" was usually reserved for completion, multiple choice, matching, and other types of items; the completely or predominantly essay-type examinations were often referred to as "subjective," as if this particular quality could be considered a virtue. In actual fact, the maximum of objectivity was sought within the free response form, meaning that questions were designed to facilitate the counting of facts or points in the marking process, often without adequate attention to qualities of originality, ability to select and organize material, and other such outcomes of a good education.

It should be recognized as a truism that teachers will teach for an external examination, particularly if the number and range of questions are so limited that there are obvious dividends from the practice of "spotting" questions on the basis of an analysis of those which have appeared on papers from previous years. To berate teachers for performing in this way is the utmost hypocrisy. If a certain type of behaviour is undesirable, it should not be rewarded. Yet otherwise sensible people used to judge schools by the percentage of their grade 13 students who passed, or won Ontario scholarships for obtaining an average of at least 80 per cent, and at the same time claimed that a good teacher made the course interesting by leading the students off the prescribed path where there was no reward to be earned in terms of marks. If the teacher did not realize the cost of these diversions from the real business of preparing for the examination, the students certainly did. It is no wonder that the grade 13 courses came to be regarded as a dreary grind from one end of the year to the other.

One of the chief sources of complaint was that the grade 13 courses were too long because they tried to cover too much ground. It was not, however, as obvious as some people claimed that the attempt to keep up with the knowledge explosion was causing a steadily increasing burden on the student. The weight of courses cannot be validly compared in terms of the number of topics or themes covered or of the number of pages in a textbook. Intensity of treatment, qualitative level of interpretation and appreciation, and other such factors must also be taken into account. An effort to shorten a course by reducing the breadth of coverage may merely result in a demand that the student be able to reproduce the more limited amount of material in greater detail. Conversely, an increase in content may be accompanied by reduced expectation of student performance. Thus the common assertion that the grade 13 courses were becoming steadily more burdensome must be discounted on the grounds that an objective comparison with the situation in earlier years was not strictly feasible. On the other hand, it is probably safe to say that the courses had little chance of becoming more inspiring because the importance of doing well on the departmental examination was not, to say the least, being reduced. In terms of university admission, the steady growth in the number of candidates made it increasingly necessary to rely on a mechanical interpretation of marks, to the exclusion of supplementary background and personal factors.

There were frequent suggestions through the 1950s and early 1960s that the grade 13 year should involve less effort at broad coverage and more treatment in depth. The student should be encouraged to develop his own lines of investigation, just as the university student did in theory and indisputably did in fact if he reached the more advanced levels. The idea was that the grade 13 year should be more like a university year. Those who made the strongest case for this type of change realized that the nature of the final examinations would also have to change. They often used as a model the existing grade 13 problems paper, which students attempted if they wished to test their ability to apply mathematical principles. Mere capacity to reproduce "book work" was of little avail.

The advocacy of a more intellectually stimulating grade 13, accompanied by an examination system that would be less mechanical and standardized, seemed to imply that the year should be limited to those who really intended to go to university. In fact, many who claimed that some of the most serious weaknesses of both program and examination stemmed from the fact that they had to serve the needs both of those who were and those who were not university-bound failed to realize what a high percentage of grade 13 students who obtained the necessary standing actually went to university. The Atkinson Study of Utilization of Student Resources showed that almost 50 per cent of the 1956 enrolment in grade 13 gained admission to university within the next five years. It is safe to assume that a substantial proportion of the remainder failed to follow them for no other reason than that they did not obtain the required standing. The proportion who left grade 13 directly for employment was comparatively small. Apart from constituting a preparation for the teachers' colleges, which performed a function that was increasingly regarded as properly belonging to the universities, grade 13 was in fact overwhelmingly a university preparatory year, and undue concern about its dual function was misplaced.

Those who were inclined in the early 1960s to advocate a more stimulating, challenging, and educationally valid grade 13 year were unfortunately too ready to suggest that the departmental external examinations should be extended to grade 12. If excessive numbers made centralized marking impossible, the papers could be marked by teachers in their own schools. No good explanation was ever offered as to how the most oppressive features of external examinations could be avoided. As explained in volume v, chapter 16, the move to reinstate grade 12 external examinations in this form was partly successful. They were soon swept away, however, in the move that also eliminated those in grade 13.

On the faulty premise that grade 13 catered to a substantial group who had no intention of pursuing their formal education in a university or in some other form, there was some distinctly questionable reasoning. In his report for 1959–60, C.T. Bissell quoted approvingly from a memorandum written by M. St A. Woodside, then principal of University College.

While it could be argued that the two purposes are, or ought to be, essentially the same, it is usually believed that they are quite different. In the case of some students, the examination determines whether or not something *has* been completed, in the case of others it determines whether or not something *should* be begun. Both purposes are very important, and although the University has a real interest in each, it must be particularly concerned with the examination as qualification for university entrance. The Grade XIII student is largely but not wholly examined on his knowledge of a certain limited amount of material, which may be found in a text-book and learned, rather than on his intellectual power. For example, the Grade XIII student who obtains 100 per cent in History may be a potentially good historian or he may be a boy with a good memory. College Registrars know that a student who has obtained 60 per cent in Grade XIII mathematics is almost certainly incapable of success in university mathematics, but they do not know whether a student with 95 per cent in Grade XIII mathematics will be a success or a failure in university mathematics. The same may be said of students in Grade XIII English. On the other hand, a student who scores 50 per cent in the Grade XIII Problems paper (usually attempted only by candidates for scholarships) is almost certain to be good or brilliant in university mathematics, because memory of standard solutions of standard theorems will not enable him to score. The reason for all this is that what the universities wish to know about a candidate for admission is the extent to which he can think as a mathematician or a scientist, or an historian, or a philologist, or a literary critic (in the widest sense), or, in other words, how effectively he can use such knowledge as he has, rather than the extent to which he can remember what he has found in a text-book.[64]

The case, as presented in this way, gives rise to two questions. 1 / Why should employers, or anyone else concerned with the student's performance after graduation from secondary school, be interested in what he had learned apart from its bearing on his potentialities? Surely the university is no different from the others in this respect. 2 / The second question is really an aspect of the first. Why should an examination that measures "the extent to which he [the student] can remember what he has found in a text-book" be regarded as satisfactory for anyone, whether bound for the university or not?

In the same report, Bissell observed the suggestion that the grade 13 student in a more consciously preparatory year might write formal examinations, similar to those at the Advanced level in Great Britain, only in areas of central relevance to his proposed field of major study in the university. The student would still be responsible for work in other fields not so directly related to his university work, but examinations in those subjects, corresponding to the British Ordinary level, would be conducted by his own teachers. The Advanced level examinations would not be dependent on the completion of a specified curriculum and thus could be given earlier in the year. Since it would be administratively difficult to assemble teachers for marking at this time, Bissell thought the universities might be persuaded to take on the task. The examinations would become, both in theory and in practice, genuine university entrance examinations.

The dominant idea of the period seemed to be that students at the secondary school level, including grade 13, should get a balanced education rather than being allowed to pursue a narrow specialty. University admission requirements ensured that there would be little deviation from a small number of subject patterns. Thus, although most subjects were theoretically optional, a student who intended to proceed to university was most often persuaded to prepare to write two papers in English, two in French (or in some cases another language), three in mathematics, and two in science. A certain number avoided mathematics and science by taking history and additional foreign languages, but they limited their university options in doing so. The rigidity of the pattern was reinforced by the fact that only one course in a particular subject was offered each year so that each candidate was theoretically working at the same level of difficulty in all subjects.

Bascom St John condemned this system in the strongest terms.

Among the reforms of the Grade 13 program, the authorities ought to consider the introduction of the major subject idea, which is used in one form or another in many of the non-Canadian school systems of the world.

This would allow a student with a special aptitude in some field – science, languages, literature, history, mathematics, geography – to emphasize this field. The method used in some school systems is to demand a certain percentage in the field of specialization, and permit a lower percentage in the other subject or subjects.

By this means, a young person might not be prevented from making a social contribution to his or her area of strength, and would not be unfairly held back by subjects for which little or no aptitude was present.

It is a crying shame that our students are forced to spend endless hours on the study of matter which they do not intend to use in later life, and, because they are forced to do so in school, are determined not to study or read about later. The feeling is that by such a refusal they are getting revenge on the school system. We have felt that way, and, silly or not, it is a potent motive.[65]

Recommendations of the Grade 13 Study Committee

The Grade 13 Study Committee of 1964, the purposes and composition of which are dealt with in volume v, chapter 15, advocated a matriculation year which would for the time being remain the thirteenth in the system beginning with grade 1, but would ultimately become the twelfth in a reorganized structure. As the committee described it, the proposed year would be characterized by a reduced amount of teaching time, more reliance on the initiative of the individual student, increased use of the library and of individual research facilities, and a freer atmosphere. There would be a less rigid prescription of courses and courses would be provided in each subject at different levels of achievement. The committee suggested the introduction of such subjects as the new Man in Society and World Politics recently introduced in the four-year program It was recognized that the individual student should take fewer subjects.

Among the immediate consequences of the recommendations of the committee was the minister's decision to remove from the grade 13 course of study in each subject, for the purposes of the 1965 departmental examinations, topics previously requiring approximately three weeks of teaching time. As the committee had also suggested, teachers were advised that the intention was not to shorten the academic year. Nor was the reduction in topics to be considered as an opportunity to cover the course of study by an earlier date and thus to have more time for drill. It was rather to be considered an opportunity to experiment with teaching in greater depth and to enable the students to read more widely. The long and detailed curriculum bulletin that specified the topics to be deleted in each subject informed the teachers that the basic pattern of the grade 13 examination would not be altered unless there was a definite indication to that effect. In other words, while a continuation of the policy of encouraging cramming was officially deplored, the rewards for that activity remained the overwhelming reality. It is hardly surprising that the step produced no change of any consequence.

Work of the Grade 13 General and Advanced and Implementation Committees

As a result of the recommendation by the Grade 13 Study Committee that instruction in the matriculation year be offered at two levels, and that a representative committee be appointed to study the implications of the recommendations, a General and Advanced Committee was duly set up. Responding favourably to the two-level idea, it submitted a report to the minister in March 1965 recommending that committees with secondary school and university representation be established in each subject field to prepare tentative course outlines as guides for experimentation and as an indication to the universities of what they might expect from students working at each level. Such committees were appointed in September 1965 for most subject fields.

The General and Advanced Committee acknowledged that the specific objectives in dividing general and advanced level courses would vary according to the subject. It suggested, however, that the following broad objectives would apply to all subjects:

(a) the provision of courses better suited to the interests, needs and abilities of all students;
(b) the provision of an opportunity for students to take a wide-ranging and philosophical approach to their studies;
(c) the development of a more effective use of oral and written communication in all subjects;

(d) the provision of an opportunity for a student to delve into specialized aspects of some subjects in which he is keenly interested; and
(e) the development of more individual student activity and responsibility.[66]

The committee believed that these objectives could be achieved by a less rigid prescription of courses and by the encouragement of wider reading and more independent study. There would need to be more use of the library, audio-visual aids, and laboratory facilities, and less dependence on the classroom lesson.

It was thought probable that the following subjects would be offered at both levels: English, Français, history, mathematics, physics, chemistry, biology, French, Latin, and geography. Subjects that should probably be offered only at the advanced level would be German, Greek, Italian, Russian, and Spanish. The committee suggested that those committees which would consider the number of students involved and the advantage the subjects offered as a background for admission to university, teachers' college, or schools of nursing should decide at which level the following should be offered: art, music, accountancy practice, secretarial practice, mathematics of investment, and subjects that might be added later, such as home economics, economics, philosophy, psychology, sociology, and electronics.

There were two possibilities with respect to the organization and presentation of the course content: to have separate and distinct courses and to set the courses up on a "core-plus" basis. The committee and most of those who submitted briefs considered the first of these alternatives the more satisfactory in that it would offer the better opportunity of keeping the two levels distinct. However, in view of the fact that many of the smaller schools would find it difficult to manage such an approach, it was thought that the decision might have to be in favour of the second alternative. Students might thus be taught together for part of the time. The committee apparently did not think that uniformity was essential but suggested rather that schools with the necessary students, teachers, and facilities should offer separate courses. Principals and teachers were to be given considerable freedom in the organization of subject content and of courses.

The committee recommended that twice as much time be allotted for an advanced level course as for one at the general level. While part of the time would be for classroom periods, much of it would be devoted to assigned laboratory periods, assigned and independent research and library work, seminars, and tutorials. The nature of the subject would determine the actual division of time: in science, for example, a major proportion of the time would be devoted to laboratory work. Each subject at the general level would carry one credit toward university admission, and each subject at the advanced level, two credits, The committee felt that the basic requirement for admission to university should be two courses at each level, or six credits in all. Its recommendations did not leave room for the student who might not wish to specialize to this extent.

The full recommendations of the General and Advanced Committee, to be carried out, if approved by the minister, under the eye of an Implementation Committee, were as follows:

1. That, in view of the general acceptance in principle of the proposal for General and Advanced Levels of instruction in Grade 13, the Minister be requested to press forward at the appropriate time for the implementation of the relevant recommendations of The Grade 13 Study Committee, 1964.
2. That certain schools be requested, in co-operation with the Department of Education, to experiment in different ways with General and Advanced Levels of instruction in Grade 13 during the school year 1965-66, and that university and other authorities concerned be asked to give immediate assurance that students in experimental programs will be eligible for admission to university and for scholarships and bursaries. (Recommendations of principals and teachers might be supplemented by other criteria at the discretion of the university concerned.)
3. That arrangements be made for extension of the experimental programs during the school years 1966–67, 1967–68, 1968–69, and 1969–70, with a view to having General and Advanced Levels of study made mandatory not later than the school year 1970–71.
4. That a special committee be appointed to study the implications of General and Advanced Levels of instruction for French-speaking students.
5. That, because of the suggestions for experimentation in the report, a representative committee be appointed immediately and charged with the task of continuous direction and evaluation of General and Advanced Levels of instruction, particularly during the experimental period 1965–70.

   This Committee would be responsible for implementing the recommendations which follow, namely 6 to 12, inclusive. It is assumed that, in view of the magnitude of the task, the Department will appoint sufficient full-time personnel to co-ordinate the experimental program and to bring it to successful fruition.
6. That Committees with both secondary school and university representation be established in each subject field under the direction of the Program Branch to study and to prepare broad tentative outlines of courses, as guides for experimentation and as an indication to the Universities of what they may expect from students taking each level.
7. That a study be made, in conjunction with Recommendation No. 6, of the appropriateness of offering core-plus or separate courses in each subject and the desirability of having two levels in each subject.
8. That a study be made of examinations for each level and that sample papers be distributed to those concerned.
9. That a substantial reorientation and updating program for teachers with respect to General and Advanced Levels of instruction be implemented and

that financial support be provided for this purpose.

10. That a study be made of changes which will be required in the physical facilities and administrative organization of schools, in order to implement the General and Advanced Levels of instruction.
11. That principals, supervisors, administrators, trustees, parents, students, and the general public be made thoroughly familiar with the changes proposed and the reasons for their introduction.
12. That a continuing study be made of the effect of the General and Advanced Levels of instruction upon the lower grades.[67]

Robert Nixon thought the recommendations of the committee were excellent.

They deal with the need for increased student responsibility, not only at the grade 13 level, but at all stages, particularly in secondary schools. Too many of our students are still subjected to spoon-feeding and are not having an opportunity to have the sense of achievement that some personal study and personal progress can bring.[68]

Nixon warned, however, that the proposal for study at the two levels was not generally accepted. He advised the minister to determine the university point of view, since he considered that university authorities must have the operative decision on requirements for entrance into university.

In accordance with the committee's recommendations, committees representing the schools, the universities, and the department proceeded under the direction of the Program Branch to develop suggestive outlines of courses at the general and advanced levels. These were distributed among schools and universities for a thorough examination and appraisal, a process on which the minister indicated he placed great importance.

As this curriculum revision proceeds, bulletins will be printed and distributed to teachers describing the progress being made. The time has passed when courses of study can be written by two or three experts and then handed to principals and teachers to carry out in the classroom. A new course of study should not come as a surprise, nor should it come to teachers who are unprepared to implement it. Effort is being made to involve the teachers themselves in the formulation of the new programme and to acquaint them with its pattern as it takes shape.[69]

After a reasonable time had been allowed for the process of appraisal, the minister asked the president of each university to let him know by April 15, 1966, whether the concept of general and advanced levels was acceptable to his institution with respect to admission requirements. Briefs were received also from university and secondary school committees on various aspects of the proposals. The verdict from the universities was overwhelmingly negative, and views from the schools were in general agreement. Thus administrative rigidities, caution, and attachment to the established patterns demolished a bold innovation that was launched with unusual enthusiasm.

The reasons offered for opposition to the proposals were given by the Grade 13 Implementation Committee as follows. 1 / Significant progress had already been made toward the goals formulated by the Grade 13 Study Committee. The year's work was being taken into consideration in determining final standing in grade 13, the number of examinations to be written by each candidate had been reduced, several of the courses had been updated, the minister had announced the phasing out of the grade 13 examinations, and there were greater opportunities for study in depth. It was thought desirable to evaluate these changes before others were introduced. It seems appropriate to ask whether the implementation of part of the reform plan of the Grade 13 Study Committee was an adequate reason for scrapping the rest of it. 2 / It was suggested that two levels of instruction in grade 13 would force students to make an earlier choice of their ultimate university course, with resultant loss of flexibility of decision. 3 / The increased specialization which the proposal would produce was contrary to the general trend to broaden rather than to narrow the first-year university program. What was being recommended was apparently a continued policy of forcing students to disperse their efforts and of preventing them from concentrating on an area of special interest. Had there been a real desire to do so, it should have been possible to work out a program and a set of university admission requirements that would have offered a choice between a broad and a specialized program. Universities have managed to devise general honours as well as specialized honours programs. 4 / The adoption of the proposal would force the universities to provide two levels of instruction in certain courses in the first year. It seems not to have occurred to their spokesmen that properly qualified students from grade 13 might have been admitted to second-year university courses. Even if there were legitimate reasons why this procedure could not have been followed, it is regrettable that administrative convenience played an important part in the decision. 5 / There was doubt whether enough secondary school teachers were qualified to teach at the advanced level. This point seems the most specious of all, in view of the fact that the advanced courses were not even to be equated with first-year university work. Furthermore, it was only a year or so later that the colleges of applied arts and technology found many secondary school teachers quite capable of giving courses up to three years beyond the grade 12 level, many of them in academic fields.

AFTERMATH OF THE ABOLITION OF THE DEPARTMENTAL GRADE 13 EXAMINATIONS

The dropping of the departmental examinations after 1967 caused rejoicing among some teachers and school administrators and a good deal of uncertainty and apprehension among others. The department undertook to ease the transition to the new set-up by outlining certain policies which the minister declared were a natural development and follow-up of changes already made. 1 / The department would continue to publish grade 13 courses of study, but the principal and staff might adapt these to meet the needs of the students as they saw them. 2 / The Program Branch would work in close co-operation with teachers in reassessing and developing the curriculum. 3 / The department would co-operate with the teaching profession in establishing a consultative service by which practising teachers would provide assistance to other teachers on request with respect to course content and student progress. The hope was expressed that more emphasis would be placed on those aspects of student performance that were beyond the scope of written examinations.[70]

COURSE REQUIREMENTS FOR DIPLOMAS AT THE BEGINNING OF THE 1970s

No attempt has been made to trace the changes in subject requirements for secondary school diplomas through the 1950s and 1960s. The result, if such an effort were made, would be an extremely long and tiresome recital, which would probably be of little value to anyone. Successive versions of Circular H.S.1 for 1969–70 and 1970–1 were divided into sections A and B. The first of these sections was designed to provide guidance for the implementation of new organizational patterns, which have been discussed in chapter 4. The second outlined an alternative that was more in harmony with practices that had prevailed in previous years. Chart 5-1 gives the obligatory and optional subjects between grade 9 and grade 12 for the "traditional" program for 1970–1.

The subjects of study in grade 13 were accountancy practice, algebra (mathematics B), art, biology, chemistry, Classical Greek, English, Français, French, geography, German, history, home economics, introduction to analysis (mathematics A), Italian, Latin, mathematics of investment, music, physical education (non-credit), physics, Russian, secretarial practice, and Spanish. Each of the languages counted as two credits, a combination of introduction to analysis and algebra counted as three credits, and all the other subjects except physical education counted as one credit each toward the Ontario Secondary School Honour Graduation Diploma. Award of the diploma required seven credits, toward which either French or Français might be counted.

The two-year program was to be conducted in close association with the four-year program in one of the branches. In a small school, it might be related to the Arts and Science Branch, but in larger schools it was usually given in conjunction with one of the others. The program consisted of English or Français, history and geography, science, mathematics, group guidance, physical education, Anglais when the language of instruction was French, and a large block of time for practical subjects. The occupations program consisted of language arts, social science, mathematics, group guidance, physical and health education, and practical work. The practical work could include art, music, science, or home economics.

DEPARTMENTAL CURRICULUM GUIDES

By 1969–70 departmental curriculum guides had departed very radically from the old prescriptive form. A brief reference to the contents of a couple of these will illustrate the point. The 1970 outline for Anglais, that is, for English for French-speaking pupils, covered the primary, junior, intermediate, and senior levels. A four-line foreword indicated that it offered a flexible plan to help teachers develop courses and made suggestions for adaptations, experiments, and pilot projects. The introduction contained the suggestion that bilingualism was a necessary objective for French-speaking pupils in Ontario, although circumstances would determine what level of competence in English was reasonable. An appropriate course in English as a second language would be designed to meet the needs of French-speaking Ontario students, rather than being a reduced version of the courses in English as a first language. The stated aims and objectives emphasized effective communication; preparation for participation in commercial, political, civic, and social affairs in English-speaking communities; preparation for advanced study in institutions using English as the language of instruction; and appreciation of English-language culture. Suggestions were offered for using a wide variety of learning materials and approaches, and for selecting the most appropriate time to begin instruction. Listed under "areas of emphasis" were listening-speaking, reading for understanding, writing as a form of expression, and exploring language and literature.

A little more than half a page was devoted to suggestions for teaching the courses. Teachers were advised to regard a course as a series of activities that would encourage students "to use English, to practice it, and to learn about it as a system of language, an instrument of communication, and a revelation of a way of life." There was to be no traditional division of language teaching into grammar, vocabulary, phonics, reading, spelling, literature, and composition. These aspects of language were to be integrated in ways appropriate to the occasion. Use was to be made of tape recorders, language laboratories, record players, film projectors, radio and television, newspapers, magazines, wall charts, and pictures. Teacher and students might themselves produce valuable materials. Learning was to be effected through plays, narrative and lyric poetry, short stories, short novels with dialogue and a narrative style, songs, games, choral speech and reading, dramatization, debates, and panel discussions, which would provide variety in the remedial work, repetition, and drills that were highly important in language learning.

Under "time allotment," no specific period was even suggested. The different requirements of individuals were to be taken into account, and

CHART 5-1

Course requirements for diplomas in Ontario secondary schools following traditional program, 1970–1

GRADE 9

Five-year

Arts and Science	Business and Commerce	Science, Technology, and Trades
←	English/Français History Geography Physical education Mathematics Science French/Anglais Group guidance	→
Any two of Art Music Industrial arts or technical subjects Home economics Agriculture-environmental science Typewriting Any authorized subject from any program or grade within this branch for which prerequisites can be met	Commercial subjects (business practice and typewriting)	*One of* Technical subjects (including agriculture-environmental science) Home economics Vocational arts Vocational music

Four-year

Arts and Science	Business and Commerce	Science, Technology, and Trades
←	English/Français History Geography Physical education Mathematics Science French*/Anglais Group guidance	→
Any two of Art Music Industrial arts or technical subjects Home economics Agriculture-environmental science Typewriting or business practice Any authorized subject from any program, branch, or grade for which prerequisites can be met	Business and commerce subjects	*One of* Technical subjects Home economics Agriculture-environmental science Vocational art Vocational music

* Under certain conditions, commercial subjects or other options may be substituted.

CHART 5-1, continued

GRADE 10

Five-year

Arts and Science	Business and Commerce	Science, Technology, and Trades
←	English/Français History Geography Physical education Anglais (French-language schools)	→
Any two of Mathematics Science A language (French, Latin, Classical Greek, German, Italian, Spanish, Russian) *Any two or more of* Optional subjects not chosen above Art Music Industrial arts or technical subjects Home economics Agriculture-environmental science Bookkeeping, data processing, or typewriting An additional language An authorized subject from any program or grade within this branch for which prerequisites can be met	Business and commerce subjects (double option), (secretarial: shorthand and typewriting; accountancy; bookkeeping; business machines and mathematics or data processing) *Any two of* Mathematics Science A language An optional subject not chosen above or any authorized subject from any program or grade within this branch for which prerequisites can be met	*One of* Technical subjects Home economics Vocational art Vocational music Agriculture-environmental science (double option) *Any two of* Mathematics Science A language Any authorized subject from any program or grade within this branch for which prerequisites can be met

CHART 5-1, continued

GRADE 10		
Four-year		
Arts and Science	Business and Commerce	Science, Technology, and Trades
←	English/Français History Geography Physical education Anglais (French-language schools)	→
Any four or five of Mathematics Science French Latin Another language Agriculture-environmental science Industrial arts or technical subjects Home economics Art Music Bookkeeping or typewriting Any authorized subject from any program, branch, or grade for which prerequisites can be met	Business and commerce subjects *Any three of* Mathematics (commercial) Science A language Art Music Industrial arts or technical subjects Additional time in business or commerce subjects Any authorized subject from any program, branch, or grade for which prerequisites can be met	Mathematics Science *One of* Technical subjects Home economics Vocational art Vocational music *One of* Art Music Agriculture-environmental science Commercial subjects A language Further time in one of technical subjects or home economics or vocational art or vocational music Any authorized subject from any program, branch, or grade for which prerequisites can be met

CHART 5-1, continued

<table>
<tr><td colspan="3">GRADES 11 AND 12</td></tr>
<tr><td colspan="3">Five-year</td></tr>
<tr><td>Arts and Science</td><td>Business and Commerce</td><td>Science, Technology, and Trades</td></tr>
<tr><td colspan="3">← English/Français
Physical education
Anglais (French-language schools) →</td></tr>
<tr>
<td>Any four of
World History, Part I
World History, Part II
World Geography, Part I
World Geography, Part II
Mathematics
Science (physics, chemistry)
French
Latin
Classical Greek
German
Spanish
Italian
Russian

One or two of
Optional subjects not chosen above
Business and commercial subjects
Industrial arts or technical subjects
Home economics
Art
Music
Agriculture-environmental science
Any authorized subject from any program or grade within this branch for which prerequisites can be met</td>
<td>Business and commerce subjects (double option)

Any four of
World History, Part I
World History, Part II
World Geography, Part I
World Geography, Part II
Mathematics
Science
French
Latin
Classical Greek
German
Spanish
Italian
Russian
Any authorized subject from any program or grade within this branch for which prerequisites can be met</td>
<td>Any one of
Technical subjects
Home economics
Vocational art
Vocational music
Agriculture-environmental science (double option)

Any four of
World History, Part I
World History, Part II
World Geography, Part I
World Geography, Part II
Mathematics
Science
French
Latin
Classical Greek
German
Spanish
Italian
Russian
Any authorized subject from any program or grade within this branch for which prerequisites can be met</td>
</tr>
</table>

CHART 5-1, continued

GRADE 11 AND 12		
Four-year		
Arts and Science	Business and Commerce	Science, Technology, and Trades
←	English/Français Physical education Anglais (French-language schools)	→
Any five or six of History (grade 11) Economics (grade 12) Mathematics Science Geography A language Agriculture-environmental science Industrial arts or technical subjects Home economics Art Music Business and commerce subjects Man in society Space and man World politics Modern literature Theatre arts Speech arts Biology Geology Any authorized subject from any program, branch, or grade for which prerequisites can be met	Business and commerce subjects *Any two or three of* History (grade 11) Economics (grade 12) Mathematics (commercial) Science Geography A language Art Music Industrial arts or technical subjects Home economics Business and commercial subjects not taken above Any authorized subject from any program, branch, or grade for which prerequisites can be met	Mathematics Science *One of* Technical subjects Vocational art Vocational music *Any two of* History (grade 11) Economics (grade 12) Geography A language Art Music Agriculture-environmental science Commercial subjects An option from the Four-year Arts and Science Program Further time in one of technical subjects or home economics, vocational art, or vocational music Any authorized subject from any program, branch, or grade for which prerequisites can be met

SOURCE: Ontario Department of Education, Circular H.S.1, 1970/71.

needed adjustments were to be made through trial and experimentation. Naturally the least flexibility in timetabling would be possible at the senior level. Under "grouping of students," it was suggested that instructional groups should be formed on the basis of competence in English as determined by testing and the teacher's personal evaluation. One page was devoted to teaching aids, with brief suggestions as to how they might be used. They fell under five main headings: the blackboard; bulletin boards, charts, and pictures; the language laboratory and the tape recorder; radio, television, and film; and pattern drills and memorized dialogue. The subsequent pages offered a model for developing a course unit, with long lists of suggested activities, book and film titles, poetry and prose selections, and the like.

Another random selection among course outlines that will serve for illustrative purposes is that for computer science at the senior level issued in 1970. The contents, covering sixteen pages, included an introduction; a statement of the scope of the course; three units entitled respectively "Problem-Solving – an Algorithmic Approach," "Programming Languages and Systems," and "Man and the Computer"; a section on the evaluation of student progress; and a section on resource material occupying the last six pages. The introduction indicated that the student was not only to secure a basic understanding of how the computer worked, and to acquire the skill to make it work for him, but also to gain a realization of how it had revolutionized methods of solving problems and, in the process, established the basis for profound social changes. The section on the scope of the course suggested that the student might pursue problems in any subject area and to any depth he desired. Because of the great range of potential problems, the course could be taken at a number of different levels. It was recommended that interest be the sole criterion for admission.

Unit 1 of the guide consisted of two pages of quite specific topics suggested under the headings Basic Arithmetic, Sequences and Series, Tabulating of Functions, Conversion of Units, Number Problems, Business-Oriented Topics, Random Numbers, Geometry, Science, Sorting and Searching, Statistics and Probability, Iterative Procedures, Two-Dimensional Arrays, Graphing and Plotting Functions, Trigonometry, Miscellaneous, and Simulation. Unit 2 followed a similar pattern. Under unit 3, it was suggested that consideration be given to such effects of the introduction of the computer as the performance of certain functions in business and industry, with the consequent threat to certain kinds of employment; the prospect of a higher standard of living through increased efficiency of production; the revolution in transportation as a result of computerized control of traffic, control of railway rolling stock, detection of mechanical trouble in aircraft engines, and the like; improvements in communication; contributions to scientific investigation, with appropriate attention to the development of lethal weapon systems; the provision of better medical service; and other aspects of life.

The section on the evaluation of student progress indicated that evaluation of work and of levels attained was to be considered more of an individual than of a class matter. Emphasis was to be placed on the student's self-evaluation, which would be aided if he kept records of his own progress. Attention was to be given to such factors as numbers of attempts necessary to find a workable solution, the ingenuity of the solution, the relevance of the documentation accompanying the solution, the quality of the solution in comparison with the alternatives, and the number of logical errors. It was suggested that the teacher should be constantly evaluating the student in other than the cognitive area.

SIGNIFICANCE OF CURRICULUM CHANGES

There is no doubt that at the beginning of the 1970s the curriculum in Ontario secondary schools was undergoing very rapid and profound changes for which there was no previous counterpart in the history of the province. There was thoroughgoing official support for a genuine effort to provide for the multitude of patterns of interest and aptitude that exist at the secondary level. There was evidence, also, of a conviction that imaginatively selected, organized, and presented material might develop and enhance interest and produce levels of achievement not previously considered attainable. While there were unquestionably many schools where the old rigidities remained, and might perhaps take some time to sweep away, attending high school was becoming a new kind of experience for young people.

Curriculum reform was having a profound effect on secondary school teaching. The teacher who expected to get by on a knowledge of a few texts and reference books, and to follow a relatively invariable pattern of presentation, was rapidly becoming obsolete. Departmental guides were making it abundantly clear that effective teaching required acquaintance with a vast range of material in a great variety of forms, as well as a continued willingness and ability to make choices in terms of the student's needs. No teacher could expect to promote growth in the student without himself growing at an ever-increasing rate. For the lovers of freedom and responsibility, it was an exhilarating time. For the timid and insecure, teaching offered no haven.

TEXTBOOKS

Importance

Throughout most of Ontario's educational history, the textbook has been a teaching aid of primary importance. In the hands of ill-trained or uninspired teachers, it has in fact borne most of the actual burden of teaching. A semblance of education has been attainable as long as a certain number of pages could be prescribed and the pupil's mastery tested by his ability to reproduce the contents. Even teachers with the capacity to keep the initiative in their own hands have relied heavily on the selection and organization of subject matter by the textbook writer. The number and quality of available books have thus been a major factor in the implementation of curriculum policy.

In pioneer days, the problem of providing textbooks was an extremely difficult one. The heavy reliance placed on the Bible was in part a reflection of the people's confidence in it as a morally uplifting influence, and in part a result of its availability for religious purposes. It was realized, however, even among the most pious, that other sources of information and inspiration were needed to provide a balanced education. Unfortunately, however, Upper Canada almost completely lacked either textbook writers or publishers. Reliance thus had to be placed on books produced in other countries.

Early drive toward uniformity

During the period before Ryerson assumed control of the educational system, there was a great variety of textbooks in common use, none of them of Canadian origin. This situation almost dictated an individualized program of a rather undesirable type. Ryerson decided on the uniform use of the Irish National series of readers, which he judged the best available. His policy was one of gradualism; superintendents were asked to let existing books fall into disuse rather than condemning them altogether. The result was that some of them were around for much too long. According to *Centennial Story*, parents insisted that younger children use handed-down books; certain teachers were wedded to the text they were used to, while others were changing texts at every opportunity.[71] Ryerson's establishment of the so-called educational depository for the purchase and resale of textbooks and other materials at low prices did as much as official fiat to exert pressure in favour of uniformity.

When the Department of Education was officially established in 1876, the minister was given the power to authorize textbooks for use in all schools receiving public grants. A new series of readers was authorized for use in 1884. Three years later, the department adopted the policy of controlling the authorship, publication, price, and copyright of textbooks. One textbook was ordinarily authorized for use in each subject.

Cost of textbooks

The Act of 1871 authorized school boards to rent textbooks at a price of not more than 20 cent a month. In 1892 Toronto initiated the practice of providing free textbooks for use in the elementary schools, followed within a few years by Hamilton and Brantford. While other city boards gradually did the same, the policy did not extend to rural areas, even though legislation in 1904 provided for grants for this purpose. Rural-urban differences in this respect constituted one of the most glaring examples of inequality of educational opportunity.

Complaints about the costs of textbooks were influential in inducing the department to set up a special commission of business men in 1906 to investigate the production of such books. A drastic reduction in prices soon followed. The boards that supplied free textbooks, as well as parents, were the beneficiaries.[72] As a matter of fact, the cost of textbooks, as compared with other types of books, has usually been low in an absolute sense, even though the burden may have been heavy on large families of modest means.

Authorization procedures and policy

When the revised program of studies for grades 1 to 6 was released in 1937, the department withdrew from the practice of having books prepared under its supervision and resorted instead to appointing committees to select suitable ones for authorization. These committees often recommended and supervised revisions to adapt books to meet the requirements of the course of study. Some lists of authorized texts mentioned two or more books for a subject or grade, leaving teachers with a certain amount of freedom to follow their individual preferences, subject to the approval of their boards. In actual practice, one or two of the optional books tended to be judged the best, thus crowding the others out. As the Royal Commission pointed out, in some subjects and grades there was not even a pretence at offering variety.

At least as far as grades 1 to 6 were concerned, the pursuit of any kind of restrictive textbook policy was almost completely at variance with the spirit of the official curricular policy adopted in 1937. That scheme depended for success on the freedom of teachers and pupils to seek information from any source that seemed to meet their needs. It might well be said that long years of obeisance to the authority of the textbook was a basic reason why the program seems to have been ahead of its time.

Recommendations of the Royal Commission in 1950

The Royal Commission's recommendations were a combination of the negative and the positive. It proposed

(a) that the present system of textbook authorization, requiring the use of only one specified textbook in certain subjects or grades, be discontinued;
(b) that the present system, whereby the Department of Education subsidizes the cost of production of authorized textbooks, be discontinued;
(c) that a system of multiple authorizations, whereby each board of trustees will be free to choose a textbook, or textbooks, for any subject or grade from a list of approved titles prepared by the Department of Education, be instituted;
(d) that school boards continue to be authorized to provide, free of charge, textbooks and other approved classroom supplies to pupils in attendance in elementary and secondary schools and in special education classes during

> the period of compulsory school attendance; and that expenditures incurred for the purchase of textbooks selected from an approved list issued by the Department, and for other approved classroom supplies, be included as a cost of operating for general legislative grant purposes.[73]

Policies of recommendation and Canadianization of textbooks

In 1950 the department abandoned the practice of authorizing readers and other texts in favour of recommended lists which gave the local authorities the responsibility of making a choice. As the Porter Plan got under way, local curriculum committees were encouraged to make suggestions to the department for additions to the list. Preference was given to books written by Canadian authors and produced in Canada. The *Report of the Minister, 1954* declared that this policy, after being in force for only a few years, had encouraged a number of talented teachers to prepare textbooks that were admirably suited to the needs of Ontario schools. The degree of success achieved appeared, however, to be rather modest in view of the fact that only a few more than 25 per cent of the books listed in the 1954 issue of Circular 14 were prepared by Canadian authors.

In sensitive areas, where Canadian authorship might be considered to be of greatest importance, the record was better. Curriculum:8, a memorandum dealing with the selection of textbooks in social studies, was published in pamphlet form in 1955 and circulated to all teachers of the junior division. It listed about forty-five recent books suitable for Canadian libraries, most of which were written by Canadians about Canadian subjects and published in Canada.

The *Report of the Minister, 1959* outlined the process by which a book got the official stamp of approval. A publisher who had a textbook which he considered better than any on the approved list, or which he thought had superior features, might present it for departmental examination. If it appeared to meet the needs of the course for which it was designed and to be suitable in other respects, it might be placed immediately on the approved list. In case of doubt, it might be submitted to specialists or to a committee established for the purpose. Any book that failed to hold up under classroom use could be removed summarily from the approved list.

The end of the 1950s and the early 1960s constituted a period of increasing activity as S.A. Watson and J.R. McCarthy in succession headed the Curriculum Branch. In 1959 it was announced that the first series of Canadian readers for the primary division and a series of spellers for all the elementary grades had been produced. It had thus become possible to remove from the approved list the books of American origin which had dominated the field for many years. In 1960 there were new books in history and geography in the intermediate division and in government for grade 10. New atlases were designed, and a dictionary was produced especially for Canadian elementary school pupils. As a substitute for texts translated from English, new history books were written in French for use in schools where instruction was given in that language.

In 1962 Robarts commented on the reliance some of the less populous provinces were placing on Ontario for books with a Canadian flavour. Like Ontario in earlier years, they did not have a large enough volume of sales to warrant the production of books for their own specific purposes. Robarts said he had been informed that only 5 per cent of the texts used in Ontario were American, or revised from American texts, and that most of these were in specialized fields such as Greek and Spanish.[74]

Government financial assistance and repercussions in the 1950s
Beginning in 1951–2 the government paid a grant of $3 per pupil per year to all school boards for the purchase of textbooks on the approved list up to the end of grade 10. This amount of money was not sufficient to meet the full cost, but it helped. It also gave rise to objections to the increasing numbers of items on the recommended list on the grounds that the cost of variety was excessive. J.F. Edwards, member for Perth, voiced this point of view in the Legislature.

We doubt with all the new courses and text books covering same if the basic truths in connection with arithmetic and grammar are changed. The same goes for correct spelling. Since 1919 I have either worked in or owned a drug-store which supplied local school books and I know that year after year, fewer dealers are left who are willing to handle these books because of the confusion resulting from the number of text books required and the change in courses. I would suggest that fewer texts are required and not so many options. I might mention one case in this connection in the primary schools. Two neighbouring schools, in different township areas, use two different texts in connection with the teaching of arithmetic, at the discretion of the teacher. This I maintain is not necessary.[75]

Similar sentiments were expressed by M. Belanger, member for Windsor-Sandwich, in 1961.

Another field of economy I believe that could be practised is that, at a recent education committee meeting it was mentioned that teachers had several sets of textbooks on one subject. This is especially true in history, arithmetic and reading. The department pays 87 per cent of the cost of these books for the elementary grades. Teachers certainly have not the time on an already overloaded curriculum to make use of all these books.

I would suggest that perhaps 2 or 3 sets at the most would be sufficient. There again, Mr. Chairman, a great saving could be made by the department.

Speaking of books, I am of the opinion that in the secondary schools books could be supplied to the students on a rental basis, thus avoiding exorbitant cost to the parents. This has been tried by some school boards and, when well administered, it can be a very successful venture.

I would also recommend, Mr. Chairman, that certain texts remain on the curriculum for a much longer period than they do today. School textbooks have become a publisher's paradise in the last few years. One book is used a year or two, then another comes on the market. There is far too much variety and not enough uniformity in the texts used in the Ontario schools.[76]

These objections to existing policy had no noticeable effect.

The issue of textbook quality in the 1960s

From time to time in the early 1960s, rather serious doubts were expressed about the general quality or the accuracy of certain textbooks. Bascom St John commented on several of these in a column on April 11, 1962, after giving space to articles by an authority on health education who had raised some pertinent questions.[77] St John offered the view that the accuracy, balance, and intrinsic interest of textbooks constituted one of the most serious problems of education next to the actual provision of teachers themselves.

The criticisms of the health textbooks were by F.J. Millar, who was then acting head of the Department of Physiology and Pharmacology in the University of Saskatchewan. He found certain of these books extremely out of date, unscientific, and grossly inaccurate. St John wrote that the examples cited recalled the teaching of hygiene in the Ontario village schools he had attended forty years earlier. The situation seemed to him to lend substance to the claim that it takes fifty years to get a new idea accepted in the schools. He was critical of the medical profession for allowing the errors in question to go uncorrected for so long and asked: "Are these majestic professionals so far above the concerns of citizenship and parenthood that they did not think these errors in the health course should have been sought out and corrected?"

The analysis of the course of study carried out under the aegis of the Joint Committee of the Toronto Board of Education and the University of Toronto a short time before had revealed what St John characterized as some astonishing failures in scientific knowledge. Important features were described inaccurately, were in the wrong place, or were not even mentioned. An explanation for the inadequacies of one particular course, covering four grades, was sought in the fact that it had been assembled by a committee of teachers and inspectors in a period of three weeks. While some justification might be found for the speed with which this work was done in the fact that the committee had presumably built on what had already existed, St John thought it an outrage that such a task had been carried out without consultation with advanced experts in the universities. Once the course had been determined, it was almost certain to dictate the contents of textbooks, since writers who did not follow it quite strictly were unlikely to have their efforts approved. As indicated in volume II, chapter 2, the department tended, as the 1960s progressed, to rely increasingly on a single well-qualified expert to work out a proposed course in the initial stages.

The content of history textbooks was a subject for discussion throughout the 1960s. Among recurrent criticisms of particular books were that they contained demonstrable errors, that their contents were inconsistent with those of others in the same field, that they perpetuated myths, that they were bland and dull, and that they contained bias either through the opinions expressed or through the particular set of facts selected for presentation. As long as textbook writing is done by individuals, there is little chance of removing the basis for the last of these charges. A teacher's only refuge is to make sure that excessive reliance is not placed on a single source. Some of the other criticisms might be softened by more insistence on greater scholarly competence in the field along with literary capabilities and a general understanding of the psychology of the child at the level for which the book is intended. One successful writer has admitted candidly that he did not even like history until he began writing textbooks in the subject. While this fact does not necessarily show that the results of his efforts were other than of high quality, one would tend to approach them rather sceptically.

Some of the findings of the study reported by A.B. Hodgetts in *What Culture? What Heritage?* called attention to the vast differences in the portrayal of the development of Canada in textbooks used by French-speaking children in Quebec and English-speaking children in other provinces.[78] To French-Canadian writers, the importance of the early French settlements has loomed very large, the initial menace posed by the British conquest to French language and culture has been stressed, and maximum credit has been given to the determination and other heroic qualities of French Canadians in preserving their vital interests. There has been comparatively little overt appreciation of what in other quarters have been assumed to be the particular virtues of British constitutional and legal forms. While English-speaking children have been introduced to the exploits of Cartier, Champlain, Laval, Frontenac, and others, they have been given the impression that the British side in the colonial wars before the final conquest of Canada was definitely "our side." They have been taught to regard the early days of British rule as consciously benign, except for a few lapses that were relatively unimportant because threats of forceful assimilation of the French-speaking inhabitants were never seriously attempted. Themes emphasized in the story of the subsequent development of the country have left them unequipped to understand or sympathize fully with the defensive quality of French-Canadian nationalism. The future of the country may very well hinge on the effect of textbooks on generations of students.

From time to time there have been complaints about the way textbooks have treated minority groups in general. In 1965 the minister announced that the department was co-operating with the Ontario Human Rights Commission to examine all the school textbooks in use, "not just for the purpose of removing material which may be offensive to any of the groups which make up our multi-national family, but more important, to make sure that our textbooks do contain the type of material which does full justice to the contribution of many peoples to the development of our province and nation."[79] Davis indicated that textbook publishers were eager to co-operate in this cause. That the effort could be regarded as entirely commendable rested, of course, on the assumption that anything that the members of a particular group regarded as offensive was really inaccurate or unjust, or that it could be suppressed without doing objectionable violence to the truth. A recital of the fine contributions of all the groups that make up Canada's multi-national family might not only be objectionable to serious historians but also unduly cloying to pupils who are encouraged to engage genuinely in man's unending search for truth.

The extension of the policy of free textbooks

Provincial grants in the early 1950s had accompanied the policy of universal provision of textbooks at no direct cost to the student up to the end of grade 8. In 1964 the same policy was extended through grades 9 and 10. The Speech from the Throne with which the Legislature was opened that year identified the measure as a step in the equalization of educational opportunity throughout the province. In actual fact, many school boards had been providing some or all textbooks for students in grades 9 and 10 with the assistance of the $3.00 grant per pupil instituted in 1951. They had thus built up a substantial supply of approved textbooks, which would facilitate the implementation of the new policy. In addition the department paid two grants of $6 each, or a total of $12 per student of average daily attendance in the previous year, to help build up the required initial stock. Grants of $6 per student were promised for subsequent years to help provide replacements for worn-out books and for additions because of increasing enrolments and new courses.

Some of the implications of the "free" textbook policy for secondary schools, many of which had of course long applied to elementary schools, were reviewed in the *Bulletin* of the OSSTF. After favourable comment on the prospect of relieving families, especially those with several children, of a considerable burden, the article continued:

> The school boards and principals can and no doubt will underwrite the additional costs (and they will be high), the enormous storage problem, the demands on teacher time, the accompanying loss of classroom instruction and the difficulties in collecting money for books lost or not returned. As time goes on and sets of books are built up, the heavy costs will decrease gradually, but the stor-

age and administrative load will increase, especially in the area of English where the stress is laid upon having students study an ever-increasing number of books to enrich their experience and appreciation.

Another problem lies in the area of languages and mathematics and probably in science. The grade nine and ten books are valuable in that they may be needed for reference in the higher grades. How can this be possible if the books are to be returned at the end of each scholastic year? Many children care for books that they have bought themselves as their personal property but will they accord so-called free books the same care? To what extent can reimbursement be forced for malicious damage? When are the books going to be returned? Will it be practical or possible to collect in an efficient manner all the books after the students have written their final examinations?

Furthermore, many teachers have students mark texts for important points, for possible corrections, and for the addition of clarifying material. Free books, by instruction, are likely to remain unmarked. If as we believe texts have a continuing value to the student does the issuing and return of free texts really further the learning process?

Many problems in this area require clarification. Co-operation, however, among all the parties concerned can lead to the solution of these difficult situations which this seemingly simple and desirable plan will present.[80]

Some of the more fundamental implications of the policy were mentioned by Duncan Green, Vice-Principal of Parkdale Collegiate Institute in Toronto, in an address to the Ontario Secondary School Teachers' Federation. He speculated that the $12 textbook grant might induce boards to buy on the basis of cost rather than of quality. He also feared that the variety of textbooks would be restricted because once a book was approved it would have a virtual monopoly. He was in favour of relief to the parents as long as the quality of education was not reduced.[81]

In April 1964 Robert Nixon suggested an ingenious scheme to the Legislature. With the co-operation of the teachers' professional organizations, a yearly book, which might perhaps be better called a workbook than a textbook, would be prepared by the department, printed in paperback form by the Queen's Printer, and supplied free of charge to all students across the province. These books would admittedly not contain all the excellent material currently contained in the good textbooks on the authorized list, with which they would not attempt to compete. They would parallel the core curriculum being produced for the Reorganized Program and provide only the essentials for each course. With the money saved, library facilities in each school would be greatly expanded. While students used the material in the paperback book for their day-to-day course work, they would be forced to rely heavily on the school library for further information. They would thus be weaned away from excessive reliance on a single textbook, which they could "clutch under their arm and memorize for examination purposes."[82]

In 1965 the free textbook policy was extended, as had been anticipated, to the end of grade 12. The department's special grant to get the program under way amounted to $20 per student of average daily attendance during the preceding year. Again, the grant for continued maintenance of the book supply was expected to be half that amount for subsequent years. A departmental announcement declared that, although the new grant might cover the total cost of textbooks in some areas, most boards would have to supplement the amount to allow for the needs of their own municipalities. It was not intended that the arrangements for distributing the books would be an additional burden on the teachers. The increased grants were expected to assist boards in providing clerical assistance to free teachers from routine clerical tasks so that they could give full attention to teaching.[83]

The departmental officials hoped that the choice of texts available to teachers would continue to be broad enough to provide suitable courses for all classes in an up-to-date school program. Flexibility was to be maintained in the selection of books in English and in the authors of other language courses. In subject areas where no texts were included in the approved lists in Circular 14, teachers might select texts, where such were required, with the approval of the principal and by resolution of the school board.

When the latest extension of the policy occurred, the Ontario Secondary School Teachers' Federation pointed fairly emphatically to some of the disadvantages. English teachers in particular were apprehensive about the possibility of restrictions on the range of books available for use. Some unhappiness was expressed that the department's action had been taken without specific consultation with the federation. Davis pointed out that there had been an earlier warning that the senior grades would be covered in due course, and that the federation had let the matter lapse until after the decision had been announced.[84] Once it made its representations, a Joint Committee on Textbooks, involving federation and department representatives, was established to inquire into and report on the results of the introduction of the special textbook grants, to identify the educational and administrative problems arising out of the implementation of the grant policy, and to recommend whatever modifications of the existing procedures might be thought necessary.[85] Davis himself suggested that the grants might prove sufficiently generous that many of the English novels could be provided in paperback form, and that they could be given to the students to keep.

Continued support for wide variety of texts

Curriculum Bulletin 5, issued in 1967, indicated the department's continued support for the use of a wide variety of books, as of other instructional materials, in each subject area. The findings of educational research were said to reinforce the view that this approach was needed to provide for the differing needs and aptitudes of the pupils. In particular, the "learning through discovery" method could best be implemented if the pupils had regular access to a number of books.[86]

The old objections to the multiple-textbook or non-textbook policy continued to be heard. For example, J.P. Spence, member for Kent East, spoke as follows on May 25, 1967.

> ... I have been approached on a number of occasions by fathers and mothers who have sons and daughters attending our elementary and secondary schools across the province, and they wonder how it is, or why it is that the teacher has choices of a number of textbooks to teach the different subjects in elementary and secondary schools. It makes them wonder, Mr. Minister, why you and the top officials that you have in your department cannot come up on one definite textbook to teach each subject. Also it makes them wonder, Mr. Chairman, when the cost of education is a burden on a large segment of our population, why The Department of Education cannot make a decision on one textbook for each subject.[87]

Davis responded by questioning whether reversion to a uniform textbook prescribed by the department would help to relieve the financial burden of education. Whether a book used in one district was the same as that used in another seemed to have little bearing on cost. While there were problems of adjustment if parents had to move, Davis observed that the percentage of the total enrolment moving in a single year was rather small. He proceeded to offer a defence of the educational value of making available more than one text and of approving a number of reference texts.[88]

In that year, the names of about 125 new textbooks appeared in Circular 14, and others were added in May and June. Grants were increased somewhat by the substitution of average daily enrolment for average daily attendance in the formula. In recognition of the increased cost of textbooks, the amount of the per-pupil grant was raised by up to $3 per pupil. Changes in the grant formula by the end of the decade ended the practice of earmarking grants for specific items, including textbooks. By this time, school board practices in supply textbooks and managing their distribution had become reasonably well established.

SIX

Significant development in certain curricular areas

As is true of so many aspects of education dealt with in *Ontario's Educative Society*, complete coverage of developments in all specific areas of the curriculum is out of the question. The subject has therefore been tackled on a selective basis, with the choice limited to a few of the main areas.

ENGLISH

Statements of objectives for the teaching of English usually relate either to technical skills of communication or to creative work and the development of aesthetic attitudes. The emphasis tends to shift somewhat from one grade level to another. The Committee on the Integration of the Creative Arts of the Ontario Curriculum Institute, which reported in 1965, found that elementary teachers placed the greatest emphasis on the development of the ability to read and on verbal expression.[1] Oral work was particularly stressed in the early grades. With increasing reliance on written expression, a knowledge of sentence structure and the rules of punctuation became necessary. As the pupils advanced, greater importance was placed on the ability to gather and organize information, the expansion of vocabulary, the use of the dictionary, and an understanding of the techniques of composition. In the senior elementary grades, the balance of attention shifted in the direction of creative expression and appreciation, although technical skills were still regarded as of major importance. Choral and interpretive reading were used to develop aesthetic attitudes. Other forms of oral expression suggested by teachers in the committee's survey were public speaking, panel discussions and debates, the conduct of meetings, storytelling, and dramatic arts. Senior pupils might be expected to develop standards of critical evaluation which could be applied to newspaper and magazine articles, advertisements, and radio and television programs. None of the teachers questioned made any reference to historical knowledge of the language.

In the secondary schools and the universities, specialized teachers of English ranked aesthetic attitudes and critical evaluation in the first order of importance among objectives, with technical skills in second or third place. Aesthetic attitude was defined, not as a mere emotional response, but as "intelligent and critical appreciation developed through understanding, participation and enjoyment."

The role of grammar

The English Study Committee of the Joint Committee of the Toronto Board of Education and the University of Toronto made a valuable contribution to clarifying the long-standing controversy over the role of grammar in language studies.

The most debated and least understood part of the programme of formal language study has to do with the study of English grammar. First of all, there are those who confuse grammar with the teaching of rules for writing correctly. Others confuse it with the analysis of empty sentences that have never been used anywhere except in grammar books. Still others find it in the learning of tables of tenses, cases, and the like which have little or no reality in English as it actually is. Each of these points of view, however, is a mistake. First, they confuse two very different types of grammar: the descriptive, which tells how language is constructed, and the normative, which tells us how we ought to speak or write. Second, descriptive grammar need not be confined to the structure of the artificial or the contrived; it can be applied to the living language in speech and writing. Nor does normative grammar have to depend on a list of artificial rules, for it can and should emanate from the active usage of the society of educated speakers and writers.[2]

During much of the educational history of Ontario, the term grammar conjured up in the minds of teachers one or more of the confused concepts which the committee identified. Sterile practices continued long after serious doubts had arisen about their efficiency in improving the ability to communicate. While attitudes toward the values of what is classified as grammatical knowledge remain far from uniform, the change since the mid-nineteenth century has been profound. At that time, the learning of detailed rules was thought to be the essential basis for the ability to speak and write correctly. It was customary to demand adherence to the rules for every sentence spoken in the classroom, and to insist that all answers be given in complete sentences, no matter how stilted. Composition was introduced very tardily as an adjunct to grammar. According to *Centennial Story*, it made its first appearance in examinations as a question asking for eight or ten lines on such subjects as Truth Will Prevail, Knowledge is Power, Toronto's Semi-centennial, The Atmosphere, An Imaginary Description of an Eruption of Mount Vesuvius, or A Collision between Two Steamers. Later additions included the writing of personal and business letters, the reproduction of a family story, and the completion of an outline suggested in class.[3]

The course of study in grammar for the public and secondary schools issued in 1936 identified its objectives as follows.

The course in Grammar should be directed towards giving the pupil such a knowledge of the functions, forms, and relations of words as will assist him in speaking and writing the language with clearness and accuracy. It should give the pupil an insight into the principles underlying the structure of the language, and thus aid him in speaking and writing correctly in a rational way and not merely in an imitative way. The course should be made as practical as possible by closely correlating it at every stage with the pupil's oral and written speech.

In Form IV, where the formal study of Grammar is begun, the pupil's reasoning powers are just beginning to develop. Consequently the teacher should not attempt to impose upon him difficult abstract distinctions in the function of words. Nor should unnecessary technical terms, or much detail in analysis and parsing be required.[4]

The curriculum revision of 1937 for grades 1 to 6 encouraged the abandonment of formal instruction in grammar in favour of incidental teaching of forms as an aspect of composition. A good many critics during subsequent years blamed what they identified as a decline in writing standards to this change. There was, however, accumulating research evidence to show that writing ability was not closely related to a knowledge of grammatical rules. Linguistic studies demonstrated that the early attempts by grammarians to force English into structures derived from and appropriate to Latin had done considerable violence to the language. These influences countered any tendency to backtrack.

What might be identified as a moderate or middle position was taken by H.S. Baker of the University of Alberta, who identified two main assumptions on which language teachers seemed to operate. One was that the way to become proficient in language expression was to study about language, especially about the rules or principles that were thought to govern its use. The alternative was simply to use the language. These distinct assumptions, according to Baker, were applicable beyond language instruction to the educative process in general. His verdict was that the definition of mutually exclusive alternatives was unnecessary.

Clearly there can be little development of language power without involvement in activities that demand spoken or written expression. But just as clearly the activities cannot be truly educative if there is not going forward, concurrently, some more theoretical process devoted to appraisal and improvement. The total process, then, is circular: we have language experiences, which provide occasions and motivations for study about language, and this study in turn enables us to have better language experiences.[5]

In *Education: A Collection of Essays on Canadian Education*, M.F. Stewart observed that, while no one had ever proved that there was a significant relationship between grammatical knowledge and competence in speaking and writing, a considerable effort was still being devoted to the teaching of grammar, whether called formal, functional, practical, or something else.[6] Although he had no sympathy for the "grade-by-grade Latino-English treadmill of unrealistic grammatical identification exercises," he saw a place for the new grammar. If students were shown the true simplicity of basic English sentence patterns and given a great deal of pattern practice or sentence building, he thought it possible that a relationship between grammatical knowledge and speaking and writing might be established. Apart from such practical results, Stewart felt that it was desirable for students to be aware of something of the best that was known about their native tongue.

Official attitude with respect to the importance of English

Courses of study issued for use in the secondary schools during the 1950s declared that English was vital to the general development of all students and was thus the direct concern of every teacher. In many schools, teachers of various courses were urged to identify errors in usage, grammar, and spelling in exercises and on examination papers and to penalize students for these in assigning marks. Such exhortations were often ignored, with the result that certain students employed something close to two different writing styles, a fairly meticulous one for the English teacher and his allies, if any, and a more casual one for those who did not care.

A memorandum issued by the Superintendent of Secondary Education in 1957 asserted that "English is without doubt the most important subject of the curriculum, and English expression – written and oral – the most obvious indication of the calibre of a secondary school pupil's education."[7] Various curriculum circulars were quoted to support the point: the course was intended to cover five full years beginning with grade 9; English was the only subject specifically required for the Ontario Secondary School Graduation Diploma; and it was one of the two obligatory courses in grade 13. The memorandum was issued because of departmental displeasure over the incidence of grade 12 students writing the grade 13 departmental examination in English composition. While they usually did so as private study candidates, it was evident that they sometimes had the approval of the school authorities. The department's objection was based on the immaturity of thought and expression and the inadequacy of preparation revealed by many candidates. The latter were warned that there might be undesirable consequences in the university or in employment if they failed to give the subject adequate attention.[8]

Studies in the 1960s

The English Study Committee of the Joint Committee of the Toronto Board of Education and the University of Toronto expressed the need for a synthesis of the whole field of English studies. It declared that the study of literature, of the structure of the language, of words and their associations, and of the art of composition were all aspects of the whole. In practice, however, these aspects often received fragmentary treatment without controlling principle. Confusion and diffusion were attributed to the difficulty of defining the scope of the subject.[9]

There was also criticism of the lack of co-ordination through different levels of the educational system.

> Teachers of the early grades do not always realize to what extent they lay the foundations for all future work with language. Teachers of the intermediate grades do not always consider to what extent the work that they do is contributing to a disciplined intelligence. Teachers of the senior grades of secondary schools do not understand how reading has been taught, often fail to acknowledge what has been achieved in the development of language, and sometimes forget to preserve the delight of reading in the emphasis on intensive study of the writer's art. University professors who make general judgments of teaching in the schools on the basis of experience with poorly prepared students do not recognize what their part has been in equipping the teachers, or how harsh judgments may affect the supply of able candidates for the teaching profession.[10]

In attempting to specify the purposes of instruction in literature, the committee faced the impossibility of formulating a definition that was universally acceptable. It declared, however, that there were areas of fairly general agreement about the nature and functions of such instruction: literature provided continuity and tradition in culture, gave form to what might otherwise be transitory insights into the nature of man and human life, stimulated the imagination, provided material for fruitful reflection, and took the reader beyond himself and made him aware of the infinite variety as well as the common heritage of humanity. Venturing on a tentative definition of literature, the committee produced the following: "The arrangement of language in significant and appropriate patterns, providing through imagination and reflection an additional dimension to the actual experience of living."[11] The purpose of an instructional program would be to realize the potentialities indicated in this definition.

The committee took a firm position in the controversy over the appropriate kind of material for use in teaching children to read. It disapproved of artificial simplicity of presentation and of controlled vocabulary. It declared that what was assumed to be simplicity was often deceptive. An adapted version of a passage might contain illogical quirks of the language that could baffle and mislead the child. The kind of control that was frequently exercised over vocabulary was said to have a highly doubtful psychological and linguistic justification. It was thought desirable to introduce the young child to myths, fairly tales, legends, and Bible stories which Northrop Frye in his introduction to *Design for Learning,* where the committee's report appeared, identified as central to our imaginative heritage. All the child needed to do to comprehend these was to listen to the story. Frye declared that this was not a passive response but a kind of imaginative basic training. The child would have planted in his mind both a sense of the structure of story-telling and a potential critical standard as well.

To describe the transition from the junior to the intermediate grades, the committee drew on analogies from Whitehead and Piaget respectively. The change was said to correspond roughly to the advance from the age of romance to the age of precision, and from the stage of concrete operations to that of formal operations. The enjoyment of the earlier period was not to be abandoned, but the "joy of freedom in play" was to be combined with the satisfaction of achievement through disciplined effort.

> The extension of his own experience through literature gives a child both pleasure and increased knowledge. It shows him new patterns of behaviour and broadens the base for his standards of judgment. It can stimulate or relax him, set his curiosity and imagination racing along new and exciting paths or let him simply sit and absorb with delight the sights and sounds portrayed by the writer. It is, if the opportunity is provided, the most important influence in his intellectual development; it gives him a chance to stop and think about what he has read, to see problems and work out solutions, to observe relationships which he had never before suspected, to contemplate as himself and yet out of himself, because he is freed from the compelling pressures of his immediate environment.[12]

As time went on, the pupil would acquire through wide reading an awareness of the different forms and recurrent themes that constituted the basic principles of structure in literature. The committee recommended that he then be taught more about these forms and about the ways in which form and content were related. He would derive increasing benefit from the technique of discussion, which involved "the combining and sifting of different impressions and interpretations leading toward fuller understanding and appreciation." A special warning was issued, however, against encouraging the pupils to engage in superficial discussions about matters that were far beyond their comprehension.

Existing practice in secondary schools was criticized because of the tendency to fragment literature into a series of individual books and poems. The committee urged that the basic themes of literature be used as a framework so that the student could observe how they were treated by different writers in different literary genres and at different periods of history. Experiments in teaching methodology might include large group instruction, individual reading and research, the correlation of studies in literature and composition through essay writing on relevant topics, and the reading and discussion of such essays in small groups.

As a means of re-establishing the synthesis among the different aspects of English study that were assumed to have existed at one time, the committee recommended careful planning and rearrangement of content for the sake of emphasis and coherence. Books might be displayed in the room where writing was practised and discussed. The examination of models and the occasional imitation of their forms were identified as integrating influences. Further study, demonstration, and experiment were recommended as means of making the relationship between language study and writing more rewarding.

The committee recognized a consensus that learning to write well was a major objective of English study. It found, however, that there was a great deal of confusion and controversy about what should be taught, at what stages, and by what methods. One problem was the lack of accepted criteria for the good writers who were supposed to emerge from the system. Some teachers allowed interesting content and freshness in observation to compensate for grammatical errors. Others encouraged a "correct" but pedestrian treatment of a subject. Still others looked for "a combination of significant content and conscious graces of style." There was uncertainty about the balance to be expected between content and style at different stages.

The schools were said to be under attack for a serious failure on the part of their graduates to be able to write completed prose with significant content, with the thought clearly developed, and without serious errors. Although the committee was hesitant about placing its unequivocal support behind the verdict that standards were declining, it was willing to concede that young people were casual about "the basic good manners of language observances." Adults were also castigated on the grounds that much of their writing was "diffuse and pretentious, vague in meaning and graceless in style." The cure for bad writing had to be sought at all stages and not only in the school. The committee did not suggest any specific course of action for effecting an improvement in the general level of expression, apart from better teaching.

Much of the confusion about teaching composition was attributed to failure to recognize the different kinds of writing.

> The motives that prompt a writer are varied: a wish or need to record or convey information, or the results of accumulated knowledge; an urge to capture some aspect of experience; a desire to release a compelling idea or emotion; a consciousness that some fragment or combination of life's many facets may be given artistic shape. The motive is often utilitarian, in business, for instance, and in much of the compiling, recording, and interpreting of information required in the process of education. Sometimes writing is in the nature of discovery, the writer finding himself as he puts into words his responses to life. For a few, writing is a form of possession, the writer driven as much as driving, loving his art and yet pursued by it, excited by the creative impulse, yet requiring of himself the most strenuous kind of discipline.[13]

Despite this great variety of motives, all kinds of writing had a great deal in common: an idea or impulse, the selection of material, form, or shape, and a choice and arrangement of words. They all required much practice to fuse the ingredients into a smooth pattern. The committee thought that most writers could develop competence and good craftsmanship in some kinds of writing, and that a few could achieve artistry in one or more forms. There seemed to be a case for attempting even those forms in which excellence was rare. An "occasional daring experiment" might prove to be a valuable experience.

Not surprisingly, the committee strongly supported the point of view expounded in departmental memoranda that, while the principles and techniques of writing had to be taught in the English classroom, practice should be carried into other classrooms. Teachers of every subject would have to accept a responsibility for the expository forms of language if students were to develop adequate skills. Assuming that this proposition was self-evident, the committee urged that teachers of English and of other subjects come together to devise means of reinforcing teaching and learning.

The committee found it necessary to take a swipe at the term "creative writing" on the grounds that it was an ill-defined term suggesting inadvisable approaches. There was everything to be said for trying to capture the directness and freshness of children's responses to experience, and a great deal had been done to achieve this objective. In certain instances, however, the expression had been equated with an unrestricted and formless flow of words. Teachers with limited imagination had reacted by over-emphasizing a "practical" approach.

> To keep alive the sense of wonder, to encourage the keen observation that sees the world afresh, and to find significance and pattern in commonplace or fantastic experiences are admirable aims that are being reflected in present-day text-books. So, too, is the development of thought through training in the accumulation of evidence, the setting of facts in order, and the drawing of conclusions. To maintain this balance in writing is a major problem for teachers of English.[14]

Among the activities that the committee believed should be recognized as intrinsic parts of formal language teaching were the development of reading skills, the teaching of spelling, word-building, the teaching of meaning (semantics), the use of the dictionary (lexicography), the sounds of English (phonetics and phonology), and grammar. Advances in linguistic theory were seen as aids to the discovery of more effective and economical ways of handling these aspects of the language program. A need was recognized for further study of some of the possible applications of linguistic knowledge to the teaching of English.

The committee recognized the claim of linguists that speech was fundamental to any kind of language analysis, and that it had to have primary consideration in any attempt to understand the differences between speech and writing. The committee agreed that a formal study of the two aspects, rather than the existing tendency to emphasize the latter and forget the former, would enrich and improve the program of language study. In illustrating the point, it stressed the value of a knowledge of the prosodic system, involving pitch, stress, and juncture in spoken English as a means of understanding why certain kinds of structures were clear and suitable in speech but led to confusion and ambiguity in writing. A knowledge of such features of speech would have a beneficial influence on the student's appreciation of poetry, dramatic literature, and prose.

Experimentation was recommended in several areas to determine how new knowledge about language and new instructional approaches could be incorporated in the English program. 1 / Teachers and linguists might co-operate to produce a school text, which might take account of the latters' insistence that language be approached as a totality and that it be described in terms of pattern and form. The committee expressed the optimistic view that there was no essential conflict between the modernists and the traditionalists, since both insisted on the formal study of grammar and both were committed to analysing and describing the language. 2 / The contemporary linguist, psychologist, and anthropologist might contribute to the refinement of teaching in the area of semantics, which had become so important with the increasing uses of the languages of advertising and public relations. Topics of vital concern to the student included how meaning was structured, how words changed meaning, and how changes in context changed meaning. The future citizen needed to acquire the means of protection against the misuse of language for manipulative purposes in politics, news transmission, and business activities. 3 / Investigation was needed to determine how to transfer the logic learned in the mathematics department to the study of language and literature.

What the committee defined as grammar was to be introduced into the school program at a very early stage. At the beginning, it might have to do with the dominant speech patterns which a child developed. In the later elementary school grades, it might involve the recognition of word classes which had concrete manifestations in structure such as the inflection of nouns and verbs for number. In the high school, it might deal with the abstract patterns of language, devices of subordination, government, concord, and the like. The study of semantics, like grammar, would begin unconsciously at a very early age.

Changes effected with the introduction of the Reorganized Program

The introduction of the Reorganized Program in 1962 gave a strong impetus to curriculum reforms in English as well as in other subjects. There was great pressure to devise new courses as the first class proceeded from one grade to another. Courses for grades 11, 12, and 13 for both the four-year and five-year programs were published in 1964. For Bascom St John, the most impressive aspect of the basic literature course was the attempt to swing the emphasis away from analysis and toward understanding and appreciation.[15] An increased amount of independent reading was prescribed, with provision for discussion in class. The hope was expressed that the students would gain a better understanding of the relationship between literature and human affairs. The basic dependence on books was to be supplemented by the use of recordings and other audio-visual aids. Students were also to be encouraged to read literary criticism.

The course for the five-year program in grade 11 included a Shakespearean play not previously studied, a modern play chosen from a long list, a longer poem and shorter ones, and in the area of prose, novels and essays. A great many of the suggested items were of extremely recent origin. The course for grade 12 in the same period was quite similar, although there was more emphasis on poetry.

The basic course for the four-year program suggested the development of discrimination in mass media through a study of magazines, periodicals, and newspapers, through dramatic performances, and through the viewing of television programs. In addition to the basic course there were three new ones that might be taken as options: Modern Literature, Theatre Arts, and Speech Arts. The first of these could be chosen in grade 11 or grade 12, or both. In the first part, students had the opportunity to compare techniques, characterization, and purpose in plays for stage and television. There was provision for the study of novels under a variety of headings such as adventure, science and fantasy, history, the sea, and mystery and imagination. At the teacher's option, autobiography, travel, and other types of contemporary literature might be included. The course in Theatre Arts emphasized performance, character study, voice training, and various aspects of production, rather than content as such. The course in Speech Arts dealt with voice production, conversation, vocabulary, speech habits, clear thinking and intelligent listening, logic, identifying propaganda, public speaking, conducting meetings, speaking on radio and television, and interpretive reading.

In 1966 an Advisory Consultative Committee on English in the four-year program was set up

(a) to examine the present English courses in the Four-Year Program, Grades 9 to 12, and assess their effectiveness in the light of
(i) new commercial, technological, industrial, and cultural developments;
(ii) opportunities for employment or further study open to graduates of the courses, and
(iii) the students' appreciation and enjoyment of English language and literature in our social and aesthetic context;
(b) to consider the implications for Four-year English courses of possible transfers within a school from the Four to Five-Year Programs, and the reverse;
(c) to request, receive, and study proposals for improving the present courses;

(d) to recommend either changes in the present courses, or new outlines of courses which, in the Committee's judgment, would better meet the needs of students in the Four-Year Program.[16]

The committee proceeded in a way that would have seemed strange a few years earlier by inviting teachers, department heads, principals, supervisory officials, and other interested people and organizations to submit written proposals for improving the courses.

As a result of its investigation, the committee recommended that the four-year English program should have its own unique character (as it was already supposed to have), and that it contribute to an education that would have meaning for young people in relation to modern cultural, industrial, business, and commercial life. It should offer "a significant, valid, and attractive" program of studies for students whose major interests lay elsewhere. It should "expand and balance the students' experience of life through language, literature, films, and other media," as well as preparing them to earn a living.

In the committee's judgment, the success of the four-year program depended more on the imaginative and sympathetic character of the teaching than did that of the five-year program. The committee therefore recommended that teachers be specially selected and prepared for four-year work. While concerned, experienced teachers were said to have the best prospects of success, alert young teachers were considered capable of performing effectively. The special preparation required might be given by the colleges of education and by in-servince training.

It was said that the aptitudes, aspirations, and special attitudes of four-year students, as individuals or in groups, demanded recognition and should form the basis for decisions on the content and presentation of the courses. At the senior level, a class or grade might establish a steering committee, which would have to justify its ideas and suggestions before the whole group. Participation in planning would presumably increase interest and help to meet the problem of student apathy.

It was suggested that the English program be renamed English Language Arts. It was considered desirable to relate the subject to other studies, an objective that was to be attained in part by encouraging students to read and study well-written works from the fields of science, history, geography, and other subjects. The program was to be characterized by electives, including topics from 1 / mass media, film appreciation, and the modern novel; 2 / theatre arts, contemporary ideas, and speech arts; 3 / the modern newspaper and linguistic studies; and 4 / modern prose and modern poetry.

The major recommendation with respect to content was that the courses must be "demonstrably relevant to the students' own lives, and represent the substance of English language, literature, and other media of communication and art which are readily available in our society." It was apparently assumed that the realization of this objective did not preclude the selection of poetry, plays, novels, and short stories for their quality as works of art, or the inclusion of works other than those belonging to the modern period. Prescriptive grammar was to be taught only as a means of understanding the structure of the language and the relationship between structure and purpose. Other avenues of study considered rewarding included the development of language and its varied components as illustrated in word origins and levels of meaning. The study of the film was recommended in its technical and artistic aspects. Students might also be expected to develop a degree of taste and discrimination in using television and radio. It was suggested that they be given the opportunity of preparing and taking part in programs designed for these media.

On the whole, the report of the committee presented a reasonably enlightened point of view. Nothing of a very novel character was, however, suggested. Unfortunately the document, brief as it was, contained a good many passages lacking any great amount of substance. It is questionable, also, whether a competent teacher would care to place this kind of sentence before a class as an example of effective communication: "The elucidation of a principle of sentence structure should imply the students' composing sentences and paragraphs that exemplify such a structure."

Special problems in the teaching of English

The attainment of aesthetic aims offers characteristic difficulties in an organized school system. Alan Proctor wrote of these in the *Bulletin* of the Ontario Secondary School Teachers' Federation in 1965. He referred to the departmental prescription in the course of study which called on the teacher to arouse a personal response to the emotional and imaginative elements of a writer's work, and responded that

> ... the way to achieve such aims is the creative way, which means activity that is exciting, personal, and richly satisfying, but also unorganized, intuitive, often done at hazard, often blind, often fruitless, in the manner of any creative activity. Thus we shun it: departments of education because they cannot set out courses of study in terms of it, inspectors because they cannot assess the effectiveness of teaching done in accordance with it, school administrators because they cannot produce meaningful sets of marks as a result of it, teachers because the resulting noisy classes can be wearing, the creative energy needed is exhausting, the goal of such lessons is neither easy to see nor readily reached. Thus understandably, but regrettably, we all regiment ourselves, organize our work, impose patterns, and extract from the students results that will fit against those patterns. But we cannot tell in all honesty what good we *really* have done for our students as a result of our planning. The good we occasionally discover in chance conversation comes too often from our accidental or incidental activity. Regimentation belongs properly to the logical, discursive, analytical curriculum subjects; is, in fact, their essence. English is not one of them. Neverthe-

less, we attempt with partial success to regiment technical matters as punctuation, spelling, major and minor errors; then literary modes such as types of essays, dramas, poems; and then even such things as themes, dominant atmospheres, poetic devices. No wonder students every year ask in confusion if the author thought in such categorical fashion.[17]

This passage contains, among other things, the essence of the reason why teachers of English are so often opposed to the use of objective tests to measure any aspect of achievement in the subject. They generally believe that the elements that can be treated in such a way are those of least importance, and that even they tend to be distorted by the process of quantification. Most of the aesthetic goals are necessarily downplayed or lost sight of. Objective testing seems to stand for empty and sterile formalism which, whatever its values for selection, has very little to do with education.

Among other participation problems of the specialist teacher of English in the secondary school is the heavy burden of essay appraisal and marking that must be borne if the students are to have the minimum amount of practice that is generally regarded as necessary for the development of adequate writing skills. The obvious solution, and one that has been accepted in an increasing number of Ontario school systems, is to give the teacher a smaller-than-average number of students. It has also been suggested from time to time that essay reading is an activity that may profitably be assigned to teachers' aides. Many teachers are not highly enthusiastic about this solution, feeling that familiarity with each student's work, including his particular strengths and weaknesses, is an essential part of understanding him and of giving him the kind of help he needs.

MATHEMATICS

General nature of recent changes

As in other places, mathematics teaching in Ontario schools underwent fundamental changes during the 1950s and 1960s. The uninitiated often insisted on assuming that the introduction of the "new" mathematics involved throwing out the old content and replacing it with something entirely different. In fact, the process was one of selecting and teaching some of the key principles of former divisions such as arithmetic, algebra, geometry, and trigonometry and relating as many skills as possible to them. In some cases, these principles were introduced at a much earlier stage than previously. An attempt was made to develop them more rationally and logically and to emphasize understanding at all levels. The process seemed mystifying to many parents and others not in direct contact with what was going on because many old ideas were represented by unfamiliar symbols.

One of the topics introduced at an early stage was that of non-decimal number systems. Among the alternatives studied were the duodecimal and the binary systems, the latter of which was of particular interest because of its application to electronic computers. Stress at all levels was placed on developing an understanding of the concept of number, including the distinction between exact and approximate numbers. Other aspects of the new approach included 1 / an emphasis on measurement, different aspects of which were studied on successive levels of the school program; 2 / an increased use of graphs as a means of developing an understanding of mathematical relationships; 3 / the introduction of sets and set terminology at an early age; and 4 / concentration on the techniques used in solving problems rather than on getting the correct answers.

Major concerns before the revolution in the mathematics program

Some idea of the concerns that were uppermost in the minds of leading teachers before the revolution got under way may be ascertained by reference to the proceedings of the sixth annual conference of the Ontario Association for Curriculum Development held in November 1956. Five topics were dealt with by the group which discussed the teaching of mathematics: 1 / the purpose of mathematics in a general education, 2 / the purpose of arithmetic in a mathematical education, 3 / methods of instruction, 4 / content, and 5 / the question "What price mathematics?" With reference to the first topic, the members of the group concluded that what was important was to develop the child's ability to do creative thinking, by which they meant his ability to discover new relationships for himself. Other objectives were to produce occupational skills and to prepare for more advanced training and for meeting life situations in general. In order to encourage creative thinking, the teacher was advised to give the child opportunities for discovery in real situations as far as feasible. Among other points of agreement were that pupils in grade 1 should begin to understand the real meaning of numbers through the grouping of objects and proceed to deal with abstract forms, that pupils should not begin number work until they were ready for it, that new concepts not be introduced too quickly, that computations be put to practical use, and that pupils be grouped, up to a point, for instructional purposes.

Recognition of the need for change

In 1959 Rev. D.T. Faught of the Department of Mathematics at Assumption University of Windsor appraised the situation in Ontario schools in an article in the *Bulletin* of the Ontario Secondary School Teachers' Federation entitled "Mathematics: Modernize or Stand Pat?" Faught observed that the idea that secondary school mathematics be taught through the use of unifying principles of the subject developed in the twentieth century had caught on in a number of places in the United States several years earlier and was being propounded in other Canadian provinces. While it was obvious that Ontario was not going to take the lead, he wondered whether the province had to be the last. According to Faught, many students and possibly some teachers felt that mathematics had all been discovered and was completely embalmed in the textbook they were using. In reality students knew nothing at the end of a four-year secondary school course that a person living in Greece in 200 BC would not have known. By the end of five years of study, they finally got about as far as 1650. Yet since 1637, when Descartes had had the brilliant idea of combining algebra and geometry, more mathematics had been discovered in each decade than was known in that year.

With a negative answer clearly enough implied, Faught posed a series of questions.

> Are the mathematics teachers of the secondary schools in Ontario best fulfilling their duties towards mathematics and other subjects by holding fast to their long-entrenched curriculum? Is the present curriculum the best tool that we have at our disposal to teach logic and order? Does it challenge our more thoughtful students, or does it lend itself to the habit of memorization?[18]

As Faught explained the situation, the fact that mathematics was continuously growing meant that it could remain manageable only through the introduction of new unifying principles. In algebra, for example, the ideas of a field or a group could systematize and simplify the subject so that, instead of dealing with a variety of rules and situations, the student could arrive at generalizations. In Europe, Faught wrote, algebra was generally approached axiomatically by the early introduction of the associative, commutative, and distributive laws through which it was synthesized. However, in Canada and the United States, the mathematician seemed to embark on a quest for the particular. Turning to Euclidean geometry, Faught pointed out that the earlier view of it as the description of the space in which we live, *a priori* true, with axioms and postulates regarded as self-evident, was destroyed forever with the creation of non-Euclidean geometries around 1830. Yet the teaching of elementary geometry remained entirely unaffected by this complete reversal of earlier views.

Exploring possibilities for making mathematics more relevant to modern life, Faught referred to the recent development of the electronic digital computer. He thought students might be interested in the symbolic logic and the calculus of propositions that had made this invention possible. While these aspects of the discipline had developed very far in the previous twenty years, and their content and literature were extensive, the basic principles were easily grasped. Faught asked: "Could not the student's interest motivate the introduction of logic into our curriculum?" Among other areas of mathematics that he thought worthy of inclusion in the secondary school curriculum were probability, statistics, set theory, induction, matrices, linear programming, and the theory of games.

In an article in the *Toronto Education Quarterly* in 1962, F.G. Robinson identified two main areas of criticism of the traditional mathematics program in the secondary schools: 1 / because the curriculum predated Newton's discovery of the calculus in 1666, the student got a completely false impression of the field of knowledge in which mathematicians were currently engaged, and 2 / the traditional curriculum too often emphasized rote learning while neglecting an understanding of the logical structure of mathematics.[19] Instead of presenting the student with a set of formulas and recipes, the reformers wanted to develop a body of mathematical knowledge by first stating the relevant assumptions and definitions and then applying logical reasoning.

There had been some objections to changes currently being introduced into the curriculum. Certain critics, for example, were opposed to the extensive terminology and symbolism of the "set" approach. They were said to believe that, while esoteric symbolism was useful at advanced levels of mathematics, set terminology was not essential to the development of mathematical ideas in the high school curriculum. There were also questions about the suitability of the axiomatic approach in the most exact sense. While it appeared likely that the bright student would benefit from the emphasis on underlying structure and logic, there was some doubt about the effect on the average or dull student. Psychological research had shown that rote learning sometimes produced a higher degree of efficiency in the academically dull. On the other hand, the value of the product of this kind of learning approach was questionable.

In 1959 W.J. Dunlop, then near the end of his career as minister, expressed cautious approval, mingled with a good deal of obvious bewilderment, of the need for change. After declaring that he did not wish to go into detail, a resolution which he might better have stuck to, he continued:

> There is talk, for instance, about something called the "theory of sets." I am told that in some aspects this involves a completely new approach to numbers from fundamental principles; that it involves a completely new language like "pronumerals" and "inequations", and an entirely different set of symbols; that, while some parts of this theory might be related to work in the primary grades and a good deal of it might be comprehensible to secondary school students, the underlying theory of it is revealed only to the advanced mathematician.
>
> That sounds like something that needs consideration, and careful trial to see whether it can be and should be pushed into a curriculum which many claim is already overcrowded.[20]

Initiatives leading to reform

The Ontario Teachers' Federation had by this time become sufficiently concerned about the lack of official interest that it seized the initiative through its Committee on Mathematics and Science. The latter recommended the formation of a commission, to consist of outstanding secondary school mathematics teachers, representatives from the universities, including the Ontario College of Education, observers from the elementary field, and representatives of the Department of Education. The achievements of the Mathematics Commission were a considerable source of pride for the organized teaching profession in subsequent years.

A very important early event in the development of this body was a workshop of a week's duration held at the Lakefield Preparatory School in 1959 under the joint sponsorship of the OTF and the Canadian Mathematical Congress, with D.T. Faught and A.J. Coleman as co-chairmen. Consideration was given to a proposed course prepared for grade 9 by D. Mumford. This course, emphasizing set terminology and the study of number systems, was tried out in certain schools in 1959–60 with the approval of the Department of Education. The effects of the workshop discussions on the program for more advanced grades in the secondary school were less immediate.

Introduction of new courses in the school system

New courses were gradually extended through the elementary school. In its annual report for 1962–3, for example, the Toronto Board of Education recorded that all the grade 7 classes in four schools were taking experimental courses. A regular in-service training program had also been held for the fifteen teachers involved in the work. There were plans to extend the program to ten schools and two thousand pupils in 1963–4. Different ideas were to be tested in different schools before changes were incorporated in courses of study for the entire system.

Early in 1963 a departmental curriculum committee was formed to produce new courses of study in mathematics for the intermediate division. By the beginning of 1964 a course for grade 7 was being distributed, and the material for the other grades was being developed. Principals were given the option of introducing the new course or of waiting until a later date. The department was making efforts to prepare teachers to make the necessary adjustment by offering summer courses and by assisting local inspectors and the Ontario Teachers' Federation to offer appropriate short courses. Several publishers were in the process of preparing appropriate textbooks. By 1964–5, 75 per cent of all grade 7 pupils in the province were reported to be using the new course and by 1965–6, 96 per cent.

At the same time that new approaches were being introduced in the intermediate division, some schools were offering a revised arithmetic program in the early grades. The Ottawa public schools, for example, reported the use of such a program in all grade 1 classes in 1963–4 and its extension into grade 2 the following year. In grades 3 to 6 some teachers were at the same time encouraged to experiment with new methods. Favourable reactions were expressed generally by teachers, and pupils were said to be understanding the underlying principles of mathematics as they never had before.

The Department of Education was kept busy devising and revising courses for each level as developments at other levels prevented the parts of the program from fitting together. In June 1965 the Senior Division Mathematics Curriculum Committee completed new courses for grades 11, 12, and 13 of the five-year program, while the Intermediate Division Committee followed suit a year later. Since the grade 11 course was designed to follow the traditional course for grade 10, and the new approach involved the earlier introduction of certain topics, a further reorganization of the courses for grades 11 and 12 became necessary. The response of the department was to set up the Grade 11 and 12 Five-Year Mathematics Curriculum Committee. The process of keeping up with changes in the mathematics curriculum promised to be extremely challenging.

Mathematics committees of the Ontario Curriculum Institute

The report of the Committee Considering the Mathematics Programme (K to 6) of the Ontario Curriculum Institute offered a set of principles for the preparation of a suitable program.

> Any mathematics curriculum suggested to-day must be prepared from all that is known in mathematics to the present time. The fact that certain topics were taught in the past is not sufficient justification for teaching them now; nor is it essential to have children follow the same path as that followed in the history of mathematics. The topics suggested must fit the overall picture of mathematics, they must suit the maturity of the child, and they must be correlated with the other topics in mathematics as well as other subjects. Every topic, old as well as new, must be carefully examined to see that it is both suitable and worthy to be included at any particular stage in the curriculum.[21]

The committee suggested topics and approaches that might be adopted for various levels between kindergarten and grade 6. Much of what was proposed was tentative, and attention was frequently called to the need for testing. A transitional curriculum would include eleven new basic topics: 1 / sets, involving recognition, matching, joining, and separating, with limited use of notation; 2 / the distinction between number and numeral; 3 / the number line to illustrate operations, with integers included as soon as feasible; 4 / number sentences and placeholders, beginning in grade 1, for use in problem solving; inequalities would be taught along with equalities, and algebraic forms would be developed; 5 / an early awareness of properties without excessive emphasis on nomenclature but with expression in algebraic form as soon as feasible; 6 / aspects of geometry, including the recognition of geometric shapes and their properties and interrelations, the development of concepts of point, line, segment, ray, angle, plane, polygon, and circle, the area of rectangles, and the production of graphs of various types; 7 / the use of ratio and rate to solve problems; 8 / factors and prime numbers; 9 / multiplication and division of fractions, including the identity element and geometric constructions;

10 / expanded notation in place values; 11 / awareness of sequences and symmetries in mathematics. Additional topics were suggested for enrichment: 1 / modular arithmetic; 2 / the history of the numeration system with attention to other bases; 3 / additional topics in geometry such as geometric constructions, scale drawings, curve and surface stitching, symmetries, three-dimensional models, construction and decomposition of polyhedrons and polygons, topological ideas, tiling (concrete), nesting (drawing), vectors, and Platonic solids; 4 / the metric system; 5 / graphs; 6 / mapping; 7 / Venn diagrams; and 8 / co-ordinate systems.[22]

The Committee Considering the Mathematics of the Four-Year Programme assembled a set of ideas and suggestions for an area that merited a good deal of attention in the mid-1960s. For students in this program, it was considered desirable to develop an appreciation of mathematical reasoning. Although a course in formal logic was considered undesirable, the committee thought the students should be able to recognize fallacies and equivalent statements. They might observe the role of assumptions, the power of implications, and the nature of logical equivalence through English sentence, algebraic, and geometric examples. The deductive approach was to be used only when it was helpful. For example, since the properties of signed numbers under multiplication were not intuitively obvious, they were to be derived through deductive reasoning. Generally speaking, while the logic implied in all the mathematics taught was to be stressed, particularly fruitful approaches were to be sought through number structure, ratio and proportion, the algebra of sets, and problem solving. In number structure, students would be expected to see the need for extension from the natural numbers to the integers and the rationals and then to the real and complex numbers for indicated solutions to quadratic equations. In ratio and proportion, they would prove those properties that were necessary for work in similar triangles, business mathematics, and technical mathematics. Geometry would involve an informal discussion of the nature of deductive reasoning and a short sequence of theorems studied deductively, culminating in the Pythagorean theorem. Three-dimensional geometric concepts would be studied wherever possible.[23]

In the area of number and polynomial structure, the committee prescribed what it considered to be reasonable achievement for students at the end of grade 12: 1 / an appreciation of the fundamental properties of the whole number as the basis of the structure of the number system; 2 / an appreciation of the need for irrational numbers growing out of experiences with numbers; 3 / a realization that each irrational number lies between some two real numbers and that the interval may be made "as small as we please"; 4 / the ability to perform the operations with real numbers; 5 / a strong conviction of the one-to-one correspondence between the real numbers and points on a line and ordered pairs of real numbers and points on a plane; 6 / a recognition of the need of a further extension of the number system beyond the reals as encountered in the roots of some quadratic equations or in factors of quadratic expressions; 7 / the concept of variable and the significance of its replacement set; 8 / an appreciation of factoring in algebra as a necessary process incidental to work in mathematics, and as an extension of the distributive property; 9 / the ability to factor simple expressions, including those of fractional form; 10 / an appreciation of the role of the distributive property in operations with polynomials and simple fractional expressions; 11 / the ability to solve graphically as well as algebraically linear and quadratic equations in one and two variables; and 12 / the ability to solve algebraically simple systems of linear equations in more than two variables. The need for practice exercises was recognized, but understanding of the concepts was said to be of prime importance and was not to be obscured by complicated or repetitive drill.[24]

Stress was placed on the idea of relation as a unifying, clarifying, and simplifying idea underlying much of the mathematics at the secondary level. The topic was to be introduced through attention to ordinary experiences with related numbers such as height and weight, age and height, time elapsed and distance travelled, and many others. A discussion of various ways of arranging data could lead to tables, ordered pairs, and graphs. Generalization of the conditions under which ordered pairs are equal might introduce references to the Cartesian co-ordinate system, with some mention of the existence of alternative possibilities. An opportunity for further exploration of the commutative property might be provided. Students might follow a series of steps involving an understanding of the connection between sets of ordered pairs, equations indicating the relationship between the elements of each ordered pair, and the graph of this set, and might proceed to the graphical solution of simultaneous equations. After the limitations of the graphical solutions become evident, an algebraic method might be employed. The committee advocated emphasis on the translation of English sentences into mathematical sentences. It was thought that all students might benefit from exposure to the intersection and union of relations involving inequalities. A good many further suggestions for topics and approaches were offered under the heading of relations.[25]

The committee believed that the study of data should be included in the four-year program both because of the inherent value of the field and because it presented an opportunity to apply arithmetic. The following topics were suggested: 1 / a detailed study of the presentation of data, either in graphical or numerical form, using the ideas of central tendency and dispersion; 2 / an elementary study of the theory of probability based on the intuitive experimental discovery of some results in probability and the initial basic terms and ideas used to discuss probability. The program would be so arranged as to produce a consumer level of competence at the end of grade 10.[26]

In the area of mensuration, pupils at the beginning of the intermediate division would do exploratory work, such as determining the perimeter, area, and volume of common geometric forms and identifying the properties of the square-cube, the rectangular prism, the parallelogram, and the triangle. Grade 8 students would extend this work to include the circumference and area of a circle and the volume of a cylinder. At the high school level, it was suggested that meaningful laboratory methods might be employed to assist the student to discover empirical formulas through test and development techniques. It was thought desirable to stress the free-hand sketching of three-dimensional figures such as the cube, rectangular and triangular prisms, the pyramid, the cylinder, and the cone. Solid geometry might be treated through models and experimental discovery.[27]

Among applications of mathematics to business, the committee thought all students should get a course on interest that was not only an application of mathematical principles but also included a discussion of some of the aspects and implications of interest rates and instalment buying. There would be specific reference to charge accounts, deferred payment accounts, revolving credit accounts, chattel mortgages, real estate mortgages, adjustments for interest accrued, and payment of interest and principal by periodic instalments. Other topics would include the advantages and disadvantages of borrowing from banks, trust companies, loan companies, insurance companies, credit unions, and private individuals, and the significance of such terms as co-signer, assignment of wages, garnishee, due date, and usury. It was said to be particularly important that students in the Business and Commerce Branch study compound interest with specific reference to bonds, annuities, and pensions.

The committee suggested that retailing be dealt with in the light of its relation to the consumer. The student would be made aware of sales and excise taxes, of the taxing authority and the level at which these taxes were levied, and of such terms as cost price, selling price, gross profit, net profit, expenses, mark-up, and cash discounts. In the area of insurance, he would learn how premiums are calculated for car insurance and fire insurance on real and personal property. He would deal with life insurance as an application of probability and statistics. The topic of commissions would include all calculations associated with commissions based on the selling of goods. Deductions from personal income might be studied along with insurance and investment. Under foreign investment, essential topics would be the currency units of countries with which Canada traded, newspaper quotations, calculations of exchange rates, the cost in Canadian dollars of foreign currencies, and foreign currency conversion to Canadian dollars. It was suggested that every grade 12 student should have a knowledge of the different types of securities, newspaper quotations, the calculations required to buy and sell securities including the brokerage commission and transfer taxes, and the determination of yield. The student might gain experience of the income tax by preparing typical income tax returns.[28]

In its references to methodology, the committee showed particular enthusiasm for the discovery method. Among its essential aspects were student interest and initiative, discussion to reveal what the students were thinking and the methods they were using, practical work involving the solution of problems arising from the environment, and computational practice succeeding practical work. It was emphasized that discovery should take different routes to truth. Great value was seen in relating mathematics to other subject areas.

Trends

A.J. Coleman, one of the outstanding leaders in the reform of the school mathematics program, undertook at the end of 1967 to predict curricular trends for the immediate future.[29] He foresaw six main developments. 1 / There would be a shift of emphasis from the teaching of mathematical facts to the more difficult task of developing an understanding of mathematical ideas. It would be necessary to use various materials and devices such as loop films, Cuisenaire rods, models of the number line, and the construction of Möbius strips and regular geometrical figures to lead the learner from concrete experience to abstraction. 2 / Within five or ten years, the idea of a group or a mathematical system would be commonplace in grade 6. 3 / In order to avoid frustrating and discouraging the slow learner and, even worse, deadening the curiosity and imagination of the able student, more flexible patterns of organization would permit each student to develop at his own pace. 4 / The main pressure for mathematics reform would come, not from mathematicians, but from the needs of society. 5 / Within a few years the "glittery attraction" of the computer would fade to leave "the substantial valid insight that the teaching of many parts of mathematics should be aimed toward the achievement of an explicit computable algorithm." 6 / Methods of training teachers and their roles would change.

SCIENCE

The direction of recent changes

The new approaches to science curriculum during the 1950s and the 1960s were to a large extent determined by the realization that content grew and changed so quickly that attempts to keep up with it were futile. The only way a student could be prepared to cope with it was to learn to think scientifically. As Wilbur Schramm wrote,

> ... what the scientists want to do with public school students is to teach them the thought patterns of mathematicians and scientists. They are not to be taught laws and theorems and relationships; they are to be taught how to *generate* and *discover* laws, theorems, and meaningful relationships. There is a neat distinction, in the vocabulary of these scientists, between what is *meaningful* and

what is *useful.* Specific laws or formulas are useful in a transient way; but the ability to think in a highly generalized way, to perceive the interconnectedness of ideas, to be able to generate new laws and relate new observations to each other, is *meaningful.* In other words, what is important in science teaching is not the products of the science, but rather its *tools.*[30]

The reform movement in science teaching got under way in the United States some years before it overflowed into Canada. Much of the impulse came from a consciousness of external threats as exemplified by the Berlin blockade and the Korean War. The Russian achievement in launching the first earth satellite jarred Americans into a new burst of creative scientific activity, although that event has been singled out so often as a turning point that one suspects that its importance is considerably exaggerated. Experiments in new science curricula attracted more financial support than any previous movement of that type in the history of education. Assistance came from various government departments, from foundations and other forms of private beneficence, from associations, and from universities. Some of the same agencies and their counterparts offered a certain amount of help in Canada, although on a comparatively minor scale. There was not enough sustained interest even to maintain a relatively modest enterprise such as the Ontario Curriculum Institute.

The Science Committee of the Ontario Curriculum Institute appraised the difficulties in bringing about genuine curricular reforms.

What is not always recognized is that the pursuit is often long (six years of writing and testing to produce the Chemical Bond Approach textbook, for instance); expensive (the National Science Foundation put about $1.3 million into the Chemical Bond Approach Project); difficult to introduce (not only must teachers be retrained, but extra preparation time is often needed for the new lessons, and this time is not always readily found); and productive of ambiguous results when the new programs are evaluated by conventional yardsticks.[31]

There seemed little likelihood that many communities would wish to invest the necessary funds to make significant efforts in science education. Because of the high development costs, only a limited number of national programs appeared to be in prospect.

In *Compulsory Mis-Education*, Paul Goodman observed that the National Science Foundation was offering more than half a dozen plausible reasons for teaching science as a major part of popular education, and proceeded to examine each one. Six of these are of particular interest.[32]

1 / It might be an aspect of the pre-training of technicians. Goodman did not consider this objective a valid one for general schooling because the highly specialized training required by certain technicians applied to only a small minority. On the other hand, many of the middle technical

skills were likely to vanish and semi-skilled technicians would require less rather than more training. He thought the ultimate employer should be responsible for various kinds of apprenticeship training.

2 / Science teachers might attempt to produce original, creative scientists. Goodman thought this idea pretentious and naïve, particularly because no one knew how the process occurred. Some thought the proper approach was the one that Dewey had prescribed for teaching any subject: "encouraging spontaneity, imagination, courage to guess; avoiding 'correct' answers and rejecting all grading and competition; maintaining continuity with emotional and day-to-day experience and having each youngster follow his own path."[33] There seemed to be little evidence, however, that these approaches were being followed. Nor had Dewey held out any promise that they would lead to a high order of creative invention.

3 / Science teaching for its own sake had considerable appeal. In this sense, the subject was to be considered as one of the humanities. Among the fundamental concepts that might be included in the handling of science from this point of view were interaction, physical system, relativity of motion, equilibrium, energy, force, entropy, and organic evolution. But Goodman observed a problem.

> Yet once we push these fundamental concepts beyond the stage of philosophical discussion, there arises a dilemma in the nature of the present state of science. It used to be that the chief excitement of science, which is the exploration and discovery of the nature of things, was easy to keep in the foreground; systematic theory was not too far from observation and experiment. Now, however, observation and experiment occur in a vast framework of systematic explanation, and ... it must be hard to convey the excitement of discovering the truth without what almost amounts to a specialist training. To get to this excitement of actual exploration requires spelling out the fundamental concepts very far; yet without this excitement, the unique contribution of science to the humanities is lost.[34]

He thought the purpose of conveying the wonders of exploring and explaining nature might, however, be moderately well served by dealing with the history of classical experiments, by repeating some of the demonstrations that scientists such as Helmholtz and Huxley once conducted, or by having students explore various natural and technical phenomena.

4 / Science might to taught to produce an appreciation of the scientific ethic – "its austere morality, accuracy, scrupulous respect for what occurs." Goodman found this objective, for the majority, almost incompatible with the acquisition of content. In a rush to cover the prescribed ground, teachers habitually condoned inexact, careless work. While the average student might acquire a system of ideas and explanations, he missed the real essence of science.

5 / Comprehension of the world one lives and works in was a purpose

that Goodman found highly acceptable. To achieve it, he advocated the study of relatively simple scientific applications.

6 / He also approved of the need to prepare people to participate in important political decisions on scientific matters. It was desirable that they should have some capacity for appraising research programs and for distinguishing between "phony cover-ups" and honest failures. If superstitions relating to science could be overcome, more rational decisions might be expected.

Early practices

In the schools of the nineteenth century, science was often referred to as natural philosophy and consisted chiefly of physics and chemistry. It was supposed to have transfer value, improving the powers of observation and developing the reflective faculty. An applied field which received early attention was the science of agriculture, a subject in which instruction was offered at the Toronto Normal School in 1847. In subsequent years, considerable efforts were made to have it taught in the common schools. In due course, textbooks were prepared and courses of study issued in both elementary and secondary schools.

According to later critics, the approach to science teaching suffered from many of the defects of teaching in general. There was too much stress on memorization and rote learning of abstract principles and too much emphasis on textbooks once these came into production. The necessity of covering a large body of content often resulted in a neglect of demonstration and experimentation. The latter term was used to describe the process by which a student followed a series of previously formulated steps to reach a foregone conclusion, as opposed to the kind of experimentation done by a real scientist in the search for new truth. Although the latter process, or anything closely approximating it, may have been out of reach of most students, there was little evidence of awareness that the learner should have an opportunity to gain insight into the joys of discovery. The legacy of those days is, indeed, far from having been dispelled. Many a student yet fails to perceive any real difference between writing up the results of an experiment according to a standardized ritual after having gone through the prescribed steps and copying the write-up of a more industrious neighbour. In terms of learning about science or acquiring a scientific attitude, it may well be doubted that there is any important difference.

Courses of study issued by the Department of Education in 1936 for different science subjects in the secondary schools emphasized the teacher's responsibility for laboratory work and for providing opportunities for observation, where appropriate, under natural conditions. The course in botany prescribed field excursions on suitable occasions. The students were to be given opportunities to engage in independent work, and a "fair proportion" of class time was to be devoted to a discussion of the results. In zoology, laboratory work involving simple morphological studies of common forms of animal life was to be preceded or supplemented by observation of living specimens. There was to be provision for suitable aquariums and vivariums where the moving, breathing, and feeding of living animals might be within view of the students. The latter were to be encouraged to collect insect larvae and to observe the stages of their development. It was emphasized that morphological studies were not to end in the study of form, but were to involve a constant effort to interpret the meaning of the form and to observe the relationship between form and function. A number of topics were suggested for general reading and discussion: the humane treatment of domestic animals, the conservation of wild animal life, destructive mammals, the relationship between plants and insects, the interdependence of the plant and animal kingdoms, and farming and fur-bearing animals. According to the prescription for physiography, notebooks were to contain records of experiments, drawings of apparatus, and observations and conclusions based on experiments and practical studies. Teachers were warned against insisting on too elaborate notes and on dictating notes.

Most of these suggestions were well designed to emphasize that the interest of the students should be aroused and maintained and that they would have plenty of experience with real phenomena. There was little evidence in the course outlines, however, that the curriculum-makers were interested in developing an understanding of the process of scientific discovery. At least, it was hard to see how the prescribed activities would in themselves help to further the attainment of that goal.

Attitudes and practices in the 1950s

At the sixth annual conference of the Ontario Association for Curriculum Development in 1956, the group which discussed "Improving the Teaching of Science (Grades VII to XIII)" produced ten aims for teaching the subject:

1. To develop the student's powers of reflective and logical thinking and to clear expression.
2. To develop a naturally inquiring mind throughout with an interest in things observed.
3. To develop powers of accurate observation and recording.
4. To show that there is pleasure in achievement and responsibility in this world.
5. To aid the student to maintain good physical and mental health by using scientific knowledge and understanding.
6. To help the student earn a good living.
7. To provide more scientists to assist our country in maintaining its position in the world.
8. To give the student an appreciation of the magnitude of the universe and what lies beyond.

9. To maintain and develop the interest the child has for things around him.
10. To give the student a respect for good citizenship (e.g., the scientists who work for the good of mankind and their country).[35]

The record of the discussion which took place gives no indication that the participants seriously questioned any of the current ideas about how these objectives were to be attained. They held the elementary school teacher responsible for covering a large amount of work, favoured maintaining some examination pressure all through school as a means of preparing students to face examinations at the higher levels, advocated having elementary school pupils make notes from blackboard outlines leading to the ability at a later stage to rely simply on a title or heading. The group considered the issue of demonstrations versus student experiments and concluded that, while experiments were desirable where time and facilities permitted, there was no need to apologize for demonstrations.

Contributions of the Science Study Committee of the Joint Committee of the Toronto Board of Education and the University of Toronto

The Science Study Committee of the Joint Committee of the Toronto Board of Education and the University of Toronto conducted a critical review of the official courses of study at different levels. The course for the elementary grades had a number of statements of purpose that were judged to be inadequate or even inappropriate. One of these indicated that the course should involve a study of the more salient features of plant and animal life – as far as possible in their natural setting. This study was defined as strictly elementary in scope and yet was to be conducted in a genuinely scientific spirit. While agreeing that the scientific study of nature involved the observation of life in its natural setting, the committee called attention to the importance of removing creatures or specimens from this setting and studying them under controlled conditions. A further purpose mentioned in the course of study was to initiate the children into "the romance and wonder of science." To this statement the committee gave cautious approval provided that it did not mean that children were encouraged to think of natural phenomena as inexplicable or mysterious.

An objection of some substance was raised about the expectation that, by observation, experiment, and inference, children would "learn much that will help to make richer and more significant their experience as children in a world governed by natural laws"; yet they were to be specifically exempted from the obligation of amassing an ordered body of scientific information. The committee pointed out that the gathering of ordered bodies of information was a major aspect of science as well as being the first step in the formation of valid generalizations about nature. It seemed improbable that unordered observation would kindle an abiding interest in science or lay the foundation for future systematic study. In the committee's view: "The discovery of order leads to the assimilation of knowledge and encourages further observation, continued search for order, and the utilization of known order as a basis for prediction."[36]

In dismissing the home or the school in favour of the "unroofed country" as the child's laboratory, where he would find things that appealed to his "primitive instincts," the course of study seemed to equate the study of elementary science with a return to a state of semi-savagery. The committee pointed out rather soberly that the objective, scientific study of nature was an activity that appealed, not to man's primitive instincts, but rather to his unique intellectual faculties. A primary aim of the science course should be to develop these faculties.

There were two statements of purpose that the committee found contradictory. One indicated that the course was expected to enhance the children's natural desire to get to know the world around them and to find an explanation for its phenomena, and the other declared that the aim was not so much to explain phenomena as to awaken the children's interest in them and to develop their powers of accurate observation and description. While it agreed that accurate observation was important, the committee declared that it was equally important to teach children to recognize what kinds of questions or problems could be investigated within the province of science, what methods were appropriate, and what kinds of solutions or explanations were acceptable.

Somewhat contradictory also was the injunction against introducing anything in the nature of a formal study of any particular branch of science while at the same time encouraging each child to follow his natural bent, to explore his favourite field, and thus to develop a genuine interest in, and perhaps a thorough understanding of, some phase of science. The committee understandably failed to see how a child could be expected to gain a thorough understanding of some phase of science unless a certain amount of formal study were undertaken.

An attempt to understand what happens in classrooms by studying the stated purposes in a course of study is always a very risky enterprise, as the committee quite definitely acknowledged. Its suspicions of the soundness of the program were, however, supported to considerable extent by the contents of the course itself, in which the same unrelated activities and superficial observations were recommended year after year. The committee based a series of specific criticisms on an examination of this course. 1 / The emphasis was almost entirely on living things, to the practically complete neglect of the physical and chemical nature of the environment. 2 / Many of the proposed activities had little or no scientific value. 3 / Some of the suggested projects could not be carried out as stated: for example, finding out why birds go south in winter and finding out why and how trees get rid of their leaves. 4 / No effort was made to encourage pupils even to begin to recognize those similarities and differences in plant and animal types which formed the basis for proper classification. In short, the defects of the course were that it centred on random observations and excluded any search for order in nature as it was revealed by observation and experimentation. The committee managed to make the course appear to be the work of fuzzy-minded, sentimental admirers of the out-of-doors with a greater propensity for poetry than for objective thought.

An examination of the program for the intermediate division which had been published in 1961 was commended because the emphasis on applications had been reduced and more stress had been placed on the treatment of topics because of their scientific importance. The committee approved of the two expressed aims: to develop an appreciation of the scientific approach to problems, and to enable the students to learn something of the discoveries, content, and problems of as many fields of science as possible. While the first seemed by far the more important there appeared to be some danger that it might be neglected in an excessively zealous pursuit of the second. The committee's view of the proper way to develop an understanding of science was to treat certain fundamental topics thoroughly, to make the basic principles clear, and to show how these principles underlay specific topics in any branch of science. Such an approach called for the removal of much of the material in the existing course.

After dealing with the existing courses at different levels, the committee offered some supplementary suggestions about how curriculum construction in science might be approached. The influence of Jerome Bruner was evident.

> Ideas required early in the study of science cannot be presented fully when first introduced. They should be used again and again whenever they assist in the development of other ideas, and their meaning should be more completely explained as the student's increasing maturity makes this possible. In this way one might hope to build up a core of essential ideas which are retained and used by the student throughout his whole career.[37]

The committee thought the fundamental ideas might be strengthened both by integrating different branches of science and by relating science to such fields as mathematics and social studies. It might be necessary to introduce some simple mathematical concepts in order to help in the development of scientific understanding. Certain advantages might be expected to accrue to mathematics if this approach were used.

The committee was not opposed to the introduction of certain topics purely because of their practical applications. It objected, however, to the inclusion of applications for the sake of interest which depended on principles that were too complex for the students to understand. The treatment of these topics necessarily entailed a superficial discussion of meaningless names and phrases, with a serious risk of developing a completely wrong attitude. "If people are to be able to make reasonable judgments of the validity of information given to them, they must not be exposed in school to inadequate or inaccurate 'explanations' of complex phenomena which they cannot possibly understand but which they must commit to memory and repeat as gospel truths in an examination."[38]

Another type of topic included for the sake of interest which elicited an expression of disapproval from the committee involved a mere repetition of what the students had already learned outside of school. It was suggested that interest be used as a starting point for further work in classifying, ordering, and extending the information previously gathered. By learning to look for order in the phenomena which they were continually observing, students could acquire the basis for a good scientific attitude.

The committee found it necessary to refute the criticism that only the bright student would benefit from the proposed approach and that the average student would be unable to grasp fundamental principles at an early stage. While acknowledging the need for experimental trials to identify the most appropriate level for the introduction of certain topics, the committee suggested that, under existing conditions, the less capable student became lost and was forced to resort to uncomprehending memorization. His salvation might well lie in concentrating on important principles and in dealing with topics chosen to form a coherent system. Although the proposed approach would also benefit the bright student, he usually managed to learn in spite of poor teaching and a poor choice of topics.

Discussion at the Ontario Conference on Education, 1961

A group discussing science education at the Ontario Conference on Education in 1961 recognized some of the weaknesses identified by the Toronto committee. It deplored the lack of a definite core of principles and concepts throughout the existing program of studies, the absence of an adequate philosophy of science education, and the failure to integrate science with topics in other subject areas. Apparently foreseeing no prospect of immediate action by the Department of Education, and demonstrating no awareness of the imminence of steps to establish the Ontario Curriculum Institute, the group recommended that the Ontario Teachers' Federation form a full-time committee to produce an integrated program for grades 1 to 13.

Comparisons with British practice

The universality of problems in science curriculum was demonstrated in *Strategy for Schools*, produced by the Bow Group in England in 1964.[39] With respect to the grammar schools, there were complaints about the rigidity of the tripartite division of physics, chemistry, and biology, with no attention given to scientific topics which fell outside the scope of these three. A few schools were reported to be attempting to integrate the sciences in a general science course offered during the first two years, but the results were dismissed as not very inspiring. In all science teaching, basic principles were obscured under a mass of facts. Chemistry was often taught as a kind of catechism. In biology, there was too little effort made to relate facts through the study of evolution, adaptation to the environment, and behaviour. Physics was "a motley collection of magnets, lenses, and tuning forks about which innumerable facts have to be learned and used as a basis for a multiplicity of problems." Some of the worst defects in the program of the grammar schools had been corrected in the secondary modern schools, where there was more teaching by topic and artificial boundaries between the sciences were less apparent.

The Bow Group offered a prescription for a productive approach to the teaching of science.

> As well as being taught elementary scientific ideas – the nature of air, water or combustion, he should be learning about the scientific issues of the day – of rockets and satellites, of atomic power stations, of oil and its uses. When a child leaves school at sixteen or eighteen he should be able, from his education, to make positive contributions to discussions on the fluoridation of water supplies, survival in space, the principles of a computer and the structure of the atom and the living cell. In our view, this is best done by forgetting completely the formalised approach to science in the first four years of secondary school and by concentrating instead on description and broad principles which will enable a child to understand scientific ideas of the world around him.[40]

The Science Committee of the Ontario Curriculum Institute

The OCI Science Committee, reporting in 1963, took positions that resembled those of its predecessor, the Science Study Committee of the Toronto Joint Committee. It agreed with views expressed on both sides of the Atlantic to the effect that science teaching should be closer to what science really was. It deplored the presentation of the conclusions of inquiry as if they were certain or nearly certain facts and the lack of attention to coherence and organization, which were essential characteristics of scientific knowledge. An appealing idea was that the student in the laboratory should be offered a number of problem situations in which he would have to work out his own solution and interpret the data, rather than verifying that some proposition was true.

The committee preferred to think of what was commonly called the scientific attitude as a number of attitudes. Despite the difficulty of arriving at explicit definitions, it offered a list of four. 1 / The student should develop a facility in analytical, critical thinking, especially that involving logical and quantitative relationships. 2 / He should acquire a readiness to accept different interpretations of the same situation from different sets of facts. 3 / He should realize that scientists often set up conceptual models such as those used to explain atomic structure which are not intended to conform to physical reality. 4 / He should understand that the scientist's approach is mainly either inductive or deductive, although there is a place for intuition or guesswork. He should grasp the importance of the search for cause and effect relationships.

During its discussions, the committee apparently gave a good deal of attention to the advisability of having an integrated science course. It considered the possible use of such unifying themes as man himself, around which the important principles of physics, chemistry, and biology could be developed. The conclusion was reached, however, that there was little advantage up to the intermediate stage in attempting an artificial fusion of the various branches of science, although some merit was seen in presenting modern physics and chemistry as a single subject at the senior level.

The committee identified three aspects of the student's development as he proceeded through his school career: 1 / a shift from teacher-directed to self-directed inquiry, 2 / a shift from a qualitative to a quantitative approach, and 3 / an increasing ability to think about abstract ideas and models as compared with the capacity to think only about concrete objects. What was described as the thread that ran through the complete science curriculum consisted of these items: qualitative classification and descriptions, measurement, the application of measurement to problems and situations, generalization from measurements, postulating theory, deductions from the theory, the use of theory as a unifying factor, and the application of theory outside the boundaries of science.[41]

While expressing its approval of the discovery method, the committee cautioned against reliance on talk about science or scientific attitudes apart from content. It devoted considerable attention to the main structure or principles of certain fields of science and attempted to indicate what the educated person, defined as the grade 12 student, should know. It concentrated on physics, biology, chemistry, and mathematics but did not find time to deal with geology or astronomy.

The principles and facts providing a basic fund of knowledge in physics were listed under four headings: 1 / measurement (kinematics), including measurement of length, time, mass, rotation, and density; measurement of position (frame of reference), linear motion, and rotational motion; the concept and measurement of linear and rotational velocity and acceleration; the concept of independent motion in two directions; equations of motion for constant acceleration; free fall from gravity and trajectories; periodic motion, the pendulum; 2 / mechanical determinism, including the concept of force and the relation of force to motion; Newton's laws; dynamics, momentum, and the conservation of momentum; friction; gravitation, near and remote, with further reference to free fall; mechanical work, energy, and power; conservation of energy; Kepler motion and satellites; 3 / atomic structure of matter and properties of matter, including atoms, molecules, Dalton's law, Avogadro's number; periodic table, nuclei; gases, pressure, the theory of a perfect gas, (Maxwell) distribution of velocities; heat as molecular motion, gas laws, and temperature scales; thermal energy, the work of expansion, and specific heat; conservation of energy (the first law of thermodynamics); changes of phase, freezing, vaporization, and latent heat energy; heat transfer, radiant energy, and thermal expansion of solids; elasticity of solids, Hooke's law, elastic potential energy; motion of weight hung from a coil spring; 4 / atomic structure of matter-electrical, including the electrical structure of the atom, Coulomb's law; ionic and covalent bonding; difference of potential, electrical field, and electrical potential energy; Ohm's law, currents, resistance, and Joulian heat energy; permanent magnets; electromagnetism, magnetic field resulting from a current; force on a charge or current in a magnetic field, induction; radiant energy, radiation of an oscillating dipole; and continuous x-rays, the electromagnetic spectrum.

The committee listed thirteen headings in a proposed outline for the fundamental content of a high school chemistry course: 1 / an introduction, including an indication of the scope of chemistry and its vocabulary, the fundamental concept of mass and energy, and the metric system; 2 / kinetic molecular theory and states of matter; 3 / atomic structure, including types of matter, atoms and molecules, and atomic weights; 4 / the periodic table; 5 / chemical reactions and bonding; 6 / simplified descriptive chemistry of common elements, including writing formulas and equations and simple oxidation and reduction reactions; 7 / chemical calculations, including related operations involving significant figures, experimental errors, and the use of the slide rule; 8 / solution phenomena, including the general behaviour of solutions and the process of solubility; acids, bases, and salts; ionization and the writing of ionic equations; electrochemistry; hydrolysis; and molar and normal solutions; 9 / reaction rates and chemical equilibrium (qualitative presentation); 10 / inorganic chemistry, including the study of selected elements and commercially important industrial chemicals; 11 / organic chemistry, including the nature of covalent bonds, the geometry of organic molecules, isomerism, the simple classification of compounds, and some typical reactions; 12 / technological applications, including metallurgy and conservation of natural resources; and 13 / nuclear chemistry. Laboratory experiences paralleling this content would ensure that the student 1 / became acquainted with the names and uses of common chemical apparatus; 2 / acquired skill in handling and assembling simple apparatus for manipulations involving the gas burner, glass tubing and bends, the preparation and collection of gases, volumetric measurements, and balances weighing to about the nearest centigram; 3 / knowledge of safe practices in the handling of common chemicals and glassware, and 4 / a desire to take proper care of scientific apparatus and respect for delicate scientific equipment.

The suggested content to be covered in a biology course fell under five headings: 1 / the construction and functioning of a living organism on the atomic and molecular level, on the cellular level, and on the organ and organ system level; the trapping, releasing, and handling of energy; the maintenance and regulation of the organism; and the kinds and causes of behaviour; 2 / reproduction, including the genetic copying device, with reference to chromosomes, genes, and DNA; the transmission of characteristics; the development of control of reproduction; and reproduction methods, systems, and cycles; 3 / variations among organisms and the consequences, including the kinds and causes of variation, with attention to recombination and mutation; natural selection and adaptation, and the origin of species; 4 / the kinds of organisms that have come into existence, including one-celled forms, the plant kingdom, and the animal kingdom, as well as the history of life on the earth and its geographical distribution; 5 / the way in which organisms live in their environment, including a description of the environment of air, earth, etc, with attention to its changing and cyclic nature; the interaction between the environment and plants and animals; food chains, energy flow, and food production; symbiosis, parasitism, and the meaning of disease; the rise and fall and succession of populations.

New programs in science

The Ontario Curriculum Institute sponsored summer courses for teachers to introduce experimental approaches to the teaching of science. Following one of these held in Toronto in 1965, the Board of Education provided $1,000 for each of two grade 5 classrooms to purchase balances, lenses, microscopes, chemicals, and test tubes so that each child could conduct individual experiments. According to the method used, the pupils were presented with a problem in science and asked to use their equipment and materials to find the answer. The teacher avoided correcting obvious errors in procedure in order to ensure that the pupils learned from their own mistakes and had an opportunity to realize that the scientist typically explores many avenues to the truth before he finds the right one. Experimental classes of this type were set up in a considerable number of centres.

New ground was broken in the same year when the department introduced a four-year high school program in chemistry with a number of options. During the first half year, the class was to concentrate on a core of basic chemistry and during the second half would deal with three or more options. There was some suggestion that the choice might be more a matter of freedom for the teacher than for the student. Adaptations were made, however, to suit the dominant features of life in various areas of the province. According to the curriculum bulletin describing the course, students in one school might be experimenting with metal plating and those from another might be learning the chemistry of petroleum products.[42] In a large city, they might see how air pollution was measured and in an agricultural area how various elements affected plant growth.

Illustrative of the development of initiative within local school systems was the introduction of a course in human biology in the schools of Hamilton in 1968–9. The course was devised by a curriculum study group which had the co-operation of McMaster University, Mohawk College, local schools of nursing, and other interested groups. Offered as an alternative to the physics course currently being taught in grade 11, it was intended as a preparation for young people considering nursing and other paramedical fields. In granting approval for the introduction of the new course, an official of the Department of Education found it encouraging to see a local authority taking this kind of initiative.

HISTORY, GEOGRAPHY, AND SOCIAL STUDIES

During the nineteenth century, history and geography were taught in such a way that a long-lasting preoccupation with facts became deeply ingrained in Ontario education. The main objectives of history were to tell the story of great men and to instill respect and affection for the great and glorious British Empire. In the lower grades, biographies were used as a source of subject matter. There were textbooks for ancient and British history long before any existed for Canadian history. The Old Testament was taught as authentic history before the influence of Darwin began to be felt.[43] There are many stories of schools where one or more battered maps were the only geography textbooks. The pupils might learn the location of every river, lake, cape, bay, county, town, city and other natural or man-made feature marked thereon.

A considerable part of the twentieth century has been characterized by an ill-co-ordinated collection of Canadian, British, medieval, and modern history courses covering various periods of time and overlapping one another in a most unsatisfactory fashion. Perhaps no area in the curriculum has more urgently demanded a careful look at the whole program to the end of grade 13. One of the greatest achievements of the 1960s was a serious effort at rationalization.

As stated in 1936, just before the famous curriculum reform, the objectives of history teaching in the public and separate schools were to interest the pupil in historical reading, to give him a knowledge of his civil rights and duties, to enable him to appreciate the logical sequence of events, and eventually to give him the power to interpret current conditions in the light of the past. The teacher was enjoined to make historical characters and events vivid and attractive. He was not to confuse the pupil with non-essential facts, nor to require him to memorize ready-made notes. Emphasis was to be placed on "the extent, power, and responsibilities of the British Empire, its contributions to the highest form of civilization, the achievements of its statesmen and its generals." The increasingly important place held by Canada among the overseas dominions was also to be stressed.[44]

The course in geography issued during the same year declared that an attempt should be made to interest the child in his natural surroundings. He was expected to gain a gradual perception of the relationship between human activities on the one hand and climate, natural features and phenomena, natural resources and products, and racial and national characteristics on the other. The early work was to be largely observational, while that in higher forms was to involve the use of more illustrative material such as globes, maps, charts, and pictures. In the secondary schools, physical features, soil, climate, economic conditions, and the national characteristics of the people were to be given special attention. In map work, the emphasis was to be placed, not on the physical divisions of the continents, but on the regions of the world as determined by their physical and economic conditions.

The impetus given to social studies in the 1937 curriculum

One of the most outstanding features of the elementary curriculum revision of 1937 was the attempt to promote the teaching of social studies in preference to an extension into the lower grades of certain disciplines, particularly history and geography, sometimes augmented by civics, a term which has acquired a rather archaic sound. The concept of social studies was not intended to be an ill-blended combination of these specific subjects. It began, rather, with the idea that the child should be given an opportunity to understand something of the physical characteristics of the world around him, of man's place in it, of the nature of human society in its various manifestations – all with reference to the temporal as well as the spatial dimension. The obvious approach was through some topic, theme, or problem. In his search for information and understanding, the pupil would be led into areas that might, for certain purposes, be defined as geography, geology, mineralogy, astronomy, sociology, economics, political science, and others in the realm of the social or natural sciences. There would be no particular concern if he failed to distinguish sharply between these last two categories. The meaningful organization of knowledge which resulted from his quest might be uniquely his own.

A fruitful approach to social studies could hardly be expected to result from teaching that adhered strictly to the textbook. It demanded, rather, a teacher with imagination, self-confidence, and a thorough grounding in a considerable spectrum of human knowledge. Since the high school graduates who were admitted to teaching with one year of preparation lacked some of the essential qualifications, it is hardly surprising that the 1937 program was not implemented with any great success. The project or enterprise method soon degenerated into busy work, and there was a reaction in favour of teaching that would produce evidence of what appeared to be solid achievement.

The curricular reforms undertaken in the intermediate division under the Porter Plan envisaged the development of a course in social studies. Courses of study produced at that time, however, showed a singular lack of imagination in that they described the subject as an integration of history and geography. Grade 9 students were to study Canada and the Americas, and grade 10 students, Canada and the modern world. What happened in many classrooms was that part of the year was spent on history and part on geography.

Reaction against social studies in the 1950s

A good deal of hostility developed toward the social studies program in the 1950s, considerably assisted by W.J. Dunlop. In part it was a reaction against the confusion attendant upon the attempt to introduce the concept without sufficient preparation of the teachers who would have to handle it. The opponents, who were concentrated in the secondary schools, were in search of excellence and respectability, which they thought could best be attained by adhering to the more clearcut traditional disciplines. Specialist teachers in history commonly objected to he prospect of having to develop a whole new approach.

Principals and inspectors were notified in 1958 of a decision of the minister to prepare separate courses in history and geography parallel to that in social studies for the intermediate division. Two new textbooks in British history were now available for examination by teachers. For grade 9, the course covered the period to the end of the reign of Queen Victoria in 1901. Stress was to be placed on those aspects of the story that had the greatest meaning for Canadians, with emphasis on the following themes: 1 / the evolution of the British people, their language and literature; 2 / the growth of parliamentary government, the evolution of the monarchy; 3 / the development of the British idea of justice, liberty, and fair play; 4 / the growth of religious toleration; 5 / the growth and nature of the British Empire; 6 / the progress of science and its effects; and 7 / conditions that led to the migration of British people to Canada, to other parts of the Empire, and to the USA before 1900. The course in geography would parallel that in history, dealing with the British Isles, Africa, Australia, and New Zealand.

Early the following year, it was announced that a two-year course in Canadian history was being prepared for grades 7 and 8, the one for grade 7 to begin with the French period and to end about 1800, and that for grade 8 to cover the nineteenth century, with particular attention to Upper Canada. The history of the local community was to be dealt with in grade 8. Apparently it did not strike anyone as undesirable to bring the story up to 1900 and then to switch to British history the following year. Of course everything was to be linked up in grade 10, which dealt with Canada, Britain, and the United States from 1900 to the present. This course was to be regarded almost as a history of the English-speaking peoples, although particular attention was to be given to Canada. There was also to be a course in government lasting from four to six weeks, which would summarize the growth of government in Canada to its current form and the steps by which the country became self-governing.

Geography was to be kept reasonably parallel to history in grade 7, when it was to deal with Canada including the Arctic, giving particular attention to Ontario and the local community. In grade 8 it was to cover the United States, Central and South America, and the West Indies. In grade 10, parallel treatment was again lost when it dealt with Europe (except the British Isles) and Asia (including the Middle East and Indonesia). Thus the world was carved up according to someone's arbitrary notion of what was important for the pupils to know.

The formation of the Canadian Association for the Social Studies in 1964 resulted from the efforts of a group of educators in western Canada, particularly centred in Alberta. This association is given credit for some of the resurgence in popularity of social studies in Ontario as well as in other provinces. Its work came at a time when progressive trends were gathering strength in Ontario, as manifested by the work of the Provincial Committee on Aims and Objectives.

Curriculum studies in the 1960s

The Social Sciences Study Committee of the Joint Committee of the Toronto Board of Education and the University of Toronto, with its heavy weighting of university professors, not unexpectedly failed to give the social studies movement any great encouragement. There was considerable value, however, in its analysis of the characteristics of certain disciplines, with particular reference to the way they were taught in the schools.

Geography, as it is now treated by its specialist teachers and by the Department, is a study whose roots are substantially, though not entirely, in some of the natural sciences. To the extent that geography is built on these natural science foundations, the objectives and the problems of teaching and learning in geography are different from the objectives and problems of teaching and learning in history. In both subjects, students should be brought to see how generalizations are reached from observed and recorded fact. Both deal, in part, with the way men are related to their physical environment. But to the extent that geography is treated as a natural science, the emphasis in its teaching must be on ensuring that the scientific concepts, facts, and laws are grasped correctly. In a natural science, correctness is an essential. In history it is not: if history is treated as a series of correct facts, or a series of correct relations between facts, it would be better not taught at all. However, the difference between history and the kind of geography now officially recognized in the schools is not as great as the difference between history and a natural science. Geography stands, in method and aims, somewhere between history and natural science: it uses some of the methods, and some of the data, of both, for it is concerned with the relation of man to his environment. It does not claim for its generalizations the degree of certainty usually claimed for scientific laws; in this respect it is nearer to history than to the natural sciences. We found, then, that history and geography did not have to be treated entirely separately. The present deficiencies, and the changes needed to overcome them, are much the same in both subjects.[45]

The report of the committee began with comments on the general design of the Ontario curricula in social studies, history, and geography and a critical statement of objectives. It then dealt with the problems of social studies in grades 1 to 4, social studies and history and geography in grades 5 to 8, and history and geography in grades 9 to 13. With reference to the first of these groups, it observed that the department had defined two main objectives: 1 / to help the child to understand the nature and operation of the social world in which he lived, and 2 / to develop desirable social attitudes. The committee expressed complete approval of the first of these, but declared the second debatable on two grounds: whether the inculcation of social attitudes should be a purpose of institutional education at all, and whether it should be a function assigned especially to social studies.

If it regarded the second of the department's purposes as debatable, there was no question which side the committee was prepared to defend. It observed that there was constant confusion between the actual and the desirable. Among the lesson concepts in the Toronto board's outline for grade 1, it found "Mother does not waste food or time," "Father cares for his property," "Policemen are always ready and willing to help people in trouble," "The teacher is the friend of *every* child in the class," and other such moral precepts presented as facts and mixed indiscriminately with properly factual propositions and properly moral injunctions. The committee was convinced that this practice was undesirable and possibly harmful in its later effects. The motive seemed to be to protect the child from the harsher realities. Yet the social universe of family, neighbourhood, community, and economic society presented in the early years was in his actual experience only partly true at best and in some cases totally false. The effect was to negate the avowed purpose of helping him understand the way society operated.

The wholly laudable design of the social studies in the primary grades – to get a pupil to look theoretically and conceptually at facts which are within his experience, beginning with the family, moving on to the neighbourhood and then to wider communities, and so to develop an understanding of social relations and an ability to think slightly abstractly – is endangered by the falsity of the society presented to him.[46]

The committee's proposals for the earlier grades, in short form, were 1 / that social studies be dropped from grade 1 and the time devoted to other subjects; 2 / that experiments be undertaken to determine the efficacy of reducing the existing social studies programs in grades 2 and

3 by one-third and spending the time on "more solid" work in geography or some other subjects; 3 / as alternatives to the first two recommendations, that experiments be undertaken to determine the efficacy of moving the existing grade 2 program into grade 1 and introducing grades 2 to 4 to more solid learning, chiefly geographical; 4 / that course outlines and textbooks abandon the "rosy cosy view"; and 5 / that the same materials avoid confusing moral precepts and factual generalizations.[47] The second and third of these recommendations typify the opinion of the committee that children were not being sufficiently challenged with respectable subject matter.

The committee approved of the narrative approach for grade 5 but recommended that the emphasis be changed so that pupils would acquire some notion of historical and geographical causal patterns. Reflecting a concern for teachers' lack of sufficient knowledge to each the course properly, the committee recommended that a manual of approximately 150 pages be prepared to give them the history and geography they needed to know to handle each of the grades from 5 to 8. There was said to be a need for an in-service program to provide further training in these subjects. In order to be effective, it would have to involve adequate time off and entail salary inducements. The in-service program could be implemented only if the number of social studies consultants was increased. The committee was strongly in favour of extending the system of rotating classes and subject specialists into the elementary schools. Nothing could better illustrate the traditionalist, subject-centred approach adopted by the committee. While one cannot quarrel with its advocacy of teachers with an adequate knowledge of subject matter, one could wish that it had shown a realization of the importance of some other aspects of elementary school teaching.

Dealing with both history and geography at the high school level, the committee complained about the lack of realization that factual knowledge was secondary. While facts were said to be only incidental to the purposes of history, including those outlined in the official statements of the department, the quality of factual information prescribed seemed to deny it.

History is treated as a body of knowledge that must be acquired by anybody who is to become a good citizen; the amount of it that can be taught in one grade up to a creditable examination level is taken as given (properly enough, since, given the type of factual examination, the amount of material it is feasible to cover can fairly easily be determined by experience or experiment); and the problem of curriculum prescription for that grade then becomes simply a matter of seeing how many chunks of history that somebody thinks important can be got in, or how few can be left out. When a curriculum is changed, it is changed by regretfully leaving out the Palace of Cnossus in order to put in the story of the United Nations.[48]

The curriculum-makers seemed to reason that the proper response to the growing complexity of the world's problems was to put more information about modern events into the curriculum. The result was to preclude any of it from being understood. Official recognition of the situation had led to certain pages of the authorized texts being prescribed for detailed mastery for examinations, other pages to be read and discussed in the classroom, and still others to be given extensive treatment, with exemption from note-making and examinations.

The committee's summary of its findings about the way history was being taught constituted a strong denunciation.

> The system now prevailing does not meet any defensible objectives. It does not train the mind; it leaves only a slight cultural deposit in the mind after a few months or a few years; it does not help the student to think abstractly, to look at evidence, or to consider relevance, which we have argued are the main contributions the study of history can be expected to make to the intelligence of the adult and the merit of the citizen.[49]

The examination pattern was the main apparent cause of the problem, but to the committee it seemed to be less a cause than a symptom. The examinations reflected, as well as reinforced, the prevailing outlook and practice of teachers. These characteristics, again, could be ascribed to the department in its role of producer of courses of study and textbooks. Any textbook seeking official approval had to have as much factual material as, or more than, the average teacher could cover. The committee speculated that the departmental view might be in itself explained by a conviction, perhaps justified, that the average secondary school history teacher in Ontario lacked the capacity and imagination to teach the subject properly.

Four research committees working under the aegis of the Ontario Curriculum Institute produced a publication in 1966 entitled *Directions: An Initial Inquiry into the Social Sciences Program for the Schools.*[50] It contained a list of questions that a teacher might ask in planning any unit in the social sciences.

(1) Does the unit have relevance and meaning in the life of the students?
(2) Does the unit enable the assembling of enough coherent and reliable data in a variety of media (printed word, pictures, artifacts, and various types of audio-visual materials) to give students a maximum learning experience?
(3) Does the unit present the material honestly?
(4) Does the unit lend itself to a broadening of the student's ideas of space, time, self, and group orientation?
(5) Does the unit provide enough flexibility or adaptability to meet the needs of each teacher and student involved in its use?
(6) Does the unit stimulate the student to continuing curiosity and personal involvement?

(7) Does the unit provide a range of alternatives by pointing out our own human behaviour patterns and those of others?
(8) Does the unit provide the student with experiences in:
Work-Study Skills – reading, writing, speaking, listening; organizing material; interpreting statistical, illustrative, and visual-aid materials.
Thinking Skills – critical thinking; statement of problems – selection, evaluation, and application of data to the problem; comparison and testing of observations; generalization and evaluation; suspending judgment when necessary or applying judgment to the solution of problems when possible.
Group Process Skills – competence in group participation and human relationships.
Social Living Skills – acting responsibly, co-operating with others, and living and working in a group setting.
(9) Is the unit organized in such a way that the student can discover concepts, think creatively, and exercise individual curiosity?
(10) Is the unit organized and presented in such a way that students can learn to recognize irrelevant data?

Although this set of principles was worked out by representatives of all levels from elementary school to university, just as were the recommendations of the Social Sciences Study Committee previously referred to, the shift toward a more progressive outlook was pronounced.

Criticism

In one of his most stimulating columns, printed on February 14, 1964, Bascom St John undertook to explain why children knew so little history. He observed at the outset that the problem was universal and thus he did not hold out the expectation of any easy solution. He was able to identify reasons, however, why the situation in Ontario was worse than it need have been.

Part of the school history problem is the dry-as-dust approach to the course of study. A pedantic curriculum committee sits down in a dusty office and decides what historical facts Ontario children should know, and this comprises the history course. It then becomes necessary by a sort of jig-saw puzzle procedure to fit together a large number of sentences which include the facts that are in the course.

The result is called a textbook. The marvel is that some of them are as good as they are. The color, vitality, inspiration, personality in history are stifled by this system. The human qualities that make events come alive are squeezed out.[51]

St John identified some deeper and more fundamental problems in the teaching of history. He observed that the concept of time, especially when it involved the passage of centuries, was a difficult one for a child to grasp because of his inadequate experience of life. He felt that history ought to be taught as a story, somewhat like the tales written by G.A. Henty. To write a history book that could recreate the colour and immediacy of the events and personalities of the past so as to grip the imagination would, he suggested, require more talent than that possessed by any existing Canadian writer in the field. Even if there was one, his work would probably be rejected as an unsuitable basis for examinations. St John was not too confident of the prospects of developing among school children a pride in being Canadian and a respect for the country's past when few adults seemed to possess or express such feelings.

G.S. Tomkins, Associate Professor in the Faculty and College of Education, University of British Columbia, wrote disparagingly in 1965 of the way geography was being taught in Canadian schools.[52] He saw no evidence that the spirit of criticism that had so strongly affected the teaching of mathematics and science had carried over to the social studies. He identified a number of the disabilities from which geography seemed to have suffered. 1 / In most people's minds, it continued to be thought of as an elementary school subject, despite the fact that it had become reasonably well established in the universities. Provincial school systems tended to insist that the whole world be "covered" by the end of elementary school, and there was an impression that there was nothing left to be done in the secondary school. 2 / Geography had suffered because of its integration with social studies, which had become "a convenient grab bag into which could be stuffed any curricular items that were impossible to classify or that were unwanted by other subject fields." 3 / There was a continuing tendency to regard geography as an inert body of facts to be memorized by the pupil. These comments were made at a time when geography was generally considered to be on the upswing. Its place had certainly improved in Ontario secondary schools. In the early 1950s, before it was recognized as a grade 13 subject, it was usually taught to students considered incapable of mastering Latin or other subjects of a more demanding nature.

The Hodgetts study

Few recent Canadian investigations of any aspect of the school program have received, or deserved, more attention than one conducted by A.B. Hodgetts and a number of assistants, the results of which were reported in *What Culture? What Heritage?* in 1968.[53] Hodgetts observed that the subjects taught in various provinces in order to pursue the customary objectives of civic education were usually grouped about history. Even in Alberta, which was making the most determined effort to pursue a social studies approach, the course for each grade included a long unit in history. In every province, the teacher of Canadian history was supposed to pursue, among other objectives, the tasks of transmitting the cultural heritage, inspiring pride in the past, developing loyalty, and producing responsible democratic citizens.

Hodgetts noted that earlier decades had witnessed a series of criticisms of Canadian studies as they were being prescribed and taught. In 1943 Charles Bilodeau of the Quebec Department of Education had found that the textbooks used by the English-speaking and French-speaking groups had both given an unbalanced impression of the contributions of the two groups. In 1945 a committee of the Canada and Newfoundland Education Association had blamed ill-founded prejudice and even antagonism on faulty teaching of history in the schools and had recommended reforms designed to foster national unity. Many years later, a study of textbooks by Marcel Trudel for the Royal Commission on Bilingualism and Biculturalism had emphasized the difference in outlook presented by textbooks in English and French. Hodgetts commented on the severity with which the Joint Committee of the Toronto Board of Education and the University of Toronto had criticized the way in which history was being taught in the schools. A few years later, the Minister of Education had not found much to comfort him in the results of an attempt to obtain advice on possible methods of improving the teaching of Canadian studies in the schools of Ontario. Hodgetts, too, found little evidence of any effective action to meet the complaints.

Yet despite this continuing criticism and the persistent evidence of deep dissatisfaction with the state of Canadian studies in our schools, no major reforms have been introduced in recent years. Some provinces have changed the scope and sequence of their history courses and introduced new textbooks; many school boards have provided generous supplies of audiovisual equipment; some faculties of education have climbed aboard various bandwagons rolling up from the United States with new teaching strategies; and some professors of Canadian history are beginning to write no longer as chroniclers but as historians. Yet, none of these reforms ... has made any fundamental change in what goes on in the Canadian studies classroom.[54]

Hodgetts' criticism of what he had observed in the schools was devastating and alarming.

Not only are the schools failing to serve the interests of the wider society, but the reasonable expectations of the individual student while he is in school – as distinct from the role he may play as a citizen after graduation – are not being fulfilled either. These expectations, of course, are not incompatible with those of society and no dichotomy is intended. But the countless hours wasted by the students each week, going through the mechanical motions of attempting unsuccessfully to find purpose in so many Canadian studies classrooms, sitting in abject boredom, and developing with each passing forty-minute lesson a deeper apathy, is a condition that should be tolerated no longer in our schools. Aside from any of the national interests we have been considering herein, this situation in itself is sufficiently damaging to command our immediate attention.[55]

There were questions of urgent current concern which Hodgetts found students from neither linguistic group being prepared to deal with as responsible citizens. While French-speaking young people in Quebec were learning next to nothing about the parliamentary system, Confederation, or the complexities of federalism, their English-speaking counterparts were confronted with such poor materials and teaching methods that, despite the great amount of time they spent on political and constitutional history, they were little better equipped to handle related problems. About all they acquired was a vague emotional feeling toward Confederation. The prospect, as far as the general public was concerned, was that "the continuing dialogue between our two linguistic communities will be conducted in an emotional and irrational atmosphere, making a stable political solution exceedingly difficult."[56]

In English-speaking Canada, the study showed that history or social studies in general ranked behind most other subjects such as mathematics, science, and English in terms of student appeal. Within the social studies area, Canadian studies proved less popular than ancient and medieval or modern European history. Twenty-five per cent of the respondents to the questionnaire stated categorically that they found no source of pride in Canada's past and another 11 per cent were unwilling or unable to name such a source. Hodgetts concluded that, while Canadian studies ostensibly tried to encourage pride rooted in historical reality, the outcome was the exact opposite. Not more than one student in seven was acquiring any feeling for the past or any realistic, reasonable pride in Canadian history. Hodgetts and his group of investigators felt that the indifference of the majority toward their past was adversely affecting their attitude toward present-day Canada. They appeared to be leaving Canadian studies classrooms with little interest in Canadian affairs and little desire to keep up with them through radio and television documentaries or magazines of opinion. Their knowledge of current events was described as pitifully weak.

Provincial departments of education generally emphasized the study of history because of its supposed aesthetic and cultural values. Some of them seemed to assume that such beneficial results would accrue almost without effort, while others recognized more realistically that teachers would have to use considerable ingenuity in order to instill in students an appreciation of their heritage and an aesthetic interest in art, literature, and science. In any case, Hodgetts found that Canadian studies did not come close to meeting these objectives, mainly because almost no effort was being directed toward that end. An extremely small amount of time was being given to many cultural aspects of human endeavour. In responding to questions dealing with sources of interest or pride in Canadian history or in present-day Canada and recent noteworthy events, 91 per cent of four thousand grade 12 students from all across Canada failed to mention anything that could be described as cultural: that is, they made no reference to developments or personalities in art, literature, music, education, religion, or any branch of science. Of the few exceptions, a large proportion were French-speaking Roman Catholics who recognized the role of their religious leaders.

In assigning responsibility for the deplorable situation which they identified, Hodgetts and associates placed a large part of the blame on the materials they found in use.

> The courses of study in Canadian history are based on the interests and concerns that preoccupied academic historians of the 1920s. These courses lack any contemporary meaning. They continue to be narrowly confined to constitutional and political history. Such things as protest and minority movements, class developments and issues, the influence of art, literature and ideas, education and religion, industrial growth and a great many other aspects of human endeavor which should be an integral part of history are virtually ignored in our schools. We are teaching a bland, unrealistic consensus version of our past; a dry-as-dust chronological story of uninterrupted political and economic progress told without the controversy that is an inherent part of history. The great debates that could bring our history to life, the natural conflicts of opinion, the new interpretations of the past by successive generations of historians, the subjective element in historical writing which produces opposing viewpoints all are grayed out of existence in our textbooks and swept from sight under the classroom desk. The great majority of students in all parts of Canada spend their time in the Canadian studies classroom trying to memorize the discrete, unpatterned and therefore all but meaningless facts of a dead past.
>
> What young Canadians learn about the structure and functioning of their government is equally outmoded. Civics classes continue to concentrate on an old-fashioned, purely descriptive account of the three levels of government, with very little analysis or realism. The psychological or sociological motives for voting, the influence of the mass media, the roles of political parties, the effects of lobbying and pressure groups, the decision-making processes, the importance of bureaucracies, power elites and other factors that bring politics to life seldom get into the Canadian studies classroom.[57]

The investigators' evaluation of the quality of the teaching they observed did not produce a more favourable verdict. In spite of all the talk of the advantages of employing material from a variety of sources, the great majority of students were using a single textbook. Also, 75 per cent of the teachers were using one of the two most universally condemned teaching methods. "In some cases, the students were 'bench-bound listeners,' lined up in rows, sitting passively, while a 'talking textbook' rhymed off material that they could have read and digested for themselves."[58] More often, the procedure consisted of mechanical, routine questions calling for answers based on the recall of factual material from a few pages of the textbook. Without a major improvement in methods of instruction, little result could be expected from an overhaul of programs.

The investigators found little to encourage them in the attitudes of principals, inspectors, and consultants. Their interviews with more than 225 principals led them to feel that teachers of Canadian studies were fighting a losing battle. Forty-eight per cent of the principals revealed that, in their hiring, timetabling, and budgeting policies, Canadian history or social studies received less attention and support than any other subject on the curriculum. At least 40 per cent expressed the opinion that Canadian studies were of no great importance and about the same percentage were entirely satisfied with the way these subjects were currently being taught. Only 6 per cent were trying to give positive leadership and special encouragement to their Canadian studies teachers. Hodgetts and his associates were even more critical of inspectors and subject consultants, among whom were some who thought that Canada had nothing unique to offer and that Canadian studies deserved no particular attention.

Recent trends

The fact that the study covered all of Canada gave complacent Ontarians the opportunity to assure themselves that things were not as bad in their own province as in some others. There was actually no basis for such an attitude. The most realistic response would be to conclude that there was a great deal to be done and that it would take many years of strenuous effort to produce a fundamental change. There could hardly be a more fruitful area for the Ontario Institute for Studies in Education than its Canadian Studies project. Observers of developments in Ontario schools in the final years of the 1960s actually did profess to see evidence of substantial improvement. Much of the impetus for change came from the abolition of the grade 13 departmental examination and from the trend away from teaching for examination purposes in general. Perhaps no subjects can be blighted more from an excessive preoccupation with measuring the outcomes than those in the social science area.

In 1968 the approval of the deputy minister was given for the establishment by the Curriculum Section of a committee to draw up a new course of study for Canadian history in the senior division which would be equally appropriate in English and French high schools. Six aims were stated: 1 / to demonstrate, through the study of evidence on crucial issues, that there are differing points of view on every public issue; 2 / by discussion of crucial issues, to encourage students to debate and to draw conclusions from evidence; 3 / by designing a bilingual course, to demonstrate that Canadians of both founding language groups have a strong basis for agreement on which understanding can be built; 4 / to provide a common historical experience by using a common course of study in English and French language schools; 5 / to provide opportunities for using the second language in reading documents and, from time to time, in classroom discussion; 6 / to provide an opportunity for students to examine emotional issues on a rational basis and to gain insights into the emotional nature of divisive issues.

It is difficult to decide what is reasonable to expect by way of adequate handling of history in the average, or even in the better, classroom. History is far from the stable, definable concept that most people assume. There is no set of objective, inclusive facts about any era in human history; all existing records are selective and incomplete. When the historian undertakes a quest for meaningful relationships, a tremendous range of interpretations becomes possible. The structure he builds is his own individual creation, owing far more to art than to rule. It will naturally bear the marks of his specific cultural group, although the less so as he transcends the trivial and ephemeral interest and advances toward the universal. While the products of all historians are not of equal value, any more than they are in other fields of endeavour, it is not easy to make comparisons among them except on rather subjective grounds. The process is especially difficult when the discovery of new data produces a radically different interpretation from the one that was previously accepted. The general movement, at least where historians make a serious objective of reducing bias and of seeking a closer approximation to the truth, is toward improvement as history is written and rewritten. There are also changes in interest as the predominant concerns of one era give way to another.

The teacher who succeeds in discarding the concept of history as an immutable body of facts and relationships to be learned faces a problem in deciding on a suitable approach. There has been some appeal in an application of the discovery method by which students seek original data and play the role of historians as they attempt to extract, organize, and interpret relevant facts. While this kind of activity can be very salutary if properly conducted, it often calls for a range and quantity of resources that the school, the library, the museum, and other community agencies cannot provide. The student is in danger of failing to realize how laborious the process of adding to historical knowledge really is and how careful the search must be to produce worthwhile findings.

There are particular problems for a teacher who makes a real effort to show that different historical writers not only vary in their interpretation of events but sometimes contradict one another's "facts." For some children, this discovery is a jolt to their security. One version at least must be careless or contain lies. It may not be easy to lead them into a healthy acceptance of uncertainty. At a certain age, it is perhaps too much to expect them to grasp the complexity of the challenge which the historian must face. It is rather easy to understand how curriculum-makers and textbook writers have been tempted to produce bland, uncontroversial versions of the past.

Another problem is really similar to that posed by the "rosy cosy" view of the world which the Toronto committee found objectionable in the way social studies was handled in the junior grades. It is often comfortably assumed that the most accurate and objective account of historical events will build up a respect for the past and a sense of loyalty toward the country. But does every country have a past that its citizens can truly respect unless it is given a few touches of varnish here and there? Will Canadian children be edified if they discover that many of the early explorers of the north and west, although undoubtedly fearless, were also drunken murderers who would not be left at large under modern conditions? Is the lack of understanding between French- and English-speaking Canadians really a matter of bias and ignorance which a more adequate knowledge of their past will remedy? Does truth necessarily produce sympathy?

FRENCH

At the beginning of the period under review, French in schools where English was the language of instruction was strictly a secondary school subject. During the 1960s it was extended progressively down through the grades as courses were developed and suitable teachers provided. This development inevitably meant increasing stress on the oral aspects of the language.

Perhaps no subject on the curriculum has demonstrated more evidence of a discrepancy between stated objectives and actual achievement. The situation is not entirely a reflection on the quality of the teaching, although a great deal of it has reportedly been inept. Much of the blame must be placed on a system where the seriousness of the effort required to attain real second language competence has not been acknowledged. It may well be asked whether a half-hearted effort in this area is really worth more than no effort at all.

Course of study for secondary schools

It is imagined in some circles that, until quite recently, a very bookish type of French instruction was officially encouraged in Ontario secondary schools. While such an approach may have been used, it was not in the spirit of departmental exhortations. The course of study for 1936, for example, stated that the first six weeks should be devoted to training the ear, and that teaching should be done without the use of a textbook. A systematic study of the sounds of the language was recommended, although not necessarily by means of phonetics. French was to be used, as far as possible, as the medium of instruction throughout the course. It must be acknowledged, despite this advice, that oral communication was not given top priority.

According to the course of study issued in March 1954, the study of French was considered to have both cultural and practical values. Under the first heading, the student was supposed to gain a broadened outlook and a sense of tolerance and good will. The practical objective was to learn to communicate with the French-speaking people of Canada. The student was ostensibly expected to understand, speak, read, and write the language. To achieve these goals, the course was to include regular practice in conversation, a considerable amount of reading, and a study of fundamental grammatical constructions.

The recommended approach for grade 9 was aural and conversational, with practice in hearing and speaking to be continued throughout the course. At the elementary stage, reading in unison was suggested, along with reading aloud by individual students. Memorizing of phrases, sentences, and passages of prose and poetry was identified as excellent practice. The use of phonetic symbols was endorsed as an aid to learning the pronunciation of unfamiliar words, although over-formalized treatment was said to be undesirable.

Dictation was considered to be a highly effective instructional approach to be begun early in grade 9 and continued through all the grades. At the outset, it would consist of a sentence or two and gradually extend into longer passages from the text. Sight passages might be written from dictation in the higher grades. It was suggested that 10 per cent of the total marks for term examinations be assigned to dictation. As an additional aid to understanding spoken French, use might be made of moving pictures, radio programs, and phonograph recordings.

The student was expected to learn to read for understanding and (optimistically) for enjoyment. There was to be intensive reading in class under the teacher's supervision and extensive reading mainly out of class. The first type was to give the student an understanding and appreciation of the subject matter, to enlarge his vocabulary, and to provide him with an opportunity of speaking the language. In order to arouse interest, teachers were authorized to introduce discussion of the story in English. Supplementary reading, at a simpler level, was to be introduced only after a considerable amount of intensive study of texts.

A careful study of grammatical constructions was said to be necessary to achieve the writing objective. The teacher was advised to use the inductive method in order to develop and utilize the student's thinking powers. Where feasible, simple explanations of points of grammar were to be made in French. If such an approach proved to be clumsy or ineffective, however, English was to be used. The student was to progress from the construction of a simple sentence to the writing of a planned free composition. It was suggested that, by the time they had reached grade 11, the better students should be able to give short summaries of passages without the aid of guiding questions.

The so-called Tan-Gau method of instruction enjoyed a brief period of interest in some quarters after 1954. In that year, Robert Gauthier returned to the Department of Education after serving on a UNESCO mission in Burma, where he had picked up the idea from Tan Gwan Leong, Director of Curriculum in the Burmese Department of Education. The name of the method was derived from Tan and the first three letters of the name Gauthier. It differed from other methods in that it divided the study of the second language into two successive stages: comprehension and expression. The student began by listening and learning to understand what he heard. When questions were put to him, he replied in his own native language. Exercises in silent and oral reading began in the second half of the second year of study. Comprehension was considered to lead naturally to expression. If the student never mastered that stage, however, he would still be able to understand radio, television, and cinema programs, to read books, newspapers, and magazines, and to understand the spoken word. The method was tried on an experimental basis in Ottawa and some other places. Most experts, however, regarded it as unsound, and it fell into disrepute.

Efforts to establish the direct method

In presenting a course of study for grade 12 in 1960, D. Steinhauer, then a secondary school inspector, declared that two basic assumptions were taken for granted: that the prime objectives in language study were communication and expression, and that the merits of direct method teaching were firmly established and required no further justification. He observed, however, that many teachers who subscribed to this view in theory found it difficult to employ the direct method because of inadequate training and insufficient mastery of the spoken language. He found it difficult to criticize them for their shortcomings because they themselves were the products of the translation method, had mastered the rudiments of grammar and syntax, and envisaged the problem of language instruction as an intellectual discipline. They had been led to believe that the objective of language study was the mastery of vocabulary, generally learned as isolated words and idioms; the skilful manipulation of intricate, irregular verb forms; and the commitment to memory of abstract grammatical rules. They trained students to translate laboriously from one language to another, always relating the unfamiliar language expression to its English equivalent instead of associating the object or idea directly with its method of expression in the other language.

Steinhauer asserted that it was important to establish the fact that the direct method did not in itself determine the objectives of language study but merely concerned itself with a methodological approach. He saw no validity in the argument that the writing objective must suffer if the direct method were used. A more comprehensive approach to language teaching, emphasizing comprehension and communication as well as writing, would produce students who were not only capable of using the spoken foreign language, but who would also be in a better position to handle translation with ease. Instead of recalling painfully memorized rules, they would depend on their ear and their linguistic intuition and would check the result by referring to the formal grammatical rules they had learned.

The question of how best to teach a second language has continued to be a matter of controversy. In an article entitled "On the Judicious Use of English in the Teaching of Modern Languages" published in the *Canadian Modern Language Review* in 1966, W.E. Kieser declared that thinking educators who had specialized in modern languages had come to the conclusion that the direct method had definite limitations and that it could even be harmful if used exclusively and with large classes.[59] He claimed that, although the method had originated in Europe, it had had a very short life in most European countries.

In the same article, Kieser reviewed some of the methods that had been successively in vogue during the twentieth century. The eclectic method, which closely resembled the old grammar-translation method, was followed in the 1920s by the reading method, which stressed pronunciation in oral work and advocated practically no translation into French. Emphasis on oral communication had emerged from the practical needs of the Second World War. The audio-lingual approach, sometimes referred to as the "new key," had developed from the crash program used to train army personnel. It was based on rote learning of structures or patterns by constant repetition. From these structures and patterns, the student was expected to infer grammatical rules. In its approach to the teaching of grammar, the method was similar to the inductive method in which the student was exposed to many examples of sentences, oral or written, which illustrated the rule, but was not required to learn them by rote. There was the added advantage in the new key that the speech patterns the student learned could be very useful in conversation in which they could be modified to suit the context. The audio-lingual method differed from the older direct method in that more effort was made to ensure that the learner understood the expressions he was repeating.

According to Kieser, teachers had identified several difficulties in the new key approach. 1 / A student who learned a pattern by heart without its grammatical synthesis might be unable to modify it by changing the tense, person, etc. 2 / There was doubt that the average student was able to deduce grammatical rules from the repetition of patterns without some questioning or prompting by the teacher. 3 / There was a question whether the memorization of expressions would not become a monotonous and boring experience without the stimulation provided by an extremely dynamic and able teacher. These problems suggested the necessity of a considerable modification of the audio-lingual approach.

The extension of French instruction into the elementary schools

In the 1950s, Wilder Penfield helped to pave the way for earlier instruction in French in Ontario schools. His observations of the physiology and operation of the human brain led him to suggest that the study of a second language should not be delayed past the age range from eight to eleven. After that time, the possibility of attaining real oral competence became increasingly remote. If the appropriate neural connections were established, however, additional languages might be learned with reasonable facility at later stages. Penfield's influence was reinforced after 1960 by a growing desire on the part of Ontario citizens to strengthen Canadian unity.

There was by no means universal enthusiasm among school trustees and officials for the introduction of French in elementary schools. C.C. Goldring, Director of Education for the city of Toronto, voiced some of the standard objections at one stage. He pointed out that Toronto pupils seldom heard French spoken and would soon forget what they had learned. Evidence from contemporary studies in the United States had indicated that an early beginning had little influence on achievement in the secondary school. Goldring was reluctant to face the administrative task of finding suitable teachers and was also apprehensive lest the time spent in studying French would encroach unduly on other subjects.

The Second Language Committee of the Ontario Curriculum Institute provided considerable support for greater emphasis on French and for its earlier introduction into the schools. In a report published in 1963, it referred to the contributions of experts from France and Norway.[60] The programs in both of these countries began earlier than the teaching of French in Ontario, involved more intensive instruction, and achieved greater success. In Norway in particular, competence in at least one foreign language, and preferably in several, was regarded as an economic and political necessity. At the time the report was written, only in Ottawa and a few other Ontario centres was there any provision for the study of French below the secondary school level. Whatever the stated aims of the secondary school program, teaching was said in fact to have emphasized reading, grammar, and translation. The result was that high school graduates had an intensive knowledge of some of the aspects of the language which were the least vital to effective communication.

The report provided a tentative outline for an integrated French course extending from kindergarten or grade 1 to university entrance. The child was to be taught by the audio-lingual method throughout the course. Reading was to be introduced only after he was able to express himself in French with a reasonable degree of fluency, and writing was to be taught only after reading was well established. From grades 1 to 5 inclusive, the committee recommended one fifteen-minute lesson a day, which might include a song, a game, some conversation, or the use of puppets, film strips, or magazine pictures. The optimistic hope was expressed that these lessons, if fast-moving and varied, would give time to develop the child's ability to understand and speak French. In grade 6, where the children were reading more extensively and beginning to learn to write, thirty minutes a day would be required. By this stage, about two-thirds of the time would be devoted to oral work.

By 1964 enough school systems had introduced French at the upper elementary level that the department found it opportune to appoint a Director of French Instruction to co-ordinate and give leadership in this area. According to the *Report of the Minister, 1965,* French was being taught to 164,145 pupils in regular classrooms and to 2,590 in special classes in schools operated by 231 public and separate school boards. There were 581 special or itinerant teachers of French only or of French and other subjects, and 537 regular classroom teachers teaching the subject.

In 1965 Education Minister Davis spoke of the worldwide trend toward instruction in a second language at the elementary school level. He mentioned several reasons for the display of interest: 1 / a conviction that the interdependence of all countries made education in one language inadequate; 2 / the fact that an earlier start in learning a new language would give more time for the development of skill in its use; and 3 / the knowledge that young children responded particularly well to oral language teaching. A reason applying specifically to Canada was that the ability to use both English and French was recognized as highly desirable both for business and cultural advantages and was an influence for unity under Confederation. According to Davis, it had been departmental policy to approve the introduction of a program in French only when it was established that the classes would be staffed by teachers who could meet a high standard of oral fluency in the language. The programs offered up to that time had been based on direct classroom teaching rather than on the predominant or exclusive use of such instructional devices as tapes and records.[61]

Davis declared that, as a result of a study conducted by teachers, inspectors, and university professors, and in the light of experience acquired in local areas, it had been decided that French would be a recognized option in the elementary school program for English-speaking pupils in grades 7 and 8 beginning in September 1966. The school boards would have the responsibility of deciding when they were ready to offer it. Their decision would depend to a large extent on their ability to obtain properly qualified teachers. Davis reviewed measures being taken to augment the supply of such teachers. There were plans for the production of courses of study for elementary schools, and those for the secondary schools would be revised to allow for the pupils' experience at the elementary level.

By September 1966 the number of public and separate schools offering French had risen to 409. There were 256,865 pupils receiving instruction in regular and 2,940 in special classes. The program was being handled by 577 special itinerant teachers and 405 regular classroom teachers. The new courses of study for grades 7 and 8 were in use, although the revisions for grades 9 and 10 were still awaited.

The subject was optional in all grades of the elementary school other than 7 and 8. A request by a board to offer it was to be made through the local school inspector to the Superintendent of Curriculum. Information to be submitted was to include the grades to receive instruction, the number of classes per week and the length of time allowed for the classes at each grade level, the name and qualifications of each teacher involved, and the total number of classes per week assigned to each teacher. An explanation was expected if special circumstances prevented the subject from being taught for at least four periods a week. If permission was granted under such conditions, it was to be for a limited period of time, and boards were not to anticipate having it renewed until a satisfactory timetable had been arranged. In this way, the department attempted to apply pressure to ensure that the classes were offered with reasonable frequency. As of September 1968, the permission of the department was no longer needed to offer a program, although relevant information about it was to be supplied to the regional superintendent.

Members of the opposition were strongly in favour of the development and based their criticism of the minister on the slowness of the pace with which the policy was being implemented. On May 24, 1967, for example, Robert Nixon claimed that only "140,000 plus" pupils in the elementary schools had access to French education (the official figure, as already noted, was 256,865). He thought that instruction could be extended with the use of language laboratories, tape recorders, and educational television.[62] The main argument against excessive speed was of course that the results of poor teaching could be very serious. Nixon had a few comments on that issue the following year, when he observed that his son, who had just entered grade 9 in a local collegiate institute, was still learning the same vocabulary lists with which he himself had had trouble in 1939 and 1940. He claimed that, while instruction had undoubtedly improved in many centres, it was, as a general rule, still archaic and inefficient, and the graduates of grade 13 had no more command of the language than they had had some years before.[63] In 1968 Nixon called attention to the fact that there were several areas in the province that needed considerable urging to adopt the program for oral French instruction. He thought the time had come to make the subject compulsory.[64] The reasons for not doing so, however, remained substantially the same.

The instalment of the report of the Royal Commission on Bilingualism and Biculturalism, Book II: Education, released in 1968, suggested that English-speaking children should begin French lessons in grade 1. French-speaking children, on the other hand, had more opportunities for exposure to English outside the school and might delay formal instruction in that language until grade 3. The report recommended the unprecedented step of federal financial assistance for public education, in this case for bilingual schools and institutions for preparing teachers to handle the second language.

The day after the report appeared, the Toronto Board of Education approved the extension of French from grade 5 down to grade 2. Some members, however, expressed opposition to the proposal to introduce it in grade 1. Barry Lowes was quoted in the *Toronto Daily Star* as saying that grade 1 pupils were busy acquiring reading skills and that it would just make for confusion if they were introduced to another language. Lowes was also critical of certain other suggestions. While he was said to have agreed that all elementary school children should learn French, he thought that only those who were really interested should carry it through high school.[65]

RELIGIOUS EDUCATION

Establishment of the Mackay Committee

Any discussion of religious education in Ontario at the end of the 1960s can hardly escape being dominated by *Religious Information and Moral Development: The Report of The Committee on Religious Education In The Public Schools of The Province of Ontario*, commonly known as the Mackay report, which was published on February 3, 1969. Established in January 1966 under the chairmanship of the Honourable J. Keiller Mackay, former Lieutenant-Governor of Ontario, the committee was given the following terms of reference:

> WHEREAS a program of religious education in the Public Schools of Ontario was established in 1944;
> AND WHEREAS there has been from time to time representations made for changes in the program;
> AND WHEREAS there is a need for evaluation of this program in the light of the experience with it and the requirements of the present day.
>
> The Honourable the Minister of Education therefore recommends that a Committee on Religious Education in the Public Schools be appointed to examine and evaluate the present program; to receive representations from all interested bodies about the effectiveness and desirability of the program; to consider suggestions for changes and improvement; to study means by which character building, ethics, social attitudes and moral values and principles may best be instilled in the young; to consider the responsibility of the Public Schools in these matters; and to make recommendations thereon for the information and consideration of the Minister.[66]

Religious observance in pioneer schools

The committee found it impossible to make a definite pronouncement about the extent to which religious instruction had been part of the program in the public schools. From one point of view, such instruction had always been given; from another, only since 1944. Any statement about it depended on the definition of terms and on "the speaker's angle of vision." It was easier to deal with the proposition that in the early years school populations were homogeneous in character and that there was no conflict over religious matters. The committee refuted this claim by pointing to the aspirations of the Church of England to occupy a dominant position, and to the opposition this ambition aroused among the Methodist settlers who came largely from the United States. The leading exponent of religious education according to the tenets of the Church of England was of course John Strachan, who became president of the provincial Board of Education in 1823.

According to the committee, opening exercises constituted the first religious observance suggested to the schools of Upper Canada. It was recommended in 1816

1. That the labours of the day commence with prayer.
2. That they conclude with reading publicly and solemnly a few verses of the New Testament, proceeding regularly through the Gospels.
3. That the forenoon of each Saturday be devoted to Religious Instruction.[67]

There was said to be scarcely any evidence of organized religious instruction. In some cases, pupils memorized verses of scripture. The Bible at a certain stage was a chief reading text. Because of its difficulty, this particular usage often caused children to take a dislike to it. According to the committee, "probably prayer and Bible reading in the public school were regarded by most people as being desirable, to some it was a matter of indifference, and ... it was objected to by a few."[68]

The recommendation of 1816 was repeated in 1846 and expanded in 1855. The school day would begin and end with scripture reading and prayer. The latter would consist of the Lord's Prayer alone or of forms provided (presumably by the Council of Public Instruction) or any other prayer preferred by the trustees and master of each school, along with the Lord's Prayer. The Ten Commandments were ordinarily to be taught to all pupils and repeated at least once a week. No pupil was, however, to be compelled to be present against the wishes of his parents or guardian. Surviving evidence is said to indicate that, although most teachers read a few verses of scripture, there was little other religious observance. Adam Crooks, the first Minister of Education and Ryerson's successor, indicated in 1878 that there was no expectation that scripture reading would be accompanied by any exposition of the text or by instruction, and that explanation should be only for the better understanding of the words used. In 1884 the opening of schools with scripture reading and prayer was made mandatory, with provision for the exemption of children whose parents wished it.

During subsequent years, there were chronic complaints about the hasty, irreverent, and perfunctory manner with which the opening exercises were performed. The regulations of 1944, however, prescribed their continuation. The scripture passages that were to accompany the repetition of the Lord's Prayer or of other prayers approved for use in the schools were to be chosen from the list of selections adopted by the Department of Education or from any other public school list approved by the minister. The exercises might include the singing of one or more hymns approved for use in public schools. The Royal Commission placed its stamp of approval on the whole procedure, as well as on religious education as a subject of instruction.

Evaluation of opening exercises

The committee conducted widespread inquiries and heard briefs on the way the exercises were being handled. In some schools, it appeared that they were elaborated "to a point constituting overt indoctrination," while in others the treatment was careless and perfunctory. In secondary schools, they were often carried over the loudspeaker and received little attention. Both the overly zealous and the lackadaisical way of dealing with them produced advocates of their abolition. Some groups felt that all devotional acts were improper in public schools, where they exerted a discriminatory and divisive influence. One group was against having Christian children pray with unbelievers. On the other hand, many briefs were in favour of the exercises and urged that they be continued. Parallels were drawn with Parliament, which was opened with prayer.

> The absence of opening exercises would indicate that religion was not an integral part of life and make the school wholly secular. Opening exercises, reverently conducted, could set the tone for the day and give strength and peace of mind. Learning to worship at the beginning of each day may initiate in the child a habit which will govern his attitudes and conduct.[69]

Other advantages were seen in the feeling of solidarity that common worship was supposed to engender and in the appreciation for the content and language of the Bible which was thought to result from hearing it read.

In general, the committee found that opening exercises were much less controversial than religious instruction. It saw sufficient advantage in them to recommend that they be continued and that they consist of the singing of the National Anthem and a prayer, either of a universal character appealing to God for help in the day's activities or the Lord's Prayer. They were to be led by the home room teacher and to involve planning and participation, where feasible, on the part of the pupils. Isolated requests for exemption might be dealt with as the need arose.

Early evidence of concern over moral instruction

Apart from opening exercises, it is possible to identify the first evidence of active concern over moral instruction on the part of the central authority with certain regulations passed in 1850. At that time, the teacher was exhorted to pay the strictest attention to the morals and general conduct of his pupils. In 1857 a further regulation authorized the clergy of any denomination, or their authorized representatives, to give religious instruction in each common school to pupils belonging to their own denomination. Such instruction might be given at least once a week after four p.m. or at any other hour of the day except during school hours. The Public Schools Act of 1896 dealt with the matter again in rather vague terms in requiring every teacher to inculcate in his pupils the principles of Christian morality.[70]

Provision for religious education, 1944

Regulation 13 provided for religious education in the public schools in and after 1944.

(1) (a) Every public school shall be opened each school day with religious exercises consisting of the reading of the Scriptures and the repeating of the Lord's Prayer or other prayers approved for use in schools.
(b) The Scripture passages, forming a part of the religious exercises referred to in 1 (a), shall be read daily and systematically at the opening of school and may be chosen from any list of selections adopted by the Department for use in schools, or from any other list approved by the Minister, as the Board by resolution may direct.
(c) If the Board does not pass the resolution provided for in 1 (b) above, the principal shall make the selection after duly notifying the Board of his intention, but such selection shall be subject to revision by the Board at any time.
(d) The religious exercises held at the daily opening of school may include the singing of one or more hymns authorized for use in schools.

(2) (a) Subject to the regulations, two periods per week of one-half hour each, in addition to the time assigned to religious exercises at the opening of school, shall be devoted to Religious Education.
(b) Religious Education shall be given immediately after the opening of school or immediately before the closing of school in either the morning or the afternoon session.
(c) Instruction in Religious Education shall be given by the teacher in accordance with the course of study authorized for that purpose by the Department, and issues of a controversial or sectarian nature shall be avoided.
(d) By resolution of the School Board, a clergyman or clergymen of any denomination, or a lay person or lay persons selected by the clergyman or clergymen, shall have the right, subject to the regulations, to give Religious Instruction in lieu of a teacher or teachers.
(e) If two or more clergymen of different denominations, upon written application to the Board, secure permission to give Religious Instruction, the principal of the school, by resolution of the Board, shall arrange for such accommodation within the school and at such prescribed times within the periods denoted above as shall be agreeable to both the principal and the clergymen concerned.
(f) Where the number of rooms in the school is insufficient to meet the needs of the groups organized for Religious Education under (d) and (e)

above, the principal of the school, by resolution of the Board, may arrange for additional accommodation elsewhere.

(3) (a) No pupil shall be required to take part in any religious exercises or be subject to any instruction in Religious Education to which objection is raised by his parent or guardian.
(b) In schools without suitable waiting-rooms or other similar accommodation, if the parent or guardian applies to the principal for the exemption of his child or ward from attendance while religious exercises are being held or Religious Education given, such request shall be granted.
(c) If the parent or guardian objects to his child or ward taking part in religious exercises or being subject to instruction in Religious Education, but requests that he shall remain in the schoolroom during the time devoted to such education, the teacher shall permit him to do so provided he maintains decorous behaviour.
(d) If by virtue of his right to be absent from religious exercises or instruction in Religious Education, any pupil is not present in the classroom during such specified periods, his absence shall not be considered a violation of the rules of the school.

(4) A teacher claiming exemption from the teaching of Religious Education as prescribed by the regulations, shall notify the Board to that effect in writing; and it shall then be the duty of the board to make such other provision as may be necessary to implement the regulations with respect to the teaching of the subject.

(5) The Minister may grant to a Board exemption from the teaching of Religious Education in any classroom or school provided the Board shall request in writing such exemption and shall submit reasons therefor.

(6) The inspector shall each year bring to the attention of the boards of trustees of his inspectorate the foregoing regulations relating to religious exercises and Religious Education.[71]

According to the program of studies, the children of Ontario were to be prepared to live in a democratic society which based its way of life on the Christian ideal. A Christian and a democratic society were apparently to be considered as closely linked together, if not actually synonymous. The regulations were intended to provide for religious education as an integral part of the school program. The foundation of the course was the study of the Bible, which was to be taught as thoroughly as social studies or science. Specific religious instruction was to be supported by an appreciation of goodness, beauty, and truth permeating all teaching. The aim was "to set up ideals, to build attitudes, and to influence behaviour," as well as to teach facts. It would be hard to imagine a stronger admonition to teachers in the Roman Catholic separate schools with respect to their religious obligations than the following: "The responsibility of the teacher for the spiritual growth of the child is just as great as for the intellectual and physical, because education is one and indivisible. If the child is to be taught well, body, mind, and spirit must be taught together."

As indicated in the regulations, two periods a week, each one-half hour in length, were to be devoted to the study of the scriptures. The scriptural interpretations were to be non-sectarian, avoiding the tenets or doctrines of any particular creed. They were to be confined to those expressions of the Christian faith upon which all Christian denominations were in substantial agreement. Those who designed the curriculum were apparently unprepared to consider the possibility that there were fundamental points in the interpretation of the scriptures on which different denominations could not agree, and that the teacher who made a genuine effort to avoid these might be reduced to dealing with trivialities.

Teachers were supplied with guides containing lesson outlines for the topics listed in the program of studies. Each lesson provided for the reading and study of a specific passage of scripture, gave an expanded story of the passage to be studied, supplied background notes with historical and other information on the setting of the story, and suggested additional class work and activities appropriate to the topic. These activities might include further reading from the Bible, choral reading and verse speaking, memory work, written work, discussion, dramatization, drawing, and handwork. Scripture study was supposed to be correlated with other phases of the school program.

Recommendations of the Royal Commission

The Royal Commission expressed considerable enthusiasm for the 1944 regulations relating to religious education in public schools. It claimed that, if the aims of education it advocated were to be achieved, religious education should be a subject of study. Among its recommendations was that certain objections raised by the Canadian Jewish Congress be considered in any revision of the existing guidebooks. It suggested that consideration be given to the use of children's Bible stories containing such parts of the scriptures as might be especially suitable for elementary school pupils. It also urged that the Department of Education seek the co-operation of the Inter-Church Committee on Weekday Religious Education in preparing a list of daily scripture readings.[72]

Changing attitudes during the 1960s

The view of the majority of the discussion group which dealt with religious education in the schools at the Ontario Conference on Education in 1961 was definitely in favour of religious instruction in accordance with Christian beliefs.

Religion is a vitally necessary ingredient in the education of the child, serving as a bulwark against the rise of juvenile delinquency, and forming an essential basis of culture. The faith of our fathers is an indispensable part of the background in any study of the humanities.

Instruction in religion is primarily the responsibility of the home and the church. Where such surveys as that mentioned in the Hope Report indicate that this responsibility is being shirked in as much as fifty per cent of the homes, the state must be prepared to remedy the deficiency, using the school as its agent. Since, by census figures, our people are ninety-five per cent Christian in belief, it follows that the religious instruction provided must be Christian. To provide for freedom of religion, the public school must allow exemption from the programme for those children whose parents so desire; this provision is, of course, unnecessary in a separate or parochial school, serving children of a single faith. Some opinion was expressed that such a course might better be termed Bible Study. In any case, it was believed that the rights of the majority ought not to be sacrificed for the rights of the minority. It was conceded that there must be no attempt to proselytize on the part of the instructor, but it was firmly believed that every child must be taught that we are children of God, and must treat others so. Some bewilderment about the recent increase in opposition to the course was expressed when it was thought that the 1944 regulations had made little change in the pattern of the last century.[73]

According to the minority view expressed at the same conference, responsibility for belief in a religion lay with the home and the church. If the school, as an instrument of the state, did not remain neutral, the principle of the separation of church and state was violated. It was said to be impossible to remain neutral on the subject of religion or objective about beliefs. The minority expressed doubts about the predominantly Christian nature of the population and suggested that an attempt to teach one religion violated the integrity of the schools. A number of injustices were pointed out in the application of the regulations. 1 / The guide books contained phrases that were offensive to Jews. 2 / While there was provision for exemption for children of dissenting parents, withdrawal was difficult in practice. 3 / Cases had been reported where thoughtless or over-zealous teachers and clergymen had embarrassed children who withdrew. The minority thought that a course about the world's different religions, taught in a factual manner and not requiring belief in any one, might be acceptable.

The arguments offered by this minority found increasing favour during subsequent years. In 1967 the North York Board of Education took action to end any pretence that the program of religious education was being carried out in the public schools. In 1968 the York Board followed suit with a resolution passed by a vote of five to two which claimed that any attempt to enforce the regulations would disrupt the school program and be a divisive influence in the community. A spokesman for the board declared that the resolution was not an anti-religious action but a recognition of the fact that many different religious groups were represented among pupils and teachers, including those who were not religious. The board members felt that the place for religion was in the church or the home.

Under the title "A vanishing problem," the *Globe and Mail* printed an editorial on May 31, 1968, giving Mackay credit for "the sheer, dogged perseverance of slugging it out for nearly three years," but suggesting that his committee might ultimately prove that problems could be solved by waiting long enough for them to go away. "What it eventually says about the issue will be of interest but there can be little hope of it recommending anything remotely resembling the religious instruction requirements that have been with us since 1944. Proselytism does not belong in a public school system that serves an increasingly pluralistic society."[74]

Recommendations to the Mackay Committee on moral and religious education

The Mackay Committee recommended the abandonment of the existing course of study in religious education, along with its aims as set out in related legislation, programs of studies, regulations, and guide books. The committee was firmly opposed to anything in the nature of indoctrination based on a specific set of beliefs. It also pointed out the futility of attempting to impose moral precepts as a means of character development. Its recommendations centred on two basic proposals: that moral education be emphasized for the purpose of stimulating the young person's capacity to make value judgments and moral decisions, and that measures be taken, including the provision of an optional course in the later years of secondary school, to enable young people to learn about the world's great religions.

With reference to the first of these proposals, the committee saw a good deal of value in Piaget's hypothesis of stages of moral development as defined by Kohlberg and Turiel and developed into a theory of moral education. Kohlberg had defined the six basic stages of development in moral judgment as follows:

1. Punishment and obedience orientation.
2. Naive instrumental hedonism.
3. Good-boy morality of maintaining good relations, approval by others.
4. Authority maintaining morality.
5. Morality of contract, of individual rights, and of democratically accepted law.
6. Morality of individual principles of conscience.[75]

The committee did not commit itself to supporting the entire theory with all its ramifications. However, it strongly approved the concept of the teacher, not as a moralizer, but as a helper of children to move from one stage of development to another.

The committee observed that the ideal approach in terms of Kohlberg's theory would require the teacher to analyse the stage of moral development reached by each pupil and to provide appropriate opportunities for him to exercise his powers as a means of reaching the next higher level. There was some doubt that this kind of approach was feasible within the practical limits of the classroom, or even that it was entirely sound. The committee was more enthusiastic about the technique recommended by Kohlberg and his associates which involved facing the pupil with situational anecdotes and realistic accounts involving genuine moral conflicts which he would discuss and resolve. If sustained mild stress were placed on his powers of moral reasoning, he would presumably advance through the developmental stages toward moral maturity. The situations and anecdotes, the committee warned, must not involve pat moralizing, nor should they be applied indiscriminately to pupils at different developmental levels. They should not, furthermore, be related to the specific moral and ethical problems of the moment. If they seemed to point to particular individuals, the effectiveness of the approach might be lost. The idea was not to arouse emotional reactions but to stimulate logical reasoning.

The point of view expounded by the committee was clarified by reference to the kind of approaches it did not consider useful.

> We are ... opposed to the use of either reading selections or anecdotes which are simply moralizing tales, holding no relevance for the young person confronted by them. Such accounts, which at one time did overload our classrooms, too seldom involved meaningful moral communication, and almost never the development of moral reasoning. When we say therefore that the basic reading program desirably should include experiences in the making of value judgments, *we mean just that*. This program does not call for the foisting of adult moral clichés on our young people through patronizing presentations that lack both moral and literary educational merit ... [76]

The process of stimulating the development of moral reasoning was not to be regarded as an exercise in debating. The approach was to be characterized by calmness, lack of rhetoric, logical thinking, and a respect for the issues involved. Each pupil's chain of reasoning, however immature or naïve, was to be treated with consideration. There was to be no effort to grade it or to criticize it specifically, although there might be opportunities to point to better courses of action.

The committee took pains to dispel any impression that the approach it was advocating would require a disproportionate amount of time. The intention was that the program would complement and reinforce all other teacher-pupil communications inside and outside the classroom and that it would be implemented through incidental, although carefully planned, teaching. Without taking large amounts of time from other school activities, the encouragement of moral development might assume a position of major importance among the school's responsibilities.

The case for the teaching of religion, including an optional course in the secondary school program designed to contribute to the student's understanding of the cultural foundations of the world's populations, was based in large part on the increasing interdependence of different parts of the globe. What was said to be needed was a forthright, honest, and objective consideration of the influence of religion on historical and social development. It was suggested that, from the early elementary school grades, steps be taken to make pupils aware that people adopt different religious customs and ways of life. The relevant information was to be presented in an objective fashion, with every effort to avoid undue emphasis on a particular form of religious practice or on the contributions of a particular creed or religion. Religion was to be associated with other cultural factors affecting human history. Information was to be provided through textbooks and class materials used in social studies, history, geography, art, music, literature, and other subjects. Stories and selections from the Bible were said to have a place in the literature program throughout the school, although care was to be taken to make sure that such material was presented without doctrinal implications.

The courses offered on an optional basis in the later years of secondary school would be presented by members of history departments, who would be as well versed in the relevant subject matter as those instructing in any other area. Such courses would involve a systematic study of the world's religions, providing "knowledge about and insight into the bases of religious doctrines, creeds, liturgical practices, and the roots from which they have sprung." Attention would be given to the lives of the leaders of the various religions and to their impact on their adherents. Within the limits of the time available, the history of different religions would be traced and their effect on modern life explored.

As a means of implementing the proposed program, the committee advocated the employment of a program consultant in each regional office. In view of the need for complete flexibility in planning and administration and for constant curriculum review, the committee orginally considered the establishment of a program advisory council to keep in touch with the ideas and attitudes of the general public. At a later stage, it concluded that such an advisory council should be incorporated in the advisory body of citizens recommended by the Provincial Committee on Aims and Objectives. As a further administrative measure, the committee advocated the appointment of a co-ordinator in the Curriculum Section of the department who would "seek to establish a general emphasis throughout the curriculum on character building, ethics, social attitudes, and moral values and principles."

Reaction to the recommendations of the Mackay Committee

When the report of the Mackay Committee appeared, it was widely praised for the nature and quality of its contents. It was obvious also that much of the province was ready for its recommendations, despite the continued existence of dissent. There promised to be difficulties, however, with French-speaking Roman Catholics who had abandoned their private secondary schools on the tacit understanding that doctrinal religious instruction for adherents of their faith in the publicly supported secondary school system would not be interfered with.

The clergy were heard from again in June 1970, when an Ecumenical Study Commission on Religious Education presented a brief to the minister urging the establishment of a course in religious education in secondary schools. This course would not be offered by the history department, but by one set up specifically to deal with the subject. Students might obtain credit, just as they did for other work. Teaching would be done by full-time specialized staff rather than by clergymen coming to the school on a casual basis. It would be the privilege of local school boards to decide whether they wished to offer a course and, if so, whether they wished to employ a teacher who had specialized in Christianity, Judaism, or secular humanism. Agreeing with the Mackay Committee that religion should be a pervasive influence, the commission felt that this objective could be achieved only if the subject had academic status.

An article by Barrie Zwicker in the *Toronto Daily Star* on June 13, 1969, reported that members of the Ontario Inter-Church Committee on Public Education, which included representatives of the Anglican, Baptist, Lutheran, Presbyterian, Greek Orthodox, Mennonite, and United Churches, along with an active observer-participant from the Roman Catholic Church, had prepared five papers, one of which condemned parts of the Mackay report for taking a "Nazi approach." The basis for this accusation was apparently that the recommended moral education would pervade every curricular and extra-curricular activity in the public school system. The committee was said to have agreed, however, that the existing program, with its strongly Protestant orientation, should be abolished.

GUIDANCE

Introduction into school system

The idea of guidance as a function requiring the services of a specially designated teacher was accepted in the early 1920s, when Central Technical School in Toronto arranged for one of its staff to devote some school time to advising students on courses and future occupations. The Department of Education began to offer guidance counsellor training courses in 1925. By the end of the Second World War guidance was a compulsory part of the grade 9 program, and the appointment of one or more teachers with part-time or full-time responsibility for guidance came to be the rule in secondary schools throughout the province. During this period, the Toronto Board of Education provided a special room for interviews and supplied clerical help to assist with record-keeping. In 1948 it opened a guidance clinic.[77]

Purposes of the Ontario program

Some idea of the nature and purposes of guidance as seen by departmental curriculum planners may be obtained from a curriculum brochure issued in 1950.[78]

Too frequently guidance has been considered as a separate entity, whereas in reality it is a permeating philosophy of service which should integrate the whole school programme. It is directly concerned with the extent to which the school fosters the development of the individual, provides exploratory experiences, broadens interests, makes available accurate and up-to-date educational and occupational information, and provides facilities for counselling so that pupils may make intelligent decisions.

The brochure recognized the different kinds of guidance needed by children at different stages of development. In the primary and junior divisions, the matters of major concern were said to be the growth of the pupil, his adjustment to the school, the promotion of acceptable ideals and attitudes, and the development of an interest in the educational and occupational worlds. In the intermediate division, the same features were identified as still relevant, but other factors were to be considered.

Young people of this age are experiencing great physical changes. Their rapid physical growth brings organic changes which require emotional adjustments. Their interests, also, are broadening and changing suddenly and violently. In fact, their entire social outlook is being transformed and is therefore presenting new demands which must be satisfied.

Modern society has created a world so complex that it challenges even the mature, the experienced, and the wise. Yet it demands of young people decisions that will affect their whole future. Guidance exists because young people must have information and help in making progress while they are at school, and help in understanding something of the occupational world into which they are going. They must learn to know something of their own strengths and weaknesses. They must have some basis for intelligent planning of a course of action. Finally they must have help in choosing, training for, and entering a field of work in which they will have a reasonable chance of success and of personal satisfaction, and in which they will also have an opportunity to make their personal contribution to society.

Any plan for organized guidance must recognize the fact that incidental guidance has always been a part of any good school programme; but it must make that incidental guidance more effective by special organization, scientific procedures, and co-ordination of all available means of help. It cannot operate successfully as an extra-curricular activity; a definite amount of time must be allotted to it during the school day. It cannot be left to chance and to the good-will of some interested person; it must be made a major responsibility of those teachers best suited for it by personality and training. A full programme cannot be built overnight; the various phases must be allowed to develop in an orderly fashion. It cannot be superimposed on a school organization; a sound philosophy of guidance must gradually permeate the whole school.

A curriculum guide issued in 1952 provided a set of detailed suggestions for establishing and operating a guidance program in the senior division.[79] Attention was drawn to the many decisions faced by the senior student with respect to his educational future. It was considered particularly important that he understand himself. The counsellor, in order to assist him, needed comprehensive information about his abilities, personal characteristics, and achievement from the time he started school. School records were the means of recording vital information and of keeping it available at all times. For this purpose, the Ontario School Record system had been developed in co-operation with a number of school boards, teachers, and school officials.

Self-determination, within certain limits, was said to be the democratic right of the individual student. The school was responsible for providing access to information on which decisions could be based and plans made. Part of this information had to do with the educational opportunities within the school and in other educational institutions. Students lacking it might choose the wrong electives and fail to qualify for further courses or for occupations which they might wish to enter. They also needed a broad and thorough background of occupational information. The Vocational Guidance Centre, as it was then called, at the Ontario College of Education performed a major role in supplying up-to-date educational and occupational information.

The aims of counselling in the senior division were defined as follows.

> Counselling is the focal point of all guidance services. In the individual interview all information is brought together in a meaningful and co-ordinated pattern. The student can thus be given valuable personal aid in making plans and decisions. The interview should be directed toward helping every pupil to develop his potentialities to the maximum, to his own advantage and in the best interests of society. This service should meet the needs of the average and above-average pupil rather than function solely as a remedial device for those who find themselves in difficulty.

At the senior level, the counsellor was advised to allow for increasing self-direction on the part of the student. It was suggested that interviews with parents were particularly helpful at this stage.

Problems experienced with guidance programs

The improvement of guidance at the early stages of the child's development was practically synonymous with ensuring a supply of well-informed, mature, and sensitive teachers. Thus the period of the teacher shortage, with its consequences in lower standards of admission to programs of teacher preparation, the influx of large numbers of immature young people into teaching, and the impossibility of enforcing any exacting standards of selection for teacher candidates, was not a happy one for the course of guidance any more than for education in general.

At higher levels, the recognition of a need for specialized guidance personnel produced a particular set of problems, some of which have been at least partially overcome and others of which, by their nature, can probably never be completely solved. One of the most important stemmed from the extraordinary and increasingly heavy demands made on the competent guidance teacher. Beginning with certain personal qualities, such as the ability to demonstrate an interest in the student's needs and to establish rapport, he must have a thorough knowledge of psychological principles and a capacity for applying them to human situations. If he is to provide sound educational guidance, he must have an appreciation of the value of different educational offerings, both at the secondary level and beyond. If he is to provide adequate vocational guidance, he must maintain up-to-date knowledge about an enormous variety of occupational opportunities in a complex technological society, including information on the kinds of interests and skills they require and their advantages and disadvantages for those with particular temperaments and intellectual capacities. While the demands made on guidance teachers point to a need for specialization within the area, actual circumstances have generally required a single individual to handle all aspects of the service. In its early stages, guidance failed, with some exceptions, to appeal to the most talented teachers. Officials who were involved with the introduction of the program observe that a considerable number of mediocre people were swept into the movement and that it took a good many years to get rid of them. Specialists in academic subjects continued to look down on guidance teachers, even those with specialists' qualifications. Only recently has it been possible to persuade any large number of the most able young people to concentrate on the guidance field. The change may be attributed in part to the growth of a particular type of idealism.

It has been the special responsibility of the guidance teacher to ensure that the whole program is a truly co-operative one, involving the co-ordinated efforts of as many as possible of the other teachers in the school. Both the teacher who is interested only in a narrow phase of the school's role and the one who himself accepts a major obligation to assist the student with broad aspects of his development have posed difficulties; the first because a larger contribution is needed from him and the second because he may easily see the guidance teacher as a rival or as a meddling busybody threatening his ability to perform as a teacher in the best and most adequate sense. Ideally, it would appear that the guidance teacher should ensure that the maximum contribution is made by other teachers, and himself concentrate strictly on those functions that require additional effort or specialized knowledge. In fact, many guidance teachers have been tempted into a short-sighted effort to enhance their own prestige by building up independent empires, the peculiar treasure of which consists of secret records containing test scores and anecdotal information which the uninitiated teacher would not understand, and which he might abuse if he were allowed access to them.

It has not been uncommon for the guidance teacher to possess a philosophical orientation differing from that prevailing among the majority of the staff. If the latter are mainly concerned with reinforcing the school's reputation for academic standards, and he is inclined to emphasize human development, a certain degree of conflict is inevitable. To insist that he conform to the prevailing atmosphere is to advocate the kind of hypocrisy that would ensure his failure to maintain his influence among the students.

The Royal Commission identified a series of problems relating to guidance.

Although we recognize the need for counselling services in our schools, and are convinced of their value, we are more than a little disquieted by the prevalence of a naive belief in their universal efficacy, and by the tendency, on the part of some teachers, to transfer to the counsellor all responsibility for assisting and advising students. It must be recognized that counselling services in schools will not answer all the questions and solve all the problems of the students and of the school. Nor is it possible, or advisable, to transfer to the special counsellor all the duties and responsibilities of the teacher in relation to counselling, which is a special service intended to supplement, not to supplant, the work of the teacher. It is not intended to weaken the relationship between the teacher and the pupil. The assistance which can be rendered through counselling is definitely limited. There are two reasons for this. Firstly, the choices made are ultimately the responsibility of the child and his parents, not of the school and counsellor. Secondly, the predictive value of any of the measures which are available at present, or are likely to be developed in the immediate future, is so low that definite and specific direction cannot be given toward any one avenue or occupation. Perhaps fortunately, the results for any particular student are seldom conclusive; in most cases they are indicative only. Hence, the task of the counsellor is to place the information, and his interpretation of it, before the pupil and his parents and, when requested, to assist them in making their decision.[80]

An article in the *ATA Magazine* recognized ways in which a counselling program could, and in some places did, become ineffective. In certain schools, there was said to be a tendency for the service to be seen as an extension of the administrative offices and the counsellor as another disciplinary agent. Counsellors were found useful by principals for scheduling classes, supervising cafeterias, and disciplining particularly stubborn students. A counselling service which aligned itself with the administration was said to be doomed to failure. Since many students' problems revolved around their inability to adhere to the rules and regulations enacted by the administration, they were hardly likely to air their grievances to one who was closely identified with administrative officers. They were even less likely to reveal their intimate thoughts about their most perplexing problems.[81]

School Record system

The Ontario School Record system, introduced on a voluntary basis in 1950, involved the use of sets of folders which facilitated the accumulation of information such as test scores and personal data over the student's entire school career. There were separate forms for the elementary and secondary levels, with provision for linkage. Each student's folder was supposed to accompany him if he moved from one school to another. Whether the system was any great success or not was a matter of opinion. There were certainly large numbers of cards kept in schools with little or no useful information on them. In any case, the department decided in 1959 to bring the last school systems into line and make the use of the cards universal. There were provisions for the revision of the forms every fifth year. A certain amount of difficulty was caused because of misuse, or fear of misuse, of the contents.

In 1967 Robert Gerrish devoted a page in *School Administration* to some of the issues in guidance record keeping. He reported the results of a poll of Canadian school boards which showed that 80 per cent of them kept student records indefinitely, and the remaining 20 per cent kept them between five and twenty-five years. He listed three reasons for the long periods of retention: the possibility that they might be needed again; the fact that they were tangible evidence of the board's product and conveyed a feeling of accomplishment; and the reluctance of any single individual to take the responsibility for destroying them. Gerrish suggested that fifteen years ought to be the maximum period of time for the retention of any student's records after he left the school system. His main reasons for this restriction were that improvements in the interpretation of behaviour tended to invalidate the contents of records as a source of information; that an increasing time lapse reduced the value of information for the prediction of behaviour; that the danger of limitations on freedom were enhanced by the existence of records of constantly declining validity.[82] The last point has rightly been causing growing concern, especially when records, often containing grossly inaccurate material, have been released to the police, to mental hospitals, and to forensic agancies. Even an assurance that the entries are 100 per cent accurate does not remove one source of objection – that the data may be used to facilitate control by governmental or other agencies.

Recommendations of the Provincial Committee on Aims and Objectives

The Provincial Committee on Aims and Objectives recommended that teachers of younger children be given more preparation for counselling in both the pre-service and in-service phases to prepare them for the general assistance and guidance they should be able to provide for each pupil. At the senior level it was suggested that the homeroom teacher, or one who knew the student through teaching him a regular subject, should handle many aspects of the guidance program such as study habits, career planning, and course selection. In order to achieve the optimum effect, the same teacher might be assigned to a group of students for more than one year, with provision for transfer of individual students in cases of incompatibility. The teacher would require some background in guidance and counselling, but need not be a specialist. In addition, the committee recommended that there be full-time counselling specialists in each school or school system, with responsibility for dealing with serious home problems, economic troubles, and emotional and social difficulties. These specialists would be expected to keep up with trends in guidance and counselling and provide leadership and assistance to teachers. Where there were several small schools in an area, an itinerant specialist might work with principals and, through them, with teachers. The committee thought that counselling should be the dominant service to students, and that vocational guidance should receive relatively less attention.

R.C. Harris, a guidance counseller, took strong exception to some of these recommendations. He claimed that the criticisms of existing guidance programs contained in the report were really based on the activities of the untrained teacher counsellors that the committee itself was advocating. Qualified counsellors, from his experience, were appalled at many of the activities being called counselling. He felt that, by definition of the very important professional role of teaching, the classroom teacher could not be a counsellor.

Guidance handled by the classroom or homeroom teacher is the very situation we are in today. It is the very thing that the pupils are complaining is so grossly inadequate. In the complex social environment in which modern man must live, skilled counseling is needed by all children – at times unique to each child. Skilled counseling does not preclude the *counsel* that adults and children afford one another. To suggest that this level of social *counsel* is adequate to the needs of youth, especially in the delightfully free learning environment proposed by the report, is a gross misunderstanding of what is involved in school counseling.

We need in our *school systems*, psychologists, social workers, and psychiatrists to handle difficult and complex problems. We need in our *schools*, counselors to work with all pupils in order that learning and growth may be maximal.[83]

Supply of guidance teachers

The Provincial Committee's recommendations demonstrated a realization of the existing scarcity of properly trained, full-time counsellors. In 1967–8 the Metropolitan Toronto area, where supporting services were much more generously provided than in many other parts of the province, had, according to estimates, the equivalent of only one full-time counsellor to approximately 820 students. Of 1,002 teachers assigned to full-time guidance duties, 53 per cent lacked certificates in guidance, 15 per cent held the Elementary Guidance Certificate, 15 per cent the Intermediate Certificate, and 17 per cent the Specialist's Certificate. Only those in the last group could be assumed to have received formal training in counselling techniques.

The Advisory Council of Directors of the Metropolitan Toronto School Board made a submission to the minister on June 19, 1968. They point out that the Toronto Board was planning to repeat the Elementary Guidance course and the North York Board the Intermediate Guidance course during the following winter. They expressed the hope that the six Metro guidance co-ordinators and the Director of Guidance in the Department of Education might meet to discuss the possibility of having local universities initiate guidance courses at the undergraduate level, which the department might recognize for credit. They also suggested that the universities be asked to establish honours courses in guidance that would lead to "an endorsed, Type A Certificate in Guidance." They supported the principle of recognizing teachers whose training had been obtained outside the province. When the teachers' colleges became affiliated with the universities, they hoped the curriculum would include an adequate introduction to guidance and counselling.

As of 1969 the Department of Education recommended that there be one full-time guidance worker for every three hundred students in secondary schools, and that at least one period of counselling per week be scheduled for every fifteen students. The comparable prescription for elementary school was one full-time counsellor for every five hundred pupils. Proposals such as those conveyed by the Metropolitan Toronto directors had obviously to be implemented if such goals were to be met in the foreseeable future.

SEVEN

The role of measurement and evaluation

GENERAL PRINCIPLES

Educational measurement involves the process of assigning quantitative symbols to various manifestations of behaviour in order to indicate the degree to which individuals possess certain traits, qualities, or characteristics considered relevant to education. Evaluation introduces the element of qualitative judgment. The rationale for both measurement and evaluation rests on the obvious fact that individuals differ from one another and that the ordinary functions of social life require that they treat one another differently. These two processes are thus inherent in all organized society.

In very simple societies, a great many decisions by and for individuals may be based largely on custom. Such measurement and evaluation as are practised may be very informal and direct. An individual is continuously exposed to most of the range of activities in which he is likely to be called upon to participate at one stage of his life or another and has adequate opportunities of assessing his own potentialities in relation to the demands he is called upon to meet. Those with the authority to assign him to certain roles have had casual opportunities to observe him and to form judgments about him. Tests of skill or courage in initiation ceremonies are not actually designed to answer a genuine question about a person's fitness for a new status, but rather to put a kind of formal stamp on the transition.

As society becomes complex, direct personal appraisals cease to be adequate to enable individuals to choose sound courses of action for themselves or for others to assign them to appropriate roles. A set of tasks is therefore designed and presented in an organized fashion, and the individual is given a tag or label to indicate how he has performed. By reading and interpreting his label, he can help to plot his own course; by reading the same label, others can avail themselves of a necessary short-cut in making decisions about him. Educational institutions are commonly assigned the task of designing and awarding appropriate labels. These may be used by the student to make educational or career choices, by the school to determine his subsequent treatment, by other institutions to decide whether or not and under what conditions to admit him, and by employers to determine whether or not to hire him.

Part of the justification for the label in the field of education has to do with the individual's own welfare. It is obviously unjustifiable to urge him to do what he cannot do or to be what he cannot be. To express the idea more positively, it is important that he identify the direction of his own most promising potentialities and pursue these as assiduously as possible. In terms of the economic realities, it becomes more and more obvious that a person cannot try out a large number of positions for which the required training is complex and expensive. The interests of society demand that funds spent on manpower development be used productively.

The United States has gone much further than any other nation in the development and use of measures of aptitudes, abilities, and other attributes. Although some of the practices relating to these measures in education are subject to more or less severe criticism, it is doubtful that any substitute could have made possible the huge educational structure that has been created in that country. It is also unlikely that the current level of industrial and commercial success could have been achieved without the use of tests for the efficient allocation of manpower.

The processes of measurement and evaluation involve questions of real concern. 1 / Is the selection of tasks that constitutes a test or examination really relevant to the decision that is to be based on the candidate's performance? In other words, is the test valid for the intended purposes? Is the resulting label genuine or spurious? 2 / Does preparation for the test or examination pervert the educational experiences or the personal qualities that it is intended to measure? 3 / Is the label read correctly, with neither more nor less reliance placed on it than it actually merits? Ideally, of course, the answers should be "yes" to the first and third of these questions and "no" to the second. The discrepancy between the ideal and the reality constitutes the challenge to theory and practice in educational measurement and evaluation. Any serious thought about the whole issue should make it clear that the abandonment of the entire process is not a credible solution. The only alternative to adequate and properly handled measurement is at least some degree of ineffectiveness in education.

There appear to be no up-to-date figures on the use of tests of different kinds in Ontario schools. The Guidance Centre of the College of Education of the University of Toronto does, however, report that sales continue to rise each year, particularly of devices for personality assessment. Nevertheless, educational measurement is perceptibly on the defensive in this province. The current decline in favour appears to cover instruments with a wide variety of purposes and values. Some of these devices, or at least the uses that have been made of them in the past, are undoubtedly identifiable with practices that leading educators are rejecting as rigid, formalistic, and outmoded. The main thrust of the Hall-Dennis report has been to emphasize the process of learning in contrast to that of assessing learning for extrinsic purposes. Also, the abuses of certain measurement procedures have been so flagrant that an ultimate antipathetic reaction has seemed almost inevitable, no matter what the predominant trends of philosophical thought. Unfortunately, there is a danger that a wave of revulsion may lead to the neglect of many techniques that can be of great assistance in the pursuit of the most enlightened objectives.

CLASSIFICATION OF MEASURING DEVICES

There are many ways of classifying educational and psychological measuring devices. Numerous periodicals, textbooks, and reference books deal with this question and should be referred to by the reader who seeks a detailed treatment. For the purposes of the present volume, reference to a few basic classification schemes will suffice to illuminate the subsequent discussion.

A primary classification has to do with the function to be measured. The functions in which educators are most interested can be divided into two groups: 1 / those calling for an indication of maximum or optimum performance and 2 / those requiring a measure of typical or habitual behaviour. The first group includes achievement, general intelligence, and aptitudes; the second involves interests, attitudes, non-intellective psychological characteristics, such as temperament and creativity, and physical states.

A second basis for categorization is the use to be made of the results of the examination or test. Again, two main subdivisions may be defined: 1 / appraisal in relation to a standard and 2 / diagnosis. A standard is a point on a scale of measures to which value has been assigned. This point is normally determined by making observations on the performance of some defined group, with statistical treatment usually required in order to make the result meaningful. A student's performance may be compared to a standard for a number of purposes: for example, to aid the teacher in planning a program, to assist the student in appraising his own efforts, to determine the fate of the student in terms of pass or failure, to assess reasonable learning objectives by indicating aptitude or capacity, and, in the area of certain psychological characteristics, to identify abnormalities or aberrations. Diagnostic tests are designed to identify specific difficulties, weaknesses, or omissions, and are generally useful only to the extent that remedial action follows their application.

A third classification scheme has to do with the approach to be used in measuring the defined function. The use of pencil and paper usually represents an indirect approach, as compared with direct observation of actual performance under controlled conditions. Either method may involve verbal or non-verbal behaviour. Pencil-and-paper verbal devices may again be subdivided into free-response and objective types. In school examinations, the former is usually referred to as the essay-type examination.

A fourth and very important distinction, at least as far as achievement examinations and tests are concerned, has to do with the auspices under which they are constructed and administered, whether by an external agency or by the teacher responsible for the instructional program. In the first case, their purpose is to classify, to describe, or to label the student with reference to a standard, usually to provide the basis for a decision about the future course of his education, whether it is to be continued in some form or terminated. External examinations tend to become the object of instruction rather than an adjunct to it. Internal examinations may, of course, fill a similar role, but one basic distinction between the two types is that the teacher and student are inclined to be in alliance in matching their efforts against the external examination, whereas the internal examination places the teacher on the other side.

MEASUREMENT OF ACHIEVEMENT

Lack of teacher preparation in measurement

There have been serious logical inconsistencies in traditional examination practices in Ontario, as well as in other provinces and countries. On the one hand, the fact that programs of teacher preparation have given little attention to the study of measurement techniques seems to imply that examinations are of little importance, whereas the strong emphasis on external examinations throughout most of the history of Ontario education suggests that they have been considered very important indeed. It is almost as if the attitude had been that constructing, marking, and interpreting the results of examinations required capacities and skills that could not be properly expected of the average teacher. And yet many teachers appear to have the diametrically opposite view that measurement is a simple process that comes naturally and without effort to any competent teacher. Every student of measurement realizes what serious misconceptions prevail as a result of these attitudes.

Undesirable practices associated with the measurement of achievement

It is easy to say, and has been said over and over again, that the first step in constructing an achievement test or examination is to define a set of instructional objectives and to put them in some order of priority. Items or questions are then devised to measure the attainment of these objectives, corresponding in number or weight to the relative importance of each objective. The work of Benjamin Bloom and associates at the University of Chicago has made a particularly important contribution to an understanding of this process. Bloom's basic categories of objectives in the cognitive domain are knowledge, comprehension, application, analysis, synthesis, and evaluation. It is hard to imagine a reputable educator claiming that examinations should require only the recall of factual information, particularly of facts in isolation. Some of the standard clichés of the era condemn this practice and exhort teachers to aim at the development of an ability to associate and express ideas, to arrive at conclusions on the basis of evidence, and generally to engage in the higher mental processes. Despite the universality of such lofty ideals, it is a continuously disillusioning experience for the onlooker to observe how often teachers fall into the practice of examining for little but factual recall based on the contents of a textbook or dictated notes. If such a practice is the result of an inability to teach for any other objective, the situation is of course far more serious than any tinkering with measurement techniques can remedy. But if more worthy purposes are really being pursued, the use of bad examinations tend to negate the effectiveness of the effort. It is difficult to persuade a student that anything is of genuine importance other than what might appear on the examination, particularly if the results are intended to label him for the purposes of promotion or admission to an institution at a higher level.

A study of measurement techniques can be very helpful, particularly in clarifying a teacher's thinking about educational objectives and the means for their attainment. But the most fundamental requirements for the good examiner are a thorough grasp of the subject or area of study involved, not only in terms of its immediate content, but also with respect to its broad implications for the educational process, and a deep understanding of its impact on the developing understanding of the learner.

Examining for the purpose of appraisal in relation to a standard consists of two distinct processes: placing the candidates in rank order of achievement from high to low and determining the position of the group, and of each individual in it, with respect to the standard. The first of these functions is a fundamental aspect of teacher competence, and any teacher accused of being unable to perform it on the basis of his own judgment might rightly consider himself under the severest condemnation. The second function is much more difficult and more subject to error than many teachers imagine. The ability to read a single, isolated paper and to place it correctly on a scale of values has so consistently failed to manifest itself under controlled conditions that researchers in the field consider it to be almost non-existent. A teacher who reads a single paper, no matter how carefully, and proclaims with assurance that it is a 70-per-center is most probably fooling himself about the accuracy of his judgment. The chances are excellent that he would identify it as a 60-per-center or an 80-per-center if he appraised it again long enough afterwards to forget his original verdict. Much the same may be said about the person who claims to be able to set an examination paper at a given level of difficulty. Time and again the grade 13 departmental examiners proved far off the mark in estimating the difficulty of the questions.

The construction of standardized objective-type tests involves no controversy. The process of standardization itself is designed to give meaning to the quantitative symbol assigned to the individual test score by making it possible to compare it with the performance of some defined group.

Scaling essay-type examination marks is a comparable process and is similarly justified.

Abuse of the terms "objective" and "subjective" as applied to tests and examinations has been widespread among Ontario teachers. The misconception is based on the opinion that an objective test is one that can do no more than measure factual recall. Many such tests, especially those constructed by classroom teachers without any specific training for the task, do actually conform to this pattern, thus helping to sustain the impression. The term "subjective," in its turn, is judged to mean the opposite. A subjective test is thus identified as an essay-type test that measures the more elusive abilities involved in organization, interpretation, application, and appreciation. In actual fact, subjective means the tendency of one person's assessment of a phenomenon to differ from that of another, or of a single person's judgment of the phenomenon to vary on different occasions. A completely subjective examination might just as well be marked by pulling a number at random out of a hat as by any process involving the exercise of human judgment. Thus subjectivity in examinations is an evil to be avoided, and objectivity a quality to be sought. Paradoxically, at least at first glance, such an assertion is not the equivalent of claiming that the ideal examination or test would be completely objective. Certain desirable qualities are often associated with some degree of subjectivity, so that it may be advisable to retain a substantial subjective element in order to get the concomitant benefits. The measurement of creative self-expression provides a good example. It is gratifying to secure agreement on the part of judges as to the degree to which a certain piece of work manifests this quality – in other words, to make its assessment as objective as possible. But a so-called objective test would be an inappropriate device for its measurement.

Not least important of the misunderstandings about the measurement of achievement, to say nothing of many other functions, lies in the tendency to overestimate the precision of the resulting marks or scores. Reputable standardized tests provide a means of estimating the amount of error in a score by specifying the standard error. The fact that most Ontario teachers lack the basic statistical knowledge to understand this measure leaves the exact interpretation of test results in the hands of guidance or other specialized personnel. When classroom teachers do attempt to deal with the test scores, they will all too often ignore the concept of measurement error, and endow them with spurious exactitude.

The corresponding abuse has been much more serious with respect to traditional examinations. Here the teacher is backed by generations of confidence in the conventional wisdom. At the middle and higher levels of education, the use of the scale ranging from 0 to 100 has prevailed despite overwhelming evidence that it provides for too many points for valid distinctions to be possible. The fact that individual teachers are willing to admit freely that they have no great confidence that the 73 they give one student really represents higher achievement than the 72 they give another does not necessarily mean that they are prepared to support the switch to a letter-grade system with perhaps five or six categories of achievement. And often where such a move is attempted, there is a rousing protest from the parents, who are thoroughly steeped in the traditions of the old scale and have no confidence that any other will tell them how their children are really doing, especially if it is very important to them to be able to make comparisons with other people's children. Nevertheless, rapid changes were made in the 1960s. J.R.H. Morgan estimated in November 1968 that perhaps 25 per cent of Ontario secondary schools would have adopted a five-point letter scale by 1969 and reported that there was serious talk about abandoning a numerical grading in favour of an expanded anecdotal report.[1] Obviously, of course, there was still a great distance to go.

There are other unsatisfactory aspects of the use of the hundred-point scale that have tended to be reinforced by tradition. For example, a mark of 50 has generally been regarded as distinguishing between success and failure. But it is difficult to assign any exact meaning to such a mark. It makes most sense, perhaps, when learning can be equated to the acquisition of very precisely defined skills. For example, if one learns to spell half the words on a list, one gets 50 per cent. But it is legitimate to ask whether the development of understanding can be treated in the same way. There is a suggestion of absurdity in the idea that an individual "passes" when he half understands a concept. Searching questions have often been asked as well about the validity of placing a stamp of approval on any performance that merits only half the total marks attainable. A bank clerk who performed only half of his transactions correctly, or even only 95 per cent, would soon be unemployed.

The variety of ways in which the scale has been used, depending on the traditions associated with a particular subject, have also been a source of difficulty. It has been common to regard a mark of 100 in English composition as ultimate perfection, not to be attained by ordinary mortals. Many teachers have regarded 85 or 90 as an actual ceiling. In subjects such as mathematics, on the other hand, a perfect mark has not infrequently been awarded. When marks have been totaled and averaged for the purposes of awarding scholarships, on the false assumption that the process involves comparable components, it has been a distinct disadvantage to have specialized in certain subjects. Beginning students in measurement have often been quite taken aback to realize the seriousness of the anomalies involved in the common practice of averaging marks in different subjects which have not in reality been marked on the same scale.

Scaling

The practice of scaling the marks on achievement examinations is essentially synonymous with the adjustment of raw scores obtained on a test. There is, however, a much greater problem of explanation and justification because of the prevalence of some of the mistaken assumptions about the traditional marking scale already referred to, particularly the idea that raw marks assigned on such a scale are endowed with immutable, absolute value. The need for scaling rests on the reality that examination marks acquire meaning only when related to the performance of some group. Even the extreme traditionalist point of view recognizes this fact, the "group" in this case being a kind of conceptual abstraction built up from the marker's experience with the performance of candidates he has dealt with in the past. His error is in believing that the standard so developed is relatively stable over a period of time and impervious to influence by the quality of the performance of subsequent candidates. The group used for reference purposes in the process of scaling may be entirely abstract. For example, the adjustment of a set of marks to conform to the normal curve is justified on the basis that observations of the distribution of various psychological phenomena in groups from unselected populations have tended to distribute themselves in a characteristically symmetrical fashion about a central point, the number of observations decreasing in a mathematically predictable fashion in relation to the distance from this point. The behaviour of scores has been generalized into a kind of law, and the process of scaling involves making a specific set of scores conform to this law. When the purpose of scaling is to decide whether students will pass or fail, or whether they will be awarded first, second, third, or lesser standing, certain "cut-off" points must be identified. The selection of such points requires a value judgment that may be based on one of a great number of criteria.

When the practice of scaling the grade 13 departmental examination marks was placed on a systematic basis in 1961, and subsequently carried out according to a scheme devised by the writer acting as an informal consultant to the Department of Education, the initial reference group was actually a composite of all the grade 13 candidates who had written each subject during the previous eleven years. Averaging the number who had obtained marks in each achievement catgory (first class, second class, etc) in all subjects combined produced the following results:

First class	Second class	Third class	Credit	Failure
(75–100)	(66–74)	(60–65)	(50–59)	(0–49)
15%	16%	17%	32%	20%

Of course, these percentages had varied from one subject to another. A decision was made to eliminate such variations over a period of three years, so that eventually the percentage in each achievement category would be the same for each subject. The writer objected to such a policy on the grounds that there was a demonstrable variation in the quality of the candidates from subject to subject. For example, it was generally realized that such subjects as German and Greek were taken as extra options by students who had shown unusual ability and application. It therefore seemed reasonable that the percentage of first-class papers in these subjects should continue to be high, and the percentage of failures relatively low. The reverse applied to geography, which at that time was regarded as a favourite option of weaker students. The original policy was reversed before it could be brought to fruition. In the later years of the grade 13 departmentals, each year's plans for scaling involved a decision as to how much variation to recognize in establishing the scaling scheme for each subject in order to take differences in ability into account.

It should be noted that the scaling of the grade 13 departmentals never involved an attempt to adjust marks to fit the normal curve. The selection of four cut-off points to produce a fixed percentage (or something as close as possible to it) in each achievement category was incompatible with such a procedure. The shape of the curve actually produced was considerably flatter than the normal, that is, definitely platykurtic.

The justification for scaling the grade 13 departmentals rested strictly on the assumption that there was negligible variation from one year to another in the capacity or in the quality of preparation of the candidates. Scaling was thought to be needed in order to ensure that a candidate with a given degree of ability and preparation would receive approximately the same mark regardless of which year he happened to write. There seemed to be no reasonable justification for a comparatively high or low proportion of failures, or a variation in the number of students receiving scholarships or bursaries based on a fixed minimum mark, simply because the paper in that particular year happened to be unusually easy or difficult. Despite all efforts to maintain a uniform level of difficulty from year to year, the earlier record showed clearly that substantial fluctuations had frequently occurred. In fact, a particularly difficult paper in one subject written before a formal policy of scaling was introduced, would have produced more than 60 per cent failures had some rather unsystematic adjustments not been made. On another occasion, the extraordinary competence of grade 13 algebra teachers was proclaimed in schools throughout the province on the basis of a paper that produced first class marks for more than 50 per cent of the candidates who wrote that year. It seemed surprising at the time, and seems even more so in retrospect, that the essential absurdity of the situation was not more obvious.

The practice of scaling the grade 13 departmentals produced attacks from diametrically opposite directions. On the one hand, there were those who claimed that the maintenance of a fixed percentage of failures tended to mask a gradual deterioration in performance over a period of years. This decline was postulated on the assumption that, since an increasing proportion of young people were completing secondary school, the lower levels of capacity must be more fully represented, and the general standard of performance must be declining. There is a persuasive logic about this view, but it fails to account for the positive influence of a rising level of aspiration on the part of the student and a more effective effort on the part of the teacher. Whether present-day students love learning any more than their predecessors is a question that would be difficult to answer. But there is no doubt that the desirability of obtaining an education is more obvious, since the available alternatives are becoming less and less satisfactory.

The contrary view about the practice was really an attack on the concept of failure. It was expressed by F.A. Burr, member for Sandwich-Riverside, after the departmental examination system had been abolished: "Until recently, our system deliberately and cold-bloodedly decreed that a certain percentage of all grade 13 students in the various subjects must be failed. Although top scholars will always be accorded their due, it is unnecessary and it is inhumane to humiliate and hurt and demean those who do not excel."[2]

The assumption that there is no sound reason for yearly fluctuations in examination results is tenable only for large groups of candidates. It is impossible to draw any definite dividing line to distinguish between a group that is large enough to be used as its own reference group for scaling marks and one that is not. There is no question, however, that the thousands who wrote each of the major grade 13 papers belonged in the former category, and that a single class falls in the latter. Where real variations in aptitude or achievement from one class to another may be expected, the application of rigid scaling schemes becomes a reprehensible abuse. It is one that has unfortunately existed in some Ontario school systems and in a somewhat different form in universities. When the writer inquired whether the abolition of the external departmental examinations and the subsequent rise in marks awarded to grade 13 graduates produced any noticeable increase in the number of weak first-year university students, he was told by more than one person that it would be difficult to tell because of the inclination of many professors to fail about the same percentage each year regardless of the circumstances. However informally, they are thus engaged in the process of scaling in one of its less desirable forms. A certain professor at the University of Toronto was notorious for years for announcing to every freshman class that each member might take a look at his neighbour on either side and tell himself that one of the three, himself included, would not be there the following year. There is a chilling determinism about this kind of performance, although it probably produced results of a kind. Referring to scaling under such circumstances, Bascom St John made the following comment in the article previously referred to: "In many schools, colleges and even in single classes, the application of this evil formula destroys honestly won standings, and in the higher levels, whole careers."[3]

In examining the question of scaling in the *Bulletin* of the OSSTF, D.A. Bristow asked: "To what extent is it reasonable to assume that teachers' marks do represent in the typical high school a fair appraisal of each student's work?"[4] In answering the question, he recognized that the standards and calibre of teachers of the same subject varied considerably, that certain subjects tended to be "high mark" or "low mark" subjects in some schools, and that the student was frequently denied a mark that related him equitably to other students in his grade and to his own record of previous years. Bristow did not, however, see any process of adjustment by rigid formula as a satisfactory answer. He felt that schools undertook, through final promotion meetings, to relieve students of the most serious consequences of inequities. In particular, he felt that teachers recognized a justification for altering marks when it appeared that a student was on the point of failing by a small margin when he was well or better prepared to do the work of the next higher grade than another student who had scraped through in all of his subjects but had shown no real strength in any one subject or group of subjects. Bristow asserted that the application of a formula did not take the place of an analysis of the individual student's performance by his teachers.

The really fundamental criticism of the whole scaling process has nothing to do with the object, entirely valid in the immediate sense, of attempting to make the results of the examinations more equitable. It refers rather to the use to which the results are put. Examinations administered to a group large enough to justify scaling are nearly always part of the mass processing of students for classificatory purposes and may have little to do with the achievement of valid educational objectives. As educators become more concerned with individual progress and development, the question of when and how to scale marks will necessarily recede in importance.

Standards of achievement

A brief definition of the term "standard" has already been offered. Its educational implications depend on whether it refers to a level to be attained by a group as a whole or by a single individual. A group standard is applied when a value judgment is made about the achievement of a class, a school, or a school system. Much of the prevailing disillusion with measurement is based on the past use or abuse of examinations and tests to determine group standards. For years even those superintendents and directors of local systems who knew better were practically compelled by the attitudes of their boards and the public to brag in their annual reports about the high percentage of first class marks and the low percentage of failures attained by their grade 13 students in the departmental examinations. Survey tests of achievement were administered in grade groups throughout a school system for the apparent purpose of demonstrating how high the average pupil stood in relation to the test norms. A norm is, of course, simply an average obtained in a special administration of a test by a reference group selected for the purpose. But many of those who were prepared to comment with pride on how many points their own pupils stood above the norm had not the slightest notion of who or what this reference norming group consisted of.

A fundamental defect in the whole process lay in the fact that it so often involved comparison of the incomparable. Officials in schools or school systems where the pupils on the average scored below the test norm were naturally careful to point out that the general level of intelligence was below normal, that many of the families in the area were culturally deprived, or that the community attitude toward education tended to be unfavourable. Where achievement was above the norm, there was seldom adequate allowance for conditions opposite to these, and complacent statements were typically made about the quality of the teaching and the effectiveness of other aspects of the educational program.

Speculation about variations in group standards over the years is a popular pastime in certain quarters. Each generation has its quota of members who recall how much higher the educational standards were in the past. On the other hand, every now and then one hears a prominent man, secure in the realization that his position in life is unassailable, proclaim in a tone of mock humility that he never would have been admitted to high school, or to university, had current high standards prevailed in his day. Strictly speaking, the situation is too complex to justify any such assertion, even if it were made in complete seriousness. The tendency for marks of a given order to change their value over a period of time, regardless of efforts to keep them stable, has already been indicated. Furthermore, it is practically impossible to find ability groups in institutions of secondary and higher education today that are comparable with those of a few decades ago because of the steady increase in the proportion of those attending from each age group.

C.E. Phillips, writing in *The Development of Education in Canada,* based his verdict on standards on circumstantial evidence.

> Perennial complaints about an alleged deterioration of education have never within the past century been supported by objective evidence covering any considerable area or period. A consideration, period by period, of such factors as general knowledge and professional qualifications of teachers, length and regularity of pupils' attendance, and quality of instructional materials makes it impossible to believe that education has not improved steadily by any criterion generally acceptable.[5]

The present emphasis is clearly and commendably on individual standards. Among those concerned with the quality of education, the view is unanimous that these should be as high as possible. And the truly humane and truly realistic are also unanimous in the view that the standards should take full account of each individual's potentialities and should be varied accordingly. The history of education presents a dreary account of practices based on the absurd assumption that every child should be assessed according to his success in clearing a common hurdle. Prizes and scholarships have typically been awarded for the highest achievement among unequal competitors. The results have no doubt seemed very gratifying to those with the capacity to win them. The effect on those who realize from the beginning that they are out of the running has seldom until recently been considered in all its destructive implications.

The rejection of the common standard for all pupils of a given age or grade has often been equated with the absence of standards. This position is illogical. If one is concerned with promoting the highest level of achievement, there is no defensible goal beyond that defined by the individual's capacities. Comparison with some other individual's maximum performance is irrelevant unless one accepts the outmoded view that competition in an unequal race is an effective way of motivating the weaker competitor. A recent Ontario Department of Education guide asserted that "external standards requiring uniformity of achievement are unrealistic at best and cruel at worst."[6] The same document illuminated the role of standards.

Standards are an integral part of the daily activities of pupils. They are implicit in the nature of the questions asked by the teacher, the quality of the textbooks being used, the behaviour encouraged by the social climate of the school, the type of problem-centred activities engaged in by the pupils, and the ability to reach levels of achievement on tests unrelated to time schedules.

There is considerable difference of opinion about the extent of the school's obligation to specify each student's level of achievement in relation to a common group standard for the benefit of potential employers and for the purposes of admission to institutions of further education. Traditionally the secondary schools have accepted a major responsibility for assisting the universities by sorting out the candidates with reasonable prospects of success, as the story of the departmental examinations, recounted in volume V, indicates. In recent years, a searching look has been taken at the price paid in terms of the distortion of the educational process involved in the assumption of such an obligation. As far as the departmental examinations are concerned, the decision was made, with considerable reinforcement provided by the growing difficulty in operating the machinery, that the price was too great.

As far as employers are concerned, it has been suggested that they might benefit more in the long run if they let the schools concentrate on improving the standard of education reached by each student and made their own assessment on the basis on such factors as interviews, tests administered under their own auspices, and performance during a probationary period of employment. School achievement has often a very tenuous relationship with success on the job in any case. Quite often a straightforward verdict on the student's reliability, general competence, and initiative would be as satisfactory as any certificate the school or the department could provide.

At specialized levels of higher education, there is a role for uniform standards that is not relevant at earlier stages. It applies particularly where the objective of study is to acquire skills to be exercised where the welfare and interests of society have primacy. The public can hardly afford to look with equanimity on the prospect of turning out inept doctors, incompetent mechanics, or poor teachers. In the general interest, a minimum level of attainment must be specified, and those who do not meet it are necessarily rejected.

With respect to general or liberal studies in universities, uniform minimum standards are defined for admission and graduation in order to maintain the specialized character of the institution. It is commonly assumed, although the assumption has been questioned in responsible quarters, that the presence of large numbers of individuals who do not meet a reasonably high uniform standard would so dilute the atmosphere of learning that the attainment of scholarly excellence would be out of reach even for those with the requisite capacity and inclination. The question is partly one of economics. Even in the present affluent age, it is doubtful that any society can afford to maintain universities that attempt to do something helpful for any individual who chooses to enter, regardless of his qualifications, without sacrificing some of the vital special functions that these institutions are expected to perform.

The concept of failure

The concept of failure is an integral part of the process of ensuring that uniform standards are maintained for the purposes just mentioned. To acknowledge its necessity under some circumstances is not of course to say that its psychological effects on unsuccessful candidates are unimportant. Some societies have experienced very unfavourable consequences from the existence of large numbers of disgruntled students trying in vain to breach the barriers imposed by an excessively rigorous examination system. Even where the creation of a revolutionary class is not an imminent prospect, and it may be noted that present-day campus revolutionaries are most likely to represent the most capable rather than the least capable students, serious questions have been asked about the value of the experience of a failed year, both from the point of view of the student's self-development and from that of the return on the economic investment involved. Most universities now take more active steps than ever before to try to reduce failures by providing counselling and psychological services.

In the elementary schools, and to a lesser extent in the secondary schools, there has been a strong shift in Ontario attitudes in recent decades with respect to the implications of failure for individual self-development. Here, as in so many other areas, the discovery of enlightened principles is no modern phenomenon. It is rather their acceptance by increasing numbers of educational leaders and the headway they have made among the mass of educational practitioners that are worthy of note.

H.L. Campbell, then British Columbia's Deputy Superintendent of Education, expressed the conventional view in one of his Quance Lectures in 1952, when he said that "given a favourable environment and good teaching, if a student with the requisite ability for a course does not measure up satisfactorily, he should be failed. Particularly should this be true where failure results from a lack of application. Only thus can the pupil learn that effort is the price of success."[7] If the first part of this assertion is interpreted in a certain way, and hedged with sufficient qualifications, it can still command general acceptance. If the learner is sufficiently stable and self-confident, if he is dealing with an area of learning where he has a true inner drive toward achievement and not merely an externally imposed and superficial incentive, and if he genuinely accepts responsibility for failure and attributes it to his own reprehensible lack of effort, as distinct from feeling that he lacks ability, then repetition of the work may not only result in much improved achievement, but may make a contribution to character building as well. The problem is that failure does not usually involve this combination of factors.

Sympathetic observation and research are convincing more and more people that failure does not teach the average pupil that effort is the price of success. On the contrary, it usually tends to produce a habit of failure and a revulsion against learning. Campbell was apparently oblivious to the fact that lack of application usually results from the pupil's inability to see relevance in the subject. Or perhaps he did not think it mattered whether the pupil saw any relevance in it or not. According to the traditionalist view, the study of a subject in school and a later recognition of its value may represent a normal sequence. There are perhaps even some surviving adherents of the belief that the study of irrelevant material has value for character building. It has been demonstrated time and again that repeating a grade normally produces little improvement in achievement unless there is a fundamental change in motivation. For a pupil for whom learning is meaningful, and for whom learning experiences are organized in a manner appropriate to his capacities and needs, the traditional concept of failure has little meaning. Looked at in this way, the term "failure" can only be applied to those who provide the content and conditions for learning.

There are unquestionably many teachers in Ontario schools who still fall back on the threat of failure as a motivating device. What passes for learning under such conditions is being recognized as of doubtful value, and the teacher who is incapable of producing more effective incentives is being subjected to well deserved criticism. But there may be certain conditions beyond an individual teacher's control which make it difficult to adopt a more fruitful approach. Despite efforts to make the curriculum more relevant to the learner's interests, there is still a great deal of material that fails to meet such a criterion. Also, many a student, because of inept handling by previous teachers or the influence of a destructive subculture, has reached the point where it is too much to expect an ordinary human being to reverse his attitudes. If the prospect of failure retains any power to produce a semblance of effort, it is all too easy for the harried teacher to reach out for it.

The elementary schools of Ontario have been moving for many years in the direction of regular promotion regardless of age. The development had gone quite far before serious consideration was being given to the abolition of the grade system and the introduction of truly individualized instruction. The elimination of the high school entrance examination in 1949 was an important step in this direction. There has of course been criticism of the whole trend on the grounds that it represents a lowering of standards. The fallacy in the argument is that the level of proficiency reached by those who have been allowed to proceed from year to year despite low achievement has not been compared with the level they would have reached had they been forced to repeat grades, but with that attained by their more successful classmates. The only demonstrable lowering of standards has perhaps been the lower average achievement for the entire class on an examination or standardized test.

Free-response and objective achievement tests and examinations

The free-response or essay-type test or examination is the traditional type in which the question permits some variation in the answer according to the respondent's knowledge, understanding, appreciation, or whatever is required, and according to his ability to express it. The objective-type test usually requires the respondent to fill in blanks, to choose the correct response from a series of two or more alternatives, to choose the preferred response from a list of such alternatives, or to match items in two complementary lists on the basis of some criterion. The test can be marked objectively if purely mechanical skills, with no necessary knowledge of the subject matter involved, are required in the process. It can be interpreted objectively if a set of norms is supplied that enables an observer to attach an unequivocal meaning to any individual score. It should be noted that some questions that are expressed in free-response form are actually objective: for example, "What are the capital cities of the ten provinces of Canada?"

Since objective testing became widely popular in the 1920s, the issue of one type of test or examination versus the other has been the subject of innumerable discussions and arguments. Perhaps the most important factor has to do with the kinds of educational objectives that can be most effectively measured by each approach. Obviously either method can elicit factual recall, although the objective test can usually be set up in such a way as to do so more economically in terms of the respondent's time. Opponents of the objective test are fond of asserting that it can measure nothing else, although many items have been devised to refute this accusation. Some of them call for skills in induction, deduction, application of principles, interpretation, organization, and appreciation on the part of the respondent. To be realistic, one must recognize that the construction of good items of this kind requires a high level of skill and a great deal of time, probably more of both than even many good teachers possess. When a limited number of objective questions were introduced into some of the grade 13 departmental papers, they turned out to be overwhelmingly of the factual recall or recognition type, perhaps not surprisingly in view of the lack of special training among those who composed them. If the average classroom teacher is to have the benefit of the more sophisticated types of items, he must either rely on outside experts or secure special training and then construct them a few at a time, either alone or in co-operation with other teachers, and store them in an item bank until he has enough so that he can employ a reasonable number on any given occasion. If he adopts the latter procedure, he is likely to be in danger of having the whole collection rendered obsolete by curricular changes. There is no doubt that, if he is interested in measuring the ability to exercise the more complex educational skills, it is easier to construct essay questions. Furthermore they can potentially elicit some types of interpretational and organizing abilities not attainable even by the best objective items. In the area of creative self-expression, the objective test has little, if any, place.

The possibility of objective marking, thus rendering a "fair" verdict on the candidate's performance, provides a major advantage for the objective test. This virtue has been reinforced by evidence of the large amount of subjectivity involved in marking essay examinations. When the unreliability of marking essay examinations is realized, sometimes the remedy applied destroys some of the greatest virtues of this form of examination. For example, the departmental grade 13 examinations in history were marked for many years on the basis of a so-called point system. Examiners drew up a list of points at pre-marking sessions, and answers were evaluated according to the presence or absence of these points. Thus a candidate who chose a few points and wove them into a well-organized and highly sophisticated interpretational presentation might do worse than another who merely presented a large number in relative isolation from one another or imbedded in a mass of irrelevancies. At a later stage, a small proportion of the maximum marks were assigned for organization, but many teachers who were concerned about the real values of history were by no means satisfied.

The advantages of highly objective marking tend to be greatest when examinations are used to compare one candidate's achievement with that of another, or with a group standard, for the purposes of promotion or certification. Errors due to subjectivity are of much less significance when the focus of attention is on individual progress, and measurement is regarded as an integral element in the learning process. Where such assessment as is needed is based on a variety of measures of performance, there is a minimum chance that a single misjudgment on the part of the teacher will go uncorrected. The increasing humanization of education is perhaps the chief factor in the decline of interest in the objective test.

A major, and to some extent irrefutable, advantage of the objective test is its suitability for sampling widely from a content area. This virtue is again most prominent when it is a matter of major importance to ensure that each candidate is judged fairly in relation to others. Broad coverage provides a guarantee that a particular individual will not receive high marks for luck in selecting those areas for study that also happen to attract the examiner's attention. It also counteracts the practice of cramming. On the other hand, there is increasing scepticism about the educational virtues of broad content coverage. This approach may sometimes, although not necessarily, be synonymous with superficial treatment and overemphasis on the acquisition of factual knowledge. Depth of understanding resulting from very thorough exploration of narrower themes may have more educational value. Perhaps the greatest advantages in the use of tests involving comprehensive sampling are in skill areas such as mathematics and foreign languages.

The type of test or examination used to measure progress has an almost inevitable effect on the educational process. This influence is much more serious when the instruments are set and marked externally than when both the program and the assessment of its effectiveness are in the hands of the teacher. There were fewer more absurd practices in Ontario education before the abolition of the grade 13 departmental examinations than the annual drill, often lasting for several weeks, on examination questions used in earlier years. While this activity was perhaps not without certain incidental values, it represented a complete perversion of priorities, with the examination dominating aims instead of the reverse. The dangers of using objective tests under the same circumstances are theoretically much less, since the extended coverage characteristic of such tests reduces the potential dividends from specific preparatory drill. There is, however, a serious problem in that it is difficult to persuade many teachers that this is so. Thus if objective tests are controlled by an external agency rather than chosen freely by teachers for their own purposes, if they are used as the sole or major criterion of assessment, and if they consist overwhelmingly of factual items, despite their capacity for measuring more sophisticated objectives, their influence on education is almost certain to be harmful. Under such circumstances, teachers are forced to neglect the most desirable objectives such as the development of thorough understanding and the capacity for creative and effective self-expression. It becomes supremely important to acquire a mind like an encyclopedia and the capacity for speedy, if superficial, response.

When the instrument is chosen and used by the teacher as part of the instructional process, it is possible to check many of its abuses and to keep it strictly subordinate to learning. Distorting effects of one type of examination can be eliminated by using a variety of types. Under some conditions, a quickly administered objective test may give a pupil an excellent idea where he stands in the development of a certain skill. The use of such a test provides no valid excuse for failing to encourage him to express his ideas in a thoughtful essay.

Critics of objective tests base much of their criticism on the ambiguous and defective items they can so easily discover, even among instruments subjected to the most thoroughgoing processes of standardization. The critics are particularly concerned about items for which one answer is correct according to conventional and superficial criteria, but for which another can be justified on the basis of advanced and highly specialized information. Thus the good candidate is credited with the right answer and the outstanding candidate with the wrong one. It is not usually claimed that any single test is likely to contain many of these items, but the psychological effect is said to be very bad on the highly sensitive individual who perceives the unfairness of the situation.

While there is certainly justification in these criticisms, they are often carried much too far. To some degree, they suggest a lack of balance, since the essay examination, reinforced by traditional use, has seldom been subjected to the same kind of rigorous criticism. It is not often even thought necessary to test the validity of the latter before it is administered. And the presence of a single badly-constructed, misleading, or ambiguous question in a set of four or five has a much greater potentiality for harm than two or three similar items out of fifty or sixty on an objective test.

The diagnostic test

One form of test, usually in objective form, that is subject to little fundamental criticism is the diagnostic test. It does not easily lend itself to making invidious comparisons among pupils of unequal capacity, but instead enables the teacher to concentrate efforts where they are most needed, that is, on the facts, processes, and concepts that the child has failed to master. The appropriate diagnostic test in arithmetic may show, for example, that a particular child has difficulty with subtraction when the subtrahend contains a zero. A diagnostic test in reading may show that his progress is hindered by certain word reversals.

Unfortunately, the teachers of Ontario have not taken to the use of diagnostic tests in a very convincing fashion. The Department of Educational Research of the Ontario College of Education long kept a stock of these tests but found much less sale for them than for survey tests. When the writer proposed, as part of his work in test construction in that department in the mid-1950s, to construct a new series for the diagnosis of arithmetic problems, an assessment of the potential market indicated that the effort would not be justified. The impression obtained at the time was that the usual teaching procedure was simply to present one topic after another, with only a general appraisal of the pupils' understanding. The accumulation of weakness on weakness would inevitably produce serious results for the pupil later, assuming that the skill area in question was of real importance.

ATTITUDES TOWARD EXAMINATIONS IN GENERAL

The charge that Ontario education has traditionally been examination-ridden has applied, not only to the confidence placed in external examinations, but to their internal use within schools as well. Although the following statement, which the royal commissioners felt constrained to quote in their report, was made with reference to Scotland, it had universal relevance.

> The influence of examinations is three-fold. It affects the treatment of the examinable subjects themselves, tending always to exalt the written above the spoken, to magnify memory and mastery of fact at the expense of understanding and liveliness of mind. It depresses the status of the non-examinable, so that the aesthetic and creative side of education, with all its possibilities for human satisfaction and cultural enrichment, remains largely undeveloped and poorly esteemed. And lastly, the examination which began as a means, becomes for many the end itself. In the atmosphere created by this preoccupation with examination success, it is difficult to think nobly of education, to see in it the endless quest of man's preparation for either society or solitude. The cult of the examination has proven all too congenial to the hard practicality of the Scot, and in excessive concern about livelihood, the art of living has tended to be forgotten.[8]

G.H. Bantock, Reader in Education, University of Leicester, reflected some of the universal concerns surrounding the role of the examination in education, when he claimed that, in spite of "all the high-sounding aims and claims of educationists, the history of twentieth-century education is, in considerable measure, the history of certain examinations."[9] He acknowledged the possibility that a person could become cultivated while preparing to pass an examination. The two objectives were not necessarily mutually exclusive, even though there was a degree of tension between them. He was not optimistic that the importance of the role of examinations could be easily reduced in view of social forces that engendered the search for status, as evidenced by the possession of a diploma. If the diploma became too common, it lost its value for certifying distinction, and new symbols had to be sought. Incentives for creating new forms of examinations continued to creep in.

Bantock pointed to what some may see as a basic dilemma for education. It revolves around this assertion, which of course involves a challengeable assumption: *"The fact of the matter is that much modern work – even at 'white collar' and managerial level – is of too trivial a nature to nurture a fully literate and cultivated population."*[10] If this pessimistic view is accepted, its implication is that the schools have no strong incentive to do other than play at providing real education, while offering a program that has little actual relevance to life's work. They must treat various subjects, as he said they did, not as complex means through which we can come to some understanding of ourselves, our society, and our world, but rather as a collection of unstructured facts. The only way that pupils can be motivated to accept such fare, indigestible as it may be, is to hold the threat of an examination over them. The idealist lives on the hope that a "fully literate and cultivated population" might not be too much of an anomaly in the modern world, and that it is an objective worth striving for.

The effect of the Mustard-Watson movement in the late 1930s and after was to downgrade the importance of examinations through the elementary grades, even though the high school entrance examination persisted until 1949. The secondary schools, however, remained largely unaffected. A continued preoccupation with means of maintaining promotion standards was long in evidence. The department's attitude was expressed in a memorandum in 1957, the tone of which was established by this statement: "Especially after the period of compulsory school attendance has been completed, it is reasonable to expect the pupil to justify by his effort and also by his attainment the privilege of continued attendance at secondary school."[11] A great deal of emphasis was placed on the desirability of imposing examinations of sufficient difficulty to ensure that the student who passed them would have a reasonable chance of handling the work of the next grade. The following suggestions were offered.

> Every endeavour must be made to maintain a reasonable standard in Grade 11 and Grade 12 tests and examinations. To this end, attention must be made to the following:
>
> (i) A comparison of recent Grade 12 percentages of passes in the various subjects with the Departmental results of the corresponding groups in Grade 13.
>
> (ii) Any Departmental "over-and-under" records of the teachers concerned.
>
> (iii) Any help which can be obtained from the study of examination papers set by experienced and capable teachers in other schools or by committees of teachers such as those recently appointed by the O.S.S.T.F. Education Committee to compile specimen sets in different subjects.

(iv) A reasonable combination of term work, including assignments, exercises, and tests, along with the results of term examinations in arriving at a mark for the year in each subject. Some schools use a weighting system such as 1:2:3 or 2:3:5 for the fall term, the winter term, and the spring term marks respectively.

The memorandum was interesting in part for what it did not say. There was no mention of having the process of evaluation arise out of a definition of course objectives, presumably these were fully defined by the course of study and the authorized instructional material.

The Ontario Curriculum Institute's Committee on the Scope and Aims of the Curriculum had some useful comments on the evaluation question in its report in 1966.

Evaluation procedures, undoubtedly, will have to be redesigned. Some standard achievement tests and most provincial and local examinations are based on the volume concept of the mind and by a sampling technique attempt to measure the amount that the mind contains. The curriculum product that we are now concerned about, on the other hand, is progress in ways of thinking. If the child does grow in ways of thinking, conceptual development through discovery of relationships in his environment is the vehicle through which his thinking moves. We need have no worry, therefore, about the usable knowledge available to the child's mind when he needs it. What we are concerned about is how far the child's thinking has gone in any given direction, how quickly he got there, and the quality of this thinking all the way along.

These are attributes that, really, only the child and teacher can know. It is not impossible, however, to work out evaluation techniques by which a teacher may check his comparative judgment of children's thought processes within a class and by which an outside observer might compare class with class and community with community. One doubts, however, whether such comparisons would be amenable to the refined statistical analyses that educational researchers have been accustomed to apply to the so-called achievement data in the past. And it would be disastrous to the new teaching project if its purposes were to be warped to fit pre-conceived notions of evaluation.[12]

What became known as Memorandum 28 showed how much departmental thinking had changed over a period of a few years.[13] General comments began wth this statement: "Assessment of student progress is an integral and continuous part of the educative process and consequently is an essential element of the responsibilty of the professional teacher." The end of the departmental examinations would enable schools to adopt a consistent philosophy of course development through all grade levels. It was suggested that assessment procedures be varied to meet the requirements of different subject areas and different groups of students. In some subjects, projects, essays, and class tests mght be stressed, while in other fields, such as technical and scientific subjects, more emphasis might be placed on day-to-day performance and on competence in shop and laboratory work. The signs of the diminishing importance being placed on final examinations were regarded as encouraging.

Serious educators have not got to the point where they are prepared to recommend that evaluative procedures be abolished. But searching questions are being asked about the value of internal formal examinations as contrasted with more casual assessment that can be linked directly with learning. One disadvantage of the formal examination is that it represents a break in what should be an uninterrupted process. It is compatible only with the idea that education can be chopped up into convenient units and administered in a mechanical fashion. Furthermore, if the value of the "knowledge" acquired by cramming is descredited, examinations represent time taken away from what ought to be constructive activities. They do not tell the learner or the perceptive teacher much worth knowing that either did not know beforehand. Their chief value, if such it may be called, is to provide something specific and authoritative that can be reported to parents. Some of these sentiments were expressed in an article in the OSSTF *Bulletin*, with the recommendation that monthly classroom tests count for 50 per cent of the mark, and that formal examinations, if they could not be eliminated entirely, should be held no oftener than twice a year.[14]

The Provincial Committee on Aims and Objectives was unequivocal in its condemnation of examinations as used for certain purposes.

> Related to grading is the use of formal examinations as the means of transition from grade to grade. Such arbitrary measures of achievement and the concepts of promotion and failure should be removed from the school – not to reduce standards, but to improve the quality of learning.[15]

The Ontario Teachers' Federation has been reflecting the same sentiments.

> Teacher evaluation of the student by the evaluation procedures that we have practised has no place in our school. If the child has not made the progress that might have been expected of him, evaluation becomes teacher evaluation of themselves – "What did we not do? What did we do wrong?" – or possibly evaluation of the home: "What's going on over there that we don't know about?"[16]

ATTITUDES TOWARD EXTERNAL EXAMINATIONS

Earlier views about examinations

A factual account of the development of the external examination system in Ontario is presented in Volume v, chapter 15. The present treatment represents an attempt to identify some of the currents of thought prevailing in different periods, particularly during the last two decades. Recent changes have been parallel to and no less profound than those in the areas of aims, curriculum, and school organization.

Referring to the high schools, Phillips defined the period from Confederation to the end of the nineteenth century as one of increasing centralization of examinations and the subsequent period as one of gradual decentralization or abolition. Between external examinations and regular tests set by teachers during the year, life for students around 1875 was just one examination after another.[17]

The emphasis on examinations in the Toronto system was described in *Centennial Story*.[18]

> For a time marks were all important; then it was realized that "cramming" might win greater success than faithful attendance; accordingly prizes were awarded on a combined basis of regular and punctual attendance, good conduct, and "perfect lessons" during the session, plus the standing at the "Combined Examinations".

The examination questions for pupils completing the Fourth and Fifth Books were drawn up in the greatest secrecy and no doubt marked with the most meticulous care. The results, used in order to obtain the maximum benefits of competition, were tabulated to show comparisons by school and sex. The Examiners' Report listed the names of prize winners, and prizes, medals, and diplomas were a highly imposing feature of public school life. There was little sign that anyone saw anything wrong with pitting children of unequal talent against one another.

In 1911 John Seath not only observed but, interestingly, deplored the role of external examinations in the system.

> The most striking feature of our primary and secondary schools is the system of uniform departmental examinations, which for over a quarter of a century have not only determined the character of the teaching, but have held in thrall the pupils, the teachers, and the public. In the case of the public and separate schools it is the examination for entrance into the high schools that dominates; and in the case of the high schools, continuation schools, and collegiate institutes, it is the examination for university matriculation and for admission to the teachers' training schools. On the results of these examinations school boards and the general public appraise the teacher's competency, and upon such appraisement depend his promotion and his salary.[19]

From these remarks, it would appear that neither the decline in the number of examinations that Phillips noted nor the weakening of their hold over the system had yet gone very far.

Changing attitudes up to the early 1960s

An early adverse reaction toward at least some types and uses of external examinations was shown by the Minister of Education, George S. Henry, in his report for 1932.[20] Understandably, considering the economic conditions prevailing at the time, his objection was partly based on economic grounds, but it included a strong element of principle as well. He pointed out that departmental examinations at the junior and senior matriculation levels were for the use of those who intended to enter the professions or the universities; but that they were being written by thousands who had no such object in view, thus putting the department to needless expense. He went on to deplore the apparent assumption on the part of employers that the departmental certificate was a better indication of the academic fitness of applicants for positions in offices, banks, and other occupations than was the school diploma, which was based on the student's school record and reflected his grasp of the subjects taught, his ability to think for himself, and his diligence and application to the duties of life. He asserted flatly that an external examination on the subjects of the course was inferior in determining fitness for a business career.

The attitude expressed in the Royal Commission report in 1950 was roughly that examination procedures should vary in role and form from one level of the educational system to another. The report recommended that no internal or external examinations should be employed in nursery schools or kindergartens, and that no system of formal, external school examinations be established in elementary or secondary schools, but that progress at those levels should be assessed entirely by internal school examinations or tests.[21] At the junior college level, the advantages of external examinations were judged to outweigh their disadvantages, and it was recommended that they be employed for admission purposes. Progress through the junior college was to be based on internal assessment. Students who wished to proceed to university would take the university entrance examinations required, but the results would not determine the granting of a Junior College Graduation Diploma, nor would the latter necessarily provide entrance to university.[22]

Some of the most serious defects of external examinations were recognized. They were identified as being outside the teaching procedure but yet capable of dominating, not only the curriculum and courses of study, but also teaching methods and practices. In extreme cases, it was observed that all efforts of a school might be directed to the task of getting as many students as possible through the examinations. In that they tended to stereotype and standardize education generally, they were to be condemned. Mass allegiance to them had "made it extremely difficult for teachers and others to adapt courses of study to the wide diversity in the abilities and needs of pupils." The situation was particularly deplorable when the examinations were designed in terms of the entrance requirements of another institution, such as a university, to which few of the students would proceed, and when no other measure of achievement or criterion of success was provided.[23]

Despite this perceptive analysis of the pernicious effects of the external examination system, the commissioners apparently accepted the view that, at the junior college level, the desirability of maintaining common standards from one institution to another was predominant. "In that they [the examinations] tend to keep schools working roughly at the same level of efficiency, they must be applauded."[24] Here we have the traditional lack of confidence that students can be induced to do their best, or that teachers will perform at their maximum level of competence, without some agency from outside wielding the whip. Nothing was said to indicate doubts about the meaning of standards achieved in this way.

In one of his Quance Lectures delivered in 1959, Woodrow S. Lloyd, at that time Minister of Education for Saskatchewan, viewed with some apprehension the pressure for more, and more stringent, central examinations. This was shortly before the introduction of the grade 12 examinations set by the Ontario Department of Education and marked locally. He pointed out that three jusifications were being offered for external examinations: 1 / that students needed the practice and challenge of facing stiff examinations because such situations would be faced later in a university; 2 / that the external examination provided some magic motivation; 3 / that the external examination could more accurately test student ability and student mastery of skills and information. With respect to the first point, he asked if there was any reason why an examination that prepared the student for university practices had to be externally set and marked. He did not deal seriously with the more fundamental question of whether the secondary schools should have a primary responsibility for introducing students to university modes of operation. In dealing with the second point, he submitted that "if the urge to learn which a school can provide has to rest on such external and, in fact, extraneous force ... we need to be concerned for the future of scholarship." He thought that the validity of the third point rested, not only on the character and quality of the teaching staff, but also on the community's willingness to leave professional decisions in the hands of a professional staff.[25]

J.R. McCarthy, who became deputy minister in 1967, was long opposed to the practice of holding external examinations. He made this attitude abundantly clear at the Ontario Conference on Education in 1961 while he was Superintendent of Curriculum for the department.

You may not agree with me on this point and this doesn't bother me at all. I happen to be in some pretty good company as I can illustrate. Whitehead has said: "A common external examination is fatal to education." Sir Richard Livingstone says, "the [external] examination system is a poison which slows down education in most cases and in some paralyses it, and no one wholly escapes its bad effects." Jeffrey puts it this way: "Let there be no mistake about it, external examinations and the complete professional freedom of the teacher are mutually exclusive."

In spite of this evidence we stream pupils to provide better for individual differences and then give them external examinations to try to keep them the same. The one contradicts the other and the latter is more likely to be achieved than the former.[26]

Bascom St John delivered a biting criticism of the uses being made of the grade 13 departmental results in 1962.

The pernicious habit of rating schools by the number of passes, honors students or scholarship students they have ought to be stopped, but this phony rating is approved and encouraged at the highest levels of the Department of Education. It is leading to many unethical practices by which students are kept from writing if it is assumed they will fail. The lengths some principals will go in diverting, discouraging or preventing average students from pulling down the pass percentage should be deemed unprofessional conduct and dealt with accordingly.[27]

He went on to point out the unfairness of judging a school by its level of achievement alone:

... in judging the honors record of a school, its location and its social environments could well be much more important than the teaching quality. It could be that in some cases many more students ought to have won honors, if they had been properly handled, or even given a chance.

Views expressed about the re-introduction of external essay-type examinations in grade 12 in 1963

The criticisms of the undesirable effects of external examinations had not made a profound dent on departmental policy or on teacher opinion in the early 1960s. The steps by which external departmental essay-type examinations were reintroduced into grade 12 in 1963 are dealt with in volume v, chapter 16. In brief, papers in certain subjects were set and marking schemes devised by committees chosen by the department and working under its supervision, while the answer papers were marked locally, and samples of these from each school were checked by the department. It is not the mechanics of this operation that need concern us at this point, but rather the attitudes expressed at the time by various individuals and groups.

The members of the Ontario Secondary School Teachers' Federation and of the Ontario Secondary School Headmasters' Association indicated in a survey that they were overwhelmingly in favour of the scheme. In general, they were strongly impressed by the desirability of maintaining reasonably uniform standards and were willing to believe that the external examination was a promising means of attaining the desired end. Some of the views expressed by the respondents among the headmasters help to reveal the prevailing attitude.

One headmaster wrote that "it would be of particular value to schools which have a high staff turn-over and which must depend on teachers of little or no experience." This was a view of paramount importance among departmental officials who were particularly concerned about the fate of students in some of the smaller and more remote high schools. A.H. McKague, then Assistant Superintendent of Secondary Education, had many distressing first-hand experiences with such schools. He knew that some students could take a subject throughout their high school career without the experience of ever having it taught by a qualified teacher. He was apprehensive that the process of education was in danger of collapsing altogether in remote areas unless every available support was provided. Another respondent commented that "the chief value of the uniform external examination at the end of Grade 12 will be to ensure that the same amount of work is covered in each school, so that students from a school which has classes only to the end of Grade 12 will not be handicapped when going on to another school for Grade 13." This was, in general, the point made most emphatically in favour of the scheme.

Many of those in favour expressed certain qualifications and reservations. One said: "Regardless of what care is taken in setting the paper, we would have to expect that sometimes we would get a paper that was either too hard or too easy and there would be no way of making an adjustment." Another hoped "that optional questions or some other suitable method would be used to allow the schools some freedom to develop their courses to meet the needs of their communities." A similar sentiment was expressed in these words: "Safeguards should be used in the setting of these papers to ensure that these examinations do not become 'cram' examinations and to allow for local differences in courses, texts, etc." One respondent emphasized what he saw as desirable measures to ensure that the examinations were properly conducted.

> I believe that rigid safeguards would be essential, such as (a) question papers arrive in sealed envelopes which are not opened until the time for the examination to begin and Principal's statement that this has been followed in each case, (b) a careful marking schedule which is comprehensive, and (c) careful spot checks, especially in schools where the same student frequently shows a substantial drop in a Grade 13 subject below his Grade 12 mark as submitted by his own school.

This type of response reveals no concern over the remoteness of the procedures described from any real process of education. While the respondent may or may not have been realistic in his recognition that steps would have to be taken to keep some principals from cheating, there was no evident inclination to blame the proposed system for putting them in a position where they would be pressured into such behaviour.

S.G.B. Robinson, General Secretary of the Ontario Secondary School Teachers' Federation, was not inclined to go along with the majority of the members of his organization. In a memorandum to the Provincial Executive on January 24, 1962, he declared that he had no objection to the decision of departmental officials to work toward uniformity of standards or to their statement that they wanted to prevent the courses of study from becoming more uniform than they were at the time. But he objected to the means they had selected to achieve these ends. He felt that the possibility that the proposed external examinations would impose a uniform standard of achievement throughout the province was remote because the existing variation in examinations was only one of the factors contributing to the variation in standards. The variation attributable to markers was substantial and difficult to control even with the grade 13 examinations. In connection with the hope of avoiding undue uniformity of courses, it seemed to him that the province-wide, essay-type examinations employed in grade 13 forced teachers to adhere to an exact course outline. He objected to an arbitrary administrative decision on the question, expressed the view that a vote was meaningless, and speculated on the possibility that research might have some of the answers needed.

Many of the headmasters and teachers recognized the threat to their initiative and autonomy in the plan but seemed to feel, unlike Robinson, that the examinations could be conducted in such a way as to avoid it. "A good plan provided all teaching is not directed toward these tests." Another expressed the hope that the papers could give some idea of the standard required by the province without having a great deal of effect on the actual assessment of the student's performance for the year.

Outright opposition took predictable forms. "I believe this is a retrogressive step. The aim should be more school autonomy in the interna of education." "'Teaching to the examinations' would rapidly return and destroy many of the valuable factors in the present grade 12 programme." "Generally speaking, if the Department is not willing to rely on the judgment of Principals, Staffs, Inspectors, we are in a sad state and the imposition of an artificial checking device isn't going to help much." "External examinations in Grade 12 would merely extend the current examination pressure on students over a 2-year period. This means that a school is, more than ever, geared to the examination system and concern for education in its broader context becomes secondary."

In view of the strong tide of feeling against external examinations only a few years later, it is rather difficult to explain why there could be so much support for them among the major groups of educators in 1962. Perhaps, as one official commented, there is little validity in counting heads. The writer recalls discussing the matter at the time with a friend who knew something of the attitudes, not only of his colleagues in the school in which he taught, but also of teachers in neighbouring schools. His opinion was that most of the best teachers were against the move, while the majority of mediocre and poor teachers were in favour.

From England came evidence that the disadvantages of external examinations were not merely attributable to the quirks of a particular system but were universal. Observers from afar who have heard of the relative freedom of English teachers to decide what to teach and how to teach it, have often assumed that their secondary schools must be a paradise for the educator with a truly professional outlook. In 1964 the Conservative Bow Group helped to dispel some illusions with this appraisal.

> Examinations have taken the sparkle out of English education at the secondary school level. Teaching becomes geared to the examinations and in most schools, so orientated, the examination syllabus is the only curriculum. Originality of approach and ideas is replaced by a column of facts to be memorised; spontaneous expression is replaced by dictated notes containing the essence of examination success. The *primary* task of grammar school staff today is to teach their pupils to pass examinations.[28]

Views expressed to the Grade 13 Study Committee, 1964

The major turning point in Ontario came, of course, with the activities of the Grade 13 Study Committee established in 1964. Most of the approximately 170 briefs it received dwelt on the adverse effects of the examinations. They were referred to as a spectre that haunted the student from the beginning of September, if not indeed much earlier. The course of study was said to be heavily charged with factual material on which the examination would be based. The language of the briefs making this point helped to establish the word "regurgitate" as something other than the performance by which pigeons feed their young. In preparing assiduously for this activity, fortunately in a figurative sense, the student had no time to explore a topic in depth or to follow lines of inquiry that attracted his particular interest. Since his motivation was external, he had no good reason to learn for retention, and the standards he attained were no indication that he had achieved much of permanent value.

The teacher was equally under the malign influence of the examination. His success also depended, although not quite to the same extent as that of the student, on its results. He could break through the narrow restraints of the course only with the guilty feeling that he might be endangering his students' chances of obtaining a diploma, winning a scholarship, or securing access to university. He was more of a robot than a professional, since he had no effective control of the course.

Despite its recognition of the faults in the existing system, the Grade 13 Study Committee did not recommend its immediate and outright abolition. A change was to be made only when proper safeguards were developed. Objective tests, which might be managed in such a way as to avoid undue influence on the curriculum, and would place no great premium on cramming, seemed to offer the promise of a suitable device for maintaining standards. Concern for standards was a very real issue among Ontario educators. They felt a sense of dismay at the prospect of the disappearance of any dependable label to identify the quality of their "product." Such a concern was behind the unenthusiastic response of the executive of the OTF to the minister's announcement that no departmental examinations would be held after 1967.

The OTF position, 1966

In its brief to the minister in April 1966, the OTF had some good things to say about the grade 13 year, thus implying that the examination system had not completely ruined it as an educational experience. To it was attributed much of the soundness of the Ontario system of education. It provided valuable direction to the whole school enterprise, it gave excellent motivation, and it established a significant educational standard. For students who looked forward to higher education, it had been a good predictor of success; for students who pursued other endeavours, it was a respected accomplishment.[29] One can sense an apprehension in the brief that the external examinations might prove to be an essential part of the structure, and that this structure might be done serious, if not indeed irreparable, damage if they were removed without the provision of an adequate substitute. Yet the brief recognized the need to extricate the secondary schools from a preoccupation with marks and to inculcate in students an interest in intellectual pursuits which had some relevance to the world in which they lived.

Attitudes expressed after abolition of the grade 13 departmentals in 1967

The immediate effect of the change confirmed the predictions of its advocates and eased the fears of its opponents. Larry Collins devoted an article in the *Telegram* to the changed atmosphere in Toronto schools in the latter part of 1968.[30] The article, entitled "Surprise! Surprise! Teachers, students glad Grade 13 exams are gone," asserted that, as far as students and teachers in top-rated schools were concerned, the experiment had already proved to be a success. He referred to some of the misgivings at the beginning. Some educators had felt twinges of panic when they realized just how much freedom had been thrust upon them. "Would they be able to maintain standards? Would the universities refuse to accept their evaluations of students? Without an external exam, how would they evaluate their students anyway?" By this time, the verdict was becoming clear: the students were performing better than ever. Under a system of continuous evaluation, they were challenged to give their optimum performance every day. They were not all unreservedly enthusiastic, of course. Some would have preferred the relatively brief and severe pressure of the final examination to the continuous low-key pressure imposed by the new system throughout the year. Some of the brightest students were getting lower marks. But most agreed that they were being offered a much more valuable educational experience.

An equally enthusiastic article by Sharon Chapman, entitled "It's happening – in Grade 13!" appeared in the *Niagara Falls Review* on May 15, 1968. Although a great deal of pressure had been removed, neither students nor teachers felt that the calibre of the work had suffered. The revised program was emphasizing a consistently high level of effort. As a result of the new freedom in the curriculum, there was time to discuss current events or to experiment with hydrogen sulphide "just for fun." During the previous week, the senior history students had been delving into Canada's racial problems. They had evaluated the causes of the issue, the demands from the French Canadians, and the possible solution. They also intended to discuss the Vietnam war and the Arab-Israeli conflict. "At any other time such a project would have been completely inconceivable."

ATTITUDES TOWARD OBJECTIVE TESTS

In comparison with their American counterparts, Ontario educators have always manifested a conservative attitude toward objective testing. To some extent, this situation has been a result of the relatively low level of prevailing knowledge about the principles of measurement, resulting in a greater confidence in the results of essay-type examinations than these devices have merited. At the same time, when amateurs have tried their hand at writing objective items, the product of their efforts has tended to reinforce adverse opinions about the whole approach. Nevertheless, the wave of interest in objective testing across the border in the 1920s did spill over into Canada. An abortive effort was made to introduce this form of test into the middle school examination system in the 1930s. The Department of Educational Research of the Ontario College of Education was established in 1931 primarily to construct a set of intelligence and achievement tests that would meet the needs of Canadian schools. The fact that this entity managed to survive through the depression years of the 1930s may perhaps be attributed partly to the conviction that such a purpose was important.

The guidance movement in the secondary schools was an influence that promoted the use of tests at the secondary level. Attention tended to be focused on intelligence and aptitude tests and on interest inventories rather than on achievement tests. The tendency to isolate guidance activity from other aspects of the school program and the generally low repute of guidance in the early years help to explain why interest in objective testing did not become more general.

The administration of survey tests in the upper elementary grades throughout whole school systems became increasingly common in the 1950s. This was the period of objectionable and unjustified bragging by local school officials in favoured areas on the basis of a comparison of their pupils' performance with unrealistic norms. Large-scale objective testing at the secondary level began with the Atkinson Study of Utilization of Student Resources. There was little antagonism expressed toward the experiment, although some administrators and teachers were not overwhelmingly enthusiastic about the loss of time it entailed. To those who were involved, the extremely naïve attitude of some of the teachers who inquired about the interpretation of test scores was a matter of concern. A much larger group of teachers became involved in mass testing when the Carnegie Study program, involving about 90,000 grade 9 students, was launched in 1959–60. At that time there was a great deal of in-service learning about percentile ranks, norms, and other measurement terms.

There was some apprehension about the introduction of objective test items into the grade 13 departmental examinations at the end of the 1950s. Assurances were offered that these would constitute no more than 30 per cent of the marks on any single paper. Some members of the University Matriculation Board were persuaded to support the move more on the grounds that it might increase marking speed and reduce costs than because they approved the principle. Others felt that the possibility of more comprehensive coverage of subject matter was a real advantage.

A Committee on Objective Type Testing of the Ontario Secondary School Teachers' Federation functioned through most of 1961 under the chairmanship of G.C. Hay.[31] Its aim was to study the implications of the increased use of objective testing for the practising teacher. In a sense, it was established to help the federation to formulate an official reaction to the testing programs initiated after 1957 by the Department of Education. The result of the committee's deliberations was a cautious acceptance and endorsation of objective testing. While recommending that free-response or essay-type testing should retain a position of primary importance, the committee pointed out that the average teacher was not taking advantage of the opportunities offered by the objective test, and urged that this type of activity receive wider acceptance. The department's external testing in grade 12 was approved on condition that it not unduly restrain the teacher from fulfilling his proper function. Support was also offered for the use of objective items on the grade 13 departmental papers. It was recommended that there be greater stress on testing in the programs of teacher training so that teachers might more adequately relate testing procedures to the objectives of courses of study.

Overwhelming approval of the departmental grade 12 testing program was expressed by the secondary school teachers at the time consideration was being given to the re-establishment of departmental essay-type examinations in the same grade. This state of affairs undoubtedly had something to do with frustrating the hopes of some of those who wanted to replace the objective tests with essay examinations. Ultimately, of course, both programs were to disappear in the wave of adverse feeling that developed after the minister's bold action in abolishing the grade 13 departmentals.

Opposition to objective testing has understandably been concentrated among teachers of subjects where creative self-expression, depth of understanding, and sensitivity in interpretation have been given the greatest stress; for example, among teachers of history and English. After the first year of the Ontario Admission to College and University (OACU) testing, the Association of Heads of English Departments in Toronto Secondary Schools presented an unusually effective case against the assumption that an objective test could do justice to the aims they felt it desirable to pursue.

The Heads believe that the emphasis in objective testing on speed and fragmentary items divorced from the context of purpose, tone and theme is opposed to the reasoned thinking and organized sequence of expression that characterized the student with ability in composition, that such testing as at present practised fails to measure the creative talent and imaginative skill required in original composition, does not permit individual difference play, rewards conformity and penalizes individual insight.[32]

The report took exception to the Ontario English Composition Achievement Test (OECAT) on the grounds both of exaggerated claims made for it and of the inadequacies of its approach. The handbook had led the candidates to expect a twenty-minute essay on a suggested topic. The department heads felt that such an assignment would have been a severe trial to the student who wished to analyse and expand his theme. After the tests, students told them that the essay had been omitted, thus effectively eliminating any valid claim that the test was one of composition. In their view, composition was a creative, imaginative, intellectual activity requiring a synthesis of many responses and many skills. They did not find that the handbook recognized this concept.

The department heads declared that an important test becomes a teaching device, reinforcing what has been taught and suggesting to teachers what should be emphasized in the future. Yet they felt that the test was in clear conflict with departmental instructions warning against textbook exercises on mechanics and emphasizing speaking and writing with a purpose. They expressed what was perhaps their severest condemnation in this assertion: "The directions and explanations, the models, and the practices required in the tests indicate clearly to teachers and students an oversimplified dogmatic concept of language, a fragmented, stereotyped, treatment that favours the literal, mediocre student."[33] In discussing the appropriateness of answers designated as correct in the handbook, they took exception to the simplistic reasoning behind some of the selections.

An understanding of the English language assumes a recognition that in any passage of writing the expression is the fusion of the writer's thought, his attitude as reflected in his tone, the language structures that he uses, and the words that he selects. Few sentences can be considered good or bad in isolation. Their "rightness" depends on the context. What is "right" in a passage that captures with concealed art the flavour of conversation, may be inappropriate in the reflections of a thinker on the tensions of our day.

There is a lack of such discrimination in the language questions.[34]

In part the criticisms applied, not exclusively to tests in English, but to objective tests in general. While studying the handbook, one student had complained that the short-answer approach did not permit a student to answer as an individual. He could not explain why he chose one answer over another. After being urged to think for himself, to form opinions on his subjects, and to support his ideas by relating them to the course of study, he found it extremely frustrating to have a question arbitrarily marked correct or incorrect without being able to argue his personal opinion. In analogy questions, for example, he felt that a logical case could be made for two or three of the given choices.

On the more favourable side, the head of the English Department in one school indicated an appreciation of the difficulty of making a test that could be marked by machine. He emphasized the importance of having any such test meet the best standards known. He believed that ingenious, interesting, and useful short-answer tests could be devised in English studies.

Some dissatisfaction could be traced to teachers' lack of understanding of basic measurement principles, a number of which have been referred to. Certain Ontario teachers have shown a particular tendency to confuse the use of tests to keep school standards in line and their employment to measure individual achievement. The first of these was the main purpose of the grade 12 departmental objective testing program from 1959 to 1968, while the second has been a major aim of the OACU and SACU programs. The former program posed much less of an inherent threat to teachers' control of the curriculum, as long as they did not attempt to give the test scores a major role in their assessment of the students' work. The department officials certainly encouraged them to keep the processes separate and urged administrators not to interfere with their freedom to assign to individuals examination marks that varied substantially from their test scores. This practice might be particularly justified in English, where an objective test might concentrate on mechanics and usage, and the essay examination on free expression. It would be perfectly conceivable that an individual's performance would differ substantially on the two measures. The department was concerned only if the general level of a teacher's marks was substantially out of line, whether on the high or low side, which was quite a different matter. The writer on occasion heard a teacher denounce the whole idea of external objective testing as an unwarranted hindrance to the teacher's exercise of professional judgment, and then in almost the next breath demand that the test scores be made available early enough so that internal examination marks could be adjusted to conform to them.

Certain important consequences have inevitably resulted in Ontario's failure to make the basic principles of measurement part of every teacher's pre-service or in-service preparation. Specialized terminology has been associated much more with objective-type than with essay-type examinations. The immediate response of the uninitiated to what appears to be an expert interpretation of some point may vary from an attempt to appear to understand what is being said to a purely negative reaction on the grounds that the whole thing is meaningless jargon. In either case, the teacher feels self-confident and at ease with the essay examination and inclined to leave the objective test, particularly the standardized test, to the specialist. The field is left wide open for those with a minimum of knowledge to pose as experts and to expound nonsense without immediately being found out. Thus we have people asserting that reliability coefficients falling anywhere within a wide range of values are "satisfactory," without ever explaining what level they would consider unsatisfactory. Or they may solemnly assure us that a validity coefficient is significant, as if that meant that it is necessarily high enough to be of any real value for predictive purposes. Eventually, of course, the truth seeps through the façade, and antitesting prejudices are reinforced.

The administration of external testing programs by the Ontario Department of Education or by any other central agency in the province seems to have gone for the foreseeable future. Those who prophesy a reverse of the pendulum do not sound very convincing. Part of the reason is the strictly practical one that these programs cost a great deal. To bear the cost is one thing where an examination system is thoroughly ensconced and maintained by a widespread conviction that it is an essential part of the educational process; it is quite another matter where the tradition has been broken and a general conviction has developed that the approach is not worth the expense or is even harmful.

The universities can probably be counted on to support any measure that will help them appraise the standards of the schools from which their applicants come. With the OACU program phased out, they must pin their hopes on the SACU program. While the Ontario government was prepared to finance its own OACU testing, it has not shown any excess of enthusiasm for playing a comparable role in the national program. The latter is likely to have to rely on students' fees, something that was considered politically unacceptable for OACU. If the SACU program does not work, the universities of Ontario will apparently face the alternatives of making their own assessment of the standards of their feeder schools by observing the performance of their graduates over a period of time, or reinstituting some kind of admissions tests of their own. That a government would allow them to use public funds for an activity of the latter kind when it refused to support a comparable program directly is rather doubtful. The universities might, of course, find it easier than a government agency to support a program by imposing fees, especially if the tests were considered quite outside the regular school program. It might appear that a university-operated admissions testing program would cost less than a departmental program designed not only for university admission, but for high school leaving as well. Experience in the United States indicates, however, and not surprisingly, that a relatively small proportion of a high school graduating class will refuse the tests on the grounds that they are certain they will never consider the possibility of going to college or university.

Speculation on the possible development of testing programs for university admission should not be terminated without a least a brief mention of some of the problems encountered in the United States. These were reviewed in considerable detail by Hillel Black in *They Shall Not Pass.*[85] Black has sometimes been classed among the adamant opponents of the whole objective testing approach, but a careful reading of the book shows him to have been in fact a critical appraiser of tests, with approval for those that were carefully produced to measure attainable objectives and denunciations for those that did not measure up. He delivered a scathing indictment of the way tests were being abused by ill-trained and incompetent people.

Black devoted a good deal of attention to the extent to which he saw school programs and students' lives being dominated by college admission tests. The worst of the evils apparently resulted from two basic conditions: attaining a high level of education was becoming a more and more important condition for success in American society and the prestige and other advantages of attending one of the small minority of outstanding institutions was generating an increasingly intense competition to get into them. Here is one of Black's most striking passages.

One of the ironies of admissions mania is that its destructive effects are felt in the very communities where a child's educational opportunities are greatest. For it is in suburbia that parents are more apt to pay dearly in taxes to make their elementary and high schools the finest in the land. Yet it is these parents and often the schools themselves that push the communities' youngsters into a debilitating marathon. Like racers chasing a mechanical rabbit, they pursue grades and test scores in an endless circle. The thrill of learning and the curiosity to know are lost in a deadly grind. In an age where all of us so badly need wisdom, many of our college-bound youth may well count as their greatest educational achievement the perfection of test wiseness. Perhaps no more telling testimony can be offered than that of an eleventh-grade boy who fought and lost what may well have been his most important battle.

"In the summer session last year," he said, "I arranged to take a biology course that I really liked. I was determined that this summer course would be for learning, not for marks. Every now and then the mark would pop into my mind, but I could pretty well get rid of it. I succeeded pretty well during the summer. It was great! I was thinking about what was actually going on in biology. But this fall I can't seem to keep this attitude. I find that I'm constantly computing averages."[36]

This kind of thing is supposed to be typical of the results of the external essay-type examination. The use of objective tests is supposed to preclude it, particularly where scholastic aptitude tests are concerned, because special preparation is said to be ineffective in raising the scores obtained on such tests. Black found the case for this claim, based on thorough research, quite convincing. Nevertheless, he discovered large numbers of coaches doing a thriving business in preparing students, and even high schools yielding to the demand for the establishment of coaching classes. Many students were simply not accepting the claims and the evidence of the ineffectiveness of such activity. The situation was aggravated by the fact that competition for admission to the most prestigious institutions was so intense that a decision might hinge on a score point or two, even though the institutions were quite properly using the test scores as only one factor among several in making their selection.

Black gave a most convincing reason why every effort should be made to promote a co-ordinated program for university admission in Canada, or at least in Ontario, rather than letting the process become fragmented. He told of one young man with a promising high school record who during his last two years in high school spent over forty-eight hours taking tests at nineteen centres in a vain effort to get into an acceptable college program. At the time the book was written, a candidate in Ohio seeking college entrance or a scholarship might have been forced to take eight different sets of tests within the state as well as the national college entrance and scholarship tests. In New York State, he might have had to take as many as ten state-wide examinations; in Pennsylvania, nine; and in Minnesota, six.[37]

There are several reasons why the danger of a similarly extreme situation developing in Ontario is remote. 1 / The universities in this province, although varying somewhat in standards, and perhaps more in prestige, do not begin to differ among themselves as much as do American institutions. Thus the disappointment of an Ontario student in failing to be accepted by the university of his first or even second choice usually does not compare with that of his American counterpart under comparable circumstances. There is not the same concentration of effort to get into a small number of institutions. 2 / It is doubtful that the relaxation of government control over school programs would ever reach the point where special classes for coaching students to take college admission tests could be set up, even though the grade 13 year did in fact gradually evolve to the point where the last several weeks were often little but coaching sessions.

REPORTING PUPIL PROGRESS

In the public view, the school's periodic reports to the pupil's parents have alway seemed to be a major aspect of the educational process. The standard comic strip joke shows the child turning parental wrath to humiliation when, in bringing home the inevitable list of Ds and Es, he presents at the same time one of his father's old report cards that he happened to find in the attic. Emphasis on reporting would be fully justified if it represented adequate and healthy communication between the school and the home. The ideal is to communicate the right things in the right way. Such an assertion covers a series of rather difficult problems.

One way of categorizing reporting procedures is according to whether they compare a pupil's achievement directly with that of others or whether they assess it in terms of his own potentialities. In the first of these approaches, which is of course the traditional one, the reference group is usually the class or grade of which the pupil is a member. Since the advent of standardized tests, the group may be that on which norms were developed, and a particular pupil at the end of grade 5, for example, would have a grade norm of 5.10, referring to five years and ten months of schooling, if his performance equalled the average of the appropriate reference group.

Virtues and faults are claimed for both types of reporting. The method involving comparison with the performance with others, appealing to the pupil's sense of competition, is thought by many educators to be desirable provided the competitors are well matched in potentiality. Competition lends zest to many of life's activities, and they ask why this should not be true of school work. They claim that a child might as well prepare himself in school to live in a competitive world. Others doubt the value of motivation that results from interpersonal competition and contrast it unfavourably with learning from inherent interest in the activity itself. On the same side also, there are many who feel that competitive attitudes among individuals and nations are a major menace in a dangerous world and that the school can perform a great service to humanity by counteracting them. Regardless of these differences, there are few thoughtful educators who would argue that unequals in aptitude should be compared in achievement, even though this practice has been prevalent and takes a long time to die out. Neither the feeling that one's natural place is at the head of the class nor the resigned acceptance of one's unalterable position at the foot is considered to be healthy or desirable. Comparison with a less personal standard of achievement has more to commend it, even without reference to one's aptitude or potentiality. The student may, for example, wish to enter a course or acquire a skill that requires a minimum absolute level of preparation. It is not enough to know simply whether or not he has done his best; it is important also to know if his best is good enough. A major question then is whether or not the indicator of potential achievement is valid for the purpose.

Some parents' motives for wanting the report giving their child's rank in class are not the most defensible. Bascom St John made this comment in 1963.

A child's progress in school is for many people a cause for boasting and a feeling of social superiority. It would sometimes seem that a family's reputation was completely dependent on a youngster's marks. The pressure on the child, in such homes, is serious.

It is for this reason that the vague report cards which are now in vogue in almost all school systems were adopted. They are kept for custom's sake, but they tell the parent little or nothing, in the somewhat vain hope that the child who does poorly will not be too badly browbeaten, or the child who does very well is not unduly praised. The purpose is somewhat negated by the children themselves, who compare cards to see who got how many A's or D's, and so the rating goes on.[38]

There is something quite disturbing in the idea that so many parents will abuse specific information about where their children stand in relation to others that this information must be denied to all. It is clearly desirable that a mature and responsible parent have the best means of deciding, at least in a general way, how far his child is likely to be able to go up the educational ladder, as well as what range of occupational choices is realistic for him. These matters cannot be dealt with in a vacuum.

Of course St John's verdict about the reason for the newer type of report card need not be accepted as the whole story, or even the major part of it, despite its undoubted elements of truth. The sensible conclusion has been adopted overwhelmingly among teachers at the earlier stages of education that the child's own potentiality ought to provide the main point of reference, if not the only one. Thus we have systems such as the OSU report card introduced in Toronto in the early 1950s, the three permissible categories being "outstanding," "satisfactory," and "unsatisfactory." Unless one insists that the child will not do his best without the stimulus of competition, and that learning so motivated is sound and desirable, there is no logic in the assertion that the adoption of this type of reporting represents a "lowering of standards," the old battle cry of those who oppose all kinds of departures from tradition. There is, however, a danger that teachers may underestimate the child's potential and may so act that the unrealistically low ceiling they place on his achievement will become his actual limit. A chief criticism of the use of intelligence and aptitude tests has been that they have contributed to this undesirable process.

Although the secondary schools were only in the early stages of abandoning marking and reporting on the 0–100 scale by the end of the 1960s, this practice has long been out of favour in the elementary schools. Ordinarily the first step away from such a scale is the adoption of a letter system with no more than half a dozen categories. While it commendably recognizes that grading is a very inexact process, the letter system is still unsatisfactory for indicating the extent to which a child is reaching his potential. It is difficult and confusing to try to put over the idea that A-standing does not refer to an absolute level of achievement, but that equal performance by two pupils may entitle one to an A and another a C. The use of letters such as O, S, and U is a further step along the way toward individualized appraisal in that these designations stand for qualitative judgments and not for sections on an underlying quantitative scale. Since parents tend to be dissatisfied with the meagreness of the information provided by a letter designation alone, or even with that supplied by marks on the 0–100 scale, it has been a practice of long standing to add additional verbal comments. It has been possible thus to combine assessment in terms of an absolute standard, assuming the latter can actually be defined, which is of course quite another question, with some suggestion as to whether or not the mark obtained represents the pupil's best work. Communication may be ineffective under these circumstances; many a parent has wondered why his child's mathematics teacher seemed unimpressed with his mark of 84, while his English teacher seemed pleased to be able to give him 67.

Once the idea of reporting in relation to an absolute standard has been abandoned, what is commonly called the anecdotal report card emerges. This is somewhat of a misnomer, however, since a report card does not normally have room for the kind of detailed observations included on an anecdotal record. Parents often feel frustrated and dissatisfied with the vagueness of the information on these cards, and fancy that they would be further ahead with something with the definiteness of numerical marks. It is probable, however, that the teacher who is incapable of making appropriate qualitative comments is no better at any form of assessment, and the gains made by shifting back to the traditional system would be spurious. In fact, a teacher may be revealing his own level of competence in a very clearcut manner by the things he chooses to comment on. The writer has seen cards that constitute a dreary whine about the child's lack of interest, his failure to pay attention, his restlessness, and his difficulty in completing assignments. The following extract from an actual report card used in 1969 demonstrates some of the kinds of things occasionally reported to parents about children mid-way through elementary school.

R. has many excellent qualities and I suggested on the previous report that I expected him to strive faithfully to improve. I regret to say this has not been the case. He is not concentrating and at times seems unconscious that instructions are being given orally. When they are written on a paper or in a book he does not read them with sufficient care to do what is required. If he's to do research he says he has no books, forgets to ask at the library, does not use the books suggested and available in our own room. Projects are seldom totally finished. Result is that a boy who should be doing very good work is producing

> very little. Reading at this time is not satisfactory, yet R. has an excellent vocabulary. Similarly Language is very poor. Spelling is reasonably well done on tests but not used in daily work. Arithmetic is only fair. We want to help R. but he must also help himself.

A parent receiving this kind of information might well wonder what he was supposed to do other than take over the direct responsiblity for educating the child himself.

The teachers who produce this kind of document apparently fail to realize what a serious indictment it is of their own work. While the school has every right to expect the constructive co-operation of the home, any parent would be merely compounding a crime if he threatened the child with unpleasant consequences if reports of such behaviour continued. In fact, it is very doubtful that he would be acting in the child's own interest if he expressed sympathy in his presence with the teacher's complaints. At its best, on the other hand, anecdotal reporting can reveal extremely perceptive insights by a good teacher, presenting the parent with some salutary means of counteracting his own biases and of co-ordinating his efforts with those of the school.

Recent advice by the Department of Education on reporting to parents emphasizes that this activity, like testing or examining, should be done primarily in accordance with definite aims and objectives and may vary with individual children.[39] The two basic categories of comparisons are recognized. Where the objective is to master a concept, the teacher is advised to report the degree to which he has mastered it in terms of an absolute standard. As far as comparisons with other children's achievement are concerned, these are to be only very general. It is suggested that some such technique as the following be used once or twice a year to help parents form an impression of their child's progress as compared with that of others.

General achievement

Above average		Average		Below average	

Check marks are to be used in the appropriate slots. A similar precedure is advocated for general effort, the criterion in this case being the child's own potentiality. Comments are to form the bulk of the report, with the possible addition of samples of the child's work. Parent-teacher discussions of the child's progress are advocated.

E.N. Rutherford, a school administrator, reported some of the ideas behind the development of an experimental report card in Fairmount Park Senior School in the mid-1960s.[40] One of these was that the card should not be returned to the teacher, but should be kept by the parent as a continuous guide to him and the child in improving school work during the subsequent term. The group participating in the development of the card felt that there was something unprofessional in the practice of demanding the card's return within a few days, since no doctor, lawyer, hospital, bank, or business made a practice of doing such a thing. It was decided also that the report would look more professional if it were typed. The basic approach involved the use of a letter grade; check lists were eliminated on the grounds that their use contradicted the recognition of individual difference. The teachers felt that they should start with the pupil and make their comments on him rather than starting with a set of standard comments and relating them to each pupil. A point they emphasized strongly was that the June report should indicate the point to which the child had progressed up to that time. They thought it anomalous to report the average of the year's work, as many schools did.

An increasing number of progressive schools have been dropping report cards altogether in favour of parent-teacher conferences. In many cases, the results have apparently been very good, especially when the process is part of a continuous relationship between the home and school rather than a contact to discuss a problem or an emergency. Some parents are not satisfied, however, with an oral exchange and persist in wanting a written record. Thus the extra work required of the teacher in arranging for and holding conferences does not obviate the effort to make out report cards. There are also certain to be parents of some of the children who cannot be reached at any convenient hour, and who can thus be approached only by the traditional method.

INTELLIGENCE AND APTITUDE TESTING

Definitions and descriptions

Intelligence testing is a very large and complex topic, only a few aspects of which can be touched upon lightly here. The emphasis in this context is on the shifting assumptions about the value of the tests and on their uses and abuses. Most references to Ontario could be made equally well to other provinces and to certain other countries, since the issues and problems tend to be universal.

Intelligence is the name applied to any one of an indefinite number of constructs varying with the ideas of the people who define them and according to the statistical manipulations they carry out on the data they select as relevant. Whatever the construct, it is centred around a quality or qualities defined in ordinary terminology as brightness, cleverness, etc. It is manifested through some form of behaviour, nearly alway conscious and overt, with perhaps some exceptions that need not concern us here. A test of intelligence consists of a series of tasks arranged in order with respect to some criterion. Differences in tests depend on the identity of these tasks, on the way in which they are arranged, and on the way in which they are scored and interpreted. Theories of intelligence testing deal with such matters as the nature of the tasks that justify inclusion in a test, the meaning of their interrelationships, and explanations as to why individuals differ in their performance on a test.

The scientist's interest in intelligence revolves around his desire to understand, classify, and explain it. The educator is in search of assistance to determine the learner's potentiality for various forms of development – intellectual, personal, physical, social. The particular theory on which a certain test is based may be of relatively little interest to him. He wants to know what the test will do or, in other words, what its validity is for his particular purposes. He is also very much concerned, or should be, with the kinds of skills he needs in order to administer and interpret it so as to derive from it whatever services it is capable of performing.

Most intelligence tests used in educational institutions call for a direct verbal or a paper-and-pencil response. For certain types of special difficulties or handicaps, other kinds of performance, such as the manipulation of concrete materials, may be demanded. Tests may also be classified according to whether they are intended for individual or group use. It is fairly well recognized that only a highly trained specialist can expect to get valid results from the former, where a considerable amount of personal judgment is required to evaluate performance of some of the prescribed tasks. On the other hand, a group test may be satisfactorily administered by a person who can be counted on to carry out a detailed set of instructions without deviating from them in any important respect. The interpretation of the results of the group test requires skill comparable to that for the individual test. Individual tests are generally assumed to be more reliable and valid than group tests, but this assumption cannot be claimed to hold for every test administration. It is ordinarily impractical to administer individual tests to more than a small proportion of a school population because of the time and expense involved. Group tests can, and frequently are, given to all pupils in a school system.

Most individual testing in Ontario has been done with the Stanford-Binet or Wechsler Intelligence Scales. The Dominion Group Test of Learning Capacity, produced by the now defunct Department of Educational Research of the Ontario College of Education, was for a long time the staple group test, although there were always numerous schools that preferred to use one or other of the better known American tests. The popularity of the Dominion tests declined with the neglect for many years of the necessary research to keep them up to date and with the relatively much greater resources devoted to the production and revision of comparable tests in the United States. The Department of Measurement and Evaluation of the Ontario Institute for Studies in Education has been directing some effort toward the updating of the Dominion tests.

Abuses of intelligence testing

Ontario has suffered from some of the universal misconceptions and abuses associated with intelligence testing. One of the worst problems relates to the widespread and mistaken notion that the tests measure a fixed characteristic that remains through life. It is undoubtedly true that individuals differ in terms of some central core of potentiality which is to a certain degree hereditary. But what intelligence tests measure is far from this quintessential factor; it is rather an indeterminate amalgam highly affected by environmental factors and innate drives, and varying by different amounts in single individuals over a period of time. Generally speaking, it is most amenable to change in the earlier years. There is considerable evidence to support the claim that losses that cannot be entirely retrieved later may occur if the child is denied a full measure of stimulation and emotional support during his first six months of life.

A most serious consequence of the notion that intelligence test scores measure an unchanging and unchangeable trait is the sharp limitation it often places on the teacher's expectation for the pupil. A number of research studies have recently emphasized the adverse effect of this expectation on the pupil's actual performance. It has even been shown that children selected purely at random show unusual gains, not only in achievement, but even in measured intelligence after a period under the tutelage of a teacher who was told at the beginning that great intellectual gains were to be expected from them.

It has frequently been the practice in Ontario secondary schools to plot the expected achievement of individuals on a chart. The point of reference is their intelligence test score. If their actual achievement falls outside an expected range based on average performance in a comparable group, they are labeled underachievers or overachievers, depending on the direction of the deviation. While this procedure cannot be condemned as inherently bad, it is subject to serious abuse. There is something ominous in a term like "overachiever," which seems to suggest that it is not altogether praiseworthy to do better than the chart indicates one should. It is true, of course, that gains may sometimes be made at an excessive cost in terms of nervous tension or the loss of opportunities for desirable activities other than study. But there have been many healthy, happy "overachievers" whose record could not be explained in those terms. It would be a disaster to imply in any way that their performance was not highly commendable simply because they did not conform to some artificial construct.

Mistaken notions about intelligence testing are reflected in the question one still hears frequently as to the minimum IQ one needs to succeed in an Ontario university. It is said that guidance teachers sometimes quote a figure of 110. There are no grounds for criticism if they say in effect that most people who are unable to score higher than that on one of the common tests will probably find it takes a great deal of dedicated effort to succeed in even the less demanding university programs. But there are too many variable factors to justify any absolute assertion. Records show that a successful high school teacher and administrator in an Ontario school was once assigned an IQ score of 96. Another teacher with an honours degree from an outstanding university has a recorded IQ of 106.

A second difficulty arises from the fact that many educators fail to realize the limited range of abilities that an intelligence test commonly measures. There is no pretence that the tests can predict success in music, art, or other special fields. Because they encourage a response based on average or conventional group behaviour, they bear no relation to certain kinds of creative activity. They are particularly ineffective in identifying qualities of genius. In general, it is risky to use an intelligence test score by itself for the prediction of any important educational outcome. In combination with other factors, however, it may be very useful.

A third and final problem, although by no means the last that might be mentioned, is that IQs, or any other types of summary measures, are not necessarily comparable from one test to another. While the middle positions do not usually vary by more than a few points, there may be a great difference near the extremes. Thus a person who does equally well on two different tests in comparison with the reference group may get IQs varying by approximately thirty points. In the middle 1950s, the writer had occasion to check the validity of the IQ scores of students in the Toronto secondary schools as predictors of first-year university success. The IQs obtained in any test administration while the students were in either grade 12 or grade 13, regardless of the particular test used, were all thrown in together. The resulting correlation with the first-year average was, not unexpectedly, close to zero. While the differences in scales were perhaps not the only reason for the lack of predictive validity in the scores, they were undoubtedly a major contributing factor.

Procedures for using test scores

The question of how intelligence test scores should be handled has been one of concern in Ontario, as elsewhere. Regulations forbid their release to anyone except principals and teachers. The implication of this policy is that students and parents have too little relevant knowledge and experience to interpret a score correctly and that their misconceptions would probably produce harmful consequences. One can see here a survival of the idea that an IQ is an unchangeable attribute. The student may be told his achievement test scores or examination marks because he can do something about them, but not his unalterable IQ, knowledge of which might result in undesirable feelings of superiority if it is high, or of hopeless despair if it is low.

David Goslin, a sociologist at the Russell Sage Foundation, observed that very little of a systematic nature is known about the effects on children of providing them with specific information about their abilities. He suggested that "the effect depends upon the information given, previously held conceptions of ability, the way in which the information is presented, the strength of competing estimates, and various other factors."[41] He urged the development of a rational policy with respect to the dissemination of test results.

Although it is possible that those who make the regulations are right in their feeling about what would happen if the policy of secrecy were relaxed, one can hardly expect the public to accept with relish the idea that educators are entitled to keep information secret from them for their own good. Teachers do not, after all, have the god-like status of doctors in our society, and even the latter receive some rather severe criticism when they refrain from providing the patient with unpalatable facts. In general, of course, it is legitimate to fear the kind of thing that grows only in the darkness and withers in the light of day. There have been direct attacks on policies of secrecy about test scores. A Long Island parent, for example, brought a suit against school officials to compel them to show him his child's records. In 1961 State Supreme Court Justice Brennan upheld his right, provided that the information was part of the official school record.

The other aspect of the same problem has to do with the relationships between guidance teachers or others who administer the tests and regular classroom teachers. There are no doubt many teachers who are no better prepared to handle IQs productively and judiciously than are the students' parents. But a policy of secrecy which excludes part of the school staff can only contribute to the intolerable isolation of the guidance people. The obvious remedy is more pre-service or in-service training in the use and understanding of tests.

Scholastic aptitude tests

Unlike intelligence tests, there is usually no attempt to relate scholastic aptitude tests to a theory of the identity and organization of mental processes. They are constructed for the purpose of predicting achievement at a later stage in an individual's educational career. Scholastic aptitude is considered to be basic capacity as developed over a considerable period of time by school experience. It may or may not be more readily modified than what is measured by group tests of intelligence. In fact, there is often no recognizable difference between items used on the respective tests. Perhaps the main real difference is that scholastic aptitude tests are interpreted with reference to quite specific groups rather than to an unselected population. The complexities and controversies surrounding the IQ are thus avoided. It has in fact been said that much of the difficulty associated with the use of intelligence tests would disappear if the term "IQ" were eliminated. Steps in this direction have been taken for some tests.

Aptitude scores for unselected groups of applicants for admission to American colleges are usually much better predictors of first-year success than the OSAT scores or the Scholastic Aptitude Test Scores administered to the Atkinson Study group in 1956.[42] In fact, typical correlations in the United States tend to fall above 0.50 and quite often around 0.55. Much depends on the variability of the statistical population used. The question of why there is such a substantial difference should be of considerable interest to those responsible for Canadian admissions programs. Canadian universities would probably not wish to accept the view that aptitude genuinely counts more toward success in American institutions. They might be more willing to attribute the difference to the type of examinations used. The high correlation between the average on the grade 13 departmentals and that in the freshman year probably reflected their common use of the essay question. In any case, the matter should have considerable further examination.

SPECIFIC APTITUDES

Specific aptitude tests attempt to measure maximum performance in areas such as musical, artistic, clerical, mechanical, and the like. The first two of these usually show very little overlap with general intelligence, in whatever way it is defined. Clerical aptitude and mechanical aptitude tests ordinarily correlate to some extent with intelligence tests. Devices of this kind are used in comprehensive guidance programs to assist a student to evaluate his potentialities and make career choices. They can serve a useful purpose provided that certain conditions are observed. 1 / It must be remembered that some of them are rather low in predictive validity. They tend to be most useful in screening out those who lack some quality regarded as essential for success in a certain field. For example, one will not go far in a musical career if he is tone deaf. Although one may legitimately wonder if a formal test is needed to uncover such an obvious deficiency, there are other traits not so subject to discovery by casual observation. When it comes to predicting outstanding achievement, the tests do not help much. A musical aptitude test may confirm a student's hope that, given the necessary motivation and facilities, he can learn to play a certain instrument with competence. What he can do beyond that remains a mystery. 2 / Success in any particular line of endeavour results from a combination of factors, of which specific aptitude is only one. A girl might show the kind of finger dexterity that would be of great value to a typist, but a typist's career might be the very last thing she would care to contemplate.

MEASURES OF TYPICAL BEHAVIOUR

Non-intellective measures include a variety of devices where the objective is to discover typical or habitual behaviour. Those of most concern to educators are interest inventories, attitude scales, and certain kinds of personality measures. The instructions that accompany these devices usually point out that there are no right or wrong answers, and that the results will be of value only if the respondent answers each question as conscientiously and honestly as possible. He can be counted upon to follow such instructions only to the extent that he is capable of identifying his own reactions, that he is interested in a valid outcome, and that he does not feel threatened in any way by the questions. Failure to ensure that all these conditions are met creates most of the problems surrounding this kind of measure.

Interest inventories

Guidance departments have made a considerable amount of use of the best known interest inventories. Whether these are ostensibly designed to identify "personal" or "vocational" interests does not seem to make a great deal of difference to the ways in which they are employed. They are given to assist students to make appropriate educational and career choices. The approach used is an attempt to overcome the difficulty caused by the fact that students' attitudes toward many occupations and positions are based on stereotypes that include varying elements of unreality. Some are endowed with a false aura of glamour, and others suffer from undeserved denigration. Instead of asking the respondent to react to broad stereotypes, the inventory identifies a large number of simple components, and demands either an absolute expression of attitude (e.g., like, indifferent, dislike) toward each one, or a statement of preference among several possibilities. According to the first alternative, for example, the respondent might be asked whether he would like, would be indifferent to, or would dislike writing short stories. According to the second, he might be asked to choose among writing a television play, operating the production machinery required to put the program on the air, and acting in the play.

One of the greatest limitations on the value of the interest inventory is that there are often major discrepancies between the career aspirations of students and their capacity to achieve the desired objective. Every teacher who has attempted to assist students to find their way through the maze of possibilities that our complex society offers has encountered this phenomenon. Despite all the strictures about not placing too much reliance on intelligence test scores, and not placing too low a ceiling on an individual's potential achievement, there are limits which it would be unrealistic and cruel to encourage him to think he could exceed. The process of guidance requires a very delicate handling of this problem.

Severe criticisms of interest inventories have been offered on several grounds. One is that they are used at too early a stage in the child's development when his interests are unstable and even ephemeral. Unfortunately there is not enough research evidence available to indicate when and under what conditions these do begin to acquire some degree of permanence, and thus provide a basis for tentative career choices. But it is not altogether fair to the two major instruments that have for many years been the staples in this field, the Kuder Professional Record and the Strong Vocational Interest Blank, to blame them if they are indeed used too early, since the instructions they provide do not encourage such a practice. In Ontario, it has been common to employ them at the grade 12 level.

There has been another side to this issue, and that is that many young people make career decisions before reaching grade 12. In fact, a considerable, although fortunately diminishing, number have already left school by that time. Thus if there really is any value in taking measured interests into account, it should be done early enough to be of some help. An important part of the program of the Carnegie Study of Identification and Utilization of Talent in High School and College was to try to clear up some problems in this area. The so-called Canadian Interest Inventory was constructed and administered to the same grade group in grades 9, 10, and 12. The intention was to determine the extent of change during this period and ultimately to validate the instrument against career choices actually made and success achieved therein. Unfortunately, adequate means were never provided to carry out this ambitious program, and it proved abortive. In a sense the issue is becoming less urgent as more and more young people remain longer in school and delay their career choices. But the need for help in making these choices certainly does not diminish. G.R. Hawes pointed out, in discussing the role of the interest inventory, that there were more than 40,000 different ways of making a living in the United States at the time of writing, according to the US Bureau of Labor Statistics.[43] Since the book offering this information was published in 1964, the number has no doubt increased substantially since that time. It can hardly be argued that Canadian young people face a much less bewildering array of choices.

A great many other abuses of the interest inventory have been described by the critics, apart from their use at what may or may not be too early an age. These centre around a mechanical, insensitive, or downright unintelligent interpretation and application of the results. Such abuses are a threat to any testing or measurement procedure, and the only remedy is to provide the right kind of teachers with the right kind of specialized training. Of course the immediate question faced by many administrators is what to do if the latter condition cannot be met. To such a question, there can be no armchair answer.

Attitude scales

Because schools have a very important stake in the development of certain types of attitudes, there would appear to be a strong incentive for the production of valid instruments to determine the outcomes of practices directed toward that end. There are in fact no well-known devices to compare with instruments widely used in other fields. The basic reason is that particular scales tend by their nature to have limited applications. There is an inexhaustible number of people, institutions, ideas, and ideologies about which attitudes may be formed. To add to the difficulty, these tend to change rapidly in terms of relevance to the educational process. It was not long after the Second World War when it began to seem rather unimportant how school children felt about Nazis. Attitudes toward the use of certain drugs have become matters of rapidly increasing concern in recent years. Anyone who wishes to measure a particular attitude may have little more than a set of principles and procedures to guide him and usually has to assume a major part of the responsibility for selecting suitable items and combining them to produce an instrument. Practising educators seldom have both the time and the training needed to go through the necessary steps. Attitude scales are most commonly employed by researchers who can afford to concentrate a great deal of effort on producing the desired result.

It is unfortunate that measurement in the attitude area presents so many problems. There are, of course, those who are apprehensive about education's role in the shaping of attitudes, feeling that misdirected efforts in this sphere can rather easily degenerate into undesirable propagandizing. But it is becoming increasingly evident to everyone that attitudes are intimately tied in with all kinds of learning. A teacher who is concerned about poor achievement might find the exploration of attitudes toward the work a very rewarding line of investigation.

Personality measures

Certain kinds of personality measures have found their way into the arsenals of guidance teachers in Ontario, although their use has typically been much more limited and restrained than in many parts of the United States. The most common have been used to assess various aspects of adjustment and to identify different kinds of emotional problems within a range of behaviour excluding the seriously abnormal. Hawes has summed up the trends as follows.

> The older type of personality inventories your child might take would attempt to measure a number of character traits – attachment to values deemed theoretical, economic, political, esthetic, social and religious on the Study of Values, for instance, or traits like "ascendancy," responsibility, emotional stability and cautiousness on the Gordon Personal Profile. Newer types of personality inventories would yield scores indicating how normal or abnormal your child seemed to be in certain areas. On the Minnesota Counseling Inventory, for example, these areas would be family relations, social relations, emotional stability, moodiness, conformity, adjustment to reality and leadership. On the California Test of Personality the areas would include sense of personal worth, nervous symptoms, family relations, feeling of belonging and antisocial tendencies.[44]

The use of instruments of this kind may be helpful in giving the student a better understanding of his own strengths and limitations. It may also assist teachers in adapting the school program to his particular needs. But the risks attendant upon the use of this type of measuring instrument are particularly great, and only under the best of circumstances can we be confident that they will do more good than harm.

It is important first of all to realize that personality inventories are relatively low in validity as compared with measurement devices in other areas. There is no substantial agreement on what constitutes a satisfactory definition of sociability, emotional stability, leadership, or other traits. Different instruments purporting to assess an individual's possession of a trait labeled in the same way often correlate poorly with one another. It has often been found that students whose performance identifies them as "maladjusted" on one instrument are designated as quite normal on the basis of another.

A second point has to do with the values assigned to certain traits. It is generally considered undesirable to be maladjusted, but there are a great many contradictory definitions of such a term, and an equal number of different ideas about what should be done about it. It has often been pointed out that a large proportion of the producers of the works of genius that have genuinely enriched human culture would have showed up very poorly on present-day instruments. There are shudders about what might have happened had a school system managed to suppress their erratic tendencies and force them into a "normal" mould. There seems to be something about the mere construction and contemplation of tables designed for the interpretation of personality inventory scores that tends to glorify the average and make an ideal of conformity. Those who deviate from the middle position are potential problems; there is an implication that something ought to be done about them. Even a well-balanced, broad-minded, and imaginative educator must struggle to avoid falling victim to this attitude. The term "adjustment" itself creates a hostile reaction in many quarters. People legitimately ask who has the right to decide what values and practices the child should be adjusted to, and what happens if he is adjusted to the wrong things.

There is also a danger that teachers with limited training may stray too far into attempts to measure severe disturbance, perhaps well within the category of real mental illness. Instruments like the Minnesota Multiphasic Personality Inventory are definitely not for use by the average teacher, or even the teacher with considerable special training. They are intended for initial diagnosis of serious disorders requiring specialized treatment. They have, it is true, been used in school populations in the United States to try to predict later delinquent behaviour, but it is hard to imagine that their positive contribution is worth the risk entailed, unless they are kept under strict control of qualified school psychologists. The increasing numbers of Ontario school systems with adequate psychological services during recent years are of course widening the range of measuring instruments that fall within the educational sphere.

One of the intangible threats in the use of inventories to discover emotional and social problems is that an excessive preoccupation with such matters can be unhealthy. Students who are too much encouraged to expect and look for abnormalities in themselves may exaggerate the importance of what they do find. The best approach is to assume that productive personality will develop in a wide range of circumstances and with a wide range of manifestations. When genuinely destructive or self-defeating qualities develop, they can be identified promptly and remedied as effectively as possible without being overemphasized.

One especially pernicious practice involves the use of measures of typical or habitual behaviour to make decisions with respect to selection, employment, or promotion. It is true that some of these devices do possess substantial validity as predictors of academic and vocational success. Innumerable studies, including some conducted in Ontario, have confirmed this fact. Examples of such research include appraisals of the effectiveness of the Brown-Holtzman Survey of Study Habits and Attitudes and the Kuder Preference Record – Personal in the Atkinson Study of Utilization of Student Resources.[45] Such measures have often shown a particular ability to add to the effectiveness of combinations of predictors because they represent dimensions that differ substantially from academic abilities. But their successful use is not only entirely dependent on the respondent's ability to give perceptive answers but also on his desire to answer honestly. The ideal condition for the valid use of the instruments exists when he sees value in them as a source of information about himself that can help make his own choices or solve his own problems. When they are employed by an external authority to classify or judge him, he is put squarely in the position of having to decide what kind of response will put him in the best light. It is reasonable then to ask who is being unethical, the person who devises the circumstances under which the respondent must choose between honesty and the legitimate objective of vocational or educational opportunity, or the respondent who chooses the second of these alternatives. In one sense, the procedure turns into an intelligence test in which the most successful candidate demonstrates the greatest ingenuity in outwitting the tester. But anyone who wishes to work successfully with employees or students might well be concerned about the quality of the relationship established with this kind of beginning. If the authority is concerned only about making a valid judgment, and not about its human consequences, he may sometimes use devices with concealed purpose. For example, a so-called test of humour, in which the respondent chooses the alternatives that he finds most amusing, may actually be designed to reveal certain personality traits. The Rorschach ink-blot test may also induce an unsuspecting person to reveal various quirks and aberrations. But all these practices are deplored by those who would like to see measurement occupy a useful and constructive place in the educational process.

EIGHT

Educational media

THE IMPLICATIONS OF TECHNOLOGY FOR LEARNING

The implications for education of the unprecedented advances in technology during recent decades include 1 / the possibility of making existing educational procedures more efficient and more effective and 2 / the necessity of adapting the purposes and the nature of the educational process itself to meet the demands of the new environment. Almost every educator has given consideration to the first; to do so is relatively easy, since it can be done without stirring from traditional attitude patterns. The second is difficult and to many people extremely disturbing, because it requires a radical departure from deeply ingrained modes of thought and action. We may, for convenience, begin by looking at the question from the first point of view.

The application of technology to the production of devices to assist in the process of education is largely, although not entirely, a phenomenon of the period since the end of the Second World War. An impressive variety of tools for learning has been produced, many with great apparent potentialities. Enthusiasts keep envisioning great improvements in teaching efficiency as a result of their widespread adoption. The fact that this revolution cannot yet be said to have occurred is not an adequate reason for predicting that it will not do so. The signs of interest have been increasing, and the rate of adoption accelerating. Some classrooms are really beginning to assume an appearance that differs in essential respects from their counterparts in Ryerson's day. In fact, in a few places where the advances have been greatest, the term "classroom" begins to appear to be a misnomer.

Progress has, in the eyes of many observers, been inordinately slow. Educators are generally considered among the relatively cautious elements in North American society. In many cases, their background and preparation have failed to make them fully aware of the role of technology in the development of modern civilization. Some have interpreted their responsibility for maintaining humanistic values as a mandate to resist the encroachments of the menacing machine. Thoreau is a more natural hero to them than Norbert Weiner. Very often their negative attitude toward the products of technology has little to do with any lofty philosophical assessment of social trends. Observers have described the reaction of many teachers to the introduction into the school of a complicated looking piece of equipment, no matter how simple its actual operation, as nothing short of downright fear. Perhaps an excessive attachment to verbalization inevitably produces a tendency to downgrade the values of "gadgets."

Slowness in applying technical devices to the process of instruction cannot be laid entirely at the door of educators. The taxpaying public has been reluctant to spend the money required for expensive innovations. In part, this attitude can be explained by the difficulty of demonstrating that the devices in question make any definite contribution. The frequent research verdict that no significant difference can be conclusively attributed to their influence does not facilitate their introduction unless they are convincingly presented as a cheaper substitute for a live teacher or the standard instructional paraphernalia. Since their case almost always rests, not on the money they will save, but on the improvement they will make in the quality of education in ways other than those that research is best at measuring, they gain little support from research. Leaving things as they are may be more expensive in terms of real gain, but the forces of inertia prevail.

Although American educators may share the same orientation as their Canadian counterparts, they are generally considered to reflect the more innovative attitudes characteristic of their society. In making this comparison in one of his columns, Bascom St John observed that the enormous wealth of American society enabled Americans to try new ideas to see if they worked, with less concern than Canadians might have about whether the money would be wasted.[1] Perhaps it is not so much the amount of money available but the attitude toward spending it that is important. In any case, while Canadians may be less venturesome than their neighbours, they are showing an increased willingness to adopt and adapt ideas that have originated and been tried out across the border.

The educational media may be categorized roughly into two broad categories according to the type of use to which they are put: 1 / those that simply supply information in some auditory or visual form, and 2 / and those that provide for a direct response on the part of the learner. The first group includes most of the devices that have been longest on the scene, such as radio, slides, and films, as well as television, the impressions carried by laser beam, and the like. In certain circumstances, they possess substantial advantages over the school's regular stand-by, the book. The information may be more easily accessible, available in more convenient form, more readily supplied in up-to-date form, or more effective and dramatic in its impact. There may even be circumstances under which it is less expensive, although this phenomenon is not yet very common. In most cases, the devices in this category are especially suitable for conveying the same information to a large group. The teletutor, with its small desk screen, can also be effective for the opposite purpose, enabling each student in a room to receive a different message.

The devices that permit a learner response include the telephone, the programmed text, the teaching machine, tapes designed to leave room for an oral response, language laboratories, computer assisted instruction, and devices from the other category, such as television, when provided with supplementary equipment. Most of them are equipped with stored information, although the telephone and some aspects of language laboratories provide for spontaneous interjections, or even the devising of the entire message by a teacher. The devices differ in convenience and effectiveness in relation to the variety and sophistication of the response they provide for in either direction. Branching programs were devised to offer improvements in these respects over programs which carried every learner over exactly the same path, whether he found the stimuli too skimpy and inadequate or boringly repetitive. The introduction of the computer has made possible a tremendous increase in the number of forms and patterns in which stored information can be supplied and in the number of ways in which the learner can pose questions or express his responses. It has also provided for the presentation of information in a more effective form. Cathode ray tubes have been found valuable for this purpose. The random access slide projector provides for the presentation of pictorial material. Considerable progress is also being made in the attempt to devise methods of speech generation so that the computer can supply a verbal response to the learner's question.

One of the main issues in the use of these devices, as seen by educators, has to do with the place of personal contact and influence in the learning process. Meierhenry and Stepp outlined the opposing views in their comments on media and education for the young child.

> At one extreme, some McLuhan enthusiasts might propose that all the world's people, including infants and young children, are really transistors being bombarded constantly by electrons, in which case all we need to do to turn on the young learner is develop the right circuitry. Others would argue that the young learner is such a fragile bit of humanity that the main prerequisite for learning is a personal and intimate relationship with other people, particularly his parents, his family, and his peer group; since media have nothing to contribute to positive personal feelings, they have no place in learning systems.[2]

These writers suggested that the answer lay somewhere in between. They felt that man's future development might involve a much-increased emphasis on the capacity to manipulate a wide range of symbols, especially mathematical symbols, rather than mainly verbal symbols, as is now the case. The media have a fundamental place in developing more fully the capacity to handle all types of symbols.

Meierhenry and Stepp referred to some of the results of recent research on the development of very young children. The necessity of a sympathetic, supporting influence from an adult is of course well known. But studies are also tending to show the great importance of adequate perceptual stimulation. Orphanage babies placed for some time in cribs covered with white sheets have been very slow in developing the capacity to differentiate among various kinds of visual configurations so necessary for reading skill at a later stage. Other infants given the opportunity to cause movement of colourful articles in the crib or to throw various kinds of flashing lights on the ceiling by bumping or striking an apparatus have developed a superior ability to perform tasks requiring visual discrimination. It has been suggested that babies would benefit from being propped in front of television sets even if only commercial programs were being broadcast, in order to obtain appropriate training in visual perception. There is also accumulating evidence of the contribution to development of other types of physical stimulation. Thus the concept of the educative influence of the warm, living human being versus that of the cold, impersonal, inhuman gadget is becoming less and less adequate.

It has often been pointed out that an effectively used combination of mechanical and electronic devices may substantially improve and enhance a teacher's personal influence. The routine and mechanical aspects of the traditional teaching function may be taken over and carried out with unprecedented efficiency, thus leaving the teacher with undiminished energy to devote to the improvement of motivation, the development of appreciation, and all the other objectives which are indisputably dependent on productive personal contact. Also, the amount of time a teacher will have to devote to each individual in a class of average size is inevitably not very great. The existence of some means of identifying each individual's weaknesses in terms of knowledge and understanding of certain essential processes enables the teacher to use his available time where it is most needed.

The challenge of technology is of course much deeper and more fundamental than merely that of utilizing new techniques to facilitate a process handed down inviolate from days gone by. The creation of new media of communication calls for such a change in approach as to be almost a new definition of formal education. In a sense, this change may be looked upon as the dethronement of print – not that there is any danger that print will be rendered obsolete, but it must make way in education, as in the rest of life, for other means of communication that serve more effectively in their own spheres. The school system has for generations centred its activities around the printed word. Alan Thomas wrote as follows:

> The ability to extract information from print with speed and ease (reading) plus the more limited ability to convey it (writing) are the major and compelling skills of the system. This focus also commits its products to certain fundamental attitudes to what knowledge is, what study is, and most important of all what learning is. The idea of *what learning is* is perhaps the single most impor-

tant idea that any school system develops in its students. That this attitude is inescapably related to the central means of communication, in this case the book, seems undeniable. If any medium has in our history attempted to replace the teacher it has been not television, but the large self-teaching text book with which we have been so copiously endowed ... Now the predominance of print is gone forever, the question is *what is the function of the school?* Should it attempt to retain its exclusive emphasis and become a specialized rather than a central institution, or to become a new central institution by means of which all our citizens learn how to learn from all these new media at their disposal?

The domination of the curriculum and the very organization of the school by print is undeniable. Any subject or faculty which does not lend itself to communication and measurement in print or writing is inevitably dubbed "a frill". Thus any shift of media will involve a much greater change in the administration and curriculum than simply the addition of a few gadgets. The change in the nature of knowledge implies a change in the nature of teaching and curriculum.[3]

There we have the challenge to the school. It can cling to the disproportionate reliance on a single medium and be relegated to a segment of cultural life of declining importance, at least in relative terms, or it can accept the realities of the communications revolution. Perhaps we shall know that the necessary adaptation is being made when "illiterate" ceases to be considered a synonym for "ignorant."

According to some assessments, the prospect of an effective adaptation of Canadian schools to the demands of the technological revolution do not seem very promising. In his report on the well-known study of the handling of Canadian studies in schools across the country, A.B. Hodgetts observed that almost all teachers in the survey could have had access to movie projectors; four out of five to filmstrip and overhead projectors, to tape recorders, and to radios; and well over half to television sets. But, with the exception of the overhead projectors, the teachers seldom used these devices. They offered as reasons the amount of time required to set up the equipment, the inconvenience of trying to fit radio and television programs into the timetable, the unsuitability of programs for their particular age group, the need to cover the required course of study, and the pressure of examinations. In classes where aids were being used, new dimensions were seldom added to the lesson.

Overhead projectors ... merely provided a substitute for blackboard outlines and mimeographed worksheets; filmstrip pictures were traced on large sheets of brown paper as another type of craft program; movies, without previewing, advance preparation or good follow-up discussions became simply a relaxed, passive diversion from regular classes or, depending on the quality of the movie being shown, another way of handing out a factual, consensus version of history.[4]

The Provincial Committee on Aims and Objectives had somewhat similar comments.

The majority of audio-visual aids that the Committee has seen in use have been employed in a narrow, didactic manner and with groups of children all presumed to be learning the same thing at the same time. Our perception of how learning takes place, and of the kind of teaching that facilitates the process, requires that the teacher understand the use of a variety of techniques in the interests of every child ... The technology to make this a reality is feasible; the dangers of thought control, passivity, and a stultifying uniformity are too grave to permit indiscriminate use of films and educational television.[5]

FILM

Films have long been a standard audio-visual aid in schools in Ontario as in other provinces. Over a period of many years, the Department of Education built up an extremely well-stocked central film library. The establishment of a regional library at Sudbury represented a step in the policy, adopted in the late 1960s, of dispersing such resources around the province.

The uninitiated often ask what the difference is between television presentation and film. F.B. Rainsberry, who served for some time as National Supervisor of School Broadcasts and Youth Programming for the CBC, undertook on one occasion to answer that question in what he described as a brief, general way.[6] 1 / Film gives the director and film editor unlimited opportunities to splice, edit, and reorganize their material, while television editing is much more limited, and is usually done by the producer switching from one camera to another. 2 / Film provides the opportunity to shoot landscape in a very spectacular fashion, whereas the use of television cameras for the same purpose is much more inflexible and expensive. On the other hand, television gives a greater sense of immediacy. The conditions under which it is viewed contribute to this effect. Television is seen in a lighted classroom, while film is viewed on a screen in a darkened room with a projector grinding at the rear. Rainsberry claimed that a good TV lesson transferred to film and shown under film-viewing conditions lost important qualities. 3 / There are different types of accessibility problems. Rainsberry thought that the distribution of films was just as difficult as adjusting the school schedule to receive television programs at the broadcast time. If this were really so, the use of video tapes would not make the contribution to flexibility in the employment of television that many people have supposed.

The differences between a film screening and a television presentation are not as evident to many teachers as they are to the experts, and it is not uncommon to find the former suggesting that the problem of diffusion of television programs would be solved very simply if they were put on film and shipped around to the schools. Such solutions are offered in complete unawareness of the cost of the proposed procedure. They also overlook the hope that television can win an integral place in the curriculum by being kept up to date. Those productions that are intended primarily to produce additions to a film library collections are mainly of the enrichment type. As such, they have tended to be treated as recreation rather than as an essential component of a formal course. The problems of educating teachers to make optimum use of films show many similarities to those applying to television.

THE TELEPHONE

Years ago the Toronto Board of Education introduced what was considered at the time to be one of the more radical post-war innovations in providing for the conduct of lessons by telephone for children confined to their homes by illness or accident. Microphones and speakers were so arranged in the pupil's bedroom that he could take a full part in the lessons. Questions could be asked and answered, and every sound from the teacher in the classroom could be heard by the pupil in the bedroom and vice versa. In describing the procedure, Bascom St John foresaw the day when telephone TV would be perfected to provide an even further degree of intimacy, enabling the child to see the classroom and its activities.[7] Something close to this procedure is, of course, actually used to enable viewers to respond to the television teacher.

Even before the development of television, there might well have been more use of the telephone in educational circles to make it possible for groups of people to confer without being in close physical proximity, as has been done so widely in business. Courses given by telephone are by no means uncommon. Much more might have been done to improve in-service teacher training, which is difficult to co-ordinate with the teacher's fulfilment of his regular responsibilities during the year, had a more imaginative use of this device been made. He could have "attended" distant conferences without actually leaving the scene of his regular activity. At present, the telephone performs a major role as an adjunct to other technical devices. It may, for example, link terminals with a distantly-located computer or serve as a link in the process of information retrieval.

PROGRAMMED LEARNING

Definition

Various terms such as "programmed learning," "programmed instruction," and "teaching machines" have been associated with a phenomenon that began to receive a great deal of attention from educators during the late 1950s. There have been attempts to identify the origins of the idea of programmed learning with techniques known and used throughout the ages. In this connection E.L. Park discussed the Socratic method of teaching by asking questions, and Descartes's approach to the solution of problems by analysing them into their smallest components.[8] He also referred to lists of questions at the end of each chapter of a textbook and the use of workbooks in which pupils had written short answers, matched items, or filled in blanks. While the new approach did evolve from existing practices, it nevertheless developed quite distinct and recognizable characteristics that gave it a clear identity of its own.

Wilbur Schramm defined programmed learning as the kind of learning experience in which a program replaces an instructor and leads the student through a set of specified actions designed and sequenced to make it more probable that he will behave in a given desired way in the future.[9] Although the program is housed in a teaching machine or a programmed textbook, these are little more than containers to hold the program. The latter is usually a series of items, questions, or statements to each of which, in order, the learner responds by filling in a blank, answering a question, indicating agreement or disagreement, or solving a problem and recording the answer. Immediately after responding, he is permitted to see the correct answer so that he can check its accuracy. In the Skinnerian type of program, the items are so written and the steps are so small between them that the learner practises mostly correct responses and avoids errors. The sequence of items is arranged to take him from responses he already knows to new responses he is able to make on the basis of previously acquired knowledge.

Origin

The forerunner of the developers of recent techniques was S.L. Pressey, an American psychologist, who in the 1920s used the procedure of breaking down subject matter into small units and presenting them at an opening in front of a machine, along with a series of possible answers in multiple choice form. The learner indicated his answer by pressing a button corresponding to one of these choices. If he pressed the right button, a new question appeared, but if he pressed the wrong one, the question remained at the opening, an error was recorded, and he tried again. The device aroused no great interest since, although it appeared at a time when substantial attention was being given to objective testing, the educational world was not ready for it.

The real beginning of the movement is identified with the appearance of *The Science of Learning and the Art of Teaching* in 1954. The author, B.F. Skinner, was a Harvard psychologist who illustrated his extreme behaviouristic theories with well-publicized experiments, including teaching pigeons how to play ping pong. He employed substantially the same method to organize and present a course in human behaviour at Harvard in 1957. This particular version was called linear or sequential programming because it involved the presentation of items of stimuli in a fixed sequence.

Skinner attributed Pressey's failure to get the movement started to such factors as the lack of adequate research and theory in the psychology of learning. This does not by any means signify that all those who greeted programmed learning with enthusiasm were convinced of the soundness of his behaviouristic theories. Many took an entirely empirical approach to what could be achieved by "operant conditioning." They were prepared to be impressed by what appeared to work and to seek practical evidence that specific modifications could make the method work better. Some observers have attributed the high degree of interest that developed to the shortage of teachers and money and the desire to find some substitute for or complement to these scarce resources. Penny-pinching members of school boards entertained the hope that they could buy more education for less money. As has been true of the introduction of other devices to facilitate learning, it was claimed that teachers feared they would be displaced.

A major early contributor to the extension of programmed learning techniques was N.A. Crowder of U.S. Industries' Western Design and Electronics Division in California, who was concerned about the inadequacies of an approach that required every user of a program to follow exactly the same path, regardless of his background, abilities, and needs. He devised the branching type of program, which gives the learner the opportunity of pursuing a variety of different paths according to his performance as he moves along. The approach does not, like the linear, seek the almost complete avoidance of errors, but gives the learner an opportunity to learn from his errors.

Developments in the United States

As far as Canadian education is concerned, it is hard to think of any development in which the movement of information across the border has been less restrained. American research has been cited and applied in Canada, American programs have been sold freely, and even in those cases where concern for Canadian identity or an obvious need for devices reflecting specific content have led to Canadian efforts in program construction, the techniques used have been borrowed practically without modification. Thus a few brief comments about developments in the United States may be assumed to have a high degree of relevance to Canada.

Within a few years of Skinner's first initiatives, hundreds of people had produced a large number of programs on a wide variety of subjects for every level from pre-kindergarten to professional school. Schramm's estimate, which he regarded as conservative, was that more than a hundred of these were commercially available in 1962.[10] Hundreds of schools and over a million students in the United States had used programs, with the prospect of rapid increases for the future. Schramm felt that there had been no corresponding increase in quality, but observed that enthusiastic comments nevertheless far exceeded complaints. Apparently the students were learning even from bad programs. The chief negative comment was that the programs were dull, and the second most common was that differences in individual progress made it difficult to fit them into a regular school year. Students who were rewarded for finishing a course early by getting some kind of fill-in activity, while others caught up, naturally tended to discount the desirability of working at maximum speed. Schramm noted that the new technique was being adopted directly into the schools, with no great effort to prepare teachers for its use.

Schramm expressed disappointment at the tendency for programming techniques to harden into a few standard approaches. Nineteen out of twenty programs were of the Skinnerian type, and within that technique fixed and mechanical methods were being used. Many of the tentative principles of programming had become requirements, even though there was no experimental evidence to justify them.

This tendency was attributed in part to the involvement of many untrained and inexperienced programmers and in part to commercial pressure to produce programs. Publishers had rushed into the field at the prospect of large profits and were encouraging the traditional approach rather than slower and more expensive experimental efforts. Schramm declared that many scholars demonstrated their veniality by engaging in unimaginative but lucrative production rather than in research and in the exploration of improved techniques. Another unfortunate effect of commercial activity was that the new approach was often oversold. The exaggerated claims about the possibility of learning "twice as much in half the time" were followed by considerable disillusionment on the part of those who had failed to appraise the programs with the proper degree of scepticism in the first place.

Although commercial interests have given little support, and to a large extent ignored the results, there has been a substantial amount of research devoted to programmed learning. Schramm said that "no teaching medium has ever come into use in such an atmosphere of research – born, as it was, in a learning laboratory, nurtured on theory, and for some years knowing no friends except scholars."[11] The general effect of the studies has been to show that the method is reasonably, if not spectacularly, effective. It has worked at all levels, among students of greatly varying degrees of ability, to teach a great variety of academic subject matter and a wide range of verbal and manual skills. Research has, however, failed to demonstrate the adequacy of Skinner's psychological theories or, for that matter, of any others. It has been found possible to dispense with some of the elements that, according to the principles of operant conditioning, should be absolutely necessary. There is no evidence to show that the constructed or consciously formulated response is any better than one selected from a list of alternatives, or than a subvocal response, or no measurable response at all. Confirmation of the correctness of a particular response has not been shown to be necessary. In some cases, the learner has done just as well by reading the programmed text with the blanks already filled in as he has by filling them in himself. Some experiments with short programs have shown that just as much learning takes place if the order of the items is scrambled as it does if they are presented in normal sequence.

Developments in Canada

With respect to the attitudes of Canadian educators toward programmed learning, F.G. Robinson characterized the period between 1960 and 1962 as one of "titillation," when imaginations were allowed to run riot.[12] He referred to a spate of national and provincial seminars and to the popularity of such slogans as "the greatest educational breakthrough since the invention of the printing press." But it was not long before disillusion, perhaps greater than that in the United States, set in. The technique could not do all that was claimed for it; there were many defective programs in circulation; the construction of items and the problem of securing access to students for tryouts were more difficult than had been foreseen; the programs did not necessarily work well for all purposes; they were not self-motivating as originally claimed. Robinson assessed the reaction as ranging from continued and undiluted enthusiasm to a tendency to reject the entire idea as a fad. The activities of those whose attitude was somewhere in between led him to identify the period after 1962 as one of quiet consolidation.

In 1963 the Canadian Teachers' Federation undertook a survey to get some reasonable estimate of the use of programmed learning material, and some appraisal of its value, from Canadian schools. A serious problem was faced in determining which of the approximately 160,000 teachers, principals, and other administrators should be approached. The method adopted was to secure lists of purchasers from commercial distributors. Using information from this source and other more casual ones, the federation compiled 325 names of potential correspondents. These people were supplied with a manual entitled *Evaluating Programmed Instruction Materials Through Action Research* as a means of assisting them to make an objective assessment of the situation. After a second approach was made, responses were secured from approximately 50 per cent of the group. Although not completely satisfactory, this result compares quite favourably with other comparable surveys conducted by mail. The data received, however, were disappointingly tenuous and incomplete.[13]

The result of the study was an estimate that about 350 Canadian teachers used programs to some extent in 1962–3 and that, of these, probably no more than half went so far as to use a complete program or a sequence of more than one thousand frames with an entire class. It was estimated that approximately six thousand Canadian students "had a brush with" programmed instruction during the school year. The general assessment was that "programmed instruction has just barely touched Canadian education."

The appraisals of the method included reports that students' interest flagged or that they were bored by the necessity of having to deal with small steps. This boredom was found across a broad spectrum of uses. There were grounds for inferring, however, that the teacher's attitude toward programmed learning, and his flexibility in using the technique, might be the chief determinants of the students' attitudes. It was thought that student interest could be sustained over a long period of time where the more flexible and imaginative teachers introduced "unit breaks," short discussion periods, live sessions, interesting side ventures for superior students, and other monotony-killers. There was a reasonable amount of enthusiasm among the respondents for the use of programmed learning in remedial work.

The Canadian Teachers' Federation immediately launched a project designed to encourage a further critical examination of the technique by teachers throughout the country. The federation arranged to provide to those willing to use and appraise them a set of units selected from commercially prepared mathematics programs, along with several short teacher-made programs in chemistry. About two hundred teachers responded to the invitation with a request for more than 35,000 programs. They also received copies of several publications for use as background for their investigation, including one that dealt with the general rationale and methodology of classroom research on curriculum and instruction. This latter document was regarded as important in that the project was not only an attempt to evaluate programmed learning but also an experiment in the techniques and effectiveness of teacher research. The appraisals included many favourable comments. About half of those who made an interpretable response reported a definite improvement in student performance.

No doubt the effects of this project help to explain why investigations by the Canadian Council for Research in Education during the next two years produced a more favourable verdict on program usage. There appeared to be a considerable and varied activity in programmed instruction in Canada, even though there was no precise estimate of the proportion of the relevant groups using the programs. The chief emphasis remained in the field testing of American programs. The surveys also indicated that there was considerable support for a national co-ordinating agency for programmed learning.[14]

The Ontario Teachers' Federation held a workshop on programmed instruction from July 8 to 19, 1963, at which the following statement was made.

It is our opinion that programmed instruction will have a definite and permanent impact on the organization of schools and curricula. It is a technique that could have a beneficial effect on education at all levels. There appears to be sufficient evidence to justify the conclusion that programmed learning is a good thing. Its proponents claim and have proved experimentally, that students learn as much in less time than they do by traditional methods. We recommend that the teachers of Ontario concern themselves with this new teaching technique, approach it with an open mind, examine it critically, and at the same time, with tolerance.

In 1964–5 the federation launched a series of studies, involving its affiliates, to determine which currently available programmed instruction materials might be most suitable for experimental use within the general framework of existing courses of study. The information was intended to assist teachers who were interested in launching preliminary trials of programmed materials. The work was of immediate interest to the Scarborough Board of Education, which approved limited trials of the method beginning in 1965–6. Provision was made for a reasonably thorough evaluation of the experiment.

In February 1965 the Technical and Vocational Training Branch of the Department of Labour co-operated with the Canadian Council for Research in Education in sending a questionnaire to training officers and to a few line officers in the federal government service, including the armed forces. The questions dealt with their activities in the programmed instruction area, their attitude toward the technique, their opinion of its future usefulness, and their recommendations as to what central services, if any, were needed. The Department of Labour sent its questionnaires to the officer in charge of staff training in each department of government and in many of its agencies, as well as to line officers known to have some responsibility for training. The fifty-two who responded constituted approximately two-thirds of those approached. No fewer than twenty-one of these, almost without exception line officers or field trainers with limited responsibility, stated that they were completely unfamiliar with programmed instruction. Three additional respondents expressed similar ignorance by the nature of their answers. The others revealed a consensus that programmed instruction had a contribution to make in the training field, mainly in conjunction with other forms of training. It was viewed with special favour for remedial training; where there were specific difficulties in relation to time, large numbers of trainees, remoteness of locality, and limitations on available training assistance; as pre-course study to impart some common background to participants; for adults; and for efforts of employees to upgrade their qualifications or effect self-improvement.[15]

During the latter half of the 1960s, programmed learning made relatively little progress in the Ontario school system. According to one informal estimate, no more than 5 per cent of all teachers were reasonably well acquainted with the method by the beginning of 1969. The Department of Education had not been persuaded to subsidize the cost of producing good programmed texts, and had shown little interest in providing opportunities for in-service training to improve teachers' understanding of their use.

The technique has been adopted with much more enthusiasm for training in industry. The goals in that area are often more clearcut than those pursued in schools, and the relevant content may be more easily defined. There is also more pressure to employ methods that produce optimum results at minimum cost. It may be of substantial advantage to have the employee work away at a program on his own time at his own speed rather than to arrange to have him attend a formal class.

Appraisal

Programmed instruction has been seen as a means of breaking down many of the traditional rigidities of school and classroom organization. It may enable individual pupils to carry their studies into areas where the teacher lacks sufficient background to guide them. Because each pupil determines his own pace, the bright ones can move at a rate that provides them with a continuing challenge. The slow ones, on the other hand, need not feel constantly discouraged and frustrated, since they are also working with material that is exactly suited to their needs. Wilbur Schramm pointed to the severe administrative problem presented by any structure that provided for individual assignments and individual rates of growth. Claiming that the only ideal way to solve this problem was to have one teacher per subject per level, he said that the nearest feasible approximation to the ideal was to "let programed instruction, where possible and appropriate, sit in for some of the teachers we don't have."[16] Schramm disclaimed any idea that students working at their own rates would do all their work in programmed instruction. He would have them read voraciously, write, explore, discuss, and experiment. The program, however, would go beyond the contribution that a book alone could make. It would guide them toward discovery in many areas rather than leaving them to move around at random looking for something new. Schramm summed up the potential contributions of programmed instruction in this way.

> ... programed instruction is essentially a revolutionary device, in that it has the potential to help free man from some of his bondage – the waste of human resources where there are no teachers or where people cannot go to school; the waste of time and talent where all students are locked into the same pace, and all teachers into the same routine; the tyranny of tradition which permits the study of a certain topic to begin only at a certain age, and expects a student to accomplish only so much as a questionable test of his ability says he can do; and the inadequacy of outmoded and inadequate curricula ...[17]

Although programmed learning could possibly do all these things, the passage shows an undue concentration of attention on a single instructional approach. Since Schramm wrote, it has become increasingly obvious that the problem is to integrate the contributions of all the media.

E.Z. Friedenberg, writing as Professor of Sociology at the University of California, expressed the view that there is very little that a good high school ought to do that could be done as well by programmed instruction. But he felt at the same time that the latter could do a great many things better than the schools actually did them. He suggested a school staffed by far fewer people that might at the same time provide students with a more sensitive, highly skilled service. Certain duties, such as "serving as a kind of room clerk and door check," could be assigned to senior tutors. The teacher would perform only those functions for which he had the necessary academic and personal qualifications. He could guide as many as sixty students in independent study by helping them plan their work and assessing their progress. For part of their time, the students would meet him in small-group seminars, and during the rest of their time they would work either with programmed instruction or in the library under the general supervision of a specialist in the area of instruction that concerned them during this period.[18]

For those who have the opportunity to undergo a reasonable amount of preparation and to engage in the serious production of programs, there may be very substantial dividends in terms of their growth as teachers. The work requires fairly precise thought about the specific objectives, the essential elements, and the soundest logical and psychological organization of the particular content with which the program deals. This process may not only result in an improvement in the teacher's grasp of the content but also, where it contains anomalies and deficiencies, in substantial pressure for the revision of the curriculum. The necessity of foreseeing the possible responses the student may make, of determining what constitute adequate steps from one point to another, of anticipating errors, of identifying the amount and type of reinforcement needed at particular points – all these constitute an excellent training course in practical psychology. The values of such an experience are increased by the need to try out frames on a particular student, to revise them, and to repeat the process a number of times until the desired standard of quality is reached.

The critics of programmed learning include some who regard the very basis of the approach as unsound or pernicious. Paul Goodman condemned programmed learning because it called upon the student to follow a pattern developed and prescribed by someone else. The programmer did all the thinking, and the learner was systematically conditioned to follow his thoughts.

> "Learning" means to give some final response that the programmer considers advantageous (to the students). There is no criterion of *knowing* it, of having learned it, of Gestalt-forming or simplification. That is, the student has no active self at all; his self, at least as student, is a construct of the programmer.[19]

Goodman felt that the approach omitted the salient virtue that most teachers had always seen in letting the student discover things for himself – the development of his confidence that he could proceed on his own initiative and ultimately strike out on an unknown path where there was no program. The programmed learning method did not fit the classical maxim of teaching, to bring the student to the point where he cast off the teacher. Goodman related programmed instruction to what he saw as the worst faults of the school.

The school system as a whole, with its increasingly set curriculum, stricter grading, incredible amounts of testing, is already a vast machine to shape acceptable responses. Programmed instruction closes the windows a little tighter and it rigidifies the present departmentalization and dogma. But worst of all, it tends to nullify the one lively virtue that any school does have, that it is a community of youth and of youth and adults.[20]

That there would be a threat to human freedom in the realization of concepts that Skinner has propounded is strongly supported by some of the things he himself has written. The following passage is disturbing for reasons beyond its obvious overconfidence in the validity of the theories expounded.

Now that we *know* how positive reinforcement works and why negative doesn't ... we can be more deliberate, and hence more successful, in our cultural design. We can achieve a sort of control under which the controlled, though they are following a code much more scrupulously than was ever the case under the old system, nevertheless *feel free*. They are doing what they want to do, not what they are forced to do. That's the source of the tremendous power of positive reinforcement – there's no restraint and no revolt. By a careful cultural design, we control not the final behavior, but the *inclination* to behave – the motives, the desires, the wishes.

The curious thing is that in that case the *question of freedom never arises*.[21]

These sentiments sound suspiciously like those one would expect to hear from a dictator who had discovered the means to make his subjects not only accept, but even love, their chains. It is fortunate that we can find benefits in programmed learning without having to swallow Skinner whole.

Most of the critics are prepared to accept programmed instruction as a productive approach provided successful efforts are made to avoid certain abuses. The report of the Ontario Teachers' Federation resulting from the summer workshop of 1963 considered the danger that the technique might be used by unscrupulous persons to manipulate attitudes and beliefs. It was observed that researchers who had used Skinner's method of shaping behaviour lent support to this view. The report warned teachers to be on guard to exclude programs carrying propaganda designed to induce attitudes and beliefs that were not compatible with the Canadian way of life. The report suggested that the basic morality of democratic and liberal education would be preserved if they assumed the responsibility for the content of programmed learning, kept control of the flow of programs into the school, and wrote their own programs. If these things were done, there was no more to fear from programmed learning than there was from radio or television.

Although generally considered a fairly enthusiastic advocate of programmed learning, F.G. Robinson has been critical of the attempt to apply an abstract psychological theory to school learning without sufficient modification. Here he recalls Skinner's ping pong playing pigeons to make his point.

> ... programmed instruction in this raw form was not noticeably successful because its assumptions did not quite fit the school situation; for example, hungry pigeons could not be equated (in motivational terms) to overfed children. Small step approximation to complex physical movements did not seem to capture the essence of the open-ended thinking characteristic of problem-solving or creative performance. The pigeon's attempt to maximize his acquisition of food pellets had no immediate counterpart in the grade-locked system where a student's rapid progress through a program is often rewarded by a lengthy sentence of boredom.[22]

For the most part, those who are interested in deriving the maximum advantage from the approach are not much concerned about what happens to the underlying theory as a result of their findings.

COMPUTER ASSISTED INSTRUCTION

As has already been suggested, computer assisted instruction is in the same general line of development as programmed learning. But it holds the promise of infinitely greater flexibility and versatility by multiplying the resources of stored information and by greatly increasing their accessibility.

R.G. Ragsdale suggested that the most fruitful classroom application of the computer might be to have it take over most of the record-keeping, information-dispensing, and drilling functions of the teacher, "freeing him for an increased number of individual interactions with the pupil."[23] He referred to a three-fold categorization of the levels of computer-student interaction – drill, tutorial assistance, and dialogue. 1 / The drill process provides the pupil with a series of problems, which he works on until he has seen them all, has answered each one at least once without error, or has done whatever else the programmer has prescribed. This form of interaction is easily programmed and relieves the teacher of one of his less creative tasks. 2 / The tutorial function involves the assistance of the computer to explain and develop some skill in the student. It differs from simple programmed instruction in that it uses varied media and variable step size and has the capacity for more sophisticated branching. Despite difficulties in programming, Ragsdale stated that at the time of writing (in

1967) there were enough good programs in existence to show that the achievement of the tutorial objective was feasible. 3 / The dialogue type of interaction allows the student to ask questions of the computer. In its ultimate form, it will not restrict these questions in terms of subject matter, difficulty, or structure. Although programs to answer some questions about small, well-defined bodies of information did exist, Ragsdale felt that the general application was "in the far distant future."

The Provincial Committee on Aims and Objectives appraised aspects of programmed learning in both its simpler and its computerized forms.

> Computerized, programmed learning is presently limited to learning tasks, such as teaching specific sets of information or skills that can be presented in sequence. Such skills must be capable of being systematically studied and described and then transmitted. The fact that a rigidity of structure exists, which seems to be inherent in programmed instruction, leads one to fear lest students feel that there is indeed only one approach and one right answer. What the student may find hard to learn is that some questions may have more than one answer – or no answer at all. Programmed instruction would appear to be antithetical to the "discovery method," as presently conceived and executed.[24]

The committee was nevertheless impressed by the views of top-ranking computer experts as expressed in a White House report on *Computers in Higher Education,* which appeared in February 1967. These experts had pointed out that, at the higher levels of education, computing enables the student or the scholar to deal with realistic problems rather than oversimplified models. By lessening the time spent in the drudgery of problem-solving and in the analysis of data, it frees time for thought and insight. It also enables the student to do old things more easily and, more important, it enables him to do things he otherwise could not.

In making these observations, the committee had considered the possible disadvantages of teaching material in a previously-established sequence by means of the computer, and then switched the discussion to the student's use of the computer as a sophisticated and highly efficient tool for the solution of his own problems. These applications are of course entirely different. In the latter case, the student may be solving a set of prescribed problems or he may equally well be tackling those that he himself has devised. Thus there are no grounds for any suggestion that the computer is necessarily an obstacle to the use of the discovery method. It depends on the particular application to which one is referring.

The difficulties in applying computer assisted instruction centre mainly around its cost. In the article previously referred to, Ragsdale mentioned a common estimate of half a million dollars for the production of a full year's tutorial course. He reported also that the rental charge for one of the more sophisticated student stations currently available was $400 a month and estimated the total operating cost at twice that amount. Even if the cost could be halved, the yearly figure would still be $4,800 per student per year, and the cost for a class of twenty would be $96,000. These estimates, furthermore, did not provide for any material for the system, which would initially cost more than the equipment. On the basis of these figures, it is not surprising that Ragsdale did not think that the day was imminent when the teacher would be replaced.

But if there is anything the recent history of the race should have taught us, it is that we should not underestimate the power of technology. If a convincing case were made for the educational effectiveness of the computer, and if present-day society demonstrated a genuine desire to implement its potentialities, it is hard to believe that it would not soon be brought within reach of the educational systems of advanced countries. For this reason, there seems to be every justification for a moderate investment in experiments to explore the dimensions of its potential role.

Ragsdale raised an interesting point on the possible effects on curriculum when the computer is put into widespread use for instructional purposes. Because of the very high costs of curriculum development, there would be pressure in favour of a Canadian curriculum rather than a number of provincial curricula (presumably excluding French-speaking areas), or even a demand for a US-Canadian curriculum. He acknowledged that this approach would defeat one of the supposed advantages of computer assisted instruction – individualization. He suggested that it might still be possible to obtain the benefits of the common curriculum if one of the variables used in branching were the regional background of the student. Whether or not different national groups will attach enough value to the peculiarities associated with their geographical environment to bear large extra costs to preserve them is a question. One of Jacques Ellul's theses in *The Technological Society* was that advancing technique inexorably erases regional differences. If he was right, we may retain these for a time but in the long run are simply fighting a rather pathetic rearguard action.

THE LANGUAGE LABORATORY

Serious efforts began to be made in the late 1950s to devise and adapt technical equipment to facilitate oral language instruction in the schools. Although some of the techniques had been known for a long time, the growth of a large potential market in the schools gave manufacturers an unprecedented motive for developmental work. The receptive attitude among educators reflected the growing enthusiasm for the development of auditory skills and oral fluency in foreign languages as opposed to the overly bookish approach which had formerly characterized instruction in this area. In Ontario, this approach has by no means disappeared at certain levels. However, the desire to make a serious response to the pressure for recognition and acceptance of French as a national language in Canada has led to a gradual extension of the subject through the elementary school grades, where the oral approach predominates. The extreme shortage of teachers capable of handling this approach has spurred efforts to develop effective substitutes. The incentive is still there, even though a relatively minor proportion of pupils are actually taught in language laboratories.

The term "laboratory" suggests a room or other specific location. For that reason, terms such as "system" have tended to be substituted, since the essence of the concept is a collection of equipment. Some of the earliest of these systems consisted of nothing more than a record player or tape recorder with an amplifier and several sets of headphones. The special contribution of the system was that a number of learners could hear the sounds of the language from a single source. Spacing of the message by phoneme, word, phrase, sentence, or some other unit enabled the learner to repeat the sound and thus gain practice. A further refinement improved the process of ear training by enabling him to hear the sound of his own voice and to compare the result with that from the recorded source. Provision was made for a teacher to monitor individual practice, to exchange comments with any one of the group, or to give instructions to the group as a whole.

Some of the systems have involved enclosed student booths with acoustic panelling. These were at first thought to be highly desirable in order to enable the student to concentrate without being distracted by classroom noise. It was also considered important to obviate the embarrassment felt by many beginning students of foreign languages over their initial inability to pronounce the strange sounds correctly and their proneness to other types of errors. The validity of this reasoning has tended to be discounted. There have also been reactions against the artificiality of studying a language, which is under natural circumstances a means of communicating between human beings, in isolation. A somewhat more convincing argument against the need for booths is that they do not really screen out neighbouring sounds. Research done by the Toronto board's Research Department has supported the view that booths do not make a recognizable contribution to the effectiveness of the laboratories.

The field has appeared sufficiently lucrative to attract a rather large number of commercial suppliers. While this development is generally desirable in that it encourages the search for improvements and ultimately tends to reduce costs, it has had at least two unfavourable consequences: the purchaser tends to be bewildered at the variety of choices open to him and there has been an undue emphasis on mechanical features, including the addition of many attachments of doubtful value. John Fielder, Associate Editor of *School Progress,* observed on this point: "The value of such items and practices as: switch-studded teacher's consoles, teacher-student monitoring from the console, a student record facility at every position, and a large (e.g. more than four) number of simultaneous program input sources, have all been questioned."[25] Too much emphasis on physical aspects tends to divert attention from the most important aspect of the system, the program.

Programs may be purchased or otherwise obtained from outside sources or produced within the school or local system. Those in the first category often have the advantage of higher technical quality but tend not to correspond closely to the curriculum. When they are used, the tapes often need cutting or other modifications demanding a substantial investment in time. Teacher-made tapes tend to have the opposite virtues and faults. The amount of professional time it takes to produce them is an important consideration.

In common with other technical devices used to facilitate learning, the language laboratory involves problems of scheduling. Fielder pointed to the difficulty in reconciling the fifteen-minute attention span of the average high school student with the rigid class periods lasting between thirty and forty-five minutes. With systems not including booths, the teacher may stop the program after the students begin to lose interest and devote the rest of the period to other forms of drill, the introduction of new points, or seatwork. Since that procedure prevents full utilization of the equipment, some schools have tried breaking the class period into two parts and changing classes in the middle. Fielder reported that few schools had sufficient facilities to meet the demand from regular classes and to allow free use of the facilities after hours.

TELEVISION

The educational role of television

Television can hardly avoid being educational in the broad sense of the term. Even when its primary purpose is to entertain or to sell a product, it informs, it motivates, it stimulates, it affects the level of taste, and although positive proof is difficult to establish, it probably has a considerable influence on the shaping of character. It does these things in a particularly effective manner, not only by its direct access to the mind through the senses of sight and hearing, but also by indirect stimulation of other means of perception. The fact that its effects are not necessarily in accord with the value systems accepted by educators is one reason why the latter have been concerned with it. They have also, and for the most part with apparent reluctance, recognized it as a possible tool for the realization of their own purposes.

The first efforts at utilizing television as part of the more formal processes of education tended to be uninspired. In accordance with the attitude that instruction could be largely equated with teacher performance, a large proportion of the programs presented a teacher giving a lecture. Where sufficient time and other resources were at hand, and where an unusually competent teacher was available, a very commendable performance was often achieved. Lester Anheim, Dean of the Graduate Library School of the University of Chicago, declared his belief in the values of this approach: "Television, by sharing the good teacher, makes it possible to have a good teacher in every subject in every school. The good teachers will be shared on a nation-wide basis ..."[26] It was the prospect of having a few outstanding teachers take over the task of many of their less able colleagues that raised the hopes of tax-conscious citizens that television might not only save money but improve the quality of educational service as well.

Many educators had the wit to realize in the first place, and many others learned from experience, that the television teacher had serious limitations. For one thing, the image of a person on the screen was quite different from the actual physical presence of a human being. For another, there was no really effective way of producing a direct interaction between the teacher and the learner, although some awkward methods were later devised. The lecture as a primary means of instruction at the elementary and secondary levels has long been discredited, and even in universities it is tending to be regarded as only one weapon in the instructional arsenal. The television lecture is even less flexible than that given by the instructor in person, since the lecturer is in no position to gauge the feeling of the group and adapt his presentation as he goes along.

On this point, C. Wellington Webb, Associate Professor of Philosophy at the University of Toronto, wrote in the *Globe and Mail* on July 14, 1967:

> It is a mistake to suppose that a good teacher can accomplish the same things with a large television audience as he can with a moderately sized class that he is addressing personally.
>
> There is a great deal of difference between the live lecturer addressing a live class and the tomb-like atmosphere of the televised lecture. Even if microphones are provided so that the student can communicate with the lecturer, a great difference will still exist. You can walk out on a television screen without offending it, or breaking up its smooth delivery. A vitally interested class will hiss a teacher who says something which offends the intelligence or sensibilities of its members. A good teacher can use the hisses to correct his own stupidities, or alternatively, to accomplish a real breakthrough to a higher level of understanding among his students.

This view of the situation, to the advantage of the live lecturer, is by no means universally shared. J.W. Sullivan, writing in the *Bulletin* of the Ontario Secondary School Teachers' Federation, identified some of the positive characteristics of the medium that distinguish it from other teaching methods. He claimed that anyone who has ever seen classes watching instructional television has observed the peculiar relation between the television image and the individual student. Each student seems to feel as if the television teacher is speaking to him personally. A girl in Michigan reputedly wrote to her television teacher: "You are the only one who really ever understood me." Sullivan speculated that this intimacy might be the result of magnification which made the speaker's head appear about the same size as one's own. "There is no need to exaggerate gestures as on the stage; what is said seems believable."[27]

Where the classroom teacher and the student watch a lecture together, there may be substantial benefits if the teacher is informed beforehand of the contents and is prepared to conduct a follow-up discussion. This type of split in the lesson has its own particular drawbacks. The students may wonder why the teacher was incapable of making the original presentation as well as leading the discussion. The effects have been particularly bad in single schools or small systems where the teacher judged to be the best has been selected to deliver the lecture, and the others, denoted by implication as inferior, have followed it up.

Two teachers in a school in New York indicated the undesirable, even devastating effects, that can result from relegating regular teachers to the position of mere monitors.

> Now look at the teacher in his classroom preparing for the TV program. What does he do? He adjusts the lights, the curtains, the TV set; sees that the handholders break it up; monitors discipline generally; and administers tests – standardized. He follows up and develops someone else's lesson; someone else's viewpoint becomes his; someone else's emphasis restrains him. The drone's degradation is complete. He hasn't even the satisfaction of expressing his personal reactions to the subject matter he learned. And this is what may have originally inspired him to become a teacher.[28]

The occasional opportunity to hear an outstanding authority is in a different category from that of listening to another teacher present the lesson and does not produce the same adverse reflection on the regular teachers.

At an earlier stage, the use of television for enrichment was seen as a clearcut alternative to direct instruction. Programs for enrichment recognize television's educational value in the extension of experience. They enable the learner to see the impressive geographical features of his own and other lands; to observe the physical appearance, actions, and habits of his fellow human beings in other nations; to watch birds, animals, insects, and other forms of life in their natural habitat; to participate vicariously in ceremonies and other significant events in national and world affairs; and to experience the best in mankind's cultural heritage. By involving more than one sense, the programs give all these phenomena a unique impression of immediacy.

The chief handicaps of enrichment programs have to do with their tendency to be dissociated from what the school regards as its business. Because they are not tied in definitely with the formal curriculum, they tend to be relegated to a level of importance far below their real merits. They are shown if time can be spared from activities judged to be more important. When such time is allotted, they are considered more as diversion and entertainment than as education. Thus the teacher tends not to make specific preparation for them, although excellent guides many be provided, nor to follow them up in the systematic way that would make them real learning experiences. Enrichment programs often come close in format and purpose to those provided by the regular public or private broadcasters. Since North American society delivers a great deal more of its wealth into the hands of private industrial and commercial agencies than it bestows on the producers of educational television programs, the latters' efforts often suffer in comparison.

There has been an increasing realization, which has by no means come as a new and startling revelation to many perceptive educators, that the effective utilization of television in education cannot be seen as a dichotomy between direct instruction and enrichment. That is, television should not be considered either as a substitute for the teacher or a kind of peripheral diversion from the serious business of covering the course of study. The teacher as a facilitator of the learning process identifies and brings to bear those influences that will stimulate and motivate the child to pursue a course of self-development. And in many cases, television is the means whereby the essential elements of reality can best be introduced. The process cannot, of course, function effectively unless the programs can be presented with a great deal more flexibility than has been possible in the past. But of all man's problems, those amenable to solution by the application of technological expertise have given him the least trouble. The Stanford report previously referred to assessed the potentialities of educational television as follows.

> Experience indicates that the most effective uses of television have been in situations where it has been combined carefully with other activities in a total learning situation; and where students were strongly motivated to learn from it. This challenges educators to make a broad review and restructuring of what happens in the classroom. Television can share the best teaching and the best demonstrations; self-instructional materials can conduct drill expertly and give the student a new freedom to work at his own best rate.[29]

In 1961 the Ontario Conference on Education assessed the uses of educational television as follows.

> 1. Television is a powerful new resource for teaching and learning. Its importance lies in the fact that it stimulates learning. It does not accomplish the total teaching job, but it can be used to provide learning situations not otherwise feasible in the classroom.
> 2. Television lessons do not guarantee learning but must be used by the classroom teacher in a similar way to classroom films. By working with the class before and after viewing the programme, the teacher makes the experience a meaningful one.

3. When television is used by itself, the amount of learning is not great but television with proper planning by the classroom teacher can make a maximum contribution.
4. Television has certain strengths: it reaches large numbers instantly; each pupil sees equally well; is provides magnified close-ups and broad coverage of the same object; it is dramatic and thus focuses attention; it is not limited to the walls of the school but can use materials from far-away lands; it can be used wherever there is a receiver.
5. Successful use of E.T.V. depends to a large degree on the teacher who helps to overcome those limitations inherent in television. There is slow interaction between studio teacher and student. It cannot be speeded up for one learner or slowed down for another. It tends to ignore readiness for the lesson content and is programmed into the classroom rather than being selected by the teacher to fit a particular need.
6. Television should be used to do those things it can do best and the teacher should do those things he can do best. Television can magnify small objects, stimulate interest because of its emotional impact, use resources, materials, and equipment not available to the classroom teacher, take students to places of historical and cultural interest, share with sick or homebound children the experiences of the class, bring current events to the classroom, and provide exchange of experiences of classes all over the country. E.T.V. should not be used to do what films can do better.[30]

These statements reflect an awareness on the part of the group involved that the effectiveness of television depends strictly on the teacher's success in integrating it into the instructional process.

The Department of Education's submission to the Board of Broadcast Governors in October 1966 dwelt on the way in which television could enhance the effectiveness of the teacher's efforts.

One objective of teaching is to communicate facts. We communicate also through the patterns whereby we present facts and skills, and through the values we attach to facts and the attitudes we have towards them. Educational television can give pupils and teachers insights into new courses, new approaches, and new ideas. Programs could be utilized to clarify difficult areas of study, to supplement regular lessons with illustrations impossible within the limitations of the classroom, to experiment with follow-up material to ascertain the effectiveness of the programming, and to involve the classroom pupils and teachers through open-ended programs.

Those who emphasize the positive values of learner activity sometimes criticize television because it leaves the viewer with too passive a role. It is quite true that he is kept relatively immobile in the physical sense, but that factor alone may have little bearing on whether or not he is learning anything. The program may or may not arouse his mind to vigorous activity depending on the approach used. The Provincial Committee on Aims and Objectives had some suggestions on this point.

Because television is essentially a one-way medium of communication, there is all too often a tendency on the part of production teams to employ basically a documentary style of presentation, whereby programs merely give information, without involving the viewer except as a passive recipient of such information. With careful planning and creative production, however, it is possible to prepare programs that involve the viewer in a variety of ways – by arousing his curiosity, by helping him to look more carefully at a subject; by transporting him, vicariously, in time and space to far-off events and places; by presenting for him various viewpoints on an issue; by creating situations leading to discussion or reflection; by showing him how to perform a skill; and by providing experiences which enable the viewer to form his own generalizations or conclusions. If educational television is to make its appropriate contribution to practices that emphasize inquiry, discovery, and the pursuit of individual interests, it will be essential that the planning and production of programs be based on this philosophy. Television programs for school use must support the teacher's goal of guiding pupils through inquiry, and must not subvert or compete with this goal by merely presenting packages of information.[31]

Bascom St John appraised the effects and uses of educational television on the basis of his own experiences.[32] He found that some programs, very interesting and informative, had as their main effect the production of a state of mind or an attitude. But too much was usually crowded into them to give the watcher the opportunity to reflect or absorb. He would have been reluctant to write an assignment on one of them. They were educative in a vague sort of way but not education in the school and college sense. He compared them with listening to a symphony; in order to make it education, he assumed one had to study its structure, its musical philosophy, and its place in a composer's work or in an era of history. Schools have, of course, been subjected to severe criticism for overemphasizing these latter aspects and failing to appreciate the educational value of cultivating the aesthetic sense for its own sake.

In asserting the role of a medium as revolutionary and pervasive as television, there is an overwhelming danger that educators will assess it from a narrow, overly restrained, and backward-looking point of view. A certain lack of vision is often demonstrated by the researchers who set up experiments to determine whether significantly more is learned by those taught by television than by those taught by a flesh-and-blood teacher, or vice versa. As a means of breaking the bonds of conventional thinking, there is no substitute for an appeal to Marshall McLuhan, who expressed these views in 1964.

If we ask what is the relation of TV to the learning process, the answer is surely that the TV image, by its stress on participation, dialogue, and depth has brought to America new demand for crash programming in education. Whether there ever will be TV in every classroom is a small matter. The revolution has already taken place at home. TV has changed our sense-lives and our mental processes. It has created a taste for depth involvement in all experience that affects language teaching as much as car styles. Since TV, nobody is happy with a merely book-knowledge of French or English poetry. The unanimous cry now is, "Let's *talk* French," and "Let the bard be *heard*." And, oddly enough, with the demand for depth, goes the demand for accelerated or crash programming. Not only deeper, but farther, into all knowledge has become the normal popular demand since TV. Perhaps enough has been said about the nature of the TV image to explain why this should be. How could it possibly pervade our lives any more than it does? Mere classroom use could not extend its influence. Of course, in the classroom its role compels a reshuffling of subjects, and approaches to subjects. Merely to put the present classroom on TV would be like putting movies on TV. The result would be a hybrid that is neither. The right approach is to ask, "What can TV do that the classroom cannot do for French, or physics?" The answer is: "TV can illustrate the interplay of process and the growth of forms of all kinds as nothing else can do."

The entire question about educational TV is like that about the "horse vote" when the motor car was new. That is, it is a mis-leading question. When the printed book was new the modern classroom was made possible. The older oral instruction by rote was dropped. And without present advocacy, it is plain that in the electric age we have re-discovered much that was liquidated by book culture in the sixteenth century. To ask whether TV is a good thing probably indicates concern about book values. Nobody could say TV was bad for books. It created the acceptance of the paperback and the "new criticism" and of reading in depth.[33]

Applications at particular levels and in particular institutions

Schools

The department's submission to the Board of Broadcast Governors suggested how television could be used to improve the learning process in specific subject areas. It could supplement literature in its close-up presentation of the human being, revealing his strengths, weaknesses, foibles, and emotions. Literature could be brought to life through the presentation of the context in which a work was written and an explanation of the personality of the author. Instruction in mathematics could be improved, for younger children in particular, by relating the visual experiences that were possible in the medium to the abstract concepts inherent in the deductive method. The processes involved in working with social science material could be emphasized through telecasts. The impact of the social, economic, and biographical aspects of history could be presented visually.

The sciences required appropriate practical demonstration and concrete illustration to emphasize the value of experience. A wide range of visual material, animated diagrams, models, and apparatus could be presented.

Universities

Universities have used television in their internal instructional programs and for extension purposes. In the first case, they have usually regarded it as a supplementary aspect of the teaching process. Some programs have proved particularly effective where demonstration of delicate and complex objects, structures, and processes is required. Not only are there opportunities to ensure that the demonstration will be planned with the greatest possible care and carried out under optimum conditions, but members of even large groups have opportunities for observation that would be impossible under other circumstances. This particular use of television is usually categorized as transmission of information. There may also be considerable additional values in terms of enhancing interest and arousing curiosity. The university does not normally assume the degree of responsibility that the school has been forced to accept for motivating the learner. The traditional attitude has been that the student wants to learn or he would not be there. But there has been a noticeable change in this view, which will no doubt be reflected in the nature of the programs that will be produced and used.

A number of attempts have been made to use television for direct instruction of extension students in their own homes. Those who wish to obtain credit must do supplementary reading, complete and send in assignments, and write a final examination. In a sense, this approach may be regarded as an elaboration of, and an improvement over, the kind of extension work begun many years ago by Queen's University, which included all the elements except the television instruction. An extension program seldom produces a large proportion of "completers" among those who enrol with serious intentions. Where the television programs are offered, the number who enrol may be assumed to be a relatively small proportion of the viewers.

Assessing the values of television in university instruction, C. Wellington Webb, in the article cited previously, recognized the superiority of television in communicating factual information and in its emotional impact. Where he saw its chief limitation, however, was in the dimension of education that deals with problems. He asserted that a teacher can present the same problem to a dozen students and find a dozen different kinds of difficulties in their attempts to understand it. "Ideally, each of these difficulties ought to receive individual attention. In small classes with good teachers, they usually do. In tutorials with excellent teachers, they almost always do. But this dimension of teaching is one that the techniques of the mass media are totally unsuited to handling." Webb offered the view that, unfortunately for the cause of educational television as a teaching procedure, the solution of problems was the most important dimension of genuine education.

Referring to proposals for the use of television to give courses leading to general arts degrees, Bascom St John expressed some well-founded scepticism about the results. He felt that there was no short-cut to educational achievement for the population at large. There were "too many diversions, interruptions, misunderstandings, and lack of background, in even the intellectually ambitious person's mental processes, to imagine that TV, assisted by some supplementary reading, could result in disciplined learning on the level demanded by Canadian universities."[34] The problem of higher education could be handled only the hard way.

Teachers' colleges

The department's submission to the Board of Broadcast Governors pointed out that a student in a teachers' college or a college of education is both a student and a teacher. In both of these roles, he can benefit from television instruction. A great deal of his education, particularly during the first few months of his course, revolves around the observation and discussion of demonstration lessons. The presence of large numbers of student teachers in demonstration classrooms may have an adverse effect on the performance of the teacher and the pupils. Some of the problems can be effectively overcome by televising the demonstration lessons, a procedure which has additional advantages in extending the number of possible observers and making possible more convenient schedules. It also provides for techniques not otherwise available, such as drawing attention to particular features, repeating significant steps, facilitating close-up examination of the work of individual pupils, and interjecting questions or points ot emphasis for viewers. Television has no parallels in its effectivness as a means of enabling the student-teacher to assess his own performance. His attention is called in a particularly convincing manner to any affectations, irritating mannerisms, and unproductive activities that detract from his performance. He is enabled to see things that a kindly master would be embarrassed to tell him for fear of hurting his feelings.

If the full potentialities of educational television are to be realized, it is obviously of vital importance that student-teachers are made fully aware of the wide range of uses to which it may be put. Thus it must be studied consciously as a tool for teaching, and experience with many types of programs must be provided. The initial preparation stage is also no doubt the best time to overcome any tendency toward "equipment phobia," which probably has more to do with many teachers' reluctance to use the medium than the feeling that it threatens their professional status or their jobs.

In-service teacher education

One of the greatest problems of providing for in-service teacher education has been the difficulty of co-ordinating the process with the exercise of regular responsibilities. An obvious contribution of television, for those who have the determination to take advantage of it, is the provision of university credit courses. There are also numerous possibilities in terms of less formal programs, which may be offered at a convenient time when it would be impossible for the participants to assemble at a central location. Television may be seen as an almost indispensable means of communication in the task of introducing educational innovations to practising teachers. It may provide direct instruction in the content and handling of new courses and teaching methods, with demonstrations of classroom lessons, research techniques, and evaluation procedures. Particular hopes rest on this approach in view of the recognized failure of traditional methods of communication, such as word of mouth or print, to induce teachers to adopt new instructional techniques.

The submission to the Board of Broadcast Governors suggested that, with the development of a network of ETV stations and production facilities in several centres, it might be possible to hold province-wide conferences of teachers on particular problems. Participation and interchange of ideas from panels or individuals in several different centres would be possible. This plan could be varied to enable teachers in various centres to ask questions of experts presenting a topic or demonstration.

Adult education

When he first announced his major foray into the area of educational television in 1965, Education Minister Davis indicated that the greatest initial impact might well be in the field of adult education. The submission to the Board of Broadcast Governors mentioned a possible contribution in three of the department's programs: the colleges of applied arts and technology, community programs, and correspondence courses. Like the universities, the colleges might use television both for internal instruction and to provide service to those unable to attend. The possibility was foreseen that some courses leading to certificates and diplomas could be given in large measure by television. Each college might even become a "school of the air" for its own area. It was also thought that services could be exchanged among colleges, and that outstanding courses, lectures, and exceptional demonstrations could be made available to all colleges.

Educational television might also contribute significantly to the role of the Youth and Recreation Branch in providing opportunities for the citizens of the province to use their leisure creatively. Among the offerings might be demonstrations of activities in the social, physical, cultural, and intellectual fields designed to create an interest and a desire to participate; courses on the effective organization and conduct of voluntary community associations; programs on particular vocational activities; and courses in music, drama, and art appreciation.

The students in the departmental correspondence courses consist mainly of two groups: children of school age who live in isolated areas and are unable to attend school, and those who have withdrawn from school before completing the formal requirements for a diploma or who wish to upgrade their academic standing. The submission to the Board of Broadcast Governors suggested the following as suitable topics for programs or courses for these groups: plays prescribed for study in English, pronunciation and conversation in French, correct grammatical usage in English and French, important events in the history course, difficult parts of the mathematics course, demonstrations of scientific experiments, and the uses of tools and machines in the trades courses.

A large proportion of Ontario's effort in adult education has been left to various associations, many of them operating partly or wholly on voluntary contributions. The Canadian Association for Adult Education has exerted particular efforts to have broadcasting facilities made available to such agencies and to co-ordinate their efforts. They have been eager to see the control of broadcasting centred in an agency that will be sympathetic to their interests. Their active involvement in educational television should help to ensure that it will present the widest variety of points of view and that it will cater to all legitimate interests.

It has sometimes been suggested that educational television should go further than the more limited purposes of adult education. Walter Pitman has proposed that it be employed to improve the quality of family life or even for preventive efforts in treating emotional instability. Such an approach would mean going far beyond its use as a replacement for parts of textbooks.[35] The idea of entrusting an official agency with the responsibility of using a restricted medium to influence public value systems arouses strong opposition in many quarters. People see the process ending ultimately in official brainwashing. On the other hand, the results of leaving the responsibility largely in a few private hands under the domination of commercial interests have been in many cases demonstrably deplorable. Many widely watched program series glorify sadistic and inhuman practices with only a token nod to conventional morality by ensuring that the villain is punished in the final scene. In some instances, even that concession is omitted, which it no doubt should be in the interests of simple honesty of treatment, if nothing else. The producers of programs that cater to debased tastes and corrupt ethical standards justify their activities on the grounds that they are giving the viewers what they want. But in the long run, particularly in view of their influence on the child almost from infancy, they are the creators of the very situation to which they must accommodate. Canadian society may be expected to increase its demand for official intervention to reverse the destructive cycle. Only public agencies can summon the financial resources to experiment with programs that run a high risk of viewer rejection.

Pre-school education

The department's submission made a very strong case for the contribution that television could make to the education of the child before the age of five. With respect to his development at this stage, it said in part:

> He learns much before he enters kindergarten because he has had many teachers. Parents, other children, objects, pictures, books and television have helped him to learn by contributing sensory, motor, and verbal stimulation necessary for his growth in skills. They have also begun to develop his attitudes towards himself and the world around him – attitudes that will govern the extent to which he can make use of subsequent learning opportunities.
>
> The many "teachers" present in the child's environment are accepted by him naturally. He seeks to learn from all of them. Television performs as one of his teachers in many ways. While it cannot take care of the need for direct experience in manipulating, tasting, smelling, moving, it can play an important role in visual-verbal stimulation. Television can bring to a home, impoverished in language, experiences with words that are most valuable. If well used it can combine language with pictures and sound, and provide a high quality of visual-verbal learning for all children ... Like pictures, stories, outings, explorations, it can bring the child into thoughtful contact with people and things, ideas and events. Television must be regarded as a "teacher" that shows some responsibility for the early concept development that goes on in the child's mind.

NINE

Education for special groups

FRENCH-LANGUAGE SCHOOLS

Early development at the elementary level

The bilingual school question made its first appearance in 1851 in what seems in retrospect to have been a rather ironical fashion.[1] Seventeen Franco-Ontarians living in School Section No. 6 in the township of Sandwich sent a petition to the Board of Public Instruction of the county of Essex protesting that the local teacher could speak only French and pointing out their right to have their children taught in English. The settlement that resulted hardly met their desires. The Council of Public Instruction at Toronto amended the regulations governing teachers' qualifications so that a knowledge of French or German might be substituted for English. Thus the county board in Essex was able to certify the teacher about whose inadequacies the local citizens had complained. Instead of an unsatisfactory unqualified teacher, they ended up with an unsatisfactory qualified teacher.

Although the use of French as a language of instruction was not legally sanctioned, it was spoken without any serious objection in common schools, mainly Roman Catholic separate schools, where it seemed appropriate in the light of the linguistic composition of the local community. Difficulties began to develop in 1885 when G.W. Ross, Minister of Education, ordered that English be taught in every school in the province. There was of course a great deal of difference between the compulsory teaching of English and the compulsory use of English as the language of instruction. The regulations issued in 1890 took something close to the latter position. They provided that, in sections where French or German prevailed, the trustees might, with the approval of the inspector, require that instruction be given in reading, grammar, and composition in either of these languages to children of parents who demanded it. This program was to be in addition to the course of study prescribed for public schools. Instruction and communications were to be in English unless the children were unable to understand the language. Inspectors were enjoined to ensure that the standard in schools where French or German was taught was equal to that in the schools where it was not. Provision was made for the establishment of model schools for the preparation of French- and German-speaking teachers.[2]

A crisis occurred over the issuance of Regulation 17 by the Department of Education in June 1912. Resulting from a study and recommendations by F.W. Merchant, although less liberal than Merchant's proposals, it limited the use of French as the language of instruction and communication to form I, except that the language might be extended further with the approval of the Chief Inspector for pupils who could not understand English. It also permitted French to be given on parental request as a subject of study in schools where it had hitherto been offered. It was to take up not more than an hour a day, unless the Chief Inspector approved an extension. The regulation did not represent the repressive intent that later critics saw in it, but rather a concern for low standards of achievement in many of the schools where French was taught, as well as a desire to meet the objections of English-speaking minorities in some parts of the province, where only French instruction was available in the local schools. While the responsible officials, by modern standards at least, showed a lack of sensitivity toward the survival of the French cultural heritage in Ontario, it would be going too far to accuse them of malice. They must nevertheless be held responsible for the development of a good deal of bitterness among Franco-Ontarians during that period.

The regulation was repeated in somewhat revised and more moderate form in 1913, with provision for more adequate inspection of the English-French schools. Opposition centred in the separate school system in Ottawa, where the regulation was tested in the law courts. While the decision was pending, all the separate schools were closed for several months in 1914. The Supreme Court of Ontario finally ruled in favour of the legal validity of Regulation 17, pointing to the fact that the British North America Act had made no mention of any right to use French in the schools.

If the intention of departmental officials had been to improve the quality of instruction in the English-French schools, the results were certainly disappointing. Further investigation was undertaken by a committee, under the chairmanship of Merchant, which reported in 1927. Sissons described the situation as follows.

> ... almost half of the pupils were in what would be known as the first and second grades where French was the sole language of instruction, and only one in ten was reaching grade eight. Little better could be expected in view of the certificates held by the teachers. Only 13.5 per cent held first or second class certificates; no less than 26.2 per cent held English-French C certificates, obtained after one year's attendance at an English-French Model School following an academic standing approximating the first year of a high school course; while 48.3 per cent held certificates classed as either "expired" or "temporary" or held no Ontario certificate at all.[3]

One might be tempted to conclude that the Franco-Ontarian population was engaging in a policy of passive resistance to coercion by rejecting learning.

A new policy, adopted in 1927, abandoned the repressive regulations. While Regulation 17 was not formally rescinded until 1944, no further pretence was made of limiting French as a medium of instruction to the first two elementary grades or of dictating the stage at which it could be studied as a subject. A resolution was made to try again to improve the quality of inspection. A special departmental committee was set up for this purpose, consisting of the Chief Inspector, a Director of French Instruction, and a Director of English Instruction. A normal school was established at the University of Ottawa to improve the quality of teachers of French and ultimately to replace the model schools, which were considered to be turning out a very inferior product.

The results of the new policy were apparently reasonably encouraging. Although Sissons suggested that the Directors of English and French Instruction might not have been entirely objective appraisers of their own handiwork, their report to the minister in 1935 included some very gratifying information. In schools attended by French-speaking pupils, the percentage of teachers who held First or Second Class Certificates had risen from 13 to 60 in a period of eight years. More pupils were completing the entrance course in form IV, although a disproportionately small number were passing the high school entrance examination.[4]

The English-French schools, which came to be called bilingual schools, customarily provided instruction in French up to the end of grade 2, including kindergarten in the few schools where it was offered. English was introduced in grade 3, and the time was divided about equally between the two languages from grade 5 to grade 8. The enrolment trends in these schools during the post-war period are shown in volume I, chapter 2 of the present series.

The Royal Commission on Education expressed rather cautious approval of the teaching of French and of its use as a language of instruction in elementary schools and recommended

(a) that, in addition to English as a subject of study and language of instruction and communication, local education authority be authorized, under specified conditions and subject to the permission of the Minister of Education, to make provision for French as a subject of study and language of instruction and communication in a public or separate elementary school or classroom under its jurisdiction;
(b) that the granting of such permission be subject to the condition that at each level of the elementary school stage the pupils attain a reasonable proficiency in English and in the other essentials of an elementary school education.[5]

The commissioners noted that, under the terms of a departmental circular issued in 1948, there was a special secondary school curriculum for "schools in which French is a subject of instruction with the approval of the Minister." The students had six periods in grade 9 and seven in each of grades 10 to 12 for the study of English, and an equal number for the study of French. To gain additional time for French, the allotment for optional subjects was reduced. While the commissioners were in favour of special courses in French for these French-speaking students as an alternative to oral French, and for other students who could demonstrate an ability to profit from them, they did not consider it necessary or desirable to have a special curriculum for French-speaking students.[6]

The majority of the commissioners recommended the abolition of the University of Ottawa Normal School on the grounds that it was inadvisable to segregate French-speaking students from their English-speaking counterparts. It was suggested that other normal schools modify their programs so as to accommodate these students. The minority report strongly opposed this recommendation, which was of course never implemented.

Many of the graduates of the bilingual schools had no opportunity to take any French in the secondary school other than the same introductory course which was offered to the English-speaking student. J.A. Belanger, member of the Legislature for Windsor-Sandwich, referred in 1962 to the situation in which some of these bilingual students found themselves.

> They are interested in teaching "basic French," which is of little value to the English student in later life. To say that this course is of value to a Grade 8 graduate of a bilingual school I would say is a misstatement. How ridiculous it is to hear from one of these graduates of a Grade 8 bilingual school who is taking the "basic French" course in Grade 9 as taught in our high schools today, come and say to his former Grade 8 teacher: "Today, sir, I learned to count from 1 to 20 in French, or else I can translate the sentence 'I am standing by the window.' " A student who speaks French, who has spent eight years of learning French spelling, French composition, French grammar, French reading and literature – and, yes, even arithmetic, history and geography lessons, were at times given to him in French – must now subject himself to learn all over again to count, to conjugate and to translate.[7]

Recent developments at the secondary level

Until the decade of the 1960s, the French-speaking student who sought an education in his own language at the secondary level had either to attend a private school or leave Ontario. The only concession, dating from 1927, was the opportunity to study an advanced version of French, in later years referred to as Français, in schools where there was sufficient demand for it. This version of the language has sometimes been referred to by students as "real" French, in contrast to the French studied by English-speaking students.

An important step was taken in 1962, when school boards could, with ministerial permission, teach Latin in French. History and geography were added to this list in 1965. The availability of suitable textbooks had a good deal to do with the manner in which the program unfolded. Later a special course in English, referred to as "Anglais," was developed to meet the particular needs of secondary school students from the bilingual elementary schools. The introduction of the new program was preceded by a general survey throughout elementary and secondary schools and by pilot courses in several locations.

An inextricable mingling of linguistic and religious factors has characterized the bilingual schools issue during most of the history of Ontario education. On April 28, 1967, H.S. Racine, member of the Legislature for Ottawa East, delivered an appeal for better provision for bilingual schools. His plea was actually for separate bilingual schools through grade 13. Racine expressed satisfaction at the constructive and liberal approach being taken by the Department of Education up to the end of the elementary school. He declared, however, that provisions were far from adequate beyond that level. In some centres, a satisfactory cultural atmosphere was being maintained up to the end of grade 10 with the aid of elementary school grants. But at the end either of grade 8 or grade 10, the French-speaking student was plunged into a totally different atmosphere from the one which he had been used to. Racine expanded on what he saw as the unfairness which forced the French-speaking population to maintain a system of private high schools while paying taxes to support the public system. The private schools were able to offer only a five-year arts and science course, without the vocational programs of the publicly supported schools.[8]

Some of the destructive effects on French-speaking students of the inadequate opportunities available to them at the secondary school level were indicated in a brief submitted to the Provincial Committee on Aims and Objectives of Education in the Schools of Ontario by five groups: l'Association canadienne-française d'éducation d'Ontario, l'Association des enseignants franco-ontariens, l'Association des commissions des écoles bilingues d'Ontario, la Fédération des associations de parents et d'instituteurs de langue française d'Ontario, and l'Association franco-ontarienne des inspecteurs de l'enseignement bilingue et des professeurs à l'école normale.

> The mother tongue is so intimately linked with all other aspects of growth of a wholesome personality that denying it in a system of education in a country where the language is official, becomes detrimental to the continuous process of learning. Experience in this province has proven that French-speaking pupils in Ontario are at a disadvantage in a system that only partly answers their linguistic needs ... To expect bilingual students to achieve equal efficiency in English and French, when French is their mother tongue, is inconceivable and definitely hampers a consistent progress in understanding, learning, psychological

and emotional development. It tends to develop in them a complex of inferiority not only in school but later on as well when they assume their position in any field of endeavour. Thence originates the complex of being a second class citizen if one is French-speaking.[9]

Volume I of the *Report of the Royal Commission on Bilingualism and Biculturalism*, which appeared in October 1967, commented on the position of the French-speaking minorities outside Quebec, 425,000 of whom lived in Ontario. The situation was contrasted unfavourably with that of the 13 per cent of the population of Quebec whose mother tongue was English. Almost without exception, it had been impossible in the other provinces for a French-speaking student to complete his education in French through the elementary and secondary public schools. The commission recognized recent efforts at improvement but found some of them rather slight. It identified French-language instruction outside Quebec as suffering from two major weaknesses.

First, it has been largely achieved through the struggles of French-speaking Canadians despite the resistance of the English-speaking majority. The toll in efficiency and vitality is readily appreciated. Second, it has not constituted a "system." There have been serious gaps and dislocations in the sequence from one educational level to another; essentials such as teacher-training, guidance, and so on, have left a great deal to be desired; a technical or scientific education has been largely unavailable. As a consequence, even where conditions have been most favourable, French-speaking children have been seriously handicapped in their education, with the result that often they were deficient in both languages. Not only has there been injustice in human terms, but these Canadian citizens have not been able to make their potential contribution to society.[10]

The commissioners declared that it must be accepted as normal that children of both linguistic groups have access to schools using their own language as the language of instruction. The extent to which this policy was implemented would depend on the concentration of the minority population. Since the English-speaking residents already had the recommended opportunities, the policy meant, in practical terms, that comparable provision had to be made for French-Canadians to receive schooling in French. Where school boards were in a position to reject a request from the minority to have a school in their own language, a formal procedure was required whereby the latter could assert their rights. The commission proposed that departments of education state the requirements and procedures for the establishment of a minority-language school at either the elementary or the secondary level. It was urged, furthermore, that such schools not be restricted to bilingual districts, but that they be provided wherever the number of potential pupils made them feasible. In some cases, it might be practical to operate an elementary but not a secondary school. Where not even an elementary school could be justified, separate classes might be organized where the minority language could be used for instruction in some subjects. It might be necessary to rely on boarding schools or television teaching where, under such circumstances, a complete minority-language program was desired.[11]

A major recommendation of the commission, apart from strictly educational considerations, was the creation or consolidation of a network of bilingual areas across Canada. In this plan, the large urban centres would act as poles of attraction for all Canadians. Educational opportunities in the French language would have to be provided in these centres if French Canadians were to feel free to leave Quebec. Their children would have to accept a certain amount of inconvenience in travelling farther than English-speaking pupils, but the compensating advantages would be considerable. Extra value might be derived from the school as part of a French-language cultural complex.

The new policy of 1967 and subsequent action

A new policy was announced by Prime Minister Robarts on August 24, 1967, at the twentieth annual conference of l'Association canadienne des éducateurs de langue française. He declared that the Ontario government would provide, within the publicly supported secondary school system, schools in which the language of instruction would be French. This decision was based on the government's sympathy with the desire of French-speaking citizens of Canada to preserve and foster their language, customs, and culture. Robarts disclaimed any intention of developing another system of French-language secondary schools, but rather supported the fullest possible range of programs and options in the French language within the existing system. English would be taught in the new schools to ensure that the graduates would be able to compete successfully in the Ontario labour market.[12]

In November 1967 the minister appointed a Committee on French Language Public Secondary schools to advise him on the provision of adequate opportunities for French-speaking students in the publicly supported system. This committee worked under the chairmanship of R.R. Bériault, a member of the departmental Policy and Development Council. At the time its establishment was announced, the minister called attention to the fact that, although some of the public secondary schools had for several years offered part of their instruction in French, he was eager to provide better opportunities for French-speaking students who were dispersed among schools where the program was entirely in English. These students had hitherto been at a disadvantage in comparison with their English-speaking colleagues. Many had dropped out or resorted to private schools where the parents had both to pay fees and to continue their tax contribution to the public system.

The committee was asked to prepare a report suggesting measures to be placed before the Ontario Legislature. Its first task, following the recommendations of the Royal Commission on Bilingualism and Biculturalism, was to study the legal requirements and procedures needed to guarantee the establishment of French-language secondary schools wherever the number of students made it feasible. The committee decided that the question of elementary education should be considered along with that of secondary education and accordingly drew up legislation applying to both levels.

The proposals of the committee were enacted by the Legislature in mid-1968. Bill 140, amending *The Schools Administration Act*, set out the procedure for establishing French-language elementary schools or classes. Strangely enough, during all the years in which such schools and classes had existed, they had had no basis in legislation, but could simply be established with the approval of the minister. The legislation made the establishment of French-language classes mandatory on the request of ten or more French-speaking ratepayers where there were at least thirty French-speaking pupils in the primary, junior, or intermediate division. If the number warranted it, a French-speaking school must be provided.

Bill 141 amended *The Secondary Schools and Boards of Education Act* to provide for the establishment of French-language secondary schools and courses. The legislation recognized three possible activities: the teaching of certain subjects in French; the creation of a French-language department within a secondary school; and the establishment of a French-language composite school. The most satisfactory arrangement was considered to be a French-language composite school, offering all available options. Such a school would be feasible only where there was a fairly substantial concentration of students. As Roland Bériault described the possibilities, in some areas it might be feasible to offer only Français and one or two other subjects in French; in others, there might be a full arts and science program, as well as some commercial subjects. French-language composite schools would be established on the same basis as those for English-speaking students. While schools of this type were for the most part being built for an enrolment of one thousand students or more, they could be provided to accommodate considerably smaller numbers. Whatever the course of action adopted in a particular area, Bériault was confident that each divisional board of education would offer the most complete program possible.[13]

The legislation guaranteed the rights of an English-speaking minority in a predominantly French-speaking area to continue receiving instruction in their own language. Where French was the language of instruction in a public or separate school, ten or more English-speaking ratepayers could petition for the use of their language for the instruction of English-speaking pupils. The same minimum number – thirty – had to be available in the primary, junior, or intermediate division before the establishment of the desired class became mandatory. Where, in the opinion of the board, there were sufficient English-speaking pupils, an English-language school was to be set up. Provision was made for an English-speaking pupil to attend a French-language class or school on the request of a parent or guardian provided that the principal was satisfied that his attendance would not be detrimental to the progress of the class.

The establishment of French-language committees by boards of education was referred to briefly in volume II, chapter 5. Such a committee was to be formed where at least ten French-speaking taxpayers made a written request that the board provide school instruction in French, or where the board intended on its own initiative to set up a program of instruction in French or to extend an existing French-language program. Each committee was to have seven members, three of whom would be appointed by the board and four elected by the French-speaking taxpayers of the area. In Bériault's words: "The most important function of the French language committees will ... be to make recommendations to meet the educational and cultural needs of French-speaking students."[14] According to the legislation, English was to be a compulsory subject taught daily to all students in grades 9 to 12. The Department of Education set about preparing English courses appropriate to the needs of French-speaking students.

The legislation did not elicit unanimous approval from all members of the government party. Syl Apps, representing Kingston and the Islands, agreed with the provision of the right to instruction in French, but urged that the pupils be kept in one school. He felt that they should be encouraged to mingle with one another in activities other than instruction in the separate languages, thus learning to know and understand one another better. In an article in the *Globe and Mail* in which the comments by Apps were reported, H. Cyr, Assistant Superintendent of Curriculum in the Department of Education, observed that principals of schools where groups were taught in two separate languages found it a complicated system.[15]

In 1968 the Ottawa Collegiate Institute Board assumed responsibility for what had been seven private French-language secondary schools. This development was part of the pattern for similar schools in other communities to be absorbed into the public system. Between 1967–8 and 1968–9, the number of private French-language high schools in Ontario was reduced from approximately twenty to four. Even though there was an understanding that the existing mode of operations, including treatment of religion, would not be too much disturbed, there were misgivings on the part of many former Roman Catholic supporters of the private schools. There was also a notable lack of enthusiasm on the part of Roman Catholic separate school supporters, who saw the development as a blow to their campaign for support of their system to the end of secondary school.

William Johnson, a staff writer for the *Globe and Mail*, asked in the title of an article that appeared on November 23, 1968, "Will The French Go Public?"[16] He claimed that there were prominent Franco-Ontarian educators who would say, "off the record and under the protection of solemn guarantees of anonymity," that it was only a matter of time before the French-speaking children of the province transferred to the public system. Part of the reason was that there had been historic conflict between French- and English-speaking Roman Catholics. Bishop Fallon of London had led the movement to prohibit the use of French in Ontario schools before the passage of the notorious Regulation 17. In 1962 a group of French-speaking parents had engaged in a sit-down strike to protest a decision by the Metropolitan Toronto Separate School Board to close a grade 5 bilingual class at Our Lady of Wisdom School in Scarborough. There was apparently a disposition to move to the public system once the equality of French as a language of instruction was guaranteed. Johnson reported that this course of action had been approved by the Ontario French-Canadian Education Association. The article concluded: "There is no movement in the province specifically aimed at bringing Franco-Ontarians into the public school system at the elementary level. But several educators who are very prominent in Ontario French education see this as the wave of the future." In view of the strength shown by the Roman Catholic separate school supporters in their drive for an extension of the system through secondary school, it is doubtful that defections by Franco-Ontarians can be considered the beginning of the end for the separate schools.

Report of the Royal Commission on Bilingualism and Biculturalism, II

The Royal Commission on Bilingualism and Biculturalism issued a second volume in December 1968.[17] Many of its recommendations with respect to education were repetitions or extensions of those made earlier. Among those attracting most attention was the proposal that federal aid be supplied to assist in the establishment and maintenance of schools for French-speaking and English-speaking minorities, possibly amounting to 10 per cent of the total per-pupil cost. Federal support might also cover teacher training colleges and universities and assist students to attend university in provinces other than their own for courses in their own language.

Two underlying principles set out in the report were that all Canadians had the right to ensure that their children were educated in the official language of their choice and that they had an opportunity to learn the second language. Arising from these principles were a number of recommendations, including the following. 1 / In bilingual districts, elementary and secondary education should be provided in both English and French. 2 / Where potential enrolment warranted it, French language education should be provided at the university level. 3 / Centres should be established for the preparation of second-language teachers for elementary and secondary schools, with machinery for interprovincial co-ordination. 4 /

In Ontario, Quebec, and New Brunswick, there should be an associate or assistant deputy minister responsible for minority schools. 5 / Canadian history texts should be revised to help transmit an understanding of the society of each linguistic and cultural group to the other. The recommendations of the commission provided the basis for federal legislation establishing bilingual districts. There was no immediate response to the proposal to use federal funds to promote the implementation of certain recommendations, nor did it appear that any positive action would be taken. The reaction of the Ontario government to the second volume produced by the commission was that most of the recommended actions within its jurisdiction were already being taken.

Franco-Ontarian cultural life

The Comité franco-ontarien d'enquête culturelle, headed by R. St Denis, released a report in January 1969 after a thorough study of the quality of cultural life among the various concentrations of Franco-Ontarians in different parts of the province.[18] While this committee identified a number of bright spots, it also found marked signs of cultural anemia. Not surprisingly, it looked to formal education to play a major role in improving the situation.

The report had words of praise for recent government actions such as the public acceptance by the Prime Minister of the guiding principles formulated by the Royal Commission on Bilingualism and Biculturalism relating to the status of the French language and the rights of French Canadians across the country. It noted with approval measures that had been taken to encourage bilingualism among higher officials in the Department of Education; the initiation of a program of cultural exchanges under the direction of Professor C.E. Rathé, which involved the establishment of beneficial links with French-speaking communities in Quebec and France; and in particular the opening of several French-language secondary schools in September 1968. There seemed grounds for hoping for the ultimate transformation of the mentality of the whole population, not only in Ontario, but in other parts of the country as well.

The committee demonstrated an unequivocal belief that it was unrealistic to talk of promoting the artistic life of a group without providing the conditions necessary for the development of all aspects of its culture. Its style of life, its particular customs, and its language, among other fundamental cultural components, had to flourish without restraint. There had to be an assurance that a person who lived fully in a French cultural environment was not seriously handicapped in making his way in life.

Little encouragement was offered for schools where French-speaking and English-speaking students studied side by side. The committee found that the atmosphere in such schools tended to be predominantly English, even where the French-speaking students were in a majority. Part of the trouble was that courses of an artistic nature, from music to plastic arts, were offered in English (a situation that might be expected to change as the provincial legislation of 1968 came into effect). French-language student organizations in such schools were rare. The situation was much better in the private French-language secondary schools, despite their scanty resources. The problem at the time, however, was that these schools were finding it increasingly difficult or impossible to continue in operation. A hope for the future lay in the transformation of secondary schools in the public system from mixed French and English to purely French schools.

The committee made 107 recommendations for the improvement of Franco-Ontarian cultural life, grouped by the institutions it hoped would carry them out: 1 / government of Ontario; 2 / the Ontario Council for the Arts; 3 / Ontario cultural exchange programs; 4 / Ontario youth and recreation service; 5 / the Ontario Department of Education; 6 / bilingual universities; 7 / normal schools; 8 / school boards; 9 / Franco-Ontarian institutions; 10 / government of Quebec; 11 / federal institutions; and 12 / libraries, art galleries and other related services. Most of these recommendations dealt with the provision of some facility, service, or opportunity to encourage the expansion of French cultural life. If even some of them were carried out with enthusiasm and vigour, there is little doubt that Franco-Ontarians would have reason to feel that they lived in a society characterized by sympathy and good will. Yet the committee failed to suggest a convincing solution to the dilemma it identified so clearly. How can Franco-Ontarians surround themselves with the authentic French environment, including education, that alone makes possible a genuine cultural contribution, and yet compete on equal terms with their fellow Ontarians in an environment that is completely dominated by economic and cultural forms that are rooted in the English language? The committee did not advocate the establishment of economically viable ghettos. Yet if Franco-Ontarians are to be so thoroughly steeped in their native culture that they can be creative in it, they can only make their way in the dominant culture without handicap by the kind of intellectual feat that is not demanded or expected of their English-speaking counterparts. Even in Quebec, where the English-language culture is represented by a relatively small local minority, there has been a wave of fear that French culture is in danger. If there is a basis for such fear, what are the long-term prospects for French culture in Ontario?

There may indeed be solutions to the problem, and if there are, it will be up to men of good will to apply them vigorously. But there is no point in ignoring what history tells us about the fate of linguistic and cultural minorities, especially those existing under tolerant conditions, whose members have attempted to participate fully in the economic life of a larger and more powerful group. The Scots who dominated the financial institutions of London left their Gaelic behind in the misty islands and glens of the north. Even the Jews, who have shown an unparalleled ability to maintain cultural cohesiveness, have retained a different language as a viable means of communication for an extended period of time only in countries where they have been ostracized from the life of the surrounding community. If Franco-Ontarians can do better, their fellow-citizens will wish them well. They will not, however, win any victories through effusions of sentimental optimism.

An education in the French language from kindergarten through university has a tremendous appeal for many Franco-Ontarians at the moment. They, and the government officials involved in providing the programs, may believe that the compulsory study of English as a subject will produce citizens able to succeed in the larger Ontario society. If such a result ensues, it will be because the French-speaking students have vastly more success learning English than English-speaking students have learning French. After the first flush of enthusiasm is over, two disappointing trends are likely to develop. 1 / The province will discover that it is educating a considerable number of its young people to swell the ranks of the Quebec citizenry, since Quebec will be the obvious place for an individual with a high level of competence in French and a serious handicap in English to seek a career. 2 / Parents with a strong desire to see their children remain in Ontario will react against a French-language school program.

EDUCATION OF INDIANS

The issues

It has been very much the fashion in recent years to deplore the poverty of the Canadian Indian population. Politicians in opposition berate the parties in power in various provinces, accusing them of neglect, short-sightedness, or worse. Provincial officials, blaming the appropriate branch of the federal government, suggest that they could solve the problems, or at least do much better, if sole responsibility were turned over to them. Nothing very much seems to be accomplished, and the general public remains bewildered as Indian spokesmen begin to threaten rebellion.

To provide more information for the public, Helen Tracy, President of the Ontario Division of the Indian-Eskimo Association of Canada, included in her report on November 20, 1966, a résumé of certain basic facts about the Indian population.[19] She dealt also with the Eskimos, so few of whom, however, live in Ontario that they may be omitted from coverage in the present context. A brief review of the most important facts about the Indians will provide a background against which educational issues may be considered.

In 1965 there were approximately 205,000 registered Indians in Canada, 51.2 per cent more than there had been fifteen years earlier. The population increased at about twice the annual rate of the Canadian population in general. About 60 per cent, as compared with 43 per cent of the general population, were under twenty-one years of age. Over 150,000 Indians lived on the 2,265 reserves, comprising almost six million acres, while another twenty thousand lived on Crown land. In addition to registered Indians, there were estimated to be about 200,000 people of Indian ancestry mingled with the general population, most of them living in settlements adjacent to towns and villages or in slum areas of larger urban centres.

There were ten traditional linguistic groupings: Algonkian, Iroquoian, Siouian, Athapaskan, Kootenayan, Salishan, Wakishan, Tsimshian, Haida, and Tlingit. Each group consisted of a number of subgroups speaking related languages or dialects which were not necessarily mutually comprehensible. Cultural and linguistic areas did not always coincide, although they might overlap. The six major culture groups were the Algonkian, the Iroquoian, the Plains, the Plateau or Cordillera, the Pacific Coast, and the Mackenzie River.

According to a housing survey conducted by the Indian Affairs Branch in 1962, about 57 per cent of Indian housing consisted of dwellings with no more than three rooms, compared with 11 per cent for the total Canadian population. Only 9 per cent of dwellings had six rooms or more, compared with 44 per cent for the general population. Indoor toilets were found in 9 per cent of Indian homes and in 90 per cent of all Canadian homes. Running water was available in 13 per cent of Indian and 92 per cent of all Canadian homes. Only 44 per cent of Indians used electricity as compared with 99 per cent of Canadians in general. The rate of construction of new housing was much below that of the population increase.

According to a survey of Indian family incomes conducted in 1962, 47 per cent of Indian families earned $1,000 or less per year, which was between one-quarter and one-fifth the national average. Three-quarters of Indian families earned $2,000 or less. The fish and game resources of the reserves were constantly dwindling. The Indian Affairs Branch had estimated that over one-third of the Indian population needed relief, compared with 3.5 per cent of the general population. Those who sought a living away from the reserve had to enter a complex industrialized society where they were poorly prepared to compete for employment because of lack of education and training. While exact unemployment figures were not available, the rate was estimated to be comparable to that in the United States – about 40 or 50 per cent.

There had been some improvement in the educational level attained by Indians during the immediately preceding period. High school enrolment had increased from 611 in 1948 to 4,065, university enrolment from nine to sixty-eight, and enrolment in vocational training from forty-one to 720. Yet about 24 per cent of Canadian Indians were functionally illiterate. The children who attended school suffered from a lack of books, poor facilities for study, and unfavourable attitudes on the part of their parents.

According to a 1968 report by E.R. McEwen, the Executive Director of the Indian-Eskimo Association of Canada, the educational situation was not improving very rapidly. About 50 per cent of Indian pupils were not going beyond grade 6, about 61 per cent were not reaching grade 8, and about 97 per cent were not reaching grade 12. There were only about 150 status Indians enrolled full time in credit courses in universities. While there were no statistics available on the educational level attained by non-status Indians, it was estimated to be no better.[20]

The 1966 report of the same association indicated that the rates of delinquency and crime were high. In Manitoba, where the Indian population was about 28,000 in a provincial total of nearly one million, a survey revealed that over half the female inmates of reform institutions were Indian. Among male Indians, the situation was only slightly better. According to the Dominion Bureau of Statistics, proportionately five times as many Indians as non-Indians went to penitentiaries. The problem was growing relatively worse, partly because of the practice among some Indians of seeking imprisonment as a means of obtaining food, clothing, and shelter.

Poverty and poor health were, as might be expected, closely related. It was estimated that Indians received hospital care at twice the rate of other Canadians. Their mortality rate was eight times the national rate for pre-school children, three times for school children, two and one-half times for teen-agers, and three and one-half for adults.

The 1966 report indicated some of the environmental and cultural factors accounting for this situation. The treaties establishing the reserves had been based on the assumption that the Indians would continue to follow their traditional pursuits of hunting, fishing, and trapping. Their reserves had separated them from the main stream of economic and social progress. Language differences and distance had reinforced their isolation. Such small amounts of education as the white man had offered had been of little value for their way of life. The lack of change in their cultural and social life, particularly in the northern regions, had left them ill-equipped to integrate with other elements of the Canadian community.

Certain characteristics of their cultural life had made it particularly difficult for them to adjust to industrial society. The report provided a particularly vivid delineation of these characteristics.

(a) Indians traditionally live in the present. They are not future-oriented. Our society is. We (individually) save and generally build up resources for the future. In the old days (before the arrival of the white man) there was always plenty of game. The Indians have always held to the belief of sharing. The exploits of a hunt in the past and even to this day are shared among all who need it. It is sin to store up resources individually when others around you are in need. Status in the tribe is obtained on the basis of what you are able to share. "The essence of life is found *in being* and not in *becoming* something we are not today. Scrimping and saving to ensure economic achievement in the future has [*sic*] never been an acceptable part of Indian culture. Further Indians have not found it necessary to change this view on life. When hunting and trapping became poor, government relief was on hand. This he accepted as a right under treaty etc. Over the years he has leaned heavily on the Indian agent, to the point he has lost a good deal of his resourcefulness.

(b) The man (or the brave), has had a role of hunter, warrior and protector in the tribe. The menial tasks have been carried by the women. Steady application to monotonous toil has not been in keeping with the tribal role. Standing up to an assembly line day after day runs counter to the grain. In the European value system there is virtue in work. Thomas Carlyle, in the 19th century, put it this way, "all work, even cotton spinning is noble. Work is alone noble. A life of ease is not for any man, nor for any God.... Even in the meanest part of labor the whole soul of man is composed into a kind of harmony at the instant he sets himself to work."

Indian women find it somewhat easier to accept the disciplines of work in modern society – simply because it required less adjustment.

(c) Indians, who decide to break with their value systems, usually lose their friends. "So the Indian way of life wasn't good enough for you – trying to be a white man", etc. This means that those who go on to higher education, face ostracism back on the Reserve.

(d) An Indian, who decides to break into the white man's world has another problem. Take the case of a young man who attains a trade or profession and gets a job in a city. Once he is on salary, has a little apartment, his relatives (brothers, sisters, uncles and aunts, in fact anyone from the band) can move in on him. His culture requires him to share his apartment and his income. It is not uncommon to have the apartment become a dormitory and eating place for literally dozens of Indians. Saving becomes impossible, and usually landlords cancel the lease. In due course he becomes discouraged and goes back to the Reserve.[21]

The Reverend James Mulvihill wrote of the "The Dilemma in Indian Education in the *Indian Record* in 1963.[22] He observed that parliamentary leaders saw integration as the key to the solution of the Indians' problems and that government officials were advocating integrated schools. Every effort was being made to have as many Indian children as possible attend such schools. There were numerous discussions on the relative value of integrated schools, Indian day schools, and residential schools, on rapid versus slow integration, on the question of welfare handouts, and on discrimination in work and play. Father Mulvihill claimed that these discussions ignored the basic fact that the Indian reserve was an insurmountable obstacle in the way of integrated education and integrated living. He saw the segregation of the Indian reserve as the main reason for the difference in IQ levels between Indian and other Canadian children and the failure of the Indians to integrate into the way of life of those around them. The schools did not really have time for individual attention, but had to treat children as a group. Most of the Indian children fell behind and remained there. Parents of other pupils in integrated schools tended to complain that the Indians held back the rest of the class.

Father Mulvihill felt that the curriculum in provincial schools, which was adapted to the particular social climate of Canada, was unsuitable for Indian children.

> The Indian child comes to school as the unfinished business of his family training on the reserve. The school then tries to take over, but will be a partial failure as long as the child remains in his family as an Indian with an Indian outlook. In Indian education, whether it is integrated or not, the Provincial curriculum is not adequate for products of reserve living so that special courses are needed.[23]

Mulvihill continued by defining the ultimate objective of education for the Indian.

> Education is one of the socializing agencies that give a richer and broader way of life to the growing adult and, in this aspect, it can be considered the process to integration. Integration then, as a social concept, means the end of the process which takes place when an outsider becomes an integral part of the community and is accepted by the community. Integration results in a mutual change; the outsider and the community are both changed. Usually, it is the outsider who is changed to a greater degree when he accepts more of the community's way of life but still retains some of his own which is accepted by the community. Integration then is achieved by the process which brings a group or an individual into society and is made part of the whole without losing all of their former ways of life and loyalties.[24]

But he saw no prospect of this type of integration as long as the Indians were prevented from sharing experiences with other Canadians. Yet the alternative, to move the Indians off the reservations without their consent, would not be sanctioned by any democratic government. This situation constituted the dilemma faced by officialdom.

True integration seemed impossible under the circumstances. Father Mulvihill argued that there was no such thing as an integrated school, except in the minds of some educators. The fact that Indian and white children sat side by side and spoke to one another meant only the illusion of integration. Thus Father Mulvihill advocated education for a pluralistic society, whereby the Indian would enrich his life at his own speed if he were shown respect and sympathy in his efforts to work out a new way of life.

It would appear that many Indians are not as patient as Father Mulvihill thought. Some have conflicting sets of desires. They would like to escape from poverty, ill-health, and delinquency but do not wish to give up as much of their culture as real integration demands. It is not a case of "I would like to be like you," but "I would like to remain my essential self but have your benefits." For many others, the issue is not the perpetuation of traditional values so much as a lack of sufficient feeling of security to enable them to leave the reserve and face the complex and unsympathetic world outside. For these, a solution may be devised by public and private agencies and by individuals who, if they cannot be moved by humanity, might consider the economic cost of having a large and growing Indian population in a constant state of deprivation.

Among the particular grievances of Indian leaders has been the use of discriminatory history textbooks, which have tended to portray the Indian as a benighted savage whom the early settlers were justified in slaughtering and whose lands they were quite entitled to steal. To the extent that these spokesmen appeal for accuracy and fairness, there can be no basis for opposition to their cause. There is some reason for apprehension, however, lest matters be carried so far that every reference to a racial minority that could be construed as unflattering may be regarded as unsuitable for texts or reference books. Children could be presented with a bowdlerized version of history quite out of touch with reality.

Assumption of responsibility by the Ontario government

Since the 1950s the Ontario government has facilitated the transfer of responsibility for the education of Indians from the federal government to local school boards. In 1957 H.C. Nixon estimated that, of the six or seven thousand Indian children of school age in the province, approximately two thousand were being educated in the provincial school system. Nixon thought that there was still an unnecessary and most undesirable duplication of services and that the federal government should withdraw from the field. Education Minister W.J. Dunlop declared that the Department of Education was ready to assume the entire responsibility provided that the federal government supplied the funds.[25] There had apparently been discussions between the federal and provincial governments, but no decisive action had ensued. The federal Department of Citizenship and Immigration, however, continued to make arrangements with individual school boards.

In an exchange between Nixon and Dunlop in 1958, there were said to be 2,000 Indian students attending secondary schools in Ontario, and 1,200 attending public schools. Dunlop had been around the province to see how they were getting along. In certain places, he thought things were working out perfectly. He admitted, however, that some Indian parents did not want their children to attend the public school.[26]

At the request of the Department of Citizenship and Immigration, the Department of Education provided inspection for Indian schools. In

1960 Robarts, then Minister of Education, reported that approximately 275 classrooms were inspected for a fee of $15 per classroom. This amount bore no relationship to the inspector's salary.[27]

During the 1960s there was a steady shift of Indian children into schools operated by local school boards. In 1968–9 there were 104 school boards in the province either maintaining integrated schools on a tuition basis or sharing capital costs of joint school buildings with the Department of Indian Affairs. An estimated 50 per cent of Indian children in Ontario were at this time attending integrated schools. Many of the remainder were prevented from doing so because they lived in isolated areas. The stage at which children entered the integrated schools varied according to the wishes of the parents and the facilities available. It might, for example, be at kindergarten, at grade 4, or at grade 9.

Dunlop's successors in the ministry of education continued to reiterate their willingness to have the department take over complete responsibility for Indian education, with federal financial assistance. One of these occasions was on June 5, 1968, when Davis said in the Legislature: "If we can provide a better educational service through agreement or in some other fashion with the boards, and the department assuming a greater area of responsibility, then I, as an individual, and I think I could [go] so far as to say as Minister of Education ... would welcome this opportunity."[28] Apparently his hesitant tone was attributable to his desire to avoid getting into any constitutional difficulty by appearing eager to infringe on an area of federal responsibility. He pointed out also that the attitude of the Indians toward their traditional church-related institutions in certain parts of the province had to be taken into account. When the report of the Provincial Committee on Aims and Objectives was released, it provided further support for the proposition that the province should assume complete responsibility, with federal financial co-operation.

In the late 1960s, the Department of Education took various initiatives designed to improve Indian education. One of these was the training of teachers for the Department of Indian Affairs in the program organized for the Northern Corps of Teachers. As Superintendent of Curriculum, a position which he occupied until he became assistant deputy minister in mid-1969, J.F. Kinlin showed a keen interest in the development of curricular materials to serve the special needs of Indians. The Curriculum Section of the department also attempted through appropriate materials to provide for a better understanding among non-Indian children of the historical development of Indians and their role in Canadian society.

In 1967 the government passed enabling legislation permitting school boards to appoint an Indian representative to board membership. Action under this legislation was taken in various parts of the province. In 1969 considerable publicity was given to the refusal of the Kent County board to follow suit. Although the proposition received a favourable vote of nine to seven when it was considered again in 1970, the motion was lost because of the requirement of a two-thirds majority to reverse the earlier decision. Some negative votes were reputed to have been cast on the grounds that it would be a manifestation of paternalism to appoint an Indian to an elected board.[29] At any rate, as a result of the board's action, there was talk of providing for mandatory Indian representation.

TEN

Special education

DEFINITIONS

The treatment given by the Provincial Committee on Aims and Objectives of Education in the Schools of Ontario to the topic of special education has been particularly commended. The committee classified children who may require special learning experiences according to the following scheme.

Children with handicaps.

(a) The intellectually handicapped:
retarded, slow learners, perceptually affected, neurologically impaired, mentally deficient.

(b) The physically handicapped:
includes impairments of vision, hearing, speech, and such impairments as disorders of bone and organs of movement, diseases of lungs and kidneys, congenital heart diseases, injuries, and physical frailties.

(c) The emotionally handicapped:
such as disturbed, including aggressive, withdrawn, shy, and severely maladjusted.

(d) The socially handicapped:
alienated and anti-social, 'misfits' and delinquents.

(e) The multi-handicapped:
any combination of (a) to (d).

Children affected by exceptional endowment or unusual circumstances.

(a) The gifted and talented.

(b) The New Canadians.

(c) The Canadian Indians.

(d) Residents with strong identification with another tongue, ethnic and religious customs.

(e) Those in need of nursery school experience.

(f) The socio-economically disadvantaged.

(g) Those undergoing severe crises:
grave accidents, hospitalization, long-term home care, pregnancy in schoolagers, death of parents or guardians, family breakdown, changes of foster home, young offenders, early marriage, school expulsion, severe economic change in family status, etc.

(h) Transfers:
from outside Ontario, from a different educational system, or within the municipality itself.
(i) Transients (short term):
children of migratory workers, wards of the Children's Aid Society, children with parents in mobile jobs.
(j) Miscellaneous:[1]

The Canadian Indians have been dealt with in chapter 9. It is possible in the present context to give specific attention only to part of the above list, in particular to those with the severest handicaps.

For the most part, educational policy in Ontario has been regarded as reasonably enlightened in terms of the provision of services for those with special needs. The most conspicuous services have been provided for children with the severest and most easily recognized physical and mental handicaps. There have been times, however, when critics have complained of a failure to respond to new or newly identified needs, such as those of the emotionally disturbed.

GENERAL DEVELOPMENT IN THE EARLY TWENTIETH CENTURY

The provincial School for the Deaf at Belleville dates from 1870, and the School for the Blind at Brantford from 1871. Industrial schools for delinquent boys and girls were first established in the late 1880s. From around 1910 the larger cities began to provide open-air classes for tubercular children, schools and classes for crippled children, speech correction classes, visiting teachers for children confined to their homes, and other special services.[2] In 1914 the Auxiliary Classes Act provided for the education of children who were unable, from any physical or mental cause, to benefit from the ordinary elementary school courses. It did not, however, apply to those whose mental capacity was below that of a normal child of eight years of age. Nor did it extend the benefits of auxiliary education to rural communities until 1930.[3] From 1921 on, there were sight-saving classes, classes for the hard-of-hearing, and speech correction classes.

These developments were not all fully recognized in the initial stages as primarily educational. For example, the Ontario Schools for the Deaf and Blind were supervised by the Department of the Provincial Secretary, which also managed prisons and asylums, until they were transferred to the Department of Education in 1905. This change helped to remove the impression that they were some kind of custodial institution.

Among the pioneers of the movement to improve facilities for special education was Helen McMurchy, the first inspector appointed to supervise services provided under the Auxiliary Classes Act. As part of her effort to encourage local agencies to develop facilities, she wrote a booklet entitled *Organization and Management of Auxiliary Classes*, as well as a book, *The Almosts*, dealing with children who had handicaps and problems. In 1920 S.B. Sinclair was appointed as Inspector of Auxiliary Classes; he was shortly joined by L. Helen Delaporte as Assistant Inspector. C.E. Stothers tells of Sinclair's work.

> Dr. Sinclair continued the practices begun by his predecessor, addressing meetings of people concerned with auxiliary education, defining procedures for establishing rural school classes, and assisting and informing school boards. These efforts instituted a period of growth and development partly due to revised regulations which required the Inspector of Auxiliary Classes to provide a survey at the request of a school board. There was an evident trend on the part of school boards to make special classes an integral part of their school systems, and Dr. Sinclair reports than in one year he made surveys of the twenty-seven school areas.[4]

In 1926–7 Sinclair conducted a province-wide survey of Ontario children to determine the extent to which the need for special classes was being met. From the distant perspective of 1970, it is rather surprising that as many as 8,213 children were attending special classes and 1,036 were in institutions. Sinclair concluded that there were 2,464 children in rural schools whose need for special classes was not being met.

Sinclair was succeeded in 1929 by H.E. Amoss who, along with Miss Delaporte, edited a manual dealing with the operation of many types of auxiliary classes, including hospital, sight-saving, oral, lip-reading, speech correction, orthopaedic, craft, opportunity, handicraft, and special vocational classes. A major part of Amoss's work involved the preparation and adaptation of intelligence tests to meet Ontario needs. In association with C.G. Stogdill, he prepared the Canadian Intelligence Examination, a revision of the Binet-Simon tests. C.E. Stothers, who succeeded Amoss in 1939, did further standardization work on the same test. At that time, there were nearly four hundred special classes in Ontario, including those for the blind and deaf. One of Stothers's leading contributions was the establishment of the Stothers Exceptional Child Foundation.

J.G. Althouse is given a great deal of credit for showing a humanitarian concern for trainable retarded children. He secured financial support for the Retarded Children's Associations in the face of opposition from departmental officials, who feared that a small concession would lead to insatiable demands for further assistance. Althouse expressed the dilemma over how far provision for certain special groups should go in his Quance Lectures in 1949.

> The practical administrative problem is to determine how much of the public funds which are raised for education may properly be devoted to the amelioration of the lot of those who can never be completely rehabilitated. This prob-

lem is rendered more acute by the fact that the per-pupil cost of training this group is many times that of educating normal children. The administrator who attempts to assess the rival claims of normal and sub-normal children to the school funds at his disposal finds his judgment strongly swayed by compassion as well as by a sense of public duty.[5]

GENERAL DEVELOPMENT IN THE 1950s AND 1960s

It might have been expected that the tremendous effort to provide for increasing school enrolment during the 1950s and early 1960s would have resulted in more serious neglect of children with special needs. However, during his ministry, W.J. Dunlop demonstrated a good deal of sensitivity to the plight of those with obvious handicaps. From 1953 on, the Special Education Branch, with H.R. Beattie in charge, developed with particular rapidity.

One particularly interesting development during this period was the establishment of an educational clinic by the London Board of Eucation in 1950. Its mode of operations was described ten years later by W.D. Sutton, then Superintendent of Public Schools and later Director of Education.[6] It was designed to provide diagnosis and remedial treatment for all kinds of problems reflected in unsatisfactory achievement in school. A child was referred there by the principal of his school with the consent of his parents. He was usually interviewed in the presence of his teacher, after which his parents were asked to provide information about his earlier development. His physical, mental, and emotional life were explored as a means of determining the course of action that would be most beneficial to him. He was given an individual intelligence test and various achievement tests. He was also given a visual survey test designed to give an evaluation of usable vision, lateral and vertical posture, stereopsis, fusion, and suppression; a test for astigmatism; a test of colour vision; a test of eye movements; a test of visual perception and visual memory; tests of lateral dominance; and a drawing test, the results of which were analysed and interpreted with reference to vision. If visual malfunction was identified as a factor contributing to his difficulties, his parents were advised to obtain the services of an oculist or an ophthalmologist. As a means of diagnosing hearing difficulties, he was given an audiometer test. If he had any appreciable speech defect, he was given training by a speech consultant. Reading disability was diagnosed by means of the Gates Battery. Attitude and interest inventories were used to help assess his feelings toward his school, his teachers, his playmates, his home, his family, and his learning difficulties.

Sutton listed a wide variety of problems which the clinic had attempted, in all but a few cases with success, to solve. There had been children with vision difficulties, children who were emotionally and socially disturbed, children with brain injury, children with schizophrenia, children who had been mishandled by their parents, and children who simply lacked the fundamental skills of reading, spelling, and arithmetic. Among the causes of their problems were poor hearing, general or specific defects in physical health, insecurity, aggressiveness, withdrawal tendencies, gaps in learning caused by frequent changes in schools or living accommodation, and defeat and failure in and out of school. The consultants were all certified and experienced teachers. As a result of the operation of the clinic, Sutton saw an increase in the interest and understanding of teachers in the diagnosis and treatment of learning problems.

The lack of special preparation for teachers of children with special needs was one of the major weaknesses of the program during this period. The length of the regular program of teacher preparation, let alone that of some of the emergency programs, left no time for specialization in the handling of atypical children. The summer courses offered by the department were of some help, but were entirely inadequate for the development of the specialized expertise that the situation called for. Nothing less than a period of preparation extending over several years could be regarded as satisfactory. A real solution to the problem awaits the integration of teacher education with the universities. As a temporary measure, reliance has had to be placed on training facilities in the United States. These have not begun to meet ordinary classroom needs but have helped to prepare consultants and other key personnel.

Departmental support for special education programs

Certain sections from Ontario Regulation 339/66 indicate in fairly specific terms the range and types of special education programs and services that the Department of Education was prepared to support. These included 1 / Braille classes for blind children; 2 / classes for children clinically diagnosed as emotionally disturbed, and who were unable to profit from a regular classroom program, but who might benefit from special classroom instruction; 3 / classes for children clinically diagnosed as neurologically impaired, including perceptually handicapped children, and who were unable to profit from a regular classroom program, but who might profit from special classroom instruction; 4 / classes for gifted children for whom a special program was provided; 5 / hard-of-hearing classes for children with hearing loss sufficient to interfere seriously with progress in school; 6 / classes for children with health problems, for whom a special program was provided; 7 / hospital classes for children confined to hospital-type residential settings; 8 / institutional classes for children in children's homes or residences; 9 / language classes for children who were newcomers to Canada and whose linguistic foundation did not permit them to take proper advantage of regular school instruction; 10 / limited-vision classes for children whose vision was limited to the extent that it interfered seriously with their progress in school; 11 / opportunity classes for educable retarded children, slow learners, or educationally retarded children; 12 / oral classes for deaf children; and 13 / orthopaedic classes for physically disabled children. A board might, with the approval of the minister, employ one or more special education teachers for the purpose of home or tutorial instruction, speech correction, pupil diagnosis, or the conduct, on an itinerant basis or otherwise, of the special classes already listed. A board might also, subject to the same condition, employ one or more social workers.

There were certain other conditions governing the establishment and conduct of special classes. The maximum enrolment was to be as follows: Braille, ten; limited vision, twelve; oral, ten; hard-of-hearing, twelve; orthopaedic, twelve; emotionally disturbed, eight; primary opportunity, twelve; junior opportunity, sixteen; intermediate opportunity, sixteen; senior opportunity, twenty; opportunity without chronological age classification, sixteen; gifted, twenty-five; health, thirty; hospital, twenty-five; institutional, thirty; language, twenty; and neurologically impaired, including perceptually handicapped, eight. The chronological age range in an opportunity class was not to exceed five years. The maximum case load for a special education teacher employed for the purpose of home instruction was to be seven, and for a special education teacher engaged in individual or small-group instruction, 150.

During a debate in the Legislature in 1967, attention was given to the question of how school boards would be induced to fulfil their obligations toward exceptional children. Davis was not inclined to concede that compulsion was needed. He preferred to wait and see what could be accomplished when sufficient personnel were available and when there was a better understanding of how the needs of the children could best be met. Under existing legislation, the school boards had an obligation to provide an educational program for all pupils within the system. When they inquired, as they did from time to time, whether they were supposed to provide classes for the perceptually handicapped, they were told that it was within their total responsibility to do so. Grants were designed to give them a strong incentive to meet this obligation.[7]

Recommendations of the Provincial Committee on Aims and Objectives

The Provincial Committee on Aims and Objectives recognized the growing importance of special education.

> The advances of sciences, the wonder drugs, better housing, and the influence of the affluent society contribute to a much greater proportion of all such children attaining school age and adulthood. These children are entitled to the same measure of opportunity as their more fortunate brothers and sisters. The neglects of the past must now be remedied, and heroic efforts, if necessary, must be made to compensate for disabilities which nature and misfortune have im-

posed. The responsibility for providing integrated services, personnel, and special facilities where needed is a Provincial one ... Only in this way can discrimination be avoided and an equal opportunity given to all.[8]

The committee was critical of past conditions which had established a pattern for special education.

It becomes increasingly clear that if the measure of success of an educational system is weighted toward pressuring children to digest a rigid, structured, graded curriculum within fixed intervals of time, many children must fall by the wayside, with some acceptable up-to-the-minute label attached to explain their unforgivable sin of failure. If a narrow curriculum is considered immutable and untouchable, it follows inevitably that those who cannot benefit from its perfection, must be put aside and separated in time and space from their peers. This was the pattern established for special education nearly a century ago, and its results will be seen when we study the complexity and ramifications of existing special education.[9]

The existing situation was criticized in rather severe terms. It was described as "a welter of complexity, divided authority, blurred responsibility, and a broad spectrum of services unevenly distributed through the province and too frequently inadequate."[10] Certain treatment practices were identified as obsolete. The large residential schools, which had been pioneers in special education, were referred to as anachronisms. The committee urged that facilities be so situated that all children with disabilities would be able to participate partially or completely in the regular school program when their development so warranted.

The committee cited psychology professor H. Carl Haywood as an authority for the claim that there was a considerable degree of overlap and discrepancy in the identification of children as emotionally disturbed, mentally retarded, or brain damaged. Haywood was said to have claimed that the way in which a clinician categorized individuals was a function of his training, philosophy, and predisposition. While psychological tests could distinguish groups of retarded, mentally handicapped and brain-damaged patients from a normal group, they had little success in distinguishing these groups from one another, and even less in diagnosing individual cases. Haywood questioned the wisdom of establishing separate special classes on the basis of each syndrome on the grounds that psychologists recommended much the same special treatment whether the diagnosis was high-level mental retardation, emotional disturbance, or perceptual handicap.

The committee observed that the emphasis was shifting from separate special classes to special teachers helping children within their own classrooms. The pattern was that children with learning disorders stayed in the regular classes with members of their own age group for activities where they were performing at or near a normal level and for recreational and social events. For one or two periods a day, they were taken to a special classroom for remedial instruction in areas of special difficulty. In the same way, children who were exceptionally competent in particular areas went to a separate schoolroom, laboratory, library, or community resource. The committee was favourably disposed to these developments.

There were some who felt that the committee's prescription was quite acceptable for children whose problems or handicaps did not differentiate them too sharply from others. They wanted to be sure, however, that there was adequate recognition of the difficulties that children with more extreme abnormalities have in adapting to ordinary life. For some, an excessively hasty immersion in a "normal" environment creates a sense of depression and despair when they are confronted constantly with the advantages which other children possess and they lack. The cruelty with which they are sometimes treated by their peers who may label them with offensive names and mock their disabilities can also have a devastating effect. It is impossible to ensure the continuous teacher supervision that might prevent these occurrences, and it would obviously be undesirable to keep children under perpetual adult scrutiny in any case.

Recent appraisal

An article by Bill Johnson appeared in the January 1969 issue of *School Progress* under the title "What Parents Expect from Special Education."[11] In it, he appraised various recent trends in the handling of special education in general. Among the points he emphasized was that new ideas and new techniques were appearing so rapidly that it was proving very difficult for teachers to keep up with them. The obvious need was for some form of continuous training. Johnson felt that administrators should give teachers more freedom to experiment and more encouragement to look into new ideas, methods, and materials. He advocated closer liaison between American and Canadian learning centres. He also expected the administration to take positive steps toward ending the existing practice of grouping handicapped children by their major disability. He believed that there should be a greater effort to integrate the disabled child, where possible, into a regular classroom. While total integration would be unwise, many children seemed to be held for too long in segregated classes.

One of Johnson's chief points of criticism was that there was often inadequate screening. Too many opportunity classes had a mixture of physically handicapped and emotionally disturbed children, along with those who were mentally retarded. The few children in such classes who might really benefit from the program were unable to do so because the teacher could not cope with the number and variety of problems presented. Johnson was convinced, despite frequent denials, that there was too much reliance on IQ scores for the assessment of children. He claimed that multidisciplined assessments were almost totally unheard of in the regular school system. All too often, a psychologist was called upon to make a reliable diagnosis in a one-hour period. What the situation required was a program of testing extending over several weeks. It seemed desirable to give less attention to testing to determine academic progress and more to identifying the causes of difficulty.

Johnson found considerable cause for concern in the lack of edequate communication. Psychologists too often made brief visits amid a swirl of tests and scores and then disappeared for another year. Regular classroom teachers were said to have almost no understanding of special education and to be unable to play an appropriate part in identifying the symptoms of learning problems. Johnson deplored the tendency of many psychologists to withhold the truth from parents and talk down to them. While he acknowledged that there were some parents who were emotional and totally non-objective, he declared that there were many who would not be satisfied with less than honest answers to their questions. There was a greater need for teamwork and co-operation than in other areas of education because the special education teacher and the parent both had a greater need for help.

THE MENTALLY RETARDED

The mentally retarded group, as observed earlier, is one of those for which Ontario, within its resources and by the standards of the time, has shown a high level of concern. Most experts have been reluctant to classify retarded children into subgroups solely on the basis of IQ because such a measure covers only certain aspects of their adaptation to their total environment. In very rough terms, however, those with an IQ below 25 are unable to look after themselves and require hospital care. Those in the 25–50 range are not considered educable in the ordinary sense, but are usually capable of personal care and of engaging in a variety of simple activities. While they have not been able to benefit from any of the regular traditional school programs, they have been trained in special classes and schools. Those in the 50–75 range, although unable to keep up with ordinary school work, have been successfully handled in auxiliary classes with specially qualified teachers.

Review of situation in 1957

A landmark address by Allan Grossman in reply to the Speech from the Throne in 1957 provides an excellent starting point for a review of recent development in the treatment of the mentally retarded. As a government supporter, Grossman could be counted on to give full recognition to the previous contributions of various departments. At the same time, he made it quite clear that there was a great deal more to be accomplished. "Even the most limited investigation of their problems and what is being done about them discloses that, although worthy efforts are being made, both by government and by private organizations, neither an adequate nor a co-ordinated programme of assistance has been evolved."[12]

Grossman commented on the slowly changing sense of community responsibility toward the mentally handicapped. The days were passing when the subnormal child was isolated or even ostracized by the family. New methods and ideas of treatment, training, and rehabilitation were being explored. While research into treatment was still in its infancy, it was becoming increasingly evident that the retarded child was subject to favourable and unfavourable influences and was definitely amenable to training measures. For example, the Surgeon-General in the United States had estimated that 75 per cent of the 1.5 million retarded children in that country were capable of rehabilitation and of becoming productive citizens.

Improved medical techniques were resulting in the survival of an increasing number of mental retardates. Because of what Grossman called an appalling lack of statistical information, no one knew how many retardates there were in Ontario. If estimates from the United States could be used as a guide, however, and 1 per cent of the population consisted of retarded children, the provincial total would be over fifty thousand. On the basis of an estimate of the Ontario Association for Retarded Children that 2 or 3 per cent of the total population were retarded, the provincial total of all ages would be over 100,000. Their age distribution was solely a matter of statistical speculation.

An adequate program had to be based on the needs of all ages, with a recognition that the handicap of mental retardation existed throughout life. There needed to be early diagnosis, appropriate school placement, suitable home management, medical treatment and therapy, and directed social and recreational activity. As the child grew, he required vocational education and guidance, job training and placement, suitable social outlets, and adequate living arrangements. Grossman saw the rehabilitation of the retarded as a many-sided undertaking involving a large number of skills and, where government was concerned, cutting across the responsibilities of more than one department. A complete program of assistance called for an array of facilities far beyond the resources of the average family.

Grossman touched on the tremendous problems confronting the parents of a mentally defective child. They lacked the numerous guidelines that assisted them in dealing with normal children, including their own experiences and those of others, the contributions of modern child psychology, and the assistance of teachers. The particular stresses and strains placed upon a family with a retarded child could lead to serious disruption. Unsympathetic and unhealthy attitudes from outside the family often created a sense of shame, guilt, and anxiety on the part of the parents. Callous advice from professional and non-professional people sometimes aggravated the difficulty.[13]

In reviewing existing government programs for the mentally retarded, Grossman first dealt with the contributions of the Department of Health, which provided diagnostic services to retarded children through its mental health clinics. There was, however, no special clinic in Ontario staffed by members of various interested disciplines which provided treatment services for the retarded. The services that existed did not, futhermore, fully cover the province. There were mental health centres in only six of the forty-two centres where the Ontario Association for Retarded Children operated schools. Grossman felt that the clinical approach was too often connected with institutional commitment. Staff of mental health clinics were required, should they diagnose a case of retardation requiring treatment, to recommend commitment to an Ontario hospital school.

At that time, the Department of Health operated two hospital schools for mentally retarded children, one at Orillia and the other at Smiths Falls, with a third for southwestern Ontario in the planning stage. These institutions provided custodial care for children between the ages of three and sixteen who were certifiable as permanently mentally retarded. As of the previous year, they were looking after a total of 4,138, with a waiting list of 2,150. The proposed new school would accommodate slightly more than the number on the current waiting list but, by the time the facilities were completed, the list would undoubtedly have grown considerably. The staff numbered 703 at Orillia and 740 at Smiths Falls. Each had a medical superintendent and a medical staff of nine. Smiths Falls had two psychologists and one occupational therapist, while Orillia had one psychologist and no therapist.

Grossman referred next to the auxiliary classes operated in the school system for pupils with IQs over 50. The percentage of retarded children of school age attending these classes and those operated by private organizations was not known. Estimates from the United States, where there had been a substantial improvement in the immediate past, had indicated that not more than 20 per cent of the retardates were in the public system. Grossman referred to authoritative opinions to the effect that adequate provision for this group in the schools might bring about a substantial reduction in the need for institutionalization.

Apart from the Department of Education, the major agency providing for the needs of the group in question was the Ontario Association for Retarded Children. At that time the local units of the association, with a membership of 3,100, operated forty-two day schools with an enrolment of somewhat under one thousand. In 1953 the government had introduced legislation providing for assistance to this association. Grants were made to its schools for children under eighteen years of age who could look after their physical needs, but who would not attain a mental capacity beyond that of an eight year old. In 1957 the grants amounted to $250 per pupil for half-day attendance and $500 for full-day attendance. Grossman acknowledged that the association did not regard the grant as sufficient for its needs, and that it had been pressing for an increase in order to provide a more adequate supplement to parental and local government contributions and charitable donations. Transportation costs were particularly high, amounting to as much as 23 per cent of the total cost and 40 per cent of the provincial grant. Grossman threw his weight behind the association's request for a higher level of assistance.

There was cause for concern that there was no standard governing teacher's qualifications in retarded children's schools. While some had regular teacher training, others lacked a certificate of any kind. Grossman supported the idea that the Ontario hospital schools might provide training grounds for teachers seeking special qualifications. He advocated also the establishment of appropriate curricula in the teachers' colleges and of a five-week summer course similar to that offered auxiliary class teachers.

Very little research was being conducted at the time in the Ontario hospital schools into the cause, preventive treatment, and rehabilitative treatment of mental retardation. Grossman referred to this situation as astonishing. At the universtiy level, there were two requests before the Departmental of National Health and Welfare for amounts between $20,000 and $30,000 to study genetics and the biochemistry of cells as they affected retardation. The Ontario Association for Retarded Children had provided $17,500 for basic research over a three-year period.

Grossman ended with a general prescription which in some ways was a blueprint for later action.

I am obliged to state that if education is the responsibility of duly constituted local authorities, then the schooling of the less fortunate must equally be theirs – for the mentally retarded are children also! I believe it is desirable to encourage, wherever possible, the integration of retarded children into the general school system.

Finally, may I say that although we have been principally concerned with the school age retardate, it would be foolish to suppose that the problem ends there. As the mentally retarded child grows into adulthood, he is unlikely to find his productive capacities put to use unless a programme is evolved to sustain him in the community under noncompetitive conditions.

The extent to which we now assist subnormals over 18 is through disabled persons' allowance. Roughly a third of the 7,600 people in the province receiving these allowances are mentally retarded – one of the few clues, incidentally to the number of adult retardates. However, these allowances are paid only to retardates who are totally and permanently disabled.

Inasmuch as the needs of this class of adult are not being considered under The Rehabilitation Services Act, our present policy would seem to lend weight to the charge that we are presuming the mentally retarded must either become fully independent, self-supporting adults or else totally disabled and dependent, a theory, of course, completely in conflict with the evidence.

If the adult retarded are to be kept in this highly specialized and competitive society of ours as useful citizens, it will be necessary to provide more private residences, perhaps to subsidize them, to provide such things as job training centres and sheltered employment workshops. It is unlikely that this need will, or can, be filled by volunteer effort alone.[14]

Schools for slow learners

An example of the way in which school boards were providing for the needs of slow learning pupils at the beginning of the 1960s was offered by Alex MacLean, who described the program in the Frank Oke School in York Township, of which he was principal.[15] The building that housed the school after January 1958 had accommodation for two hundred boys who were taught in groups of twenty. There were five classrooms, five shops, and a gymnasium. Applicants were screened by an admissions board made up of the superintendent, inspectors, the Medical Officer of Health, the Supervisor of Special Classes, and the principal of the school. The Medical Officer of Health participated in order to identify physical handicaps such as poor hand-motor co-ordination. The criteria for admission were IQ and age. It was intended that at least 75 per cent of the pupils should have an IQ of 80. The minimum chronological age was twelve, and the minimum mental age, eight and a half. Boys over thirteen were accepted only under unusual circumstances, since they were not considered likely to remain long enough in the program to make it worthwhile.

The school was classified as elementary so that shop teachers with a background of elementary teaching with the addition of an industrial Arts Certificate could be employed. The students were divided into two groups, junior and senior, which rotated through five periods each day. The juniors had three academic periods and two shops, while the seniors had two academic periods and three shops. Placement was according to mental age and achievement. The filmstrip method, and in some cases the kinaesthetic method, were used for reading instruction. The reading program utilized school publications and periodicals, while the spelling program was based on words from shops and trades. Knowledge of the fundamentals of arithmetic was extended by application to practical situations. The industrial arts department provided a wide variety of experiences with materials, tools, and machines in the industrial arts field. There were introductory courses in leather, plastics, sheet metal, and ceramics. MacLean described the equipment as follows.

Three well-equipped shops have been set up for the senior school. A representative sample of modern machines including a planer, radial saw, table saw, jointter, gap-bed lathes, band saw, and drill presses make the senior wood shop well fitted for courses in advanced woodwork. Courses in sheet metal, electronics and auto body repair are offered in the second shop. Oxy-acetylene welding equipment, spray equipment, and the various body tools and jacks permit the boys to work on actual cars. The third senior shop is equipped for advanced work in machine shop, forge and welding. The milling machine, shaper, lathes, and metal-cutting saw give scope for a variety of experiences in machine work. Gas and coal forges, oxy-acetylene, arc and spot welders provide facilities for many types of metal fabrication. A special spray room has been included for finishing. Modern barbering equipment enables this trade to be taught to a limited number, and helps to maintain a high standard of grooming.[16]

Recent trends favour keeping pupils with widely varying abilities in the same school, while providing appropriate programs to suit individual needs. MacLean, however, felt that, for boys of limited ability, a special school was a relief from the feeling of isolation they experienced in a regular class or in a special class in an ordinary school. They could experience success on their own terms and thus developed a new interest. Parents of the boys were said to be commenting favourably on the results being achieved.

Hospital programs

In 1961 the Minister of Health, Matthew Dymond, provided a sketch of the educational and training programs at the hospital school at Orillia. The fundamental purpose was to prepare the child for a useful, purposeful, and happy life in accordance with his ability. The program was "not intellectualization, but socialization."

Administratively, the school is organized into a number of departments centring their attention on the individual's emotional and physical needs, in an attempt to make the programme of treatment, care and training an effective one. Utilizing procedures of study, periodic evaluation and programme planning, the school endeavours to promote, whenever possible, the individual's ability to meet the problems of everyday life through improving social adjustments, broadening interests and skills, stabilizing emotions, learning useful tasks and understanding self. The institution is a community striving to provide for each individual a happy home, opportunities for training, health of mind and body and rehabilitation for those with capacity and social adequacy for community life outside.[17]

There were three main divisions of the training program: pre-school, academic, and occupational and trade training. In the first of these, the child was taught to walk and talk, to control elimination, to dress and feed himself, and to play with others. The academic program was conducted in lower and upper departments. The lower department was for children with the capacity for kindergarten, ultimate self-care, and return to their own homes. Sense training dealt with taste, sound, smell, colour and form. Many of the children had difficulty learning to co-ordinate their muscles. Skills in this area were developed through stringing beads, cutting, sewing and weaving on cards, pasting, colouring, and cutting out paper dolls. At the end of kindergarten training, emphasis was placed on the development of language. Very beneficial results were attained through musical games. In the upper academic department, the course consisted of simple arithmetic, exercises in reading a ruler, the use of weights and measures, changing money, reading simple material for enjoyment, writing simple compositions including letters, and a certain amount of geography, history, and civics. (In view of the level of achievement that some of these children could apparently reach, one recalls Grossman's suggestion that fewer children would need to be institutionalized if adequate facilities of other types were available.) Music in the form of singing and rhythm bands was relied on heavily.

At the stage where manual training was appropriate, there was a reasonably well-equipped room where boys learned to use and care for tools and made toys, bird houses, and other articles for the institution itself. Each year a hobby fair was held, and prizes were awarded. Domestic science classes were held for the girls, with cooking taught by the hospital's dietitian. In the class corresponding to that offering manual training for the boys, the girls also studied sewing, eventually having an opportunity, if they made good progress, to use power machines.

Puppetry had been found to have considerable educational as well as recreational value. The children had begun by fashioning fist puppets in their classes and later had been provided with a puppet stage where they could express themselves with a measure of confidence. Children with speech problems were encouraged to take part. Tape recordings were sometimes made and played back to the group to arouse interest in self-improvement.

At the conclusion of the period spent in the academic school, where the children might reach the grade 5 level, some continued in the junior vocational program where they spent part of their time in school and part in some occupation or trade. The next phase was trade training, where the sexes were separated for the first time. Unitized operations in industry were considered ideally suited for the trained defective, since he never tired of the most routine tasks. Dymond offered a long list of occupations in which he could engage. A placement officer helped to smooth the transition from the hospital school to employment.

Support for schools for retarded children

A great many people could see no good reason why school boards, with adequate provincial grants, should not assume the entire responsibility for mentally retarded children. In 1960 V.M. Singer, member for York Centre, pointed out that parents, as members of local associations, got about 30 per cent of the approved costs of the necessary school buildings from the government and had to raise the balance of the capital costs themselves. While operating grants covered 90 per cent of regular costs, they still left the high transportation costs to be raised by voluntary effort. In some parts of the province, service clubs had generously and devotedly filled the gap, but in many places there were no such clubs, and it was impossible to find the required funds.[18] While Robarts, as Minister of Education, expressed sympathy with the idea of having the department and the local boards assume the entire responsibility, the objective was not achieved for some years.

When Robarts was taken to task in 1962 for failure to move the retarded children completely into the public school system, he declared that the delay was not because the government was unwilling to spend the necessary funds, but because there were other problems that were proving difficult to solve. There was no agreement on the part of members of the Ontario Association for Retarded Children that the proposed course of action was the proper one. Since the association was made up almost entirely of parents of the children, it did not seem desirable to force the issue. What would happen to the sensitivities of these parents if the local school systems took over? Under existing conditions, only 50 per cent of the retarded children in Metropolitan Toronto were attending schools of any kind. Many of the rest were tucked away in back rooms from which their parents were reluctant to have them emerge. Among other difficulties was that the attendance areas of the schools did not correspond to any political boundaries.

In April 1964 Davis reviewed progress from the time, eleven years earlier, when the department had begun to make grants to local associations. More than forty new schools had been constructed, and over four hundred teachers had received summer course training. Eighty-four associations were currently operating eighty-seven schools with a total enrolment of approximately 2,750 children.[19]

Studies were undertaken in 1963 to develop a plan by which the schools could be operated by legally constituted bodies and the departmental grant could be a percentage of approved cost, including that of transportation. A detailed analysis of the financial situation was carried out, and consultations were held with various organizations, including the Ontario Association for Retarded Children. As a result, legislation was introduced in 1964 to provide for the establishment of Retarded Children's Education Authorities to assume responsibility for the operation and financing of the schools. A local association affiliated with the Ontario Association for Retarded Children might petition the council of a municipality in which there were at least ten resident retarded children to establish an authority, an action that it might take with the approval of the minister. In order to ensure their continued involvement, the local associations were given two representatives on each authority, while the council appointed the other four. They also retained title to their buildings and property. Beginning in 1965 the authorities received departmental grants amounting to 80 per cent of their total budget, including the cost of transportation. The remainder was raised from that time on entirely through municipal taxation, with no further need to rely on charity drives. The department at the same time raised its contribution to capital expenditure to 50 per cent of approved costs.

In the Legislature, K. Bryden took exception to the solution reached by the government.

> We believe that the administration should be the responsibility of the school boards, not with the idea that there will be an integration necessarily into the regular school system, but that the same people will be responsible for the administration of this phase of educational effort. After all, for school boards, education is the sole preoccupation; that is the sole thing they are concerned about. Municipal councils are only secondarily interested in education. They have before them many problems which in terms of their responsibility are more pressing than educational problems. That is why we feel that the people who spend all their time, in their capacity as elected representatives, concerning themselves with educational problems are the people who are best qualified to deal with this matter.[20]

Two years later, according to a report made by the minister in 1967, the number of schools for trainable retarded children had reached ninety-seven, and the enrolment was 3,753. A second summer course had been provided to augment the program for teachers of such children. By comparison with the two-week course available ten years earlier, substantial progress seemed to have been made. In any absolute sense, however, provisions for teacher training were still grossly inadequate. Behind the scenes, Davis was searching for a means of providing more effective measures.[21]

The Department of Education was co-operating with the Department of Health in providing educational programs in institutions. In September 1966 the engagement of five principals and fifty teachers had brought the total number of staff involved in this activity to 101. Classes for educable children were kept to a maximum of fifteen pupils, those for trainable children to ten, and those for children with multiple handicaps to five or six. The total enrolment of 1,054 in 1966 consisted of 620 educable children, 290 trainable children, and 144 children with multiple handicaps.

Davis was able to report gratifying progress in meeting the needs of those with a lesser degree of retardation. In the populous parts of the province, and in the county and township school areas where central schools were being built, school boards were being encouraged to provide special education classes for slow learners in the elementary schools, special classes for the emotionally disturbed who had the prospect of returning to regular classes, and occupational and service trade classes in secondary schools for students who were transferred from grade 8. Almost every city with four or five secondary schools had a special vocational school, and all composite schools outside the cities included occupational classes as a matter of course.[22]

When the divisional boards were created, they were made responsible for the operation of programs for trainable retarded children, and the Retarded Children's Education Authorities were dissolved. According to the legislation, each board was to establish an advisory committee on schools for these children. Of the six members, three were to be appointed by the board from among its members and three by the local association for retarded children. Funds for the operation of the program, both current and capital, were raised in the same way as those for secondary schools. Thus the schools were supported by both public and separate school taxpayers. The representatives of the separate school supporters on the divisional boards for separate school purposes were also representatives with respect to the programs for trainable retarded children.

According to the regulations, a child below the age of ten years could attend only the morning or afternoon classes in a session lasting between two and one-half and three hours. Between the ages of ten and eighteen, he might attend for the full day provided that he had the approval of a legally qualified medical practitioner and of the admissions board. Admission to the school was contingent on an intellectual assessment conducted by a person considered competent by the admissions board and a medical examination conducted by a qualified practitioner. The admissions board had the right, after a hearing, to dismiss a child who was judged incorrigible or unable to profit from instruction.

THE PHYSICALLY HANDICAPPED

Part of the story of how Ontario has provided for the education of physically handicapped children has to do with the Ontario School for the Blind at Brantford and the Ontario Schools for the Deaf at Belleville and Milton. The origin and functions of these institutions were dealt with in volume II, chapter 2. The Brantford school has at times looked after a considerable number of children from other provinces. In 1956 W.J. Dunlop reported that of the 182 in attendance twenty-six were from Manitoba, twenty-three from Saskatchewan, and thirteen from Alberta, for each of whom the respective provincial government paid $750 a year. Ontario had a similar arrangement with institutions in Montreal to provide for its French-speaking children.

At the Belleville school, the children were given an academic program carrying them about a year beyond grade 8, after which they spent another year in vocational work. Those at Brantford were first taught Braille, and then given an opportunity to go as far as the end of grade 12. They often remained at the school until they were twenty-one, after which the Canadian National Institute for the Blind assisted them to find suitable occupations.

Early in the twentieth century, children with the same types of handicaps in varying degrees began to be taught in regular schools. Observation of the ways in which those with impaired sight could be helped led to measures to assist children with other handicaps. Urban systems, and even some of those in rural areas, began to set up special facilities. After 1918 the Canadian National Institute for the Blind assisted with the care of children who could not, for various reasons, be admitted to the Ontario School for the Blind. Some of these were able to attend regular classes, and others were given instruction at home.

One of the first measures to serve the malnourished and sickly was taken in Toronto in 1908, when the Hospital for Sick Children established an open-air class on Toronto Island. This class was later taken over by the Toronto Board of Education, which opened forest schools for similar purposes in High Park and Alexandra Park in 1912. Health classes were also set up within a number of schools.

The Ontario Society for Crippled Children, formed in 1922, worked for the establishment and improvement of facilities for the group referred to in its title. Among these were the cerebral palsied, for whom classes or schools were established. The organization also conducted surveys of the cerebral palsied in such places as Chatham and Windsor. The Cerebral Palsy Association was later organized and performed an active role after the Second World War.

Sunnyview School in Toronto pioneered in the education of physically handicapped children, whom it admitted with the approval of an orthopaedic surgeon from the Hospital for Sick Children. They had to be considered educable as determined by a test of learning capacity administered by a psychologist. Apart from special measures to deal with their handicaps, the curriculum was the same as that in the regular schools.

An example of a full-time physiotherapy treatment centre designed to assist with the rehabilitation of handicapped children was the Orthopaedic Unit opened in Sault Ste Marie in September 1952. Three years later, the program was extended to include pre-school children whose deformities were corrected, where possible, before they reached school age so that they could attend regular classes. The unit was supported by federal and provincial grants, by the local board of education, and by the Rotary Club. The board provided the building, its upkeep and maintenance, and the salaries of teachers and other staff members. The Rotary Club paid for the transportation of the children by taxi, for the services of the therapist and matron, for special equipment such as braces, crutches, and wheel chairs, for beds and bedding for the rest room, and for part of the individual treatment and hospital care. In 1961 the staff included a teacher, a physiotherapist, a matron, and two assistants.[23]

A very impressive program has been carried on by the Ontario Society for Crippled Children, which was reported in 1968 to be providing a variety of services for more than sixteen thousand crippled children. It maintained five rehabilitation centres, four centres for crippled children, thirteen cerebral palsy centres, four orthopaedic classes, and one orthopaedic school. With the co-operation of the Variety Club of Toronto, it operated a vocational school for orthopaedically handicapped boys between sixteen and eighteen years of age who had successfully completed grade 8 and were unable to secure training elsewhere. Where the society provided educational services, the Department of Education assisted with grants that covered 80 per cent of the teachers' salaries.

In a review of the problems of the perceptually handicapped in an address to the Legislature in 1965, Stephen Lewis defined the group as those who had suffered damage to the central nervous system by accident, infection, or unknown cause, whether before, at, or after birth. Many of them had multiple handicaps, such as speech and hearing disorders. It was common to find emotional disturbances in addition to special handicaps. As a group, they were primarily categorized by hyperactivity, by distractibility, and by lack of motor control. The ones Lewis was most concerned with were those with normal intelligence for whom it was possible to develop programs to reinstate them in the school system. He illustrated their problems for the members.

> As an example, imagine a telephone switchboard that went out of order and all the incoming messages were relayed at once over the same receiver at top volume, six times the normal speed and with every other word left out. The confusion, frustration and panic of the child who lives constantly in this world of loudly distorted images can only, I suggest, be imagined. It is not surprising that he is hyper-distractible, since so many stimuli enter his brain at once, unfiltered and at top volume you might say, that he cannot help but be hyper-active.
>
> This is further complicated in that many of the children have difficulty in controlling their physical actions and reactions. In addition to hyper-activity there can be sudden bouts of laughter, sudden uncontrollable bouts of crying, sudden shifts in mood. They may be clumsy physically, the difficulties in school are enormous. Where another child may see a drawing of a house, the perceptually handicapped child may look at the same picture and perceive only a chimney or a single detail of the door. The ticking of the clock may be as forceful to his ears as the teacher's voice.[24]

Lewis indicated that the incidence of perceptual handicaps was extremely high. In February of the same year, the Ontario Association for Children with Learning Disabilities had estimated it at 5 per cent of the population. An American expert had claimed that at least 10 per cent of the children of average intelligence in schools in the United States suffered from severe reading disorders originating from disturbances of perception. A similar percentage of the population in Denmark had been found to have a specific reading disability. Lewis pointed out that only a small percentage of the children with perceptual problems needed special classes, but even between 0.5 and 1 per cent of the children of school age in Ontario amounted to over ten thousand.

Lewis went on to say that there were well-developed methods of treating such children. The basis of one approach was to eliminate all distractions. The room was painted in a uniform colour, all the cupboards were enclosed, the windows were frosted, and the floors were carpeted. There were no clocks or decorations and as little furniture and equipment as possible. In some cases, the temperature and humidity of the room were strictly regulated. The classroom schedule was tightly ordered. In many respects, the approach was the opposite to that used for emotionally disturbed children, for whom all the apparatus and techniques of the modern classroom were often important parts of the treatment.

Again Lewis referred to a small number of classes in the larger centres in Ontario, but emphasized the tremendous unfilled need. As in the case of the emotionally disturbed, experiments had demonstrated that treatment could be successful. A number of examples from various places in the United States were cited to prove the point. A class had been introduced in London, Ontario, in 1960, with teachers sent to Syracuse for the training that was not available in Ontario. Out of a total of twenty-four children, fourteen had been returned to regular classes, and only one was unsuccessful. Under ordinary circumstances, they would have been unable to fit into the main stream, and would probably have ended up by being expelled.

In a departmental memorandum issued in 1967, principals of secondary schools were urged to assist their teachers to understand the needs of perceptually handicapped students so that they would derive maximum benefit from their program. The perceptually handicapped were defined as those who suffered from a specific deficiency attributable to a malfunction of the central nervous system. They were said to require the same understanding as those with more obvious handicaps such as blindness, deafness, and cerebral palsy. Many possessed the intellectual capacity to benefit from a secondary school program leading to university entrance. The memorandum suggested that, since vocational or occupational programs were not suitable for some of those with perceptual problems, they be offered a modified program in the Arts and Science Branch. An individualized program was to be devised for each student allowing for his specific type of dysfunction. When necessary, special arrangements were to be made for the student to work alone in a quiet place, to take a longer period of time than usual to write examinations, or to dictate answers to assignments and tests.[25]

The following year in another memorandum regarding perceptually handicapped children, elementary school officials were warned that such children, whether or not they had good intellectual potential, usually had undue difficulty in learning to read, spell, and do arithmetic, in following directions, in controlling their behaviour, and in concentrating on or performing tasks that required physical co-ordination. Planning was recommended on the basis of multi-professional diagnosis. It was suggested that segregated classes might be necessary for those who were highly distractible in large groups. On the other hand, if consultative help and special materials were available to the teacher, regular class placement might constitute the best approach. School officials were urged to hold frequent conferences to consider the pupil's academic, social, and behavioural progress and to co-ordinate planning between the home and the school.[26]

Children with a variety of handicaps have been provided, in the more progressive systems, with home instruction. The Department of Education assisted this type of activity until the end of the 1960s with special grants. Regulations made such a subsidy dependent on each child's receiving a minimum amount of instruction per week.

THE EMOTIONALLY DISTURBED

A definition of the emotionally handicapped originating with E.M. Bower referred to five typical characteristics: 1 / an inability to learn that cannot be satisfactorily explained by intellectual, sensory, or health factors; 2 / an unsatisfactory relationship with peers and teachers; 3 / a tendency to exhibit inappropriate behaviour under normal circumstances; 4 / a feeling of general unhappiness or depression; and 5 / the development of physical symptoms or fears with respect to school or personal problems. All five symptoms are not necessarily manifested in every emotionally handicapped child. Underachievement is the most common and obvious symptom, and the one that most often leads to a request for professional assistance.[27]

R.G. Stennett, a professor and educational administrator in London, Ontario, delineated certain manifestations of emotional disturbance, with a description of the background against which they develop.

> The social and emotional immaturity that form the basis of the underachievement syndrome are produced by a variety of special circumstances. Among the more common are those in which a child has been overindulged because of his favored position in the family as an only child, an only boy or girl, or one who is the "baby" in the family. Some of these children display the "vulnerable child syndrome". In these cases, the child has suffered some prolonged, serious or life-threatening physical illness in his early years. This has provoked intense parental anxiety which has persisted beyond the point justified by the physical condition. The parents, continuing to regard the child as fragile or vulnerable, tend to be overindulgent. This constitutes a special problem for the physician, who must take care that he does not unwittingly communicate to the parents a conviction that their child is unusually vulnerable.
>
> Whatever the immediate cause of the parents' tendency to indulge their youngster, or to make insufficient demands on him for control and responsible behavior, the usual outcome is inconsistent discipline. This, in turn, produces a defect in the child's ability to inhibit his impulses, make decisions and persist at activities which do not please him; i.e., he does not mature. This poor self-control is accompanied by underlying insecurity, weak or spotty conscience devel-

opment and a failure to develop adequate skills. Therefore, the child does not receive the usual satisfactions and self-enhancement that come from development of skill. These deficits produce thinly veiled feelings of inadequacy which lead him to make inappropriate bids for attention ...

The typical adult response to such a youngster is to remind him repeatedly of his responsibilities and scold continually in vain. This generates resentment in the child which further interferes with his already weak motivation for constructive work. The child often retaliates by passive-aggressive behavior against what he perceives as "mean" adults. This in turn, provokes additional negative attention from the supervising adult. Thus, a downward spiral is set in motion: underachievement; nagging and ineffectual disciplinary methods; poor application with discouragement, and increased hostility on the part of the youngster. The long-term effect of this cycle is usually reflected in consistently poorer grades as the child moves over the elementary school years.[28]

In the same paper, Stennett reviewed evidence that children who display visible signs of behaviour disorder early in their lives are reasonably amenable to treatment. If they are not treated, however, they cannot be counted on to outgrow their difficulties. As they proceed through school, they commonly encounter more problems and tend eventually to drop out. Many of them are later diagnosed and institutionalized or otherwise treated as delinquents, schizophrenics, psychosomatics, etc. The importance of early diagnosis and treatment is, therefore, difficult to exaggerate.

The Out-patient Department of the Toronto Psychiatric Hospital offered the first psychiatric consultation service for children in 1926. Four years later, the Department of Health established travelling psychiatric clinics and in 1945 began to provide area consultants in clinics in general hospitals. Legislation authorized the school to seek the services of a psychiatrist to deal with an educational problem. The service was available to the school rather than to the parent. As a result of consultation with a psychiatrist, ordinarily involving an examination of the child, the principal might inform the parents of the nature and degree of a disturbance and might recommend that the family take measures to obtain treatment.

The Thistletown Hospital in Etobicoke was purchased by the provincial government in 1957 to serve as a residential treatment centre for emotionally disturbed children under the Department of Health. Provision was made for the admission of children in the same way that patients were admitted to a public hospital. Applications for admission were submitted from mental health clinics, private practitioners, social agencies, or parents. Applicants were considered by an admissions committee representing the various interests involved in treatment, and admitted if it was felt that a diagnostic or treatment service could be provided that was not available on an out-patient basis. In 1961, when the maximum number of children the hospital could accommodate was 65, there were 175 staff members performing administrative and professional tasks. The psychiatric staff consisted of a superintendent, two staff psychiatrists, and two senior post-graduate psychiatrists enrolled in a course in child psychiatry at the University of Toronto. The psychological department consisted of a chief psychologist and two other full-time psychologists. There were also two full-time social workers, five nurses, and approximately ninety-five child care workers under the direction of a chief child care worker. One of the main functions of the hospital was to provide for the training of child care workers. A research program of increasing importance was developed as the hospital became established.[29]

In 1963 the Ottawa School Board tried a new procedure for helping emotionally disturbed children in the public schools. The idea was that many of these children might benefit from periods of individual attention from a sympathetic adult. The services of members of the University Women's Club were utilized for the purpose. Each participating member was assigned a particular child by the school psychologist. At least twice a week, she took him out of his regular classroom to give him individual attention and instruction. With some guidance from the psychologist, the principal, and the teacher, but mainly on her own initiative, she devised ways of winning the child's confidence, restoring his self-respect, and helping him to learn to the limit of his capacity. By the end of the second year, when ten regular workers had helped approximately thirty children, the project was considered an established feature of the Ottawa public school system.[30]

In 1964 the Ontario Association for Emotionally Disturbed Children presented a brief to the Minister of Education urging better provision for the group of children toward whose welfare its efforts were directed. The brief indicated that only a small proportion of emotionally disturbed children were discovered early enough, and that, even when they were identified, treatment was often neglected. The following recommendations were made: 1 / that educational legislation be changed to make provision for special education by school boards compulsory rather than optional, as it was under existing conditions; 2 / that the Department of Education assume leadership in helping school boards provide educational opportunities for emotionally disturbed children; 3 / that emotionally disturbed children be educated, as far as possible in the same schools as normal children in preference to special institutions; 4 / that the Department of Education sponsor surveys to determine the number of emotionally disturbed children in the province and the percentage of such children who were educable; and 5 / that the department assume greater responsibility for the education of these children in remote areas and in other areas where the school boards were unable to provide for them. The minister expressed sympathy with these recommendations but, as far as the first one at least was concerned, found it impossible to move too quickly because of the shortage of teachers with the kind of training that would be needed. A summer course was, however, scheduled for 1965. Davis indicated that a survey was being conducted by the department to try to determine the dimensions of the problem.

In the address to the Legislature already mentioned, Stephen Lewis recognized that there had been special emphasis, special financing, special classes, and special attention for blind, deaf, retarded, and crippled children. He declared, however, that the educational system had not yet begun to understand or respond to the emotionally disturbed child.[31] With respect to this type of disability, he reported an estimate that one per cent of the school-age population should have special classes or special attention within the regular school stream. The number would amount to over twenty thousand children, adolescents, and young adults in Ontario. Reviewing the existing situation, he contended that there were many children in opportunity classes who should not be there. The problem was not that they lacked normal intelligence, but that their intelligence did not function properly. Serious damage might result from their retention in such classes if these were not properly organized. Lewis asserted that psychological services were desperately thin. Even in the city of Toronto, there was only one psychologist for every four or five thousand pupils, although UNESCO, the American Psychiatric Association, and similar organizations had estimated that one for every thousand was needed. While there was permissive legislation for special classes, it was hardly operative. There was one class in North York, one in Etobicoke, and one in Toronto. Scarborough was planning to set up two classes in the following year to serve twelve children with emotional disturbances and perceptual handicaps. The total school population of the municipality at that time was about 48,000.

Experiments with special classes, both in Ontario and elsewhere, had apparently been profoundly successful. Etobicoke was returning children to the regular stream, and North York's efforts at rehabilitation were equally productive. In Elmont county in New York, volunteer mothers from the community had worked successfully with schizophrenic and autistic children on a one-to-one basis, developing a learning procedure to suit each individual child and placing great emphasis on love and affection. During a three-year period, twenty-seven out of fifty schizophrenic children diagnosed as ineducable had been returned from the League School in Brooklyn to the main stream of the educational system.

Lewis made the following series of suggestions for the prevention and treatment of emotional disturbances in children: 1 / that the most highly qualified teachers, preferably with university degrees, be assigned to teach primary school children, who were at the most critical and vulnerable stage of emotional as well as physical development; 2 / that the Department of Education asume responsibility for the education of all educable children, including the emotionally disturbed, which would involve "open grants" to local school boards and the development of special programs such as sheltered classes, special classes, home teaching, and maladjustment services; 3 / that in any central bureau in the department with the responsibility of overseeing special education projects, no particular profession or clinical discipline be allowed to dominate, but that variety and experimentation of every kind be promoted; 4 / that school boards be encouraged and directed to investigate and establish liaison with mental health services in their communities; 5 / that problem case conferences involving school supervisors, social workers, clinical personnel, citizen groups, and local mental health agencies meet at regular intervals; 6 / that the Ontario College of Education and the teachers' colleges provide standard courses in human growth and development, child behaviour, the detection of abnormal behaviour, emotional aspects of learning, and the fostering of mental health in the classroom; 7 / that the department provide funds and encouragement to any approved and interested group wishing to start a day nursery for emotionally disturbed children; 8 / that more guidance counsellors be provided for both elementary and secondary schools, and that they have no educational duties other than counselling; and 9 / that the Department of Education underwrite the cost of day schools for in-patient and out-patient emotionally disturbed children.[32]

Continuing his campaign a year later for greater effort on behalf of the same group, Lewis estimated that, at a ratio of one trained person for every two thousand students, it would take 836 such people to meet the need. This would mean one to every seventy-four teachers and one for every eight schools. By his reckoning, the province fell short by over seven hundred people. The result, as the Select Committee on Youth had noted in travelling around the province, was that emotionally disturbed children were suspended from school, and a sense of despair and frustration was widespread.[33]

The plan of 1967

In 1967 Matthew Dymond tabled a white paper outlining the principles and policies of a co-ordinated program to provide additional services and facilities for the treatment of children suffering from mental and emotional disturbances. The paper was the result of more than a year's work by the deputy minister and senior officials of the Departments of Health, Education, Public Welfare, Reform Institutions, and the Attorney General. Dymond indicated that steps were already being taken to implement various aspects of the program.[34]

The plan would involve close collaboration among the five departments mentioned, and maximum participation on the part of voluntary agencies. Co-ordination of the program would be the responsibility of the Department of Health. First priority was to be given to additional facilities for assessment and treatment, for which the participating departments would provide staff and arrange adequate follow-up. Regional diagnostic, assessment, and treatment centres were to be established by the Department of Health throughout the province to provide out-patient, day-care, and in-patient services. Local agencies would receive technical advice and financial assistance. Pilot projects would be encouraged and supported. Bursaries would be offered to assist students entering the field of children's mental and emotional health care. Seminars, workshops, and institutes would be provided to improve the qualifications of the people involved.

An educational campaign would be conducted to apprise parents and others working with children of the symptoms of mental and emotional disturbance. Training programs would be undertaken among service organizations and agencies to improve the ability of their staffs to meet the needs of such children. Existing community resources would be fully identified and utilized. The basic services required by children with mental and emotional disturbances would be available to all residents of the province free of charge.

Regional centres would be established at Ottawa, Kingston, Toronto, Hamilton, London, Windsor, Sudbury, and Port Arthur. The capital cost for new construction and renovation at these centres was estimated at $7.5 million. The Ontario hospital schools at Cedar Springs, Orillia, Smiths Falls, and Palmerston would, in addition, function as regional centres. Also, an assessment centre would be established by the Department of Reform Institutions in Metropolitan Toronto. By the time the plan was fully implemented within three to five years, the annual cost would be over $12.5 million.

As evidence that the plan was already being carried out, Dymond mentioned the following developments: a fifteen-bed unit for emotionally disturbed children had been opened at the Children's Psychiatric Research Unit in London; renovations were nearing completion on a twenty-two bed unit in a separate building at the Ontario Hospital in Kingston; approval in principle had been given for a forty-bed children's centre at the community psychiatric hospital in Windsor, and for one hundred beds at the Chedoke General and Children's Hospital in Hamilton; there was to be a further expansion of the psychiatric facilities at the community psychiatric hospital in Ottawa, where the existing out-patient and day-care program was being augmented by an eighteen-bed in-patient unit; the expansion program also included the construction of a new building to accommodate a larger regional centre of sixty-five beds for children at the same Ottawa hospital; the Clarke Institute in Toronto, opened in June 1966, included a twenty-bed in-patient unit for children and an expanded out-patient and day-care program; a mental retardation centre to provide seventy beds had been established in the former Toronto Psychiatric Hospital building and would offer services for emotionally disturbed children as the program developed; the Toronto Mental Health Clinic was constructing a twenty-two bed in-patient unit with expanded facilities for out-patient and day-care services for children and adolescents; an out-patient building had been completed at Thistletown Hospital to augment its facilities for treatment and research; a 150-bed unit for younger patients was being included in the reconstruction of the Ontario Hospital in Toronto; negotiations had been undertaken to reorganize diagnostic and assessment services of the juvenile and family court of Metropolitan Toronto under the direction of the Clarke Institute in co-operation with the Attorney General's Department; the responsibility for the care of children at the Warrendale centre had been assumed by Thistletown Hospital; a new program for adolescents was to be established at the Lakeshore Psychiatric Hospital the following month; increased financial assistance had been provided to the local health authorities of Hamilton and York in support of their programs.

Dymond reported an expansion of the training facilities at Thistletown, where the number more than doubled to approximately 130. A separate training program for such workers had also been established at the Children's Psychiatric Research Institute in London. Salary scales for child care workers and for various other categories of professional personnel had been increased to assist in recruiting.

The white paper indicated that, during the 1966–7 school year, the Department of Education would appoint a consultant who would

(A) create and implement within the Teachers' College and in co-operation with those masters teaching psychology, an orientation and training focus which will alert the teacher-in-training to the characteristics and needs of the mentally and emotionally disturbed pupil;
(B) work with school boards and school officials and mental and public health units to create professional development seminars and workshops for teachers which will emphasize the importance of mental health practices within the classroom, the identification of the mentally and emotionally disturbed child and referral procedures;
(C) initiate the design of long-term planning which will structure a developmental approach on the part of education to the question of the mentally and emotionally disturbed pupil.[35]

In the same document the department declared its intention to

(A) inform every school inspector in the province that specific aid is to be given to educational jurisdictions to design, in partnership with medical services, public health, the welfare service, the Children's Aid Society, and the courts and law enforcement, a directory of community services and a communication pattern whereby such services can be utilized effectively;

(B) inform every school principal of the school-community technique of analyzing through case procedures the diverse needs of the mentally and emotionally disturbed child.[36]

The department promised also to appoint education officers to the regional diagnostic and treatment centres established by the Department of Health. Their duties would be to conduct an educational diagnosis for each referral, relate the results of the diagnosis to a school program and work with the teachers to implement it, and follow up the educational progress of the pupil.

On December 3, 1968, Davis referred to the reorganization of the special education resources of the Department of Education which had taken place in August of the same year in order to provide consulting services to the local school systems. There was a program consultant in each of the regional offices, and seven provincial supervisors at the central office of the department, one of whom, Joan E. Bowers, was specifically responsible for programs for emotionally disturbed children. Davis hoped for a great improvement in meeting the needs of these children when the new divisional boards of education were in operation. He pointed out that it had been simply impossible for a board operating a single six-room or eight-room school with a minimum number of students to provide a class for the emotionally disturbed.[37]

In February 1969 J.L. Brown, member of the Legislature for Beaches-Woodbine, launched an attack, by no means the first, on the practice of sending emotionally disturbed children to training schools. Before he entered politics, Brown was the centre of a controversy over a method of treatment he encouraged at the Warrendale centre. He strongly advocated uninhibited displays of warmth and affection toward the children on the part of the staff. The Departments of Public Welfare and Health initiated action to displace Brown and his staff, after which the group established a private centre referred to as Brown Camps, and later as Browndale. Whatever the rights and wrongs of the case, the public generally gained the impression that the struggle was one of rule-quoting bureaucracy versus unrestrained, and perhaps somewhat disorderly, humanity.

In his 1969 address, Brown expressed general disapproval of large institutions, including large orphanages, of which there were a few left, and large hospital schools. He declared that it was a kindness to these institutions to suggest that they dehumanized children. "The graduates of these centres now fill our prisons and adult mental hospitals and have passed on one, two, or three generations of maladjusted children in their wake."[38] Brown objected particularly to the practice of sending emotionally disturbed children to training schools on the pretext that they were limited in their capacities and aspirations. He said that it was assumed that they were all going to become artisans regardless of whether they had the capacity for other work.

Brown referred to the procedure by which children were brought to a correctional institution as "perhaps the cruelest of all their experiences."

To be brought before a juvenile court, which is modelled on the adult court, and having one's maladjustments laid out like crimes, and having the judge consider them and sentence the child to a training school for problems and acts which are perhaps the result of the maladjustment, is the most dehumanizing treatment that the child can possibly get.[39]

In defence of his department, Allan Grossman introduced a testimonial from an editorial in a publication of the Ontario Association for Emotionally Disturbed Children in which the blame for any stigma attached to training schools was placed on public misunderstanding. These schools were said to be hardly distinguishable from the best of modern treatment centres and on a much higher level than the homes from which many of the children came.

THE DISADVANTAGED

The disadvantaged child has suffered from inadequate sensory training and experience in an intellectually poverty-stricken environment. One of his most obvious and serious handicaps is a lack of communication skills. He tends to have difficulty in learning to read and finds little enjoyment either in reading or in conversation. Thus he is unable to take full advantage of the potentially richer and more challenging environment that the school provides. His parents' lack of knowledge of, concern for, or ability to provide proper nutrition may result in his being undernourished and lacking in energy. Typically, he has been aware of the low expectations others have of him and his own self-respect is correspondingly low. A combination of adverse factors is likely to have produced some measure of emotional disturbance. An insensitive teacher who expects too much of him and holds him directly responsible for his deficiencies may do much to aggravate the situation.

The disadvantaged child tends to come from the downtown area of a large city or from an impoverished rural area. In the first of these instances, the growth of the city has sorted the population on the basis of economic and related factors, The more prosperous have moved to the suburbs in search of a relatively pleasant and presumably healthier environment. The inner city is left to low-income families, many of them on welfare, who must accept deteriorating housing and generally undesirable living conditions. Their ranks are augmented by those migrating from unprosperious rural areas and by immigrants from foreign countries who fail to adapt to the economic milieu and join the exodus to the suburbs. The children are often presented from their earliest years with scenes of hopelessness and despair. Such resources as their parents have are frequently squandered on alcohol or other means of escape.

A number of compensatory education programs began to appear in the United States in the 1950s. One of these, called Higher Horizons, developed from a demonstration guidance project set up in 1956 to compensate for deficiences in the home and community by improved services in the schools. The assumption was that the child's progress in school could be improved by raising his own and his family's educational and occupational aspirations. The first task was to elevate the child's self-concept. A good deal of attention was concentrated on the teacher, whose belief in and enthusiasm for the program were considered vital for its success. Every participating teacher had to be concerned with guidance, reading, and other aspects of language. In addition, specialist teachers in these areas, as well as social workers and psychologists, were added to the staffs of the schools concerned. Results of the concentration of effort in these schools were very encouraging.

The Head Start program undertaken in the mid-1960s represented a recognition of the fact that the effects of cultural deprivation began very early in life. It was hoped that substantial improvements could be made if counter-measures were also taken at an early stage. While certain positive results were achieved, they proved not to be as long lasting as some of the proponents of the program had hoped. Among the explanations offered for the rather disappointing results were that the program was introduced too hastily and without proper preparation, that there were not enough teachers with the special training required, that classroom facilities were inadequate, that there were too few ancillary personnel, and that the procedures for screening the children and evaluating their progress were not entirely satisfactory. Perhaps the most important lesson to be learned from this type of approach is that the destructive forces of an impoverished and hostile environment can effectively counteract the efforts of formal education. It is also evident that the enthusiasm and fervour that can often be aroused for an experimental program on a small scale are too soon dissipated when a general application of a promising approach is attempted. While a call for more research in the treatment of the culturally disadvantaged is no doubt justified, there is already plenty of evidence that a positive manifestation of human sympathy and concern will produce results. But there is no magic that will make human uplift easy, and no substitute for that vital human ingredient – sweat.

The school boards in some of the larger Ontario cities have made a very commendable effort to provide special educational opportunities in their inner-city schools. In a pattern that is not too typical in North America, they have been spending more per child in the deprived than in the prosperous areas. Examples of particular efforts are presented in volume VI of the present series.

THE GIFTED

Special concern for the gifted child developed rapidly during the 1950s.

The general view was that he represented a valuable human resource in that he was a probable future leader in some area of human society. It thus seemed particularly important, in terms both of his own interests and those of his fellows, that his capacities and talents be developed to the fullest possible extent. There was a great deal of discussion about the means by which this objective should be achieved.

The problems of definition were considerably more difficult than they were with respect to the mentally retarded. It was natural, perhaps, in a period when excessive confidence was placed in the IQ as a determinant of future achievement, to attempt to make the distinction on the basis of this measure. An IQ of 130 or higher which, if obtained on a commonly used individual test, characterized about 1 per cent of children, was often accepted as the crucial factor. Where a segregated class was to be set up, however, supplementary measures had to be taken into account for two main reasons. 1 / Differences in drive, temperament, emotional development, and other factors often produced widely differing levels of achievement among those with approximately equivalent learning capacity. 2 / It often seemed desirable to make special provision for those with unusual talent in areas related only moderately, or hardly at all, to intellectual capacity.

To some, it seemed entirely reasonable to establish classes for those with a previous record of superior achievement. The problem, of course, was that some children who fell in this group were already exerting their utmost effort, and a greater challenge might constitute no particular kindnes to them. It thus seemed desirable to take account of both measured intelligence and achievement in order to select a special class. A practice that was sometimes adopted was to rely on achievement as the fundamental criterion, with a minimum IQ level as an additional screening device. Most classes during the 1950s, however, were established on the basis of IQ.

At the height of interest in the subject in 1956, one of the discussion groups of the Ontario Association for Curriculum Development was devoted to the topic "How to Treat the Gifted Children." The members of the group expressed their dissatisfaction with the term "gifted," but failed to discover one that suited them better. They arrived at the definition of a gifted child as one whose performance in any line of endeavour is consistently remarkable. They added two qualifications: 1 / that the performance must be at a socially acceptable level and 2 / that in some instances undeveloped latent ability must be recognized. Presumably the first of these riders was intended to ensure that an expert forger or thief was not included. The group recognized three categories of gifted children: 1 / the intellectually gifted, 2 / the culturally gifted in such fields as art and music, and 3 / the physically gifted. Whether or not the decision was based on a judgment of relative importance, the discussion was concentrated on the first of these categories.

The intellectually gifted were identified according to the criterion already mentioned as those with an IQ of 130 or higher. They were said to have certain distinguishing characteristics observable in the classroom, such as their performance, their ability to make sound judgments, their success on standardized tests of achievement, their facility in expressing themselves, their ability to learn rapidly, their originality, their general knowledge derived from private research, and their curiosity and eagerness to learn. It was observed that they were occasionally non-conformists and antagonistic toward authority, perhaps because of boredom in a regular class.

The group felt that the greatest problem in dealing with the gifted was to present an adequate challenge to their ability. It was considered advisable to provide them with time, opportunities, and materials to pursue their special interests. This meant the freedom to select certain topics for individual study. A good deal of the discussion apparently centred on the need to develop their social conscience and their realization that they had an obligation to contribute to the general welfare. It was also suggested that other pupils should be taught to appreciate the special abilities and potential of the gifted.

Three possible methods of dealing with the gifted were considered: acceleration, enrichment in the regular classroom, and segregation. With respect to the first, most members of the group apparently felt that a gain of one or two years during the whole period of school life was not likely to have harmful effects. It was considered probable that there would be social and emotional as well as intellectual benefits from the removal of frustrations resulting from inappropriate grade placement. Gains in productivity were also seen as a result of early graduation from university. The approach that apparently aroused the most enthusiasm among the group was that of enrichment in the regular classroom. Among the specific activities that were suggested were individual assignments with reports to the class, panel discussions, the use of the three-level type of textbook, development of special talents in art and music, club activities, and visits outside the school. There was no consensus among the group on the question of segregation. Some saw an advantage in that it would encourage competition among the bright children. Obstacles were seen in possible objections from parents and in the extra cost of equipment and transportation.

A second discussion group at the same conference apparently showed more enthusiasm for segregation into special classes. The list of advantages distilled from the discussion contained the following points: teachers could be specially selected and trained; a more suitable curriculum could be used; creativity was stimulated; administration and organization were easier; and leadership was more likely to develop in the groups from which the gifted were removed. Among the disadvantages were that the children had to be taken out of their home community; intellectual snobbery might develop; and leadership was removed from the regular group. Where special classes had been organized, the results were said to have been very satisfactory. It was considered undesirable to establish them before the grade 4 level.

Acceleration was a common but extremely variable practice in Ontario schools during the 1950s. A questionnaire administered by the Canadian Education Association in the middle of the decade revealed that 70 per cent of the pupils in the Ottawa public school system had been accelerated by one year by the time they finished the sixth grade. The corresponding percentage in London was 40, in Hamilton, 20, and in Windsor, 12. There were some systems where only a negligible number were given such treatment.

In the late 1950s, the Toronto Board of Education established classes for highly gifted children in grades 7 and 8 and later extended the program to grade 6. The group involved those with IQs over 144 drawn from a large number of schools in different parts of the city. The program offered exploratory short courses in special subjects which avoided ground that would be covered in the regular courses in the secondary school. Assistance was sought from people with special interests outside the school system. While there was a good deal of emphasis on the pursuit of cultural goals, the children had opportunities to gain insight into certain occupational fields. Among the subjects dealt with were mathematics, mineralogy, meteorology, art, and current events. Field trips were related to these areas of study.

The 1960s were marked by an obvious decline in the earlier preoccupation with the gifted. One reason for this trend may be found in the growing sense of embarrassment that many educators feel in espousing any cause that might identify them as elitist. The danger that children identified as gifted and isolated for special treatment might develop an undesirable sense of superiority has been more strongly emphasized. Not a few members of the older generation have been repelled by the social attitudes and habits developed by many of the brightest young people, who have absorbed certain college subcultures, and have become more reluctant to invest extra resources to provide special privileges for potential members of this group. Correspondingly more attention has been focused on the needs of those whom cultural deprivation has prevented from realizing their potential.

The main reason for the change, however, has been an increasing realization that the sources of difficulty for the gifted in the school program have affected children at all levels of ability: rigid organization, standardized curricula, uniform timetables, mass testing, and practices of promotion and failure designed more to categorize than to promote growth. As individualized learning has become a goal that the Department of Education has actively supported and administrators and teachers have begun to make a real effort to attain, the prospects are that the gifted will thrive as they could not have done under earlier conditions.

ELEVEN

School buildings, facilities, and equipment

BUILDINGS

The importance of environment to education

In a search for the simplest environment in which formal education can take place, we can probably go no further than the stereotype of the teacher sitting on one end of a log with the pupil on the other. Apart from teacher and pupil, there is nothing but the log. Or is there? Perhaps there are also leaves rustling in the breeze, insects scuttling under twig and stone, birds chirping in the shrubs. The sun may be shining or hidden under sombre clouds. If the teacher is not enslaved by some academic fixation, he may draw his theme from the environment or illustrate from it. Unless the learner is abnormally insensitive, he is influenced by it. In inspires him, uplifts him, irritates him, or distracts him. As he listens, recites, or writes, his surroundings may even contain the chief educative influences impinging upon him, not excepting the teacher. Or they may reinforce the effect of the lesson so that background and stimulus are merged in one harmonious whole.

In historic succession the school presumably succeeded the log. Generations of children were herded for instructional purposes into box-like structures with barren walls relieved by little but a blackboard and filled with evenly-spaced, uniform desks. If more than one class had to be accommodated in one building, an equally barren corridor was required to link the boxes. Windows were provided to admit light but tended to be high enough on the outer wall to exclude external distractions. All that was asked of the environment was that it be dry and warm, that there be sufficient light and fresh air to preserve a minimum of health and promote the necessary physical functioning, and that, if possible, the distraction of external noise be kept to a minimum.

This type of school was necessary in a near-subsistence economy where the investment of resources in school buildings meant skimping on the bare necessities of life. The building had to be plain and austere because the cheapest available materials had to be employed. Space had to be utilized to the fullest extent. During this stage in pioneer Upper Canada, the prevailing educational philosophy rather conveniently suited the spartan accommodation. Education meant mainly the inculcation of moral principles and the storing of minds with useful knowledge. These aims were pursued through abstract verbalization with a minimum of textbooks or other aids. The environment was seldom thought to be important. It would have been considered a character-destroying indulgence to provide children with any kind of luxury, especially of the type that their parents could not have afforded in their own homes.

Even when the province became wealthy beyond the imagination of the pioneers, many members of the public (commonly referred to as "taxpayers," or as "overburdened taxpayers" when the possibility of expenditure for doubtful purposes is raised) continued to insist that essentially the same type of accommodation was called for. The attitude of less prosperous people involved a certain amount of jealousy. They did not care to see their children provided with anything bordering on the luxury that they could not afford at home. Many felt that, if they had any surplus to spend on conveniences beyond what was considered strictly essential, they should be permitted to spend it in their own way rather than have it taken from them in taxes to pay for educational "palaces."

Buildings and facilities have tended to become more elaborate and expensive for the obvious reason that educational aims and objectives have become more varied, complex, and sophisticated. If the student is to be given a vocational background or taught a vocational skill, appropriate equipment must be provided. The more directly usable and up-to-date the skill is intended to be, often the more expensive the machinery, models, specimens, tools, and the like with which he must work and the more elaborate the buildings required to accommodate them. If physical education is desirable, there must be gymnasiums, swimming pools, and a wide range of sports equipment. Music requires special rooms where the expensive instruments may be used to advantage. If science is to be taught effectively, it must be taught in laboratories, or at least specially designed classrooms. All this is generally accepted, and the necessary taxes are paid, although not without grumbling.

The development of new concepts of teaching has called for a great deal more flexibility in buildings. If the potentialities of modern methods are to be realized, rooms of greatly differing sizes must be available. It must be possible for walls to be moved, for desks, seats, and tables to be set up and put aside conveniently and at short notice, for screens to be pulled down and rolled up, for projectors to be put in place and removed. It is as if, in a half-way step toward the abandonment of the school for the open classroom of society, the traditional solidity and stability of the school were being destroyed.

A considerable amount of psychological research has been done on the effects of certain kinds of sensory stimuli. The findings of this research have disproved the notion, however logical it may have seemed, that the best learning takes place where visual, auditory, and other distractions are most completely removed so that teachers and students may concentrate most completely on the lesson. Paradoxically, the student may gaze out of the window in order to attend more single-mindedly on the teacher when his eyes focus again on matters close at hand. He may absorb the spoken message more completely if it is conveyed against a moderate background of street noise. A slight breeze flowing through an open window may make him feel more alive to impressions provided for his education than he would be in an atmosphere with even temperature control.

Consideration has been given to the sense of well-being and to learning receptivity of such features as sloped walls, which some people like to lean against. One architect permitted himself the wild speculation that a pile of large boulders on which students might lean, climb, or lie would provide more relaxation than an abundant supply of chair and sofas. It is possible that random variations in light, sound, and temperature will make a positive contribution. In a civilization that rapidly becomes more complex and artificial, an increased effort will have to be made to identify the factors that contribute to mental health as part of the process of learning.

Apart from the contribution of the environment to the instructional process is the educative effect of the environment itself. It is only in recent decades that serious attention has been given to the influence of a wide variety of factors that are only vaguely or indirectly connected with instruction: colours and colour combinations; texture of walls, floors, and furniture; types and variety of decoration; size and form of enclosures; provision for privacy; the impression of contact with or seclusion from life outside the school. It has occurred to many people that existance in beautiful surroundings, even for part of the day, may do more to elevate taste than a course in art appreciation. It is possible that a child may develop a more fundamental respect for property if he is surrounded with things that are worth preserving than if he is only offered exhortations. Physical surroundings may have much to do with determining how effectively he learns to function as a social being.

The school as a community asset

An attractive school building is a tangible asset of great importance. In order to convey the impression that the community is vigorous and lively, a good place to bring up children, and a favourable location for a new industry, the structure should be of modern design, and the newer the better. Canadians have little regard for such mementos of the past as desks carved with the initials of their ancestors. An old desk is a source of embarrassment that one discovers with relief that the poor children in the Caribbean might be able to use. Ivy on external walls probably means that the bricks are deteriorating, or that they were not all they should have been in the first place. Young parents on their way up in the world put a good deal of stock in the kind of educational facilities the community offers. Faced with the difficulty of assessing the quality of the teaching, or other elusive factors, they undoubtedly base their judgment to be a considerable extent on the appearance of the buildings their children will attend. Increasingly, also, they tend to consider the extent to which the school is the centre of social, recreational, and cultural activity for the community.

Bascom St John dealt with this issue in his column in the *Globe and Mail* in 1961. The occasion was a reputed comment by the chairman of the Ontario Municipal Board that the schools in the Toronto area were costing more than they should. St John declared that too many municipal councillors and government officials lacked the common sense to see that public investment was the basis of growth and that it returned many times the amount of money invested by the increased assessment it created. He wrote of the implications of schools for community growth.

> A community with a reputation for poor schools, rundown buildings and underpaid teachers does not grow. Nobody wants to live there. A good, well-designed school has a very strong influence on property values in the area where it is located. If the Municipal Board succeeds in forcing inferior standards of construction or inferior educational programs on school boards ... it will be striking a body blow at one of the main elements of assessed values, and therefore of municipal prosperity.[1]

The significance of the post-war building boom

During the entire post-war period, schools have been built at a remarkable rate all over the country. It is doubtful that, in relation to the population, the amount of such construction has been exceeded anywhere else in the world. The major reasons have been fairly obvious. The depression and war years had almost called a halt to such activity, with the consequence that there was a large backlog of obsolete buildings waiting for replacement. The high birth rate after the war and the huge influx of immigrants with children of school age called for the multiplication of existing accommodation. The rural-urban shift and the general increase in population mobility aggravated the problem still further. The improvement of roads and of means of transportation led to the abandonment of local elementary schools, many consisting of one room, in favour of new central schools.

When George Drew held the portfolio of Education, a Committee on Planning, Construction, and Equipment of Schools in Ontario was established to inquire into the planning and equipment of schools, standard methods of school construction, standards for mechanical services, and the useful life of school buildings. Bascom St John later gave this committee credit for a great deal of influence on the design of school buildings in the province. According to him, it "broke for good the old pattern of ugly and commonplace rural schools, and the factory-style architecture once used for school buildings in Toronto and other Ontario cities."[2] In the mid-1940s, encouragement was offered for large sites, administrative suites, staff rooms, special rooms for the conduct of the school health program, landscaping, art and music rooms, auditoriums, up-to-date ventilating equipment, and other amenities.

There was a rather drastic change in the atmosphere in the 1950s, when provincial grants for construction covered little but classrooms. This attitude was partly explainable in terms of the enormous amount of building, and thus also the tremendous cost, as compared with the previous decade. The prevailing philosophy expounded so effectively by W.J. Dunlop also tended to make a virtue of austerity. While a kind of blight settled over building in many areas, some of the larger school boards continued to search for and provide amenities that made a positive contribution to the process going on within school walls. Fortunately architectural effectiveness and beauty did not necessarily mean large increases in cost.

The 1960s witnessed a great deal of concern over both cost and quality. Departmental provisions for building control and for research into construction were mentioned in volume I, chapter 2. The Metropolitan Toronto School Board attracted world-wide attention with its Study of Educational Facilities, which showed how very substantial savings might result from the mass purchase of components and supplies, without sacrificing individuality. It is not too much to say that Ontario has become a world leader in the area of school architecture.

Major developments in building in the 1960s

Effect of the Technical and Vocational Training Agreement

One of the chief influences on building during the 1960s was the Federal-Provincial Technical and Vocational Training Agreement, which gave the province approximately two years before March 31, 1963, to build as many vocational schools and extensions as possible with a federal contribution of 75 per cent. After that date, this contribution was to fall to 50 per cent. With the provincial government making up the difference, and thus leaving local boards with no fund-raising obligations, there was a tremendous building rush. While there were no doubt many beneficial consequences, the whole affair is an example of the kind of waste that can result from an ill-co-ordinated effort on the part of federal, provincial, and local authorities. The principle that buildings and facilities must be designed to fit the program was violated. Plans were assembled hastily to meet deadlines. Demand grew so quickly that the suppliers of equipment could not keep up with it. Because of the importance of the deadline, some boards were said to be making poor choices of what was actually available. There was a risk that some of the equipment, particularly in the electronics field, would be obsolete before the students taking new courses in the Reorganized Program had advanced far enough to make full use of it. That there were not more complaints was probably attributable to the failure of local taxpayers to realize that the money was coming out of their own pockets just as surely as if it had been raised by their own school boards.

Monarch Park Secondary School, Toronto

The construction of Monarch Park Secondary School by the Toronto Board of Education represented a step forward in the move to provide more adequate accommodation. There was considerable criticism from the public over plans to include, not only an auditorium, a cafeteria, and a swimming pool, but also some air conditioning, an additional small auditorium seating three or four classes, an extra-large library located so that it might be kept open for separate use at night, offices for teachers, and an elevator for the handicapped and for moving supplies. Perhaps the strongest objection was over the proposals for air conditioning and for teachers' offices. The former was defended on the grounds that there would be a number of inside rooms without windows, which would constitute an economical use of space, and that the summer classes recently begun would not be able to function efficiently without special provision for temperature control. Offices for teachers represented a recognition that there were aspects of professional performance other than standing in front of a classroom. They included interviews with students and parents, the use of spare periods for preparation of lessons and for self-improvement, and even the availability of privacy for an occasional moment's rest. The small auditorium represented a recognition of the need for variable space for techniques such as team teaching and for the more effective use of educational media.

Franklin Public School, Kitchener

Representative of another type of innovation was Franklin Public School, opened in Kitchener in 1963. It consisted of eleven hexagonal classrooms located at the ends of the arms of a Y-shaped corridor. The rooms were grouped around a small assembly area instead of along corridors. On one side of the stem of the Y was a playroom, and on the other side, two kindergartens. The cost was somewhat less than that of a building of the conventional form because the hexagonal shape of the classrooms kept circulation walls and total wall area to a minimum. There were said to be other advantages in the shape of the rooms. The chalk-board, extending along two walls, formed an angle at the front of the room which, because it sloped away from the windows, avoided glare caused by natural light. Also, since the classroom was wider and not as deep as one of the conventional rectangular shape, pupils were brought closer to the teacher and the boards.

Some of the advantageous features of the school, as listed by the first principal, D.A. Kraft, and reported in *School Progress,* were as follows. 1 / The circular arrangement of the classrooms ensured that there would be a minimum distance to travel from any classroom to the administrative area, which included the principal's office, the health room, the supply room, the auditorium-gymnasium, and the teachers' workroom. 2 / Future additions could be made without limiting the time-saving features. 3 / Kindergarten pupils were completely isolated from the rest of the school population. They could enter the building by way of a private entrance and assembly area and play in front of the school in safety. 4 / Because most corridors were short, and all classrooms opened into the circular assembly area, hallway supervision was simple and effective. 5 / Since exits were close to all classrooms, children could enter and leave the building quickly for recess and fire drill. The limited amount of hallway used by pupils moving to and from classrooms kept dirt from being tracked through the entire school. 6 / Segregation of the playground for different groups of children was facilitated. 7 / The circular hall space provided a good assembly area and a place to hang art displays.[3]

Trend toward variable-sized internal spaces

One of the more radical innovations developed in the United States during the 1960s was the school without interior classroom partitions, which was particularly appropriate for non-graded team teaching. It provided areas of unbroken space housing from three to five groups of ordinary class size. A pupil could move from one group to another according to his ability in the subject being dealt with. Sound-proofing ensured that irrelevant noise would not be excessively distracting. Most of the schools built according to this idea were not completely committed to large open spaces. There was provision for movable partitions which could be installed to wall off a section in order to isolate particularly noisy or messy activities or those that called for an unusual amount of physical activity.

William G. Davis School, Pickering Township

The William G. Davis Public School, built in 1966 in Pickering Township Public School Area No. 2, consisted of hexagonal classroom units around a centre where the auditorium and administrative offices were located. In the initial phase, there were eight classrooms within two hexagons separated by acoustically insulated partitions in standard sizes with chalkboard and tackboard on each side. A large, trapezium-shaped classroom could be partitioned into two smaller study areas. Provision was made for the enlargement of the school by the addition of other hexagonals. The kindergarten was in an independent room with its own entrance.

The Ryerson Senior Public School, Brantford

The Ryerson Senior Public School, opened about the same time in Brantford, was essentially an octagonal ring of five standard-sized classrooms, one library-classroom, and two larger classrooms surrounding a core containing a stage, washrooms, the teachers' room, and storage space. The two larger classrooms and the stage, which was used part of the time for small-group instruction and audio-visual purposes, could be opened up to form an auditorium. It was used for group teaching, student assemblies, family nights, and certain community activities. The seating arrangement in the five-sided classrooms consisted of three or more semicircles, which gave the teachers better access to pupils and improved viewing angles for audio-visual devices and television.

General trends at the end of the 1960s

In its December 1968 issue, *School Progress* reviewed architectural trends as indicated in more than one hundred entries in the exhibition of school architecture at Canadian Education Showplace.[4] Frank Nicol, who had been Chairman of the CES Architectural Advisory Committee for six years, had commented that the entries got better each year. There was no comparison between those of the current year and those submitted three years earlier. The improvement was attributed in part to the expanded effort to include the potential users in the planning. Teachers were being questioned about how they wanted to teach, what audio-visual aids they wished to employ, and how equipment and space could be used most effectively. School boards were said to be getting good value for their money. It was not realistic to make direct comparisons on cost per square foot because of the many variables affecting the design solution for a particular school.

The *School Progress* writers noted that the trend to open-space planning continued, and school boards were stressing a need for flexibility in the use of space. Many educators were hedging their bets by insisting that the open-plan design permit conversion back to traditional classrooms if the open-teaching area concept did not appear to be working. Since this teaching approach had not yet been attempted over an extended period or on a large scale, a considerable period of uncertainty was to be anticipated. In some open-area plans the perimeter corridors formed a part of the carpeted teaching space. One entry stated that the multi-use of corridor space that stood idle most of the time in conventional schools resulted in a reduction of building size.

Many entries took advantage of different types of interior partitions. Some of the movable walls permitted the junior grade pupil to change the shape of the learning area in a few seconds. Such walls might be mounted on the ceiling or the floor. Other systems of relocatable walls were intended for weekly or monthly changes. A good deal of use was made of movable furniture and fixtures such as chalkboards, tackboards, bookshelves, and closets mounted on casters, which could provide readily accessible storage and work areas. Group mobility was also afforded by the use of movable desks and chairs. Carpet flooring had come to be regarded as an acoustic building material, and was recognized as a standard requirement for open teaching areas and libraries. Another design feature, once considered a frill but now winning acceptance, was air conditioning. It was most often provided in shop areas, but was likely to be extended to the whole school as summer classes became more common.

The resources centre was being referred to as the "centre of gravity" of the school. The library was often located so that students had to pass through it to get from one part of the school to another. It tended to be a working area for group projects. In addition to being a repository for books, tape, and filmstrips, it often housed a sophisticated array of electronic gadgetry.

There were indications of a growing belief that school buildings should be designed to facilitate community use of the gymnasium, the cafeteria, and the auditorium. A small comunity in British Columbia wanted a separate gym block for community meetings, drama presentations, and sports events. In a Quebec community, a two-schools complex, a municipal cultural centre, and a sports arena surrounded a central area and shared parking areas and athletic facilities. The library addition to the District Collegiate and Vocational Institute at Orillia was designed for convenient access by the students during the day and the public in the evening.

There was particular evidence of an attempt to make the schools as pleasant as possible. In some elementary schools, the design stimulated the child's imagination, the building was scaled to his size, and bold use of colour in friezes and wall murals broke the monotony of long corridors. There was increasing awareness of the psychological effects of particular colours and colour combinations. One group of architects declared that vivid colours sharpened attention, while white counteracted tiredness.

The search for higher quality at lower cost

The demand for standardized plans

Education Minister Davis showed his early concern for the possibility of improving school buildings, and providing them at minimum cost, by calling a conference on school design in Toronto in September 1963. Approximately five hundred architects, trustees, administrators, teachers, and officials gathered to discuss various aspects of the issue. The gathering was marked by a good many accusations of lack of ingenuity and even of incompetence. Architects blamed school trustees for having an unclear idea of what they wanted before calling on an architect. The department was accused of enforcing regulations that placed too much emphasis on maintenance and made the schools places for janitors rather than for children. Architects were blasted by administrators and contractors for being incapable of designing a one-room school. Fruitful consequences were seen even from the more acrimonious exchanges in that communication among the varied interests was begun. Some of the later developments in the department were dealt with in volume II, chapter 2.

It has frequently been suggested that the architect's fee, amounting to something like 6 per cent of the total cost of the building, could be saved if the Department of Education prepared standardized plans for use by school boards. Davis dealt with this possibility in the Legislature on April 1, 1966.[5] He was doubtful that there was much to be saved by this approach. He pointed out that it would still be necessary to retain an architect for the supervision of the work, even if he did not design the structure. This task in itself accounted for a substantial proportion of the fee under existing conditions. If the service had to be provided by a government agency, the cost, although indirect, would not be less and might easily be more.

Davis indicated further that it would become increasingly difficult to standardize plans and that it was somewhat undesirable in any case. The tendency was toward greater flexibility. At the secondary level, he asserted that it would be almost impossible to use a standardized plan for the major schools. Presumably he was referring to the wide range of sizes required and the variety of purposes that these schools had to serve.[6]

The case from the architect's point of view was presented at about the same time in an article in *School Progress* by D.M. Blenkhorne of the firm of Shore & Moffat and Partners, Architects and Engineers.[7] He mentioned the same factors that Davis had referred to and added a number of others. In order to produce a stock plan of universal applicability (the usual suggestion was, not that there be a single plan, but rather a small number), the department would need a large staff of architects to spend a few years conducting preliminary research in an attempt to devise the plan that would be acceptable to the largest number of boards and educators. Decisions would have to be made with respect to building and finish materials, types of mechanical and electrical services, hardware, colours, landscaping, and parking arrangements. Because of the inordinate number of possible combinations of items, he did not think agreement could ever be reached.

In some respects, there could not be complete standardization. A building constructed initially for a given enrolment had to have certain design features if there was a possibility that it might later have to be extended. One could not simply tack on a number of standard classrooms, but had to provide for the increased heating and electrical load, additional administration and washroom accommodation, site adaptation, and other factors. A stock plan would require a stock site, or else an experienced architect would have to be employed to make adaptations to the building plans.

Once prepared, a stock plan would be dated from the beginning. There would have to be an intensive effort to adapt it in the light of rapid improvements in building methods and materials and changes in teaching concepts. Many schools opened at the time of writing would never require any further expenditure for exterior painting or caulking, and would cost little more than half as much to heat as buildings constructed ten years earlier. Blenkhorne felt that architects working in competition had a much more effective incentive for keeping up with the latest developments than would the employees of a large government department.

The Study of Educational Facilities

The Study of Educational Facilities, referred to briefly in volume II, chapter 7, was undertaken in the 1965–6 school year by the Metropolitan School Board in Toronto, with the support of the Department of Education, the National Research Council, and the Ford Foundation. Its purposes were to promote 1 / the development of systems and components designed for school use, 2 / the more effective application of modular construction principles, and 3 / the attainment of better value for initial and long-term expenditures by school boards. Two main reasons for the study were the large construction program that would have to be conducted in Metropolitan Toronto during subsequent years in the face of steadily rising costs and the need for structural flexibility to accommodate team teaching and curricular changes. The study was carried out by a group of architects, engineers, educators, and administrators.

The SEF researchers were able to build on techniques developed in other parts of the world to achieve similar objectives. Under the sponsorship of the Educational Facilities Laboratories Incorporated, a non-profit organization supported by the Ford Foundation, new techniques for standardizing construction components had been developed in California in 1961. It had been found necessary to interest a considerable number of school boards in order to provide a large enough market to produce the desired savings and to encourage interest in research and development by manufacturers. The findings resulting from the project, which applied to conditions in California, did not meet Ontario needs.

In the SEF method lists of requirements for each school were drawn up and construction functions were divided into ten main systems: structure, atmosphere, lighting-ceiling, interior walls, vertical skin (outside walls), plumbing, electric, casework (cupboards), roofing, and interior finishing. All items for each school were to be standardized according to common specifications and manufactured to fit together automatically. Tender specifications simply indicated what each component would be required to do, rather than giving details of design. Each bidding firm had to co-operate with bidders for other subsystems. There was some initial question as to whether the industry would perform as required if the approach were to work, but fortunately it responded favourably. After the bidding was completed, a computer was used to determine the cheapest possible combination of contractors. The method was said to produce buildings with features that would ordinarily cost 30 per cent more than the Metro formula at an actual cost of 10 per cent less than the formula.

Publications issued as a result of the SEF were permeated with the idea that the school of the future should house a lively, mobile, active process with an underlying order like that of organic life. There would have to be a continuous reorganization of space to facilitate the pursuit of changing purposes. This did not mean an extreme emphasis on large open areas. An individualized learning program would call for small enclosed zones to enable the learner to engage in certain activities in relative privacy.

What appeared to be the impressive achievements of the SEF did not satisfy all the critics. As late as February 1969 George Ben, member of the Legislature for Humber, was urging the government to save architects' fees by using standardized designs.[8] He proclaimed his progressive outlook by expressing relief that the little red schoolhouse era had been left behind. He also thought that schools should be bright, comfortable, and airy, as well as being aesthetically pleasing. Yet in his view a classroom was just a classroom and not of much importance in relation to what was taught. The wide range in physical characteristics in schools built in recent years seemed to be useless. He advocated the building block type of construction like that demonstrated by Expo's Habitat. A school could be extended at minimum cost simply by adding more standard-sized classrooms.

Schools in apartment buildings

An idea developed in the United States and arousing some interest in Canada is that of combining apartments and schools in joint-occupancy buildings. There is some appeal in the possibility that rentals for apartments in the upper part of the building may help to repay the capital cost of the original investment. Advantages are also seen in bringing the school to the pupils, assuming that the apartments are of the type that will tolerate or even welcome children. The development is most attractive in urban areas of high population density. It is thus not surprising that the scheme has been pioneered in New York.

Educational park concept

The educational park concept, introduced in Scarborough, involves a group of schools of all levels at a single site. The Stephen Leacock complex consists of a junior public school, a senior public school, and a collegiate institute on a twenty-five acre site adjoining a park. They share common recreational and educational facilities and are served by central utilities. The project was developed in co-operation with the authorities responsible for parks and recreation and provides for access to facilities by the general public.

Size of schools

There are no particular pressures to increase the size of elementary schools, although there appears to be growing support for the idea of school complexes to blur the distinctions between levels and to emphasize the idea of continuous progress. At the secondary level, it is considered necessary to have a fairly large enrolment in order to provide the wide variety of offerings that make it possible to cater fully to individual aptitudes and interests. There is no doubt that a point may be reached beyond which there are serious psychological as well as economic disadvantages. In April 1970 Douglas Heath of Haverford College in Pennsylvania spoke of this problem in an address to the Federation of Women Teachers' Associations of Ontario. He claimed that there was considerable evidence that students in large schools participate in fewer extra-curricular activities, hold fewer positions of responsibility in the schools, cheat more often, are more dissatisfied, and feel less responsible for their school. The bureaucratic structure of the large school gives the impression of an impersonal system. Heath even suggested that there was no proof that a wide variety of courses or available lab facilities really contributed to a student's education. In his view, the irony of the past decade was that more students were educated, but that increasing numbers of them were less open to further growth. It would be somewhat risky, of course, to apply generalizations based on American experience too directly to Ontario, since even the largest schools in this province are very small in comparison with those in certain major centres of population in the United States; yet Heath's observations deserve to be taken seriously.

Extended use of school buildings

Year-round use

The increasing investment in school buildings has inevitably been accompanied by complaints over the large proportion of the day and of the year during which many of them have stood idle. It has appeared to be an unjustifiable waste of community resources not to take full advantage of them. Some criticism has centred on the fact that the number of days in which classes are held amounts to considerably less than 60 per cent of the total in the year. It would theoretically be possible to stagger attendance in some way so that the same accommodation could provide for many more pupils. The long summer vacation offers particularly enticing possibilities for exploitation. The point is frequently made that the original reasons for such an extended period of time off have disappeared. Few children are needed any longer to help their parents during the busiest season on the farm. The increasing prevalence of air conditioning is removing any valid excuse for excessive lassitude because of summer heat. Despite these factors, however, there has as yet been no significant progress toward any kind of trimester system at the elementary or secondary level. Administrative complexity and ingrained habits have proved to be forbidding obstacles.

A related idea has been that vacations, or at least long ones, are lost opportunities for learning. School is supposed to have become such a pleasant place that children need no urging to attend for a more extended period of time. Anyone who thought this attitude was prevalent at the grade 13 level must have been disabused of the notion by the screams of protest that were raised over what appeared to be a decision to extend the school year by a few days in 1969. There have, however, been two sets of circumstances under which considerable numbers of children have attended summer schools in certain of the larger systems. 1 / Some will accept the opportunity, no doubt frequently under parental pressure, to attempt to make up some academic insufficiency in order to win the promotion that eluded them during the previous year. 2 / There has been a growing interest in offering opportunities for learning at advanced levels, for studying subjects not offered in the regular school curriculum, or for participating in classes conducted under unusual conditions of freedom. Much of the attraction of such classes may no doubt be attributed to the fact that compulsion to attend is absent. The opportunity for innovation may result in the development of techniques that find a reflection in regular classroom practice during the year. As Deputy Minister of Education, J.R. McCarthy was on record as offering strong encouragement for the use of schools during the summer for this type of activity.

It is probable that there will an increasing number of schools open during the summer for voluntary purposes. Teachers can probably be persuaded to spend some summers, or at least parts of some summers, in this type of activity provided that they are adequately recompensed. Any considerable increase in the period of compulsory attendance is another matter. As long as the summer is the customary vacation period for parents as well as children, public resistance to a change would probably be decisive. Apart from those whose personal interests are directly involved, there are many who would wonder at the validity of adjusting the educational program primarily to fill up empty schools.

In answering a question in April 1968 on the possibility of operating the schools on a regular basis through the summer months, the minister expressed concern about the effect on the economy of the province. He speculated on the consequences for the tourist business, which was so important for the prosperity of a number of areas. The disadvantages would have to be weighed against a gain of only thirty-six or thirty-seven additional teaching days. Another point he emphasized at the same time was that a large proportion of teachers counted on using several weeks of the summer to upgrade their qualifications.[9]

Another possibility is that of using the schools for a longer period each day. During times of rapid growth, many communities have had to operate a double shift, with part of the student body attending from 8:00 a.m. to 1:00 p.m., and the remainder from then until 6:00 p.m. This system has usually been regarded as an unsatisfactory emergency measure, to be dispensed with as soon as construction catches up with need. Some teachers and students, however, have felt that the advantages outweigh the disadvantages, and that the scheme should be adopted on a permanent basis.

Community use of schools

At one time, it was almost considered an affront in certain communities for an outside group to request the use of the school, or part of it, when it was not being employed for instructional purposes. The school board felt justified in following a restrictive policy on the grounds that extra use meant additional costs for caretaking services. Even when the suppliants were prepared to pay for these, there was always the possibility of damage to property. Buildings were typically constructed so that it was difficult to provide access to the auditorium, the gymnasium, or the swimming pool without leaving the remainder open to intrusion. Even when the obstacles were not extreme, and considerable use was made of the building by community groups, the attitude often tended to be one of toleration rather than of encouragement. The situation was often attributed in part to the existence of school boards looking after only the educational facet of community service, while other aspects were handled by the municipal council or other agencies.

The situation has called forth frequent comment in the Legislature. For example, B. Newman, member for Windsor-Walkerville, said in 1965:

> I would like to suggest at this time to The Department of Education that in all new school construction the gymnasium, auditorium and library facilities be so placed or constructed that these facilities could be used after school hours by the community. Many of today's schools do not lend themselves satisfactorily to evening use. Some more progressive centres build their schools adjacent to parks so that they end up with an educational–community centre–parks complex. The school facilities are used by the school boards until, say, 4 p.m., and then they are taken over by the parks and recreation department for a community programme for recreational, cultural and educational purposes.[10]

At a School Design Workshop held in Toronto in November 1968 T.L. Wells, then Minister without Portfolio, explored the issue.

> There are many today who tend to isolate our schools from the community, to build chain-link fences around them and lock them up at 5 o'clock in the evening. Occasionally a gym, an auditorium or, if the community is lucky, a swimming-pool is open to the public. A few youth groups may be allowed to use the building regularly but, unfortunately, all too rarely is an integrated attempt made to use the whole school plant as a community facility. This should not be and I am equally certain that it is not what the majority of our citizens intend be done. At the Conference of Leisure called by the Minister of Education in November, 1966, Mr. Davis said, "Co-operation between the school and recreation authorities in a community needs to be continuous so that the best and most

dynamic program of recreation and continuing education is available to the citizens. All publicly-owned buildings must be used for program development. Facilities are of little consequence unless they are used to the maximum".[11]

Wells referred to the work of a committee that had been established in the Department of Education in 1964 to look into the matter. It had produced the following list of common barriers to community use of schools: the grant structure; liability in case of an accident; high rental fees caused by union agreements; the difficulty of disciplining adult groups; the ban on smoking; interference with books, blackboards, and cupboards; equipment not returned to its proper place; and maintenance and operational control. He identified these as merely administrative and mechanical matters that could be annoying at times but might be resolved in a rational and easy way.

The school system of Flint, Michigan, has often been cited as an example of the development of an effective community-school participation program. This program was begun in 1935 with financial assistance from the Mott Foundation. It involved keeping the schools open until 10 or 11 p.m. five days a week through the year, and half a day on Saturday. The schools offered classes for adult education, occupational upgrading, hobbies, crafts, high school credit, and adult reading. There were said to be more adults in the school after 3:30 p.m. than there were children during the school day. Even before that hour, mothers took hobby-type courses in one part of the building, while the children studied in another. In addition to educational courses, there were recreational activities such as dancing, card playing, chess, basketball, and badminton.

Among Ontario school boards, the Toronto Board of Education has had a particularly commendable record in making its educational facilities available to the community. The policy has been in effect for at least twenty-five years. The annual report of the board for 1967 indicated that, over the previous five years, community use had been increasing at the rate of 10 per cent a year. In 1967 over 1.5 million residents had used Toronto schools for a total of 65,000 separate events. The Building and Plant Division had issued over three thousand permits for the use of classrooms, auditoriums, gymnasiums, swimming pools, and playgrounds. Over sixty schools and twelve swimming pools were being used by the Metropolitan Toronto Parks Department for its summer and winter recreation program. Eleven ethnic groups had board permission to hold Saturday morning classes to teach children their native tongue and cultural heritage.

INSTRUCTIONAL MATERIALS CENTRES

In *Curriculum Bulletin 4*, issued in May 1966, the Department of Education took note of the development of instructional materials centres, of which there were twenty-eight in urban school systems in Ontario.[12] These centres were described as an ever-expanding outgrowth of audio-visual centres, teaching aids centres, and local film libraries. Initial services included the supplying of films, filmstrips, recordings, and tapes of school broadcasts to classroom teachers. At a more advanced stage, secondary services of the workshop type were added, including such activities as the preparation of transparencies and slides, the use of photocopying equipment, and the production of tapes. A major function of the centres was said to be in-service teacher training. Consultants attached to the centres spent a major part of their time in classrooms demonstrating good utilization techniques. Specialists in audio-visual aids within each school co-ordinated the school's program by selecting materials, training operators, and recommending purchases of new equipment.

The instructional materials centre operated by the Scarborough Board of Education under the direction of C. Wilkinson was singled out as an example of what might be accomplished. Beginning with a staff of two in 1955, Wilkinson had organized the basic film library and a system of distribution to Scarborough schools. In the interval, the staff had grown to ten, and the centre occupied two separate buildings. Maximum use of the stock of over seventeen hundred films was ensured by weekly delivery service to ninety-five schools. Catalogues were prepared for each grade level, correlating the films with the course of study and supplying a lesson guide for each title. Films for use at the secondary level were divided into three subject groupings, with a catalogue for each.

The centre provided a preview service to enable teachers to borrow filmstrips for trial use. Filmstrips were, however, purchased by each school on the recommendation of its own staff members. Instructional pictures were handled on the same basis. Teachers could obtain copies of tapes in the collection at the centre by sending blank tapes along with instructions about what was required.

Expert technicians were employed to maintain equipment in good working order. The several types of projectors in the possession of each school were supplemented by machines at the centre which could be sent out when regular equipment was being repaired. A reduction of lost time through breakdowns was achieved through standardization of types of equipment, a complete stock of spare parts, and good training in operation.

The Department of Education claimed a part in the establishment of each of the instructional materials centres in the province. Each school board creating a centre had received a number of films on a permanent loan basis. Boards had also received advice and guidance in surveying the requirements of the local area, in obtaining qualified people to direct the program, and in dealing with administrative details having to do with organization, equipment, distribution, and storage. Technicians had also received training in servicing film at the department's Audio-Visual film library. Members of the staff of the Audio-Visual Section visited all the centres twice a year and were available on request for consultation. Teacher training in audio-visual utilization was provided at annual summer courses.

SCHOOL LIBRARIES

Changing role of libraries

Secondary schools

A brief characterization of the pre-war secondary school library was given by W.A.T. Perrins in the *Bulletin* of the Ontario Secondary School Teachers' Federation in 1963.[13] It was thought of chiefly as a collection where students could find some of the books to supplement their reading program. The librarian was attached to the English department and ordinarily had some classes in that subject. This particular situation was still fairly common in the early 1960s. Perrins anticipated two major developments. 1 / The librarian would be recognized as head of his own department, and 2 / the library would be recognized as "a social and educational institution in our culture." The librarian would organize the materials of the library to serve the needs of all departments in the school.

Among the most important of the aims of the school library identified by the American Library Association, Perrins listed the following:

(1) To meet the reading and research needs of teachers and students.
(2) To provide students with materials and services essential to their growth and development as individuals.
(3) To stimulate and guide the students in their reading so that they find enjoyment and satisfaction and grow in critical judgment and appreciation.
(4) To provide an opportunity for students to develop helpful interests, to make satisfactory personal adjustments, and to acquire desirable social attitudes.
(5) To help young people become skilful and discriminating users of libraries and of book and non-book materials.[14]

The American Library Association standards suggested that the librarian co-operate with teachers in these ways:

(1) By building systematically the collections of the school library to meet curricular and other needs of students.
(2) By providing a variety of professional material for teachers.
(3) By assisting teachers in the development of effective techniques for using the resources of the school library.
(4) By helping teachers in the preparation of bibliographies and reading lists.
(5) By locating information and other reference services for teachers.
(6) By working with teachers to motivate students to use the library frequently.[15]

Among improvements during the immediately preceding period, Perrins noted that increased budgetary allowances had made possible a good reference collection in every secondary school to enable senior students to carry on research. More materials had been provided for teachers to enrich their courses. The Ontario College of Education had been offering a library option as well as summer courses dealing with the use of the library as a teaching instrument. Robarts, who had given up the education portfolio a short time before, had supported a move to give all students in grades 9 and 10 instruction in the use of the dictionary, encyclopedia, card catalogue, periodical indexes, and other reference materials.

In another article in the *Bulletin* approximately three years after the one just referred to, Perrins observed some substantial progress in the directions he had foreseen.[16] While it would no doubt be unrealistic to suppose that these applied throughout the province, there were at least grounds for gratification that the better schools were showing the way. Perrins saw the school librarian becoming a kind of information officer and director of research. He had to know the curriculum and the courses of study for all departments in order to stock the library with needed materials and to prepare bibliographies for all subject teachers. He kept in touch with department heads and attended department meetings to keep the members informed of what books and magazines were available. By keeping up with changes in the curriculum, he was able to weed out obsolete materials.

In an informal paper, S.D. Neill of the School of Library and Information Science of the University of Western Ontario indicated some of the peculiar problems faced by the school librarian. For example, his work required a high degree of selectivity. Ideally he should know everything published that might have an application to any part of his school's program. In actual fact, he seldom had time to devote full attention to more than one or two reviewing journals. If he were given enough time to do the job properly, his fellow staff members were irritated with the apparent contrast between his leisurely reading and their own harried lives. In defence against complaints, the principal might yield to pressure and overload his timetable with classes. Thus selections must be made with excessive haste, and ordering done through jobbers. Members of the teaching staff had to make their choices without sufficient guidance, and a good deal of money was spent unwisely.

Elementary schools

Until comparatively recently, libaries in elementary schools were uncommon. A few shelves of books in a cupboard in the corner of the classroom were all that was commonly offered. In the early 1960s, the Department of Education began to pay grants for libraries in schools of twelve rooms or more. In his annual report for 1964, the Superintendent of Public Schools in Ottawa reported that the practice there had been to build libraries in new intermediate schools and, where possible, to adapt a classroom in each elementary school for library purposes. The latter arrangement was not, however, proving satisfactory.

In the same report, the Ottawa superintendent offered a concept of future library development in elementary schools.

> The library of the future will be more than twice the size of the regular classroom, for it will have the usual reading area for a class, and in addition a small group teaching area, a workshop area and a reference area. The library will play a greater part in the future in the entire curriculum than it has in the past. It will be more than a mere reading room or a book circulating depot. It will be the centre for the school of resource materials in all subjects, a place to which pupils will go, unscheduled, at times as individuals, at times as groups to do research for a study project.
>
> It will be the depository of reference books, film strips and slides, flat pictures, records and all sorts of material aids. It will be staffed, I hope, by a trained teacher-librarian able to assist pupils to find source material for their studies in all subjects. Thus in the expanded library of the future one may see on any given day a class of pupils in the reading room on a scheduled visit with their own teacher, a group of pupils from another class under pupil leadership in the workshop area, and the teacher-librarian helping an individual pupil from a third class find some specific item of information, and a picture or a slide or a film strip to illustrate it.[17]

Integration of libraries and instructional materials centres

Perrins took note of the type of instructional materials centre that was developing in the United States, where the library was being augmented by audio-visual equipment and materials. He thought this was a logical development, which would ensure maximum usage of the various items. It was in accord with the increasing emphasis being placed on independent study.

Audrey Taylor of Thornhill Secondary School dealt with recent trends in an article in *School Administration* in February 1968.[18] She felt that the term "library" was rapidly becoming obsolete, although it was hard to shake loose from the current vocabulary. She regarded the blending of libraries with resource or instructional materials centres as sufficiently advanced to rely wholly on the latter designation. The librarian might also be appropriately called a media specialist. The resource centre would contain the major collection of instructional materials and would be considered "the hub of all activities directed towards the spirit of inquiry." It differed both in physical structure and contents from the older concept of the library. In the first respect, it provided specialized areas for differing types of pursuits, including seminar rooms for small group discussions, "dry" carrels for independent study, "wet" carrels for listening and viewing, and lounging areas for relaxed, leisurely reading.

Taylor stressed the importance of the resource centre as an integral aspect of the attempt to individualize instruction, enabling the student to progress at his own rate and according to his individual needs. The student had to accept more responsibility for the organization of his own learning and to make effective use of blocks of time for independent work. The possibility of learning by discovery depended on the availability of the widest possible variety of materials and of an environment where they could be put to good use.

In 1968 Canadian Education Showplace presented a demonstration of the resource centre concept, with expert consultants on duty to answer questions. The centre, consisting of a carpeted area with dimensions of one hundred by twenty-four feet, suggested the kind of materials needed for a comprehensive library program. The Scarborough Board of Education organized a workshop for the preparation of audio-visual materials in an adjoining area. Among the impressions gained by the consultants at the exhibit was that many teachers and librarians who made enquiries had no idea of the amount of work that confronted them in establishing resource centres.

Departmental assistance in planning

In 1968 a booklet entitled *Library Resource Centres* was prepared by the School Planning and Building Research Section of the Department of Education in conjunction with the Departmental Library Committee. It was intended as a guide for those planning elementary school library resource centres, which were recognized as being in the initial stages in many areas. The suggestions were intended to be general and to avoid inhibiting the initiative of the school board, the superintendent, the architect, the principal, and the teaching staff in adapting the centre to meet the special needs of the school.

The booklet declared that library resource centres would need to be built to accommodate more pupils, to house larger collections, and to provide facilities for the newer learning media. Since it was difficult to adapt or enlarge old library quarters, new construction would be called for in most cases. Books were still to be the mainstay of the library. As a minimum, it was suggested the five thousand volumes would be needed for schools with an enrolment up to five hundred and that, in larger schools, there should be a minimum of ten books per pupil. As library use increased, it was said that many schools would need to enlarge their collections to twenty or thirty volumes per pupil. Between twenty and twenty-five titles were a suggested minimum of current periodicals. Other recommended equipment included pictures, pamphlets, disc and tape recordings, filmstrips, film loops, and other non-textual materials. The quarters were to be constructed, if possible, so that pupils could use the resources individually, in small groups, or even in large class groups.

A similar publication was released a year later under the title *Library*

Materials Centres to provide guidance for secondary schools. Drawings suggested ideas for the arrangement of spaces and facilities. Circular H.S.1 also offered suggestions for the use of libraries, some of which may be summarized as follows. 1 / The library was to be open continuously from 8:30 a.m. through the lunch periods until at least one hour after the end of classes. If it was the wish of teachers and students, it might also be opened for service and study during the evenings and on Saturday. 2 / It should be available for use by class groups, seminar groups, and individual students as much as possible during class hours. It was not to be scheduled as a subject classroom. / A library program conducted by a trained librarian was to be regarded as essential for all first-year students. This program was to introduce them to the materials, the organization, and the services of the library, and to emphasize reading, experience with subject resources, and instruction in research techniques. One library period a week was suggested for optimum results. Grade 9 classes were not however, to monopolize library facilities at the expense of students in the higher grades. 4 / It was recommended that students with spare periods, particularly grade 13 students, be permitted to use the library for research but not for doing routine homework.

Levels of training for school librarians

The report of Francis R. St John Library Consultants, which will be dealt with in more detail in volume V, chapter 20, indicated the desirability of having secondary school libraries operated by librarians with at least the BLS degree. Their professional services would be extended by ensuring that they were not burdened by the tasks of cataloguing and of classifying and printing cards and labels. For the elementary level, it was considered unrealistic to expect that any except the largest consolidated schools could be staffed by fully trained degree holders. The recommended solution to the problem of providing improved services was to have area supervisors with the BLS and teaching experience as minimum requirements. Individual libraries would be staffed by teacher-librarians who had completed the minimum number of courses given at the Ontario College of Education. The area supervisors would be responsible for the supervision of school library operations, for advice to teacher-librarians, for in-service training, for guidance in books selection, and for liaison between libraries and curriculum planning.[19]

As the idea of the library as a resource or instructional materials centre has gained currency, the problems of finding adequately prepared staff has taken on new dimensions. The requirements include, not only the conventional librarian's training, with a particular knowledge of curricula and psychology in order to be able to understand the needs of school children, but certain mechanical skills as well. Individuals with all the necessary qualifications are so uncommon that the only realistic hope is to attempt to find an administrator with a reasonable amount of each, with particular emphasis on organizing ability, and to have the centre staffed with several people of varying abilities. While the growing importance placed on the resource centre may be making this arrangement possible in the larger schools, it is not likely to be realized soon in those of medium or smaller size.

A development of some promise is the appearance of programs for the training of library technicians in the colleges of applied arts and technology. These programs have not been under way for long enough to indicate the kind of role the graduates will ultimately play. Since they lack teaching experience and library training at the professional level, it would appear to be essential that they work under adequate supervision.

CANADIAN EDUCATION SHOWPLACE

Canadian Education Showplace, a combined convention and exhibition originated and sponsored by *School Progress*, has been held annually in Toronto since 1965. When it was launched on February 5 and 6 of that year, it attracted over seven thousand delegates from all parts of Canada. They were superintendents, inspectors, principals, teachers, trustees, school business officials, school architects, and student teachers. Besides listening to a number of prominent speakers, they had the opportunity of comparing and evaluating over $1 million worth of school equipment. The program was intended to give them an opportunity to exchange practical ideas of all kinds.

One of the main features was an exhibition of school architecture, where twenty-nine elementary, secondary, and university buildings were portrayed graphically on panels. The display consisted of a wide variety of design concepts and ideas. Members of a Showplace Architectural Advisory Committee discussed school design and construction with visitors and answered their questions. Another exhibit showed a working miniature of the Toronto Education Centre Library, with a demonstration of information retrieval and of a telephone-tape system. About three hundred new professional books and hundreds of educational periodicals were on display. Over thirty classroom television receivers carried continuous programming from a live studio in the main hall of the Queen Elizabeth Building. In this way, it was hoped that the potential uses of television in education might be demonstrated. A.F. Knowles, an expert on educational television, was available to give authoritative explanations of the applications of the medium.

In 1966 the Showplace was moved to the Automotive Building at Exhibition Park to allow for a major expansion in displays. About 250 exhibitors occupied more than four hundred booths to demonstrate the latest equipment, supplies, and services. Attendance rose to 13,514 – nearly double that of the previous year. There was a particularly large representation from school trustees because of the fact that the Canadian

School Trustees' Association held its mid-winter conference to coincide with the Showplace dates. As a result of popular demand, the program was extended to cover a three-day period. Again, major features were an exhibition of school architecture and a wide range of audio-visual equipment. T.L. Wells headed the Program Advisory Committee for the second successive year, while the Architectural Advisory Committee was chaired by F.J.K. Nicol.

Each successive year, suppliers of products and services continued to be attracted in increasing numbers. By 1969, 475 exhibitors occupied 642 booths and, as *School Progress* put it, offered "the widest selection of school needs ever assembled, from pencils to portable classrooms, filmstrips to floor cleaners." The Canadian Association for Children with Learning Disabilities sponsored a series of seminars stressing the teacher's role in special education. There were slides of remedial programs and a display of new publications on the subject. Educational television seminars were presented each day by the Educational Television and Radio Association of Canada. In one session, a panel of leading Canadian ETV and educational radio specialists dealt with cost, staffing, equipment, utilization, presentation, and other television problems. Films presented in the Showplace Theatre included *English with Impact*, showing a language arts program designed to arouse the interest of the uninvolved student; *A Lover's Quarrel with the World*, a documentary on Robert Frost; *The Library Is*, dealing with the development and contribution of libraries; and *To Be a Librarian*, showing the work of acquiring, cataloguing, and processing library books. There were demonstrations on such subjects as Film Loops, New Medium for Art & Vocational Demonstrations; Modern Techniques in Preparing Visual Aids; Proper Care and Handling of Videotape; Shortcuts in Spirit Duplicating and Preparing Projection Transparencies, and Instructional Modular Servo Systems. An exhibit on individualization in a totally flexible school, arranged by the Ontario Institute for Studies in Education, was based on a project in an elementary school where teachers were using a variety of media to accommodate individual differences. An exhibit with films, slides, pictures, brochures, and printed material showed the scope and activities of community colleges across Canada. Six half-hour colour television programs produced by Ryerson Polytechnical Institute dealt with problems of student unrest. The exhibition of school architecture for the year included fifty-six plans and models.

PROBLEMS OF THE EQUIPMENT REVOLUTION

The great increase in the amount of certain types of equipment used in the schools has posed very serious problems for school business officials and for the school boards which must take the ultimate responsibility for their decisions. It is not enough that they can appraise needs and make cost/value judgments with respect to conventional items such as desks, chairs, tables, blinds, cleaning equipment, and the like, where the need is fairly readily definable and where standards of quality exist. They are now confronted increasingly with pressure to purchase equipment designed to further the learning process. Here they have great difficulty in determining the importance of variations in the products of different manufacturers, since cost is in itself meaningless without some basis for estimating effectiveness.

Undoubtedly the audio-visual equipment field offers the best examples of the kinds of problems that are being confronted. In an article in *School Progress* in October 1966, Morley Patterson wrote that no one knew exactly how much was being spent in Canada for this type of equipment, but the estimate was $4 for every $100 of educational costs. It is probably safe to assume that the proportion is rising, and that, in a rich province such as Ontario, it is higher than the national average. In any case, even on the basis of estimates considered by Patterson, the sales value of audio-visual equipment was between $15 million and $35 million a year, depending on what was classed as an audio-visual product.

What Patterson called "traditional" audio-visual products have included motion pictures, strips, slides; opaque, overhead, and special-purpose projectors; radios, tape recorders, record players; and various specialized devices and accessories. Later additions are secretarial labs, video tape recorders, closed circuit television, teaching machines, and information storage and retrieval systems components. The US Department of Audio Visual Instruction of the National Education Association began the practice of publishing guidelines for elementary and secondary schools and for post-secondary institutions indicating what traditional audio-visual equipment could be classified as weak, good, or superior. According to Patterson's illustration, a school that had one projector for every twelve "teaching stations" would be considered weak, while if it had one for each four stations it would be considered good, and if it had one for each station it would be superior.

This kind of quantitative evaluation is based on extremely doubtful assumptions about the educational contribution of different kinds of equipment. No one actually knows what, if anything, any particular item contributes to learning. A really adequate appraisal would hinge on a large number of factors relating to teacher attitude and capacity; to the instructional approach employed; to the background, interests, and ability of the pupils; to the subject area being dealt with. There is a temptation to take refuge in a call for research. In a sense, this is a valid position to take. A massive research effort, if sufficiently concentrated and pursued consistently over a period of time, should be able to unravel some of the complexities of the situation and provide some tentative answers. To be realistic, however, one must concede that there is little immediate hope that substantial relief will come from this direction. School business officials are forced to rely on the opinions of educators and on information or propaganda from equipment suppliers.

Of the two sources, unquestionably the greater reliance must be placed on the first. If educators have no dependable judgments to make, there is no basis for deciding what to purchase other than pure guesswork or the notion that whatever is new and shiny must have merit. Of course the purchasing officer can be guided by a flat negative reaction. There is obviously no point in buying an item if the teachers indicate emphatically that they have no intention of using it. However, things are seldom that easy. A teacher or administrator, in the face of uncertainty, or where the contribution of certain equipment is unproved, is likely to favour its acquisition. He does not see it as his concern to lean over backwards to ensure that the school board takes no financial risks. This does not mean that he is extravagant but simply that his first obligation is to provide education of the highest quality. Where there is a strong presumption that the item is at least of marginal value, his judgment as to the amount of money that should be invested in it is particularly likely to need scaling down. If educators without financial responsibility establish guidelines indicating that a school with one projector for each teaching area is superior, while one with a projector for each twelve teaching areas is weak, it is quite likely that they have not taken into account the possibility that, beyond a certain point, money spent on projectors would produce greater benefits if spent on something else. Indeed, educators seldom have the knowledge required to make valid cost/benefit comparisons among alternatives any more than purchasing officers can determine the educational value of the so-called hardware. Thus whatever hope there is of investing wisely rests on close co-operation between the two.

Relying on the producers of the equipment for an appraisal of its value entails risks that are so obvious that they hardly need to be mentioned. While competitors can be depended on to point out the specific defects in one another's products and the superior qualities of their own, they tend to offer little assistance in defining the general educational role of the item in question. Practice varies, however, according to the desire and ability of any particular firm to take a long-term view of the market. A great deal of harm was done, for example, in the area of programmed instruction by the efforts of certain firms to make a quick profit on unnecessarily elaborate teaching machines and on hastily constructed and inadequately tested programs. On the other hand, while the large firms that produce and sell computers and other data processing equipment employ all the wiles at the disposal of business enterprises to edge one another out of the market, they realize that the sale or rental of an expensive piece of equipment does not contribute to their ultimate interests unless the customer really needs it, knows how to use it, and has some hope of obtaining ultimate satisfaction from it. Their representatives sometimes feel that they are forced to violate this principle because if they do not supply the customer with what he thinks he needs, others will do so.

THE "BUY CANADIAN" POLICY

From time to time, the minister urged, although he did not absolutely insist upon, a policy of buying materials produced by Canadian manufacturers for the construction of educational facilities. A recent statement of the position was as follows.

The department does, and I do, make an effort to encourage the boards to buy Canadian where they can. The decision, of course, rests with the local board but I would read to the House a directive that was sent out by myself on May 31, 1968.

"The support of the Canadian economy is a responsibility that each of us must share and I regard it as particularly important that the authorities and officials of the educational institutions of the province keep this constantly in mind.

It is suggested that boards, officials and administrators of our many educational institutions should encourage the policy of "Buy Canadian" by advising architects and consultants to specify Canadian goods and manufactured products whenever possible and by instructing purchasing departments to adhere to the practice of buying Canadian-made goods where price and quality are comparable."[20]

TWELVE

The role and status of teachers

LEGAL POSITION

At the beginning of 1970, the rights and obligations of teachers were specified in considerable detail in *The Schools Administration Act*. Like so much legislation remaining on the books, a number of the provisions had a distinctly quaint tone. If the year were specified in which each item was added to the list, the result would no doubt be a kind of history of the problems and difficulties encountered by teachers in dealing with school boards, inspectors, principals, pupils, and other individuals or agencies, since much of the legislation seems to have been designed to prevent or settle some particular type of controversy.

Part II of the act dealt specifically with teachers. Section 17 was concerned with a number of aspects of their contract and salary rights. A memorandum of a contract between either a permanent or a probationary teacher on the one hand and a school board on the other was to be made in writing on a form prescribed by the regulations, signed by both parties, sealed with the board's seal, and executed before the teacher assumed his duties. The absence of such a written memorandum for any reason did not, however, prevent a contract from being in force. An unwritten contract was assumed to contain the terms and conditions of the form prescribed for a permanent teacher, which made provision for the teacher to be paid in ten equal instalments. In the case of a separate school board, a contract might provide for board and lodging for the teacher.

In a very legalistic sounding subsection, a teacher was guaranteed the right to receive his salary, unless otherwise agreed, "in the proportion that the total number of days during which he teaches bears to the whole number of teaching days in the year." That is, if he taught for 90 per cent of the teaching days, he was entitled to 90 per cent of his salary. This provision was, however, modified to the extent that he was entitled to payment for twenty days during any one school year while he was ill, as certified by a physician, or suffered from an acute inflammatory condition of his teeth or gums, as certified by a licentiate of dental surgery. A board could, if it wished, pay him for more than the minimum of twenty days because of one of these conditions. A temporary teacher could claim remuneration for two days "in respect of" each month because of absence for the same reasons, but again, a board was authorized to be more generous. Similarly, an itinerant teacher was entitled to sick leave payment for at least 10 per cent of the periods of instruction and supervision specified in the agreement for his employment in any one school year.

A teacher was entitled to full salary despite absence from duty because of quarantine or other conditions imposed by the medical health authorities and despite absence to appear as a witness in a court to which he had been summoned in any proceedings to which he was not a party or one of those charged. A dispute between a board and a teacher over salary or other remuneration was to be settled in the division court of the division in which the dispute arose. If the judge in the dispute had reason to think there was not reasonable ground for the board to dispute its liability, or if its failure to pay the amount in question seemed to stem from an improper motive, he might award up to three months' salary as a penalty. The absence of a written memorandum of agreement did not in itself constitute an excuse for the board's failure to meet its obligation. Sufficient time was to be allowed for an appeal against the judge's decision by either party or by the Minister of Education. The judge might award costs against the party on whose behalf an unsuccessful appeal was made. The minister might, however, pay such costs and charge them as contingent expenses of his office.

Section 19 of the act dealt with teachers' qualifications and certificates. Subject to *The Department of Education Act,* a teacher employed in an elementary or secondary school had to be qualified in accordance with the regulations. A qualifying certificate could be awarded only to a British subject of good moral character who was physically fit to perform the duties of a teacher, who passed the examinations prescribed by the regulation, and otherwise complied with the regulations. The provisions of *The Department of Education Act* that modified these conditions were contained in section 11, which authorized the minister to accept the equivalent of a requirement prescribed for a teacher, department head, director, supervisor, supervisory officer, or inspector in terms of evidence of experience, academic scholarship, or professional training. The same section empowered him to grant a temporary or interim certificate to a person who was not a British subject, but whose application to become a British subject was pending or who made a declaration that he intended to become a Canadian citizen when eligible under the *Canadian Citizenship Act.* The minister could also grant a letter of permission to a board authorizing it to employ an unqualified person as a teacher if he was satisfied that no qualified person was available. A letter of permission was valid only for the period of time specified by the minister, but not for more than one year. The minister could cancel any certificate or diploma granted under *The Department of Education Act* or the regulations made under it.

Section 20 of *The Schools Administration Act* was particularly out of tune with the trend toward greater freedom for the teacher in terms of curriculum selection. It sternly forbade him to use or permit the use of any book not approved by the minister or the regulations as a textbook in a prescribed subject in an elementary or secondary school. If the minister received a report from an inspector that this stricture was being violated, he might withhold part or all of the legislative grant for the school where the offence was being committed. The guilty teacher might, furthermore, be suspended and the amount of the legislative grant lost because of his offence might be deducted from his salary. With the written approval of the board, a teacher might substitute for a textbook in actual use any other approved textbook on the same subject. Perhaps an even more heinous deed than using an unauthorized textbook was that of refusing to deliver to the board any visitor's book, school register, schoolhouse key, or any other school property. The offender lost his status as a qualified teacher until restitution was made and forfeited any claim he might have against the board.

The duties of the teacher were set forth in section 22 of the act as follows:

(1) It is the duty of a teacher

(a) to teach diligently and faithfully the subjects in the course of study as prescribed by the regulations;

(b) to encourage the pupils in the pursuit of learning;

(c) to inculcate by precept and example respect for religion and the principles of Christian morality and the highest regard for truth, justice, loyalty, love of country, humanity, benevolence, sobriety, industry, frugality, purity, temperance, and all other virtues;

(d) to maintain proper order and discipline in his classroom and while on duty in the school and on the playground under the direction of the principal;

(e) in instruction and in all communications with the pupils in regard to discipline and the management of the school, (i) to use the English language, except where it is impractical to do so by reason of the pupil not understanding English, and except in respect of instruction in a language other than English when such other language is being taught as one of the subjects in the course of study, or (ii) to use the French language in schools or classes in which French is the language of instruction except where it is impractical to do so by reason of the pupil not understanding French, and except in respect of instruction in a language other than French when such language is being taught as one of subjects in the course of study.

(f) to see that the classroom is ready for the reception of pupils at least fifteen minutes before the time of opening in the morning and five minutes before the time of opening in the afternoon ...

(h) to conduct his class in accordance with a timetable which shall be accessible to pupils, principal and inspector;
(i) to attend regularly the teachers' institutes of the inspectorate;
(j) to notify the board and the inspector of his absence from the school and the reason therefor; and
(k) to deliver the register, the schoolhouse key and other school property in his possession to the board on demand, or when his agreement with the board has expired, or when for any reason his engagement has ceased.

Part III of the act dealt with school trustees' and teachers' boards of reference. Section 25 provided that a board could dismiss a teacher or terminate his contract only by notice in writing stating the reasons, and in accordance with the contract. By the same token, a teacher could resign only by giving notice in writing according to the terms of the contract. Either a teacher or a board that was not in agreement with the dismissal or termination by the other party might, within fifteen days of receiving notice of the disputed action, apply to the minister for a board of reference. On the same day, the applicant was obliged to send a copy of the application to the other party to the disagreement. A board was forbidden to make a permanent appointment to replace the teacher who was dismissed or whose appointment was terminated in a manner not agreeable to him until 1 / the time prescribed for applying for a board of reference had elapsed without action on the part of the teacher; or 2 / the teacher had notified the board in writing that no application for a board of reference would be made; or 3 / the minister notified the board in writing that an application by the teacher had been withdrawn; or 4 / the minister had notified the board in writing that he had refused the teacher's application; or 5 / the teacher had not assumed his legal obligation to name a representative on the board of reference; or 6 / the minister had taken legal action to have the contract discontinued. Similarly, a teacher who terminated a contract in a manner not agreeable to the board was forbidden to enter into a contract of employment with another board after receiving notice that the board with which he had terminated the contract had applied for a board of reference until one of the following things had happened: 1 / the minister had notified the teacher that the school board had withdrawn its application for a board of reference; 2 / the minister had notified the teacher that he had refused the board's application; 3 / the minister had notified the teacher that the board had failed to name its representative on the board of reference; 4 / the minister had notified the teacher that the contract was discontinued. Any of these actions was to be in writing.

On receiving an application for a board of reference, the minister was to notify the other party to the disagreement by registered mail. Within thirty days, he was to inquire into the disagreement and either refuse the application or grant it and direct a judge to act as chairman. Before taking the latter step, however, he might require the applicant to furnish security for the action. Again, after designation of the judge, both parties to the dispute were to be notified, and each was to be requested in the notice to name a representative other than the teacher involved or a member of the board, and to inform the minister of the nomination within ten days of his sending the notice. Failure by either party to take this action signified abandonment of the case, and the minister would direct that the contract be continued. If the representative of either party failed to appear at the hearing, the chairman of the board of reference was to name a substitute. The chairman was to hold a hearing within thirty days, after suitable notice to the parties in a convenient court house, municipal building, or school building. Meetings of the board of reference were to be held in camera. When the hearing was completed, the board of reference was to notify the minister within seven days and direct either the continuance or discontinuance of the contract. It might also make such recommendations as it considered advisable. The minister was to have a copy of the decision sent to the school board and teacher within seven days of receiving the report and was to see that it was implemented. The minister could force compliance by a reluctant board by withholding any funds payable to it under the authority of the Legislature. If a teacher failed to comply, the minister could have his certificate suspended for whatever period he considered advisable.

From time to time the Department of Education has found it necessary to forbid teachers to engage in practices not specifically condemned in the regulations. For example, the following memorandum went to inspectors in 1963 under the signature of G.A. Pearson, Superintendent of Elementary Education.

Re: *Teachers Acting as Agents or Salesmen*

1. The Department recognizes and appreciates the high ethical standards maintained by most teachers and the co-operation of the Ontario Teachers' Federation and its affiliates in maintaining such standards. However some exceptions on the part of individual teachers have recently been brought to the attention of the Department, and it has been considered necessary that the following directive be issued.
2. The Department considers that it is unethical for a teacher to take advantage of his position to sell any materials, books, maps, globes or any teaching aids to pupils or to parents of pupils of the school or schools in which he is teaching, or of schools in neighbouring areas where he is known and respected as a teacher and where this fact would give him an unfair advantage because of his position of trust.
3. Each inspector is hereby directed to advise each teacher in his inspectorate that this conduct is considered to be unethical and improper, and to warn

each teacher who may be engaged in this practice that he is to desist from so doing. It will be the responsibility of each inspector to report to the Department on each case where a teacher has been given fair warning and has continued with such activity.

4. Each inspector is hereby directed not to supply to commercial firms the names of teachers who may be considered for such activity either during the school year or during the vacation period.[1]

THE TEACHER'S RIGHT TO SERVE ON A SCHOOL BOARD

As of 1970 *The Schools Administration Act,* section 49, contained the following provisions.

(1) A school trustee is not eligible for appointment as an inspector or as a teacher by the board of which he is a member.

(2) A teacher is not eligible to be a member of the board by which he is employed.

Teachers have, however, frequently been elected to serve on school boards other than those employing them. For a time before 1967 the Etobicoke board was sometimes described as being teacher-dominated. The legislation establishing the new educational structure for the area as of the beginning of that year prevented a teacher employed by any board in the area from serving on any other area board. The reason for the provision was that it was felt that a teacher trustee who served on the Metropolitan Toronto School Board would be subject to conflict of interest when financial matters, for example, were dealt with. The teachers of the area were, however, most unhappy about the arrangement.

In accordance with a request by Prime Minister Robarts on May 10, 1967, the Minister of Municipal Affairs set up a committee under the chairmanship of C.W. Yates to study the question of conflict of interest of public employees. Its terms of reference included the following:

1. The consideration of the best interests of the public in having any employee of a municipality or a local board serve as a member of a municipal council or of any local board and to determine appropriate safeguards respecting conflict of interest.
2. The means by which the knowledge and abilities of an employee of a municipality or a local board may, in the public interest, be made available in elective or appointive office.
3. The extent to which other persons presently disqualified by statute should be permitted to participate in public office and to determine appropriate safeguards respecting conflict of interest.
4. The consideration of the application of these matters to governing bodies of universities.[2]

The committee's recommendations called for amendments of legislation in accordance with the following principles, along with others that are less relevant here.

A. An employee of the corporation of a municipality is no longer disqualified from sitting on council.
B. A member of council or a local board is now required to disclose an interest in any contract or proposed contract which may be affected by a decision of the council or local board.
C. A person failing to comply with section 36 [i.e., failing to make the required disclosure] forfeits his seat and is ineligible as a candidate at any election for five years thereafter.
D. Officers of a municipality are required to give notice in writing to the council of their interest in a contract or proposed contract.[3]

A specific provision recommended that "a teacher should be allowed to sit on the Divisional Board which employs him, provided he has no say or vote in any matters involving the school by which he is employed, and the number of teachers on a Divisional Board constitutes the minority."

The Department of Education has not been receptive to the idea that any change should be made. There has been a feeling that conflicts of interest for certain municipal employees are fairly readily identified and isolated. A teacher's involvement in education is seen, however, as all-pervasive rather than confined to matters of pecuniary interest and thus is likely to be the source of continual conflicts. There has been no great enthusiasm, furthermore, for an arrangement whereby Metropolitan Toronto teachers would be eligible for election to area boards other than those employing them but barred from service on the Metropolitan Toronto School Board.

CERTIFICATION

Since teacher preparation and certification are for the most part intimately linked, the two topics will be treated together in volume v, chapters 1 and 6, which deal with elementary and secondary school teachers respectively. The present section is confined to a limited review of some of the historical highlights; to reference to a few aspects not covered in volume v, particularly those with salary implications; and to a brief treatment of some of the issues involved.

Significant early developments

During the nineteenth century, the central authority imposed increasingly exacting certification requirements as a principal means of improving the quality of the work done in the schools. Before the middle of the century, certificates were granted by county boards. From all accounts, political factors were often given as much consideration as academic achievement. The licence granted by the board was valid only in the area within its jurisdiction, and teachers who wanted to move out of the county had to repeat the process. From the time of its establishment in 1847 until 1853, the Toronto Normal School issued only statements indicating the standing of graduates in various subjects, and certificates had to be secured from county boards. The latter made a practice, however, of granting certificates to these graduates without examinations. The central authority entered the field of certification in 1853.

For a considerable period of time, both county boards and normal schools granted certificates. The role of the former was reduced when their rights were limited to the granting of Third Class Certificates. When the county model schools were abolished in 1907, the boards disappeared. After that time, certificates were issued by the Department of Education on the recommendation of the normal school staffs.[4]

Financial incentives were offered by the central authority to induce the school boards to hire teachers with certificates of higher grade. The existence of several grades facilitated the process of improvement, while maintaining an adequate supply of teachers. During the twentieth century, however, the survival of the lower grades offered an easy means of descent to lower standards when local authorities objected to the increasing cost of hiring those with the best qualifications.[5]

Perhaps the most important development in secondary school teacher certification in the nineteenth century was the establishment of the academic specialist's certificate as a qualification for teaching in a collegiate institute. By the 1890s the university honours course had become clearly recognized as the basis for the award of this certificate. The position of the honours course was, as a result, firmly reinforced, with profound implications for later university development. Another significant consequence of the existence of a large group of academic specialists was the emergence of the senior matriculation year in the secondary schools. The academic specialist, with his unassailable position at the top of the status hierarchy among secondary school teachers, did much to orient the secondary school curriculum toward academic goals. He also helped to emphasize the distinction between the elementary and secondary school levels.

The special status of the academic specialist was protected by the fact that a general or pass degree could not be converted into an honours degree by the in-service courses for which provision was increasingly made over the years. Few teachers could contemplate making a new start at the early stage in university work that the honours course required. It was regarded as a major achievement when the OSSTF made an arrangement with the University of Waterloo to guarantee that honours programs would be offered during the summer over a long enough period of years that those who began them would have an opportunity to complete them. The number of teachers who have taken advantage of this provision has not, however, been a very large percentage of the number eligible.

During its early years, the Ontario College of Education made provision for a considerable number of certificates at the elementary, intermediate, and specialist's level in a variety of areas such as physical education, guidance, and art, most of which required additional summer courses after completion of the pre-service program. These specialties reflected the greater variety of programs offered at the secondary than at the elementary level. When formal provision for the preparation of vocational teachers was first made in the 1920s only one grade of certificate was offered. In 1928, however, a distinction was made between ordinary and specialist's certificates, offering considerable incentive to vocational teachers to improve their formal education.

Major effects of the post-war teacher shortage on elementary teacher certification

In very brief summary, to avoid undue repetition of material presented in volume V, chapter 1, the major changes made in elementary school teacher certification as a result of the teacher shortage in the final years of and after the Second World War were as follows. 1 / Rejecting the possibility of a general revival of the Second Class Certificate, which was still being offered at the University of Ottawa Normal School, the authorities chose to debase the academic standard of the First Class Certificate by reducing the grade 13 subject requirements for admission to the one-year course and by awarding the certificate after programs of teacher preparation covering two years, or two summer courses plus one year, after grade 12, in neither of which there was any pretence that the academic rigour of grade 13 was maintained. 2 / In 1953 the department dropped the requirement of in-service courses for the permanent First and Second Class Certificates; thereafter, all that was demanded was pre-service training and successful experience. 3 / Measures were taken to facilitate the admission of teachers educated in other provinces and countries. Before 1953 those from Great Britain and other provinces might be given a Letter of Standing enabling them to teach in Ontario for one year, at the end of which they had to write the final examinations at a teachers' college. At that time, the examination requirement was dropped, and a certificate was issued on the basis of successful experience.

Certification by the OSSTF

A major development at the secondary school level occurred in the 1950s, when the OSSTF undertook to classify its members according to their qualifications and to grant or withhold its stamp of approval. The complexity of the situation gave the Certification Committee a considerable amount of work over a period of several years. In the spring of 1957, this committee presented a report proposing three levels based on the High School Assistant's Certificate, the Endorsed Certificate (which had just been introduced), and the Specialist's Certificate. After further work, a fourth level was added. In rough terms, the four levels came to be defined as follows. Group 1 required the Interim High School Assistant's Certificate, Type B, or the Permanent High School Assistant's Certificate, or the Interim Vocational Certificate, Type B, or the Permanent Vocational Certificate. Group 2 required the Endorsed Certificate in an academic subject, or an Intermediate Certificate in guidance, music, art, commercial work, or another subject where the requirements might be met through attendance at departmental summer courses. Group 3 required a Specialist's Certificate not based on an honours degree, or an honours degree or equivalent with at least second class standing but without the requirements of a Type A or Specialist's Certificate. Group 4 required a four-year honours degree with at least second class honours and a Type A or Specialist's Certificate, or a Specialist's Certificate without an honours degree but with at least five additional university courses with an average of at least 66 per cent in each, or more than one Specialist's Certificate, or a Vocational Specialist's Certificate with any acceptable university degree. After a time, provision was made for a seal stamped on a Group 4 Statement indicating that the holder had one or more graduate degrees in addition to the regular requirements. Similarly, a special stamp indicated work done toward an extra undergraduate degree.

This category system was not given any official status. It became very important, however, in that local school systems came to accept it as a basis for the establishment of their salary schedules. Different minima and maxima, designed to encourage upgrading, were defined for each group. Although as a matter of form the single salary schedule was successfully resisted by the secondary school teachers, school boards began to recognize seven levels when the Elementary School Teacher's Certificate with four standards was established to recognize successively higher levels of preparation based on university or departmental summer courses.

Some of the secondary school teachers hoped that the provincial government would eventually be prepared to turn over the responsibility for official certification to their federation. Many saw this step as an essential aspect of full professionalization. In a study paper prepared for the Canadian Conference on Education in 1962, J.M. Paton observed that nowhere in Canada did the organized teaching profession control, or even have an important voice in determining, the conditions under which candidates entered its ranks, obtained certificates, had their certificates made permanent, or lost them.[6] These powers were exercised exclusively by officials who tended to be slow to advocate change and reform and who readily bowed to the slightest community pressure to lower standards. The study contained a provisional conclusion worded as follows.

Every provincial teachers' association in Canada today has the power by law to enrol as active members all teachers in publicly controlled schools and to subject them to its discipline. It therefore has the organizational potential to accept delegation to it of some or all of the provincial department's power over the preparation and certificating of teachers. In practice, of course, the actual work of teacher-education would be assumed by the universities ... Certification could, however, be the responsibility of the profession. But the issuing of the license to teach could remain the prerogative of the department of education, thus protecting the state from excessive demands by the profession. If the organized teaching profession had the power of certification, it could justifiably be given the responsibility for maintaing high standards of competence and ethical conduct by its members.

H.O. Barrett spoke on the question of teacher certification at a summer conference of the Provincial Executive of the OSSTF in August 1967.[7] On that occasion, he declared that he considered the goal of complete federation responsibility for certification both unrealistic and undesirable. Referring to parallels frequently drawn with the medical and legal professions, he expressed the opinion that these two professions had too much control and that each would ultimately have to yield some of its power. According to his "ideal" solution, the universities would maintain their existing responsibility to conduct courses and to confer degrees on those who successfully completed them. Admission would be at the discretion of each college of education rather than being centrally directed. Each college would grant its own certificate, which would not, however, confer the automatic right to teach. The Department of Education would maintain its licensing role by issuing a single type of licence permitting the holder to teach in the schools of Ontario. The OSSTF Certification Board would have the task of evaluating both academic transcripts and teaching qualifications bestowed by the colleges of education, and of placing each individual at an appropriate level. Barrett thought this board might face up to the difficult and unpleasant responsibility of comparing the quality of programs offered by different universities.

In the Legislature in June 1968, Robert Nixon spoke in favour of granting to the teaching profession the right to control admission to its ranks. He used the familiar examples of the medical and legal professions and offered some suggestions for safeguards against abuse.

Naturally, The Department of Education would have some supervision. It might act in this regard as a resource centre. It might act as an ombudsman for anybody who felt that the teachers' professional organization was not acting in fairness and justice. I feel sure that if the Minister were to look at the report authored by Mr. McRuer he would find ample justification for granting under suitable legislation to a properly established teachers' professional organization the right to grant certification, and to police and patrol and develop professionally and otherwise the attitudes of the teachers of the province. I do not agree with the Minister at all that it is essential for the control of the system that he retain in his own hands the requirements that certificates be authorized by himself.[8]

The Provincial Committee on Aims and Objectives expressed the view that control over certification should remain with the minister only for an interim period. It suggested that the responsibility be shared ultimately by the university and the teachers' professional organization. The university would grant the degree or diploma indicating the type of preparation, and the teachers' professional organization, operating through a College of Teachers of Ontario, would issue the licence permitting the qualified graduate to teach.[9]

TEACHER RECRUITMENT

The shortage of teachers which characterized most of the period after the Second World War was a cause of persistent concern to Department of Education officials, local authorities, trustees' organizations, and the teaching profession. Measures taken to deal with the problem by lowering standards of admission to pre-service courses and by offering special programs are recorded in the early chapters of volume v. Efforts were also made to lure the maximum number of young people from the appropriate age group into teaching. These efforts were supplemented by recruiting campaigns in Britain and other Commonwealth countries where salaries were lower and an incentive for emigration was presumed to exist.

There is some question about how far it is desirable to attempt to promote teaching careers among young people. They have without exception had an opportunity to observe teachers at work over a period of many years, and by the time they reach the end of secondary school have usually formed very definite opinions about the advantages and disadvantages of teaching. If they have not already decided to become teachers, it is doubtful that promotional activities designed to glamorize the teacher's task will have much effect. The potential candidates whose uncertainties are overcome at this stage may well be among those who are not long retained in the teaching ranks. Yet a number of recruiting activities have been organized on the assumption that benefits may be expected from the promotion of teaching as a career.

In 1950 a committee of selection was organized at each of the normal schools to ensure, not only that undesirable candidates were excluded, but also that promising ones were persuaded to enrol in the teacher preparation course. One or more members of these committees, which consisted of the principal of the normal school, other members of the staff, an inspector, and a representative of the Ontario Teachers' Federation, visited secondary schools around the province to interview prospective applicants. Advertisements were placed in daily and weekly newspapers stating the requirements for entrance to normal school and providing information for those interested in an interview with the committee of selection. It would be impossible to get a satisfactory estimate of the effect of these measures on the supply of teachers.

Early in his career as Minister of Education, before he became excessively reluctant to acknowledge the existence of a shortage of teachers, W. J. Dunlop assessed the seriousness of the rapidly developing problem. At a Niagara zone conference of the Ontario Urban and Rural School Trustees' Association, he admonished the trustees that they had a definite responsibility to recruit more teachers. He admitted, however, that at a time when there were so many other professions and occupations competing for the high school graduates, he did not know the answer to the recruiting problem.

During the latter half of the 1950s the Teacher Recruitment and Service Council, later called the Teacher Recruitment and Service Foundation, concerned itself with the shortage of teachers for the secondary schools. Organized mainly through the efforts of S.G.B. Robinson, General Secretary of the OSSTF, it brought together representatives of the Department of Education and of school trustees and administrators along with federation members to plan strategy to cope with a common problem. Between 1956 and 1959 the writer prepared a series of projections of teacher supply for the organization. These fluctuated considerably from one year to another, but generally reinforced the impression that the situation was serious and would remain so for a number of years. The council encouraged the preparation of a brochure entitled *Time of Decision*, which was financed by the OSSTF and circulated widely among the secondary schools.

The Superintendent of Secondary Education, S.D. Rendall, commended the work of the Teacher Recruitment and Service Council in a memorandum issued to principals of secondary schools in January 1957. The memorandum also referred to other activities in the same area.

It is understood ... that many of the District Teachers' Organizations are making it their special concern this year to bring to the attention of their members their responsibility for presenting to senior students the legitimate claims of the profession.

Doubtless all Principals will be making arrangements for group meetings of pupils who may be attracted to teaching in secondary schools. In planning for speakers to address such groups, it is suggested that possibly an interchange of Principals, Vice-Principals, or Guidance officers in neighbouring schools, or an invitation to a suitable person outside the profession, might have some merit in supplementing the efforts of the local personnel.[10]

Some of the larger school boards conducted recruiting campaigns in Great Britain during this period. Their efforts were complemented by those of the department which in 1957, for example, arranged for W.R. Stewart, Assistant Superintendent of Secondary Education, to visit Britain to interview teachers, assess their qualifications, and on behalf of Ontario school boards to engage those who were considered suitable. Prior information from interested boards was secured on forms specially prepared for the purpose. This kind of mission was not regarded with great enthusiasm in Britain, which was having its own problems of maintaining an adequate supply of teachers. Similar feelings were aroused in Australia and New Zealand which, however, suffered more from the depredations of the western provinces than from those of Ontario. The teachers' federations generally welcomed the arrival of well-qualified teachers from abroad until the supply began to exceed the demand in larger centres in the late 1960s. Objections were sometimes raised on the ostensible grounds that school board recruiters were wasting the taxpayers' money in making visits abroad.

In its report to the 1957 Annual Assembly of the OSSTF, the Teacher Training, Certification and Supply Committee offered a number of observations and recommendations. Reference was made to the dissemination of information among high school students and to direct counselling for those interested in becoming teachers. While these measures were considered effective in recruiting for teachers' colleges, it had been impossible to overcome the effects of the time lag between the student's decision to teach in secondary school and his graduation from a university three or four years later. Efforts had been made to persuade the universities to undertake the necessary counselling. The committee deplored the failure of the Department of Education to provide filmstrips or movie shorts about teaching in Ontario. Those prepared in the United States were not appropriate for the province.

The committee felt that better financial assistance could make a substantial contribution to improving the supply of teachers. At that time, a student at the Ontario College of Education could obtain a dominion-provincial bursary part way through his one-year course. For his first few months, however, the only help available consisted of loans from the OSSTF. During the previous winter, these had amounted to $7,975, and in the previous summer to $18,405 – amounts which the organization did not feel it could exceed. Despite pressure from the federation and other sources, the department had declined to eliminate fees for attendance at the college, nor was there any move to provide residence accommodation at the lowest possible rates.

The federation made repeated and unsuccessful efforts to persuade the Teachers' Superannuation Commission to permit some superannuated teachers to return to teaching without loss of pension. Economic necessity was given credit for forcing boards to repeal by-laws requiring compulsory retirement before the age of sixty-five. Little success had been recorded in having married women teachers return to the classroom or in having teachers over sixty-five resume teaching on a half-day basis. School administrators seemed to find it more convenient to get teachers on Letters of Permission.

During the 1960s, recruitment efforts largely involved a continuation of procedures developed in the previous decade. Some attention was directed at the uncertainties involved in trying to persuade young people to become teachers. A private firm defined certain areas which would benefit from a long-range research program on the part of the Department of Education. The following were suggested: 1 / a study of attitudes toward teaching among high school students, university students, parents of school children, elementary and secondary school teachers, and guidance teachers and student counsellors in high schools and universities; 2 / an analysis of teacher records by the Department of Education to determine the characteristics of teachers and to compare those who stayed in the profession with those who did not; 3 / a study of factors influencing teachers to leave the profession, particularly those withdrawing voluntarily to seek other work or to continue teaching in other provinces; 4 / a long-range follow-up study of high school and university students to identify changes in attitudes and influences relating to teaching and other career choices; 5 / a study of teachers' attitudes to their profession and of the processes by which they reached a decision to teach.

In 1967 Davis referred to two measures in particular which had been taken to improve the supply of teachers in the secondary schools. 1 / Admission requirements had been changed to permit university graduates from a wider spectrum of courses to enter teaching. 2 / The availability of Letters of Standing had been extended to include graduates from any part of the world who could meet Ontario standards and had the necessary language and citizenship requirements.[11] At that time, approximately 30 per cent of the graduates from arts and science faculties in Ontario universities were going into teaching.

THE PROBLEM OF QUALITY

The importance of good teachers

The Provincial Committee on Aims and Objectives declared: "A child's best guarantee of a good education is an inspiring teacher, a vigorous, informed, friendly person who likes children, who is able to establish a cheerful, social, permissive climate for learning, and who maintains creative and democratic relationships."[12] Most elements in this statement would elicit general agreement, even from those with a substantially different philosophical orientation from that expressed in the report. Some would prefer to see a strong emphasis on the word "informed." Certain implications of the term "permissive" arouse opposition in some quarters, and there are those who would wish to see "democratic" defined in such a way as to ensure that ignorance, inexperience, and poor judgment are not given equal status with their opposites. On the whole, however, the general tone of the passage would be widely acceptable.

The potential supply

A good deal of talk about education seems to be based on the assumption that an adequate supply of paragons available for teaching exists somewhere in the background. Salary campaigns are conducted on the basis that better and better incomes will soon fill the ranks of the profession with such people. Methods of instruction are appraised as if they would never be used except by outstanding teachers. Media such as television are judged in relation to exceptional teaching performance. Those who advocate raising standards for admission into the profession often seem to assume an inexhaustible reservoir of talent at the desired level.

The value of a report such as that produced by the Provincial Committee might be immeasurably enhanced if it were possible to make at least a rough calculation of the extent of Ontario's resources of people with the potentialities of good teachers who might be enlisted to conduct education in the recommended manner. One might concede the maximum allowance for the capacity of rather ordinary individuals to catch a higher vision of excellence and to reach levels of performance beyond normal expectations. After the most generous estimate had been made of the extent of the contribution to be anticipated from these individuals, some super-researcher might determine how many teachers of mediocre talents would be needed to fill the remainder of the province's classrooms. If that could be done there would be, for the first time, a sound basis for determining how far it would be advisable to attempt to replace teaching power by other educative forces in society. It is quite possible that logic would point to fewer hours in the classroom for each child as a means of distributing fairly a recognizably limited teaching resource. The desirability of reducing the time spent by talented teachers in non-teaching duties would compel recognition. There would, futhermore, be a minumum of difficulty in ensuring that teaching talent would receive adequate financial reward. Above all, there would be some basis for estimating to what extent educational ideals were attainable.

Incalculable social waste results from the supposition that poor teachers contribute some proportion of the benefits that are conferred by good teachers. Schools are actually run as if one and one-third bad teachers were equivalent to one good one. In fact, many children would probably be better off without ever seeing a classroom at all than being subjected to a rigid, compulsive, unimaginative individual whose chief message is that learning is a boring, unpleasant experience to be got over as soon as possible.

The ranks are protected by the assumption that the worst possible situation would be to have empty classrooms. During the 1950s W.J. Dunlop and others who were placed in an exceedingly awkward spot by a badly unbalanced age distribution used to express satisfaction over the statement that no classroom in Ontario was empty for lack of a teacher. The attitude of an undiscriminating public no doubt made it politically essential that they be able to do so. During that period, however, inspectors were calling some of the so-called teaching they witnessed "execrable." Because the expectations of the public outran the possibility of fulfilment, officials were forced to be part to a sham and a pretence. While the pronounced shift in the age distribution and the great increase in the general level of education promise the possibility of real selection among future candidates for the teaching profession, there is a danger, corresponding in a sense to that in the 1950s, that the recommendations of the Provincial Committee may promise an education that will be beyond the capacity of society to deliver. While the inadequate ingredient could be money, it is even more likely to be human resources. The educational establishment may once more be forced into a pretence.

Motives for entering the profession

Those applying for admission to an institution of teacher preparation are usually well advised, when asked their reasons for wishing to enter the profession, to stress the altruistic motives such as their love for children or young people, their desire to make a positive social contribution, the inspiration provided by their own teachers, and the like. It would be depressing indeed if one were forced to conclude that these reasons did not have a certain degree of validity. There are, however, a good many other occupations that offer outlets for most of these commendable impulses. Something more specific is demanded in answer to the question, "Why teach?"

In earlier days, many young women would have been forced to answer, if the absolute truth were exacted, that their range of choice was extremely narrow. Teaching might be selected on the grounds that it was merely less unattractive than office work or nursing. At one time also, the influence of a parental occupational choice was much greater than it is today. It would appear that the choice of teaching is made against an increasingly wide variety of possible alternatives. One factor of indisputable importance is of course remuneration. A substantial shift of young women toward teaching and away from nursing accompanied a change in salary levels in favour of the former. A second factor is that many young people, despite vigorous protests to the contrary on the part of those already in the profession, assume that teaching is easy. They are particularly impressed by the numerous holidays and the long summer vacation. The truth is that teaching *can* be undemanding, or it can be one of the most arduous of occupations. There are teachers who expend enormous amounts of nervous energy in the classroom; who supplement their daytime efforts with long hours of preparation and marking exercises, essays, and examinations; who pass their summers working for degrees, diplomas, and informal upgrading. There are others who get by without doing any of these things. As long as they have no greater ambition than that of earning their annual salary increment, they remain undisturbed.

There are some distinctly undesirable traits that attract certain individuals to teaching. One of these has been epitomized by the following interchange.

> "Why are you a teacher?" asked one of my students.
>
> I answered, "When I was younger the neighbourhood gang never selected me as their leader. Now I have a gang of my own."

The school offers a captive gang. The teacher is a leader who cannot be ignored. He can express his long-frustrated desire to dominate. If his problem is really deep-seated, he may become more dictatorial, more oppressive, and more autocratic as the years pass. The less willingly his subjects accept his dictates, the more he demands the obeisance that he regards as his due.

In an appraisal of American teachers as a class early in the 1960s, Margaret Mead noted that entry into the teaching profession was regarded by both men and women as a suitable way to move from lower-class to lower-middle-class status or to cling to endangered middle-class status. The lower-middle class was said to be characterized as having "clear, firm and unadventurous standards of prudence, cleanliness, neatness, caution, carefulness."[13] Its members were the kind of safe, respectable people to whom landlords gladly rented houses, whom merchants welcomed as instalment buyers, and to whom civic duties and neighbourhood activities were confidently entrusted. By their choice of profession, teachers had bettered themselves and achieved a position in society from which they had no over-powering ambition to move.

In the classroom these teachers were confronted with children who varied extraordinarily in background, intelligence, originality, expectations, and hopes, and who were ostensibly supposed to be encouraged to develop their creative powers – to be original, spontaneous, and free to move and think in unusual ways. By their nature, creative children did not accept things as they were and did not readily settle down to the lessons that were given to them. Mead wondered how it was possible for a young woman whose purpose was to keep twenty-five or thirty children well-disciplined, cheerful, and successful in conventional terms to welcome a creative child. Everything she stood for seemed to be antithetical to the required values.

The appraisal issue

Even if there were general acceptance of the proposition that bad teachers are a luxury that no system can afford, there would be very serious problems in weeding out more than a very small proportion of them. While the teaching profession in Ontario supports the exclusion of a few of its least creditable members, given adequate evidence of conspicuously poor performance, any attempt to go beyond the fringes would arouse a strong defensive reaction. Many would suggest that there was something underhanded or disreputable in implying that the overwhelming majority in their ranks were anything but highly capable and conscientious. Furthermore, a very real obstacle to effective screening would be evident – that of evaluation. Unless indisputably efficacious methods of appraisal were used, the process could not help but arouse widespread apprehension and insecurity.

It is not necessary to repeat at this point the rather convincing evidence that even trained and experienced administrators and supervisors show surprisingly little ability to reach consistent verdicts about the quality of teacher performance evidenced in a single lesson. In fact, the attempt to do so should by now have been almost completely discredited, although the approach may be defended as a means of detecting very blatant faults. There are those who would go further and say that there is no valid procedure for appraising teachers. Whatever grounds there are for this statement are mainly to be traced to the fact that there are many different criteria on which to base a judgment. Lloyd Dennis would presumably look primarily for warmth, humanity, concern, sensitivity, and other related qualities. But Dennis has not persuaded all his fellow citizens that order, obedience, and respect for one's elders are not among the primary goals of education. Given sufficient time and opportunity to observe a teacher performing under a variety of circumstances, a competent person who placed a high value on these qualities should have no more difficulty in determining whether or not the accepted goals were being attained than Dennis would in identifying the kind of performance that met his criteria. With their contradictory orientations, the two would naturally be expected to place a particular teacher at different points on a qualitative scale. It would not be the means of effective rating that were lacking, but rather the ability to agree on what was wanted. Yet Dennis and his opposite number would probably not find themselves in total disagreement. The strongest contrast in the eyes of both of them might be between the teacher who seemed capable of attaining defined goals, whatever their nature, and the teacher who was not.

In an article in the *Phi Delta Kappan* in February 1969, Don Hamachek deplored the oft-repeated contention that it was impossible to distinguish good teachers from bad.[14] He noted that this claim continued to be made despite the fact that no issue in education had been so voluminously researched as teacher effectiveness. His paper was devoted to an effort to demonstrate the contrary. He began by singling out four dimensions of teacher personality and behaviour that had been most frequently probed: 1 / personal characteristics, 2 / instructional procedures and interaction styles, 3 / perception of self, and 4 / perceptions of others. This list was presented as representative rather than exhaustive.

The first series of studies Hamachek referred to revolved around the question of what characteristics students liked best in teachers. Not surprisingly, they were most attracted by those who were helpful and competent in the way in which they expressed their desire to help. A sense of humour was looked upon with favour. Hardly more startling was the fact that unpopularity resulted from the opposite qualities, along with arrogance, partiality, ill-humour, and a propensity to sarcasm. Somewhat less expected was the discovery that mastery of subject matter received a very low ranking. A cynic might conclude that the students expressing their opinion appeared to be more interested in being entertained than in learning. As if to deal with this point, Hamachek examined the question of whether or not a teacher with attractive personal qualities got better results. He was able to cite a number of studies to support the view that they did.

I think the evidence is quite clear when it comes to sorting out good or effective from bad or ineffective teachers on the basis of personal characteristics. Effective teachers appear to be those who are, shall we say, "human" in the fullest sense of the word. They have a sense of humor, are fair, empathetic, more democratic than autocratic, and apparently are more able to relate easily and naturally to students on either a one-to-one or group basis. Their classrooms seem to reflect miniature enterprise operations in the sense that they are more open, spontaneous, and adaptable to change. Ineffective teachers apparently lack a sense of humor, grow impatient easily, use cutting, ego-reducing comments in class, are less well-integrated, are inclined to be somewhat authoritarian, and are generally less sensitive to the needs of their students. Indeed, research related to authoritarianism suggests that the bureaucratic conduct and rigid overtones of the ineffective teacher's classroom are desperate measures to support the weak pillars of his own personality structure.[15]

Hamachek dealt next with instructional procedures and interaction styles of good versus poor teachers. Studies in this area showed that results were best where teachers' behaviour demonstrated the following characteristics: 1 / flexibility, varying from directness to indirectness as the situation demanded; 2 / ability to perceive the world from the student's point of view; 3 / ability to "personalize" their teaching; 4 / willingness to experiment; 5 / skill in questioning; 6 / knowledge of subject matter; 7 / provision of well-established examination procedures; 8 / provision of definite study helps; 9 / demonstration of an appreciative attitude by means of nods, comments, smiles, and other gestures; 10 / use of an informal, easy, conversational style in teaching.

Research into the self-perception of good and poor teachers showed that the former perceived their own dominant traits as self-confidence and cheerfulness; that they identified themselves with people; that they felt themselves to be trustworthy, reliable, and capable of coping with events; that they considered themselves to be wanted; and that they regarded themselves as worthy. These were the essential characteristics of good mental health. Related to such qualities were the views effective teachers held of other people. They had relatively favourable opinions of students, of administrators, and of colleagues, a propensity for personal contacts, and an inclination toward democratic classroom procedures.

The value of the research is hardly that it shows that good teachers are in general good people. It is rather that certain definable and recognizable teacher characteristics can be related to student performance. The process of evalution cannot, of course, be made simple. One reason is that desirable and undesirable qualities occur in a great variety of combinations and, despite the tendency for certain traits to cluster together, it is often difficult to determine what kind of total they add up to. How many virtues, for example, does one serious fault cancel out? Despite such problems, however, there are considerable grounds for the belief that teachers can be effectively evaluated. Whether the process occurs or not depends both on the existence of people with the knowledge and skill required to do so and the existence of a genuine desire on the part of those involved to have it done.

The idea that students at the secondary school as well as the post-secondary level might participate in the process of teacher evaluation has often been suggested. Sometimes the case is made in sentimental terms replete with assertions that education is, after all, for the benefit of the students and no one else, and that young people are more perceptive and responsible than they are usually given credit for being. It is also pointed out that they are in a much better position to observe the teacher's behaviour under a wide variety of conditions than any outsider could possibly be. Some objective studies have shown that they can quite accurately assess the extent to which a teacher's personality and competence meet specified criteria. They can certainly be depended on to say whether or not their relationship with a particular teacher promotes or inhibits their own success in learning.

In an article in the *Bulletin* of the Ontario Secondary School Teacher's Federation, J.M. Cameron suggested that students rate teachers on a five-point scale with respect to each of the following questions: 1 / Does the teacher show an interest in the students as individuals and communicate well with them? 2 / Does the teacher appear to have a knowledge of the subject? 3 / Does the teacher make the subject interesting to the student? 4 / Does the teacher have the respect of the class? 5 / Does the teacher have an interest in the world outside the classroom and help the student find out more about this world? Cameron advocated that teacher evaluation be based one-third on inspectors' reports, one-third on principals' reports, and one-third on students' reports.[16]

Objections to allowing students to have a part in teacher evaluation are often made on the grounds that teaching should not become a popularity contest. From this point of view, it is assumed that the highest ratings would go to teachers who maintained a circus atmosphere and never exerted pressure on the students to do anything unpleasant, such as work. In fact, it has been demonstrated repeatedly that students whose vital concerns have been correctly identified appreciate the opportunity to do hard, constructive work. There is everything to indicate that the teaching qualities they assess favourably are those most valued by adults as well. The main reason why many teachers would be unwilling to let students have any vital part in evaluating them is that they would find it demeaning and inconsistent with the superior status which they feel is rightfully theirs. Apart from these considerations, there are valid grounds for opposing formal student evaluation (as opposed to informal evaluation, which is of course inevitable). They are the same as those for objecting to it when conducted by inspectors or administrators.

Even though it may be accepted that quite specific criteria for the evaluation of teachers can be defined, and that the qualities of individuals and their performance can be measured against these criteria, there still remains the very vital problem of determining how, if at all, the process of appraisal can be applied without producing destructive effects outweighing any possible gain. The presence of a superintendent or inspector sitting at the back of the room watching the teacher's actions for the purpose of assigning a rating has been seen increasingly as incompatible with a full recognition of human dignity. The existence of a superior implies an inferior, a relationship which the pupils cannot help but sense. The effect might be salutary if they perceived the difference solely in terms of knowledge or skill, but they are all too likely to identify the teacher as an inferior person, less worthy of inherent respect than his administrative superiors. Such an attitude is inimical to true learning.

The effect of inspection on a teacher might be beneficial if education could be equated largely with mechanical drill, as it once was. Fear of an adverse rating, provided that the consequences were immediate and sufficiently unpleasant, might spur a lazy teacher to greater effort and efficiency. But inspection can do nothing to make an insensitive teacher more humane or a plodding teacher more inspiring. On the contrary, it can produce destructive fear, hypocritical pretence, and an attempt to conceal weakness rather than bringing it into the open where it can be effectively remedied. The teacher who kept a model lesson handy for the inspector's visit was notorious in the days when departmental inspection was a major event in Ontario schools. The inspectors were not nearly as good at detecting this practice as they often claimed, and many a teacher looked much better as a result of a neat bit of specially prepared showmanship than he would have if he had proceeded with some of the less inspiring tasks that inevitably were part of his classroom work. The deplorable aspect of the subterfuge was not, however, that the teacher got a better rating than he deserved, but rather that he demeaned himself before his students, and that they demeaned themselves by their willing and often sympathetic participation, which meant engaging in deceit.

It is trite to observe that teaching ought to be regarded as a means to an end and never as an end in itself. Yet the rating of teaching almost inevitably concentrates attention on the means and, in doing so, tends to distort them. The inspector with the responsibility of assessing the teacher finds himself frustrated if he arrives to find the students working quietly on projects. He cannot be satisfied to observe that they are demonstrating an intense interest in what they are doing and to conclude from that evidence that the teacher deserves to be classed as excellent. He must see an organized lesson, with the teacher asking questions, stimulating discussion, making a presentation, or in some other way occupying the centre of the stage. It is not hard to see what he regards as important. By contrast, some of the most productive learning activities which do not involve overt intervention by the teacher are made to seem inconsequential. It is true, of course, that this effect can be avoided, especially if plenty of time is allowed for repeated classroom visits. In actual practice, however, things seldom work out that way.

The effect of inspection for the purpose of rating is something like that of the external examination. While a good teacher should in theory be able to concentrate solely on the goals of education, both the rating score and the examination mark tend to become independent objectives. It is unfair to the teacher to expect him to resist the pressure that diverts him from his proper task. This fact was implicitly acknowledged when the Ontario Department of Education converted its inspectors into program consultants. The idea that they could combine appraisal and assistance was entirely abandoned. Not only was a visit from one of them dependent on the teacher's invitation, but the consultant was forbidden to make any report whatever on the quality of the performance he observed.

The critics of the educational establishment are far from ready to see the abandonment of overt appraisals of teaching performance. There remains a strong feeling that formal evaluation is an essential guarantee that standards will be maintained. In actual fact, however, such a belief is largely illusory. Once in the profession, and past a brief probationary period, only an infinitesimal percentage of teachers are driven out against their will because of poor performance. Evaluation that almost never leads to expulsion, but only to classification by some quantitative or qualitative label, makes no significant contribution to education, although it may assist favourably situated and well-endowed school boards to conduct successful raids against those in a poorer position to compete.

There are more effective ways to elevate the quality of teaching performance. The obvious basic requirement, of course, is to ensure that incentives such as salaries, working conditions, and social prestige are adequate in comparison with other occupations which might attract potential teachers as alternatives. Assuming that this condition is met, extreme care can be taken to ensure that those who do not have an excellent chance of being a credit to the profession are not admitted in the first place. Although no existing device or approach can offer an absolute guarantee that the occasional misfit will not breach the barriers, there is no question that the effectiveness of screening procedures could be vastly improved. At the risk of excessive repetition, it may be suggested again that, if the supply of potentially good teachers is inadequate to meet the assumed need, or if the community is not prepared to offer the incentive required to attract them to teaching, it would be better to utilize other educative devices and influences rather than enlist people with inadequate talents.

In teaching, as in other professions, there is a danger that a certain percentage of those who begin with enthusiasm and vigour will eventually sink into a state of torpid complacency. Perhaps the only effective way to counteract this tendency is provide an abundance of stimulating opportunities for continued growth. Conferences, workshops, seminars, short courses, summer courses, and other such activities, while not without the capacity to create boredom and disgust, have substantial potentialities for arousing and maintaining interest. A vigorous Department of Education can direct a stream of innovative ideas into the school system. Research agencies with a commitment to the actual improvement of the educational process can be a powerful stimulating force. Professional associations can do much to ensure that the teacher who is not only good but constantly becoming better earns the regard and appreciation of his fellows. Administrators, backed by enlightened school boards and an understanding public, can ensure that the teacher's obligations are not so burdensome that he is unable to take advantage of opportunities for improvement. If these measures cannot produce a high standard of teaching performance, it is quite certain that the inspector with his little black book can never do so.

TEACHER FREEDOM AND RESPONSIBILITY

The quality of education is directly and chiefly dependent on the effective utilization of teacher resources – resources of knowledge, skill, understanding, and sympathy. The extent to which the learner will benefit from these resources is largely a matter of the teacher's freedom to choose, to act, to give, to withhold, and in general to control the learning environment. Every rule imposed by an authority outside and beyond the teacher reduces that freedom. Power within any organizational structure is a limited commodity. To the extent that the Department of Education, the school board, and the administrative hierarchy share power, the teacher's power and freedom are reduced. Every time a new layer is added to the bureaucratic structure, power is subtracted from some other part, and the teacher is all too likely to be a loser. The chances are that the ultimate loser will be the pupil.

It must be conceded that in no sphere of human society can a single class or group be safely entrusted with absolute power. Teachers are corruptible, just as any other group. Education is the public's business, and it is perfectly right that the public interest be expressed through provincial and local government structures. It is all too easy to forget, however, that teaching resources are wasted if the balance of power shifts too far toward controlling agencies. Unfortunately, it seems to be an almost irresistible tendency, as society grows more complex, for the power to move in that direction. Leaders in the Ontario Department of Education have wisely realized that a diminution of central control is essential if creative teaching forces are to be released. In certain areas, it may be that major responsibility will land and remain in the lap of the individual teacher. There is a considerable danger, however, that a good deal of the authority being abandoned by the department will be seized and exercised by the administrative hierarchy in the enlarged school divisions and that the teacher's freedom will not be enhanced, but may even be curtailed. It is a paradox, also, that the construction of larger secondary schools to provide the range of opportunities that a modern education demands tends to work against the exercise of teacher initiative and the expression of teacher individuality. Creative teaching is simply incompatible with the sense that one is part of a huge, impersonal machine.

Professor Oswald Hall of the University of Toronto wrote of this development in a booklet entitled *New Developments in Society* prepared for the second Canadian Conference on Education in 1962.[17] He pointed to efforts of high school teachers during the previous two decades to establish their professional status by specifying the proper training for a teacher, classifying themselves in various levels (a debatable contribution to professionalization), establishing a strong association, adopting a licensing system, and gaining some measure of control over their conditions of employment. They were no longer helpless in the face of a dominant school board or department of education. But Hall found some of this autonomy illusory. While teachers were escaping from the control of external agencies, they were becoming victims of a new form of bureaucracy. As the schools grew larger and more complex, principals became administrators rather than teachers or teacher-administrators. As the gap between teacher and principal widened, the vice-principal stepped in and widened it still further. The organization of departments with department heads extended the process.

The wording of Hall's summary statement is significant. "In escaping from the controls of the troublesome School Board teachers have continued a new and cumbersome bureaucracy to plague their work." He rightly implicated the teachers themselves in the proliferation of levels of authority. In supporting the creation of new positions to which their more ambitious or worthy members may be promoted, with appropriate salary increments, they have overlooked the implications for the regular classroom teacher. They have reinforced the pervasive assumption that administrative functions are more important than mere teaching and thus have contributed further to the debasement of teaching. By supporting the extension of the ladder of promotion, they have helped to ensure that they will be co-ordinated out of much of their independence and spontaneity. There is little hope that the classroom teacher in a large school will ever become an innovator unless the administrative superstructure is kept within bounds. If drastic pruning is ever undertaken, it will of course be met by screams of protest from the administrators that they are already overworked, a claim that may very well be true. What will be needed will be a cold appraisal of administrative activities in terms of their real contribution to education. Much of what survives such an appraisal will be found to be within the competence of employees with a good deal less training than that required by a teacher. The number of high-level decisions that must be made in a school, apart from the educational decisions, which ought to be the teachers' business, is much smaller than commonly supposed.

Despite progress made in the 1960s, the Provincial Committee on Aims and Objectives found that the situation deserved rather severe criticism.

> Unfortunately, the educational system itself often equates the classroom teacher with the laborer on the working team. The more the levels of gradation, the farther policy-making is removed from the classroom. Instead of the pupil being the focal point, he is often forgotten, lost in a maze of policies, procedures, memoranda, reports, and surveys that filter down to the classroom, usurping teacher energy and time that belong to the pupil. It is not surprising that in this process teachers lose much of their initiative and enthusiasm, and learn to place emphasis on the disciplinary, custodial, and recording functions that comply with instructions from the central office. Enthusiastic young teachers learn quickly to submit to the operational doctrine by which schools are run. Lip service is often given to the child-centred curriculum, but in the machinery of education the system, the school, and the organization of the school often take precedence over the best education of the pupil. It is ironical that the very system which was set up to assist the child frequently loses sight of him and of his teacher.[18]

The committee contrasted curriculum trends in evidence at the time it made its report with the situation in which teachers found themselves.

> The modern curriculum places its focus on the child. It respects his interests,

his dignity, his individuality. It grants him freedom, understanding, and acceptance. It involves him in planning programs and making decisions about his school experience. To this Committee it seems paradoxical that many teachers who are expected to provide their pupils with such a curriculum are themselves denied the same conditions. Such teachers are given little freedom or autonomy, have no share in policy, are not encouraged to experiment, and receive little recognition as individuals or as vital forces in the educational system.[19]

In early 1969 James Bethune, an assistant secretary of the Ontario Secondary School Teachers' Federation, wrote an article entitled "The Urban Teacher's Hang-up" in which he discussed the reasons for widespread dissatisfaction among teachers in large urban centres. Much of the difficulty he traced to what he saw as the teacher's peculiar status as an element of lower-middle-class society. Since he identified secondary school teachers among the top 10 per cent in terms of income, "middle class" might have constituted a more appropriate placement in the social structure. At any rate, the general theme was that teachers lacked status, a feeling of identity, a sense of contribution, as manifested by "passionate voices demanding confrontation, revolution, rebellion and an end to frustration." While in general Bethune held urban society responsible for the dissatisfaction, he had some sharp words for the bureaucratization – inevitable as it was – of large school systems. He declared that in a school with a hundred or more teachers the process was intensified geometrically. Administrators seemed to have spent little or no time considering the fact that teachers required encouragement and stimulation just like anyone else. Their needs were those of the ego and the soul. If these were not satisfied, salary campaigns often provided a forum for the release of tensions and frustrations. Bethune presented a picture of the urban teacher as "a dedicated but frustrated, reasonably well paid cipher, whose working environment is poor and whose labor-management relations are lamentable." The fact that he could speak of "labor-management relations" epitomizes the teachers' lack of responsibility and power.[20]

A very important distinction must be made at this point between individual and group power. Teachers' organizations have been an inevitable and on balance no doubt a highly beneficial aspect of the evolution of the profession. They may, indeed, have made a major contribution to the exercise of individual power and responsibility. But the strength of the organized teaching body is by no means synonymous with that of the individual member, and could in fact be inimical to it. In his article, Bethune acknowledged the danger that the urban teacher might come to see his own federation as part of an antagonistic bureaucratic structure. The vastly greater freedom of the university professor as compared with the secondary school teacher has never been backed by an organization with the power possessed by the Ontario Secondary School Teachers' Federation.

Alan Brown of the Ontario Institute for Studies in Education earlier put part of Bethune's case in more general and universal terms.

The teacher militancy movement, already in evidence in several large Ontario cities, springs from several sources; one is the increasing degree of professionalism on the part of teachers. Research shows this phenomenon to be a growing one; as teachers improve their qualifications and begin to feel a sense of self-direction in the practice of their profession, they begin to chafe – and justifiably so in most instances – under the restrictions of a bureaucratic establishment ... This militancy is directed toward several ends, which are frequently only indirectly identified with bureaucracy. Educational leaders find this frustrating. They applaud the improvement in teacher qualifications and initiative, but are unable to cope with the "side effects."[21]

While there seems no question that highly educated teachers chafe at a lack of individual freedom and responsibility, it cannot be safely assumed that the possession of these prerogatives will inevitably lead to a highly innovative educational system. In *Strategy for Schools,* the Bow Group mentioned that teachers in England and Wales allegedly had more freedom to decide what they would teach and how it would be taught than their colleagues in any other country. Yet the schools were said not to be a source of fruitful and exciting experiment in curricula and method but rather places characterized by dull uniformity. One of the most important reasons for excessive conformity was identified as the exaggerated respect given to tradition.[22] While teacher freedom would seem to be a necessary condition for educational innovation, there is a complementary need for a stream of ideas, not all of which in the normal course of things will be good ones, to be generated from outside and directed toward the schools. Ontario's system of departmental program consultants and its attempt to provide for organized research and development on a large scale are examples of this type of approach.

THE CONCEPT OF PROFESSIONALISM

Teachers are rather fond of discussing such questions as whether or not they are really professionals, in what respect they fall short of being fully professional, and how they compare with others who consider themselves to be members of a profession. In exasperation with some limitation on their individual or collective privileges, someone from their own ranks is constantly asserting that they have no justification for a claim to professional status. The problem, of course, is largely one of definition. Many attempts have been made to distinguish the essential factors that dignify an occupation as a profession. J.M. Paton identified six of these in a preparatory study for the Canadian Conference on Education in 1962.[23] In abbreviated form, his list was as follows. 1 / A professional has superior competence and skill in a field normally unfamiliar to most laymen. 2 / His paramount consideration is service to others. 3 / He is self-reliant, largely self-motivating, and requires little or no close supervision in his work. 4 / He is well-educated, with at least some measure of higher education in his professional preparation. "He remains intellectually curious and engages in a continuing search for new knowledge and skill." 5 / He belongs to and participates in the work of an organized group of professional colleagues with the responsibility of "attaining and maintaining high standards of admission to, and of competence and ethical behaviour in the practice of, his chosen profession." 6 / The community accepts his superior intellectual attainment, contribution to the well-being of society, and probably economic status.

There are some technical problems about applying a list of this kind to any occupational group. For example, is every one of the conditions essential? Where they are a matter of degree, what level of attainment confers professional status? For example, how much more competence and skill does a member of the group have to have than the layman? How much more devoted does he have to be to the general welfare? Do all the members of the group have to meet all the criteria in order to keep the occupation classified as a profession? Since this is an obvious impossibility, what would be a satisfactory proportion? Two-thirds? One-half? Are not the implications of this question that no occupation can be classified unequivocally as a profession, but rather that an individual may earn the distinction of being a professional, and only in relative rather than absolute terms? These questions may perhaps be labeled picayune. Possibly it is sufficient to establish the validity of the term "profession" according to the performance generally expected of the members of the group in question, with the assumption that most of them make a reasonable effort to meet the recognized criteria.

Apart from these considerations, a number of problems revolve about Paton's list. With respect to the first item, a majority of laymen may be willing to concede superior teaching ability to most teachers. The population of parents, however, includes a rather large proportion of ex-teachers, or even of active teachers, who are not prepared to admit that their child's teacher knows more about handling their child than they do. They feel quite justified in constantly looking over his shoulder and offering criticisms without any inhibitions. And, especially where the minimum level of teacher preparation is low, this attitude may be quite defensible, although possibly somewhat upsetting for the child. Another cause of difficulty is that aims of education offer grounds for legitimate disagreement. In a democratic society, a parent cannot be expected to leave the definition of aims to any special group, whether it considers itself professional or not. Further, even where there is reasonably close agreement on aims, there is so much uncertainty about techniques for achieving them, and so much disagreement among teachers themselves, that the "lay" population can hardly be expected not to take a hand. Matters would be very different if there were a science of education that could identify one practice as right and another wrong, one good and another bad. The contrast with the medical profession is very striking. Although there is lively controversy about such matters as the morality of abortion, for the most part physician and laymen are completely agreed that the objectives are to preserve life and to relieve suffering, as embodied in the Hippocratic oath. Furthermore, medicine is such a highly developed science that the physician's superior competence in diagnosing and treating illness is not seriously disputed.

There is less difficulty with Paton's second point. It is impossible to teach effectively without genuine devotion to the welfare of the pupil. The individual who places a high value on service does not, of course, have to achieve the kind of sainthood that totally despises material comforts and security. The teacher may, however, be expected to keep these in their proper perspective. By the third criterion on the list, teaching has not in general achieved the status of a profession, although in Ontario the Department of Education has given it a strong push in that direction. While quality of performance will and should be recognized, the practice of close supervision identifies the person subject to it as incapable of the kind of self-motivation that characterizes other recognized professions. The fourth criterion identifies a characteristic that can be defined in specific terms only to the extent that it refers to formal qualifications. A diminishing number of people are prepared to accept as professionals those without at least some university education. Continued learning and growth are also being increasingly recognized as essentials for good teaching. By the fifth criterion, no group of teachers in Canada can claim full professional status, since none controls admission to its own ranks. Elected officials have not been persuaded to give up ultimate control over a function for which they believe they are responsible to the public. Some fear is expressed also that the teaching body would restrict admission in order to create an artificial scarcity and thus force up salaries. On the other hand, many feel that the possession of power would enhance the teachers' sense of responsibility. Those teachers who believe they should control entry to their ranks point to comparable privileges held by professions such as medicine and law. The record of such groups has not, however, been entirely exemplary. Unless subjected to considerable outside pressure, they tend to demonstrate a remarkable capacity to persuade themselves that their own selfish interests are synonymous with those of the community at large.

The status of the teacher in the community is a very intangible factor and, furthermore, varies a good deal according to local conditions. The pioneer view of the teacher was partly shaped by the traditional respect for the great teachers of the past, but owed most to the fact that teaching was a function performed mostly by those who were too weak, crippled, old, or addicted to drink to help meet the more fundamental needs of the community by clearing the land, farming, transporting logs, or engaging in other manly pursuits. Matters were not helped much when this kind of teacher was largely replaced by the young woman who, however superior as a person, regarded teaching as a temporary and short-term pursuit on the way to marriage. Identification of teaching as a stepping-stone to something else has always been a major factor in keeping its prestige rather low. A further influence on the popular attitude toward teaching has been its association with the church. Paton wrote rather sarcastically: "Even in the second half of the twentieth century it is not difficult to find people whose picture of the ideal teacher is that of a dedicated spirit, separated from the world, a learned ascetic who must not be expected to behave like a sensible business man, and who should not be corrupted with offers of too much money."[24]

Influences in recent decades have been rather contradictory. When educational requirements were quite high in comparison with the general community level, the teacher might be credibly regarded as "one who knows." But, in Ontario at least, the educational level of the population rose while that required for admission to institutions for teacher preparation at best remained constant and at worst fell substantially. On the other hand, rising salary levels have contributed to teacher prestige, and a demonstration of the ability to fight vigorously for improved salaries has established teachers as a group to be reckoned with. On the whole, the social status of teachers in Canada strikes most observers as being noticeably higher than that of their counterparts in the United States.

A report resulting from a study conducted for the OSSTF, released in January 1969, threw some light on the questions of professionalism in that it indicated the attitudes of various groups toward teachers. The general view, as reported in *InterCom*, was that teachers had yet to win a professional image in the mind of the average man in the street.[25] They had more prestige than nurses, social workers, chiropractors, and librarians, but less than doctors, lawyers, dentists, and druggists. While an overwhelming proportion of the people interviewed agreed that the teacher was second in importance only to the doctor, this opinion seemed to go no further than lip service. Although upper-class people showed a greater awareness of the teacher's importance, lower-class people ranked him higher on the professional scale. Of considerable comfort to the OSSTF was the finding that other professional people did not look down on teachers because of the aggressiveness of their federations. It was also encouraging to find that most people thought teachers worked hard, although they found it rather difficult to define what this work involved.

Arthur E. Salz, in "Formula for Inevitable Conflict: Local Control vs. Professionalism," *Phi Delta Kappan*, February 1969, identified teachers' lack of autonomy as the glaring deficiency in their claim to being members of a profession. He noted that when they acted to remedy this deficiency, that is, when they attempted to define the conditions within which they would provide their services, they came into direct conflict with the public, which had traditionally been in control of education. Teachers who were demanding professional status, and the local, lay public, who controlled education, were on a collision course. The illustration provided by Salz was the conflict in New York City between the organized teachers and local leaders who were attempting to exercise newly designated powers to hire and fire teachers within city-wide standards. The struggle between the Ontario Secondary School Teachers' Federation and the elected boards in Metropolitan Toronto in 1970 over the issue of student-teacher ratio was a manifestation of the kind of clash that Salz described.

The long-term prospects for the professionalization of teaching are not good. The tide in modern society is running strongly against the right of members of other professions as organized groups to determine their own conditions of service. The chain of developments is easily recognized. Humanitarian concern focuses increasing attention on the injustice of denying adequate medical, legal, or other such service to those of poor or modest means. A large proportion of these people are unable to pay for such service – partly because the cost rises more quickly than that of most other goods and services as knowledge accumulates and practitioners require increasing levels of skill and sophistication. The government steps in with support from the public treasury. As the costs rise, usually to a far greater extent than initial forecasts indicate, the public exerts pressure for controls. Members of the profession may have enough strength to fight an impressive rearguard action, but ultimately they must submit. It appears inevitable that any service that comes to be regarded as a necessity for all citizens, regardless of social or financial status, will sooner or later come to be provided under publicly regulated conditions. If the teachers' organizations win a clearcut victory over local school boards, they will eventually have to deal with a more powerful provincial government, however dedicated the latter may be to the principle of local responsibility.

APPRAISALS OF THE TEACHING FORCE

Objective assessments of the quality of the teaching force in Canada as a whole, or in Ontario in particular, are difficult to find. Those who are in a position to obtain the necessary information are, as a rule, biased in favour of the group. In view of their responsibility for defending their members' interests, the federations cannot be expected to make, or at least to publicize, any evaluation that runs the risk of being too harsh. Administrative and supervisory officials, whether locally or provincially employed, have risen from the ranks of the teachers and are hardly more likely to turn a cold eye on their former colleagues as a group, however straightforwardly they may admit the existence of individual members who are unworthy. To turn to outsiders is not much more productive simply because they do not have enough facts. Even university professors, who share the responsibility for education, can demonstrate the most astonishing lack of awareness of the conditions under which schools are conducted.

When groups of teachers have occasion to identify deficiencies among their fellows, they often show an extraordinary ability to find plausible excuses. For example, the Social Sciences Study Committee, which contributed a major section to *Design for Learning*, commented unfavourably on the way social sciences were being taught in the schools.[26] It declined, however, to attribute the inadequacies it observed to inherent defects in the average teacher as currently recruited, but rather blamed many of them on pressures exerted by the established school system, which directed the teacher away from scholarship. The teacher was said to be in the classroom for seven forty-minute periods a day on the average, with additional administrative tasks and extra-curricular responsibilities. Marking papers and assignments or reading essays encroached heavily on his evening time. The committee wondered where there was time in such a day, even if there was an incentive, to look at historical journals or to read a new book.

By Frank MacKinnon's recent assessment, about a third of our school teachers, presumably in Canada as a whole, are very good, a third mediocre, and a third poor. MacKinnon's reading of the Macpherson report in the University of Toronto indicated that, of five university teachers, a student could be considered fortunate if he got one good one and no more than one very bad one. Differences in quality were, of course, common to all occupations. However, MacKinnon thought the matter more serious in teaching because, while it was possible to vote against politicians, refuse to listen to clergymen, and stop employing carpenters, school children consigned to a poor teacher were helpless to do anything about it. As MacKinnon said: "A year with a poor teacher is a pretty harsh punishment for a youngster; the best he can do is learn not to imitate by example; the worst is to get bored with education."[27]

In his report on the state of Canadian studies in schools across the country, A.B. Hodgetts indicated that the group conducting the investigation found a great deal to deplore. After trying to point out all the extenuating circumstances that made the teacher's work more difficult, he posed the questions: "What kinds of people ... are entrusted with the civic education of young Canadians? What special qualities, if any, do they have for this important responsibility?"[28] His answers were not at all inspiring or encouraging. Although he referred to a specific area of study, it is hard to believe that whatever validity his appraisal had did not have substantial general application.

The investigating group discovered that the most academically inclined students were not attracted to the teaching of Canadian studies. Of the 50 per cent of those in the survey who were working in elementary schools, the great majority had fulfilled only the minimum requirements in their respective provinces. While a number of them were engaged in extramural degree work, they seemed not to be particularly interested in selecting courses that would improve their teaching of Canadian studies. Their main purpose seemed to be to get any kind of degree that would enable them to secure advancement in position and salary. Among the secondary school teachers surveyed, almost 80 per cent had second- or third-class degrees from a general arts or an integrated education course. Many of them seemed to lack the self-motivating force that would have enabled them to excel in their studies. Hodgetts declared that they also frequently lacked the other qualities that might have compensated for a weakness in scholastic drive and attainment. Their academic deficiencies suggested deeper difficulties. As indicated by their responses to questionnaires and their performance in interviews, they did not seem to be very dynamic, outgoing, or socially or politically involved. They had not participated in cultural, social, political, or athletic activities. In entering the teaching profession, they had avoided more competitive and superficially more demanding occupations. At a time when demand had exceeded supply, they had found the profession easy to enter and secure. Over 80 per cent of them had been born and raised in one province and were teaching within a hundred miles or so of the place where they had gone to school. Reasons for entering the profession given by fully 59 per cent were that they were attracted by the long holidays, good salaries, and pension plans, and because they could think of nothing else to do.

One of the most devastating passages Hodgetts included on the topic was the following.

> On paper, a great many Canadian studies teachers appear to be the kinds of people who will quickly become stratified. Without a deep involvement in what they are teaching, they will not be motivated to read and keep up with the latest developments. The evidence suggests that, as teachers of difficult subjects in a complex society, their thinking will be fuzzy and superficial. They will follow the rules and regulations so rigidly that, in actual fact, they will be misinterpreting and abusing some of the good advice they have received at teacher-training institutions. Despite the absence of externally set examinations and the urging of supervisors, they will dutifully try to follow the course of study from one end to the other. The textbook is a convenient crutch; the doctrine that it does not matter what we teach provides a golden excuse to play around with teaching tactics divorced from content; or conversely, the simple, unimaginative question-answer technique of the assignment method is an easy escape from quality work in the classroom.[29]

The majority confessed that they made little effort to improve their knowledge of Canadian history and current affairs. Among the respondents, 23 per cent admitted frankly that they had no interest in outside reading associated with Canadian studies, and another 43 per cent claimed not to be able to find or make time for such activity; a further 14 per cent claimed they did some outside reading, but could not name anything specific. Only 20 per cent were making a real effort to keep up with the literature in their field. The reading habits of the teachers in general showed a surprising resemblance to those of the grade 12 students involved in the survey. They seldom read any of the scholarly journals of culture or opinion, but concentrated on news and light entertainment magazines, mainly of American origin.

Hodgetts and his associates were quite unable to justify what they called the incompetent handling of subject matter and the continued use of antiquated teaching methods which they observed. They asserted that graduate practising teachers had a great deal more freedom than most of them used. If they had a stronger conviction of the importance of what they were doing, they could improve their academic background and devise more effective techniques. Yet hundreds of them had been observed standing with their thumbs in the same textbooks they had been using for many years. To a significant proportion of the students, the teachers seemed as bored as they were.

Most of the preparatory work of the teachers in the survey was devoted to designing rigidly structured lesson plans based on the authorized textbook. This practice was seen by the investigators as a perversion of the instructions offered in institutions of teacher preparation, where the development of such plans was intended as a stepping stone to more flexible approaches. Sixty-five per cent of the Canadian studies teachers were judged to be over-organized. No amount of stimulation from their classes could induce them to depart from their previously determined course of action. Some of the weaknesses observed were traced to teachers' personality difficulties. The investigators described 11 per cent of those in the survey as domineering martinets who seemed to get some kind of satisfaction from lording it over their classes. In such an atmosphere, learning seemed impossible. Another 8 per cent were judged incapable of keeping any kind of order. While some of the difficulty could be attributed to the toughness of the classes and the inadequacy of teaching materials and techniques, much of the fault lay in the teachers' lack of force and self-confidence, in their inability to command respect, in their extreme nervous tension, and in their negative and distracting mannerisms. The investigators felt that a great many teachers in these two groups did not belong in any classroom.

On the classroom personality scale used in the investigation, 39 per cent of the teachers were placed in the two highest categories. They were described as in varying degrees "warm, resonably confident and friendly people; they obviously were interested in their students and knew how to communicate with them; they had the respect of their classes; discipline was no problem, it flowed naturally from the easy rapport that had been established." Even those who had obvious academic deficiencies seemed to have a good effect on their students. When desirable personal qualities were combined with academic competence, as they were in about 7 per cent of all cases, truly good teachers were the result. They were almost universally characterized by the successful use of dialogue techniques.[30]

The investigation placed about half the observed teachers in the middle range of the personality scale.

> These were teachers without any identifiably good or bad personality traits. In class, they were ordinary, neither attractive nor unattractive persons, apparently capable of little real communication with their students, plodding along using the textbook and the assignment method. Discipline in their classes depended on ... external factors ... or quite often on incessant nagging: "Now class, you must pay attention"; "Mary, turn around and stop talking"; "Tommy, sit still, stop shuffling your feet"; "Put that book away"; "Keep your legs under the desk" Close textbooks, sit up, stand up, and so on. This constant scolding, interspersed from time to time with biting sarcasm, deadly gimlet-eyed silences and desk-pounding, is a poor substitute indeed for quality teaching.[31]

The investigators expressed some hope that people of this personality type could become effective teachers if self-confidence, feelings of competence and social adequacy, a sense of purpose in life, and professional pride were developed during their students days.

Hodgetts was evidently eager to avoid the impression of one-sidedness in his treatment of the teaching profession. He mentioned some of the unsympathetic and unflattering references to teachers in the press, based on "hasty newspaper research," and wondered how they could be expected to retain their self-confidence in the face of such treatment. He identified teaching as one of the most difficult of professions and speculated that society, overlooking some of its own shortcomings, expected too much of the teacher.

> Why should teachers spend hours of extra work outside the classroom – as a great many of them do almost every evening – when the employed population of this country have their eyes on the time-clock and shed their responsibilities with the five o'clock whistle? Why should conscientious teachers bother to watch the documentary and public affairs programs while others relax in front of Jackie Gleason? Why should they strive for excellence when planned obsolescence has become a way of life and the makers of cars or houses have so little regard for quality? Why, in this materialistic world, should teachers' federations not be trade unions bargaining for every dollar they can get when this is what goes on all about them? In asking these questions, we do not infer that teachers should drift with the popular currents. Teachers are indeed in positions of special trust and responsibility and the general public has every right to expect the profession to strive for standards of excellence. But the public, in

turn, should recognize that all the pressures of modern living make the teachers' task an increasingly difficult one.[32]

An example of the type of diatribe that Hodgetts may have had in mind when he mentioned some of the trials faced by teachers was contained in a short article by Hugh Garner which appeared in the *Telegram* on September 13, 1965, under the title "Teaching: Ready Haven For The Second-Rate." Garner acknowledged that it would be unfair to denounce all teachers, since there were some who deserved the praise that had been "heaped on the whole gang with unthinking indiscrimination." This concession, however, hardly restrained him.

The overworked adjectives used to describe the schoolteacher include overworked, underpaid, self-sacrificing, exploited and dedicated, an assessment that is greeted with approving affirmative roars at service club luncheons and like gatherings of the perennial pupil ...

The quasi-profession of teaching school, like that of the ministry, is too often the second choice of second-rate students. Teaching school attracts the dull, the college dropout and the child-hating spinsters of both sexes who fall into teaching as a socially acceptable white-collar job with short hours, ridiculously long vacations and a salary range generally much too generous for the people it attracts.

The dedicated schoolma'am belongs with those other beloved characters of modern mythology like the nun who coaches a Little League baseball team, the scruffy but sharp-as-a-tack old family physician, and the muscular village preacher who would just as soon help raise a barn as preach a sermon ...

And judging by the teachers that middle-aged ex-pupils or students do remember, their only claim to fame at all seems to have been their sadism, stupidity or eccentricity. The self-sacrificing, underpaid, overworked, dedicated teacher of our folklore belongs, with few exceptions, to mythology.[33]

The mature teacher realizes that outbursts of this type may come from those with inferiority feelings arising from a lack of schooling. What ought to be a cause for very serious concern among responsible teachers is the influence of child-hating sadists, some of whom do practise, as Garner suggested, in their midst. Some of these teachers try to disguise their real attitude under a mask of solicitude. The rage that can build up in the mind of a child who is helpless to defend himself against them may be sufficient to last a lifetime. It takes very few teachers of this kind to cause serious damage to the image of the entire profession. As suggested earlier, the only really effective way of dealing with such people is to exclude them in the first place.

TEACHERS' ASSISTANTS

An increasing number of school boards were employing "lay assistants" or non-professional aides at the end of the 1960s. This policy has never been looked upon by the teaching profession in Ontario with as much enthusiasm as it has to all appearances in some parts of the United States. For example, at the fortieth annual meeting of the Federation of Women Teachers' Associations of Ontario in 1958, Miss Ruby McLean, who was then president of the organization, was quoted as saying that Ontario teachers did not want or need volunteer assistants. Among the reasons given were that volunteers would disrupt the classrooms, and if they were not paid, it would not be easy for teachers to control their activities. Miss McLean doubted that there were enough duties for them to perform that they would actually relieve much pressure on the teacher. Mrs. Florence Irvine, the first vice-president of the federation, voiced the opinion that it was the sole responsibility of the teacher to keep attendance records and to vouch for their accuracy. She also felt that it was unwise to relieve the pupils of the responsibility of tidying up after themselves in the classroom. As to playground supervision, it gave the teacher an opportunity to observe the children and to get to know them better. Their behaviour on the playground often provided clues about psychological problems that needed to be dealt with.

In 1968 Davis noted the differences of opinion among members of the teachers' federations with respect to the value of assistants. He himself saw a role for such people in the performance of certain tasks.[34] A departmental memorandum to school officials in 1968–9 referred to courses offered in some of the colleges of applied arts and technology leading to diplomas for audio-visual technicians, business assistants, laboratory assistants, library assistants, and recreational assistants. While these diplomas were not necessary for employment by a school board, they were said to be an indication of specific training for a definite service position. The memorandum suggested that teachers could benefit from the employment of these assistants, the degree of their usefulness depending on the size, location, and type of school. Departmental policy was as follows.

> The use of such specially trained personnel in schools does not change the present policy that a person who is employed to fulfil an instructional role in a classroom shall be qualified as a teacher and under contract. It is assumed that where such an assistant is employed, more effective use may be made of the services of the professional teacher. Careful consideration must be given to the pupil-teacher ratio if the cost of education is to be stabilized.
>
> Boards are reminded that where they give permission for persons without teaching certificates to do work of any kind with students in a school, it is the function of these assistants to help and not to replace the teacher who will be in the classroom and in charge of the class, or extra-curricular activity, at all times. Only where persons in charge of a class or a school activity are employed under the Departmental Acts and Regulations is a board protected in case of accident or complaint.[35]

THIRTEEN

Teacher welfare

SALARIES

Some statistics on salary trends in the elementary public and separate schools and in the secondary schools of Ontario during the post-war period were presented in volume I, chapter 6. These showed the changes in absolute levels, both for ranges and for average salaries, from year to year. After a rather slow rise in the late 1940s, there was a consistent and fairly rapid upward trend.

Basis for determining reasonable salary levels

Immediately after the war there was general agreement both inside and outside the teaching profession that salaries were much too low. Had they responded more quickly to changing conditions, the shortage of teachers that was soon to develop would have been less severe. As matters improved during the next two decades, there was a growing feeling that teachers as a group, in relation to the amount of prior preparation required for their work, were reasonably well paid. Certain people claimed that they were over-paid, although such critics were ordinarily considered to be the bilious types who were not to be taken too seriously. In fact there was no real progress in devising an objective basis for determining reasonable or fair levels of remuneration.

Ideally, it would appear that the case for high salaries should be based chiefly on the importance of the contribution made by the teacher, or at least on the importance assigned to this contribution by the taxpaying public. Some observers claim that this is exactly what has happened. According to such a view, when teachers were paid a miserable wage the public in fact considered their work as simply that of purveying some rather simple and superficial skills that almost anyone could offer with practically no special preparation. The very substantial rise in salaries during the post-war period has corresponded quite closely to the increase in value placed on education as a means of surviving economically in a technological society. Even those who doubt that schools have much to do with education have been forced to fall into line because of the unique value of the certificate attainable only through a formal school program. In the long run, teachers can demand only what society really believes they are worth. If it is willing to pay its physicians several times as much, it is because a higher value is placed on the relief of suffering and the preservation of life.

Within certain broad limits, salaries are determined by supply and demand. As shown in volume I, chapter 6, Ontario has had to pay teachers with a given level of preparation at a higher level than has been customary in most parts of the United States. The main reason has been that the pool of those with the requisite amount of education has been smaller. As the proportion of those with an education at the post-secondary level increases, there are two chief possibilities: 1 / that salaries will rise less rapidly than those in other fields; 2 / that higher qualifications and stricter selection will keep the pool of eligible candidates relatively small, and that tight supply will exert the same influence on salaries as in the past. Of course these two developments are not mutually-exclusive alternatives. The value the public places on education will largely determine the nature of the trend.

In their campaigns for higher salaries, teachers find themselves handicapped by the fact that there are a great many of them, and that their number in relation to the population as a whole rises rapidly as the public demand for education increases. When the amount of individual increments demanded or awarded in a large system is announced, the size of the total bill is immediately calculated and usually deplored on the grounds that it would be unreasonable to expect the public to contribute such a large additional sum.

There has been a strongly-held feeling among teachers that their long-term interests will be damaged if they appear to be too grasping and mercenary, or if they show a willingness to sacrifice the interests of their pupils for selfish advantage. According to this view, their ultimate strength lies in their fitness for moral leadership, which provides the best assurance that the community will continue to offer adequate financial support. In certain circles it has become common to assert that the public accords its chief respect to those who stand up for their "rights," and that teachers have nothing to lose by being just as greedy as practically every other organized group. The federations have obtained results from public opinion suveys that seem to offer considerable support for this position. The long-term effects of pursuing policies that the public regarded as outrageously selfish might, however, be seriously adverse.

Apart from the problem of establishing a reasonable over-all level of remuneration, there is the question of how an individual teacher's salary should be determined. It is usually assumed that the quality of a teacher's performance improves on the average for a period varying between ten and fifteen years, since salary schedules typically allow for a number of increments somewhere in this range. In fact, any investigations into the validity of such a belief have tended to suggest that a distinct improvement over this entire period of time is exceptional and that actual deterioration is much more common than teachers would like to think. The case for a large span between initial and maximum salaries cannot be supported solely on grounds of identifiable variations in the quality of the contribution over a period of more than a few years.

The Royal Commission on Education studied the situation at a time when salary scales with regular increment to a maximum much higher than the starting salary were the exception rather than the rule. While declaring complacently that salaries of teachers in general compared favourably with those paid for service in professions and occupations requiring comparable training, it claimed that there was not the same opportunity in teaching to rise to high salaried positions. Both experienced teachers and those in administrative and supervisory positions were said to be inadequately paid. The case was based on the greater efficiency and effort of these groups. At that time, also, there were grounds for the perennial complaint that supervisory officials in the Department of Education were receiving less than those employed by local boards and in some cases less than those whose work they supervised.[1]

Comparison between elementary and secondary school teachers

C.E. Phillips estimated that secondary school teachers in English-speaking Canada were paid about twice as much as elementary school teachers in 1900 and about 50 per cent more in 1950. The trend reflected the narrowing gap between the levels of qualifications required of the respective groups. The period after 1950 saw an increasing acceptance of the principle of salaries based on qualifications and experience regardless of the level at which a teacher was employed. The Ontario Secondary School Teachers' Federation would, however, have nothing to do with the single salary schedule, but insisted on the right to bargain separately. If school boards and the federations representing elementary school teachers could agree on a scale that provided the same remuneration for equivalent experience and qualifications for those who chose to teach at the elementary rather than the secondary level, that was their own affair.

The attitude of the OSSTF was mainly based on the fact that the secondary teachers as a group were easier to mobilize and hold together in the salary campaigns that were conducted throughout the period. They were generally considered to have a greater sense of commitment to professional betterment. Apart from the Ontario Public School Men Teachers' Federation, of course, the OSSTF had a smaller proportion of young women who regarded teaching as a brief interlude before they embarked on a more or less permanent career of home-making. The rapidly growing tendency for married women to return to the classroom eventually made a considerable change in this situation, although the image of the OSSTF as the most militant of the federations did not disappear.

A frequent topic in secondary school staff rooms has been the supposedly more difficult and burdensome task of teaching at the secondary than at the elementary level. Facing a series of classes in the rotation system is said to be more demanding than that of dealing with a single class. Those who have faced both situations are frequently prepared to agree that the teacher who wishes to get by with minimum effort can fare better in an elementary classroom. But for one who expects to throw himself enthusiastically into his work, whatever the level, the argument seems irrelevant. If secondary school teachers actually thought themselves at any considerable disadvantage in terms of the burdens imposed upon them, there would undoubtedly be a much more substantial move into elementary schools. The effort needed to secure the different qualifications required has never been excessive. Part of the reason why few have transferred in this direction has been the continued advantage in prestige generally associated with secondary school teaching, although particular school systems have had considerable success in counteracting it.

Every now and then, someone calls attention to the fact that opportunities for influencing the child for good or ill decrease steadily as he grows older; it is proclaimed that, as a consequence, the best teachers should be assigned to beginners. The implication of this argument is that such teachers should receive the most thorough preparation and the greatest incentives in terms of prestige and probably also of salaries. The idea has had to contend, without too much success, however, with the deeply ingrained impression – a survival from pioneer days – that the teacher need only be a grade or two ahead of the class in order to pass on the knowledge he has acquired.

Pay by merit

The concept of paying teachers according to merit involves a variation in their salaries for a specific position on the basis of an evaluative judgment of their performance. It does not include evaluation for initial appointment, promotion, or tenure. It contrasts with the customary practice of providing increments for level of preparation, experience, and additional responsibility. When teachers as a group express themselves in favour of pay by merit, they usually have in mind a modification of this scheme whereby standard increments are determined by these latter factors, and a special bonus is awarded to some proportion of the group for particularly creditable service.

Few topics having to do with teacher remuneration have been debated more frequently than that of pay by merit. The literature on the topic has been voluminous and extremely repetitious. Although some participants in the controversy claim that changing conditions of service and salary levels call for a re-evaluation of the arguments, and perhaps for a reversal of a previously held position, it is difficult to identify any really new points on either side. Having stated a position against the practice of formal teacher rating, not because it is impossible if a specific set of criteria can be agreed upon, but rather because it is on balance damaging to effective teaching, the writer has by implication sided against the principle of pay by merit.

From a certain point of view, one of the strongest arguments in favour of pay by merit is that teachers indisputably differ in their ability, effort, and efficiency. It seems a matter of simple justice that salaries should be related to these differences. Those who assess their own contribution quite accurately, and realize that they are rendering greater service than many of their colleagues, can be forgiven if they feel a sense of frustration when they are paid at the same rate. It would be understandable if a number of them left the profession for this reason, although no one seems to have made a serious effort to gather relevant statistics to determine how many actually do so. The weakness in the argument is that it puts the emphasis in the wrong place. Education is conducted for the benefit of the pupil rather than for that of the teacher, and teachers' salary schemes should be determined in this light. "Justice" to good teachers cannot be defended if it can be achieved only at the expense of good education. The vital question is whether the favourable effects of a pay-by-merit scheme on the educational atmosphere of the school are on balance favourable or unfavourable.

Proponents of pay by merit claim that increments based on merit provide an incentive and a reward for effort. It is suggested that teachers are entitled to be regarded as human, and that they respond to the same motivating devices as the rest of the population. The opponents are repelled by the idea that a teacher gives or withholds part of his maximum contribution because of salary considerations. They also point out that recent trends in educational philosophy and methods increasingly emphasize the importance of intrinsic motivation as opposed to competition for extraneous rewards. They ask why a set of principles regarded as outmoded for pupils should be thought appropriate for teachers.

The opponents claim that a merit scheme would destroy the possibility of fruitful co-operation among teachers as their competitive impulses were sharpened. However, there is no reason why the propensity to co-operate could not be regarded as one of the chief criteria of meritorious performance, and undue competitiveness penalized. It should not be overlooked, however, that a scheme that fostered ill-will among staff members might adversely affect the possibility of co-operation, even though such behaviour was rewarded.

Comparisons are made between teaching and other occupations. It has frequently been claimed that pay by merit is the rule in business and industry, in government service, and in other spheres of life, and that teaching should be brought into line. There are, of course, examples of pay by piecework, although the conditions of modern industrial production have eliminated many of these. Salesmen typically work for commissions. On the other hand, much of what appears to be pay by merit turns out on closer examination to involve differentials based on variations in the nature of the task and in the extent of responsibility assumed. Increments in the public service typically depend on these principles. There are comparatively few examples of systematic differences in remuneration according to the degree of competence with which individuals perform a comparable task.

Teaching as it concerns different individuals is not, of course, the same task. Within any particular school, there is an infinite number of variations depending on the size of classes taught, the total number of pupils assigned, the extent of behaviour problems, the amount of preparation required, and other factors. The administration cannot be expected to equalize these from one teacher to another. Yet how would a teacher react if a colleague, whose burden he rightly regarded as lighter than his own, were given a higher salary because of superior competence? Obviously the destructive effects of teacher resentment could be minimized only if both competence and teaching load were taken into account. This task would be extremely, if not impossibly, complex since load is in itself a very difficult factor to assess and control.

The question of evaluation procedures is one of the most crucial. Advocates of pay by merit rather effectively ridicule the contention that the quality of teaching cannot be measured. They correctly point out that, if this claim were really valid, there would be no justification for selecting candidates for the teaching force in the first place. The schools might as well be staffed completely at random. The opponents more frequently assert, not that variations in quality are impossible to identify, but that existing instruments for assessment are much too crude to justify the reliance that would have to be placed on them if they were used to determine salaries. They point to innumerable studies showing low correlations among ratings by principals, supervisors, and students and among results obtained by different approaches. As was suggested earlier, reasonably successful measurement is possible provided that a sufficiently exact set of criteria of performance can be established. Something much more is required, however, than general agreement on acceptable criteria, difficult as these are to define, if a scheme is to secure the support of teachers. Each individual must be able to relate his own behaviour to the criteria. He must be willing to accept the possibility that his endearing little quirks or his own highly individual techniques do not earn him high marks in terms of standard expectations. The rating procedure must then, not only be valid but also palatable, or it will produce destructive reactions. The teacher who feels himself under a cloud of injustice is not likely to have a salutary influence on young people.

A *Toronto Daily Star* editor tried to settle this question in the following fashion: "to put it as gently as we can – the morale of poor teachers is not the public's first concern when it considers the education of its children."[2] If identification as a poor teacher were to involve immediate removal from the classroom, this position would be valid. Pay by merit would be in fact "retention by merit" if such a practice were followed. But a teacher who remains in the classroom with damaged morale because of a label of inferiority may do incalculable harm to those in his charge. To suggest that this fact is not a matter of major public concern is a serious mistake.

The most satisfactory basis on which to determine teacher merit might appear to be some measure of the progress of the pupils. Although payment by results has not been applied in Ontario to individual teachers, a brief experiment in tying school grants in part to the pupils' success in examinations was attempted in the 1870s and 1880s. The consequences are considered to have been distinctly unfortunate. The exaggerated stress placed on external examinations is thought to have lasted for decades, and much of what was called education became a mechanical process of trying to meet a narrow and limited set of objectives. While it would be unrealistic to deny the importance of those outcomes that are amenable to measurement, the intangibles may be of even greater significance. To ignore them in an assessment of teacher effectiveness would be to identify them as of no great consequence.

A major problem in applying the "ultimate" criterion of pupil success is that it is impossible to disentangle the contributions of individual teachers. Pupil success is also dependent on a variety of influences apart from that of any particular teacher, or of all of a particular pupil's teachers combined. This idea was expressed by the British Columbia Teachers' Federation in 1962.

> No teacher is entitled to sole credit for the achievement of the pupils who are temporarily under his jurisdiction. His apparently meritorious record may be due in various measures to the effective preparation of the youngsters by excellent teaching in earlier grades, to the inspiration they may gain from other teachers in the current grade, to the care with which the principal has matched the teacher's assignment to his particular talents, to the efficiency of the school's administrative organization, to the principal's success in establishing a good school tone, and to constructive influences exerted by home and community environment. It seems manifestly unfair that a teacher should receive, or be denied, individual merit recognition on the basis of a record which has been influenced by so many factors which are beyond his control.[3]

Teacher evaluation for any purpose tends to militate against eccentricity, non-conformity, and innovation. Where anything as important as a decision on a salary increment is involved, the effect might be expected to be magnified. Since teachers are widely accused of being too conformist in their attitudes and practices, it would seem highly undesirable to push them further in this direction. The only way to ensure the maximum of initiative is to offer assurances that it will not be penalized. While absolute protection cannot be given, it is advisable to come as close to it as possible.

Parents are under no delusions about the fact that teachers vary greatly in competence and effectiveness. If their children enrol in the publicly supported system, they must accept what they are given. If teachers were more specifically identified in terms of their ability, dissatisfaction among parents whose children were taught by those at the bottom of the merit scale would certainly increase. If the result were to bring pressure on the poorest teachers to seek some other occupation, the result might be beneficial. There is no assurence, however, that the process would work with sufficient selectivity.

Rating for salary purposes is often defended, or even declared to be essential, if the public is to be induced to support the increasingly heavy costs of education. Some of the newspapers in Ontario continue to make this point. Their editors appear to regard teacher resistance to rating as a kind of feather-bedding, or as a manifestation of a totally unjustified desire to protect the weak and inefficient in the teaching ranks. They usually overlook two important factors with respect to merit rating plans that have been seriously proposed or tried out: the plans do not involve any overt device for getting rid of a substantial proportion of the least effective teachers, and they do not purport to reduce the cost of education by any significant amount. It may be that members of the public would feel better about the high level of taxes for education if they knew the funds were being distributed more fairly. The chances are, however, that the realization that they were getting the best possible quality in education would be more appealing, especially if they understood that the two propositions were not necessarily synonymous.

The Royal Commission on Education weighed the argument on either side of the issue and expressed itself in favour of "promotions based upon a combination of years of experience and merit." The reference was apparently to salary increases rather than to promotions involving greater responsibility. The commission acknowledged that teaching efficiency was difficult to assess, and that no device developed up to that time constituted an adequate and valid measure. It offered the inconsistent opinion, however, that a local education authority might accept the judgment of its supervisory officials.[4]

Frank MacKinnon's advocacy of pay by merit in *The Politics of Education* was one which he was able to reconcile with his emphatic and eloquent support of the maximum of freedom, dignity, and control of the educational process for the teacher. His case was based on a number of the arguments already reviewed.

> There are, of course, many teachers and trustees today who do not like "merit rating," and who emphasize only seniority, hours of work, and credits in training schools. They need to remember that no other profession relies on these criteria alone, and that ability must be recognized above all else if teaching is to be respected and paid. Teachers' fear of the possible prejudice of trustees and principals is no more justified than fear of an employer, bank manager, regimental commander, or anyone else who pays or recommends for promotion.

Certainly it should be far less of an obstacle than the impersonal computations of distant politicians and civil servants and the hampering influence of incompetent teachers who hold back the able. A recognized practice with a necessary degree of flexibility would, under conditions of freedom, gradually evolve and it would be bound to result in the end in generally higher salaries.[5]

Perhaps it is sufficient to point out the danger of using bank managers and regimental commanders as models for supervisory officials in education.

A curious case of an apparent reversal of position was that of I.M. Robb, who retired as General Secretary of the Ontario Secondary School Teachers' Federation at the end of 1967. Early in the very same year, he contributed an article in the *Bulletin* under the title "The Philosopher's Stone on Education," in which he likened the advocates of pay by merit to the alchemists of old and claimed that their enthusiasm seemed to vary inversely with their knowledge and understanding of the problems involved.

The educational world seems destined to face ever-recurring waves of enthusiasm for some scheme that will financially reward those teachers who in someone's opinion are meritorious or, conversely, that will penalize financially those who are not. This enthusiasm flourishes until the protagonists of the particular scheme put it into practice; then enthusiasm begins to wane and eventually dies out. The scheme is then abandoned only to be re-proposed with a new twist to it by another group of alchemists in some other locality. Perhaps their reason for this is that whereas in half a century of experimentation and research no one has succeeded in devising a pay-by-merit scheme that will work with teachers, no one has proved conclusively that some such scheme can not work. Like the medieval alchemists, their modern educational counterparts keep trying.[6]

Robb took note of the claim by the advocates of merit pay that, with the incentive of increased financial rewards, good teachers would become better and mediocre teachers would become good. He asserted, however, that none of the studies of pay-by-merit plans had offered any evidence that this was what happened. The most favourable verdict had been produced by the so-called Utah Study, which had taken ten years and a quarter of a million dollars to carry out. It had concluded with a cautious statement that a merit salary program would result in improved teaching performance with higher morale and job satisfaction among teachers provided that the school system adopting it had met certain basic conditions. There were eleven of these, including such requirements as the development and acceptance of evaluative standards that could be applied to individual teaching performance with reliability and objectivity, a generally accepted basic salary schedule before merit payments were added for those who could qualify, and supervisory personnel in the ratio of one to fifteen teachers. One comment on the Utah Study was that any school system that could meet all the basic conditions would be asured of top grade teaching and would not need a merit plan.

Robb cited James Bushong, Superintendent of Schools at Grosse Pointe, Michigan, where pay by merit had been tried and abandoned in favour of an earned increment program designed to encourage long-term professional growth, who had expressed the view that, while a merit plan might improve teaching on the part of the few who were rewarded by a superior rating, it was likely to damage the morale of the many who failed to achieve such standing. The effect on balance was reduced efficiency. Since at the secondary school level, at least, the education of each student depended on the co-operative efforts of a number of teachers, it seemed more important to Bushong to try to improve the over-all efficiency of teachers as a group than to single out individuals for reward.

Robb next dealt with the impression by some of the advocates of the approach that there would be economic benefits. There was more than a trace of sarcasm in his treatment of this point of view.

> They argue that if a school system has a salary schedule which offers bonuses for superior teaching, every teacher will strive mightily to earn such a bonus, but only a few will succeed. Thus because high salaries are paid to the few, the many will be content to labour on at mediocre wages, eternally inspired by the hope that some day they will gain the financial rewards now given to the chosen elite among their confreres. In the meantime the over-all cost of teachers' salaries is kept low, and to those who protest there is always the answer that good teachers are paid well and that those who feel their salaries are inadequate have only themselves to blame. The fallacy in this position lies, of course, in the fact that teachers are not donkeys and refuse to pursue the elusive carrot indefinitely.[7]

Robb declared that reports on pay-by-merit schemes that had been tried were agreed that they cost more than conventional types of salary schedules. If they were to produce positive results, they had to be superimposed on basic salary scales that were competitive locally, and the merit bonuses had to be within reach of a large proportion of the teachers. Another factor that tended to push up the cost was the need to employ supervisory personnel to do the rating. These people would have to be paid at least as well as those they rated.

The third argument to which Robb turned his attention was that of fairness to the good teachers. He found it difficult to take a contrary position because to do so seemed to brand a person as an opponent of justice. The essence of his case was the lack of valid measures for rating teacher quality. "Merit rating of teachers can mean no more than a measurement of the extent to which an individual teacher conforms to the ideas and ideals of the rater, and those ideas and ideals will vary just as much between individuals as do the performances of teachers." Robb suggested that pay by merit might be appropriately termed "pay-by-opinion." He asked who would rate the raters in the inevitable cases of differences of opinion about a teacher's performance.[8]

The fourth argument which Robb described as among those most frequently encountered was that large merit bonuses would help to prevent first-rate teachers from leaving the classroom to earn higher salaries in administrative positions. If superior teachers were to be kept in the classroom, he wondered whether administrators were to be recruited from among the second best, the third best, or those who had never taught. He asked if such administrators were to be the ones to determine which teachers deserved merit raises.

Since he rejected pay by merit as an effective means of achieving the worthwhile objectives sought by its proponents, Robb felt it necessary to suggest alternatives. One of these was a more rigorous screening of those wishing to enter the profession. He admitted that it was futile to talk of rigorous screening while there was a serious shortage of well-qualified applicants. Teachers' organizations had maintained continuous pressure for improved salaries in the hope of remedying this deficiency. A second suggestion was that teachers be encouraged to achieve their highest professional potential through a program of sound personnel policies. A third was that definite levels of qualifications be established and incentives be provided to encourage teachers to work toward higher levels.

Robb's new position was articulated before the end of the same year and presented in the February 1968 issue of the *Bulletin*. He made what he thought were certain practical and easily attainable suggestions.

> First, I am convinced that school boards are prepared to offer substantially higher salaries in return for a relinquishment on the part of teachers of some measure of the security of tenure they now enjoy.
>
> Second, the adoption by O.S.S.T.F. of a policy favouring an earned, but not necessarily uniform, increment as opposed to the present automatic and uniform increment, would inevitably put more money in the pockets of those teachers who should be our primary concern – namely the good teachers.
>
> Third, the relation of our minimum salary to the teacher who obtains a permanent contract rather than to the beginner who may be not only inexperienced but also unqualified, would strengthen our position in bargaining for professional salaries.
>
> Fourth, the establishment of a policy which would enable a first rate teacher to earn as much as a teacher as he or she could hope to earn as an administrator, would provide for the profession prestige salaries and thereby attract to the profession a higher calibre of people than is possible under the present system.[9]

The only justification Robb could offer for the adoption of a point of vew that he himself had so effectively demolished was that the old policies were out of date. The earlier policies were labeled as appropriate fifteen years earlier when the salaries paid to high school teachers had been by common agreement extremely low, and when there had been a measure of equilibrium between teacher supply and teacher demand. One searches in vain for some relationship between these conditions and the issues dealt with in the article of the previous March. What had suddenly made it acceptable, for example, to keep the good teachers from seeking higher administrative salaries? Why was it now less objectionable to recruit administrators from among the inferior or from among non-teachers?

As might be expected, Robb's flash of enlightenment made him the darling of some of the newspapers. The *Globe and Mail* expressed the following sentiment in an editorial entitled "Truth, from an expert" on December 30, 1967: "He has given a new challenge to the teaching profession in Ontario (a legacy, one man said) and he has begun the arduous task of lifting it from a plateau where it has rested too long."

Barry Lowes, first Chairman of the Metropolitan Toronto School Board, attracted a good deal of attention in 1967 by advocating special financial rewards for merit. He was quoted as saying that the teaching profession should endeavour to attract the best minds into teaching, and that a young person must know that with ability, desire, and perseverance, he could attain the same heights of prestige and remuneration as in other professions. Lowes confused the issue by referring to the need for variations in pay corresponding to differences in teaching assignments, some of which involved areas in which it was more difficult to teach. As some of those responding pointed out, this idea was not pay by merit but pay for special responsibility, a policy which the teachers' federations approved. Lowes was influential in encouraging investigation of the question of what constituted quality teaching, but it is doubtful that this activity contributed much to a settlement of the controversy over pay by merit.

Experience with pay by merit

When Robb was in his "philosopher's stone" mood, he cited an American report produced a short time earlier which indicated that only eighty-one of 3,805 urban school districts in the United States had a merit-pay plan. Only 6.2 per cent of those districts in the United States with a population over thirty thousand which had a merit plan in 1938 had one at the time of the survey. Although almost every centre with a population over 100,000 had tried a merit plan, not one of them still existed. No existing merit plan had been in operation for as long as ten years.

The Etobicoke Board of Education took steps as early as 1960 to implement a merit scheme, labeled the master head plan, which involved stacking merit increments on those awarded on the usual basis. When a teacher had received a permanent certificate awarded after a minimum of two years of successful teaching, he might apply for inclusion in the master head plan. His principal and the assistant thereupon evaluated his work and, if they decided that he met the required standard, he was appointed as assistant head, and given an extra increment of $200. Receipt of this increment for three years in a row placed him $600 higher than he would have been on the regular salary scale. An assistant head who aspired to become an associate head went through the same process and, if successful, gained three more annual increments of $200 each. A teacher who had spent a minimum of ten years in Etobicoke schools, at least five of them as a department head, might apply for promotion to master head, with the prospect of seven extra increments of $200 each.

There were a good many enthusiasts for the scheme within the Etobicoke system. If there was evidence of damaging effects from the resentment of those who applied for and were refused promotion to the higher level, it was never publicized, Teachers might be expected to be reticent in expressing adverse feelings because it could always be pointed out that, at worst, they were as well off as teachers in systems where the customary salary scheme was in effect. One experienced teacher was quoted as objecting to the requirement that application be made for the higher status. He thought he had been around long enough for the quality of his work to be recognized.[10]

The Etobicoke scheme had little in common with the concept of substituting merit for experience and qualifications as the basis for determining salaries. It could not, furthermore, be regarded as an indicator of what would happen if extra increments for merit were incorporated into salary scales in local systems in general. It owed much of its effectiveness to the fact that it was a successful ploy in the competition among school boards to get the best teachers. Since it did perform that function, the citizens of the community might be expected to regard the extra cost as money well spent. If the same approach were widely adopted, and the competitive advantage lost, it is conceivable that taxpayer reactions might be less favourable, although the argument that the most deserving teachers were receiving a fair deal would undoubtedly continue to have an appeal.

Most of the strong advocates of pay by merit expect to see some absolute savings in comparison with a scheme involving uniform annual increments to fixed maxima varying only in terms of qualifications and degrees of responsibility. This result would be achieved by keeping automatic increases rather small and within a strictly limited range. The *Toronto Daily Star* seemed to be suggesting such a plan in an editorial on March 6, 1967.

... the salary schedules should be put on a rational, permanent basis.

This can be done by agreeing upon a fundamental scale, adequate but not lavish, with say, $300 annual increments up to 12 years. On top of that, provision for a percentage increase related to the cost of living. Then merit pay additions for superior teachers.

Such a salary framework would have stability – a quality of value to both teachers and trustees – and would allow taxpayers to feel they could pay their best teachers highly without overpaying for mediocrity.

Support for what the editor had in mind could not be reconciled with the Etobicoke scheme.

It must be said in fairness that the *Star* did not make absolute savings a fundamental condition in its case for merit pay. Thus in 1968 its editors were able to rejoice in the fact that 2,300 separate school teachers had accepted a new salary scale that would "allow school boards to reward their finest teachers with pay raises to match their classroom performances." After five years of experience, the teachers would be eligible for a $600 annual raise instead of the automatic $300 written into their contracts. Teaching performance was to be assessed by principals and other school officials.[11]

In March 1969 the OSSTF, at its annual convention, endorsed the principle of pay by merit in the sense of extra allowances above the basic salary schedule, although it remained opposed to any scheme that would involve replacement of the basic schedule. This decision placed the stamp of approval on a number of schemes in operation in various parts of the province which had been tolerated unofficially by the federation. Ross Munro reported in the *Globe and Mail* that a scheme instituted in one community the previous fall was already in disrepute. Selection of candidates for merit bonuses was in the hands of a committee, consisting of a teacher, a trustee, a vice-principal, and a principal. They chose four department heads and the teacher on the committee. A plan in another community was said to be working well. A teacher who had reached the maximum of the basic scale might submit a brief indicating the special contributions he had made in teaching, research, or extra-curricular activities.[12]

Negotiations in Metropolitan Toronto in 1970

The negotiations between the teachers' federations and the trustees in Metropolitan Toronto in the spring of 1970 aroused particular interest. The OSSTF pinklisted all of the six school boards in the area and seemed for a time prepared to submit the resignations of a large proportion of the members to back up its demands, the chief of which involved 1 / a contractual arrangement over the student-teacher ratio and 2 / salary increases that went far beyond the limits that the federal government recognized as reasonable in its campaign against inflation. In the face of the success of the Ontario School Trustees' Council in maintaining a policy against hiring anywhere in the province, and in view of the lack of overwhelming support among teachers for mass resignations, the teachers continued to serve the following year without having attained their objectives.

The *Telegram* printed a series of articles in February to indicate the issues as seen by the teachers and the trustees. An abbreviated review of the contents of these articles is presented here in the order in which they appeared. The secondary school teachers' case was outlined first by their chief negotiator at that stage, Ralph Connor. He was followed by Bruce Bone, Chairman of the Metropolitan Toronto School Board, who gave the trustees' point of view. Gary L. Richardson, who spoke for the elementary school teachers, had the opportunity to rebut Bone's arguments.

In his case for the secondary school teachers, Connor first called attention to the statement by the former Chairman of the Metropolitan Toronto Council, William Allen, to the effect that the area had the most productive, well-to-do, exciting two million people on the planet. If that was the case, the teachers had failed to benefit in terms of either their pocketbooks or their teaching conditions. Yet they had a major responsibility for creating the community so enthusiastically described. Connor evoked a stereotype of the teacher

> somewhere between Mr. Chips and the nice-nice teacher of Latin with the bun hairdo whom you *think* you remember from the past.
>
> ... God-fearing but rather impractical idealists, smarter than the average fellow in their subjects but not too smart for their own good, so devoted in their calling as to bypass wordly or economic goals.

He intimated that teachers had too readily accepted this image of themselves in the past. Two things were different, however, in the current negotiations: 1 / teachers would no longer accept whatever their boards were prepared to offer and 2 / they were concerned about a steady erosion in teaching conditions. In connection with the first point, he declared that increases had been low in the previous two contracts while raises of 15 or 20 per cent were "not uncommon" in organized labour. With reference to the second point, there were 2,800 classes in the city of Toronto and two thousand in Scarborough with more than thirty-one students in them. More than one-third of the vocational and occupational classes had eighteen or more students. Connor declared that no one knew better than the classroom teacher what contributed to quality teaching.

The increase in the basic scale in 1969–70 had ranged from 5 to 6.25 per cent, and the year before from 3.7 to 5 per cent. At the same time, the Department of Labour was reporting increases of 7 to 8 per cent in practically all other sectors of the economy. A police constable in Metropolitan Toronto received $7,884 after a thirteen-week training period with a minimum educational qualification of grade 10. In comparison, a secondary school teacher required three more years of high school, three years of university, one year of professional training, and three years of teaching experience before reaching the same salary level. The previous year, the Metropolitan Toronto School Board had granted an allowance for the extra living costs in a large centre, but had withdrawn it.

The board's original offer had involved no increase in the maxima in the four salary categories, but instead a $500 merit payment for those who reached those levels. It would be paid only on application, and might or might not be granted. One unfair feature of this proposition was that teachers in Group 1 took only twelve years to reach their maximum, and thus to become eligible for the merit bonus, while those in Group 4 took sixteen years. The teachers' research indicated that the offer would leave them with less spending power than during the previous year because of the 4 per cent rise in the cost of living.

Bruce Bone began his case with the declaration that the teachers' proposals were astronomically high and beyond the community's capacity to pay. Elementary teachers were asking for a 25 per cent adjustment to the scale, while their secondary school colleagues wanted upwards of 39 per cent. In addition, they wanted a Metro living allowance of $800 per teacher, which in itself would amount to $5,990,000 for secondary teachers alone. The latest requests would give a secondary school principal an increase of $7,500. The total cost of the secondary teachers' proposals was estimated at $50 million in extra funds for the 1970–1 school year. To raise that sum would require a tax increase of about ten mills. These estimates did not include parallel adjustments for elementary school teachers.

As a result of research into starting salaries for those with comparable levels of education in other occupations, the board was convinced that the 1969–70 schedule was fair and competitive. In order to maintain this position, it had offered teachers other than those at the maxima of their categories increases, including the regular increment, ranging from $600 to $1,600, or an average of 10.2 per cent of their 1969–70 salaries. For those at the maxima, an increase of $300 to $600, or 4 per cent, was offered to compensate for the rise in the cost of living. The merit plan would provide an additional $500 for those who qualified. Apart from amounts for merit promotions and increases for improved qualifications, the average increase would be 8.35 per cent. Bone offered "random examples" to show 1 / that a teacher who started in 1966 with grade 13 and one year of teachers' college would be receiving an increase of 70.7 per cent for the four-year period; 2 / one who had an honours degree and fourteen years of experience be receiving an increase of 53.6 per cent in the same period; and 3 / one with a three-year pass degree and nine years of experience would be receiving a corresponding increase of 55.1 per cent. Teachers at the maxima of the third, fifth, and seventh levels at the beginning of the four-year period had received increases averaging 33 per cent.

Bone referred to the teachers' frequent complaint that their friends in industry and commerce could move to far higher salaries than were available to them. He pointed out that such employees generally lacked tenure, a published salary scale, and automatic annual increments. Only a very few earned the extremely high salaries, which they had to earn on merit in competition with fellow employees. Launching into a case for merit pay, he pointed out that the administration evaluated staff continuously for promotion to administrative positions and proposed that this process be extended so that the best teachers could be rewarded financially while remaining in the classroom.

The school boards in Metropolitan Toronto were proposing to introduce the merit plan in stages, since it would be impractical to apply it to twenty thousand teachers in a single year. Teachers at their maximum in levels three to seven would be eligible to apply for a "professional excellence allowance" of $500 the next year. The boards hoped to extend the plan to teachers with less experience thereafter until it was in force throughout Metropolitan Toronto as it had been in Etobicoke for some time.

In addition to its salary proposals, the boards were also offering substantial fringe benefits. These included group life insurance, 60 per cent of the premiums to be paid by the employer; OHSC and OHSIP, 50 per cent of the premiums to be paid by the employer; and sabbatical leave, special leave, sick leave, and retirement plans that could be compared favourably with others in teaching and industry.

Bone acknowledged that teachers should be increasingly involved in the development of policies affecting their welfare, as they were in their schools, with the administration, and in board-staff committees. The boards were concerned, however, about increased militancy leading to demands for the negotiation of a host of items including class size, teacher-pupil ratio, number of teaching periods per day or week, number of periods of preparation, and length of the school day. The boards were persuaded that the quality of education would suffer if such items were included in teachers' contracts. With the development of new approaches to curriculum and teaching, the greatest possible flexibility in staffing and deployment was required. Various circumstances would call for team teaching, large lecture-style classes, and small seminars. Trustees and administrators agreed that staffing decisions had to be made board by board and school by school and not dictated at the Metro level. They recognized the value of teachers' experience in arriving at decisions in this area, and had invited them to share in the development of a pupil-teacher ratio formula. The teachers had refused, however, unless the final formula became a negotiable part of their contract. In Bone's words:

> To build for pupils a series of educational experiences from school entry to school leaving is a complicated business which involves many components – class size, number of periods, teacher-pupil ratio, size of staff, kinds of schools, staff qualifications, options, time-tabling, concepts such as non-grading and team teaching, to name but a few.
>
> These cannot, and should not, be isolated and converted, one by one, to mathematical formulae, under the pressure of negotiations. Suppose the bargainers write into an agreement that no class shall have more than 30 pupils. Does this mean that a principal who organizes a class of 31 pupils might bring on a grievance, a breach of contract, or a strike?

Gary Richardson wrote in rebuttal that the elementary school teachers of Metropolitan Toronto were simply seeking economic justice, which meant the establishment of a salary scale that would attract and retain a professional staff of highly-qualified, competent teachers. This scale, based on the measurable criteria of qualifications and experience, would provide an incentive for teachers to improve their academic and professional qualifications and would compare favourably with salaries paid to similarly qualified people in industry and other professions. Richardson asserted that a year of teachers' college following high school graduation was an inadequate base for elementary teachers. Since the profession did not control entrance requirements, the best alternative open to it was to support a salary scale that limited the progress of teachers who were unwilling to improve themselves. The proposed scale allowed only four yearly increments to the teacher who did not advance beyond Level 1, but offered as many as fourteen increments for the one who maintained a process of continuous academic and professional improvement.

Richardson's interpretation of the boards' most recent offer, which had been made on February 12, differed substantially from the one Bone had presented, mainly because he declined to count regular increments as an increase. The scale adjustments, which ranged from a low of 2.6 per cent to slightly more than 5 per cent, were in some instances less than half the increase in the cost of living. The offer did not compensate for increasing productivity and taxes, for the removal of the Metro living allowance, or for the fact that teachers' salaries had not kept pace with the average industrial settlement over the previous two years. The boards' merit proposal was available only to 14 per cent of the teachers.

Richardson stated the teachers' opposition to merit pay on the grounds that few such schemes tried in North America had succeeded for long, that the criteria for teacher selection were vague and subjective, and that the scheme, however beneficial in industry, would not be conducive to a harmonous relationship among those working with children. He wondered if the boards' merit proposal was an admission that they were retaining unsatisfactory staff beyond the probationary period. If this was the problem, merit pay would not solve it. The answer was to establish a basic scale that would attract the most highly talented people into the profession.

The fringe benefits being offered by the boards were mainly intended to make common the plans already existing in various forms throughout Metro. Since they were not substantially changed, they involved no great increase in costs. The only new aspect was the proposed insurance scheme. The elementary teachers, however, wished to keep their existing schemes with no change except at the local level.

Unlike the secondary school teachers, the elementary school teachers were not proposing to negotiate at the Metro level such items as pupil-teacher ratio, unassigned preparation time, and other such items. They agreed that these matters should be determined by area boards in consultation with teachers and administrators. Their success in local consultation would determine their future position. They were not, however, particularly optimistic about the outcome of this exercise. Current trends in educational thought stressed attention to the needs of individual children. With a class of thirty, each child got an average of ten minutes a day, with no time set aside for teacher preparation. Yet there were still classes of nearly forty. Elementary teachers got closer to 10 per cent of their time in unassigned preparation periods than the 25 per cent available to secondary school teachers. If the needs of the teachers could not be met by compromise in each area, they would insist that conditions of work be negotiated at the Metro level. Richardson was not prepared to accept the "militant" label as applied to the elementary school teachers in view of their stand on this issue.

Richardson recognized that the inadequate tax structure placed heavy burdens on the local taxpayers and most particularly on those with fixed incomes. The teachers were not, however, prepared to continue to subsidize education. If society expected the highest quality, it had to be prepared to pay for it.

MISCELLANEOUS WELFARE BENEFITS PROVIDED BY SCHOOL BOARDS

The kind of welfare benefits available to teachers in 1969–70 may be illustrated by reference to policies implemented by the Sudbury Board of Education. The board assumed 50 per cent of the cost of plans offered by the Ontario Hospital Services, Blue Cross, and Physicians' Services Incorporated for single employees and heads of families. In the case of married women who were not heads of families, it paid 50 per cent of the single rate. A sick leave credit system was in effect in accordance with the provisions of *The Schools Administration Act.* An employee of the board on September 1, 1969, was entitled to a credit obtained under a plan operated by a board which had come under the Sudbury board up to a maximum of two hundred days. If the board or boards previously employing him did not have a sick leave plan, he was given an initial credit of 50 per cent of his unused statutory sick leave for the period of such employment. The maximum credit allowed by the Sudbury board was two hundred days. A teacher might be required to submit a certificate from a qualified medical or dental practitioner for three or more consecutive days of absence because of illness.

Leave of absence was granted under the following conditions: 1 / As provided by *The Schools Administration Act,* the teacher was not subject to loss of pay or sick leave credit for absence because of jury duty, subpoena, or quarantine. 2 / The same conditions applied when he was absent for up to five consecutive teaching days because of the death of a member of his immediate family, including a father, mother, brother, sister, son, daughter, husband, wife, grandfather, grandmother, father-in-law, mother-in-law, or guardian. 3 / Similarly, he would be granted one day's leave on account of the death of any other person. 4 / The same conditions applied for absence for professional purposes approved by the board. 5 / Absence for personal reasons approved by the board might be granted for a maximum of ten half days without loss of pay, but subject to deduction from sick leave credit. 6 / Absence for the purpose of writing an examination for credit toward a university degree or a higher professional certificate, or for the purpose of attending convocation ceremonies where a degree was conferred on a son, daughter, husband, wife, mother, or father might be granted for up to one day without loss of pay or sick leave credit. On retirement, each employee was eligible for a gratuity equal to 50 per cent of the unused portion of accumulated sick leave multiplied by one year's salary. In the event of his death before or after retirement but before recovery of the full benefits of the accumulated sick leave, the remaining benefits would be paid to his estate.

Maternity leave was granted subject to the following stipulations. 1 / Leave was to be requested, if possible, to coincide with the legal contract year. 2 / At the board's request, the teacher might return at any time, but should not expect to resume duties at a time other than September 1 or January 1. 3 / Leave should be requested early to give the board sufficient time to obtain a replacement. 4 / A teacher was expected to leave when pregnancy interfered with efficiency or at the end of the term. 5 / Leave should not exceed two years.

The Sudbury program for sabbatical leave was designed to recognize teachers who were giving outstanding service and to offer them an opportunity for enrichment that would benefit the Sudbury school system. It was not intended to be a means of obtaining higher qualifications. In order to qualify, a teacher had to be employed by the Sudbury board or one of its predecessor boards for at least ten years. Sabbatical leave involved the payment of two-thirds of the teacher's regular annual salary, which might be augmented by a maximum of 75 per cent of his accumulated sick leave provided that the total received was not more than his normal salary. Superannuation deductions were to continue during the period of leave, and on return to full duties he was to have the option of contributing the difference between the amount of superannuation deducted and the amount that would have been deducted had he remained on the staff and drawn full salary. Anyone returning from a sabbatical leave was to be eligible for any increment or increase in salary resulting from a revised schedule that he would have received had he not been on leave. The statutory sick leave allowance was not to apply while he was on leave. As a condition of leave, he agreed to teach in the system for three years after his return. If he failed to do so for reasons other than ill health, he was expected to reimburse the board on a *pro rata* basis for payments received while on leave. The board's policy was that the number of applications granted in any year would not require an expenditure for sabbatical leave salaries greater than 0.5 per cent of the total budgeted for salaries during the year before the one for which the leaves were requested.

TEACHER EXCHANGE

Teacher exchange programs received the support of the Department of Education for many years as a means of enabling teachers to improve their professional knowledge and competence and as a contribution to national and international understanding. In 1960, for example, the Canadian Education Association and the United Kingdom Branch of the League of the British Commonwealth and Empire co-operated to arrange exchanges between Ontario teachers and those in other provinces of Canada, the United Kingdom, the United States, and New Zealand. While on exchange, the Ontario teacher's salary was paid by his own school board, while corresponding arrangements were made for his counterpart in the other country. If the exchange was made with a teacher in the United Kingdom, he had to pay the latter $250 to compensate for lower salaries in that country and for loss of exchange on the pound. The exchange teacher had to pay his own travel and living expenses. A candidate for exchange had to be at least twenty-five years of age, to have had a minimum of five years' experience, and to be rated by his inspector as an above-average teacher. Although the number of exchange teachers increased during the subsequent decade, conditions under which the arrangements were made did not change radically.

In September 1966, following a proposal by the Canadian Education Association and l'Association canadienne des éducateurs de langue française, the ministers of education set up an exchange program for English-speaking and French-speaking teachers in Canada. As was true of other exchange arrangements by this time, the minimum length of experience required was three years for a teacher with a degree and five years for a teacher without one. Although the upper age limit was fifty years, consideration might be given to an older teacher who was especially recommended by a supervisor. Applicants were warned that they were expected to adapt themselves to conditions as they found them. They might, for example, have to teach larger classes or higher or lower grades than they were used to. Travel expenses were paid, not only for applicants themselves, but also for their wives and dependent children. An allowance up to $200 for unmarried teachers and $400 for married teachers was provided for one trip home per year and smaller amounts were included for travel within the province visited to improve their insight into the other culture. There were also additional special allowances.

SCHOLARSHIPS FOR STUDY OUTSIDE ONTARIO

The Department of Education for a number of years also provided scholarships to enable teachers to study outside Ontario. Up to 1966–7 these amounted to $2,000 for the year, payable in two instalments of $1,000 each. In 1967–8 the amounts were raised to $2,500 and $1,250 respectively. The applicant had to have a university degree qualifying him for admission to the course leading to the Interim High School Assistant's Certificate, Type B, at an Ontario College of Education, or acceptable for the purpose of obtaining an Interim Elementary School Teacher's Certificate, Standard 4. The program of study followed by the recipient had to be one prescribed by a school, university, or other institution and approved by the minister. A teacher accepting a scholarship had to sign an agreement promising at least three years' service to the province of Ontario in educational work on completion of the course.

SUPERANNUATION PROVISIONS FOR TEACHERS

Early developments

Steps were taken to establish a superannuation fund in Canada West in 1853 for the benefit of "worn-out common school teachers." At first participation was voluntary, and the annual contribution was only $4 per member. The initial pension was $2 for each year of service, averaging $26.54 per year per recipient in 1860.[13] In 1871 contributions were made compulsory for all male public school teachers; provision was made three years later for female public school teachers, high school teachers, and inspectors to become voluntary contributors and beneficiaries. In 1873 the pension was increased to $6 per year of service, with those holding First Class Certificates eligible to receive a corresponding rate of $7. The allowance was awarded on the basis of infirmity to those under sixty years of age and to all those retiring at or after the age of sixty.[14]

When teachers requested in 1881 that a half pension be provided for widows and suggested that the amount of the pension could be augmented by increased contributions from members, the reply of the Minister of Education was, in the opinion of Phillips, typical of nineteenth-century thought.

> The minister was against making pensions compulsory, especially for women, and was also against giving a higher pension to those who remained for more than twenty-five years of service, for fear that teachers who had outlived their usefulness would continue teaching in order to get a larger pension.[15]

It must not be thought that all the teachers of the day were necessarily in favour of the scheme. According to Guillet, at the meeting of the Ontario Teachers' Association in 1871, the prospect of compulsory payments was called tyrannical, and a motion against it was passed unanimously.[16] At subsequent meetings, recommendations for increased benefits were usually accompanied by objections to the compulsory feature, although the teachers were realistic enough to recognize that voluntary contributions would have to be increased if the benefits were to be worthwhile.

In 1885 the government ceased to make any further payments, and contributions were again made voluntary. After 1886 no new contributors were allowed, and the fund was gradually phased out. The dissatisfied members of the Ontario Teachers' Association had a committee studying the matter and pressing for the adoption of a new scheme for many years thereafter.

In 1904 urban boards were given the power to establish superannuation funds for their own teachers. Some did so, with varying provisions for contributions and benefits, and with the inevitably restrictive effect on teacher mobility. The OTA continued to appeal to the government for a provincial fund. In 1909 R.A. Pyne, Minister of Education, gave the organization some hope when he expressed himself in favour of a bonus to teachers of $50 to $100 a year for the rest of their lives after they had given fifteen or twenty years of service. It was not until 1914 that steps were taken to prepare an appropriate bill for the Legislature, but action was further delayed. Finally, at Convocation Hall in the University of Toronto, where the OEA Convention was held in April 1917, the Superannuation Committee made a triumphant report of "complete success"; they had "every confidence" that *The Teachers' and Inspectors' Superannuation Act* would prove "the best on the statute books of any country."[17]

Although the basic structure of the original act has remained, there have been numerous revisions of both act and regulations incorporating many changes, most of them of a minor nature designed to remove anomalies or to plug loopholes. Some of the main features of successive versions of the act and regulations from 1936 to the present are reviewed in the following pages. The year 1936 has been selected because it represents the period of the bleakest economic outlook, a kind of welfare watershed. Generally, although not necessarily in all respects, the trend since then has been toward higher contributions and more generous benefits. The very word "generous" suggests an old-fashioned concept of benevolence in contrast to the view that adequate pensions are a right earned over the years by a combination of direct payments and contributions of service to the community.

Structure of the Teachers' and Inspectors' Superannuation Commission

The act of 1917 provided for the administration of the fund by the Teachers' and Inspectors' Superannuation Commission, which was composed of five members, three of whom were to be appointed by the Minister of Education, including the chairman and an actuary, and two elected by the teacher and inspector contributors who belonged to the Ontario Educational Association. The election was to take place at the annual meeting of the association. In 1938 the number of members was raised to seven, four appointed by the minister and three by the OEA. Of the latter, one was to be elected by the secondary school members, one from the public and separate school male members, and one from the public and separate school female members. After a staggering of initial appointments, the term of office was to be three years. From 1949 on, there were nine members, five chosen by the minister and one each by the Federation of Women Teachers' Associations of Ontario, the Ontario Secondary School Teachers' Federation, the Ontario English Catholic Teachers' Association together with l'Association de l'enseignement français de l'Ontario, and the Ontario Public School Men Teachers' Federation. In 1950 the name of the commission was changed to the "Teachers' Superannuation Commission." In 1959 two more members were added to make a total of eleven: six appointed by the minister and five by the teachers' organizations. The Ontario English Catholic Teachers' Association and l'Association de l'enseignement français de l'Ontario now elected one each.

Eligibility

The problem of defining eligibility for superannuation has been a result of the rather complex structure of the Ontario educational system, with its many categories of educators to be covered. In 1936 there were three main groups: 1 / teachers in public and separate elementary schools, in secondary schools of all types, in institutions for teacher preparation and attached observation and practice schools, in special provincial schools such as the Ontario School for the Deaf and the Ontario School for the Blind, and in a miscellaneous group of institutions certified by or supported to some degree by the province; 2 / locally employed inspectors; 3 / provincially employed inspectors, supervisors, or officials requiring the professional qualifications of teachers and officers of "any association or body of teachers approved by the Minister as engaged in advancing the interests of education."[18] There were also certain categories of voluntary membership, including teachers qualified in Ontario who were employed by the Canadian government or by combinations of federal and provincial agencies in schools or classes for veterans of the First World War.

In 1946 those teaching in or inspecting classes for veterans were added, while the rest of the categories of eligibility were left substantially unchanged. Those not eligible were, however, specified in more detail; they included 1 / members of the staff of a technical or vocational school, not considered to be teachers, who pursued some other occupation, 2 / those engaged part time to teach certain special subjects such as music, art and crafts, etc, 3 / those regularly engaged outside Ontario who were performing services in Ontario under an exchange arrangement, and 4 / those contributing to the Public Service Superannuation Fund. In 1948 an amendment to the act granted eligibility to those in the first of these categories and removed it from the staff of the Ontario College of Education and the University of Toronto Schools. The act of 1949 however, specified that those on the instructional staff of any normal school in Ontario, the Ontario College of Education, the University of Toronto Schools, the Ontario School for the Deaf, the Ontario School for the Blind, the Province of Ontario Correspondence Courses, or the Royal Ontario Museum who had been contributors to the fund before 1946 should be entitled to continue as long as they remained on such staff and did not contribute to any other government-supported superannuation fund. An amendment of 1950 mentioned all these groups, along with teachers in railway-car schools, as unequivocally eligible for membership, provided they were qualified as teachers under the acts and did not contribute to any other fund supported by the government. Teachers in railway-car schools had to have contributed to the fund for at least one year previously before they were eligible under this amendment. The amendment of 1954 specifically included teachers of members of the armed forces or veterans in schools maintained by the Canadian or Ontario government. Teachers in provincial technical or polytechnical institutes were recognized in 1957. At the same time, eligibility was granted to teachers in private non-profit institutions giving instruction equivalent to that offered in elementary or secondary schools in the public system.

In the 1960s several changes were made to recognize the appearance of new categories of teachers and the creation of new institutions. The minister ruled in 1962 that a full-time or part-time teacher under program 5 of the Federal-Provincial Technical and Vocational Training Agreement who was qualified to teach in an elementary or secondary school in Ontario must contribute to the fund and was eligible for benefits. Qualified employees of the Ontario Curriculum Institute were added in 1964. Institutions recognized in the 1966 amendment included, among others, colleges of education, the Elliot Lake Centre for Continuing Education, the Moosonee Education Centre, the Institute of Child Study of the University of Toronto, Retarded Children's Education Authorities, the Ontario Institute for Studies in Education, and a number of training schools. In 1963 it was provided that a person on, or who subsequently joined, the staff of a college of education must irrevocably opt to continue to contribute to the fund or to join the university plan for which he was eligible. In 1966 a corresponding arrangement was made for the Ontario Institute for Studies in Education and Lakehead University; in 1967, for members of the staff of the colleges of applied arts and technology and the Ontario Council of Regents for Colleges of Applied Arts and Technology; and in 1968, for members of a teachers' college staff who might transfer to a university.

Contributions

In 1936 every eligible teacher, inspector, or official was required to contribute 3 per cent (formerly 2.5 per cent) of his annual salary to the fund. For the purpose of deductions, any salary less than $550 per year was to be treated as if it were that amount. According to the regulations, payments for extra service such as night school teaching were not treated as salary. As long as the legislative grant payable to the board or other agency employing the contributors was greater than the amount of the contributions, there was no actual transfer of money from the board; the Department of Education merely deducted that amount from the grant and credited it to the fund. A teacher or inspector who had been granted leave of absence with salary for acceptable purposes or who was employed by a board that neglected or refused to make the deductions might make the appropriate payments directly to the fund. The regulations defined the limits of the period of leave of absence as one year. Not more than once in three years, a member who had been without salary for up to six months in a school year because of absence on account of illness might make contributions and receive credit for that period. Contributions might be made for teaching service outside the province under the League of Empire or under the authority of the minister, and credits would be obtained accordingly. Incoming visiting teachers or inspectors could not, however, participate in the fund. Years of service in the Boer War or in the First World War which interrupted either the professional career of a contributor, or his preparation for such a career, might be counted as years of teaching, and contributions could be made for them.

Contributions might be withdrawn only after five years of service. A member who resumed service after withdrawing his contributions had to repay them with compound interest at a rate of 4.5 per cent, and was then fully reinstated in the fund. Temporary, occasional, or substitute teachers who taught fewer than twenty days in a year were entitled to a refund of their payments.

In 1940 the individual contribution rate was raised to 3.5 per cent of the annual salary. Contributions could now be made for a year's leave of absence with or without salary on the basis of the year's salary previous to leave for acceptable purposes, provided, as before, that the payments were made within a specified period of time. Three years later, an amendment to the act brought the contributions made by the province up to the level of those of the members.

Continuing the upward trend, the contribution rate was increased to 4 per cent in 1945. At the same time, any salary of less than $800 per annum was to be treated as if it were that amount for payment purposes. Cost of living bonuses were recognized as salary, but not extra earnings for special services, in accordance with earlier arrangements.

Evidence of greater liberality is found in regulations which came into force in 1946 by which service up to five years before April 1917 in another province of Canada or another part of the Commonwealth might be counted in computing a pension, even though no payments had been made for those years, provided the claimant had credit for at least fifteen years of service in Ontario immediately prior to retirement. He might count any time in excess of five years for service before 1917 under the same conditions, provided that he made appropriate payments into the fund. It is hard to imagine that any great number of people or amounts of money were involved. Much more important was the provision for credit for service outside Ontario after 1917 on payment by the contributor of an amount equal to that accumulated in the fund on behalf of a teacher of the same age with corresponding service in Ontario.

The regulations under the act of 1946 made provision for credit for active service or related service during the Second World War on more generous terms than those that had applied to earlier wars. As before, those whose teaching or inspectoral careers were interrupted by the war might receive credit for their years of service, provided they made contributions based on their last year of professional service or on the salary they would have received had they not left for war service; such payment had to be made within two years of the cessation of war service. In addition, those who became teachers subsequent to war service could obtain credit for years of war service with appropriate payments. At about the same time, these provisions were made applicable to veterans of the First World War, and they were given a year to pay for credit not already claimed. They might also count time subsequent to discharge for treatment of injuries sustained during war service. Provisions for credit for war service were later extended to subsequent wars.

The rate of contributions was raised in 1949 to 6 per cent of annual salary, where it remained until modifications were required by the integration of the Canada Pension Plan. The rate of actual superannuation contributions on the part of the individual has not, however, been affected by the CPP. The province's contributions as of 1949 were to be two-thirds of the total contributed by the members. According to the act of 1949, a salary of less than $1,000 a year was treated as $1,000 for contributory purposes. Twenty years later, this minimum was raised to $2,000 a year. On January 1, 1956, the government's contribution was raised to equal that of the membership.

An arrangement was worked out in 1960 whereby a contributor to the Teachers' Superannuation Fund who transferred to the University of Toronto Pension Fund might on retirement from the university also receive a pension from the former based on his total length of service and calculated on the last ten years on which he contributed to the teachers' fund before transferring from it. Presumably his allowance from the two funds at the time of his retirement would add up to an equitable total. An arrangement was also made for transfer in the reverse direction. In 1966 the seven best years were substituted for the last ten.

The act of 1966 established full transferability of credits back and forth between the Teachers' Superannuation Fund and the Public Service Superannuation Fund for those qualified for transfer. The government's contributions as well as those of the individual could be transferred, and an equal period of service was recognized provided the years of service as a teacher were continuous. Transfer to any other fund would involve the individual's credits with compound interest, but not those made by the government on his behalf.

The establishment of the Canada Pension Plan, which came into operation on January 1, 1966, created some complexities. While the legislation was being prepared, the OTF considered it necessary to ask the government to assure the teachers of Ontario that the benefits they currently expected would continue. Their apprehensions were relieved with the decision to integrate the two plans. The result was that the contribution remained at 6 per cent, with part going to the Canada Pension Plan; ultimate benefits, also shared by the plans, would not be less than under the previous scheme. Initially the school boards deducted the 6 per cent of the teachers' salaries, out of which the Superannuation Commission made the appropriate payment to the Canada Pension Plan. As of January 1, 1969, for some apparently perverse reason, the boards were required, on the basis of a directive received from the Department of National Revenue, to remit this contribution directly to that department. This change provided the boards with additional and, to the observer, seemingly unnecessary obligations.

Transfer of credits

The question of transferability of credits is important to teachers considering the possibility of moving from one province to another or of leaving the country altogether. In general, arrangements have not been such as to encourage mobility. There is a general arrangement applying to all other Canadian provinces, the Commonwealth, and any school maintained by the government of Canada for children of members of the armed forces, for Indians, or for inmates of penal institutions for anyone who is not or will not be receiving a pension from another fund for that period of service. In essence, he can pay into the Teachers' Superannuation Fund the amount he would have contributed had he been a regular participant, based on the salary he received on beginning employment in Ontario following his outside service or, if he does not return to employment in Ontario, the salary he received during his last year of service in the province, with a minimum base of $2,000. He must also pay the amount the Ontario government would have contributed on his behalf, plus compound interest on both sums. The complete payment must be made within ten years of the date of his termination of employment outside Ontario. He can count the years of service outside Ontario only if he serves for at least ten years within Ontario.

For those employed in Ontario before September 1, 1940, there is another provision, of rapidly diminishing importance as the years pass. The pension is calculated both with and without counting the extra-provincial service. The applicant may then choose one of the two bases for his allowance. If he chooses the second, he must pay a lump sum into the fund composed of the difference between the two funds multiplied by an actuarial factor which takes into account his life expectancy and the current rate of interest used by the actuary in his valuation of the fund.

There are also reciprocal arrangements with British Columbia, Alberta, Saskatchewan, England and Wales, the Canadian government, and Ryerson Polytechnical Institute, which involve the possibility of a genuine transfer of credit rather than a mere opportunity to purchase credit for outside service. The conditions under which advantage may be taken of these arrangements are rather complex and need not concern us here.

Payments from the fund

As of 1936, a member who retired after the end of 1916, and who had given at least thirty-nine years of service, was entitled to the maximum pension allowable, later called the A pension. The annual payment amounted to one-sixtieth of his average salary for the full number of years during which he had made contributions to the fund multiplied by the number of years during which he had been employed. Since the fund had existed only since 1917, and he had made no payments to it previously, his years of service before that time were normally counted as half years; however, if he had made payments to a municipal or school board fund that was transferred to the new fund in 1917, the years during which he had made such payments could be counted as full years. The situation was approximately equivalent to saying that he was given credit for contributions that the government would have made on his behalf prior to 1917 had the fund existed, but not for those he himself had been unable to make before that time. If the total annual pension, as calculated according to the formula, was less than $365, the amount paid might be at the rate of $20 per year of service up to $365. The act specified that the maximum pension could exceed $1,000 a year only if the contributor had paid into the fund a sum sufficient to purchase at Dominion government rates a life annuity yielding an amount greater than that, in which case his pension would equal that amount. But the act also authorized the minister to grant additional benefits when the condition of the fund seemed to warrant it. Thus, by regulation, the actual ceiling in 1936 was $1,250 per annum. There was an overriding provision that the pension could not exceed three-fifths of the annual salary over the period of service. If the recipient of a pension resumed regular service, his pension was suspended. If he engaged in occasional teaching, the pension was reduced by one-half of 1 per cent for each day of such service. Upon his return to retirement, the additional service was to be taken into account in determining his revised pension. If he preferred to convert his pension claims into an annuity payable to himself and to his wife or heirs after his death, a contributor might arrange to do so within a specified period before his retirement.

A second category of pension, later called the B pension, might be claimed after thirty years of service. It was to be actuarily equivalent to that provided in the case of a contributor retiring after thirty-nine years of employment, with a reduction based on the difference in length of service and the earlier age at which it became payable.

There was also a total disability pension, claimable after at least fifteen years of service and calculated with regard to the same factors as the thirty-year pension. What was later called the C pension became distinguished from the CB pension on the basis that the former was awarded on evidence of total and permanent incapacity for any employment, and the latter for incapacity to perform teaching or inspectoral duties. Anyone who was granted a disability pension and subsequently returned to service not only forfeited the pension, but also had to repay the amount received before any subsequent pension, whether based on service or disability, could be approved.

If a contributor died in service, his estate received a sum equal to the total of his lifetime contributions plus interest compounded half-yearly at the rate paid by the Province of Ontario Savings Office at the time of the refund. In 1940 the rate of interest was 3 per cent. The heirs of a deceased pensioner became entitled to a sum equal to his contributions to the fund at the rate paid by the same office compounded semi-annually. The act of 1946 specified that this amount was to be reduced by the total of the allowances already paid to him with compound interest at 3 per cent.

According to the act of 1936, amounts paid into the fund during a total period of more than five years could be refunded at 4 per cent interest compounded semi-annually to anyone ceasing to be employed but not eligible for a pension. In the act of 1949, this rate of interest was fixed at 1 1/2 per cent if the period of service was less than fifteen years, and 4 per cent for a period of fifteen years or more. The right to withdraw contributions at compound interest was the only one open to a person who reached retirement age before accumulating enough years to be entitled to a pension. If the period of service was less than five years, contributions remained part of the fund. In 1949, however, provision was made for the withdrawal of such funds by the heir of a contributor who died within two years of termination of a period of employment lasting less than five years. A temporary, occasional, or substitute teacher who taught fewer than twenty days in the school year was entitled, until 1967, to obtain a refund on contributions made for that period. The recipient of a pension who returned to teaching could not withdraw his contributions for the new period of employment, although on his death such contributions were counted in the total payable to his heirs, minus the amount he had received in pension, with due allowance for interest.

A person who withdrew his contributions and then resumed employment could reinstate himself in terms of credit toward future benefits. In 1957 the chief conditions under which he might do so were as follows:

1 / the second period must be longer than twenty days; 2 / within five years of resuming employment, he must return to the fund all the contributions previously refunded to him with compound interest at 4.75 per cent; 3 / subsequent to reinstatement, he was not eligible for any disability allowance until he had been employed for two school years after his return to employment; 4 / his dependents were not eligible for an allowance under the disability pension until the same conditions had been met.

Until 1954 a person who resumed employment after withdrawing his contributions was unable to withdraw the contributions he made for the later employment if the period amounted to less than five years. In other words, he was treated in this respect as a newcomer to the profession. In 1954 it was made possible to withdraw all such contributions, regardless of the length of the second period of employment, with compound interest at 1.5 per cent and a deduction to allow for the interest his earlier contributions would have earned for the fund had he not withdrawn them.

The strictures against anyone who received a total disability allowance and subsequently returned to service were quite severe from the beginning. In 1953, however, it was specified that anyone who lost the right to such a pension might still receive a refund of his contributions with compound interest minus the amount he had received in allowances plus compound interest. He was, however, subject to the loss of all his claims under the act if he failed to notify the commission forthwith upon resuming employment either inside or outside Ontario.

In 1940 measures were taken to restrict eligibility for the permanent disability pension to those who met certain standards of health upon entry into an institution for the preparation of teachers. A person in whom some condition was identified that did not prevent him from teaching at the time, but might totally incapacitate him from further employment at a later date, had to sign a "consent" form. Incapacitation after fifteen but less than thirty years would entitle him only to an annual allowance equivalent to the Canadian government annuity that his payments and those of the provincial government would have purchased during his years of service had they been so invested. After thirty years of service, he was pensionable just as if he had not signed the waiver. In 1950 this period was reduced to twenty-five years. The amended act of 1954 provided that a member who had waived his claim to a disability pension on entering service might be re-examined after fourteen years of employment and the waiver cancelled if his physical condition justified such action. In 1966 the minimum period after which a disability pension might be granted was reduced to ten years. After 1967 the requirement of a waiver of eligibility for such a pension on the basis of an adverse medical report was no longer required, and all consents previously signed were automatically cancelled.

As a result of modifications in 1946, the total period of service required to be eligible for the maximum pension was thirty-six years for a male member who had reached the age of sixty-five and for a female who had reached sixty-two. After forty years of service, the maximum pension might be claimed regardless of age. The pension was calculated by dividing the average salary for the years for which contributions had been made after April 1, 1917, by sixty and multiplying the quotient by the number of years of employment up to thirty-six. As before, years of service before 1917 were counted as half years except that years in which contributions had been made to a municipal or school board fund were counted as full years. If the average salary for the contributory years was $800 or more, the minimum pension was $500; if it was less than $800, the minimum pension was 60 per cent of this amount. The maximum pension was $1,500 per annum unless payments into the fund would have purchased a Dominion government annuity worth more than that amount, in which case the annual yield of such an annuity became the actual pension.

The pension claimable after thirty years' service bore much the same relationship to the maximum payment as had its counterpart under previous legislation. Such a pension could not be less than the number of years of employment multiplied by $7 – not only a pittance by today's standards but a very small amount in 1946 as well. The disability pension that might be awarded after fifteen years of service was also calculated according to a formula similar to that of the maximum pension, with an appropriate reduction on account of age and length of service. It could not be less than $240 per annum plus $10 for each year by which the applicant exceeded sixty years of age when he ceased to be employed.

A recipient of a pension after at least thirty years of service who resumed employment ceased to receive any allowance during such time as the new period of employment lasted. If this period was less than two years, there was no alteration in his pension when he reclaimed it, but if more than two years, the pension was recalculated with recognition of the extra period of service.

The regulations made in 1949 declared the interval from then until June 1952, a "period during which there is urgent need for the services of persons in receipt of allowances." As encouragement for retired teachers to return to service, they could teach at a reduction of one-quarter of 1 per cent of their pension for each day of employment beyond twenty days.

The period of urgent need was the normal situation until August 31, 1968. In 1966 an amendment to the act made it possible for a pensioner to receive salary for teaching to the point that the salary plus the annual pension equalled the rate of salary he was receiving during his last year of employment before his pension began. This provision was not likely to affect many of those who returned to regular full-time teaching, but encouraged pensioners to engage in supply teaching. In 1968 the teaching regulation was amended to permit a pensioner to teach for 100 days in a school year and draw full pension. For each day of teaching in excess of 100, the pension was reduced by 1/200th of the annual pension.

The act of 1949 modified the procedure for calculating the maximum pension. The average salary for the last fifteen years of contributions was divided by fifty and the quotient multiplied by the number of years of credit in the fund, but not exceeding thirty-five. Provisions for the years before 1917 remained unchanged. The minimum allowance was to be $600 and the maximum was $3,000. There was a new scheme for those who retired with between twenty-five and thirty years of credit who had been employed for five years after reaching the age of fifty-five and had retired after the age of sixty-two. Such a pension would be reduced in terms of the claimant's length of service, but must also henceforth, like the permanent disability pension, be between the limits of $600 and $3,000. It was also provided that, on the death of a male contributor with at least fifteen years of credit, his widow or dependent child or children would receive half the pension he was entitled to or was being paid. This pension became known as the D pension. The same applied to the male recipient of a pension. Under this clause, the widow must have married the claimant before he reached the age of sixty or began receiving the pension. Payment ceased if and when the widow remarried or when the dependent child reached age 18. Payment to the widow was reduced according to the amount by which her deceased husband's age exceeded hers by ten years. Similar provisions applied to the completely dependent widower of a female contributor or pensioner, provided that the marriage had taken place at least ten years before she went on pension, and to any wholly dependent children. The minimum payment of this type of allowance was $300.

In 1950 the dependent's allowance was made available to the widow or underage children of a person who died within two years after ceasing to be employed on account of ill health or within one year for any reason other than ill health. He must, however, have demonstrated to the commission that he expected to return to teaching. It would appear that the exercise of this right must have required considerable foresight.

In 1960 it was provided that a dependent's allowance being paid to a deceased pensioner's widow devolved, upon her death or remarriage, on any dependent children and continued until the youngest reached eighteen. The marriage must have taken place before the recipient of the pension reached sixty years of age, and was reduced in accordance with any period by which his age exceeded his wife's by ten years or more. A similar arrangement applied in the case of the husband of a deceased female pensioner if he were permanently incapacitated and wholly dependent financially upon his wife at the time she went on pension.

An amendment in 1953 took out all reference to a maximum pension of $3,000. Considerable pressure from the Ontario Teachers' Federation had helped to bring about this change. There was henceforth no ceiling on the amount of allowance that might be paid.

In 1953 conditions were made less favourable for the person who withdrew his contributions after five years but before fifteen years of service in that even the tiny interest rate of 1.5 per cent on those contributions was eliminated, unless he had retired before March 31, 1949. The consequences of this situation came to the attention of Donald MacDonald, who referred to the matter in the Legislature on April 16, 1962. He pointed out that a group of older teachers had come back into the profession, on the urging of school boards and other agencies, to meet the desperate need for teachers. Not only would many of them be unable to contribute to the Superannuation Fund for the twenty-five years that would entitle them to a pension, but a considerable number would also fail to serve for the fifteen years that would enable them to claim interest on refunded contributions. He pointed out the unfairness of the situation.

For teachers teaching to retirement without completing the long period of 25 years of service these regulations, first, compel such teachers to contribute to a superannuation fund from which they cannot draw a pension; second, deny such teachers any benefits from Ontario government grants paid to the fund on the basis of their contribution; third, result in considerable loss of interest for those who do not attain 15 years; fourth, may result in increased income tax payments because of the lump sum rebate at the time of retirement; fifth, prevent such teachers from using their own funds to make adequate arrangements for their future; sixth, deny to such teachers the right granted by the federal government to use 10 per cent of their income, tax free, to provide for their retirement. This percentage is reduced to four per cent for these teachers because of the forced contribution of six per cent to a superannuation fund from which they can never receive a pension.[19]

Robert Nixon echoed many of the same sentiments, using many of the same words, nearly two years later.[20] In 1966 provision was made for the refund of all contributions on retirement for full-time, supply, or part-time service, with interest compounded semi-annually, where no pension was payable.

The amendment of 1954 provided for larger payments to most teachers by reducing the period on which the allowance was to be calculated from the last fifteen to the last ten years. The teachers' federations later began to urge further modifications. At its annual meeting on August 21, 1963, for example, the Federation of Women Teachers' Associations of Ontario passed the following resolution: "Be it resolved that FWTAO ask OTF to continue to press for the seven best years of teaching service to be used to compute pensions for retiring teachers." The request of the teachers' federations was met at the beginning of 1966. Existing pensions were not, however, recalculated on the same basis. Tim Reid protested this omission in the Legislature in December 1968, pointing to relative poverty of some retired teachers. He did not feel that any great amount of money would be involved if the adjustment were made.[21] The minister had already indicated that 5,400 pensioners were involved, and that the award of allowances on the recalculated basis would cost about $1.5 million in the first year, involving a capitalization of over $16 million.[22] In a subsequent letter to the minister, one of the pensioners involved wondered why an increase in benefits such as that proposed would have to be funded. He asked if the amount could not be paid from revenues that were rising and showed every prospect of continuing to do so. He suggested that, if funding were necessary, it might be done by instalments of $3 million per year with partial interim benefits until the required amount was reached. Unfortunately, the financial situation was not such as to add persuasiveness to the case during that particular year.

Superannuation was a matter of constant concern to the teachers. Generally, they were not much interested in benefits or refunds claimable by those who served for short periods of time. They were more sympathetic toward the teachers who contributed a lifetime of service. At its annual meeting in October 1961, the FWTAO passed a resolution that benefits be available at age fifty-five. The members were willing to pay for this privilege by increasing their contributions from 6 to 7.5 per cent of their annual salaries. During the discussion, one of the members, Miss Payne, objected to the following aspects, among others, of the existing provisions:

(1) That a teacher who contributed for 35 years and retired at 62 years gets the same pension as a teacher who started younger and taught for forty years.
(2) That a widow gets half her husband's pension but a widower receives none of his wife's pension unless he is permanently and totally incapacitated. Yet the contributions paid are identical.
(3) That a mother for whom a teacher is entirely responsible will receive no pension should the teacher die unless she, too, is totally and permanently incapacitated.
(4) That there is a penalizing clause which reduces a teacher's pension by five per cent for each year she is under 62 years if she has not completed 40 years' service.

At the annual meeting of 1963 the same federation passed a resolution that a teacher should have the privilege of retiring on full pension after thirty-five years of service regardless of age.

In 1964 *The Pension Benefits Act* of Ontario required further protection for those aged forty-five or more. The consequence was the following arrangement, worked out in subsequent years. 1 / A person with less than ten years' credit upon retirement might claim a refund with interest regardless of age, but was not entitled to any other benefits. 2 / A person who was retiring from teaching with ten or more years of credit before the calendar year in which he turned forty-five had the option of claiming a refund of this credit with interest or of leaving his money in the fund to provide the basis for a deferred F pension payable after he reached the age of sixty-five or, with an appropriate reduction for each year, as early as age fifty-five. The right of withdrawal of contributions up to age forty-five was rather paternalistically regarded as a reasonable one, since a person younger than that was considered to be in a good position to begin a new retirement arrangement. If he decided that he had made a mistake in withdrawing his credits, he was not, however, permitted to repay them and regain his former standing. 3 / A person who contributed ten or more years to the fund before December 31, 1964, and had not been in service for more than twenty days subsequently, might withdraw his contributions with interest regardless of age. He was not entitled to an F pension, which represented a privilege only for later contributors. 4 / A person with ten or more years of credit on cessation of employment who contributed for twenty days or more of service after December 31, 1964, and after the year in which he reached the age of forty-five, might not claim a refund of contributions made after that date. He was thus protected against the temptation of withdrawing the funds and leaving himself relatively unprotected in his old age. The contributions were "locked into" the fund as credit toward an F pension. In 1967 the requirement that he must have contributed at least twenty days of service after reaching the age of forty-five was removed.

Decline in pensioners' relative financial position

The improvement in benefits over recent years in accordance with an increasingly liberal attitude toward such matters and in view of rapidly rising salaries has tended to leave pensioners of any particular period in a decreasingly favourable position in relation to their successors. The act of 1936 authorized special payments, from sums appropriated by the Legislature for that purpose, to teachers and inspectors who had retired before 1917. The act of 1949 arranged for all pensioners to be brought up to a minimum of $600 annually, and removed the ceiling imposed on them by the act of 1946. An amendment to the act of 1949, passed in 1955, provided for the re-computation of all allowances based on earlier periods of employment in accordance with the current act and regulations. After continued appeals by retired teachers with very low pensions, the minimum was raised to $1,200 in January 1967. The cost of the adjustment was not charged against the fund, but was a direct payment from the provincial government.

In 1955 provision was made for an E pension to look after the widows of male pensioners and male teachers who died with fifteen or more years of credit in the fund but before dependents' allowances became available on April 1, 1949. It was a flat allowance of $300 a year, raised to $600 effective on January 1, 1967.

Recent pressures from the Ontario Teachers' Federation for further pension improvements have centred on the interests of retired teachers. Recommendations sent to the minister in early 1969 included the introduction of an escalation clause related to the average or median salaries of practising teachers, the provision of an increase of 2.5 per cent of the original pension multiplied by the number of years it had been in force, and an increase in the minimum A, B, C, and CB pension to not less than $2,100 a year. The federation also wanted an amendment that would provide for the 5 per cent reduction factor clause to be applied either to years under age sixty-two or to service under forty years, whichever was less. There was also a request that the unmarried spouse of a deceased teacher of either sex be eligible to receive 50 per cent of the deceased's pension regardless of the survivor's past or present employment or personal pension.[23]

An order-in-council, effective January 1, 1970, raised the minimum A, B, C, and CB pensions to $2,100, reduced by any amount received from the Canada Pension Plan based on contributions to it from January 1, 1966, to the date of retirement. The F pension was also raised to a minimum of $2,100, but the amount was reduced at the rate of 5 per cent for each year the recipient was under the age of sixty-five at the time the allowance began. The reduced minimum also included any receipts from the Canada Pension Plan. At the same time, the minimum D and E pensions were raised to $1,050 per annum. As in similar circumstances in previous years, the cost of the increases was met directly by the Ontario government rather than from the fund.

Administration of the Ontario Teachers' and Inspectors' Superannuation Fund

The 1936 revision of the act named the Treasurer of Ontario as the custodian of the fund and specified that funds not required to meet current expenses were to be invested in securities of the province of Ontario, with interest thus earned to be paid into the fund. For the period up to 1942, the remainder of the ten-year period covered by the 1936 revision, these securities were to earn interest at 4.75 per cent, compounded half-yearly. On maturity in 1942 they were to be replaced by a new issue paying interest at the same rate and maturing forty years later, in 1982. By November 1942 the commission and the province were to agree on a rate of interest to be paid by the latter on securities purchased with funds available for investment during the subsequent ten-year period. A similar process was to be repeated in 1952 and every ten years thereafter. In 1949 the rate of interest established was reduced to 4.5 per cent for 1952, and provision was made for it to remain at the same level for the decade ending in 1962. The rate for the decade 1962 to 1972 was 5 per cent. In a certain sense it does not seem to be a matter of any great importance how much money is transferred from the province to the fund in this way, since the province provides a large part of the fund's income in any case and, further, the province assumed formal responsibility in 1949 for making up the deficiency from the Consolidated Revenue Fund in any year when payments into the fund might be insufficient to meet obligations. The significant fact about the arrangement is that the fund has provided the province with a reliable source from which it may borrow against future income.

Regular provincial contributions to the fund have increased rapidly. At the end of the Second World War, they were approximately $1.4 million; in 1950–1, $2.6 million; in 1958–9, $11.8 million; and in 1966–7, $29.1 million. The Ontario Committee on Taxation projected this amount to $65 million for the 1975 fiscal year.[24] An additional supplementary payment of $1 million was also paid into the fund by the province each year from 1952 to 1965. J.N. Allan, provincial treasurer, explained to the Legislature in 1959 that government payments relieved school boards of the necessity of paying a share of the teachers' superannuation and might be regarded as provincial assistance to education.[25]

Legislation requires a triennial actuarial valuation of the fund, although the minister may direct an additional valuation to be made at any time. The most recent of these was completed in 1967. It showed net income of over $87.5 million in 1966 and over $98.4 million in 1967. For the same years, the corresponding allowances paid were approximately $18.7 million and $22.1 million, and the refunds approximately $4.9 million and $4.4 million. Mainly because of Canada Pension Plan instalments of $18.9 million in 1967, for which there were no counterparts in 1966, total expenditure was $46.2 million in 1967 as compared with $24.6 million in 1966. Thus the excess of revenue over expenditure declined by over $10 million from 1966 to 1967.

The report of 1967 referred to the earlier actuarial liability of the fund. In 1961 the deficit had been reported as nearly $293 million; that is, the fund fell short by that amount of being able to meet all existing claims on it, including those of pensioners and current contributors. The auditors were concerned about the size of the discrepancy, although they did not suggest that actuarial soundness was a reasonable goal. The 1967 report indicated that there was no reason to think that the situation had improved substantially.

It would of course be quite possible to have a pension plan operated on a pay-as-you-go basis, with no accumulated fund at all. New Brunswick has apparently found it quite practical to operate in this way. Any deficit between revenues and payments can be met out of the Consolidated Revenue Fund of the province. During a period of rapid expansion of the teaching force, the possibility of having such deficits would be small unless the contributions required of participants were grossly out of line.

FOURTEEN

The Provincial Committee on Aims and Objectives of Education in the Schools of Ontario

The report, *Living and Learning*, appeared in 1968 as a result of approximately three years of effort on the part of the Provincial Committee on Aims and Objectives of Education in the Schools of Ontario or, to give it its more popular and convenient title, the Hall-Dennis Committee. It may well deserve the judgment that it is the most important educational document ever produced in Ontario. Whether this enthusiastic verdict will hold up over a period of time is an impossible question to settle and, no doubt, a futile one to pursue. In any case, the report merits at least the chapter devoted to it in the present series, if not considerably more. It is not dealt with in close conjunction with aims of education because it differs widely from the usual treatise on the subject. Most of its contents are in fact devoted to issues, ideals, values, and opinions about how learning should be promoted, along with many specific suggestions for the improvement of the school system.

ORIGIN AND PURPOSES OF THE COMMITTEE

The actual machinery was set in motion by an order-in-council of June 10, 1965, which read:

The Committee of Council have had under consideration the report of the Honourable the Minister of Education, dated the 10th day of May, 1965 wherein he states that,

Whereas it is deemed expedient to revise the courses of study for children in the age group presently designated as Kindergarten, Primary and Junior Divisions.

And whereas it is deemed expedient to appoint a Provincial Committee to make a careful study of the means whereby modern education can meet the present and future needs of children and society.

The Honourable the Minister of Education therefore recommends that there be established a Provincial Committee on Aims and Objectives of Education in the Schools of Ontario for the purposes hereinafter mentioned:

–to identify the needs of the child as a person and as a member of society
–to set forth the aims of education for the educational system of the Province
–to outline objectives of the curriculum for children in the age groups presently designated as Kindergarten, Primary and Junior Divisions

–to propose means by which these aims and objectives may be achieved
–to submit a report for the consideration of the Minister of Education.
That the Committee be empowered to request submissions, receive briefs and hear persons with special knowledge in the matters heretofore mentioned.
That the Committee be empowered to require the assistance of the officials of the Department of Education, in particular members of the staff of the Curriculum Division, for such research and other purposes as may be deemed necessary.
That members of the Committee be empowered to visit classrooms in the schools of Ontario, by arrangement with local school systems.
The Committee of Council concur in the recommendation of the Honourable the Minister of Education and advise that the same be acted on.[1]

A statement from the Department of Education dated April 14, 1966, undertook to explain some of the thinking that went into the minister's decision to set up the committee. It referred to a widespread and growing public awareness that the province's educational system must be kept responsive to the social, economic, and technological changes of the period. The need for a full-scale review of the system was compared with that of the time fifteen years earlier when the report of the Royal Commission was published. In anticipation of some of the themes the committee expounded so effectively, it was stated that the educational programs of the future would be largely determined by three factors: 1 / flexibility, to satisfy the changing requirements of society; 2 / diversity, to meet a variety of interests and aptitudes among students; and 3 / continuity, to do justice to the ethical and democratic traditions of the province.[2]

At the earliest stages, the stress on objectives for the kindergarten to grade 6 curriculum was intended to be quite strong. It was rather quickly realized, however, that whatever aims and objectives were formulated would be valid only if they applied to all levels of the school system. Thus the emphasis soon came to be placed more on the second and fifth purposes referred to in the order-in-council by which the committee was established.

Justice E.M. Hall of the Supreme Court of Canada, who had recently chaired the Royal Commission on Health Services, was named chairman of the committee. Robert Nixon paid tribute to him in the Legislature.

I must say that I have the greatest respect for Mr. Justice Hall ... if his survey of the educational needs of the society of Ontario is as extensive and useful as his survey of the medical needs of Canada, then it is going to be a very useful report indeed ...

I presume that the hon. Minister was as impressed as I have been with Mr. Hall's work in the past in a capacity such as this.[3]

While those who worked with Justice Hall on the committee gave him no particular credit, at least at the outset, for a great deal of detailed knowledge about educational matters, they found him constantly ready to support positions that emphasized the dignity and rights of the individual. He thus had a great deal to do with establishing the general tone of the report.

As of 1968, additional members of the committee were Lloyd A. Dennis who, at Hall's request, was named co-chairman when the exploratory activities of the committee became onerous; Sister Alice Marie; G.W. Bancroft; E.J. Brisbois; E.J. Checkeris; J.K. Crossley; J.E. Duffin; M.J. Fenwick; Reva Gerstein; H.G. Hedges, Co-ordinator of Research and Production for the committee; R.E. Ingall; J.F. Leddy; D.W. Muir, Deputy Chairman of the Committee; G.A. Nash; M.P. Parent; M.B. Parnall; C.E. Phillips; E.J. Quick, Secretary and Research Director of the Committee, 1967–8; Ola Reith; M.G. Ross; L. Séguin; Mrs. R.W. Van der Flier; and Mrs. J. Woodcock. Members serving on the committee at earlier stages were Sister Stanislaus, deceased in 1965; R.H. Field; and F.B. Rainsberry.

The committee conducted a very active search for pertinent information. As a result of an invitation to interested individuals and organizations, 112 briefs were submitted, a number of which were very relevant and of high quality while others, naturally, were mainly exercises in axe-grinding. Public hearings were held in Ottawa in December 1965, in Sudbury and London early in 1966, and on a number of occasions in Toronto in 1966 and 1967. Presentations were made by experts, research studies were commissioned, and visits were made to schools, universities, and colleges of education in several places. Studies were made of innovations already instituted in Ontario and in other provinces. Teams were sent to the United States and to several countries in Europe to study educational systems and programs.

REVIEW OF THE CONTENTS OF THE REPORT

Style and tone

There have been too many sweeping statements about the style and tone of the report. Just as one might expect from the fact that several different individuals participated in the writing, it was an unblended mixture of styles of greatly varying quality. Much of the earlier part was hortatory and inspirational – a sermon, in fact. At its best, it was eloquent and even poetic. In many passages, the language was clear, forceful, and pungent. On the other hand, the critic could easily find examples of clichés, flawed images, and the jargon that writers on educational topics seem unable to avoid. The latter part of the report reverted to the more prosaic style commonly used for expository purposes.

The writing style naturally reflected the committee's concept of its task. A set of values was articulated and agreed upon, partly, no doubt, as a result of the investigations and hearings that were conducted, and even more, one suspects, through the influence of such powerful exponents of the progressive point of view as C.E. Phillips. Then, with a sense of mission well developed – and it must have permeated the group, since there was no minority report – the committee set out to expound an approach in harmony with these values for the many facets of education. A great many references to the results of research were cited, but this reader feels that, in much of the report, those findings were selected which buttressed the accepted philosophical position. For example, prominent psychologists are by no means unanimously prepared to give discovery as all-inclusive a role in learning as were members of the committee. The report was the antithesis of the approach of the scientist, who seems so often to sit hesitant and cautious until the weight of evidence pushes him off the fence. While there is something very appealing in following the dictates of the heart, one must in so doing, however, be prepared for some mistakes.

The report was anything but a model of logical organization. Certain topics were dealt with and returned to one or more times, often with the same material or ideas repeated in somewhat different wording. While the effect may not be wholly bad in that the reiterated points are impressed strongly on the mind of the reader, it is difficult to locate everything said on any specific theme. The content review in the present chapter, moving from section to section as it does, demonstrates the same repetitive quality.

The preamble

The report contained a kind of introductory summary or preamble, the contents of which receive attention in some detail in the following pages because it indicated and summarized the committee's views on a number of issues. This preamble, entitled "The truth shall make you free," opened with the following paragraph.

> The underlying aim of education is to further man's unending search for truth. Once he possesses the means to truth, all else is within his grasp. Wisdom and understanding, sensitivity, compassion, and responsibility, as well as intellectual honesty and personal integrity, will be his guides in adolescence and his companions in maturity.[4]

This ringing beginning set the tone for the whole report. Although it did define an aim, it was compatible with Dewey's position that there are no aims of education, but only the individual's aims *in* education. It differed in a fundamental fashion from superficially similar assertions that the aims of education are to produce wise, understanding, sensitive, compassionate, responsible individuals in that it implied that desirable human qualities are products of man's own inner drives, nourished and encouraged by education, rather than features stamped upon him or moulded into him by external influences. It was thus in harmony with the educational philosophies of Comenius, Rousseau, Pestalozzi, Froebel, and others, as well as that of Dewey. One might say that the first sentence itself was sufficient to identify the report as progressive with reference to the progressive-essentialist antithesis.

Following the opening statement, the report continued with a sweeping declaration of faith. Once the child possesses the means to truth, which seem almost as tangible as a pen, a shovel, or a computer, everything else follows.

> This is the key to open all doors. It is the instrument which will break the shackles of ignorance, of doubt, and of frustration; that will take all who respond to its call out of their poverty, their slums, and their despair; that will spur the talented to find heights of achievement and provide every child with the experience of success; that will give mobility to the crippled; that will illuminate the dark world of the blind and bring the deaf into communion with the hearing; that will carry solace to the disordered of mind, imagery to the slow of wit, and peace to the emotionally disturbed; that will make all men brothers, equal in dignity if not in ability; and that will not tolerate disparity of race, color, or creed.[5]

It is probably both charitable and fair to assume that the committee let the last clause get by unintentionally, and that it really meant something like "and that will not tolerate discrimination because of race, colour, or creed." More than one critic seized on the passage as evidence that the committee was inconsistent and illogical rather than treating it as a minor error in editing.

What followed was a statement of satisfaction with the past achievements, not only of Ontarians but of all Canadians as well, and a call for even greater deeds in the future. The philosophical orientation was definitely the optimistic one that enjoyed its heyday in the Victorian era but which has been shattered in so many minds by the bloody and destructive events of the twentieth century. Man, in this view, is not a Sisyphus, condemned to strive forever in utter futility; his efforts can make a cumulative contribution toward his own betterment and that of the society in which he lives. The fact that this outlook has been challenged by so many twentieth-century thinkers does not mean that it is not true. It is nevertheless salutary to observe that the validity of the report rests on unproved and unprovable assumptions.

Comments followed on the advantages enjoyed by Canadian in the struggle to build a good life for all. Climatic conditions were viewed in a favourable light; resources and know-how were seen as the means of meeting material needs. Reference was made to the theory of education as investment as well as a universally recognized right.

The preamble referred to the educational system of Ontario with a mixture of praise and criticism. Ryerson established a commendable system that worked well, but only fragmentary changes were made in the subsequent century. The people of Ontario had reason to be proud of their past educational achievements; from time to time, and in certain aspects, the province had been in the forefront of progress. But the committee found a rising demand for change and apparently good reason for it. The impression that the report was a denunciation of the system as it existed at the time the investigations of the committee were made was based on passages such as this.

> The Committee was told of inflexible programs, outdated curricula, unrealistic regulations, regimented organization, and mistaken aims of education. We heard from alienated students, frustrated teachers, irate parents, and concerned educators. Many public organizations and private individuals have told us of their growing discontent and lack of confidence in a school system which, in their opinion, has become outmoded and is failing those it exists to serve.[6]

After this criticism, the report returned to the rosy future that was within the grasp of Canadians, and Ontarians in particular, if they followed certain recommended courses of action. They were urged to work for harmony between the two founding peoples, with due attention to newcomers and to the original Indian inhabitants. An appeal was made to their pride in the way the country had developed. "We determined to build our nation through an evolutionary movement upon the irrevocable recognition that French and English were here as a fact of history" is the kind of statement that writers insert for emotional effect. A historian would find it difficult to discover the "we" who made any such sweeping decision.

A means by which Ontario could perform what might be a decisive role in holding Canada together was said to lie in encouraging the teaching and use of the French language. While the existing difficulties in administration and personnel were recognized, the report urged that all pupils be given the opportunity to become conversant with both English and French so that members of the next generation might be able to converse with their fellows in their mother tongue in Quebec or elsewhere. "If this is part of the price of national unity then let Ontario pay it gladly, for, in so doing, it will not only do justice to all citizens, but its people will also reap rich dividends culturally and economically, far beyond the cost in facilities and personnel needed to accomplish this result."[7]

While this objective may very well be entirely justifiable, or even necessary, from the social point of view, the recommendation pointed up the contradictions between the committee's philosophical position and some of its specific recommendations. It certainly is naïve to think that the "unending search for truth" conducted by children all over the province will lead them to a voluntary study of French to the point where it becomes an effective means of communication, especially in areas where it is almost never heard under ordinary circumstances. The situation might be different if they lived in communities where realistic incentives for learning to communicate in the language existed. However, leaving aside the question of whether or not students en masse can be expected to master the oral aspects of a language in the artificial environment of the school, it would appear that the only way the committee's recommendation could be achieved would be to use some form of extrinsic motivation or compulsion. While the committee did not advocate letting every child follow his whims without restraint, its main case definitely rested on the necessity of ensuring that his learning experiences were in harmony with his own perception of his needs. Thus there was no room for authority to step in and say that he must spend a major part of his efforts acquiring a skill to serve a social purpose but not, as far as his understanding carried him, a personal one.

The preamble gave brief attention to the role of different levels of government in education. While recognizing the primacy of provincial responsibility, it asserted that the federal government had a vital interest in co-operation with the provinces to ensure the adequacy of their resources and to equalize educational opportunity throughout the nation. Similarly, the provincial government was said to have an ever-increasing responsibility for educational costs at a time when the price of education was completely beyond the resources of local communities.

Coming back to the theme that the educational system of an earlier era made a great and necessary contribution to the welfare of the province, the report paid tribute to the one-room school, to the dedicated and underpaid teachers who made the system work, and to the local school boards, the members of which made a corresponding contribution. Small schools and boards, however, were said to have outlived their usefulness. The trend toward larger units of administration, including the announcement of further consolidation in 1969, was referred to in favourable terms.

> Such changes in accommodation and administration are inevitable if the system of education is to provide all students with access to the numerous and varied aids to learning that are now available. The changes will make great demands. They will require an expansion of local loyalties, a high degree of co-ordination among the agencies administering services, and a diversity of those services according to the needs of particular environments. But only in meeting such demands can education offer the reward of equal opportunity to all the students in Ontario's schools.[8]

A brief paragraph on the existence of a dual system of public tax-supported "non-confessional" and Roman Catholic separate schools demonstrated the determination of the committee not to repeat the mistake of the earlier Royal Commission by letting disagreement over the separate school question damage the impact of its recommendations. The system was recognized as having been in existence before Confederation and having been a condition of the union. Since the pattern would continue unless the constitution was changed, the report urged its operation in a spirit of co-operation, understanding, and good will.

Reference was made to the growth of vocational and technical education as a result of the industrial revolution. It was recognized as extremely important that pupils be given opportunities to study in these areas. A warning was issued, however, that the decision to shift emphasis from the academic to the commercial or technical must not be made arbitrarily or too early in the child's career. The importance of competent counselling and consultation with parents or guardians was emphasized. "The welfare of the individual child must be paramount in making decisions, and no stereotyped attitude, or condition of class, economic status, or environment should prejudice such decisions."[9]

Suggestions with respect to areas of particular pupil interest, such as music, art, or drama, were strictly in harmony with the report's fundamental theme. The child was to be encouraged to advance in these regardless of whether or not he had a particular talent for such academic disciplines as mathematics and science. No one was to insist that he conform to someone else's idea of a balanced program. The typical tactic of a critic of this proposition is to imply that potentially good students in the academic disciplines will be encouraged to abandon them in favour of "easier" subjects, but this is not, of course, what the report advocated.

A similar approach was suggested for the slow learner. He was to be accommodated by the curriculum so that he emerged from school with his capacities developed to the maximum in an atmosphere of self-respect and dignity, without the stigma of failure. The report affirmed the province's responsibility toward children with special disabilities, deplored past neglect, and urged that remedial action be taken at once. Services were to be provided in such a way as to permit these children to enter a regular school program when their development so warranted. In the light of existing knowledge, the large residential schools were identified as anachronisms, unsuited to educate and prepare children for today's world. This verdict was judged in some quarters as being too sweeping. There were those who felt that more emphasis should have been placed on the qualification "when their development so warrants," with more recognition of the inhumanity involved in placing a handicapped child in a situation that is normal for most children when his development does not so warrant.

A series of declarations followed, most of them revolving around the theme that education was a function of growing importance, that it required the best co-operative efforts of many agencies, and that it could best be conducted under certain specified political conditions. A passing reference was made to the responsibility of the universities to prepare teachers in the light of the content and philosophy inherent in the curriculum of the primary and secondary schools. While approval was given to the system whereby education was the responsibility of a minister who was answerable to the Legislature, education was identified as a non-political exercise. In order to ensure that it would continue to be kept out of the partisan arena as successfully as it had been in the past, the report recommended the establishment of "an autonomous, non-political advisory body of citizens, representative of the various interests of the people in Ontario."[10] Among the interests it would represent would be education, business, labour, industry, the arts, and parents. It would keep policy and practice under constant review and make reports and recommendations to the Legislature. The administration of education would also be improved by reliance on expert short-term and long-term forecasts. Planning would be based on a co-ordinated, systematic approach to the identification of society's goals.

Attention was next directed at the conditions for successful classroom learning.

> The lock-step structure of past times must give way to a system in which the child will progress from year to year throughout the school system without the hazards and frustrations of failure. His natural curiosity and initiative must be recognized and developed. New methods of assessment and promotion must be devised. Counselling by competent persons should be an integral part of the educational process. The atmosphere within the classroom must be positive and encouraging. The fixed positions of pupil and teacher, the insistence on silence, and the punitive approach must give way to a more relaxed teacher-pupil relationship which will encourage discussion, inquiry, and experimentation, and enhance the dignity of the individual.
>
> The curriculum must provide a greater array of learning experiences than heretofore. Classes must be more mobile, within and beyond the local environment, and the rigid position of education must yield to a flexibility capable of meeting new needs. These and other innovations will be aimed at developing in the child a sense of personal achievement and responsibility commensurate with his age and ability, to the end that going to school will be a pleasant growing experience, and that as he enters and passes through adolescence he will do so without any sudden or traumatic change and without a sense of alienation from society.[11]

The report referred to the school's obligation to meet the pupils' health and emotional needs by providing such services as psychiatric assessment and counselling. Resource personnel were to be called upon for assistance in such matters as family and community relationships, physical and emotional growth, and sexual ethics, and in dealing with the dangers of excessive smoking, alcoholism, and drug addiction. The importance of recreational pursuits was to be recognized in the curriculum, with emphasis on the aesthetic, social, and physical rewards rather than on team engagement and spectator participation. In short, the idea that the school should accept responsibility for the development of the whole child was advocated in a most enthusiastic manner.

New educational aids and facilities, with particular emphasis on television, were greeted with favour, and educators were urged to take the fullest advantage of them. The committee felt it necessary to mention at this point that, according to its observations, most audio-visual aids were being used in a narrow, didactic manner, on the apparent assumption that all the children involved were learning the same thing at the same time. An appeal was made for the adaptation of the media to meet each child's individual needs. The committee warned that "the dangers of thought control, passivity, and a stultifying uniformity are too grave to permit indiscriminate use of films and educational television."[12]

Efficient use of the student's time through improved conditions for learning was said to justify the phasing out of grade 13. The report suggested that twelve years after kindergarten was a long enough period of time to prepare students adequately for universities, community colleges, and other forms of post-secondary education. There would be the added advantage of bringing Ontario's school structure into line with that of most other Canadian provinces. At the other end of the school program, access to kindergarten was urged for all children throughout the province.

The time was said to be coming close for the extension of compulsory education beyond the age of sixteen. Many felt that this suggestion was out of tune with the main thrust of the report. The successful implementation of the stimulating procedures for facilitating learning that were so strongly advocated, and the provision of a multitude of attractive facilities, ought theoretically to make the school such a pleasant place that every child and young person should wish to attend, and compulsion should be unnecessary. For students who, despite the most enlightened efforts of the school, have reached the point where formal education has ceased to be relevant, compulsory attendance seems to be part of the dictatorial, punitive approach against which the report constantly inveighed and, given the assumption that intrinsic motivation is essential to successful learning, ought to be futile. Furthermore, many teachers fear to introduce the free and uninhibited atmosphere so strongly recommended by the report for no other reason than they doubt their ability to control those who have come to regard the school as a kind of prison, except by employing the kind of regulations that a prison demands. It is no comfort to them to say that the kind of ideal approach to education that the committee defined would prevent the development of destructive and antagonistic attitudes on the part of a few young people. Some mistakes of the past are beyond the school's immediate power to remedy, and it seems vastly better to give other educative elements in society a chance. There may, of course, be a case for compelling parents to send their sons and daughters to school, assuming that the latter wish to attend, beyond the age of sixteen. Such a measure might well be essential to ensure equal educational opportunity for all. But if that is what the committee meant, it surely had an obligation to say so at the point where the subject was brought up.

A special plea was made for assistance to the Indian citizens of the province, whose traditional cultures were said to have become increasingly inoperative, but who had not acquired the technological, economic, and political skills needed to share in the affluent society. Education was given a two-fold objective: "To make it possible for the majority of Indians, young and old, to become self-supporting and participating citizens in our present-day society, and to identify themselves as a respectable and valid cultural entity within the fabric of the Canadian community."[13] That is, it was the optimistic hope of the committee that Indians could both avoid all-out assimilation and deal successfully with the economic, social, and political conditions of the dominant group. At best, this solution requires that they bear a much heavier burden than the average citizen. The committee recommended that the provincial government provide educational services for all Indians within the province, including those living on reservations, with the federal Department of Indian Affairs continuing to be responsible for the costs assumed under existing conditions.

Rather abruptly, the report switched to school premises and school architecture. A plea was made for more flexible and functional design. It was said that planning would include attention to such matters as the number and location of schools, the provision of nursery schools, and the transportation of pupils. There would have to be "a new look at school construction as well as provision for the sharing and integration of services as measures of economy and efficiency."[14]

The body of the report

For those who wish to gain a real appreciation of the contents of the report, there is of course no substitute for reading it. The comments and quotations that follow are necessarily sporadic, designed mainly to indicate the general character of the work and to provide a concrete basis for a discussion of its impact on Ontario education in the period immediately following its release.

Elaboration of the basic theme

The educational approach advocated was linked to the freedom and responsibility that constituted the essential basis for a democratic society: "It [democracy] can thrive and flourish only when its citizens are free to search continually for new ideas, models, and theories to replace outmoded knowledge ..."[15] Opportunities were to be provided for science, philosophy, the humanities, and the fine arts to flourish side by side. All aspects of learning were to be given support. Learning and ideas were not the exclusive property of an elite, but must be shared by all elements of society.

At the same time the social responsibility of the educated was strongly emphasized. "Commitment to preserving a free society is of the highest order."[16] This objective was contrasted with the worship of intellectual pursuits and scientific endeavours for their own sake. It was said that the individual must develop the capacity at every stage to make value judgments.

Discussion of national and provincial problems

A substantial section of the report was devoted to an analysis of the Canadian cultural environment, with reference to some of the chief national problems. Some readers might be disturbed at the juxtaposition of highly inspirational passages with the mention of situations that seem to require an unemotional and objective eye if they are to be productively appraised. For example, we have this paragraph.

> But more important than the land are the Canadians who bend her to their will; who seed her; who tunnel for her riches; who build upon her, and who, in establishing their centres of population, do so in a ribbon of settlement that stretches along her southern border from the Atlantic Provinces to the Pacific. It is in the soul of the people that the Canadian identity can be found; and despite frequent self-evaluation, sometimes positive though muted, and frequently negative and banal, Canadians sense an identity that is not rooted in Britain, France, or America, but in themselves and their own land.[17]

It is debatable whether the mood established by these words is the one that should have been evoked just before the report launched into a discussion of the problem of foreign ownership of Canadian resources.

The report went on to deal with the internal divisions of the country. While seemingly recognizing the seriousness of the threat, it did so in the optimistic tone characteristic of so many school textbooks, in which it appears that nothing more serious than misunderstanding need be overcome to settle the matter. A great deal of effort was devoted to paying tribute to those elements in the population whose background was neither English nor French, and to proclaiming the value of their economic and cultural contributions.

Among other topics and issues dealt with were the rural-urban population shift, the changing distribution of occupations, the economic value of education, the challenge of leisure, the geographical distribution of various ethnic groups settled in Ontario, the degree of religious commitment of the population, changing patterns of morality, the outlook of young people, the problems involved in developing appropriate national and international attitudes, the question of how to deal with the powerful cultural pull of the United States, the challenge of providing equal opportunity for all classes of people, the problem of poverty, and the devices for handling conflict within socially acceptable forms.

The role of the school

The role of the school as a transmitter of culture was described in these terms:

> ... to make the student aware of the customs and procedures which have developed through long periods of trial and error; to acquaint him with the institutions and organizations through which these flow, to make him knowledgeable of the values for which his predecessors fought, and that determine the common purpose; and to give him experience in making decisions that touch on his and his society's destiny.[18]

Here again, there appears to be some inconsistency in philosophical orientation. One must ask whether every child is expected to choose to learn these things under ideal permissive circumstances, or whether in some case they will not have to be imposed on him.

The implications of change

The report made the familiar effort, on the heels of innumerable after-dinner and conference speakers and writers of casual articles, to define the nature of the changes that have transformed the world, particularly the child's world, since 1945. In this endeavour, it succeeded to a remarkable extent, despite the odds, in creating a dramatic effect. From the inevitable reference to the rate of accumulation of scientific knowledge, it proceeded to comment on the transformation of the everyday vocabulary by the acceptance of the scientist's terminology; the creation of new values and ideas, new concepts of time and space, new freedoms and restraints; and the extent to which the skills and service of the world were at the child's fingertips. Attention was drawn to the multitude of sensory stimuli that impinged upon the child, and to the challenge he faced in coming to terms with them.

> ... very quickly he has learned to watch passively scenes of violence and beauty, as well as commercials designed to mould his desires and excite his appetites. Subliminally or directly all kinds of messages get through to him. The extent to which he is affected by or prepared to act upon them is highly dependent upon his ability to evaluate, to discriminate, to be consciously aware of hidden or obvious persuaders.
>
> With every season come revolutions in fashions, hair styles, jargon, dances, music, colors, and gadgets. Every day Johnny's attitudes and values undergo a shake-up. Faced with the presence of hallucinatory drugs, wars, violence, sex, and social pressures, he often finds himself on a turbulent sea of experience for which there are no charts.[19]

Social problems

There was a discussion of the special circumstances affecting childhood, some characteristic of Ontario children in particular and others of a universal nature. The existence of poverty was deplored. "We ... have children in this rich province who are starving for attention, receiving inadequate diets, living in filthy, crowded rooms, lacking privacy, and destined to be losers in our society from a very early age."[20] The report referred in complimentary terms to attacks being made on this problem by a few inner-city schools, where poorly dressed children could be seen "talking and moving about easily in colorful classrooms, stimulated and taught with the most technical and sensitive skills by dedicated and patient teachers who are guided and supported by crusading principals."[21] The implication was, however, that a much greater effort was to be made if the situation was to be adequately dealt with.

The particular needs of immigrant children, especially those without a substantial knowledge of English, were again referred to. So also were those of 100,000 children who left French-language elementary schools and were suddenly expected to cope with instruction in English when they reached secondary school. Children from affluent neighbourhoods had their own peculiar problems. They had no guarantee of growing up in an intellectually and emotionally healthy environment. Further, they were subjected to particularly strong pressure to succeed in university – with the likelihood of being branded as failures if they did not.

A section dealt with the confused and contradictory definitions of childhood and adulthood, as demonstrated by the different ages at which the individual was eligible for family allowances, and was entitled to leave school, to vote, to consume alcohol, to be tried in an adult court, to drive, to marry, and to go to war. Reference was made to the familiar theme of the growing gap between attainment of physical maturity and the achievement of independence from parental support and control. There was passing mention of parents' confusion and uncertainty about how to handle their children in an age of confused values.

Identification of educational needs

Particular attention was called to the importance of the early childhood years. The evidence supplied by research and clinical studies was cited to support this emphasis. Needs were defined in terms both of emotional security and intellectual stimulation. Bruno Bettelheim's support was sought for the view that, while it might be possible to compensate for early emotional deprivation, the effect of intellectual starvation were likely to be irremediable.

Adolescence was identified as "one of the most critical" ages of man.

> During this period, the child begins to explore himself seriously. He searches to find out what kind of person he is, how to relate to other people, and what to believe in. Patterns of behavior are solidified. Decisions have to be made about his education, his future life's work, about sex, courtship and, later, about mar-

riage. Adolescents push out for discovery everywhere. They ask themselves searching questions, such as, "Who am I?" and "Why am I here?" Because of the complex, impersonal, and changing environment in which most of them function, it is little wonder that many young people lose their way."[22]

The school drop-out was identified as the most visible and alarming symptom of youth in difficulty. Most, although not all, drop-outs were said to be alienated youth. They tended to follow a typical pattern of cumulating difficulties in school, eventually reaching a stage of hopelessness and despair. They paid a high price for dropping out in terms of limited job opportunities, low earnings, and lifelong job insecurity.

The report suggested a kind of collective soul-searching with respect to drop-outs.

We must ask ourselves, "Who failed? The young people?" Or dare we ask, "Where did *we* fail them?"

This is no doubt idealism at its finest. It has also been the cause of considerable disquiet to those who are eager to find some constructive practical step beyond the expression of personal understanding and good will. An individual teacher may feel helpless to counter the ill effects of certain aspects of a system and equally incapable of initiating, or even of making any perceptible contribution to, the massive organizational changes that are needed to change the system. When he has done his best, he asks whether it is fair to blame him individually, or as part of a collectivity, for failing anyone.

The report was at its most lyrical in defining the non-utilitarian needs of the child.

The needs of the child are simply stated. Each and every one has the right to learn, to play, to laugh, to dream, to love, to dissent, to reach upward, and to be himself. Our children need to be treated as human beings – exquisite, complex and elegant in their diversity. They must be made to feel that the world is waiting for their sunrise, and that their education heralds the rebirth of an "Age of Wonder". Then, surely, the children of tomorrow will be more flexible, more adventurous, more daring and courageous than we are, and better equipped to search for truth, each in his own way.[23]

Discussion of the learning process

At the heart of the whole report was the section entitled "The Learning Experience." Psychological, biological, and educational knowledge were said to be giving us an increasing understanding of the child's mind, and to be emphasizing its complexity. The shift in emphasis from content to experience was singled out as a factor of overriding importance, an assertion that would indeed have pleased Dewey. A list of characteristics of learning was given as follows. 1 / It involves many processes. 2 / It is a very personal matter which parents and teachers may only encourage and stimulate. 3 / Its limits are not rigidly established at birth, but may be expanded or contracted by the nature of the living-learning experiences in which the child is born and develops. 4 / It is continuous, although varying in pace, throughout life. 5 / It is not always visible to an observer. 6 / It does not follow a set daily timetable. 7 / It requires personal effort, which no one person can make for another.

The ideal environment for the young child was described thus.

Talking with children, playing games with children, providing stimulating and diversified learning experiences in the home – all of these are important platforms for learning. Teaching children simple numbers, counting, helping them become aware of time, naming parts of the body, concepts of color and direction; these are some of the countless words and games that most middle-class parents take for granted and teach almost unconsciously. Feeling objects, finding words for experiences, talking about events and things out of sight, or from yesterday, anticipating the future, are the subtle ways in which a child in a loving-caring atmosphere acquires the foundation upon which a school can build.[24]

By contrast, children in deprived homes were said to lack opportunities to build up the vocabulary they required. They were denied a variety and quality of stimulation. Ideas were not presented to them in the kind of sequence that would expand their comprehension. They arrived at school unable to understand and act upon ideas presented to them by strangers. Their already unfavourable self-image was lowered even further. The report expressed hope that some of the disadvantages of a poor beginning might be overcome by remedial action, begun as early as possible. It appealed for more research into the learning process to help to determine what happened to a child who was exposed to stimuli which were perceptually, intellectually, or emotionally inappropriate to his age, his state of development, or his individuality; for more study of the question of when the first sign of emotional or intellectual awareness appeared, and when the child first showed a readiness to embrace new sets of concepts or enter into new relations.

The committee did not attempt to deal in detail with the learning theories propounded by adherents of different psychological schools. Note was taken of two main categories: 1 / approaches involving the observation of behaviour in the traditional behaviouristic, stimulus-response, or modified Pavlovian conditioning tradition and 2 / approaches emphasizing the "holistic, Gestalt, perceptual activity of the mind, and particularly recognizing that the total response of the child to a barrage of stimuli is more than the mathematical reactive sum of its parts."[25] It was suggested that the findings of adherents of the two seemingly contradictory positions might contribute to school learning, given certain precautions. The committee emphasized a theory of dynamic learning, while acknowledging the role of rote memory experience and drill as the basis for some further learning. In view of some of the later criticisms of the committee's position, its opinions in this area are particularly worthy of attention.

Facts, formulae, definitions, songs, poems, medical terms, names, vocabulary, and so on are all conducive to such memory skill and practice. Our quarrel is not with the fact that some things should be committed to memory, but that too often in the past such practices were meaningless and out of context, and were considered as the foundation of education. Data to be memorized or skills to be acquired should be evaluated in a total context in relationship to the needs of a child and the task at hand.[26]

The committee recognized that ostensibly worthwhile results could be obtained by immersing children in learning situations and "blitzing" their minds with information and stimuli. This approach was being advocated by certain experts as a means of upgrading disadvantaged children. Some doubt was expressed that the price to the child was really known or that it was worth paying. The report indicated, however, that members of the committee were prepared to have their apprehensions laid to rest by further evidence.

Elaborating on the recommendations provided in the preamble, with respect to classroom organization and management, the report described existing conditions.

At the present time, in most schools many rigidly controlled stipulations must be accepted by everyone who enters their portals. Basically, the school's learning experiences are imposed, involuntary, and structured. The pupil becomes a captive audience from the day of entry. His hours are regulated; his movements in the building and within the classroom are controlled; his right to speak out freely is curtailed. He is subject to countless restrictions about the days to attend, hours to fill, when to talk, where to sit, length of teaching periods, and countless other rules. Often the rules of the game can be just as mystifying to the child and his family as the English language to a newly-arrived immigrant.

In a real sense, the basic school stage for learning is set long before any child makes his entrance. In some instances, curriculum content dates back more than fifty years, with fragmentary changes made from time to time in answer to the pressures of local boards, parents, principals, and teachers. Less frequently are the changes related to the needs of children. Too often in the past, we have ignored the children who have been inadequately fed, are heavy with fatigue, mentally stunted, socially alienated, emotionally warped, economically deprived, slightly deaf, or partly blind. Too often, when recognized too late, these children have been segregated with labels, splintered into special groups or classes, or dropped by the wayside. The child arriving on the school scene in too many instances has been treated not as a major actor, but as an intruding spectator at a command performance. In many situations the child has been expected to learn, memorize, mimic, regurgitate, and duplicate the pearls of wisdom to which he is exposed. He is expected to be stuffed or programmed like a computer at any hour of the school day, and to be filled with enthusiasm for every golden nugget cast in his direction. If the child fails to benefit from the curriculum provided, the assumption often made is that the fault lies with him, and that he is a misfit.[27]

This indictment was followed by an acknowledgment that many schools were breaking this pattern and entering an era of child-centred education.

Teachers were urged strongly to pay attention to the natural sequence of learning experiences. This sequence had both universal features and variations for each individual child. If it was taken fully into account, children would be presented with the underlying specifics before they attempted to deal with abstractions. They would thus avoid mouthing undigested, uncomprehended words. Among the general factors related to learning sequences were the differences in rates of early development between boys and girls. A plea was made in the report for the breaking down of "ghettos for learning," which existed because certain areas were labeled "for girls only," "for boys," "for adults," or "taboo."

In dealing with the characteristics of the effective teacher, the report acknowledged that it was probably unrealistic to expect him to express love to every child. But it was said that all children would respond to a teacher who was genuinely interested, well-informed, kind, patient, and dependable.

Children respond to inquiring, imaginative people. They enjoy adults who attempt to match their mental vitality, adults who are discovering, trying out new ideas, and demonstrating their joy in using their imagination. What could be more delightful as a teacher, or teammate, than a mind that is playful, fanciful, and original in the relationships it perceives, that connects things as they are with things as they might be, that pokes into nooks and crannies and comes up with refreshing ideas which excite laughter and wonder. Such human beings are in tune with the minds and hearts of children. In an age when so many are seeking a reason for being, what better cause could an imaginative adult espouse? Such people have a sense of worth and style, and recognize and contribute it to all those who come in contact with them. Imaginative people are exciting, enthusiastic, vital people – they are contagious and can infect a child with their characteristics by loving demonstration.[28]

The good teacher was described as one who recognized the problems, trials, and crises in the child's life, who identified the different thresholds for stress within individuals, and who knew just how and when to offer the needed word of encouragement and emotional support. The report declared that such teachers could fill the desired role without trying to be amateur psychiatrists or substitute parents. Yet they could also be expected to recognize disturbing behaviour as the child's cry for help.

The report did not claim that the child should be protected from all kinds of failure. It did, however, condemn the failure that resulted in public stigma or that gave the individual an image of himself as a failure. Children were said to be able to learn to cope with the stress of real failure if their differences were understood, if they were loved despite their inabilities, and if they were given the courage to try again. They must also be given a chance to succeed at something within their capacities. Physical discomforts in the form of deprivation or punishment were said not to make a positive contribution to learning. External rewards in the form of marks, stars, and other awards were questioned. It was pointed out that the children who most needed the incentive of good marks were least likely to get them. There was considered to be no substitute for building on an intrinsic interest in learning and leading children to learn for themselves.

The prescription offered for the curriculum of the future was that it be child-oriented, providing opportunities for choice within broadly defined limits. At every level, teachers and counsellors would combine their efforts to guide the child along the path where his needs would best be met. In order to discharge their functions, they would require a general knowledge of child development and a detailed observation of the characteristics of each individual with whom they dealt. The signs of readiness would have to be discovered for all aspects of learning. When these signs appeared, rich and varied materials and solutions would be offered.

Rigid division of the curriculum into subjects was condemned as an obstacle to children's perceptions of order and pattern in experience. It was said to hinder them from realizing the common elements in problem-solving. This was a point which tended to arouse opposition among a number of secondary school teachers. It was not that they would have insisted that divisions be rigid, or that they would not have been prepared to support the drawing of new boundary lines in certain places, but they were agreed that knowledge could be handled successfully only if it were treated in a more structured and orderly manner than the committee seemed to believe necessary.

The committee recommended that the process of curriculum development be less formal and structured.

> A child-centred emphasis heralds a demand for imaginative, resourceful, and qualified teachers to create a curriculum of learning experiences on the spot. Remote curriculum constructors should wither away as anachronisms, and

qualified consultants on child development, methodology, program aids, field experiences, and special learning problems should take their place as supporters and stimulators of teachers in their daily work.[29]

The learning environment

An indirect challenge was offered to those who deplored the expenditure of public funds on anything but the plainest and most utilitarian buildings for schools and labeled anything beyond that as "palaces."

> The school environment sends messages to all children. The space that invites, the color that warms, the parkland that lures, the human accents of the planning of the school and its surroundings are intuitively grasped by every child. Children thrive when they can touch, breathe, see, hear, and feel beauty. Early sensory awareness can mark significant first steps in the never-ending joy of discovery and appreciation of the aesthetic. Works of visual art, sculpture gardens, fountains, and trees should be part of the integral planning of every school, for the bricks and mortar of the schools are themselves the "silent teachers." Through the personal experience of beauty one of the most significant dimensions of humanity is added to a child. He who has known beauty as a growing child is never again complacent about the ugly and he becomes a lifelong devotee and advocate of the aesthetic wherever he finds it.[30]

Issues related to aims of education

The section of the report entitled "On Aims of Education" might seem of singular importance in view of the name given to the committee and the terms of reference within which it was expected to work. What was presented, however, was not a discussion of aims according to the traditional approach, but rather a review of a number of issues on the basis of which certain procedures must be established.

The most important of these was said to be the relative importance of the individual and society. This issue was said to be of recent origin, since the demands of society were dominant until the nineteenth century. "What was provided was, in one way or another, conducive to and subordinate to the stability of society."[31] Dewey was claimed to have proposed a solution to the conflict of the child versus society, or the child versus the curriculum as society's instrument, by his formula "the child in society." The committee declared its acceptance of this concept, recognizing that the child should not be treated as an isolated entity but educated for life in a society which recognized his individuality. If any question of conflict remained, the decision was to be made in favour of the individual.

One of the most frequently voiced criticisms of Dewey's educational approach is that he overstressed the importance of socializing the child. His emphasis on this objective can be understood in terms of the strong individualistic trends that were prevalent during the period in which his ideas were developed. The threats to non-conformity have loomed larger as the twentieth century has advanced. The committee wisely made allowance for this change.

A second issue was stated in the form of a question: "In so far as the pupil must be educated to fit in with the social environment, should emphasis be given to living in society as it is or to adaptation to rapidly changing conditions?"[32] This again was seen as a problem of relatively recent origin. Not surprisingly, in view of the general tenor of the report, the verdict was as follows.

This Committee expresses its inclination toward education for adaptability to a changing world and less insistence on conformity to past and present. But it also urges that highly valued parts of our inheritance be polished and enlivened for inclusion as material likely to be encountered in appropriate opportunities for learning.[33]

The third question, in view of other views included in the report up to this stage, appears to be a straw man set up only to be knocked down. "Should there be different types of education for children of different social classes?"[34] The report indicated that the issue was a lively one by pointing to the continued existence of the practice in Ontario of maintaining separate classes for the intellectually superior, separate schools for vocational and academic students, and separate curriculum categories, all of which tended to perpetuate the idea that the academically endowed were superior to those with vocational inclinations. The committee deplored survivals of class distinction and advocated schools that would accommodate students without invidious distinctions.

The fourth issue was whether the school should remain aloof from society or be actively engaged in matters of current social importance. The committee naturally supported the second alternative. Among the problems that seemed to merit attention were the preservation of world peace, the type of patriotism needed, the role of Canada in world affairs, world government, air and water pollution, and threats to national resources.

An issue relating to the individual was said to be whether the school should be concerned chiefly and almost exclusively with intellectual development, or whether it should be concerned with the whole child.

Among modern philosophies of education there is a school of thought called New Realism which assigns clear-cut and distinct functions to social institutions such as the church, home, and school. As one might expect when this is done, an almost purely intellectual function is assigned to the school. On the other hand, another school of thought called Pragmatism does not regard the school as having a separate entity quite distinct from and unaffected by other institutions in the social environment. As might be expected, therefore, any division of functions is regarded as a matter of convenience or necessity. If the school is faced with problems that compel it to do what the home was ordinarily expected to do, the school simply does what it must. Furthermore, within the child, such qualities as the physical, intellectual, and emotional are not distinct and independent but interrelated, according to Pragmatists. For these reasons the school should and must educate the whole child.[35]

There is something unfortunate in the effect created by the passage in that it ties the conclusion more closely than necessary to adherence to pragmatism. One need not accept the whole system of pragmatic thought to approve of the particular definition of the school's role.

The report proceeded to relate the opposing views on the question to different levels of education. Teachers of academic subjects in senior high schools, as well as those engaged in higher education, except in departments or faculties of psychology and education, were identified as predominantly supporters of the restricted view of the school's function. Kindergarten and elementary school teachers were largely on the other side. The committee found that this conflict of views made it difficult to accommodate at the higher levels those pupils who were not academically inclined. While leaning toward the whole-child concept, the committee felt that the differences in views could be reduced drastically, while opportunities for students to take structured academic intellectual courses were preserved.

A related issue identified in the report had to do with the nature of knowledge. A conflict was seen between the traditional view that knowledge was something that could be transmitted and the opposing idea that the latter was "only information couched in words which may or may not influence the learner to acquire knowledge."[36] According to this concept, knowledge is what the pupil gets to know through his experience. A related question was stated as follows. "Should we continue to think of education as the acquisition of knowledge by the pupil by whatever means, or should we be concerned more with the pupil's ability to get knowledge when needed, to interpret it and collate it, and to use it?[37] The committee, of course, favoured the latter alternative.

The next issue was whether or not all pupils should be taught through logically organized courses in separate subjects, such as reading, spelling, arithmetic, history, science, literature, and grammar. The report's reasons for a negative answer were that, while some teachers handled structured subject matter so that pupils had the satisfaction of learning by discovery, "more often formal, traditional courses lead to a deadening routine; to real or imagined pressure on the teacher to cover the course; to pressure on the pupil to memorize for tests and examinations; to lack of time for discussion or learning by discovery; to inert rather than lively ideas; and to an end of creativity."[38]

As a final issue, the report tackled "the antithesis between indoctrination and complete freedom to discover, evaluate, think and decide." Indoctrination was defined as "to get a pupil to accept something as true by some other means than allowing him to make up his own mind after free critical inquiry." The committee was against this kind of activity. Much of the criticism of the report was based on the proposition that this attitude was unrealistic.

Rather than defining what C.E. Phillips referred to in a discussion of the report after its appearance as the aims of the many groups of people engaged in education, the report presented about three dozen outcomes of a good curriculum arranged in four groups, headed by the following statements. 1 / "The curriculum must ensure that pupils have the basic necessities for education." 2 / "The curriculum should help pupils acquire desirable interests, abilities, skills, attitudes, dispositions, and understandings." 3 / "The curriculum should educate the pupil in ethical values and ensure his moral development." 4 / "A good curriculum must meet the needs and expressed desires of pupils."[39]

The basic necessities of education, to refer back to the first of these headings, were defined as the physical and mental health of the students and the essential skills of communication. Under the second heading, the report included a continuing desire to learn, a feeling of security and adequacy, the ability to manage one's own affairs, social competence, an understanding of man and his world, positive attitudes toward change, the ability to solve problems and overcome difficulties, the acquisition of a purpose in life, preparation for the world of work and leisure, and the acquisition of opportunities to acquire interests and abilities that give lasting satisfaction. The third area included an understanding of other people, especially groups or nations with different characteristics or points of view; consideration for others, compassion, empathy, and responsibility; a disposition to serve the good of one's fellow man; responsible parenthood; respect for law, willingness to use lawful means to correct injustices, and interest in desirable changes in the law; patriotism and ethical attitudes toward international relations; a desire to overcome problems and dangers in society and bring about a greater measure of social justice. Under the fourth heading were included the creation in the school of a pleasant and friendly environment where society and its institutions were dealt with realistically and objectively; where students were encouraged to ask questions, to contribute further information, and to express their opinions freely; and where teachers were encouraged to answer pupils' questions truthfully as often and as fully as possible.

The learning program

The curriculum was described as a dynamic process, reflecting the personalities of the teacher and pupil and their interests, skills, and abilities. It was claimed that ideally the pupil should choose his own content under the teacher's guidance. Apparently conceding indirectly that this was not always possible, the report asserted that he should at least have some voice in curriculum planning. A primary requirement was that the curriculum be flexible, providing learning experiences adapted to meet the needs of pupils at every level. "Although many classes under many different teachers may share one course of study, every class, every group within a class, and every pupil may have a unique curriculum."[40] Two innovations, already indicated in the preamble were recommended: the complete abolition of the graded system, and the use of individual timetables at the senior level.

While disclaiming any responsibility for providing a detailed description of a proposed school curriculum, the committee offered a number of what it called fundamental conditions as the basis for the general design of curriculum and school organization. One was that there should be a learning continuum designed for an essentially unified school period of thirteen years, including kindergarten, with no horizontal or vertical division of pupils into such groupings as elementary, secondary, vocational, academic, above average, or below average. Groups might be formed for special learning situations, but there would be no segregation into categories as a regular practice.

Pursuing the proposition, mentioned earlier, that the traditional subject organization was inappropriate, at least for the young child, the report appraised the situation in this way.

> From an early age, the student probes the frontiers of understanding, and it is only in the later stages of his learning experience that these frontiers crystallize in the form of a discipline of study with clearly defined structure and content. Thus there is a place in the more senior elements of the curriculum for subjects of instruction, at least as long as these are required for admission to higher institutions. But generally speaking, subjects, with their adjuncts of textbooks and the like, should be used primarily as resources for knowledge. They should be so used freely in designing learning activities which suit students' needs, systematically in planning studies for older children, and often selectively in topical studies which include content from several subjects.[41]

The report suggested three "organizing centres or areas of emphasis within the human experience, each of which is a common denominator to certain fields of learning."[42] 1 / Communications would include all aspects of learning relating to the interchange of thought: the ability to speak, listen, read, write, record, film, paint, and dance. In terms of traditional subjects, it would take in certain aspects of social studies, mathematics, business and commerce, manual arts, and other activities involving the transmission and reception of ideas. 2 / Man and his environment would include the sciences; the geographical elements of social studies; much of applied mathematics; the practical aspects of agriculture, manual arts, home and consumer economics, and much of vocational training. 3 / The humanities would include the "search for the ideal, the constant probing of the unknown, the seeking for truth, the intuitive effort toward unity."[48] In terms of traditional subjects, the area would cover the fine and practical arts, physical education, philosophy, and religious studies. The committee expressed reluctance to list the subjects that would appear in each area on the grounds that to do so would defeat the purpose of the intended thematic approach.

The report outlined a school program from pre-school to the end of secondary school, indicating the kinds of services and opportunities that should be available at each level. This material is too detailed for specific review in the present context. Its presence is noted, however, in view of the fact that some critics complained that the report consisted only of vague generalities. In order to make its suggestions as specific as possible, the report offered a number of examples of how its broad design might be applied in school situations.

Facilities

The case for having attractive school buildings was complemented by a later section in which some of the desirable features, facilities, and equipment were listed. These included adequate libraries of books, films, tapes, programmed materials, and other resources; spacious areas for study; well-equipped learning laboratories; TV and motion picture projection rooms; music rooms; cafeterias; areas to which individuals or groups might go in spare time or for special purposes; an auditorium; a gymnasium; "perhaps" a pool; rooms large enough to permit team teaching; carpeting on the floor; rooms with a small platform for drama; costumes, masks, and puppets; a classroom library of books, magazines, special lamps, and pictures; a typewriter; picture-making equipment for sketches, murals, and posters; still and motion-picture cameras; projection equipment, including a screen and drapes to darken the room; radio and television; a tape-recorder and tapes; a record player and records; duplicating equipment, a workbench and sink; scientific equipment; and adequate storage space for material and supplies.

No matter how well equipped, the school was not to be regarded as a self-sufficient educational institution. The child's own experience with the wider world was to be supplemented by conducted tours to such places as museums, art galleries, government buildings, theatres, institutions of higher education, weather stations, and unspoiled natural settings.

Students' appraisals

A section of the report presented some of the students' appraisals of the school system. The area they mentioned most often was guidance. Ex-pupils of many secondary schools were said to have believed that it was not taken seriously by the staff and that it was poorly handled. There was a great feeling of need for expert counselling about vocations, higher education, and personal problems. Although the young people may have been asking for greater certainty than was possible in estimates of their own future success in certain areas, there was said to be no uncertainty about what they wanted.

There were complaints about methods of instruction used in the schools. A large number of teachers engaged in routine presentation of content to be memorized or mastered for examinations. There was a demand for content related to life. "Many respondents could find nothing of significance or interest in academic subjects remote in time or application to the modern world or of no apparent help to pupils conscious of their own problems, immediate and imminent, in the world familiar to them."[44] Many expressed a desire for more individual attention from teachers. There were suggestions that the school should offer a wider choice of options but demand a smaller total from each student. There was a demand for subjects such as psychology, sociology, philosophy, and economics. Regret was expressed that there was not more time for cultural subjects.

Special education

The section called "Special Learning Situations" elaborated on the plea referred to earlier that children who were handicapped physically, emotionally, mentally, environmentally, or in more than one of these ways should be integrated if at all possible in regular school programs. The roots of the existing unsatisfactory situation were found in some of the fundamental faults of the school system.

> It becomes increasingly clear that if the measure of success of an educational system is weighted toward pressuring children to digest a rigid, structured, graded curriculum within fixed intervals of time, many children must fall by the wayside, with some acceptable up-to-the-minute label attached to their unforgivable sin of failure. If a narrow curriculum is considered immutable and untouchable, it follows inevitably that those who cannot benefit from its perfection, must be put aside and separated in time and space from their peers. This was the pattern established for special education nearly a century ago ...[45]

But, the report continued,

> ... if primary emphasis is placed on the learning and progressive development of each child as an individual, it becomes easier – as well as imperative – to take in a far greater number of children with a variety of personal strengths and weaknesses under the umbrella of the regular school program. Except for the very severely impaired, such a rationale would make what was formerly considered 'special education' an integral part of general education.[46]

The specific ways in which Ontario had provided for the learner with special needs were criticized in rather strong terms. Everything seemed to be designed to isolate him from the mainstream: acts, regulations, the grant structure, and teacher preparation. Special education, discussed in chapter 10, was described in the report as "a welter of complexity, divided authority, blurred responsibility, and a broad spectrum of services unevenly distributed through the province and too frequently inadequate."[47]

The committee urged a co-ordinated approach to the child's total needs, including health needs. Among the measures advocated in the report was a registry of all high-risk infants in the province. Such a registry would involve taking the information already gathered by hospital authorities at the time of the infant's birth and making it available to departments and agencies that had subsequent responsibility for his welfare. He would be followed up systematically to detect disabilities before symptoms might be obvious to parents. The committee emphasized the need for remedial physical therapy, as well as for counselling of parents, in the early years of childhood. Particular reference was made to eye and dental health.

The home and the school were described as the primary social institutions for preventing and treating emotional problems. The importance of the school was said to be based on its close contact with the child over a long period of his life and on its commitment to health goals. Manpower shortages in the health professions also contributed to throwing the burden on the school. A great deal of confusion was identified in the way the school went about dealing with its obligations.

The report commented with approval on the growing tendency to assess the child demonstrating learning or emotional difficulties through a comprehensive battery of tests and team conferences and to construct a profile of his strengths and weaknesses. On the basis of this assessment, remedial programs could be worked out in anticipation of problems that were likely to develop, such as difficulties in learning to read. The existence of these profiles was said to make diagnostic labels of less importance, except where particular sensory or orthopaedic handicaps made specific treatment imperative. "The fifteen to eighteen different areas of exceptionality now served in the school system could probably be reduced to a very small number, the largest group relating to children with major learning disorders."[48]

The report was critical of the occupational program in secondary schools on the basis of the underlying assumption that what was appropriate for slow learners was early school leaving, early work experience, and an early assumption of adult responsibilities.

> Many slow learners, culturally deprived pupils, and others, find the move from school to full-time employment a difficult experience. These pupils pass through a typical cycle of a few years of unemployment, several part-time or short-term low-paid jobs, and finally a succession of full-time unskilled and semi-skilled positions. This is the segment of the work force which becomes increasingly

battered by shifts in our economy and the resulting displacement of industrial personnel. It is the group which reaches a plateau as a productive force early in its work experience and declines rapidly thereafter.[49]

Rather than turning this type of individual out into the labour force at a relatively early age, the report urged that he be retained longer in the school system and given more experiences to enable him to meet the challenges of work and society in a mature fashion.

The position of the committee was unequivocally against "specially labelled classes for the intellectually elite." An appropriate learning program, carried out by competent teachers working with children individually, was considered sufficient to provide for the full development of the brightest as well as of the slowest learners. Extra opportunities would be provided for those who needed them to "reach beyond the confines of their school, family, community, and country" without being treated as showpieces or made the victims of exploitation.[50] The report acknowledged that there might be some children who, because of their all-round intellectual, emotional, and physical development, should advance more rapidly than their peers and be with older children who were closer to their intellectual level, but this pattern was not seen as desirable for the majority of gifted children.

Attention was given in the report to the special needs of immigrant children, particularly those who arrived in school with little or no knowledge of English and who found

themselves severely handicapped without adequate means of communication. Teachers cannot communicate with parents; parents are unable to ask questions to which they need answers. The obtaining of simple information about the child's age, birthplace, and medical history can become a very difficult task. Misunderstandings can multiply, become exaggerated, and lead to anxiety.[51]

Note was taken of several approaches employed in Ontario schools to meet the needs of immigrants. These included nursery schools and language classes for parents established by voluntary centres, intensive crash programs where children were taught English in special classes or schools, and programs for teaching English while the children remained with their regular classes. English was said to be picked up most readily where children were encouraged to have young "teacher-buddies" and where the classroom atmosphere was conversationally permissive. The committee predictably favoured teaching English in the regular school environment. Although the report conceded that children might master the language quickly in a special centre, the program was said to do little to integrate them into their own community.

Teachers were urged to make special efforts to establish contact with the parents of immigrant children. Special efforts must often be made to overcome their fear of the school's authority. A recommended approach involved the use of teachers of various cultural and ethnic backgrounds, supplemented with well-trained volunteers who were acquainted with the languages and customs of the newcomers.

Teaching

Several pages devoted to "The World of Teaching" elaborated on the vital importance of the good teacher in educational reform, on the qualities of such a teacher, and on his functions in the approaches to education advocated in various parts of the report. His changing responsibilities for inculcating, instructing, and guiding were seen as stages in a historical sequence.

> The modern professional teacher is a person who *guides* the learning process. He places the pupil in the centre of the learning activity and encourages and assists him in learning how to inquire, organize, and discuss, and to discover answers to problems of interest to him. The emphasis is on the process of inquiry as well as on the concepts discovered.[52]

Factors which led to the changing status and role of the teacher were discussed. Children and teachers were said to have been influenced by the nature and pace of change in scientific discovery, technology, communication, and social values. There was "a greater inclination to question, discuss, and criticize; to challenge the significance or relevancy of traditional disciplines; to demand a share in curriculum planning; to relate traditional problems to current matters; and to identify and assert individual needs and interests in the planning of school experiences."[53] There had been a growing awareness of the uniqueness of each child and an improved understanding of child development. As a result of a better understanding and application of learning theory, there had been changes in classroom methods and a shift from teaching to learning. The process had been assisted by a greater variety of new techniques, audio-visual devices, text and resource books, and procedures for organizing classes. Research in education was acknowledged as having brought about some changes. So also was the presence of more teachers with university education, including graduate degrees.

Questions with respect to the future of teaching as a profession were asked.

> How quickly will a university program of teacher education become a basic requirement for all teachers? When will teaching truly become a profession with the status, recognition, and salaries granted to other professions? Can the most able and dedicated teachers expect to receive opportunities, recognition, and remuneration in keeping with their abilities and contribution in the schools? Will teachers as professionals be given, and will they accept and make effective use

of, a greater degree of autonomy? Will the role of supervisory, consultative, and administrative personnel become one of service to teachers and pupils rather than one of directing and inspecting them? Can the teacher expect to be freed from many non-professional tasks which could be handled by school assistants? Will teachers be given a greater voice in the development of curricula and in the preparation, selection, and use of teaching aids and other resources?[54]

The problems experienced by the province in recruiting teachers during much of the post-war period were reviewed sympathetically. Recognition was given to the effects of the high birth rate, the influx of immigrants, and the small supply of young people in the age groups from which the teachers had to be drawn. The report observed that these conditions had forced a postponement in the attainment of the generally approved goal of improving teachers' qualifications. Tribute was paid to the efforts of the staffs of the colleges of education and the teachers' colleges, as well as of large numbers of associate teachers, during the period of difficulty. This gentle build-up led to a strong expression of disapproval of the practice of requiring only one year of preparation beyond grade 13 for elementary school teaching and of the special summer courses for the professional aspects of the preparation of secondary school teachers.

The committee found that there was often justification for the criticism of programs of teacher education. Such education was frequently conducted in antiquated buildings according to inflexible schedules carried on in a traditional manner with limited experimentation. Even in newer buildings, there was such overcrowding that shifts had to be employed. Lack of time and facilities had hindered experimentation and plans for specialization, even when these had staff support. Departmental control, while contributing to the the maintenance of a respectable minimum standard, had deterred the development of flexible programs.

Notice was taken of the report of the Minister's Committee on the Training of Elementary School Teachers, which was submitted to the minister in 1966. The Provincial Committee on Aims and Objectives gave whole-hearted support to the major recommendations of this report and to most of the minor ones. Approval was expressed in particular of the idea of having several accepted routes to teachers' qualifications under university auspices.

Attention was given in the report to a number of differences in the treatment of the teachers' colleges and the colleges of education, despite the financing of the two types of institutions from the same ultimate sources. The former had a much greater ratio of students to staff, more limited facilities and equipment, and lower staff remuneration, including that paid to associate teachers. In keeping with the concept of a continuous program from kindergarten to grade 12, the committee recommended that teachers for all levels be prepared in the same university faculties and that they be treated as one group for all areas of study except those designed for specialization in particular subjects or in the work of particular levels. The program would emphasize child development, and would be conducted through such procedures as group discussion, seminars, team-teaching sessions, television, individual and group projects, analysis of research findings, and field trips.

Great stress was placed on the importance of continuing in-service education for teachers, both to remedy the inadequacies of initial preparation and to maintain a steady process of upgrading. The report suggested that the most effective measures for improvement were consultation, discussion, and demonstration involving department heads, principals, consultants, and teaching teams. Also mentioned were service on curriculum committees, attendance at conferences sponsored by the teachers' federations and the Ontario Educational Association, participation in teacher exchange programs, visits to demonstration classes and "lighthouse" schools, private reading, travel, participation in action research, attendance at research seminars, and the study of reports on research findings. School boards were urged to recognize these activities as part of teachers' regular responsibilities and to make maximum provision for participation in them during the regular working day, as well as helping to defray expenses. It was suggested that the appropriate educational authorities make research findings available in comprehensible and usable form so that teachers could apply them, where they were relevant.

It was observed that the more formal courses would be offered by the proposed faculties of education, other faculties of a university, school boards, the Department of Education, and other unnamed institutions and agencies. A plea was made that these courses be adequately recognized for purposes of improved certification and salary. It was also urged that there be some system of co-ordinating academic and professional courses for the purposes of granting credit. The committee found that, under existing conditions, a teacher who planned to obtain a degree handicapped himself in terms of lost time and salary if he let himself get involved in professional courses first. It was foreseen that much of the problem would be eliminated eventually when university programs of teacher education were fully developed.

A rapid expansion in the number and variety of graduate courses in education was advocated. Such a development would involve the growth of the program offered in the Ontario Institute for Studies in Education, as well as an early entry into the field by the faculties of education in other universities. School boards might contribute by making the necessary provision for sabbatical leave.

Mention was made of the service network supporting the provincial system of education, the largest group of which included directors, superintendents, inspectors, consultants, co-ordinators, supervisors, remedial teachers, principals, and vice-principals. The past role of these people was said to have been directive rather than supportive, but to be changing as the teacher increasingly filled his rightful place as the key agent of education. Recognition was also given to an ancillary group, including psychiatrists, psychologists, doctors, social workers, counsellors, nurses, secretaries, business administrators, caretakers, and school assistants. A special appeal was made that teachers be recognized as giving the highest professional service by remaining in the classroom, and that they not be forced to assume administrative positions to advance in their profession. It was suggested that this objective would be achieved "only when the teacher is allowed to move from the fringe to the heart of professional decision-making, and when educational planning becomes a product of consultation among equals rather than of direction by superiors."[55] Value was seen in posting more men teachers to work with children in the early years of school, a recommendation that was not enhanced by the report's adoption of the obnoxious habit of referring to the teacher in general as "she" instead of by the common pronoun "he," thus implying that the male teacher was a kind of intruder in a female preserve. The report rightly recommended that women be given more consideration for promotion to higher administrative positions.

A strong plea for teacher autonomy centred on the following passage.

> The modern curriculum demands that curriculum control be centred in the classroom. In spite of this demand, many teachers find that courses of study, timetables, specific textbooks, standard report cards, system-wide examinations, and many other determinants and controls on the curriculum are prescribed by authorities who cannot possibly understand the program in each classroom for which these factors are prescribed. Until teachers have a large measure of autonomy and a share in policy-making, the modern curriculum cannot become a reality.[56]

Contradicting an earlier optimistic assertion about the direction in which things were moving, the report continued:

> Through the years, as educational systems have become larger, various hierarchies of administrative personnel have been allowed, or even encouraged to assume control. As more and more administrative and supervisory levels become established, policy-making moves farther and farther away from the classroom.[57]

It was said that the educational system often equated the classroom teacher with the labourer on the working team. This analogy was challenged on the grounds, first, that the administrators "are teachers by profession, and should be placed in specialized roles, not to direct the teacher, but to assist him," and, second, that the teacher was both a professional and a technician – "a director, a planner, and an engineer in the educational work team."[58] When the stage was reached at which most of the decisions that related to the school's program were made by teachers, the report suggested that the various levels of outside supervision should either disappear or be transformed into new patterns of service to the teacher.

The committee dealt with a sensitive area in appraising the structure and role of the teachers' federations. The report observed that, while *The Teaching Profession Act* of 1944 brought the various federations together in a loosely knit organization, it did not end disunity, because each affiliate retained its former membership and most of its autonomy and continued to represent a group of teachers identified by sex, level, or phase of education.

> ... these groups have not submerged their individual loyalties for the common good of education. The one reason that the separate groups have been able to act as effectively as they have is that the educational system itself was stratified, with the various affiliates representing the teachers of different divisions.[59]

The committee found it difficult to envision the successful integration of the existing elementary and secondary school levels by teachers whose primary loyalties were to a particular level. It declared that a unified federation would be essential if the professional organization was to provide leadership in implementing the new curriculum.

School assistants

The report estimated that a third of the teacher's day went into clerical and other non-professional tasks, and an hour or more into work that could be performed by technicians and automated devices. To increase his capacity to discharge his essential teaching responsibilities, the employment of school assistants and technical assistants was advocated. It was suggested that the qualifications and duties of such assistants be as little defined by regulation as possible, that they be assigned to schools rather than to individual teachers, and that they serve where most needed according to decisions by the principal and the staff. Among their contributions would be keeping certain records, some aspects of supervision, assembly and dismissal, distribution of materials, routine checking of books, marking tests, supervising seatwork, and preparing and arranging materials and laboratory equipment.

The growing need for school technicians was seen as arising from the introduction of television and other devices on a large scale. These assistants would be responsible for maintaining, delivering, and setting up equipment, for ordering audio-visual materials to meet teachers' requests, for taping and playing television programs, and for other such activities. Their contributions would be to "ensure a better economic return for the large budgets spent on audio-visual apparatus and materials, by proper inventory and maintenance, by more efficient ordering and operation, and by a greatly increased utilization by the teachers who would be spared the mechanical aspects of using modern communications media in their teaching areas."[60]

The report explored the possibility of using the services of a variety of types of volunteers from the community, many of whom had professional, clerical, and library experience. It was suggested that their recruitment and encouragement would give new impetus to Home and School and Parent-Teacher Associations. Among the areas in which they might contribute, the report mentioned vocal and instrumental music, ballet, art, drama, introductory psychology, science, economics, politics, oral French, and commercial and technical topics.

New technical tools

The importance of technological advances was recognized by the use of the familiar expression "the technological revolution that is taking place in our schools."[61] Attention was drawn to a future need for teachers and pupils, not only to use technical tools, but also to have a greater share in the production of films, slides, television and sound tape programs, and transparencies for overhead projectors. Certain devices were identified as both aids to learning and the subjects of study as forms of communication. The problem of obtaining and maintaining a supply of suitable materials was said to be on the way to being overcome. It was recommended that the selection of appropriate materials be aided by the constant updating of film catalogues and the issuance of a single master television schedule integrating the schedules of several producing agencies. The increased emphasis on individualized instruction was said to require greater flexibility in the selection and use of teaching materials as well as moving the processes of production and distribution closer to the classroom level. The committee's recommendations with respect to television production are discussed more fully in volume v, chapter 19. It appears to the writer that the committee failed to see the value in the production, necessarily by a well-equipped central agency, of television programs of high quality, not as a substitute for local effort, but as a supplement to it.

While saying comparatively little about computers, the report foresaw a role of profound importance for them. It speculated that they might "eventually serve the pupil's individual needs for educational materials more effectively than any existing material or resource centre."[62] Because of their probable value, the committee suggested the setting up of a provincial committee consisting of interested and competent scientists, technologists, and educators to conduct a periodic assessment of the ways in which computers could contribute to education.

Team teaching

Treatment of the topic of team teaching followed the section on tools for teaching and learning. Team teaching was identified as the latest and potentially most far-reaching of the procedures designed to make maximum use of the contribution of each teacher.

... this in general is a system whereby two or more teachers, sometimes with school assistants, plan for, teach, and co-operatively evaluate two or more class groups of students within a flexible timetable, with facilities for organizing them into groups of various sizes, depending on the particular learning experience. From the student's point of view, team teaching tends to provide a greater variety of experiences, more skillful presentation and more effective organization of some aspects of the lesson, greater opportunity for discussion, and greater attention to his individual requirements. For the teacher, this plan tends to provide more time for preparation, more communication with colleagues, a more co-operative atmosphere, and greater opportunity to make use of special skills. It also lends itself to long-range planning, careful analysis of objectives, more use of films, television and other tools for learning, and presentations by persons in the community who can relate their background to topics under study.[63]

As conducted at the elementary level, the approach was described as typically involving a number of teachers and classes working together in one large area, with a flexible timetable and the children grouping and regrouping on the basis of interest, ability, subject, or activity. The teaching team organized the program for each day, and the members consulted informally as the need arose. The report pointed out that the widespread adoption of this approach would necessitate modifications in existing school buildings and in the design of new ones.

Recognizing the fact that team teaching at the intermediate and senior levels usually involved only one subject area, the report advocated that it increasingly cut across traditional subject lines. As described, the approach at these levels would involve the presentation by a single teacher of a point of view or a body of knowledge to up to 150 students, often with the support of audio-visual aids. A visiting specialist might participate or a panel discussion might be employed. After the presentation, smaller groups of from fifteen to thirty students would be formed for individual study or discussion. Small group discussions were said to have the advantages of enabling teachers to identify and stimulate interests, to get to know individual students, to measure individual progress, and to encourage all students to take an active part in the lesson. The committee's over-all verdict was favourable.

By directing the co-ordinated attention of teachers toward the individual student and his learning experience, and by demanding and recognizing special competence in teachers, new patterns in the organization of instruction may contribute, more than any other proposed educational change, to the achievement of that professional status which has long been the aspiration of teachers and which is the brightest hope for the students in their care.[64]

The role of the principal

The committee's observations confirmed the impression that the tone of the school was largely set by the principal. He was found to be in a position where he was able to exercise too much power. He could, for example, control promotion, marks, grading, and examinations; assign pupils by whatever philosophy and plan he chose, subject only to the degree of uniformity imposed by higher authority; and control the discipline and morale within the school. At the same time, the committee found him paradoxically at the bottom of an administrative hierarchy of considerable proportions, from the Department of Education down.

The report advocated for the principal the role of curriculum leader of the school, in which he acted as consultant, adviser, and co-ordinator, and "spends most of his time with children and teachers in psychological, sociological, and curricular activities. He subscribes to the theory that the aims of education are determined philosophically, and he realizes that striving for uniformity through standardized tests, external examinations, and other devices and controls has little to do with the attainment of objectives in education."[65] The committee found that the performance of these functions was seriously hindered by the activities of the superimposed administrative hierarchy. One solution offered was to have enough secretarial assistants with enough business training to relieve the principal as much as possible from purely administrative or organizational responsibilities. The committee also advocated that he be encouraged to visit other schools and to participate in policy formation across his own school system. One of his major responsibilities was considered to be that of maintaining links with the community. The formation of a school committee was recommended for each school, with members elected at a meeting of the school community.

The purpose of such a committee would be to aid the principal and his staff in interpreting the school to the community, to keep the principal and staff informed and aware of the needs of the community, to support their school in its relationship to the school board, and generally to provide for and maintain a degree of local interest in the school among people whose school trustees will be more remote than formerly.[66]

The committee advocated the re-examination of the principalship in favour of what appears to this writer to be a very questionable form of leadership: that a team of teachers take over the role. Such an arrangement was said to be particularly suitable for a campus-type school in which several buildings formed a single school complex. In the writer's judgment, placing the responsibility for the management of any institution in the hands of a committee is a recipe for chaos.

Size of schools

On the question of the ideal size of schools, the report noted with concern the impersonal attitudes and regimentation often associated with large schools. While agreeing with the argument that larger units of administration were needed for maximum efficiency, economy, and flexibility of program, the committee did not feel that this implied that the schools themselves needed to be extremely large. The report advocated groupings that would enable students and staff to have a relatively close relationship. Only under such conditions was it considered possible to have the kind of effective counselling required by many of the committee's recommendations.

Community use of schools

Community use of schools was referred to as a much-discussed but seldom-accomplished goal of education. The problem was seen as one of divided administrations, undefined responsibilities, restricted finances, and outdated legislation. The committee asserted that school buildings were expensive resources, and that the public was entitled to make the widest possible use of them. Employment of the library resource centre, the swimming pool, the gymnasiums, and the classrooms was seen as part of a regular community program.

Several pages of the report were devoted to comments and views on the organization of administrative units, finance, the role of the provincial Department of Education, and other such matters. Reference is made to a number of these in various parts of *Ontario's Educative Society* and need not be repeated here.

RECOMMENDATIONS

The report contained 258 recommendations, grouped to answer certain questions. It would not be a productive use of space in the present context to reproduce all the questions and the individual recommendations. In many parts of the present series, references are made to these, either singly or in groups, sometimes with observations on their prospects of implementation.

APPRAISAL

The report did not contain any philosophical discourse on the nature of truth, although the reader has every ground for expecting a definition of the term when he is told that the child's unending search for it is the key aim in education. It may be assumed, however, that the committee had no alternative but to leave the subject alone, since there are few better ways of ensuring discord than to raise the question of whether or not there is such a thing as absolute truth. There are many who will accept a set of propositions about the aims and processes of education which Dewey and others have promoted as long as they need not feel that in so doing they must identify themselves as pragmatists. There is little doubt that a number of the members of the committee were in that category. There were some, indeed, who were willing to go along with the whole report, provided that their own particular axe received a touch of the file, and provided that they were not pushed too patently into an uncomfortable philosophical position.

It could hardly have been expected that the essentialist position had vanished in just a few years, and that Ontario educators were unanimously prepared to embrace progressivism. The committee may have acted from necessity in avoiding labels, but the strategy would have been excellent in any case. Also, the report contained so many excellent specific suggestions that it was difficult to launch a wholesale attack on it on philosophical grounds without appearing churlish or reactionary. The essentialist reaction did come, as we shall see, but it was surprisingly mild and sporadic.

Review of representative commentaries on the report

One way of identifying the contentious aspects of the report is to consider what certain analysts wrote about it after they had had time to give it careful consideration. Enough articles, essays, and booklets have appeared to make possible the selection of a variety of points of view. The three which have been selected for treatment in the present context, while far from exhausting the possibilities, are sufficient to give some idea of the range of viewpoints from which the report was appraised.

Essay by G.T. Evans

G.T. Evans was a contributor to a publication of the Ontario Institute for Studies in Education consisting of a series of essays under the title *Means & Ends in Education: Comments on Living and Learning.*[67] His own section was called "Attitudes, Ends, and Means." Some of his points are valid in terms of essentialist assumptions. He may also be said to represent those who seek to establish theories on the basis of verifiable observations.

Evans's attitude was that of the scientist who would prefer to suspend judgment, and necessarily also action, until he had assembled and interpreted more facts. Although the point was not made explicitly, Evans seemed to imply that the committee had not derived any excessive benefit from all the information it collected, or that it was offered, during the course of its investigations. He doubted that the report presented enough facts about Ontario, its people, its educational system, the children of Ontario, children generally, how children learn, the content of what might be learned, and Ontario teachers in a sufficiently systematic way to provide the basis for educational planning.

The caution of the scientist was in evidence as Evans referred to the immature condition of most psychological theories of learning. He suggested that none of these provided a very specific guide to classroom practice. As an example of the dangers of being emotionally attracted to a particular theoretical position, he referred to the committee's emphasis on discovery learning, an approach which he did not feel was sufficiently supported by evidence. The solution he offered was the conduct of more classroom experimentation. To the extent that this position suggests delay until a greater assurance of sound action is provided, it will not appeal to those who feel that reforms are needed now.

The same attitude was evident in the assertion by Evans that the committee did not ask if the methods it recommended were really appropriate means of attaining the specified goals. In this sense he felt the report was incomplete. In his elaboration of this point, Evans split the recommendations into two groups: those referring to the provision of education and those dealing with its content. Declaring his primary interest in the latter, he then proceeded to elaborate on a description of the process of learning that differed substantially from the way in which the committee saw it. Instead of emphasizing the innate drive to learn, which presumably would look after many of the methodological questions, provided that plenty of opportunities were available and a supportive atmosphere existed, Evans's procedure leaned much more heavily on an organized process with attention to the specific requirements of each successive step. In the classification of performances into hierarchical levels in the manner of Bloom and Ausubel, the first level of response was said to be associationistic. Associations might be formed in a number of ways, ranging from rote learning to that requiring a great initial effort of understanding. The second level of response was identified as a result of the application of "understanding" to a situation with at least some novel elements. Further, attention was drawn to situations that went beyond the requirement of an understanding of the basic principles to a need to reanalyse and resynthesize the problem. If the search among a variety of possibilities led to a unique solution, the process was called problem-solving, and if it led to a variety of novel productions, it was called creative thinking.

Evans sympathized with the committee's reaction against the traditional subject compartmentalization of curricula, which inhibited the assembly of information and ideas from a variety of sources and thus impeded problem-solving. He evidently believed, however, that much more attention must be given to the necessity of providing sufficient background information, to the determination of what particular background information was needed to solve particular problems, to the relative importance of each type of performance involved in the process of problem solving, and to the best way for each type of child to attain satisfactory performance at each level. Evans asserted that each teacher had a clear responsibility to organize and plan learning in the classroom so that the desired outcomes would occur.

He demonstrated something of the essentialist orientation where he raised the question of the means of selecting the basic content that every student was to be required to learn. He pointed out that the committee did not propose to give the learner complete freedom of choice, but that it did recognize general areas that it regarded as necessary. However, he implied, that, by advocating that local boards, principals, and teachers have the responsibility for curriculum construction, the committee had assigned them most of the task of determining the essentials. The writer does not get this impression from the report. Rather, it seems that while boards, principals, and teachers were expected to provide a wide variety of opportunities for learning, and competent guidance to assist the learner to make wise choices, it was the learner himself who was to decide, within very broad limits, what was essential for him in the light of his own needs.

That Evans was unequivocally opposed to letting educational goals be selected in this way came out clearly in this statement: "The problem [of determining the essentials] ... certainly cannot be solved by consulting only the expressed interests of students, for there is no guarantee that these will encompass the core of essentials."[68] He considered the problem a national or provincial rather than a local one, demanding careful study of the society, the developmental characteristics of children, and the educational characteristics of different types of knowledge.

A strong point was made of the committee's failure to justify its position with respect to the values which the school should support. There does indeed seem to be a facile assumption that if the child is assisted in his search for truth, he will inevitably accept as virtues most of those attitudes, beliefs, and behaviours that society subscribes to. There is no real consideration of the possibility that he will not. As Evans pointed out, the maintenance of a coherent social system demands that people all make the same choice with respect to certain crucial matters such as the priority of democratic government and law. He implied that a common set of core values must be based on an initial socialization process which depends on indoctrination.

In emphasizing that sound choices must rest on adequate knowledge of the alternatives, Evans doubted that the learner's own initiative in the learning field would provide him with an adequate basis for choosing wisely. He stressed the development of knowledge.

The first task of the school ... is to help its students gain knowledge – knowledge at various levels of response, and knowledge in each of the main skill and value areas. It is a value judgment of this writer that such knowledge should meet the needs of society, the needs of all individuals in the group, as well as the personal needs of the child. It should also ensure the passing on of those cultural achievements that allow people to know the depth and beauty of mankind's creativity and achievement. The particular kind of knowledge which eventually leads to commitment to values needs special care. The price of an inflexible *ex cathedra* type of value teaching may be student rebellion or moral stupidity. The price of a vaguely defined value system could be eventual social chaos. Values are not necessarily good because they are new, popular, or emerging, nor because they are traditional. They are not necessarily good because they are invented by children, or because they are agreed upon by a majority of adults.

The last two sentences leave the whole matter up in the air, since they imply that the school has no defensible means of determining what values it should inculcate. Why, for example, should the school have any right to define a value system that does not have majority approval?

When Evans went on to state that what the school could do was to give children the ability to think about their own value structure, he could very well have been using one of the most crucial sentences from the report itself. Committee members might assert that they had proposed an educational system to do exactly what he advocated, and in the most effective way possible. In fact, although Evans identified one of the most serious difficulties encountered by the committee in trying to formulate a viable approach to education, his solution was much less clearcut that that of James Daly, whose treatment of the same issue is dealt with later.

The essentialist point of view was nowhere more clearly expressed in the article than in the assertion that educational planning must begin with the content of what is to be learned and the kind of performance desired, and that these contents and behaviours could be considered the aims of education. Evans asserted that many of these aims referred to a remote future in the child's terms. He regarded it as unfortunate that in planning there was a tendency to disregard life outcomes, since they could not be observed in school, and to focus attention instead on the process of education, as was done in the report. He regarded such an approach as a mistake, as of course it is for those who accept his philosophical orientation. The progressives, however, make the refusal to separate process and goal one of the keystones of their position.

Evans considered it self-evident that no amount of study of process could in itself give any information at all about the quality of the product. There are, in fact, a great many people who regard this proposition as anything but self-evident. The process of learning what the learner deliberately and consciously chooses in the light of full information and under the non-prescriptive guidance of sympathetic and able teachers is considered to be an expression of healthy and constructive innate forces. The kind of individual produced by this process cannot but be better as a result of it. Learning becomes destructive only when the natural and normal drive for mastery is distorted, repressed, or subverted through lack of love and encouragement. These aspects of process are entirely open to study if one feels it necessary to examine them.

To his proposition that the proper approach is to define aims in the form of behaviours, knowledge, and attitudes, and then to devise processes and evaluate them in terms of the extent to which they contribute to the attainment of such aims, Evans offered only three alternatives. 1 / One can claim that education is no more than the activities carried on in the school and judge them rather than their outcomes. 2 / One can agree that outcomes vary in quality with reference to some set of standards, but hold the view that so many of them are good that it is sufficient to let the child participate in them without too much concern about which he chooses. 3 / Certain life goals are regarded as so important that the school accepts a major responsibility to direct its teaching toward their attainment. Within this approach, there is room for individual differences in goals and in methods of their attainment. Evans declared that the committee reacted against a type of teaching that did not correspond to any of these but was most like the last. He suggested that an acceptable alternative to "an education which is narrowly conceived as training to produce a rote response in prescribed fields of content or subjects" was to plan as far as possible to have children achieve outcomes judged as good.

Evans proceeded to discuss several alternative ways in which the school could provide for individual differences. Since the suggested procedures were all based on the assumption that goals should be determined by forces at least partly external to the learner, they differed considerably from those proposed by the committee. In fact, given Evans's underlying assumptions, it is difficult to see why the efficiencies of homogeneous grouping should be rejected. This section of Evans's essay helps to demonstrate that much of the confused thinking about individualized instruction would be cleared up if more care were taken to distinguish between a situation where the learner establishes the goals and one where he does not.

An impression of teacher-centredness and learner passivity, which are admittedly rather loaded expressions, particularly after the emotion-arousing effect of the Hall-Dennis report, hung over the elaboration Evans provided of a classroom approach to individual differences.

> It is supposed, for example, that some children learn best by means of group discussion, others by individual assignment and discovery opportunities, others by clear expository teaching. It may further be assumed that the effectiveness of these methods varies according to whether facts, understandings, or problem-solving skills have to be acquired. The teacher is faced with an impossible number of possibilities and it can only be expected that he will choose one or two of these as his modal classroom procedure. What needs to be considered is the question of whether it is worthwhile to use different methods for different types of students. It is well known, of course, that children's motivation is increased

if the teacher uses a variety of approaches on different occasions and for different kinds of tasks. This is not the same as varying methods on any one occasion for different groups or individuals. Research in this area has barely started to answer the question of when and whether this should be done.[69]

This approach is obviously completely different from the kind of learning situation envisioned by the committee. No doubt it is one with which a great many Ontario teachers would be more comfortable.

In dealing with what he felt was an inadequate and over-simplified treatment in *Living and Learning* of different forms of learning, Evans called on Ausubel to help define four categories of methods of teaching for initial learning: rote-reception, rote-discovery, meaningful-reception, and meaningful-discovery. He suggested that the report adopted the common practice of comparing only the first and last of these four. Identifying the two rote methods as useful only for the attainment of a very limited number of objectives, he asserted that the real rivals as teaching methods were those in which learning was meaningful: that is, where the new information or mental creation could be attached to or interpreted in the light of previous knowledge. Evans felt that the committee slighted meaningful-reception teaching in favour of the meaningful-discovery variety. He agreed, however, that meaningful application constituted more effective practice than did repeated recitation of a set of words, although much depended on the type of material.

Evans supported the committee in its insistence on the need to provide training and practice in the problem-solving and the opportunity for creative acts. He went on, however:

Not only are discovery, problem solving, and creativity seen as goals of school learning, but they are also seen as favored methods of learning. It is at this point one should be cautious. For a start, it is obvious that there just isn't enough time for anyone to learn much by pure discovery. We are at once constrained by circumstances to a compromise, to "guided discovery." We have to ask whether all learning doesn't involve some kind of discovery, even if we just internalize in our own unique way what other people say or write. The real job that needs to be done is not to sell discovery learning as a method, but to become aware of the great range of available teaching techniques in which students are led both to be involved in what they are learning, and to organize the knowledge they have so that it is readily available for problem solving.[70]

When the question was viewed in this light, Evans felt that much of the point of the argument about the relative values of meaningful-discovery learning and meaningful-reception learning disappeared. He pointed out that the available experimental evidence on the two approaches was equivocal. He suggested that guided discovery learning would prove "tremendously useful" for the acquisition of meanings, but once that step had been achieved, it might prove very much inferior to a carefully sequenced teacher exposition.[71]

Although his paper contained no specific statement to that effect, Evans seemed to play down the importance of the motivation that impels the individual to attempt to gratify his own self-perceived needs. Guided discovery and receptive learning seem to be compared in terms of their value as methods of mastering subject matter defined for the learner by the school. Thus it hardly seems surprising that research cannot deliver a straightforward verdict between them. The real message of *Living and Learning* appears to be that discovery learning is particularly appropriate for the attainment of goals which the learner establishes for himself, whereas receptive learning is much more likely to be suitable for the attainment of externally imposed goals. A common research technique requires that motivation be equalized when the effectiveness of different methodological approaches is being compared, whereas the committee was not prepared to accept the proposition that this was possible. It is evident that much of what Evans had to say and the arguments he offered against the committee's recommendations hinged on this fundamental difference in basic assumptions. Furthermore, if these assumptions cannot be reconciled, there appears to be little use in appealing to research for answers. Nor does it help to call on Ausubel, Gagné, and Bruner for support.

Essay by C. Bereiter

In the collection in which Evans made his case, Carl Bereiter offered "A Proposal to Abolish Education."[72] The sharpness of his attack on the very foundations of the Hall-Dennis position was somewhat clouded by his insistence on the unfamiliar use of common terminology to distinguish between what he called educational goals and learning goals. The latter were said to differ from the former in being terminal and in being attainable by almost anyone, as well as being of a less lofty nature. Examples of educational goals taken from the Hall-Dennis report were the capacity to apprehend and practise basic virtues; the power to think clearly, independently, and courageously; the talent to understand the views of others and to express one's own views effectively; and inventiveness, adaptability, and creativity. Educational goals were defined as ideals to which people might aspire but could never hope to achieve in their entirety. Learning goals, on the other hand, included the mechanics of reading, writing, and arithmetic, fluency in foreign languages, many fundamental concepts and principles of science, and basic cognitive schema which would enable children to organize and interpret new facts as they encountered them.

The Hall-Dennis report was condemned for advocating educational goals that the majority of children could not achieve. According to Bereiter, to insist that they do so was to condemn them to "failure, disillusionment and corruption." He proposed alternatively that schooling should be limited to attainable goals, which amounts to the abandonment of virtually all of the goals that are properly considered educational. Rather than giving up on the values these goals represent, however, I propose that we embody the values in other, non-educational provisions for children.[73]

Before elaborating on his proposal, Bereiter devoted some attention to establishing his claim that children failed to attain educational goals by telling what had happened in certain schools run on Hall-Dennis principles. The criteria of success and failure were said not to have been eliminated but merely to have been made less explicit. Parents and teachers continued to hold normative expectations of what children should achieve. The latter thus remained in constant danger of falling short of these expectations and thus of experiencing personal failure. The problem intensified in high school, where achievement expectations were associated with university and occupational requirements. In brief, there was no use talking of permitting the child to pursue self-defined goals as long as the social forces around him insisted on specific outcomes.

Bereiter pointed out that, in the conventional school, the child was expected to behave acceptably and to carry out assigned tasks. When he did not do these things, he did not necessarily feel a sense of failure, since he might perceive himself as one who chose not to obey the rules rather than as one who was incapable of living up to expectations. In the child-centred school, he did not have this way out.

[He] is also expected to comport himself civilly and apply himself – to self-assigned tasks. In addition, however, the child is expected to show initiative, independence, curiosity, a creative urge, an autonomous desire for competence, and a large measure of responsibility for the productive use of his own time. That these are desirable traits of behavior is not to be denied. And that all children by nature possess these traits to a certain degree may also be acknowledged. But all children do not possess them to the same or, necessarily, to a sufficient degree, and the child who falls short in any of them cannot do much about it. Such a child, therefore, is likely to perceive himself as a failure, as an inadequate human being ...[74]

Bereiter characterized the Hall-Dennis report as full of glorified assumptions about the nature of children which ensured that they would disappoint the expectations of their teachers.

While he acknowledged that society could conceivably change sufficiently that all children, except those who were mentally defective, could meet its expectations, Bereiter did not see any imminent prospect of such a development occurring. Nor did he see the Hall-Dennis report making a contribution in this direction. He identified as a "critical flaw" in it the assumption that whatever was generally considered a worthwhile goal should be a goal of the school. His own counter-proposal was that the school should accept only goals that it could reliably achieve through teaching.

Under his scheme, children would pursue some of the learning goals already mentioned as examples. With reference to the functions of the schools, Bereiter elaborated further.

They could teach specific study habits and particular tactics for digging out the meaning of written material, but they would not presume to turn children into self-motivated scholars or critical thinkers. They could teach children to understand a variety of problems in mathematics, science, and social studies, but they would not hold out expectations that children become broadly competent problem-solvers. They could teach practical skills and perhaps even develop intelligent judgment within limited practical areas (as, for instance, in driving a car and in handling money), but they would not expect to develop skill in coping with novel situations.

More generally, the schools could teach procedures and ways of applying them, but they would not expect thereby to enhance intelligence ... The school's job would be to decrease the range of situations in which the child did not know what to do, thus to make intelligence ... less rather than more essential for success in school and in life.[75]

The school could discharge the functions so defined and limited during a much abbreviated school day, varying possibly between one and three hours, depending on a child's speed of learning. Admitting that the school program would be rather barren, Bereiter proposed to permit the child to spend the rest of the day doing what he wanted, wherever he wanted. During this time, it would be society's responsibility, and not the school's, to provide him with opportunities for a rich cultural life. As an alternative, some children might choose to undertake more demanding learning tasks within the capacity of their own subgroup.

Bereiter had great confidence in the educative influences impinging on the child from society at large.

We have banished creative writing, literary appreciation, mathematical discovery, extensive factual learning, independent scholarship, critical thinking, and intelligence in coping with novel situations from the school. All of these can enter the lives of young people, however, through newspapers and journals produced by young people, drama groups, Great Books clubs, mathematics clubs, laboratories, museums, films, television broadcasts, tours, field trips, libraries, political and social action groups, religious activities – along with concerts, musical performing groups, organized and individual sports, and service projects.[76]

The critical difference between the projected situation and the child-centred school would be that all these activities would be conducted as an integral part of daily living. None would have any ulterior goals and none would be compulsory.

There is, unfortunately, too little space here to do justice to Bereiter's outline of the constructive possibilities for the healthy growth of the child under the scheme he envisioned. Apart from the school, which would play a minor, if necessary, part in childhood life, the implications of the freedom of choice of experience so strongly advocated in the Hall-Dennis report would seem to be followed with considerably more logic. The problem of unrealistic expectations would certainly be dealt with effectively.

Objections to the scheme were seen and discussed in the essay. Many of them related to a lack of confidence that children could safely be left without custodial care during so much of the period in which they were supposed to be acquiring the competence to cope with the demands of modern life, particularly adult life. Bereiter recognized that "a number of fears leap to mind: that they will get into trouble of various sorts, that they will be drawn to low-grade activities and amusements (however defined) to the exclusion of more desirable kinds, that peer-group fads and cliques will dominate their lives, or that parental guidance will take over if school guidance ceases, thus perpetuating the socioeconomic disadvantages of low-status social groups."[77] Bereiter pointed out that these problems also confronted the Hall-Dennis committee, with its plan of freedom within an educational context. His essential answer was that constructive plans were at least as likely to be implemented within a framework emphasizing the values of current life as within one emphasizing educational goals. He noted the need to devote great efforts and resourcefulness to the provision of a cultural life for the young. An essential aspect of his proposal would be an open cultural market as opposed to the monopoly and the captive clientele of the school. There might be a kind of public body with the responsibility of providing cultural activities for the young, but without exclusive rights. The basic characteristics of the open market would be 1 / that it would be competitive, which would ensure that an enterprise could survive only on its merits; 2 / that it would be pluralistic, "allowing children to devote themselves to activities of disputed value or minority appeal";[78] and 3 / that it would make the fullest possible use of the rich and varied talents found in a modern society.

Anticipating criticism from the libertarians on the grounds that the school should be eliminated from the scheme altogether and the children left to learn everything that they really need while in the process of living, Bereiter claimed that there was sufficient evidence to show that this happy expectation was unrealistic. Further, he saw no good reason why the formal pursuit of learning goals he defined should be dull or boring, given good teachers using really effective methods.

Bereiter conceded that there was little chance that his scheme would be adopted. Its implementation would require educational institutions to acquiesce in the diminution of their own role, with fewer teachers assuming reduced responsibility. He saw some sign, however, that pressures for reform would come from practical-minded people exasperated at the way the school was performing its assumed task, from talented people in many fields who felt that they had as much or more to offer to the cultural life of children than the professional teachers, and from the young people who were increasingly realizing the extent to which the school was frustrating their desire to learn and live.

A fundamental difference between Bereiter and the committee is in their contrasting assessments of the capacities of the average child. If Bereiter is right, and the committee wrong, which might well be the case, then the structure developed by the latter is seriously defective. Which basic position is essentially sound must for the time being, at least, be taken on faith. It is unlikely that research will soon be able to demonstrate the final and absolute limits of human capacity as developed under the most ideal conditions. Bereiter did acknowledge that the ill effects he saw in an attempt to implement the committee's recommendations would be mitigated in a society that ceased to press unrealistic demands on the child. The committee was also apparently prepared to acknowledge that a truly educative society might be a superior cultural medium for children than a school, however humanely and intelligently conducted. Neither transformation, however desirable, is imminent.

Booklet by J. Daly

James Daly produced a really sharp frontal attack on the report in a seventy-nine page booklet entitled *Education or Molasses? A critical look at the Hall-Dennis Report.*[79] The history professor found the intentions of the report good, some of its statements admirable, and many of its recommendations praiseworthy. But he accepted the view of the authors that it could not be judged piece by piece. When looked at as a whole, he could only conclude that it was at best a bad report with some good in it. That he found the bad aspects very bad indeed he made completely clear at the outset. "Its besetting fallacies have dangerous consequences far beyond the schools. The general public would be the eventual victims of what one must regretfully call an assault on civilization as we know it."[80] He did not think there was any chance that its prescriptions for revolutionary changes in the relations between children and adults, or for revolution in the school, the family, and society itself, would be adopted. He warned, however, that the report might, in failing, do a great deal of harm along the way.

Daly devoted a considerable amount of attention to the format and style of the report. He gave the format much of the credit for the favourable impression the report had made on the public, and found it sad that the aesthetic skills employed were put to such dubious uses. He considered that the abundant illustrations of active and happy children were designed to produce a sentimental reaction in the reader and to dull his critical faculties. He described the subliminal message:

See the good children. Aren't they lovely? Aren't they pure? Aren't they helpless? Do you want to hurt them? Do you want to make them sad? See Dick. Dick is sad. Teacher told Dick he has failed. Isn't teacher cruel? Are you cruel? Do you want Dick to be sad? Do you want him to develop *Angst*, and drop out of society? See Jane. Jane is happy. Jane is enjoying a healthy learning experience. Jane doesn't know very much, but she knows how to learn. Jane slapped Nancy in the face and spat at teacher. Teacher loves Jane. Teacher loves all children. And teacher loves her job. So teacher did not punish Jane. Punishing is nasty. Instead, teacher smiled. Principal smiled. Principal asked Jane if her father drinks too much. Principal did not punish Jane. Jane is happy. Aren't teacher and principal good? Don't they love children? Don't you love children?[81]

Daly asserted quite unequivocally that real children ranged in conduct from very good to horrid, but that the report was not about real children.

Daly ridiculed the members of the committee for trying to show that they were "with it." While acknowledging that much of the report was written straightforwardly and without notable defect, he concentrated on the part that was not.

It reads like a badly written sermon of the new lay theocracy, the progressively-oriented educrats. Like most bad sermons, it is full of truisms mixed with outlandish assertions, good sense tumbled together with bathos and shallow moralism. One mark of poor thinking and bad writing is the failure to distinguish between stirring eloquence and pompous pretension. In the Report, no cliché is forgotten, no platitude overlooked. Relentlessly the verbal molasses pours out.[82]

When he turned to the content of the report, he flayed the committee for its assumption that children must learn democracy by practising it. He accused it of implying that a system that does not encourage free expression on the part of its children is not likely to produce scientists or poets either. He found it easy to cite all kinds of historical examples to prove the contrary. He weakened his attack on the shallowness and lack of historical knowledge of the members of the committee by statements like this: "The Greek schools that produced Socrates, Plato, Aristotle, Sophocles, Hesiod, and, in the dimmer past, Homer himself, were not very democratic."[83] There is in fact not a scrap of evidence that any kind of school, democratic or otherwise, had anything whatever to do with the production of Homer. As far as the others were concerned, it is probable that the schools they attended were a relatively minor aspect of the social environment in which their greatness flourished and were in no real sense their producers. Daly was right, however, in suggesting that an appreciation of history seemed to have had little influence on the content of the report. One could wish, however, that his own case had been watertight.

The report did not claim that no great scientists or poets would emerge if the schools were not run democratically. It simply did not pay much attention to the nurture of genius, but rather sought a way to release and develop the creative and productive abilities of the great mass of ordinary children, whom a delicately-poised civilization dare not leave in a state of ignorance. A critic does the committee an injustice if he does not recognize this central fact and keep his attention on it.

One can agree with Daly that the committee apparently regarded democracy as a self-justifying set of beliefs, after the manner of Dewey, rather than as a system of government and social organization accepted and defended on the basis of an objective analysis of its merits and defects. It thus rather easily fell into the practice of throwing the term around without defining it. Furthermore, it failed, as Daly says, to examine the assumption that children are sufficiently like adults that they can appropriately be prepared to operate a democratic system in their maturity by imitating the same form of experience during school life. There is also justification for the more general charge that "the authors take positions which presuppose philosophical or political analysis which is not found in its pages."[84] This charge, of course, applies just as much to Daly. And what would he have had the committee do, given its desire to influence the public and the teaching profession to work for constructive reform? The committee might be given credit for realizing that the readership it desired to reach would soon have tired of an exhaustive analysis of the foundations of its beliefs.

Daly's essentialist position was emphatically stated when he finished blasting the committee for insulting thousands of devoted teachers by the derogatory terms in which it described the way most schools were operated. He had no argument with the committee in its assertion that children involved in exciting learning experiences do not have the time or inclination to get into trouble. But he did not even recognize the thesis that, where interest in the experience ceases, so also does any learning that deserves the name. He claimed quite correctly that achievement involves drudgery, discouragement, disgust, and the occasional disappearance of any desire to press on. But he acknowledged no distinction between the inner drive that leads a person to cope with these feelings and the kind of external motivation imposed by the school. The assumption that subjection to irrational authority will develop self-discipline and a willingness to sweat and suffer to attain a worthy goal is just as much an article of faith as anything in the Hall-Dennis report. In fact, more and more people are realizing that a mockery of education often results when such an approach is used. The reaction against the attempt to impose learning, and not the attractive packaging of the report, is the reason why the latter has had such widespread appeal.

Daly's confidence in the value of compulsion was stated without equivocation.

He [the learner] must acquire the habit of continuing to work when he does not "feel like it". He can only do so if he has been compelled often enough that he acquires the *habit* of continuing past the "pleasure-point". An adult grows in love by forcing himself (or herself) to wash the diapers, and finds his love the better for it. But young people simply do not have as much will-power as adults, on the whole, and must be helped form these habits by a certain amount of stern direction. After a period of years, the student will indeed learn the "characteristics of the learning curve of performance". He will treasure his moments of zestful enquiry – and not be discouraged by those of thankless drudgery.[85]

Daly attacked the committee for forcing a choice between content and method of learning. In support of this accusation, he quoted the report. "Should we continue to think of education as the acquisition of knowledge by the pupil by whatever means, or should we be concerned more with the pupil's ability to get knowledge when needed, to interpret it and collate it, and to use it? The committee favors the second alternative."[86] It is difficult to see any basis for the conclusion, in this statement or elsewhere, that the committee felt that the learner did not need to acquire knowledge. In fact, if his drive for growth was nurtured, and if he was shown how to search efficiently, he would learn much more than he could in any other way. And, most important, his knowledge would become a real part of him rather than a piece of superficial baggage that he would unload as quickly as possible after he had passed an examination.

Daly indeed touched on what may be a serious weakness in the committee's treatment of subject disciplines. To the extent that it challenged the idea that there was any sanctity in the existing organization of content, the Hall-Dennis report was on the side of the most vigorous and enlightened elements in the university. At that level, new specialties are constantly being defined and redefined, and formerly separated areas are being combined as new foci of interest develop. But the committee left itself open to the charge of fuzzy and unrealistic thinking when it proclaimed that what confronted the learner would not be exclusively or mainly subject matter prearranged to meet requirements of adult logic. It is one thing to suggest that the learner should have the opportunity to select subject-matter sequences in line with objectives and purposes that have meaning for him, and quite another to advocate that he assemble a coherent body of knowledge by piecing together innumerable fragments that he can identify as having interest or value. If the committee really meant the latter, as it seemed to in the passages that Daly criticized, it was being unrealistic. If, on the other hand, it was fully aware of the need for experts to devote their best scholarship, sense of logic, and whatever other powers it requires to structure and restructure knowledge so that it can be employed to serve real human needs, the message should have been delivered in an unmistakable fashion. High school teachers have every reason to be alarmed at the prospect that they may be expected to assist each student to construct his own individualized disciplines from the innumerable components of three broad areas such as communications, environmental studies, and the humanities.

It is easy to support Daly's approval of Bruner's position as outlined in *The Process of Education.* As Daly said, "he finds that the structure of subject-matter is a *sine qua non* of that method [i.e., of the discovery method], that the sudent can only profit from a sense of enquiry and a zestful curiosity if material placed at his disposal clearly conveys the internal laws and characteristics of the discipline, as worked out by the most distinguished scholars in the field."[87] There is no question that this proposition is acceptable to people of many shades of opinion.

Like Evans, Daly found the committee's treatment of measurement and evaluation superficial and prejudiced. He did not think it gave an honest appraisal of the part examinations played in modern schools. He berated the committee for leaving fundamental questions unanswered.

> Is profound comprehension really detected by three hours at a table? No sensible teacher can answer such a question lightly, or with unbounded confidence. But the Committee can. It is quite certain that the answer is "NO". It does not waste much time exploring the pros and cons; it merely states the cons, over and over again.[88]

He went on to challenge the report's position on promotion and failure. He approached a key point in Bereiter's position when he asserted that, unless standards were eliminated altogether, a system of concealed failure would develop. The child would realize that he had in fact failed if he could not proceed to the next unit of work.

Daly questioned the committee's antipathy to competition and accused it of begging fundamental questions in this area.

> Is competition really that bad? If the pupil does not meet it in school, how will he be prepared for it in life? If he is protected from failure in youth, how will he face it later – as the Committee admits he must? Is it not playing with words to say that a child cannot fail, so long as he is learning a little bit?[89]

If Daly himself had wished to be a little less dogmatic, he might have considered the possibility that, given the reality of competition in the larger society, there might be better ways of preparing the child to deal with it than insisting that he practise it at an early age. To consider a similar situation, it has come to be realized that infants are far better prepared to cope with the harsh realities of later life if they are surrounded with warmth and support than if they are deliberately subjected to a taste of the hardships that adults must face. Daly might have drawn a parallel from his doubts about the proposition that children need to practise democracy in order to be able to participate effectively as adults in a democratic system.

Daly was concerned about the committee's attempt to promote egalitarian objectives by opposing specially labeled classes of the intellectual elite, as well as separate curriculum categories and different schools for vocational and academic classes. He saw a good deal of merit in this position, but asked how achievement could be rewarded and discipline inculcated without creating invidious distinctions. Members of the committee might answer that gratification from learning should be the only reward, and that it would prove entirely satisfactory if there were no derogatory comparisons among children on the basis of the line of development they pursued. If each learner is doing his best, the case for external rewards is irrelevant.

With respect to differences in the value of various human talents and activities, Daly's point rested on the validity of the assumption that external forces were responsible for, and capable of, determining the line of development that the learner would follow.

> Especially in a democratic society, the problem is to distinguish between intellectual and human values, *both* of which have their legitimate claims. Philosophy is better than auto-mechanics, but the philosopher may not at all be better than the auto-mechanic. All men are equal in human rights and human dignity, but not in the contribution they can make to the common life. Everyone who has ever thought seriously about democracy realizes that one of its besetting perils is the temptation to think that because all men are of equal value, the things they say and do are of equal value too.[90]

All this may be quite true – and important. But it is irrelevant to an educational system based on the idea that each individual's own particular talents are of supreme value to him, and that they will neither be changed nor improved by a comparison with those possessed by someone else. To stress to a learner at any stage that philosophy is better than auto mechanics can only increase the supply of bad philosophers and decrease the number of good auto mechanics.

Daly defended the use of various disciplinary methods, including the strap. His memory of its liberal application for all sorts of shortcomings in the grim old country schools included the fact, which provided a strange justification for it indeed, that there was competition among the tougher boys to see who could take the most punishment. He also recalled the terror which the threat, or even the thought, of its use caused among some of the more sensitive. While conceding that there were abuses, he vented most of his displeasure on those who exaggerated these. In considering the positive case, he went further than those who supported the use of corporal punishment as a necessity if the unruly were to be restrained, and expounded its virtues as a correctional device. As an effective answer to those who would dispute the validity of these points, he criticized the committee for closing the escape hatch of expulsion, and for saying in effect that sweetness and light simply must work – that the school could have no alternative. If the committee could be accused of sloppy sentimentality at any point, this was surely it, and Daly made the most of it.

Like Evans, Daly was concerned with the problem of how the child was to acquire the values which the adult world regarded as basic. He credited the committee for the recognition that education could not escape having a moral dimension. He pointed out that it faced this dilemma: "How can there be moral education without indoctrination, and how can there be indoctrination without hampering that free intellectual development which is the main purpose of education?"[91] He was somewhat more indulgent than usual toward the committee for its failure to produce any adequate answer, since the problem was so difficult, and at least gave it marks for perceiving that there was a problem. But he did not gloss over its failure.

> ... it clearly laid out a scheme of indoctrination, and then refused to take responsibility for it. What it did, with some honourable embarrassment, is what progressives usually do. It tried to disguise the indoctrination as discovery. The teacher is supposed to help students discover ethical principles for themselves, and certain "values or principles emerge in the process." (173, 96) Suppose the wrong values "emerge"? Suppose cruelty, bigotry, xenophobia and selfishness emerge instead of the Report's assumed "respect for and consideration of others and a commitment to truth, honesty, and fairness?" Knuckles will get rapped, that is what will happen. And so it should. The choice is not between indoctrination and no indoctrination, but between frank indoctrination and phoney discovery.[92]

It would be surprising if members of the committee were willing to admit that Daly's "wrong" values would be espoused by children brought up in a sympathetic, loving, stimulating atmosphere where they were encouraged to discover and develop their inherent talents in a stimulating and challenging environment. Thus it may be assumed that they did not see the problem in Daly's terms.

Daly took a clearly different view of the nature of the child and his needs, of the rights and obligations of adults, of the relationship between the individual and society. His vituperative language and his success in holding up various aspects of the report to ridicule remove any claim he might have to objectivity. Yet even those whose enthusiasm for the committee's work is genuine will find at least some validity in many of his points.

FOLLOW-UP

Several of the members of the committee made numerous addresses to groups of teachers, parents, and miscellaneous public gatherings throughout the province. They explained and defended the report among perceptive and informed people and among thousands of others who had only the vaguest notion of what it was all about. They debated with critics who were prepared to appraise their position with an open mind, as well as with those who reacted with catchwords or slogans such as "warmed-over Deweyism." Whatever the degree of acceptance or rejection, there was no doubt that the report aroused unprecedented interest.

An awesome promotional burden was borne by Lloyd Dennis, who was employed for the purpose until April 1969 by the Department of Education. Dennis used a vigorous, dramatic style to emphasize the stupidities in the operation of the schools which the committee claimed to have uncovered during its hearings. Some idea of the kind of approach he used may be gleaned from a newspaper article, one of a multitude which appeared during the months following the release of the report, in the *Globe and Mail* on September 14, 1968. It was headlined "Fire your incompetent teachers, Dennis challenges school trustees," and opened with his assertion that a class of eighty students taught by a good teacher was more fortunate than two classes of forty, each taught by an incompetent. Offering some interesting insights into the committee's deliberations, he reputedly said that there had been serious question as to whether schools were actually needed, whether school attendance should be optional, and whether education should be wholly under provincial or federal government control. (In the light of the second of these points, one wonders how the committee could have brought itself to suggest that compulsory education should eventually be extended beyond the age of sixteen.)

Dennis's style of presentation was described in the article.

> Joking, gesturing, striding up and down the centre aisle, Mr. Dennis tried to sell his audience on his philosophy of education.
>
> He played the part of an old-style teacher who looks upon his pupils as empty-headed idiots:
>
> "I'll pour in some facts and periodically stick in a dipstick, called an exam, to see how I'm doing."
>
> Mr. Dennis abruptly stopped, pointing at an adult in the audience and barked: "You're talking. Write 300 lines."
>
> He paused. "Now wouldn't that be ludicrous? Then why do we subject young people to such treatment?"

If teachers treat young people in this juvenile fashion, he said, they are saying that they have nothing better to do than control them.

"What else can you expect from such circumstances except an irresponsible, selfish teen-ager?" he asked.[93]

One of the audience reportedly said during the question period that Dennis's ideas were fine, but that it would take a race of superteachers to implement them. Dennis responded that the report was in part pointing the way to the unreachable star, but that everything recommended was being implemented somewhere in the world.

RESPONSE OF POLITICIANS, THE PRESS, AND THE PUBLIC

In the political area, reactions to the report mostly ranged from cautious approval to expressions of strong enthusiasm. The *Toronto Daily Star* quoted Davis as saying that the report would be "extremely helpful in future planning by the Department of Education."[94] On the same date, the *Telegram* used a headline "Cheers all round for new Ontario education plan" for an article reviewing a variety of opinions.[95] Walter Pitman reputedly called the report a "magnificent document" and was described as "virtually ecstatic" about it. Robert Nixon, considerably more restrained, thought many of the recommendations were progressive but pointed out, quite correctly, that the report broke little new ground in educational philosophy. The committee had, of course, made no claim that it was attempting to do so and hoped that its work would not be evaluated in those terms. Among the recommendations that appealed to Nixon was that for French instruction in the first four years of school, as well as that for including nursery school facilities in the educational system. Both Pitman and Nixon foresaw tremendous costs in implementing the recommendations.

There was a great deal of favourable response to the report from columnists and editorial writers. One editorial, entitled "Space-age education," in the Toronto *Telegram* on June 14, 1968, caught and expressed the essential message with remarkable perception.

Literacy has assumed a new meaning – a meaning which leaves many, who know how to read, write and figure, still illiterates in a world that demands an understanding of the purposes of man's journey and of the nature of the new forces that man has trapped but not yet tamed and domesticated.

In such a world, learning can no longer be commanded, if indeed it ever could be. No one has ever instilled discrimination, appreciation or sensitivity to ideas by compulsory measures. Today these qualities are essential in the face of rapidly expanding knowledge in every field.

From the beginning of organized education, teachers have known that a child progresses more quickly if he finds satisfaction in learning. Now the realization has come that unless the child has a sense of mastering something worthwhile, he is not learning very much, certainly not in an age where the demands increase daily.

The content of education is becoming tougher and more complicated, and there is no hope of mastering it unless a student, from kindergarten years, can identify with it. That means catering more to his interests and needs, stimulating him to learn by doing, challenging him to discover himself by trying himself out.

It means recapturing the natural joy of learning in the same sense as a child instinctively absorbs language from his environment without the drudgery of drill and formal exercise.

The *Globe and Mail* contrasted the format of the report with that of the Royal Commission of 1950, much to the disadvantage of the latter. *Living and Learning*, with its style and rich illustrations, was said to be aimed at coffee tables, while the implication was that the earlier "encyclopedic tome," bound between conservative blue hard covers, was meant to sit on library shelves. In particular, the form in which the recommendations in *Living and Learning* were presented seemed much more attractive than the sober approach employed by the Royal Commission.[96]

Harold Greer, writing in the *Montreal Star* on June 15, 1968, combined enthusiastic praise of the report with a number of comments about its unflattering implications for the provincial government, along with speculations about the possibility of its being implemented. Under the first heading, he described it as in many ways an incredible document, brilliantly written and psychedelically designed. It was notable for its rejection of the idea that mass education in a technological society could amount to no more than the training of servants for industry, commerce, and the professions. It had struck a hearty blow for the liberal and humane tradition in education.

The report was said to be, by implication, a damning indictment of Ontario's schools and the government's education policy. But it was labeled a political masterpiece in that it had avoided criticism like the plague in favour of unabashed idealism that the government could only cheer. Its main thrust was identified as running directly counter to the Robarts Plan, which the government had adopted only six years before, and which it would find difficulty in admitting had been in error.

This interpretation of the report's implied condemnation of the provincial government's educational policies was decidedly exaggerated or even seriously faulty. Such an impression is strengthened by some of Greer's further observations. He drew attention in the article to the committee's assertion that progress in education is accomplished not so much by new ideas as by getting enlightened ideas broadly accepted and put into practice, and went on to comment that "it is now up to the government." He added that, judging by the record, progress would be at a snail's pace.

This verdict ignores a number of important facts about the nature of educational progress in general and about progress made during the Robarts-Davis years in particular. 1 / While the government plays a key role, it cannot do more than provide leadership to put into practice ideas generally acceptable to the public at large. If the report was a "damning indictment" of anything, it was an indictment of the society that had got essentially what it wanted in its educational system. 2 / To imply that the government would have to be pushed or pressured into acting in the spirit of the report ignores the fact that exponents of the report's approach had gradually been assuming a position of dominance in the Department of Education. Several of these very officials had had key roles in the production of the report itself. Also, some of the most fundamental recommendations in the report, such as the abolition of external examinations and the breaking down of structural rigidities in the grade system, were completed or well under way before the report appeared. 3 / The Reorganized Program or Robarts Plan, far from being regarded as an error, is considered by some of the most enthusiastic supporters of the Hall-Dennis approach to have been a defensible step toward a more satisfactory system in that it built up courses and programs in the technical-commercial area so that they might attract students as appropriate fields of study when a greater freedom of choice began to be offered. In private discussions with the writer, a prominent political opponent of the government avoided what might have seemed to offer a tempting opportunity for criticism in favour of this very point of view. Furthermore, contrary to predictions, the government has not shown any sign of clinging to the Robarts Plan as a consequence of being unable to admit an "error" or for any other reason.

An editorial in the *Globe and Mail* found the report a severe criticism of the existing order, but assigned responsibility more reasonably. It grouped the new document with the Glassco report on government organization, the Carter report on taxation, and the McRuer report on civil rights in these comments.

The reports coming down the pike of late have gone way out ahead of governments to recognize the need for overwhelming change in our society. They have clobbered our tradition-hallowed institutions, exposed the creaking obsolescence of our thoughts and actions. They have been most devastating because they have not been the products of radicals or mavericks, but of people themselves identified with the establishments they battered.

... Judge Emmett Hall and his crew have set education on its ear, exposed the failures of every educational institution in the province, plunged eagerly and creatively into the future, and undoubtedly occasioned the eruption of fountains of cold sweat throughout the educational establishment.[97]

The editorial writer, while identifying the revolutionary nature of the report, saw fit to point out that some of the changes advocated were already under way.

There were, it is true, signs that certain aspects of the report did bruise some official feelings. The signs were discernible, not so much in references to the report as "a bunch of sentimental slop," as an unnamed official is reputed to have called it, but rather in the lack of a strong affirmation of its general principles, even though they seem to harmonize so well with the government's orientation in recent years. Naturally, of course, one could hardly expect that any government would give unequivocal support to 258 recommendations, many of them of a quite specific nature. To do so would be almost an abdication of its own responsibility for the continuous process of policy-making. Yet a more general expression of satisfaction might have been forthcoming if there had not been, figuratively, a somewhat plaintive, "Couldn't you have given us a little higher mark for effort?"

Education reporter William Reid of the *Kingston Whig-Standard* demonstrated how completely views on the critical implications of the report could differ by producing an article entitled "A pat on back for Ontario educators."[98] In it he claimed that many of these educators were being given "an overwhelming vote of confidence." He noted that there had been, during the immediately preceding years, a strong undercurrent in support of a large number of the report's recommendations. The new approach had been reflected in recent actions by the minister and by programs introduced into Kingston schools. Among the latter were moves to abolish the grade system, attempts to integrate handicapped children into regular classes to the greatest possible extent, the introduction of conservation education, and the extension of French instruction through the public school grades.

Greer, in the article previously referred to, raised the quite valid question of costs, and suggested that, although the committee had put no price tag on its recommendations, they might involve as much as a doubling of existing expenditures. He observed that the committee's only solution was that Ontario and the other provinces try raiding the federal treasury while keeping the federal government from infringing on provincial rights in education.

The *Globe and Mail* raised the same question of costs in an editorial on June 15, 1968, under the suggestive title "Costly, but worth it." The first point made was that, although the committee's recommendations could not be implemented immediately, the concept could be accepted and appropriate planning could be undertaken. The old box-type schools might not be ideal, but the report had placed more emphasis on what went on inside than on the architectural structures. As new schools were added, they could be designed to suit the new program. "As for staff, that will come much more readily to an educational system that is quick with the creativity of today and tomorrow, instead of moldering in the frustrations of yesterday." It was pointed out that, of the approximately $2.1 billion being spent on education at all levels during the current year, some was not being spent purposefully. In certain respects, the new approach would mean redirecting funds rather than additional expenditure.

In the Legislature on June 18, Pitman again expressed his enthusiasm, but also dwelt on this problem of costs. While agreeing that the implementation of some of the recommendations, such as the removal of grade 13, the abolition of the lock-step system of grades, the emphasis on exploration rather than the acquisition of facts for examination purposes, the reorganization of the disciplines, the giving of greater initiative to students, and the abolition of corporal punishment would not call for increased expenditure, he asserted that the idea that cost would not rise to any great extent ought to be dispelled immediately. Among the factors that would produce this result were the demand for smaller classes, for better trained teachers, for a whole new system for the retraining of teachers, for expanded and more sophisticated educational facilities, for increased health and psychological services, for an extension of the system into the pre-school area, for the use of musicians, artists, and actors to participate in school affairs, for the pursuit of different language studies, for the development of experimental schools, for better provision for special education, and for field trips and other forms of education outside the classroom. Pitman used the occasion to press for a change in existing procedures for raising funds for educational purposes.[99]

The *Ottawa Journal*, taking a sceptical line, editorialized that the report did not merit all the "exciting rhetoric" being applied to it. Most of the ideas it propounded were said to be the current orthodoxy of schools of education in Canada and the United States. "The philosophy is John Dewey's, warmed over and revised by his latter-day disciples." The recommendations were described as including about every educational fad and fancy enjoying current critical respectability. There was considered to be no particular ingenuity in advocating gradeless schools, the abolition of grades and marks, visual aids, television, and health services, since most high school principals who attended an annual convention and read their journals could have made similar proposals.

Referring to the committee's belief in the perfectibility of pupil and teacher, which was labeled naïve, and to the vision of a classroom where the fixed position of pupil and teacher, the insistence on silence, and the punitive approach gave way to a more relaxed teacher-pupil relationship, the editorial writer accused the members of living in a dream world if they thought such an ideal could be realized in a public school system that had to accept every pupil who came to its doors.

> We can strive for the ideal. It would be flattering to human nature to believe that students do not need discipline nor the spur of competition to make them excel. An examless, gradeless school would have a better social climate; perhaps some would benefit academically. But it is a pure act of faith to believe such educational utopia is possible.

The theme that the use of force is a suitable method of dealing with troublesome pupils was expounded by the *Brantford Expositor*.

How many teachers are capable of performing, or would want to, in so permissive an atmosphere? What is the effect of a complete lack of discipline likely to be on pupils? The crying need of this age is for discipline. The report recommends doing away with corporal punishment entirely. A good teacher maintains discipline not just for the sake of keeping the unruly in order but to ensure that those who want to learn will not be prevented by the irresponsible actions of those who do not. Is the time of the rest of the class to be sacrificed while the teacher "reasons" with a trouble maker?[100]

One can imagine the feelings of members of the committee on hearing that they had recommended "a complete lack of discipline."

Where newspaper reaction was adverse, it often took the form of a regretful sigh that the beautiful world envisioned by the committee did not, alas! correspond too well with realities. The *Hamilton Spectator* followed this line in an editorial which appeared on August 17, 1968, under the title "Abstract Delight." The report was called beguiling and received praise for "its prose, smooth, polished and occasionally reminiscent in its elegant phrasing of the famous Massey Report."[101] The ideals of education which it presented were said to be beyond dispute. The editorial singled out for criticism recommendation 29, which advocated the abolition of corporal punishment. The viewpoint was much like that of James Daly, which has already been discussed. Tribute was paid to this recommendation as an ideal, but the editorial went on to assert that corporal punishment could not be replaced by an abstraction.

Just as no society can exist without ideals and perishes as it discards them, so no society can exist without discipline. It is the backbone of everything. If we are to discard the harsher methods of imposing discipline that were commonplace in past generations, then we must find effective substitutes. To fob off this challenge with an idealistic abstraction is not intellectually courageous, it is dodging the issue.

The editorial went on to describe the very real difficulties which teachers often encounter.

A teacher often finds himself faced with recalcitrants, "tough guys," insolent and defiant; deliberate trouble-makers who hold up work and carry their campaign to the limit. What does the teacher do? Take him to the principal. What does the principal do? Well, he has to think of parents who believe their little Johnny is perfect, who will phone not only him but also a member of the board of education and generally make his life miserable.

... A high proportion of some teachers' time is wasted merely in keeping order. Nor is this a reflection on their ability or dedication. It is merely because they have been deprived of authority and, what is more, their tormentors know it well.

It is regettable that the editorial writer did not concern himself with the issue of why a teacher should be expected to act as a jailer for young people who have reached the stage where the school no longer offers the possibility of real learning. It is too bad he did not suggest what benefits he saw in confining the youthful tormentors of teachers to the classroom. Might he not have gone even deeper and estimated the ultimate cost to society of turning out individuals who have adopted a purely destructive attitude in their adolescence?

A familiar critical point of view was taken in an editorial in *School Administration.*[102] The report was said to have made two fallacious assumptions which "only when made true, will allow its realization":

that every child who comes to the school system is of a nice, stable, middle-class, relatively problem-free background, who will bring to the teacher, principal, and rest of the education structure a propensity to absorb willingly the values of the school system, if not the overt ability;

that all organizations in the education mosaic (teachers' federations, trustees' organizations, school boards, provincial superstructures) all have the clear-cut single-minded aim of the improvement of education.

Despite the committee's endeavour to emphasize the importance of the individual, its position was either unclear or unconvincing to some people. A correspondent wrote to the *Globe and Mail* on September 4, 1968, as follows:

... the basic philosophy of the Hall-Dennis recommendations ... is totalitarian and immoral in spirit because it envisages a system in which the State conditions our children to become "well-adjusted", "non-competitive", "co-operative" participants in a world of team teaching and group enterprises, of careful manipulation of "development profiles" and lordly assessment of "potential" by all-too-fallible "experts".

No doubt there will always be some people for whom any kind of intervention, from whatever motive or by whatever means, into the life of the child represents an intolerable threat.

Among the doubters about the validity of the approach advocated in the report were many who felt that its implementation would surround the growing child with influences that would constitute a poor preparation for the hard realities of life. Mrs Norma M. Lynes articulated these views in a letter to the *Telegram*. She offered as examples of magnificence in defeat the performance of Duff Roblin and Dalton Camp, who had shown the grace and toughness of character to lose well in their political struggles, and asked:

Will the child who has never been allowed to fail, has tried no examinations, who knows not the exhilaration of competition, who has not been taught to accept discipline while young, grow to be the man who can stand the hurly-burly of political competition, who is willing to give his time, strength and purse for his country?

Will he be a man who can accept a failure or defeat and rise from it a better man than before? ...

Will the child who has only to learn what he likes and does well and learns it in a luxurious, air-conditioned school under nearly ideal conditions (far better than most people have at home) be the man who can endure the physical and mental challenges of the competition that oils the wheels of industry and commerce?[103]

Mrs Lynes's answer was "Hardly likely."

This position was, of course, expounded at length by Daly. People who hold it are very numerous and include many parents whose concern for the welfare of their offspring cannot be doubted. It may be suspected that they will be the strongest obstacle to the implementation of the report.

There has been particular apprehension among parents about the strong de-emphasis on job training. Whether the opinion is expressed openly or simply implied, many regard this as the chief end of education. They are not quite prepared to believe that the flexibility, the urge to learn more, and the capacity to think, which the proposed curriculum is designed to develop, are sufficient to permit a young man or woman to get a foot in the door of the occupational world. They are not at all certain that a kindly social system will ensure that deficiencies in vocational skills, which they think it is the school's business to develop, are compensated for.

RESPONSE FROM TEACHERS AND ADMINISTRATORS

The response from elementary school teachers and administrators was reported by those who delivered addresses and participated in discussions on the report to be generally favourable, while that from their secondary school counterparts was ordinarily negative. These generalizations leave room, of course, for many exceptions among the two groups. They are not too easy to reconcile with the findings of a survey by Dormer Ellis and J. Rosaire Cloutier, reviewed later in the present chapter.

P. Miller, an elementary school principal in Etobicoke, was quoted in the *Educational Courier* as saying:

The appealing aspect of the report is the degree of flexibility felt to be necessary for schools to contribute to the education of each individual child. This may not make for so much tidiness from the external point of view but our lives are mostly untidy. The general tone of the report says to me: we can enjoy learning, and there is a joy to life (a feature which seems somewhat diluted as the child advances in school).

Have we the courage to be honest with ourselves, readily accepting the children with all their imperfections, and flexible enough to acknowledge they will not always develop according to the neat little framework adults often visualize as success in school? I have faith in my colleagues.[104]

One of the criticisms most frequently heard from secondary school teachers and administrators was that the point of view expressed in the report was appropriate for the elementary level but not for the secondary or higher levels. I.M. Robb, during his final year as General Secretary of the Ontario Secondary School Teachers' Federation, put the case this way.

The first flavour I wish to mention, and one which, with my background I find less than palatable is a definite orientation toward, or bias toward the junior grades of the elementary school. This, of course, is not surprising when you recall that the committee was originally established (and here I quote from the Order in Council setting up the Committee) "to outline objectives of the curriculum for children in the age groups presently designated as Kindergarten, Primary and Junior Divisions and to propose means by which these aims and objectives may be achieved". Naturally there were chosen as members of the committee persons with a dominant interest and background of experience in this area of education. When the terms of reference of the committee were expanded to include secondary education – and no-one seems to know quite how this happened – the committee naturally tended to see in secondary education no more than an extension of elementary education with the same aims and therefore the same techniques applicable. I know this may be an oversimplification of what happened but I still maintain that the flavour of the junior grades of elementary schools permeates the whole report.[105]

Robb put the case more effectively than did some others who suggested that the committee was too heavily weighted with people whose background and interests were primarily at the elementary school level. But it was easy to point out, in refutation of this claim, that a number of members, including some of the most powerful, had a reasonable claim to being able to speak for the secondary and higher levels. C.E. Phillips asked, also, how it was possible to treat the individual as an entirely different type of creature after he passed a certain level of development. On the assumption that a truly educational experience must be based on the individual's innate tendency to grow, and to learn as part of growth, it does indeed seem to make little sense to switch tactics at some arbitrary stage and begin to impose learning on him.

J.R.H. Morgan, identified in some quarters as the most outspoken critic of the report, was one of those who objected that a psychological approach which might be appropriate for the pre-adolescent was being foisted on the senior grades. He felt that the child was a natural learner only up to the age of puberty, at which time he became introverted, self-centred, and lazy. Left to his own devices, he would learn nothing. Although this theory is in harmony with the observations of many secondary school teachers, who find it difficult to believe that the inclination to learn is so often killed merely by the wrong approach and not by some inherent developmental factor, there seems to be no reputable psychological support for it.

The adverse reaction of some of the more articulate secondary school teachers was thought to have a good deal to do with the challenge the report posed to their sense of intellectual security. Their university preparation presumably conditioned them to think in terms of specific subjects – more rigidly than many university scholars, who are currently showing a strong interest in breaking down interdisciplinary barriers. The theory is that they have concentrated on learning to teach these subjects, and the achievement of excellence has been defined in terms of teaching one or two subjects well. The honours graduate with the specialist's certificate has long been at the top of the status hierarchy among secondary school teachers. The prospect of having to begin again on some basis other than the assumed value and importance of the subject is considered a disturbing, if not frightening, prospect. For teachers whose specialty retains its position in the curriculum because some agency external to the student thinks it is good for him, or defines it as a prerequisite for something that is to come later, there is thought to be an apprehension that students who are given freedom to select content in line with their own interests will reject it. Remarkably few secondary school teachers participating in curriculum committee work where the importance of their own subject has had to be evaluated have ever concluded that it ought to be given a position of lesser importance on the timetable.

To offer this proposition, even if valid, as the sole reason for scepticism or opposition on the part of secondary school teachers would be to oversimplify the situation. On the same occasion on which he identified in the report an orientation toward the junior grades of the elementary school, I.M. Robb made two other major points which, if not necessarily typical of secondary teachers' views, were probably in accord with those of many.

> The second flavour of the report that I find somewhat less than palatable is its obsession with change, an obsession which implies if it does not actually state, that for anything to be good it must be flexible, fluid, different from what it was. Anything that is inflexible, static and permanent obviously has its origin in the proverbial inertia of bureaucrats and therefore is probably bad. Of course we live in a time of constant and rapid change. Of course the boundaries of knowledge have expanded tremendously. Of course man has developed new techniques for dealing with his environment and modifying it to meet his needs.

This does not mean that there is any virtue in change itself and that we can afford to ignore the static, the immutable, the past. It may be pertinent to point out that while society has undergone many changes in recent years, the components of society, people themselves, have not changed significantly in the past millenium [*sic*]. Men still love and hate, are generous or greedy, ambitious or lazy, honest or deceitful in just about the same degree as they have been through the course of recorded history. We are no nearer a practical acceptance of Christ's commandment to love thy neighbour as thyself than was mankind when this commandment was first propounded. What I am trying to say is that in the report there is lacking a counter balance to the emphasis on change – an equivalent emphasis on the need to preserve unchanged the best of our heritage of the past, to keep before our students at all times examples of the best man has achieved so that they may develop as part of their educational experience the ability to make critical judgments. This is surely one of the prime aims of education and in my opinion has received scant attention in the report. I believe wholeheartedly in the philosophy behind the television commercial which says "Nothing stays the same longer than it takes to improve it". Unfortunately I get from the 'Living and Learning' report the feeling that the committee would word this commercial "Nothing stays the same longer than it takes to change it".

The third flavour of the report that I find unpalatable, and this will be the last one I shall mention, stems from a host of items that seem to indicate that the committee sees education as a glorious romp for the student, learning by discovery and inquiry, pursuing the discovery with inquiry only "if interest and enthusiasm" is aroused by the former, abandoning it and looking for another discovery if no interest is aroused. Permissiveness is a key word and at no stage must the student be coerced into the pursuit of inquiry. He makes the decision. It is the obligation of the school to provide an ever-widening range of experiences so as to ensure that every pupil regardless of background or ability will discover plenty of interesting experiences to stimulate earnest enquiry. Failure and frustration must be avoided at all costs since they restrain the child in his progress toward self-development and ultimate full self-realization. No external pressures, either in the form of punishment or rewards can be allowed to impede or to accelerate the child's rate of progress. He is to go about the business of getting himself educated in his own sweet way and in his own sweet time. And provided he does this for twelve years after kindergarten he will have acquired a general education – new Ontario style – and will be ready, even eager, to cope with whatever problems the tough, hard, highly competitive, frequently unsympathetic, work-a-day world of adults will throw at him. He will probably cope with his problems by joining organized protests against them rather than by coming up with the effort, the sweat, and the tears that will produce a solution.[106]

Some of the sharpest of the documented criticisms of the report emerged from a gathering at the College of Education of the University of Toronto, dubbed a "teach-in" by someone apparently determined to show that the institution was "with it." Among his observations as a panelist, J.R.H. Morgan suggested that there was much to be lost and little to be gained by spelling out 258 recommendations. He thought that it was possible to adopt them all and still have a very structured and sterile type of learning situation. A stupid and unimaginative teacher might be as much a slave to one set of shibboleths as to their opposite. Under the old regime, the inspired teacher found his way around restrictive regulations. Morgan did not, apparently, explain what value he saw in regulations that the good teacher had to find his way around. They may perhaps have been there to restrain or prop up the teacher who was not so good.

Morgan also raised a point that has bothered a number of people who have not been able to base a judgment on direct observation of a large number of schools ranging from the best to the worst, as he had been doing as a secondary school liaison officer for the University of Toronto. He was shocked at the committee's conception of the modern secondary school. The report had conveyed to him a description of the school he had attended in the 1920s, but not of the one where he had taught in the 1930s, or of the ones he had seen in the 1950s and 1960s. The same view was expressed on that occasion by R.E. Saunders, an official of the Ontario Secondary School Teachers' Federation, who reportedly said that "the image of the present school system that one gets from the report is that of a rigid, inflexible bureaucracy devoted to the bending, breaking or trimming of students in order that they may be fitted to the procrustean bed of diploma requirements."[107] Saunders charged that the authors of the report appeared to have been describing education practices that disappeared after 1910. Yet the committee conducted widespread investigations and solicited opinions from large numbers of people. One cannot help but wonder which observations on the part of the committee or its critics were conducted in selected classes in selected schools, which side had been listening to what it wanted to hear and seeing what it wanted to see, which side had been blinded by prejudice or complacency, or indeed whether either side had a very accurate impression. It is certainly difficult to believe that both had been looking at the same school system.

SURVEY OF TEACHER OPINION

There may be a considerable difference between the general opinion a teacher will express about a report such as *Living and Learning* and his reaction to specific recommendations. In an effort to ascertain something of the true situation, the Ontario Teachers' Federation and the Office of Field Development of the Ontario Institute for Studies in Education co-operated in 1969 to carry out an opinion survey among Ontario teachers. The work was done under the supervision of Dormer Ellis and J. Rosaire Cloutier.

A committee of the Ontario Teachers' Federation selected 210 of the

258 recommendations of the report for use in the survey. Since it was considered unrealistic to expect individual participants to react to all of these, they were divided at random into seven groups of thirty each. The same five general statements expressing the underlying philosophy of the report were included in each form. Chance determined which of the seven forms an individual teacher received. The response options enabled the teacher to indicate whether he strongly agreed, agreed, had no opinion, disagreed, or strongly disagreed. The forms were distributed to a 10 per cent random sample of teachers in the publicly-supported elementary and secondary schools of Ontario categorized according to the following factors: 1 / geographical area (using the ten Department of Education regions); 2 / size of school (using numbers of pupils and teachers); and 3 / type of school (including, in proportion to their numbers, Roman Catholic separate schools, French-language schools, K–6 public schools, junior high schools, district high schools, and other types).

The opinionnaires, sent out in May 1969, elicited a very favourable response. The fact that forms were returned by over 70 per cent of those who were approached justified considerable confidence in the validity of the results.

Over 90 per cent of the respondents expressed agreement or strong agreement with each of the five statements of principle. It was also considered impressive that most of the items elicited a much higher proportion of agreement than of disagreement. It would, however, be easy to draw the conclusion that there was more support for the really fundamental aspects of the report than was actually the case. General principles with an idealistic, humanitarian cast are extremely easy to endorse. So also are individual recommendations that promise to make life easier for the teacher, such as that para-professionals be employed to release teachers from non-professional tasks. Again, many matters that affect some aspect of the educational system that has little bearing on the work of the classroom teacher are more likely to receive a favourable than an unfavourable vote, especially if the report has made a generally good impression.

On the extremely vital question of corporal punishment, more than half the respondents disagreed with the proposition that it should be abolished, along with other degrading forms of punishment. It is questionable whether anyone who reacted in this way could really be considered consistent in claiming to support the general spirit of the report. Also, 40 per cent were opposed to the removal of the horizontal and vertical divisions of pupils such as elementary, secondary, academic, vocational, and commercial. This recommendation, again, may be considered a keystone of the whole educational structure proposed by the committee. A large number of the other recommendations would be meaningless or impossible to implement if it were rejected outright.

A few scattered recommendations, along with the general nature of the teachers' responses, have been selected for comment in the present context. These are sufficient to give a slight indication of the general attitude.

Recommendation 2 advocated phasing out the grade 13 year and absorbing its curriculum areas within the twelve-year continuum as quickly as possible. Among elementary teachers, 58 per cent indicated agreement or strong agreement, and among secondary teachers, 53 per cent. There was little difference of opinion between those of five years' experience or less and those of ten years' experience or more.

Recommendation 5 advocated organizing learning experiences around general areas, such as communications, environmental studies, and the humanities. The percentage of agreement and strong agreement among elementary teachers was 78, and among secondary teachers, 68. Only 12 per cent of the latter disagreed or strongly disagreed – a result that did not support the view that teachers at this level were firmly attached to traditional subject organization, unless one concludes that the respondents did not understand the full implications of the recommendation.

Recommendation 10 advocated designing the senior years of schooling to accommodate the different needs of students by offering a wide variety of courses open to all students without restriction by year or arbitrary sequence. Among secondary teachers, 36 per cent agreed and another 36 per cent strongly agreed, while the combined percentage of those who disagreed or strongly disagreed was only 18 per cent. This result again belied the idea that secondary teachers were particularly attached to traditional structures and procedures. The more experienced group, combining elementary and secondary teachers, expressed almost as high a percentage of agreement (80) as did the least experienced (82).

Recommendation 15 advocated placing training programs for specific types of employment in post-school institutions. Among elementary teachers, 78 per cent agreed or strongly agreed as compared with 68 per cent of secondary teachers.

Recommendation 28 advocated the abandonment of the practice of assigning homework as a regular curriculum activity in favour of long-term assignments that invite pupils to make responsible decisions regarding their use of time. While 70 per cent of the elementary school teachers agreed or strongly agreed, only 48 per cent of the secondary school teachers did so. This evidence of paternalism on the part of the latter again offers a hint of conflict between a liberal attitude in general and a traditionalist attitude on specifics.

Recommendation 39 advocated integrating the development of school libraries with community library services. On this one, 76 per cent of all teachers agreed or strongly agreed.

Recommendation 50 advocated the provision of instruction in conversational French for all pupils during the first four years of schooling. Of the elementary teachers, 70 per cent agreed or strongly agreed, and of the secondary teachers, 71 per cent. Of those with less than five years' experience, 73 per cent were in this category, as compared with 66 per cent of those with ten years or more.

Recommendation 74 advocated the abandonment of the use of class standing, percentage marks, and letter grades in favour of parent and pupil counselling as a method of reporting individual progress. While 68 per cent of the elementary teachers agreed or strongly agreed with this recommendation, only 34 per cent of the secondary teachers did so, and 54 per cent were opposed or strongly opposed. There was very little difference in response on the basis of length of experience.

Recommendation 83 advocated that decision-making related to curriculum design and implementation be located at the school board level and in particular at the individual school level. There was agreement or strong agreement among 69 per cent of the respondents, with little difference on the basis of level or length of experience.

It was only to be expected that there would be general approval of the idea of providing complete health services for all children, including periodic medical examinations. There was no overwhelming enthusiasm, however, for going as far as providing food services including breakfasts, "where the need is apparent," according to recommendation 103. While 52 per cent of all teachers agreed or strongly agreed, 22 per cent had no opinion, and 26 per cent disagreed or strongly disagreed. Some of the critics who wrote to the newspapers singled this item out as implying that the teachers were expected to become glorified cafeteria operators.

Recommendation 137 would have a Teaching Profession Act enacted which would make teaching a self-governing profession, with powers to license and to discipline its members through a College of Teachers of Ontario. It might be supposed that such a proposition would receive an overwhelming endorsement. However, only 34 per cent of teachers at both levels agreed strongly and another 36 per cent agreed, for a total of 70 per cent in favour, with 19 per cent having no opinion and 11 per cent opposed or strongly opposed. There was a substantial difference according to level; 65 per cent of elementary teachers agreed or strongly agreed, as compared with 81 per cent of secondary teachers.

Recommendation 138 advocated the consolidation of all teachers' organizations into a single association to be known as the Ontario Teachers' Association. There was an expression of strong agreement from 37 per cent of the respondents, and of agreement from another 21 per cent, for a total of 58 per cent. While 66 per cent of elementary teachers were favourably disposed, only 44 per cent of secondary teachers were of the same mind. Even so, however, the latter overbalanced the 38 per cent who disagreed or strongly disagreed. Such a finding creates a certain degree of awkwardness for those who consider the secondary teacher group as an immovable obstacle to the unification of the teaching profession.

Recommendation 140 was that the validity of the teachers' licence should be made contingent on a demonstrated record of professional development to be reassessed at intervals. This idea appealed to 59 per cent of the respondents, while 17 per cent had no opinion, and 24 per cent were opposed. Secondary teachers were more strongly in favour than were elementary teachers, and teachers with less than five years' experience than those with more than ten.

Recommendation 144, which proposed the implementation of basic recommendations of the *Report of the Minister's Committee on the Training of Elementary School Teachers*, must have been difficult to respond to, since it consisted of three separate parts which would not necessarily all elicit the same reaction. A related recommendation, no. 146, advocated the establishment of 1972 as a target date by which all candidates for teaching must either have a university degree or become enrolled in a degree program. Only 45 per cent of elementary teachers agreed or strongly agreed, as compared with 59 per cent of secondary teachers. Many others at both levels would undoubtedly have to be counted as favourably disposed to the general principle but opposed to such a close deadline.

Recommendation 173 apparently was an endorsement of merit pay. It advocated salary policies that would recognize the capabilities demonstrated by teachers and encourage outstanding teachers to remain in the classroom. Whatever their interpretation, the teachers were very much in favour of the idea. Among the elementary teachers, 74 per cent agreed or strongly agreed, as compared with 86 per cent of secondary teachers. Opinions differed little on the basis of the respondents' length of experience.

A great many of the later recommendations had to do with matters of departmental organization and school board administration about which the average teacher could hardly have been expected to feel strongly. Recommendation 216 came rather close to home in that it advocated the establishment of a parents' school committee in each school district to assist the school staff in interpreting the school to the community, and to aid in keeping school staffs and trustees aware of the schools and their programs. Only 56 per cent of all respondents, with little difference according to level, agreed or strongly agreed. There was apparently a good deal of feeling that the parents should be held at arm's length.

On the whole, despite the point made earlier that it is easier to be in favour of vague principles expressed in benevolent sounding terms than it is to accept specific changes in an established routine, there are grounds in the survey for feeling that the teaching force in Ontario is a reasonably enlightened group. Given administrative support and imaginative leadership, they can be expected to make considerable headway in implementing the spirit of the report.

IMPLEMENTATION

A consideration of the question of implementation must begin with a recognition of the existence of two quite different types of recommendations: those which call for some specific and recognizable decision or action on the part of an identifiable agent and those which advocate a more enlightened attitude on the part of educators or other social groups. In the first case, no one would have any difficulty in determining whether the recommendation had been implemented. In the second, the change, if any, might always be a matter of dispute.

As suggested earlier, no attempt is made in the present context to undertake a systematic review of the recommendations or to discuss in an exhaustive way what their prospects are for implementation; when appropriate action is likely to occur, if it has not already occurred; and with what consequences. Individual recommendations are dealt with in various chapters dealing with specific aspects of education. Comments at this juncture are confined to the prospects for a significant move toward the ideals held out in the report.

In a convention address entitled "The New Philosophy," some of the contents of which have already been referred to, C.E. Phillips tried to place the report in historical perspective.[108] He pointed out that, in recent centuries, almost all those who had distinguished themselves in educational thought had pursued such objectives as making education more congenial and pleasant for the child and giving life and meaning to the content. Such Canadian figures of comparatively recent prominence as W.J. Dunlop, Hilda Neatby, and Sperrin Chant were, he thought, of quite ephemeral importance.

Phillips declared that "progress in education, from the progressive point, is marked not by the appearance of novel ideas, but by more widespread adoption in practice of mainstream thinking." The success of the report, along with a comparable one produced in British Columbia under the title *Involvement – The Key to Better Schools,* would ultimately be measured by the effectiveness with which it enabled more teachers to move more rapidly and further in the progressive direction. He found most of the omens favourable: at the time the committee was set up, a large proportion of the curriculum staff in the Department of Education had graduate degrees in education and the minister and deputy minister had advanced views. The original edition of twenty thousand copies of the report had soon been sold out, and a new one had to be printed. Lloyd Dennis had been unable, even by speaking two or three times a day for six days a week, to keep up with the demand for further information. The over-all assessment was that most of the interested public approved the report and its recommendations. The same could be said for most teachers, although not of most secondary teachers.

There were certain reasons for apprehension which Phillips found it necessary to consider. He referred to an article by Guerney Chambers in the January 1969 issue of *School and Society* entitled "Educational Essentialism Thirty Years After" in which the writer had maintained that essentialism not only became the dominant educational philosophy in 1957, but remained so at the time of writing. As evidence, Chambers cited the existing emphasis on ability grouping, gifted students, advanced placement programs, foreign languages, national curriculum reforms, and mathematics. Phillips found some comfort, however, in the possibility that progressives were still somewhat intimidated in the United States. Many of them seemed to be hiding behind "cloudy bombast." He did not find any comparable timidity in Canada.

Despite the undeniable interest in and enthusiasm for the report, there are many who see it, not as a return to mainstream thinking after a temporary sojourn in the wilderness, but as a rather inexplicable and certainly regrettable dying gasp of the progressive movement. A man with long experience as a teacher and administrator wrote to the minister in August 1968 warning him against the influence of the permissive educators. He had been beguiled thirty years earlier by Thornton Mustard's description of the new approach which was to "eliminate all present and future problems of learning and teaching." Everything was to be taught by the project method, with arithmetic, science, history, geography, and other subjects introduced as the situation demanded. The word recognition approach was to replace the phonic method. The result, according to the correspondent, was several generations of elementary school graduates who were poor in reading, spelling, and arithmetic and deficient in knowledge of history and "good old fashioned political geography." He was grateful that progressive methods never gained much of a foothold in the secondary schools.

The educational crisis occasioned by the launching of the first Russian earth satellite was treated as an awakening on the part of the public to the existence of a public school that had grown too soft. As a result of pressure for a more demanding curriculum and higher standards, a number of important improvements had been brought about, and Ontario currently had "what is perhaps, the best educational system on this continent." The correspondent acknowledged that further changes were necessary and inevitable, but did not want "the total replacement of the tried and true with the far-out proposals of educational hippies."

The educational approach of the progressives was seen as an aberration that had been tried in other countries and abandoned after its deficiencies were realized. The Russians, during the heady days immediately following the Bolshevik Revolution, were said to have tried letting children hold meetings to decide what they would learn for the day, establishing equality between pupils and teachers in the classroom, maintaining discipline by committee, and abolishing marks and examinations – only to find the whole scheme unworkable. In many parts of the United States, they were trying to return to a more rational pattern of education after the educational chaos that had been caused by the permissive brand of education which had been rampant there for many years. Canadians were exhorted, in effect, not to be so eager to pick up ideas that others had discarded.

Whatever the ultimate effects may be, there is no doubt whatever that, for the time being at least, the traditionalists have been placed on the defensive. Many an unenthusiastic comment on the report has been prefaced by some such remark as, "I hate to sound like a reactionary, but ..." or "I may be old-fashioned, but ..." In the present era, to be old-fashioned is not considered among the major virtues. Yet the enthusiasts for the spirit that suffuses the report should keep reminding themselves that it is much easier to raise an emotional wave than it it to produce a fundamental alteration in attitudes and values in an entire population. It will take a great deal more than a single report to accomplish such an objective.

Notes

CHAPTER 1

1 George S. Counts, "Dare the School Build a New Social Order?" in Ronald Gross, ed., *The Teacher and the Taught* (New York: Dell Publishing, 1963), p. 180.

2 Paul Goodman, *Growing Up Absurd* (New York: Random House, 1956), pp. 81–2.

3 John Dewey, "My Pedagogic Creed," in Gross, ed., *The Teacher and the Taught*, pp. 142–3.

4 John Dewey, "Traditional vs. Progressive Education," *ibid.*, pp. 152–5.

5 Bertrand Russell, "The Negative Theory of Education," *ibid.*, p. 213.

6 Ontario, *Programme of Studies for Grades I to VI of the Public and Separate Schools, 1937* (Toronto, 1937), p. 5.

7 *Ibid.*, p. 6.

8 *Ibid.*, p. 7.

9 *Ibid.*, p. 9.

10 *Ibid.*, p. 10.

11 *Report of the Royal Commission on Education in Ontario, 1950*, J.A. Hope, chairman (Toronto: King's Printer, 1950), p. 23.

12 *Ibid.*, p. 24.

13 *Ibid.*

14 *Ibid.*, p. 25.

15 *Ibid.*, pp. 25–6.

16 *Ibid.*, p. 27.

17 *Ibid.*, p. 28.

18 *Ibid.*, pp. 29–30.

19 *Ibid.*, p. 32.

20 *Ibid.*, p. 33.

21 J.G. Althouse, *Structure and Aims of Canadian Education*, Quance Lectures in Canadian Education (Toronto: W.J. Gage, 1949), p. 61.

22 Ontario, Department of Education, *Report of the Minister, 1953*, p. 1.

23 Charles E. Phillips, "Effective Aims in Public Education," in Freeman K. Stewart, ed., *The Aims of Education*, Conference Study No. 1 (Ottawa: Canadian Conference on Education, 1961), p. 3.

24 *Ibid.*, p. 6.

25 *Ibid.*, p. 9.

26 *Ibid.*, p. 12.

27 John Francis Leddy, "The Aims of Education," *ibid.*, p. 16.

28 *Ibid.*, p. 17.

29 *Ibid.*, p. 22.

30 Northrop Frye, "The Critical Discipline," *ibid.*, pp. 27–8.

31 *Ibid.*, pp. 26–7.

32 Ontario, Legislative Assembly, *Debates*, 28th leg., 1st sess., 6 June 1968, p. 4018.

33 Jacques Maritain, "The Seven

Misconceptions of Modern Education," in Gross, ed., *The Teacher and the Taught*, p. 169.

34 Father Marcel de Grandpré, "Training and Education," in Stewart, ed., *The Aims of Education*, p. 36.

35 *Ibid.*, pp. 36–7.

36 *Ibid.*, p. 37.

37 *Ibid.*, p. 40.

38 Neville V. Scarfe, "The Aims of Education in a Free Society," in Fred W. Price, ed., *The Second Canadian Conference on Education: A Report* (Toronto: University of Toronto Press, 1962), p. 65.

39 *Ibid.*, pp. 82–3.

40 F. Henry Johnson, "Amidon: A Return to Essentialism?" and "Intellectual Discipline or Life Adjustment: A Symposium," *Toronto Education Quarterly*, II, 4, Summer 1963, pp. 13–16, 17–25. Published by the Toronto Board of Education.

41 Carl F. Hansen, *The Amidon School: A Successful Demonstration in Basic Education* (Englewood Cliffs, NJ: Prentice-Hall, 1962), as cited by Johnson, "Amidon," *ibid.*, pp. 13–14.

42 William C. Bagley, "An Essentialist's Platform for the Advancement of American Education," *Journal of Educational Administration and Supervision*, April 1938, pp. 242–54.

43 "Intellectual Discipline or Life Adjustment: A Symposium," *Toronto Education Quarterly*, II, 4, Summer 1963, p. 17. Published by the Toronto Board of Education.

44 Ontario, Legislative Assembly, *Debates*, 27th leg., 1st sess., 2 June 1965, p. 3585.

45 Seymour L. Halleck, "Why They'd Rather Do Their Own Thing," *Think*, XXXIV, 5, September-October 1968, pp. 6–7.

46 Bruno Bettelheim, "The Class of '84," *Toronto Education Quarterly*, III, 3, Spring 1964, p. 12. Published by the Toronto Board of Education.

47 Brock Chisholm, "Changing Values," in John P. Kidd and D. Carlton Williams, eds., *New Developments in Society*, Conference Study No. 4 (Ottawa: Canadian Conference on Education, 1961), pp. 9–15.

48 *Ibid.*, pp. 11–12.

49 *Ibid.*, p. 13.

50 Committee on Religious Education in the Public Schools of the Province of Ontario, Report of the Committee, *Religious Information and Moral Development*, J. Keiller Mackay, chairman (Toronto: Ontario Department of Education, 1969), pp. 46–54.

51 *Ibid.*, p. 47.

CHAPTER 2

1 Charles E. Phillips, *The Development of Education in Canada* (Toronto: W.J. Gage, 1957), p. 179.

2 Honora M. Cochrane, ed., *Centennial Story: The Board of Education for the City of Toronto, 1850–1950* (Toronto: Thomas Nelson & Sons, 1950), p. 5.

3 *Ibid.*, p. 15.

4 Phillips, *Development of Education in Canada*, p. 128.

5 Cochrane, ed., *Centennial Story*, p. 37.
6 *Report of the Royal Commission on Education in Ontario, 1950*, J.A. Hope, chairman (Toronto: King's Printer, 1950), p. 53.
7 Ontario, Legislative Assembly, *Debates*, 27th leg., 3rd sess., 2 June 1965, pp. 3582–3.
8 Ontario, Provincial Committee on Aims and Objectives of Education in the Schools of Ontario, *Living and Learning* (Toronto: Newton Publishing, 1968), p. 114.
9 Ontario, Legislative Assembly, *Debates*, 28th leg., 1st sess., 5 June 1968, p. 3979.
10 *Ibid.*, 28th leg., 2nd sess., 5 March 1969, p. 1884.
11 J.M. McCutcheon, *Public Education in Ontario* (Toronto: T.H. Best, 1941), p. 151.
12 C.B. Sissons, *Church & State in Canadian Education: An Historical Study* (Toronto: Ryerson Press, 1959), p. 11.
13 Phillips, *Development of Education in Canada*, p . 198.
14 Robin S. Harris, *Quiet Evolution: A Study of the Educational System of Ontario* (Toronto: University of Toronto Press, 1967), p. 48.
15 Edwin C. Guillet, *In the Cause of Education: Centennial History of the Ontario Educational Association, 1861–1960* (Toronto: University of Toronto Press, 1960), pp. 80–1.
16 Committee of Presidents of Provincially Assisted Universities and Colleges of Ontario, Supplementary Report No. 1, *The Structure of Post-Secondary Education in Ontario* (Toronto, 1963), pp. 6–7.
17 Harris, *Quiet Evolution*, p. 51.
18 This account, from Sissons, *Church & State in Canadian Education*, pp. 78–9, differs in some points from the account given in the report of the Royal Commission of 1950.
19 Harris, *Quiet Evolution*, p. 116.
20 Ontario, Department of Education, *Report of the Minister, 1953*, pp. 9–10.
21 William M. Alexander, "The New School in the Middle," *Phi Delta Kappan*, L, 6, February 1969, pp. 355–7.
22 "Traditional Junior High Still Predominant Form," *Phi Delta Kappan*, L, 7, March 1969, p. 415.
23 Hamilton, Senior Public Schools, Principals, *A Study of the Principles and Practices of the Senior Public School* (Toronto: W.J. Gage for the Board of Education for the City of Hamilton, 1965), pp. 1–2.
24 McCutcheon, *Public Education in Ontario*, p. 184.
25 Harry Pullen, "A Study of Secondary School Curriculum Change in Canada with Special Emphasis on an Ontario Experiment" (Ed D thesis; University of Toronto, 1955), pp. 76–7.
26 Harris, *Quiet Evolution*, p. 53.
27 Cochrane, ed., *Centennial Story*, pp. 211–12.
28 John Seath, *Education for Industrial Purposes* (Toronto: King's Printer, 1911), pp. 282–3.
29 McCutcheon, *Public Education*

in Ontario*, p. 185.

30 J. Bascom St John, "Lost: 50 Years of Technical Education Progress," *Globe and Mail*, 17 June 1963.

31 Seath, *Education for Industrial Purposes*, p. 283.

32 McCutcheon, *Public Education in Ontario*, p. 187.

33 Pullen, "A Study of Secondary School Curriculum Changes in Canada with Special Emphasis on an Ontario Experiment," p. 76.

34 Harris, *Quiet Evolution*, pp. 54–5.

35 McCutcheon, *Public Education in Ontario*, pp. 191–2.

36 Dominion Bureau of Statistics, Education Division, Research Section, *The Organization and Administration of Public Schools in Canada* (2nd ed.; Ottawa: Queen's Printer, 1960), pp. 129–30.

37 Ontario, Department of Education, Memorandum to Principals of Secondary Schools and Secretaries of Secondary School Boards re Advanced Technical Evening Classes, 1958–59: 8, 2 September 1958, C.W. Booth, Deputy Minister.

38 DBS, *The Organization and Administration of Public Schools in Canada*, pp. 129–30.

39 Ontario, Legislative Assembly, *Debates*, 28th leg., 1st sess., 18 July 1968, p. 5953.

40 J.F. McGivney, "The Need for Junior Vocational Education," *Bulletin*, XLIV, 6, 10 December 1964, p. 509.

41 G.E. Price, *The Director Reports .... A Year of Change: Scholastic Year 1965–1966* (Board of Education for the City of Hamilton), p. 11.

42 Phillips, *Development of Education in Canada*, p. 297.

43 Ontario Alliance of Christian Schools, "A Brief Submitted to the Cabinet of the Province of Ontario," July 1968, pp. 5–6. (Mimeographed.)

44 Parents Committee of Jewish Day Schools of the Province of Ontario, "Submission to the Prime Minister of Ontario and the Minister of Education for the Province of Ontario," January 1968, p. 3. (Mimeographed.)

45 Independent Secondary Schools in Ontario, "Brief to the Ontario Committee on Taxation," 1963, p. 2. (Mimeographed.)

46 Eric LeBourdais, "The Case for Private Schools," *Toronto Life*, I, 10, August 1967, p. 19.

47 Parents of Students Attending Independent Secondary Schools, "Brief Directed to the Minister of Education of the Province of Ontario Requesting Aid on Behalf of Parents of Students Attending Independent Secondary Schools." (Mimeographed.)

CHAPTER 3

1 J.G. Althouse, *Structure and Aims of Canadian Education*, Quance Lectures in Canadian Education (Toronto: W.J. Gage, 1949), p. 38.

2 W.W. Worth, "Motivating Teachers: Guidelines for Principals," *School Progress*, XXXIV, 5, May 1965, pp. 28–30.

3 Frank MacKinnon, *Relevance*

and Responsibility in Education, Quance Lectures in Canadian Education (Toronto: W.J. Gage, 1968), p. 23.

4 *Revised Statutes of Ontario*, 8–9 Eliz. 2, 1960, chap. 361.

5 Ontario, Legislative Assembly, *Debates*, 27th leg., 3rd sess., 3 June 1965, p. 3656.

6 Ontario, Department of Education, Secondary School Principals' Course, 26 March 1957, S.D. Rendall, Superintendent of Secondary Education.

7 Ontario, Department of Education, Memorandum to Officials Concerned with Secondary Education re the Secondary Principals' Course, 1965, 1964–65:14, 21 September 1964, W.R. Stewart, Deputy Minister.

8 Ontario, Department of Education, Memorandum to Elementary School Inspectors re 1. Engagement of Unqualified Principals and Supervising Principals, 2. Engagement of Unqualified Teachers, 3. Engagement of Graduates of University of Ottawa and Sudbury Teachers' Colleges, and 4. Letters of Standing, 1964–65:17, 16 March 1965, A.H. McKague, Superintendent of Supervision.

9 Ontario, Department of Education, Memorandum to School Officials re Elementary and Secondary School Principals' Courses, 1965–66:29, 3 December 1965, H.E. Elborn, Assistant Deputy Minister.

10 H.L. Willis, "Is the Canadian Superintendent a Leader or Paper-shuffler?" *School Administration*, January 1968, p. 16.

11 Don O'Hearn, "Today in Queen's Park," "Small Classes Costly," *Windsor Star*, 29 May 1968.

12 Paul Goodman, *Compulsory Mis-Education and The Community of Scholars* (New York: Random House, Vintage Books, 1962, 1964), p. 28. (*Compulsory Mis-Education* is also available in a hardcover edition from Horizon Press. *The Community of Scholars* is available in a hardcover edition from Random House.)

13 B.L. Cox, "Issues of Class Size," *Bulletin*, XLVI, 2, 31 March 1966, p. 87.

14 "First Hall-Dennis – and Now the Crunch," *OSSTF Intercom*, III, 3, March 1969, pp. 1–2.

15 T.W. McConaghy, "Highlights of the Annual Assembly," *Bulletin*, XLVI, 1, 31 January 1966, p. 18.

16 "O.S.S.T.F. Policy on Conditions of Work for Quality Teaching," *Bulletin*, XLVII, 4, October 1967, p. 196.

17 Ontario, Legislative Assembly, *Debates*, 28th leg., 2nd sess., 16 December 1968, p. 685.

18 *Ibid.*, p. 704.

19 Emerson Lavender, "Classroom Discipline," *Bulletin*, XLIV, 4, 5 October 1964, p. 281.

20 Edgar Z. Friedenberg, *Coming of Age in America: Growth and Acquiescence* (New York: Random House, 1965), pp. 41–2.

21 Betty Lee, "4 Rs and a Whack!" *Globe Magazine*, 8 June 1968.

22 Ontario, Legislative Assembly, *Debates*, 28th leg., 2nd sess., 3 December 1968, p. 305.

23 "Private Schools May Stop Caning," *Toronto Daily Star*, 30 December 1968.
24 "Says Strap Needed to Curb Chaos in Class," *Toronto Daily Star*, 6 December 1968.
25 "Strap Use Revived in Renfrew Schools," *Globe and Mail*, 23 May 1970.
26 *Toronto Daily Star*, 7 December 1968.

CHAPTER 4

1 Ontario, Department of Education, *Courses of Study for the Public and Separate Schools, 1936*, p. 3.
2 *Report of the Royal Commission on Education in Ontario, 1950*, J.A. Hope, chairman (Toronto: King's Printer, 1950), p. 78.
3 Robin Harris, *Quiet Evolution: A Study of the Educational System of Ontario* (Toronto: University of Toronto Press, 1967), pp. 49–50.
4 *Ibid.*, p. 50.
5 *Report of the Royal Commission on Education in Ontario, 1950*, p. 48.
6 *Ibid.*, p. 83.
7 J. Bascom St John, *Globe and Mail*, 23 April 1963.
8 Ontario, Legislative Assembly, *Debates*, 26th leg., 3rd sess., 10 April 1962, p. 2177.
9 Ontario, Department of Education, Memorandum to Members of Secondary School Boards, Members of Advisory Vocational Committees, Secretaries of Secondary School Boards, Directors and Superintendents, Principals of Secondary and Private Schools re Information Pertaining to the Reorganization of Secondary School Programmes Commencing September 1962, 1961–62:37, 2 February 1962, F.S. Rivers, Chief Director of Education.
10 Ontario, Legislative Assembly, *Debates*, 26th leg., 3rd sess., 10 April 1962, pp. 2176–7.
11 *Ibid.*, 30 November 1961, p. 128.
12 Ontario, Department of Education, Memorandum 1961–62: 37.
13 Ontario, Legislative Assembly, *Debates*, 26th leg., 3rd sess., 10 April 1962, p. 2180.
14 *Ibid.*, pp. 2199–2200.
15 *Ibid.*, pp. 2142–3.
16 *Ibid.*, 27th leg., 2nd sess., 27 January 1964, pp. 229–30.
17 Gertrude M. Fatt, "They All Belong," *Toronto Education Quarterly*, III, 2, Winter 1963–4, p. 8. Published by the Toronto Board of Education.
18 *Report of the Grade 13 Study Committee, 1964*, F.A. Hamilton, chairman (Toronto: Ontario Department of Education, 26 June 1964), terms of reference.
19 Ontario, Legislative Assembly, *Debates*, 27th leg., 2nd sess., 24 April 1964, p. 2559.
20 Ontario Teachers' Federation, "Brief to the Grade 13 Implementation Committee and to the Grade 13 General and Advanced Committee," 12 January 1965. (Mimeographed.)
21 E.M. Davidson, Secretary, Senate Committee on Admission Standards, and Director of Ad-

missions, to James R. Thomson, Chairman, Grade 13 Implementation Committee, 6 March 1967.

22 Ontario, Legislative Assembly, *Debates*, 28th leg., 1st sess., 5 June 1968, p. 3994.

23 *Ibid.*, p. 3995.

24 *Ibid.*, p. 3998.

25 W.H. Swift, *Trends in Canadian Education*, Quance Lectures in Canadian Education (Toronto: W.J. Gage, 1958), p. 71.

26 "Notes and Ideas," *Toronto Education Quarterly*, III, 3, Spring 1964, p. 28. Published by the Toronto Board of Education.

27 "Continuous Progress Replaces New Brunswick Grade System," *School Progress*, XXXVI, 12, December 1966, p. 13.

28 "Non-grading: A Misunderstood Concept," *OTF Reporter*, XIII, February 1969, pp. 8–11.

29 Ontario, Department of Education, *Programme of Studies for Grades 1 to 6 of the Public and Separate Schools*, 1937, cited in Ontario, Department of Education, *Curriculum P1, J1, Interim Revision, Instruction and Guide*, 1967, p. 12.

30 "They're Either Too Young or Too Old," *Curriculum Bulletin, No. 1*, 1965, cited in *Curriculum P1, J1*, 1967, p. 12.

31 *Curriculum P1, J1*, 1967, p. 12.

32 Ontario, Provincial Committee on Aims and Objectives of Education in the Schools of Ontario, *Living and Learning* (Toronto: Newton Publishing, 1968), pp. 75–6.

33 K.N. Craig, "Individual Subject Promotion and Shorter Units of Work," *Bulletin*, XLVI, 6, December 1966, pp. 473–5.

34 Ontario, Legislative Assembly, *Debates*, 28th leg., 1st sess., 4 June 1968, p. 3884.

35 "Patterns for the Future," *New Dimensions in Education*, IV, 2, May 1969, pp. 3–5.

36 Ontario, Department of Education, Memorandum to Secondary School and Private School Principals re Admission of Secondary School Pupils from Other Provinces, Circular 550, 4 March 1963, F.S. Rivers, Chief Director of Education.

CHAPTER 5

1 J. George Hodgins, *Documentary History of Education in Upper Canada, I: 1790–1830* (Toronto: Ontario Department of Education, 1894), p. 166.

2 Charles E. Phillips, *The Development of Education in Canada: An Historical Study* (Toronto: W.J. Gage, 1957), p. 150.

3 Honora M. Cochrane, ed., *Centennial Story: The Board of Education for the City of Toronto 1850–1950* (Toronto: Thomas Nelson & Sons, 1950), pp. 42–3.

4 *Ibid.*

5 *Ibid.*, p. 66.

6 *Ibid.*, p. 197.

7 J.M. McCutcheon, *Public Education in Ontario* (Toronto: T.H. Best, 1941), p. 105.

8 Edwin C. Guillet, *In the Cause of Education: Centennial History of the Ontario Educational Association, 1861–1960* (To-

ronto: University of Toronto Press, 1960), p. 472.

9 Cochrane, ed., *Centennial Story*, p. 194.

10 McCutcheon, *Public Education in Ontario*, p. 157.

11 Cochrane, ed., *Centennial Story*, pp. 195–6.

12 Harry Pullen, "A Study of Secondary School Curriculum Change in Canada with Special Emphasis on an Ontario Experiment" (Ed D thesis; University of Toronto, 1955), p. 71.

13 McCutcheon, *Public Education in Ontario*, p. 106.

14 John Seath, *Education for Industrial Purposes* (Toronto: King's Printer, 1911), introduction.

15 Cochrane, ed., *Centennial Story*, p. 203.

16 Ontario, Department of Education, *Courses for the Public and Separate Schools, 1936*, p. 7.

17 Seath, *Education for Industrial Purposes*, p. 263.

18 C.A. Brown, "Ontario's Grade 13 – Guidelines from the Past," lecture delivered at the Ontario College of Education as part of the Centennial Series, "Between High School and University in 1967," Toronto, February 1969, pp. 9–10.

19 Pullen, "Study of Secondary School Curriculum Change in Canada with Special Emphasis on an Ontario Experiment," p. 70.

20 *Ibid.*, pp. 79–80.

21 Brown, "Ontario's Grade 13 – Guidelines from the Past," pp. 10–11.

22 Pullen, "Study of Secondary School Curriculum Change in Canada with Special Emphasis on an Ontario Experiment," pp. 82–4.

23 *Ibid.*, pp. 101–2.

24 Ontario, Department of Education, *Programme of Studies for Grades I to VI of the Public and Separate Schools, 1937*, p. 60.

25 *Ibid.*, *1941*, p. 5.

26 *Ibid.*, p. 6.

27 Pullen, "Study of Secondary School Curriculum Change in Canada with Special Emphasis on an Ontario Experiment," pp. 88–93. The dates for the introduction of the Ontario Secondary School Graduation Diploma and the Ontario Secondary School Honour Graduation Diploma have been changed to conform to official records.

28 Phillips, *Development of Education in Canada*, p. 436.

29 Pullen, "Study of Secondary School Curriculum Change in Canada with Special Emphasis on an Ontario Experiment," pp. 77–8.

30 *Report of the Royal Commission on Education in Ontario, 1950*, J.A. Hope, chairman (Toronto: King's Printer, 1950), p. 106.

31 *Ibid.*, p. 107.

32 Pullen, "Study of Secondary School Curriculum Change in Canada with Special Emphasis on an Ontario Experiment," p. 112.

33 *Ibid.*, p. 156.

34 *Ibid.*, p. 212.

35 Ontario, Legislative Assembly, *Debates*, 25th leg., 1st sess., 14 March 1956, pp. 1018–19.

36 J. Bascom St John, "Mending the Split in School System," *Globe and Mail*, 2 April 1964.
37 Ontario, Department of Education, *Report of the Minister, 1956*, p. 8.
38 Ontario, Legislative Assembly, *Debates*, 25th leg., 4th sess., 11 February 1958, pp. 86–7.
39 *Ibid.*, 12 March 1958, p. 777.
40 *Ibid.*
41 *Ibid.*, 25th leg., 1st sess., 14 March 1956, p. 1020.
42 W.H. Swift, *Trends in Canadian Education*, Quance Lectures in Canadian Education (Toronto: W.J. Gage, 1958), pp. 63–4.
43 Jerome S. Bruner, "The Process of Education," in Ronald Gross, ed., *The Teacher and the Taught* (New York: Dell Publishing, 1963), p. 259.
44 J.R. McCarthy, "Curriculum Crossroads," in Ontario Association for Curriculum Development, Report of the Ontario Conference on Education, Windsor, November 1961.
45 Northrop Frye, ed., *Design for Learning*, Reports submitted to the Joint Committee of the Toronto Board of Education and the University of Toronto (Toronto: University of Toronto Press, 1962), p. 66.
46 W.R. Wees, "For Whom We Teach," address to the Second International Curriculum Conference, in Brian Burnham, ed., *New Designs for Learning: Highlights of the Reports of the Ontario Curriculum Institute, 1963–1966* (Toronto: University of Toronto Press for the Ontario Institute for Studies in Education, 1967), p. 20.
47 Ontario, Department of Education, Memorandum to Directors and Superintendents, Principals of Secondary Schools, Secretaries of Secondary School Boards, Principals of Inspected Private Schools re Progress Reports on the New Options of the Four-Year Programme, 1963–64:45, 5 February 1964, S.D. Rendall, Superintendent of Secondary Education. (Attached progress report on "Man in Society.")
48 *Ibid.*, attached progress report on "World Politics."
49 *Ibid.*, attached progress report on "Speech Arts."
50 *Ibid.*, attached progress report on "Modern Literature."
51 M. Doyle, "Man in Society," *Bulletin*, XLVII, 3, May 1967, p. 138.
52 Ontario, Legislative Assembly, *Debates*, 27th leg., 3rd sess., 11 February 1965, p. 441.
53 Walter Chlystyk, "New Occupational Classes in Secondary Schools," *Bulletin*, XLIII, 1, 31 January 1963, pp. 25–6.
54 Ontario, Department of Education, Memorandum to School Officials re 1. (a) Services Course in the Occupational Program, (b) Apprenticeship from the Occupations Course; 2. Forms to be forwarded to Elementary School Principals by the Federation of Women Teachers' Associations of Ontario; 3. Ontario Red Cross Youth, 1965–66:88, 2 June 1966, H.E. Elborn, Assistant Deputy Minister.

55 Ontario, Legislative Assembly, *Debates*, 26th leg., 3rd sess., 10 April 1962, pp. 2165–6.
56 *Ibid.*, p. 2167.
57 J. Bascom St John, "A Proper Job in Revising the Curriculum," *Globe and Mail*, 3 December 1962.
58 J. Bascom St John, "Piecemeal Course Revision," *Globe and Mail*, 4 December 1962.
59 Ontario, Department of Education, *Report of the Minister, 1964*, p. 11.
60 Ontario, Department of Education, Memorandum to School Officials re Kindergarten and Grades 1 to 6 Curriculum Revision, 1965–66:77, 10 May 1966, H.E. Elborn, Assistant Deputy Minister.
61 Ontario, Department of Education, *Curriculum Bulletin 5*, I, 5, January 1967, p. 6.
62 Ontario, Department of Education, *Interim Revision. Introduction and Guide. Curriculum P1, J1, 1967*, pp. 11–12.
63 "Teaching Reform Pressed in Nation: Educators Think Trend In 3R's Is Just Starting," *New York Times*, 5 September 1966.
64 University of Toronto, *President's Report for the Year Ended June 1960* (Toronto: University of Toronto Press, 1960), p. 11.
65 J. Bascom St John, *Globe and Mail*, 11 June 1963.
66 Ontario, Department of Education, *Report on the Proposal for General and Advanced Levels of Instruction in Grade 13*, 18 March 1965, p. 4.
67 *Ibid.*, pp. 21–2.
68 Ontario, Legislative Assembly, *Debates*, 27th leg., 3rd sess., 3 June 1965, p. 3612.
69 *Ibid.*, 2 June 1965, p. 3576.
70 *Ibid.*, 27th leg., 5th sess., 17 May 1967, p. 3536.
71 Cochrane, ed., *Centennial Story*, p. 198.
72 *Ibid.*, p. 207.
73 *Report of the Royal Commission on Education, 1950*, p. 149.
74 Ontario, Legislative Assembly, *Debates*, 26th leg., 3rd sess., 16 April 1962, p. 2406.
75 *Ibid.*, 24th leg., 4th sess., 23 March 1954, pp. 674–5.
76 *Ibid.*, 26th leg., 2nd sess., 20 February 1961, p. 1282.
77 J. Bascom St John, "Keeping Errors Out of Textbooks," *Globe and Mail*, 11 April 1962.
78 A.B. Hodgetts, *What Culture? What Heritage? A Study of Civic Education in Canada*, Report of the National History Project, Curriculum Series No. 5 (Toronto: Ontario Institute for Studies in Education, 1968).
79 Ontario, Legislative Assembly, *Debates*, 27th leg., 3rd sess., 2 June 1965, p. 3588.
80 "In Our Opinion," *Bulletin*, XLIII, 6, 10 December 1963, p. 500.
81 "Ontario's Free Textbook Plan," *School Progress*, XXXIII, 4, April 1964, p. 59.
82 Ontario, Legislative Assembly, *Debates*, 27th leg., 2nd sess., 28 April 1964, p. 2556.
83 Ontario, Department of Education, Memorandum to Officials Concerned with Elementary and Secondary Education re

Provision of Textbooks for Students in Grades 11 and 12, Effective September 1965, 1964–65:69, 26 March 1965, H.E. Elborn, Assistant Deputy Minister.

84 Ontario, Legislative Assembly, *Debates*, 27th leg., 3rd sess., 3 June 1965, p. 3663.

85 Ontario, Department of Education, *Report of the Minister, 1965*, pp. 6–7.

86 Ontario, Department of Education, *Curriculum Bulletin 5*, I, 5, January 1967, p. 9.

87 Ontario, Legislative Assembly, *Debates*, 27th leg., 5th sess., 25 May 1967, p. 3811.

88 *Ibid.*

CHAPTER 6

1 Committee on the Integration of the Creative Arts, Report, *The Creative Arts: A Survey of Professional Opinion* (Toronto: Ontario Curriculum Institute, 1965), pp. 18–19.

2 Northrop Frye, ed., *Design for Learning*, Reports submitted to the Joint Committee of the Toronto Board of Education and the University of Toronto (Toronto: University of Toronto Press, 1962), p. 48.

3 Honora M. Cochrane, ed., *Centennial Story: The Board of Education for the City of Toronto, 1850–1950* (Toronto: Thomas Nelson & Sons, 1950), pp. 198–9.

4 Ontario, Department of Education, *Courses of Study for Public and Separate Schools, 1936*, p. 17.

5 H.S. Baker, "Teaching Composition in the Elementary School," in *Education: A Collection of Essays on Canadian Education*. II: *1956–1958* (Toronto: W.J. Gage, 1959), p. 1.

6 M.F. Stewart, "English Grammar: Retrospect and Prospect," in *Education: A Collection of Essays on Canadian Education*. V: *1962–1964* (Toronto: W.J. Gage, 1965), pp. 39–40.

7 Ontario, Department of Education, Memorandum to Secondary School Principals and Teachers of English, 1957–8: 12, 15 October 1957, S.D. Rendall, Superintendent of Secondary Education.

8 *Ibid.*

9 Frye, ed., *Design for Learning*, p. 22.

10 *Ibid.*, p. 23.

11 *Ibid.*, p. 30.

12 *Ibid.*, pp. 34–5.

13 *Ibid.*, pp. 39–40.

14 *Ibid.*, p. 41.

15 J. Bascom St John, "Course Stresses Independent Reading," *Globe and Mail*, 18 June 1964.

16 Ontario, Department of Education, Memorandum to School Officials re 1. Discontinuance of Advance Staff Information form (Secondary), 2. Advisory Consultative Committee on English in the Four-Year Program, 3. Error in Item 3(j) Memorandum 1965–66:65 "Procedures with Regard to Library Book Grants and Selection of Books for Secondary Schools," 4. Booklet "The National Flag of Canada," 1965–66:74, 6 May 1966, H.E. Elborn, Assistant Deputy Minister.

17 Alan Proctor, "How Not to Teach Poetry," *Bulletin*, XLV, 6, 10 December 1965, p. 526.
18 D.T. Faught, "Mathematics: Modernize or Stand Pat?" *Bulletin*, XXXIX, 1, 31 January 1959, p. 25.
19 F.G. Robinson, "New Dimensions in Mathematical Teaching," *Toronto Education Quarterly*, II, 1, Autumn 1962, p. 17. Published by the Toronto Board of Education.
20 Ontario, Legislative Assembly, *Debates*, 25th leg., 5th sess., 18 February 1959, p. 429.
21 Committee Considering the Mathematics Programme, K to 6, Report of the Committee, *Mathematics* (Toronto: Ontario Curriculum Institute, 1965), p. 3.
22 *Ibid.*, pp. 30–1.
23 Committee Considering the Mathematics of the Four-Year Programme, Report of the Committee, *Mathematics* (Toronto: Ontario Curriculum Institute, 1965), pp. 11–12.
24 *Ibid.*, pp. 12–13.
25 *Ibid.*, pp. 14–15.
26 *Ibid.*, p. 17.
27 *Ibid.*, pp. 18–20.
28 *Ibid.*, pp. 20–2.
29 A.J. Coleman, "Future Reflections of Mathematical Reform," *Bulletin*, XLVII, 6, December 1967, pp. 473–4.
30 Wilbur Schramm, *Programmed Instruction Today and Tomorrow* (New York: Fund for the Advancement of Education, 1962), pp. 23–4.
31 Brian Burnham, ed., *New Designs for Learning: Highlights of the Reports of the Ontario Curriculum Institute, 1963–1966* (Toronto: University of Toronto Press for the Ontario Institute for Studies in Education, 1967), p. 67.
32 Paul Goodman, *Compulsory Mis-Education* and *The Community of Scholars* (New York: Random House, Vintage Books, 1962, 1964), pp. 95–6. (*Compulsory Mis-Education* is also available in a hardcover edition from Horizon Press. *The Community of Scholars* is available in a hardcover edition from Random House.)
33 *Ibid.*, p. 96.
34 *Ibid.*, pp. 97–8.
35 Ontario Association for Curriculum Development, Proceedings of Sixth Annual Conference, Toronto, 8–10 November 1956, p. 24. (Mimeographed.)
36 Frye, ed., *Design for Learning*, p. 122.
37 *Ibid.*, p. 134.
38 *Ibid.*, p. 135.
39 Bow Group, *Strategy for Schools* (London SW1: Conservative Political Centre, 1964), pp. 22–3. (Pamphlet.)
40 *Ibid.*, p. 57.
41 Science Committee, Interim Report of the Committee, *Science* (Toronto: Ontario Curriculum Institute, 1963), p 32.
42 Ontario, Department of Education, *Curriculum Bulletin 2*, I, 2, May 1965, p. 8.
43 Cochrane, ed., *Centennial Story*, p. 191.
44 Ontario, Department of Educa-

tion, *Courses of Study for Public and Separate Schools, 1936.*

45 Frye, ed., *Design for Learning,* p. 82.

46 *Ibid.*, p. 92.

47 *Ibid.*, p. 96.

48 *Ibid.*, p. 88.

49 *Ibid.*, p. 110.

50 *Directions: An Initial Inquiry into the Social Sciences Program for the Schools* (Toronto: Ontario Curriculum Institute, 1966), pp. 7–8.

51 J. Bascom St John, "Why the Children Forget History," *Globe and Mail*, 14 February 1964.

52 G.S. Tomkins, "Geography in the Elementary School," in *Education: A Collection of Essays on Canadian Education.* v: *1962–1964*, pp. 15–16.

53 A.B. Hodgetts, *What Culture? What Heritage? A Study of Civic Education in Canada,* Report of the National History Project, Curriculum Series No. 5 (Toronto: Ontario Institute for Studies in Education, 1968).

54 *Ibid.*, p. 6.

55 *Ibid.*, p. 16.

56 *Ibid.*, p. 72.

57 *Ibid.*, pp. 115–16.

58 *Ibid.*, p. 116.

59 W.E. Kieser, "On the Judicious Use of English in the Teaching of Modern Languages," *Canadian Modern Language Review,* XXII, 2, January 1966, pp. 13–23.

60 Second Language Committee, Interim Report of the Committee, *French as a Second Language* (Toronto: Ontario Curriculum Institute, 1963), pp. 4–5.

61 Ontario, Legislative Assembly, *Debates*, 27th leg., 3rd sess., 2 June 1965, p. 3578.

62 *Ibid.*, 27th leg., 5th sess., 24 May 1967, p. 3740.

63 *Ibid.*, 28th leg., 1st sess., 21 February 1968, p. 121.

64 *Ibid.*, 5 June 1968, p. 4006.

65 "Grade 1 Pupils Not Ready for French Is City View," *Toronto Daily Star*, 10 December 1968.

66 Committee on Religious Education in the Public Schools of the Province of Ontario, Report of the Committee, *Religious Information and Moral Development*, J. Keiller Mackay, chairman (Toronto: Ontario Department of Education, 1969), p. vii.

67 *Ibid.*, p. 31.

68 *Ibid.*, p. 32.

69 *Ibid.*, p. 34.

70 J.M. McCutcheon, *Public Education in Ontario* (Toronto: T.H. Best, 1941), p. 76.

71 Regulation 13, General Regulations, Public and Separate Schools, "Religious Exercises and Religious Education in the Public Schools."

72 *Report of the Royal Commission on Education in Ontario, 1950*, J.A. Hope, chairman (Toronto: King's Printer, 1950), pp. 126–7.

73 Ontario Association for Curriculum Development, Report of the Ontario Conference on Education, Windsor, November 1961, pp. 124–5.

74 "A Vanishing Problem," *Globe*

and Mail, 31 May 1968.

75 Committee on Religious Education in the Public Schools of the Province of Ontario, *Religious Information and Moral Development*, p. 59, quoting Lawrence Kohlberg, "Development of Moral Character and Moral Ideology," in Martin Hoffman and Lois Hoffman, eds., *Review of Child Development Research*, I (New York, 1964), p. 400.

76 Committee on Religious Education in the Public Schools of the Province of Ontario, *Religious Information and Moral Development*, p. 63.

77 Cochrane, ed., *Centennial Story*, p. 206.

78 Ontario, Department of Education, *Guidance in the Intermediate Division, Grades* VII–X, April 1950, introduction.

79 Ontario, Department of Education, *Guidance Services in the Senior Division, Grades* XI–XIII, March 1952, "Suggestions for Implementing Guidance Services."

80 *Report of the Royal Commission on Education in Ontario, 1950*, p. 99.

81 H.W. Zingle and W.J. Winship, "Crucial Issues in Our Guidance Program," *ATA Magazine*, XLVII, 6, February 1967, pp. 23–4.

82 Robin Gerrish, "Probe. Student Guidance. The Should and Should Not of Guidance Record Keeping," *School Administration*, III, March 1967, p. 23.

83 R.C. Harris, "A Counselor Looks at the Hall-Dennis Report," *Canadian Counsellor*, III, 2, April 1969, p. 39.

CHAPTER 7

1 J.R.H. Morgan, "The New Look in the Secondary Schools," November 1968, p. 7. (Mimeographed.)

2 Ontario, Legislative Assembly, *Debates*, 28th leg., 1st sess., 2 April 1968, p. 1532.

3 J. Bascom St John, "The World of Learning," *Globe and Mail*, Toronto, 5 April 1963.

4 D.A. Bristow, "Should Marks Be Adjusted?" *Bulletin*, XLIV, 1, 31 January 1964, p. 27.

5 Charles E. Phillips, *The Development of Education in Canada* (Toronto: W.J. Gage, 1957), p. 524.

6 Ontario, Department of Education, *Interim Revision, Introduction and Guide, Curriculum P1, J1, 1967*, p. 13.

7 H.L. Campbell, *Curriculum Trends in Canadian Education*, Quance Lectures in Canadian Education (Toronto: W.J. Gage, 1952), p. 73.

8 Scottish Education Department, *Secondary Education* (Edinburgh: His Majesty's Stationery Office, 1947), p. 43, cited in *Report of the Royal Commission on Education in Ontario, 1950*, J.A. Hope, chairman (Toronto: King's Printer, 1950), p. 89.

9 G.H. Bantock, *Education in an Industrial Society* (London: Faber and Faber, 1963), p. 70.

10 *Ibid.*, p. 74.

11 Ontario, Department of Education, Memorandum to Secondary School Principals re Standards of Promotion and Recommendation, 1957–58:14, 4 October 1957.
12 Committee on the Scope and Organization of the Curriculum, Report of the Committee, *Children, Classrooms, Curriculum, and Change* (Toronto: Ontario Curriculum Institute, 1966), pp. 25–6.
13 Ontario, Department of Education, Memorandum to School Officials re Policy and Suggestions re Grades 12 and 13, 1968, and in Future Years, 1967–68: 28, 5 December 1967.
14 "Eliminate Examinations," *Bulletin*, XL, 1, February 1968, pp. 45–6. (Reprinted from the District 6 Courier.)
15 Ontario, Provincial Committee on Aims and Objectives of Education in the Schools of Ontario, *Living and Learning* (Toronto: Newton Publishing, 1968), p. 76.
16 *Pattern for Professionalism*, Report of the OTF Commission to the Board of Governors of the Ontario Teachers' Federation, August 1968, p. A19.
17 Phillips, *Development of Education in Canada*, p. 516.
18 Honora M. Cochrane, ed., *Centennial Story: Board of Education for the City of Toronto, 1850–1950* (Toronto: Thomas Nelson & Sons, 1950), p. 74.
19 John Seath, *Education for Industrial Purposes* (Toronto: King's Printer, 1911), p. 264.
20 Ontario, Department of Education, *Report of the Minister, 1932*, pp. vii–viii.
21 *Report of the Royal Commission on Education in Ontario, 1950*, p. 93.
22 *Ibid.*, pp. 94–5.
23 *Ibid.*, p. 90.
24 *Ibid.*
25 Woodrow S. Lloyd, *The Role of Government in Canadian Education*, Quance Lectures in Canadian Education (Toronto: W.J. Gage, 1959), pp. 46–7.
26 J.R. McCarthy, "Curriculum Crossroads," address delivered at the Ontario Conference on Education, Windsor, Ontario, November 1961.
27 J. Bascom St John, "The World of Learning," *Globe and Mail*, 16 October 1962.
28 Bow Group, *Strategy for Schools* (London, SW1: the Conservative Political Centre, 1964), p. 19. (Pamphlet.)
29 Ontario Teachers' Federation, Submission to the Minister of Education re Grade 13 Examinations, April 1966, pp. 1–2.
30 Larry Collins, "Surprise! Surprise! Teachers, Students, Glad Grade 13 Exams Are Gone," *Telegram*, 16 March 1968.
31 The fact that the writer was a member of this committee may have led him to place undue emphasis on the resulting document.
32 Association of Heads of English Departments in Toronto Secondary Schools, Brief submitted by the Association on the Testing of Composition as Pre-

sented to Students of Grade 13, 1967, in the Student Handbook, Ontario Tests for Admission to College and University, July 1967, pp. 4–5.

33 The punctuation is reproduced strictly as it appeared in the original document.

34 Brief submitted by the Association of Heads of English Departments in Toronto Secondary Schools, p. 8.

35 Hillel Black, *They Shall Not Pass* (New York: William Morrow and Company, 1963), pp. 11–25.

36 *Ibid.*, pp. 24–5.

37 *Ibid.*, pp. 29–30.

38 J. Bascom St John, "Standards of Achievement," *Globe and Mail*, 21 January 1963.

39 Ontario, Department of Education, *Interim Revision, Introduction and Guide, Curriculum P1, J1, 1967*, p. 14.

40 E.N. Rutherford, "Experimental Report Card," *Toronto Education Quarterly*, IV, Spring 1965, p. 9. Published by the Toronto Board of Education.

41 David A. Goslin, *Teachers and Testing* (New York: Russell Sage Foundation, 1967), p. 136.

42 When the range of aptitude among those admitted is narrowed by a policy of stricter selection, the correlation coefficient falls because of the way the variance component operates in the formula.

43 Gene R. Hawes, *Educational Testing for the Millions* (New York: McGraw-Hill, 1964), p. 128.

44 *Ibid.*, p. 152.

45 H.W. Savage, *An Evaluation of the Brown-Holtzman Survey of Study Habits and Attitudes for Use in Ontario* (Toronto: Department of Educational Research, Ontario College of Education, University of Toronto, 1961); John F. Flowers, *An Evaluation of the Kuder Preference Record–Personal for Use in Ontario* (Toronto: Department of Educational Research, Ontario College of Education, University of Toronto, 1961).

CHAPTER 8

1 J. Bascom St John, "The World of Learning," *Globe and Mail*, 4 October 1963.

2 W.C. Meierhenry and Robert E. Stepp, "Media and Early Childhood Education," *Phi Delta Kappan*, L, 7, March 1969, pp. 409–11.

3 Alan Thomas, "Education and Communications," in *New Developments in Society*, Conference Study No. 4, John P. Kidd and D. Carlton Williams, eds., (Ottawa: Canadian Conference on Education, 1961), p. 34.

4 A.B. Hodgetts, *What Culture? What Heritage? A Study of Civic Education in Canada* (Toronto: Ontario Institute for Studies in Education, 1968), p. 61.

5 Ontario, Provincial Committee on Aims and Objectives of Education in the Schools of Ontario, *Living and Learning* (Toronto: Newton Publishing, 1968), p. 15.

6 F.B. Rainsberry, "T.V. a Challenge to Teachers," *Toronto*

Education Quarterly, III, 2, Winter 1963–64, pp. 14–15. Published by the Toronto Board of Education.

7 J. Bascom St John, "The World of Learning," *Globe and Mail*, 4 October 1963.

8 E.L. Park, "A Teacher Evaluates Programmed Instruction, *Bulletin*, XLV, 4, 30 September 1965, pp. 252–5.

9 Wilbur Schramm, *Programmed Instruction Today and Tomorrow* (New York: Fund for the Advancement of Education, 1962), p. 1. Additional aspects of the definition are also substantially those supplied by the same writer.

10 *Ibid.*, pp. 5–6.

11 *Ibid.*, p. 11.

12 Four Canadian Surveys of the Utilization of Programmed Instruction and Attitudes Concerning Its Future Role. A joint project of: Canadian Council for Research in Education, Canadian Education Association, Canadian Teachers' Federation, Department of Labour (Technical and Vocational Training Branch), Ontario Society for Training and Development (Canadian Council for Research in Education, 1965), p. 1. (Mimeographed.)

13 *A Survey of the Use of Programmed Instruction in Canadian Schools, 1962–3*, Research Memo No. 12 (Ottawa: Canadian Teachers' Federation, September 1963), pp. 8–9.

14 Canadian Council for Research in Education, Four Canadian Surveys of the Utilization of Programmed Instruction and Attitudes Concerning Its Future Role, August 1965, p. 3.

15 *Ibid.*, p. 58.

16 Schramm, *Programmed Instruction Today and Tomorrow*, p. 31.

17 *Ibid.*, p. 38.

18 E.Z. Friedenberg, *Coming of Age in America: Growth and Acquiescence* (New York: Random House, 1963), p. 259.

19 Paul Goodman, *Compulsory Mis-Education* and *The Community of Scholars* (New York: Random House, Vintage Books, 1962, 1964), p. 80. (*Compulsory Mis-Education* is also available in a hardcover edition from Horizon Press. *The Community of Scholars* is available in a hardcover edition from Random House.)

20 *Ibid.*, p. 87.

21 B.F. Skinner, *Walden Two* (New York: Macmillan, 1962), p. 262.

22 F.G. Robinson, address to the Second International Curriculum Conference, Toronto, February 1966.

23 R.G. Ragsdale, "Computer-Assisted Instruction," *School Administration*, IV, 4, April 1967, pp. 51–4.

24 Ontario, Provincial Committee on Aims and Objectives of Education in the Schools of Ontario, *Living and Learning*, p. 61.

25 John Fielder, "Language Labs," *School Progress*, XXXVII, 2, February 1968, pp. 31–9.

26 Lester Anheim, "A Survey of Informed Opinion on Television's Future Place in Educa-

tion," *Educational Television – The Next Ten Years* (Stanford: Institute for Communication Research, 1962).

27 J.W. Sullivan, "Towards Enriched Teaching," *Bulletin*, XLVIII, 1, February 1968, pp. 37–9.

28 Arthur A. Delaney and Fabian A. Glassman, "Let's Take Another Look at ETV," reprinted from the *Clearing House* in *Toronto Education Quarterly*, III, 2, Winter 1963–64, pp. 11–12. Published by the Toronto Board of Education.

29 *Educational Television – The Next Ten Years*, p. 5.

30 Ontario Association for Curriculum Development, Report of the Ontario Conference on Education, Windsor, November 1961, p. 111.

31 Ontario, Provincial Committee on Aims and Objectives of Education in the Schools of Ontario, *Living and Learning*, p. 159.

32 J. Bascom St John, "The World of Learning," *Globe and Mail*, 11 March 1963.

33 Marshall McLuhan, "Understanding Media: A McLuhan Sampler," *Toronto Education Quarterly*, III, 4, Summer 1964, p. 21. Published by the Toronto Board of Education.

34 J. Bascom St John, "The World of Learning," *Globe and Mail*, 11 March 1963.

35 Ontario, Legislative Assembly, *Debates*, 28th leg., 1st sess., 6 June 1968, p. 4044.

CHAPTER 9

1 J.M. McCutcheon, *Public Education in Ontario* (Toronto: T.H. Best, 1941), p. 84.

2 C.B. Sissons, *Church & State in Canadian Education: An Historical Study* (Toronto: Ryerson Press, 1959), p. 76.

3 *Ibid.*, pp. 92–3.

4 *Ibid.*, p. 94.

5 *Report of the Royal Commission on Education in Ontario, 1950*, J.A. Hope, chairman (Toronto: King's Printer, 1950), p. 439.

6 *Ibid.*, p. 116.

7 Ontario, Legislative Assembly, *Debates*, 26th leg., 3rd sess., 10 April 1962, p. 2135.

8 *Ibid.*, 27th leg., 5th sess., 28 April 1967, pp. 2790–2.

9 L'Association canadienne-française d'éducation d'Ontario, *et al.*, Brief to the Provincial Committee on Aims and Objectives of Education in the Schools of Ontario, Ottawa, December 1965, p. 6. (Mimeographed.)

10 *Report of the Royal Commission on Bilingualism and Biculturalism*, I (Ottawa: Queen's Printer, 8 October 1967), pp. 122–3.

11 *Ibid.*, pp. 127–8.

12 *Report of the Committee on French Language Schools in Ontario*, R.R. Bériault, chairman, 28 November 1968, pp. 9–11.

13 Roland R. Bériault, "French Language Schools in Ontario," *Dimensions in Education*, II, 8, August 1968, p. 4.

14 *Ibid.*, p. 5.

15 "PC Opposes Schools to Teach French Only," *Globe and Mail*, 12 June 1968.

16 William Johnson, "Will the French Go Public?" *Globe and Mail*, Toronto, 23 November 1968.

17 *Report of the Royal Commission on Bilingualism and Biculturalism*, II (Ottawa: Queen's Printer, December 1968).

18 *La Vie culturelle des franco-ontariens: Rapport du comité franco-ontarien d'enquête culturelle* (Ottawa, Janvier 1969).

19 Indian-Eskimo Association of Canada, Ontario Division Annual Meeting, Fort William, 20 November 1966, President's Report.

20 Indian-Eskimo Association of Canada, Report of Executive Director to the 9th Annual Meeting of Members, Toronto, 28 September 1968, submitted by E.R. McEwen.

21 Indian-Eskimo Association of Canada, Ontario Division Annual Meeting, Fort William, 20 November 1966, President's Report. Attached statement re historical sketch, pp. 4–5.

22 James Mulvihill, "The Dilemma in Indian Education," *Indian Record*, XXVI, 2, March-April 1963.

23 *Ibid.*

24 *Ibid.*

25 Ontario, Legislative Assembly, *Debates*, 25th leg., 2nd sess., 18 February 1957, pp. 425–6.

26 *Ibid.*, 4th sess., 12 March 1958, p. 778.

27 *Ibid.*, 26th leg., 1st sess., 28 March 1960, p. 1858.

28 *Ibid.*, 28th leg., 1st sess., 5 June 1968, p. 3990.

29 Rudy Platiel, "Kent County School Board Branded Racist, Paternalistic to Indians," *Globe and Mail*, 20 April 1970.

CHAPTER 10

1 Ontario, Provincial Committee on Aims and Objectives of Education in the Schools of Ontario, *Living and Learning* (Toronto: Newton Publishing, 1968), p. 108.

2 Charles E. Phillips, *The Development of Education in Canada* (Toronto: W.J. Gage, 1957), p. 370.

3 J.M. McCutcheon, *Public Education in Ontario* (Toronto: T.H. Best, 1941), pp. 141–3.

4 C.E. Stothers, "The Development of Services, Agencies, and Materials to Provide for Handicapped Children in Ontario," in Ontario School Inspectors' Association, *The Sixteenth Yearbook, 1960–61: The Education of Children with Handicaps* (Toronto: Copp Clark, [n.d.]), p. 11.

5 J.G. Althouse, *Structure and Aims of Canadian Education*, Quance Lectures in Canadian Education (Toronto: W.J. Gage, 1949), pp. 35–6.

6 W.D. Sutton, "The London Educational Clinic," in Ontario School Inspectors' Association, *The Education of Children with Handicaps*, pp. 209–12.

7 Ontario, Legislative Assembly, *Debates*, 27th leg., 5th sess., 25 May 1967, p. 3855.

8 Ontario, Provincial Committee on Aims and Objectives of Education in the Schools of Ontario, *Living and Learning*, p. 13.

9 *Ibid.*, p. 101.
10 *Ibid.*, p. 102.
11 Bill Johnson, "What Parents Expect from Special Education," *School Progress*, XXXVIII, 1, January 1969, pp. 64–5.
12 Ontario, Legislative Assembly, *Debates*, 25th leg., 2nd sess., 14 February 1957, p. 359.
13 *Ibid.*, p. 361.
14 *Ibid.*, p. 368.
15 Alex MacLean, "The Frank Oke School," in Ontario School Inspectors' Association, *The Education of Children with Handicaps*, pp. 139–42.
16 *Ibid.*, p. 142.
17 Ontario, Legislative Assembly, *Debates*, 26th leg., 3rd sess., 14 December 1961, p. 470.
18 *Ibid.*, 26th leg., 1st sess., 11 February 1960, pp. 300–1.
19 *Ibid.*, 27th leg., 2nd sess., 23 April 1964, p. 2371.
20 *Ibid.*, 5 May 1964, p. 2969.
21 *Ibid.*, 5th sess., 17 May 1967, pp. 3544–5.
22 *Ibid.*, p. 3540.
23 Ashton S. Upper, "The Education of the Orthopaedically Handicapped," in Ontario School Inspectors' Association, *The Education of Children with Handicaps*, p. 92.
24 Ontario, Legislative Assembly, *Debates*, 27th leg., 3rd sess., 3 June 1965, p. 3679.
25 Ontario, Department of Education, Memorandum to School Officials re Perceptually Handicapped Secondary School Students, 1967–68:32, 6 November 1967, G.L. Duffin, Assistant Deputy Minister.
26 Ontario, Department of Education, Memorandum to School Officials re Perceptually Handicapped Elementary School Pupils, 1968–69:2, 15 August 1968, G.L. Duffin, Assistant Deputy Minister.
27 R.G. Stennett, "Chances Are He Won't Grow Out of It," *Canada's Mental Health*, XVI, 1 & 2, January–April 1968, p. 3, citing E.M. Bower, *The Education of Emotionally Handicapped Children* (Sacramento, California: California State Department of Education, 1961).
28 *Ibid.*, p. 4.
29 Ontario School Inspectors' Association, *The Education of Children with Handicaps*, pp. 205–7.
30 Beatrice Wockett, "A Program of Volunteer Assistance for Emotionally Disturbed Children," CEC Convention Papers, 1967, p. 67.
31 Ontario, Legislative Assembly, *Debates*, 27th leg., 3rd sess., 3 June 1965, pp. 3677–83.
32 *Ibid.*, 9 February 1965, pp. 366–8.
33 *Ibid.*, 4th sess., 9 March 1966, p. 1349.
34 *Ibid.*, 5th sess., 27 January 1967, pp. 43–6.
35 Ontario, Committee of Officials of the Departments of Health, Education, Welfare, Reform Institutions, and Attorney-General, "Services for Children with Mental and Emotional Disorders," [n.d.], p. 13.
36 *Ibid.*, p. 14.
37 Ontario, Legislative Assembly, *Debates*, 28th leg., 2nd sess., 3 December 1968, p. 314.

38 *Ibid.*, 18 February 1969, p. 1338.
39 *Ibid.*, p. 1343.

CHAPTER 11

1 J. Bascom St John, "School Costs and Quality," *Globe and Mail*, 26 October 1961.
2 J. Bascom St John, "Keeping Schools Behind the Times," *Globe and Mail*, 19 February 1962.
3 "Franklin Public School," *School Progress*, XXXIII, 4, April 1964, pp. 43–5.
4 "Is the Message Getting Through," *School Progress*, XXXVII, 12, December 1968, p. 32.
5 Ontario, Legislative Assembly, *Debates*, 27th leg., 4th sess., 1 April 1966, p. 2162.
6 *Ibid.*
7 D.M. Blenkhorne, "Architect Argues There's No Real Saving in Standard Plans for School Construction," *School Progress*, XXXV, 3, March 1966, p. 56.
8 Ontario, Legislative Assembly, *Debates*, 28th leg., 2nd sess., 11 February 1969, pp. 1182–3.
9 *Ibid.*, 1st sess., 25 April 1968, pp. 2109–10.
10 *Ibid.*, 27th leg., 3rd sess., 11 February 1965, p. 456.
11 Thomas L. Wells, Remarks to the Opening Session of the School Design Workshop, Toronto, 18 November 1968.
12 "Instructional Materials Centres: Their Organization & Development," *Curriculum Bulletin 4*, I, 4, May 1966, p. 3.
13 W.A.T. Perrins, "The School Library," *Bulletin*, XLIII, 1, 31 January 1963, p. 23.
14 *Ibid.*
15 *Ibid.*, p. 48.
16 W.A.T. Perrins, "The Changing Role of the School Librarian," *Bulletin*, XLVI, 2, 31 March 1966, pp. 77–8.
17 Ottawa Public Schools, *Superintendent of Public Schools Annual Report, 1964*, p. 5.
18 Audrey Taylor, "Resource Centres? Trouble is We Don't Really Know How to Use Them!" *School Administration*, February 1968, pp. 24–6.
19 Francis R. St John Library Consultants, *A Survey of Libraries in the Province of Ontario, 1965* (Toronto: Ontario Library Association through the co-operation of the Ontario Department of Education, 1965), p. 131.
20 Ontario, Legislative Assembly, *Debates*, 28th leg., 2nd sess., 28 November 1968, p. 212.

CHAPTER 12

1 Ontario, Department of Education, Memorandum to the Inspectors re Teachers Acting as Agents or Salesmen, 30 April 1963, G.A. Pearson, Superintendent of Elementary Education.
2 "Draft Report of the Committee on Conflicts of Interest," F.W. Callaghan, chairman, December, 1968. [Unpaged. Owing to the extended illness of Mr. Yates, Callaghan was requested to chair the committee.]
3 *Ibid.*, pp. 53–4.
4 J.M. McCutcheon, *Public Education in Ontario* (Toronto:

T.H. Best, 1941), pp. 221–2.

5 Charles E. Phillips, *The Development of Education in Canada* (Toronto: W.J. Gage, 1957), pp. 559–60.

6 James M. Paton, *The Professional Status of Teachers*, Conference Study No. 2 (Ottawa: Canadian Conference on Education, 1961), p. 64.

7 H.O. Barrett, "Who Should Certify Teachers?" *Bulletin*, XLVII, 6, December 1967, pp. 455–6.

8 Ontario, Legislative Assembly, *Debates*, 28th leg., 1st sess., 6 June 1968, p. 4053.

9 Ontario, Provincial Committee on Aims and Objectives of Education in the Schools of Ontario, *Living and Learning* (Toronto: Newton Publishing, 1968), p. 133.

10 Ontario, Department of Education, Memorandum to Principals of Secondary Schools re Recruitment in Our Schools of Prospective Secondary School Teachers, 1956–57:21, 4 January 1957, S.D. Rendall, Superintendent of Secondary Education.

11 Ontario, Department of Education, *Report of the Minister, 1967*, p. 7.

12 Ontario, Provincial Committee on Aims and Objectives of Education in the Schools of Ontario, *Living and Learning*, p. 121.

13 "Creativity in the Schools," *Toronto Education Quarterly*, II, 3, Spring 1963, pp. 3–4, citing Margaret Mead, *Think*, 1962. Published by the Toronto Board of Education.

14 Don Hamachek, "Characteristics of Good Teachers and Implications for Teacher Education," *Phi Delta Kappan*, L, 6, February 1969, p. 341.

15 *Ibid.*, pp. 341–2.

16 James M. Cameron, "Teacher Evaluation by Students," *Bulletin*, XLVIII, 2, March 1968, p. 108.

17 Oswald Hall, "Some Pitfalls of Bigness," in John P. Kidd and Carlton Williams, eds., *New Developments in Society*, Conference Study No. 4 (Ottawa: Canadian Conference on Education, 1961), p. 23.

18 Ontario, Provincial Committee on Aims and Objectives of Education in the Schools of Ontario, *Living and Learning*, p. 136.

19 *Ibid.*

20 James Bethune, "The Urban Teacher's Hang-up," *OSSTF InterCom*, III, 2, February 1969, pp. 2–3.

21 Alan F. Brown, *Changing School Districts in Canada* (Toronto: Ontario Institute for Studies in Education, 1968), p. 13.

22 Bow Group, *Strategy for Schools* (London SW1: Conservative Political Centre, 1964), p. 9. (Pamphlet.)

23 Paton, *Professional Status of Teachers*, pp. 6–7.

24 *Ibid.*, p. 3.

25 "Teachers' Image High with Young People, Survey Shows," *OSSTF InterCom*, III, 1, January 1969, p. 4.

26 Northrop Frye, ed., *Design for Learning*, Reports submitted to the Joint Committee of the To-

ronto Board of Education and the University of Toronto (Toronto: University of Toronto Press, 1962), p. 113.

27 Frank MacKinnon, *Relevance and Responsibility in Education*, Quance Lectures in Canadian Education (Toronto: W.J. Gage, 1968), p. 31.

28 A.B. Hodgetts, *What Culture? What Heritage? A Study of Civic Education in Canada*, Report of the National History Project (Toronto: Ontario Institute for Studies in Education, 1968), p. 106.

29 *Ibid.*, p. 107.

30 *Ibid.*, p. 109.

31 *Ibid.*

32 *Ibid.*, pp. 96–7.

33 Hugh Garner, "Teaching: Ready Haven for the Second-Rate," *Telegram*, 13 September 1965.

34 Ontario, Legislative Assembly, *Debates*, 28th leg., 1st sess., 5 June 1968, p. 3953.

35 Ontario, Department of Education, Memorandum to Regional and Area Superintendents, Program Consultants, Municipal Directors and Superintendents, Principals of Schools, Secretaries of School Boards, and Principals of Private Schools re The Use of Non-Professional Personnel in the Schools, 1968–69:20, 27 November 1968, G.L. Duffin, Assistant Deputy Minister.

CHAPTER 13

1 *Report of the Royal Commission on Education in Ontario, 1950*, J.A. Hope, chairman (Toronto: King's Printer, 1950), p. 625.

2 "Better Pay for Better Teachers," *Toronto Daily Star*, 13 January 1967.

3 "Merit Pay For Teachers – the B.C.T.F. Stand," *BC Teacher*, September-October 1962, pp. 12–13.

4 *Report of the Royal Commission on Education in Ontario, 1950*, p. 628.

5 Frank MacKinnon, *The Politics of Education* (Toronto: University of Toronto Press, 1960), p. 164.

6 I.M. Robb, "The Philosopher's Stone on Education," *Bulletin*, XLVII, 2, March 1967, p. 81.

7 *Ibid.*, pp. 82–3.

8 *Ibid.*, p. 84.

9 I.M. Robb, "Some Observations," *Bulletin*, XLVIII, 1, February 1968, p. 13.

10 David Menear, "A Teacher's Merit Pay System That Works," *Toronto Daily Star*, 7 February 1968.

11 "Let's Reward Classroom Ability," *Toronto Daily Star*, 1 May 1968.

12 Ross H. Munro, "Teachers Endorse Merit Pay," *Globe and Mail*, 21 March 1969.

13 Charles E. Phillips, *The Development of Education in Canada* (Toronto: W.J. Gage, 1957), p. 559.

14 Edwin C. Guillet, *In the Cause of Education: Centennial History of the Ontario Educational Association 1861–1960* (Toronto: University of Toronto Press, 1960), p. 150.

15 Phillips, *Development of Education in Canada*, p. 559.

16 Guillet, *In the Cause of Educa-*

tion, pp. 59–60.
17 *Ibid.*, p. 275.
18 *The Teachers' and Inspectors' Superannuation Act and Regulations* (rev. ed.; Toronto: King's Printer, 1936), section 1.
19 Ontario, Legislative Assembly, *Debates*, 26th leg., 3rd sess., 16 April 1962, p. 2444.
20 *Ibid.*, 27th leg., 2nd sess., 27 January 1964, pp. 393–4.
21 *Ibid.*, 28th leg., 2nd sess., 16 December 1968, pp. 712–13.
22 *Ibid.*, 28th leg., 1st sess., 21 February 1968, p. 108.
23 Nora Hodgins, "From the Secretary's Desk," *O.T.F. Reporter*, XIII, February 1969, p. 4.
24 Ontario, Committee on Taxation, *Report of the Ontario Committee on Taxation.* I: *Approach, Background and Conclusions* (Toronto: Queen's Printer, 30 August 1967), p. 188.
25 Ontario, Legislative Assembly, *Debates*, Budget Address, 25th leg., 5th sess., 25 February 1959, p. 611.

CHAPTER 14

1 Ontario, Provincial Committee on Aims and Objectives of Education in the Schools of Ontario, *Living and Learning* (Toronto: Newton Publishing, 1968), p. 4.
2 "The Provincial Committee on Aims and Objectives of Education in the Schools of Ontario," 14 April 1966. (Mimeographed.)
3 Ontario, Legislative Assembly, *Debates*, 27th leg., 3rd sess., 3 June 1965, p. 3614.
4 Ontario, Provincial Committee on Aims and Objectives of Education in the Schools of Ontario, *Living and Learning*, p. 9.
5 *Ibid.*
6 *Ibid.*, p. 10.
7 *Ibid.*, p. 11.
8 *Ibid.*, p. 12.
9 *Ibid.*
10 *Ibid.*, p. 14.
11 *Ibid.*, pp. 14–15.
12 *Ibid.*, p. 15.
13 *Ibid.*, p. 16.
14 *Ibid.*, p. 17.
15 *Ibid.*, p. 21.
16 *Ibid.*
17 *Ibid.*, p. 23.
18 *Ibid.*, p. 34.
19 *Ibid.*, p. 39.
20 *Ibid.*
21 *Ibid.*
22 *Ibid.*, p. 44.
23 *Ibid.*, p. 47.
24 *Ibid.*, p .50
25 *Ibid.*, p. 52.
26 *Ibid.*
27 *Ibid.*, p. 54.
28 *Ibid.*, p. 56.
29 *Ibid.*, p. 60.
30 *Ibid.*
31 *Ibid.*, p. 67.
32 *Ibid.*
33 *Ibid.*
34 *Ibid.*
35 *Ibid.*, p. 68.
36 *Ibid.*, p. 69.
37 *Ibid.*
38 *Ibid.*
39 Charles E. Phillips, "The New Philosophy," in *Education and the Innovative Society*, Report of the 46th Conference of the Canadian Education Association, 24–26 September 1969, Halifax, Nova Scotia (Toronto: Canadian Education Association), pp. 33–4.

40 Ontario, Provincial Committee on Aims and Objectives of Education in the Schools of Ontario, *Living and Learning*, p. 75.
41 *Ibid.*, p. 76.
42 *Ibid.*, pp. 76–7.
43 *Ibid.*, p. 77.
44 *Ibid.*, p. 98.
45 *Ibid.*, p. 101.
46 *Ibid.*
47 *Ibid.*, p. 102.
48 *Ibid.*, p 106.
49 *Ibid.*, p. 108.
50 *Ibid.*, p. 109.
51 *Ibid.*
52 *Ibid.*, p. 122.
53 *Ibid.*, p. 123.
54 *Ibid.*, p. 128.
55 *Ibid.*, p. 134.
56 *Ibid.*, p. 136.
57 *Ibid.*
58 *Ibid.*
59 *Ibid.*, p. 140.
60 *Ibid.*, p. 143.
61 *Ibid.*
62 *Ibid.*, p. 144.
63 *Ibid.*
64 *Ibid.*, p. 145.
65 *Ibid.*, p. 149.
66 *Ibid.*
67 G.T. Evans, "Attitudes, Ends, and Means: A Comment on the Hall-Dennis Report," in Brian Crittenden, ed., *Means & Ends in Education: Comments on Living and Learning*, Occasional Papers 2 (Toronto: Ontario Institute for Studies in Education, 1969), p. 43.
68 *Ibid.*, p. 48.
69 *Ibid.*, pp. 51–2.
70 *Ibid.*, p. 56.
71 *Ibid.*
72 Carl Bereiter, "A Proposal to Abolish Education," in *ibid.*, pp. 62–70.
73 *Ibid.*, p. 62.
74 *Ibid.*, p. 65.
75 *Ibid.*, p. 66.
76 *Ibid.*
77 *Ibid.*, p. 68.
78 *Ibid.*
79 James Daly, *Education or Molasses? A Critical Look at the Hall-Dennis Report* (Ancaster: Cromlech Press, 1969).
80 *Ibid.*, p. 1.
81 *Ibid.*, p. 4.
82 *Ibid.*, p. 5.
83 *Ibid.*, p. 12.
84 *Ibid.*, p. 13.
85 *Ibid.*, p. 19.
86 *Ibid.*, p. 20.
87 *Ibid.*, pp. 22–3.
88 *Ibid.*, p. 28.
89 *Ibid.*, p. 31.
90 *Ibid.*, p. 32.
91 *Ibid.*, p. 46.
92 *Ibid.*, p. 48.
93 "Fire Your Incompetent Teachers, Dennis Challenges School Trustees," *Globe and Mail*, 14 September 1968.
94 "Davis Hails Hall's Blueprint to Change Education System," *Toronto Daily Star*, 13 June 1968.
95 *Telegram*, 13 June 1968.
96 *Globe and Mail*, 13 June 1968.
97 *Ibid.*
98 "A Pat on Back for Ontario Educators," *Kingston Whig-Standard*, 13 June 1968.
99 Ontario, Legislative Assembly, *Debates*, 28th leg., 1st sess., 18 July 1968, pp. 5951–2.
100 "Education in Utopia," *Brantford Expositor*, 18 June 1968.
101 "Abstract Delight," *Hamilton Spectator*, 17 August 1968.
102 "The Hall-Dennis Report – A

Study in Succinct Obscurity," *School Administration*, July 1968, p. 4.

103 "Gracious Canadians in Defeat," *Telegram*, Toronto, 2 July 1968.

104 *Educational Courier*, March 1969, p. 22.

105 I.M. Robb, "On the Report 'Living and Learning'," paper presented at the Ontario Secondary School Headmasters' Council, Northern Region, Fall Conference, 8 November 1968.

106 *Ibid.*

107 "Hall-Dennis – 'The Impossible Dream'?" *OSSTF Inter-Com*, III, 1, January 1969, 2.

108 Phillips, "The New Philosophy," in *Education and the Innovative Society*, pp. 31–41.

Contents of volumes in
ONTARIO'S EDUCATIVE SOCIETY

General index

Index of persons

www.ingramcontent.com/pod-product-compliance
Lightning Source LLC
LaVergne TN
LVHW090756070826
844660LV00022B/1001

* 9 7 8 1 4 8 7 5 9 8 6 2 4 *